CLASSICS
OF THE
AMERICAN
PRESIDENCY

Edited by   HARRY A. BAILEY, JR.
Temple University

MOORE PUBLISHING COMPANY, INC.
OAK PARK, ILLINOIS

Library of Congress Cataloging in Publication Data

Main entry under title:

Classics of the American presidency.

    1. Presidents—United States—Addresses, es-
says, lectures.   I. Bailey, Harry A.
JK516.C5   353.03'1   80-61
ISBN 0-935610-10-3

Classics of the American Presidency, First Edition

Moore Publishing Company, Inc.
701 South Gunderson Avenue, Oak Park, Illinois 60304

For Mary Lee Howard Bailey

Topical Contents

Chronological Contents

Preface

The selections in this volume were chosen on the basis of their enduring value. Some have already had considerable longevity. Others are more recent, but their lasting value seems already certain. Still other selections were chosen with an eye toward their potential enduring value. The editor may be faulted for the latter if his prognostication is wrong. But overall, it seems fair to assert that practically all of the significant writers and views on the study of the American presidency are contained in this volume.

That many of these "classics" are of rather recent vintage indicates something of the dearth of early quality writing on and insights into the presidency among the plethora of materials which have been written. A good deal of writing on the presidency has faded rapidly into obscurity. The simple goal of this effort is to make available, in a single place, the insights into the presidency that were valuable in the past, that have utility presently, and that are likely to be equally useful on the morrow.

My criteria for including a selection involved asking three questions. First, does the selection provide an important understanding into a main concern about the American presidency—the way in which it was created, has developed, has operated over considerable stretches of time, and endures? Second, has the author of the "piece" included been generally recognized as having made a significant contribution to the study of the presidency? The third and final criterion for including a selection was: Does it have relevance to students seeking to understand the "modern" presidency? I believe the selections included will serve students of the American presidency, rather well, into the third century of the Republic and beyond.

I am most indebted to Professor Jay M. Shafritz of the University of Colorado at Denver for having first suggested and encouraged me to do this book. I am happy to have Jay as a colleague and friend. I am indebted also to Temple University colleagues, Aryeh Botwinick and Richard Joslyn, and to graduate students, Dennis Ricci and David Risser, for giving me their ideas at the initial stages of this work. I am further indebted to my undergraduate assistant, Virgie Pogue, for her resourceful library assistance, and especially to the graduate and master of public administration secretary, Betty Seidman, for the many items which she graciously and expeditiously typed to make this project possible.

Finally, my debt to Mary Lee Howard Bailey, wife and friend, is, as it has been for a long time, immeasurable.

HARRY A. BAILEY, JR.

I
Origins and Creation
of the Presidency

Introduction. Of all the issues confronting the framers of the Constitution, the nature and form the presidency would take ranked as a concern of highest priority. The earliest holders of executive power in America were the provincial governors. Many of these executives incurred widespread enmity, because they looked to the crown, rather than to the people, for policy guidance. Reacting to the negative experience of the provincial governors, the framers of state constitutions, after the Revolution, had with few exceptions (New York state, for example) created weak executives and strong legislatures. This had not been a particularly rewarding political experience. Thus, the question: Should the new nation adopt a weak or a strong executive?

The fifty-five delegates who assembled in convention at Philadelphia in 1787 to draw up a new constitution brought with them conflicting viewpoints. One popular alternative was a plural executive in which power would be shared by a council or committee. Rule would be collectively, perhaps by majority vote. Another alternative was the single executive who alone would rule the executive branch of government. For many of the delegates, however, a single executive could constitute the fetus of monarchy.

Thus, although the framers wanted to avoid the weaknesses of a plural executive, which they visualized as "government by committee" and which they had experienced under the Articles of Confederation of 1781 (which provided only for a Committee of the States to rule while Congress was not in session), they were also attempting to avoid the abuses they had endured before the American Revolution under the rule of the British king, George III.

Political scientist Charles Thach's essay, "The Creation of the Presidency," shows much of the sharp division among the delegates over how the executive power ought to be organized under the new constitution and provides the most fruitful starting point for an explanation of the creation of the presidency.

1

James Madison—a leading spokesman for a thorough reorganization of the existing government, one of Virginia's delegates to the convention, and later the fourth president of the United States—in a letter to Thomas Jefferson, summarized many of the views aired in the convention as well as his own. In this letter, "James Madison to Thomas Jefferson," Madison discussed many of the problems raised by the presidency, such as the nature of his duties, the method of his election, and his tenure in office.

The Constitution's antagonists, the antifederalists, felt that the new constitution granted considerably more power to the executive than had been the case at any time during colonial rule. The ghosts of tyranny loomed large in the minds of the antifederalists and accounted for their vehement opposition to the new document.

George Clinton, the first governor of New York after Independence and an ardent antifederalist, opposed the federal Constitution. He was particularly concerned that vagueness in the Constitution could result in a president easily establishing himself in office for life.[1] Clinton's arguments, expressing his fears about the presidency and the redundancy and superfluity of the vice presidency, a view bandied about in recent years, were written under the pseudonym, "The Letters of Cato." His essay is addressed to the voters of New York under the title, "To the Citizens of the State of New York."

Emanating from the challenge of the antifederalists, the Federalist Papers, the most carefully articulated defense of the Constitution, were to become a cornerstone of American political thought. Alexander Hamilton, one of three New York delegates and later secretary of the treasury under George Washington, wrote Federalist No. 69 as an answer to Governor Clinton's charge that the presidency would differ little from the British monarchy. Hamilton made clear the political differences between the republican executive with limited powers of governance, which he wanted to see in the United States, and the hereditary monarchy of Great Britain with virtually unlimited powers of rule. Hamilton's Federalist No. 70, also reprinted here, discusses the merits of a unitary executive. For Hamilton, only a single vigorous executive, not a council nor committee, was essential for successful republican government.

NOTE

1. Interestingly enough, Clinton's fears on this point seemed never to have had any chance of materializing. Although no limit was placed on a president's term of office by the 1789 Constitution, the myth of the two-term tradition developed soon afterwards. Upon close examination, however, that tradition turns out to be more myth than reality. The American presidential tenure in office has been more nearly a one-term tradition. For the evidence, see Harry A. Bailey, Jr., "Presidential Tenure and the Two-Term Tradition," Publius 2 (Fall 1972), 95-106.

1. The Creation of the Presidency*

CHARLES C. THACH

The fundamental purpose [of this essay] will be . . . to trace the evolution of the ideas which the conservative class ultimately attained concerning the part which the executive department ought to play in governmental life, and also to ascertain the principles of executive organization which in 1787 were regarded as necessary for it successfully to take this part. This point is worthy of some insistence. To consider a department of government, in this case the executive, as a mere arithmetic sum of individual powers, without taking into account the fact that it is an integral part of an organic whole, is to fail correctly to visualize the problem. In a study of the present sort, we must go behind the bare words of constitutions and seek the actual relationship of the executive officers, state and national, to other governmental organs, the part they played in political life, their successes and failures. A mere cataloguing of powers is not enough. We can attempt to discover the lessons which governmental philosophy gleaned from contemporary experience only when we understand what that experience really was.

If the triumph of the natural rights, individual liberty philosophy, in which the Revolutionary movement found its theoretic justification, operated strongly to reduce executive prestige, practical considerations of long standing had contributed strongly to the same end. Much of colonial history had been a repetition in little of the struggle for self-government in Great Britain, a struggle to whose traditions the American Whigs were coheirs with their British fellows.

The responsibility of the royal governor to the home government had placed him in much the same relation to the local assemblies as that in which the Stuart kings had been to the Commons. It had therefore seemed necessary to the colonists to utilize every agency, and especially the control over the purse strings, to force concessions from the executive branch. The aim was always to control those powers of the government which, by virtue of the royal instructions, were in the hands of the executive, in exactly the spirit that British Parliaments had shown. In these struggles the popular assemblies were the bulwark of popular liberties, the executive departments the instrumentalities of British control. This attitude of mind could not fail profoundly to affect the original American concept of republican executive power.

Relieved of all external constraint, the makers of the first American constitutions were free to translate these predilections into positive enactments. There was no longer need to concoct methods of controlling the executive. Powers could be bodily transferred to the legislature. The executive could be organized in such a fashion as to ensure complete subordination. And such, in general, was the process followed. In the words of James Wilson:

> The executive and the judicial as well as the legislative authority was now the child

*Source: From *The Creation of the Presidency* by Charles C. Thach, pp. 26-54. Copyright © 1922 The Johns Hopkins University Press. Reprinted by permission. Footnotes omitted.

of the people; but, to the two former, the people behaved like stepmothers. The legislature was still discriminated by excessive partiality; and into its lap, every good and precious gift was profusely thrown.

An analysis of the state constitutions formed during the Revolution, and especially those constructed in the years 1776-1778, affords abundant confirmation of the truthfulness of Wilson's statement. With one exception, that of New York, they included almost every conceivable provision for reducing the executive to a position of complete subordination.

Short terms, strict limitations on reeligibility, and election by the legislature were the outstanding characteristics of the chief magistracy. Nor was the principle of executive unity adopted, for in the exercise of his power the chief executive was controlled by the necessity of acting in accord with the advice of an executive council chosen, save in Pennsylvania, by the legislature. The exact degree of conciliar control varied, but the general result was the same. The chief magistrate was, as Governor Randolph denominated himself, only "a member of the executive."

An even more fundamental weakness was the common practice of expressly submitting the exercise of either certain enumerated powers, the field of enumerated powers, or even the whole of the executive power to the legislative will. There was no opportunity for a real claim to executive independence to be made when the executive held his powers under the terms, for example, of the Virginia constitution, which declared:

> He shall, with the advice of a Council of State, exercise the executive powers of government, according to the laws of this Commonwealth; and shall not, under any pretence, exercise any power or prerogative, by virtue of any law, statute or custom of England.

Language like this fairly invited legislative interference, for it was possible for the legislatures to claim, with a show of reason, that the Constitution intended that all matters concerning the executive were subject to legislative determination.

The spirit of these state conventions was precisely that of the French National Assembly, and their concept of executive power was well expressed by the latter body's spokesman, Tom Paine, who declared:

> With respect to what, in Europe, is called the executive . . . it is either a political superfluity or a chaos of unknown things. . . . [The executive] can be considered in [no] other light than as inferior to the legislative. The sovereign authority in any country is the power of making laws, and everything else is an official department.

It was in complete accordance with this spirit that the new constitutions functioned, the legislatures refusing even to keep within the liberal constitutional limits set them, which were, in Madison's phrase, "readily overleaped by the legislature on the spur of an occasion."

Jefferson described conditions in Virginia in the following language:

> All the powers of government, legislative executive and judiciary, result to the legislative body. . . . The convention, which passed the ordinance of government, laid its foundations on this basis, that the legislative, executive and judiciary departments should be separate and distinct, so that no person should exercise the powers of more than one of them at the same time. But no barrier was provided between these several powers. The judiciary and executive members were left dependent on the legislative for their subsistence in office, and some of them for their continuance in it. If therefore the legislature assumes executive and judiciary powers, no opposition is likely to be made; nor, if made, can it be effectual; because in that case they may put their proceedings in the form of an act of assembly, which will render them obligatory on the other branches. They have accordingly in many instances, decided rights which should have been left to the judiciary controversy: and the direction of the executive, during the whole time of

their session, is becoming habitual and familiar.

To the same effect, and without contradiction, Edmund Randolph declared in the Virginia ratification convention:

The history of the violations of the constitution extends from the year 1776 to the present time—violations made by formal acts of the legislature: everything has been drawn within the legislative vortex.

To be sure, Jefferson contended that the Virginia situation was a special case, due to the fact that the Virginia convention had no special mandate from the people to form a government and that consequently the constitution was on the same footing as any other legislative enactment. But this view was by no means generally admitted in Virginia, and certainly was not the true explanation.

Thus Richard Spaight writing of the condition of affairs in North Carolina, where there was no question of the convention's mandate, even though strongly reprobating the doctrine of judicial control, admitted that "it cannot be denied that the Assembly have passed laws unjust in themselves, and militating in their principles against the Constitution in more instances than one," and also that "it must be acknowledged that our Constitution, unfortunately, has not been proved a sufficient check to prevent the intemperate and unjust proceedings of our legislature.

The significance of this legislative disregard of the constitution with respect to the position of the executive department is splendidly illustrated by the protests of the Pennsylvania council against legislative interference, a protest the more interesting as the council was chosen by the people and was vested with its powers in unequivocal language. One protest sets forth:

We should be wanting in duty to ourselves, as well as regard to the interests of the State, if we did not express our concern at the interference of your Hon'ble House in matters merely of an Executive

nature, and which have been already under the cognizance of this Board, and received a full determination.

The importunity of the petitioners has doubtless operated upon the indulgence of the house, but we flatter ourselves they rely upon the wisdom and spirit of Council in refusing their applications, where they appear inconsistent with plain positive law, or the rights of the Council, as declared by the Constitution.

Another runs:

The Council having exercised the powers vested in them by the laws of the Commonwealth, with respect to sundry persons who have withdrawn themselves from the troubles of the country, and reside with the enemy, we observe sundry petitions on those subjects, defending, and resolutions calculated to rescind the determination of this Board. We have no desire to intercept the kindness and liberality of the House to petitioners of any character, but apprehend that the introducing special and particular laws to repeal the acts of the Executive branches of Government, without any conference with, or information from the Board, of the reason or ground of their proceedings, must necessarily lessen the weight of the Council, and disturb the harmony of Government.

A third declares:

A desire to preserve the harmony so essential to the public welfare, has kept us silent under the various measures adopted by your House, which we conceive prejudicial to the State and derogatory to the Constitutional rights of this Board. But as we perceive a system to be adopted and steadily pursued, which evidently tends to annihilate the powers and usefulness of the Executive part of government, our duty to our constituents, and a due respect to the sacred obligations we have entered into, oblige us to speak with freedom, and to declare that as we will never make a voluntary surrender of our privileges, so we will not tamely and silently submit to any invasion of them. In the station assigned us in the government we do not apprehend ourselves obliged to take notice of any deviations from the Constitution which do not touch our own rights; but of these we conceive ourselves, in the first instance, the special and natural guardians, and when we can no otherwise prevent Legislative encroachments it is our duty at least to make a solemn appeal to the people, our mutual constituents, the true source and fountain from whence all our authority is derived. When the Constitution of this State placed the Legislative power in a single branch, with certain checks upon rash and hasty determination, it was never supposed that any House of Assembly would by special laws made for the purpose, assume the Executive powers, and by blending Legislative and Executive, unite what the Constitution had wisely and decisively separated; much less that such laws should pass without even a decent regard to those salutary restraints of time and publication, which were intended to provide against intemperate and indigested measures. It has been one of the greatest objections made to this Constitution, that it has left too little power in the Executive branch; and yet we see daily attempts to make that little less. We cannot suppose that it is intended practically to shew the people what mischief and abuse a single Legislature may do, and yet we are at a loss otherwise to account for those proceedings which are particularly the objects of this message.

The communication then proceeds to specify the acts in question which had produced this vigorous protest. In the first place the salaries of the judges had been reduced, with the effect, as the council demonstrated, to "make them dependent upon the Assembly for their daily subsistence, and subject them to the strongest temptations of yielding to every veering gale of politics or party." "We conceive," they continue,

> the independence of the Judges, both of the Executive and Legislative, as a point of the greatest importance to the good people of the State, and as their commissions are for seven years, unless convicted of misbehavior, it is clear that their support ought to be equally fixed and irrevocable during that period.

Again, the assembly had drawn money directly from the treasury by officers other than the council, to whom the power had been given by the constitution.

> The giving this power to any other persons, by a special law, is a violation of the Constitutional privileges of the Council—an

unjust and unnecessary wound to their feelings, and calculated to lessen their influence and utility.

Special commissioners, the message shows, had been appointed with powers to draw upon the treasury and to manage and conduct the defence of the Delaware. The fact that the constitution expressly declared that it was the right and duty of the council to expedite the measures of the assembly was ignored, inasmuch as the law expressly provided that "other persons [should] expedite the execution of [legislative] measures." This action, the council declares,

> plainly encroaches on the rights of the people, who have elected you for the purpose of devising measures, and us for that of executing them; and so far as we attempt to legislate or you to execute, so far we depart from the principles of the Constitution, usurp the rights of each other, and do injustice to the people.

Another law removed the incumbents of the office of auctioneer without any complaints being lodged against them. "We cannot but consider it as a part of a system to increase your own power and lessen the weight of the Council in the eyes of the world." The council's judgment was doubtless correct.

In short, in actual operation, these first state constitutions produced what was tantamount to legislative omnipotence. The executive departments, constitutionally weak, proved even weaker in actual practice, since they were defenceless. The legislatures kept them under close supervision and control, interfered with them in their constitutional spheres, dictated to them what they should do by laws which they were unable to oppose. Separation of powers, whatever formal adherence was given the principle in bills of rights, meant the subordinate executive carrying out the legislative will.

We have excepted the constitution of New York from this discussion because of the very different state of things that resulted in that commonwealth. It is to be noted that the constitution was not completed immediately upon the outbreak of the war, going into effect only in the early spring of 1777. Governmental experience in neighboring states and in the national government had had an opportunity to make itself felt, an influence which could have reached New York, even though it did not affect, as it manifestly did not, the constitutions of South Carolina and Georgia, made in 1777 and 1778 respectively. It is also to be noted that the dangerous nature of the military situation of the state, the conservative nature of its population, and the fact that the individuals most influential in the construction of the constitution, Jay, Livingston and Gouverneur Morris, were, and remained, leading conservatives were all factors which contributed to establish a feasible assumption that the cause of executive strength would fare better here than in the other new states.

An analysis of the executive provisions of the constitution confirms this assumption. An extremely important departure in this direction is found in the fact that the executive department was made to consist of a governor in whom was vested "the supreme executive power and authority of the State." There was no privy council of the kind set up elsewhere in America, the sole remnants of the idea being found in the senatorial council of appointment and the council of revision.

It will be admitted that the addition of a senatorial council in the one case, and of a certain number of judges in the other, savors of that jealousy of the executive already observed. But it is easy to overemphasize this aspect of the matter. With the exception of the Maryland governor, the tool of the legislature and the executive council, and of the Pennsylvania council, which had proved so feeble, the power of appointment was uniformly in the possession of the legislature or the people. Nowhere, except in the temporary South Carolina government of 1776, was the veto power admitted. Nor is

evidence lacking, indeed, that the admixture of the judges sprang from a different source than executive jealousy, namely, a proposal to allow judges a seat in the Senate. At any rate, there was a very great difference between the privy council idea and that of the individual executive who should possess the whole executive power, subject to the participation of other members of the government in the exercise of two functions only. For the first time we have a real example of the single executive head.

Nor was the step taken without a purpose. The first draft of the constitution provided for an executive entirely of the same kind as those of the other states. But the conservatives delayed completion of the document and mustered strength enough to eliminate the privy council entirely, while, at the same time, making important additions to the governor's powers.

These powers were far more completely defined and more extensive than those in any other constitution save that of Pennsylvania, from which many of them were taken. The relevant portions of the constitution were as follows:

Art. XVIII. . . . The governor . . . shall by virtue of his office, be general and commander in chief of all the militia, and admiral of the navy of this state; . . . he shall have power to convene the assembly and senate on extraordinary occasions; to prorogue them from time to time, provided such prorogations shall not exceed sixty days in the space of any one year; and, at his discretion, to grant reprieves and pardons to persons convicted of crimes, other than treason and murder, in which he may suspend the execution of the sentence, until it shall be reported to the legislature at their subsequent meeting: and they shall either pardon or direct the execution of the criminal, or grant a further reprieve.

Art. XIX. . . . It shall be the duty of the governor to inform the legislature at every session of the condition of the state so far as may concern his department; to recommend such matters to their consideration as shall appear to him to concern its good government, welfare, and prosperity;

to correspond with the Continental Congress and other States; to transact all necessary business with the officers of government, civil and military; to take care that the laws are executed to the best of his ability; and to expedite all such measures as may be resolved upon by the legislature.

To these, of course, are to be added the important powers of qualified appointment and qualified veto. It is to be observed also that there is no question of the interposition of the law of the land to regulate these powers. They are the governor's, by direct grant of the people, and his alone.

Another distinguishing characteristic, equally important, is the fact that the governor was to be chosen by a constitutionally defined electorate, not by the legislature. He was also to have a three-year term, and there were to be no limitations on his reeligibility to office. In short, all the isolated principles of executive strength in other constitutions were here brought into a new whole. Alone they were of slight importance; gathered together they gain new meaning. And, in addition, we have new elements of strength utilized for the first time on the American continent.

The proof of the pudding is the eating, and the New York constitution stands the test. For the first eighteen years of its existence the chief magistracy was in the hands of one man, George Clinton. From the standpoint of executive vigor, it could not have been in better, for he was, as Governor Morris characterized him, a man "who had an aversion to councils, because, to use his own words, the duty of looking out for danger makes men cowards."

The spirit of his long administration found prophetic expression in his first gubernatorial message to the legislative houses:

> The late convention, having in their plan of government, manifested the most scrupulous attention to the freedom and happiness of the people, and by marking the line between the Executive, Legislative and Judicial powers, wisely provided for

the security of each, it becomes our duty to second their endeavors; and as our conduct will in some measure be a rule for those who are hereafter entrusted with the administration of government, let us remain within the several departments in which the constitution has placed us, and thereby preserve the same inviolate, and repay the trust reposed in us by our constituents, when they made us the guardians of their rights.

> I do not urge this, gentlemen, because I conceive the caution necessary to you; but to shew you the important light in which I see this object, and to convince you (however unequal I may find myself for the task) that it shall always be my strenuous endeavor, on the one hand, to retain and exercise for the advantage of the people the powers with which they have invested me; on the other, carefully to avoid the invasions of the rights which the constitution has placed in other persons.

A study of the Clinton Papers, the gubernatorial messages to the legislature and the records of the council of revision reveals that Clinton kept his word. From the time when he exercised his independent control over the militia to rush reinforcements to relieve the critical military situation that existed when he was sworn into office (July 30, 1977), until he surrendered the reins of office, his administration was characterized by a vigorous use of the powers with which the constitution invested him. He constantly suggested matters for legislative action, and generally laws were passed in accordance with his suggestions. When the evacuation of New York left the southern part of the state without government, his actions in the direction of restoring and maintaining law and order were of such a kind that even Alexander Hamilton, in a caustic campaign attack, found in them little to criticise. A legislature that threatened to surrender what he regarded as New York's just claims in the Vermont region was threatened with proroguement. The so-called "Doctors' Riots" in New York City were put down by the militia, and remnants of Shay's insurrectionists who fled to New York were routed out. And, what was more important still, as a member of the council of revision, Clinton joined in vetoing no fewer than fifty-eight legislative enactments in the ten years prior to the convening of the federal convention alone.

While thus abating no whit the ideals of executive power which he had enunciated in his first message, Clinton was able at the same time to rise to the position of dominating the political life of the whole state, and this despite the fact that he lacked the support of the most influential leaders of the state, such as Schuyler, Hamilton, Jay and Morris. The vigor, as well as the lack of success, of the campaigns of 1789 and 1792 testify to the importance that the office had attained in the constitutional system and political life of the state. One need only read the campaign documents prepared against Clinton by Hamilton in 1789 to see the evident importance that the author of them attached to the office, as one needs only follow the course of the anti-impost, anti-national party in New York prior to 1787 to understand that it was Clinton who was its head and front. "It is seriously to be deplored," Hamilton wrote,

> that dissension reigns in the most important departments of the State, and as dissensions among brethren, so destructive to the happiness of families, are often appeased by parental influence, so there is good reason to flatter ourselves that a Chief Magistrate, sincerely desirous of re-establishing concord, may without much difficulty effect it, especially if he should owe his exaltation to the votes of both contending parties.

One doubts whether the parental comparison could, or would, have been used in any other commonwealth on the continent.

In fact, by 1789 Hamilton was ready to charge that the governor had, through the control that he exercised over the council of appointment, built up a party machine that enabled him to retain his hold on the office and at the same time control, in large measure, the legislative branch. Modern researches have disproved this charge to a considerable degree, and doubtless Hamilton's accounts were exaggerated for party purposes, but one can not fail to see the significance of the fact that the charges could be made with at least a show of reasonableness, nor to believe that, in a day when clamor for public office was the equal of any that has since been known, the control of the patronage could have failed to be of tremendous influence. It was to experience, at any rate, that Hamilton appealed when he wrote:

> Whether an improper or excessive influence has in fact been derived from the use of that engine [the council of appointment], those who have been attentive to the progress of public affairs must decide for themselves. Appearances must be carefully consulted, and if there are instances in which members of the Legislature have been seen to change one party or system disagreeable to the Governor, for another system agreeable to him, and if that change of conduct, has been observed to be speedily followed by the reception of lucrative appointment the conclusion from such a fact would be irresistible.

As effective a weapon in maintaining the independence of the executive as the patronage was the veto power, a power which the council exercised in full accord with the spirit of the constitution. The constitutional reason assigned for its creation was because "laws inconsistent with the spirit of this constitution or with the public good may be hastily or inadvisedly passed." With this constitutional justification, the council proceeded to object to laws on either ground with complete freedom. By far the larger portion of these objections were, however, based on constitutional reasons. The result was that in New York alone, prior to 1787, there was built up a body of constitutional interpretation, in which, indeed, may be found some of the most important of American constitutional principles.

The importance of this can be hardly overrated. For the first time we have in practice a legislature actually limited by the constitution. Constitutional limitations become something more than pious wishes, and constitutional provisions for separation of powers pass from the realm of governmental theory into positive law. The executive and judiciary gained in proportion as the legislature lost. The interests of both were enlisted in keeping the legislature in bounds, and there is no evidence of friction.

The practical value of the veto obtained one striking illustration. One complaint of the Pennsylvania executive council had been, as we have seen, that the legislature created special bodies to which were assigned various functions vested by the constitution in the council, and which were independent of it. This was carried out in New York on a large scale immediately after the inauguration of the new government. The recently convened legislature resolved itself into a convention and created a council of safety, of which the governor was only a member with a casting vote. In this council it vested practically unlimited and uncontrolled power and adjourned.

The new government, in an almost unorganized condition, was unable to prevent this highly unconstitutional procedure. As soon as possible, however, the governor reconvened the legislature, though not without objections from at least one member of the council, and restored the regular constitutional processes.

The council of revision made vigorous attempts to prevent the recognition of the legal validity of any action of this irregular body, but the legislature overruled them. The day of the executive was yet to come. In 1780 a second attempt was made to create a council with both legislative and executive powers. The council promptly vetoed the measure, and this time were upheld.

The constitutional reasons assigned for this veto were of the utmost significance. They were:

Because to take the several measures in the bill directed to be taken, the person administering the Government, with the Council therein provided, must exercise the power of legislation; which, by the Constitution, is vested in the Senate and Assembly, and cannot by them be delegated to others. 2nd. Because the person administering the government is by the bill subjected in the exercise of his office, to the control of a Council, when by the Constitution, it is expressly ordained, determined, and declared, *that the supreme executive power and authority of this State shall be vested in a Governor.*

Constitutional government in New York and constitutional government elsewhere thus meant quite different things. In the other states we find legislative supremacy, executive subordination, a non-controlling constitution. Whatever the theory, there was legislative omnipotence of exactly the type found today in continental countries possessing written constitutions. The legislature was sovereign. In New York the council of revision made the constitution, in reality as in theory, a controlling instrument, the people's charter to government. Executive independence and executive equality with the legislature became a fact. The one man who possessed the executive powers vested in him by the constitution exercised them in accordance with his own judgment. Since he gave satisfaction to the people, he was returned to office. With the power of popular approval and the patronage at his disposal, he was able to become the dominant political force in political life, until by the period of the making of the federal Constitution possession of the governor's chair and control of state policy had become synonymous. In short, here was a strictly indigenous and entirely distinctive constitutional system, and, of course, executive department, for the consideration of the Philadelphia delegates.

It was an easier task for this concept of executive power to take root in conservative New York than in two such typical New England commonwealths as Massachusetts and New Hampshire, especially since in both the completed constitutions were submitted for popular ratification. It is the more significant, consequently, that even there a distinctive trend towards executive strength is observable.

At the outset of the Revolution, Massachusetts had been content to revert to the governmental forms provided by its suspended charter. Since there was no longer a royal governor, executive power was placed in the hands of a council of twenty-eight.

The success of this body was but slight. A contemporary observer described the situation as follows:

> There is great expectation of a new form of government in our state. I hope it will be a good one, and an executive power will be lodged somewhere; at present, if there is any, you would be puzzled to find it; hence the chariot wheels drive so slowly.

These expectations were, however, grievously disappointed. The concept of a strong executive was evidently no favorite of those responsible for the document submitted by the convention in 1778 for popular ratification. Election was to be by the voters, but with this exception, all of the familiar evidences of jealousy of the executive were included. The governor was to hold office for only a single year. He was to be controlled in the exercise of his functions by the upper chamber or the legislature as a whole. He was, for example, to exercise the military power "according to the laws . . . or the resolves of the General Court," while the advice of the senate was required to call extra sessions, declare embargoes, or make such appointments as were placed in executive hands. When the advice of the senate was required, the governor had only a single vote. The pardon power was vested in the governor, the lieutenant-governor and the speaker. There was no provision for a veto power, or any other organic control of the legislature.

But this constitution failed of ratification, and in the process of rejection the various towns drafted addresses in which were included the objections which led to their action, and also constructive recommendations of principles which they desired to see embodied in a new instrument. Easily the most important of these was the so-called "Essex Result." This document, from the pen of a future state chief justice, may be fairly considered as representative of conservative Massachusetts opinion.

Its criticisms of the proposed executive department are illuminating. It was objected that the governor ought not to be a member of the senate (he was its president); that the property qualifications of the office were too low; that the executive powers were too small; that the senate's control over the executive was improper—in the words of the Result, "the supreme executive office is not vested with sufficient authority . . . and an independence between the executive and legislative authority is not preserved"; that the method of making appointments was exceptionable; and that the pardon power was improperly divided.

The positive recommendations of the Result were moderate, but significant. The participation of the senate as such in the business of the executive department should be eliminated, but in its place an advisory privy council should be installed. The governor should possess the power to appoint and remove all militia officers. Subject to the advice of his council, he should have complete control of calling the armed forces into service and of regulating them. The appointing power of the governor should be extended to include judges and the attorney general. And, most important of all, the veto power should be given him.

The arguments in behalf of these changes will illustrate the influence of the experience of those states which enjoyed the doubtful blessing of uncontrolled popular assemblies. Full quotations seem justified. Concerning the veto power, the Result argued as follows:

> We now want only to give the executive power a check upon the legislative, to prevent the latter from encroaching on the former and stripping it of all its rights. The legislative in all states hath attempted it where this check was wanting, and have prevailed, and the freedom of the state was thereby destroyed. This attempt has resulted from that lust of domination, which in some degree influences all men, and all bodies of men. The Governor therefore with the consent of the privy council, may negative any law, proposed to be enacted by the legislative body. The advantages which will attend the due use of this negative are, that thereby the executive power will be preserved entire—the encroachments of the legislative will be repelled, and the powers of both properly balanced. All the business of the legislative body will be brought to one point, and subject to an impartial consideration on a regular consistent plan. As the Governor will have it in his charge to state the situation of the government to the legislative body at the opening of every session, as far as his information will qualify him, therefore, he will now know officially all that has been done, with what design the laws were enacted, how far they have answered the purposed end, and what still remains to compleat the intention of the legislative body. The reasons why he will not make an improper use of his negative are—his annual election—the annual election of the privy council, by and out of the legislative body—His political character and honor are at stake—If he makes a proper use of his negative by preserving the executive powers entire, by pointing out any mistake in the laws which may escape any body of men through inattention, he will have the smiles of the people. If on the contrary, he makes an improper use of his negative and wantonly opposes a law that is for the public good, his reputation, and that of his privy council are forfeited, and they are disgracefully tumbled from their seats. This Governor is not appointed by a King, or his ministry, nor does he receive instructions from a party of men, who are pursuing an interest diametrically opposite to the good of the state; and he knows he must soon return and sink to a level with the rest of the community. The danger is he will be too cautious of using his negative in the interest of the state. His fear of offending may prompt him, if he is a timid man, to yield up some parts of his executive powers.

The arguments for gubernatorial control of the militia and exercise of the power of appointment are equally illuminating:

> Was one to propose a body of militia, over which two Generals, with equal authority, should have command, he would be laughed at. Should one pretend, that the General should have no control over his subordinate officers, either to remove them or to supply their posts, he would be pitied for his ignorance of the subject he was discussing. It is obviously necessary, that the man who calls the militia to action, and assumes the military controul of them in the field, should precisely know the number of his men, their equipments and residence, and the talents and tempers of the several ranks of officers, and their respective departments in the State, that he may wisely determine to whom the necessary orders are to be issued. Regular and particular returns of these requisites should be frequently made. Let it be inquired, are these returns to be made only to the legislative body, or a branch of it, which necessarily moves slow?—Is the General to go to them for information? intreat them to remove an improper officer, and give him another they shall chuse? and in fine is he to supplicate his orders from them, and constantly walk where their leading-strings shall direct his steps? If so, where are the power and force of the militia—where the union—where the despatch and profound secrecy? Or shall these returns be made to him? when he may see with his own eyes—be his own judge of the merit, or demerit of his officers—discern their various talents and qualifications, and employ them as the service and defence of his country demand. . . . It may be further observed here that if the subordinate civil or military executive officers are appointed by the legislative body or a branch of it, the former will become dependent upon the latter, and the necessary independence of either the legislative or executive powers upon the other is wanting. The legislative power will have that undue influence over the executive which will amount to a controul, for the latter will be their creatures, and will fear their creators.

Such is the temper of mankind, that each man will be liable to introduce his own friends and connexions into office, without regarding the public interest. If one man or a small number appoint, their connexions will probably be introduced. If a large number appoint, all their connexions will receive the same favour. The smaller the number appointing, the more contracted their connexions, and for that reason, there will be a greater probability of better officers, as the connexions of one man or a very small number can fill but a very few of the offices. When a small number of men have the appointment, or the management in any particular department, their conduct is accurately noticed. On any miscarriage or imprudence the public resentment lies with weight. All the eyes of the people are converted to a point, and produce that attention to their censure, and the fear of misbehavior which are the greatest security the state can have, of the wisdom and prudence of its servants. This observation will strike us when we recollect that many a man will zealously promote an affair in a public assembly, of which he is but one of a large number, yet, at the same time, he would blush to be thought the sole author of it. For all these reasons, the supreme executive power should be rested in the hands of a small number, who should have the appointment of all subordinate executive officers.

The constitution finally adopted in 1780 embodied many of the conservative ideas of the New York constitution in respect to executive strength. Annual choice by the voters, a privy council "for advising the governor in the executive part of the government," and for "ordering and directing the affairs of the commonwealth, according to the laws of the land," the possession by the governor of the military powers, subject to the law, of the pardon power, a considerable portion of the civil appointing power, and, most important of all, the qualified veto power,—these were the chief features of the new executive. It was evidently a compromise product of conservative wishes and popular prejudices.

The same rise in prestige in the executive department in conservative circles which is apparent in Massachusetts is revealed by the constitutional history of New Hampshire, and also the same enduring popular jealousy of the chief magistrate. In January, 1776, temporary governmental arrangements—there was nothing that deserves the name constitution—were made, which included no formal provision for an executive department at all, the omission being supplied by an extra-constitutional council of safety. As in Massachusetts, this worked badly. The expense of so large a body and "the delay necessarily occasioned by the business of the executive department being intrusted to so great a number of persons, have been too sensibly felt to require arguments on our part, to convince you that an alteration in this respect will promote the interest of every individual in the community," declared one of the addresses that accompanied a proposed constitution.

Exactly the same note was struck by these addresses as in the Essex Result. The growing importance of a well-constructed executive department is eloquently evidenced, for example, in the following excerpt, in which it was declared to the voters:

This power is the active principle of all governments: it is the soul, and without it the body politic is but a dead corpse. Its department is to put in execution all the laws enacted by the legislative body. It ought, therefore, to have the appointment of all the civil officers of the State. It is at the head of the militia, and therefore should have equally the appointment of all the military officers within the same. Its characteristic requisites are secrecy, vigour, and despatch. The fewer persons, therefore, this supreme power is trusted with, the greater probability there is that these requisites will be found. The convention, therefore, on the maturest deliberation, have thought it best to lodge this power in the hands of one, whom they have stiled the GOVERNOR. They have, indeed, array'd him with honours, they have armed him with power, and set him on high. But still he is only the right hand of *your* power, and the mirror of *your* majesty. Every possible provision is made to guard against the abuse of this high be-trustment and protect the rights of the people. He can take no one step of importance without the advice of his privy-council; and he is elected annually. But as this was too little, no one person is capable of being elected oftener than three years in seven. Every necessary and useful qualification is required in him, in point of age, religion, residency, and fortune. In addition to all which, he is liable for every misconduct to be impeached, tried, and displaced, by the two legislative branches; and is amenable to the laws besides, equally with the meanest subject of the State. Thus controlled and checked against himself the Convention thought it reasonable and necessary, that he, in turn, should have the right of objecting to and suspending, tho' not the absolute control over the acts of that body; which they thought indispensably necessary to repel any encroachments on the executive power, and preserve its independency.

Democratic forces in New Hampshire were too strong to permit either the adoption of the veto clause or even the retention of so hated a title as that of Governor. For the rest, ultimately the provisions of the Massachusetts constitution were adopted. But in conservative circles new language was being spoken concerning the importance of the executive, the desirability of one-man rule, and the role of this individual executive in state life.

The experiences with the state governments during the period following the cessation of hostilities served further to confirm these tendencies towards increasing confidence in the executive and increasing distrust of the legislature. A review of those practical factors enumerated . . . as the active causes of the convening of the Philadelphia convention reveals the state legislatures as the main instruments of evil. It was these bodies which had originated and multiplied most of the difficulties which the Constitution was intended to remedy. From them came the paper money and debtor laws. It was also they who adopted the retaliatory commercial restrictions which played havoc with

commercial prosperity. Especially was it true that the lower house proved the stronghold of the popular party.

The experience of Massachusetts during the insurrection is a case in point. Governor Bowdoin acquitted himself well, from the standpoint of the conservatives. His executive measures were vigorous, albeit moderate. The senate supported the action of the executive wholeheartedly, but the house of representatives proved a haven of refuge for the discontented. To this effect writes the contemporary historian of the insurrection:

While the Supreme Executive was employed in making the necessary military arrangements, for supporting the administration of justice, the House of Representatives remained in the same pacifick disposition towards the insurgents. Nothing of consequence was suffered to pass them, but what was connected with the grievances of the people. . . . Such delays taking place in the effecting of a vigorous system for the authority of the laws, occasioned very great alarms among those who were most opposed to the insurrections. . . . They began to lose confidence in the General Court, and to wish that means might be found to adjourn them, before the publick cause should be injured by a feeble system, which might tend to hold up their divisions and want of energy.

There also began to arise another class of men in the community, who gave very serious apprehensions to the advocates of a republican form of government. These, though few in number, and but the seeds of a party, consisted of persons respectable for their literature and their wealth. They . . . were almost ready to assent to a revolution, in hopes of erecting a political system, more braced than the present, and better calculated, in their opinions, to promote the peace and happiness of the citizens.

Indeed, the injustice, mutability and multiplicity of state laws brought home to the conservatives even the truth, which Mill was subsequently to elucidate, that legislative bodies are incompetent legislators. In his thoughtful analysis of the causes of the second revolution, Madison wrote:

As far as the laws are necessary to mark with precision the duties of those who obey them and to take from those who are to administer them a discretion which might be abused, their number is the price of liberty. As far as they exceed this limit, they are a nuisance, a nuisance of the most persistent kind. Try the Codes of the several States by this test, and what a luxuriancy of legislation do they present. The short period of independency has filled as many pages as the century which preceded it. Every year almost every session adds a new volume. . . .

We daily see laws repealed or superseded, before any trial can have been made their merits, and even before a knowledge of them can have reached the remoter districts within which they are to operate.

The spoliation of the "College" in Pennsylvania and the bitter attack on the Bank of North America indicated only too well the animus of many of these laws, namely, the destruction of vested interests. The following tax law of New York, of whose purpose we may approve, points in the same direction, and shows even more plainly the validity of the complaints against the legislature:

Whereas, many persons in this State, *taking advantage* of the necessities of this country, *have,* in prosecuting their private gain, amassed *large sums* of money to the great prejudice of the public, and ought therefore to pay an extraordinary tax, and it will be impossible for the assessors, with any degree of certainty, to ascertain the profits made by such persons in manner aforesaid, be it therefore enacted . . . that the assessors shall . . . assess *all such persons* . . . at such rates . . . as they, the assessors shall . . . think proper.

John Marshall could well say, with customary lucidity:

In the state governments generally no principle had been introduced which could resist the wild projects of the moment, give the people an opportunity to reflect, and allow the good sense of the nation time for exertion. The uncertainty with respect to measures of great importance to every member of the community, the instability of principles which ought if possible to be rendered immutable produced a

long train of ills. . . . The direct consequence was the loss of confidence in the government and in individuals.

Executive strength was such a principle. This was, in fact, the chief teaching of state experience. It could not have been otherwise, for the cause of executive power and executive independence had been too often identified with the cause of representative government as opposed to the rule of popular committees, with the cause of orderly governmental processes as opposed to legislative disregard of constitutional principles, with, and this was vital, the whole cause of property and established rights, for that department not to rise in the scale of conservative esteem. In short, the change of emphasis from liberty to authority had meant a corresponding change of emphasis from the legislature to the executive.

State experience thus contributed, nothing more strongly, to discredit the whole idea of the sovereign legislature, to bring home the real meaning of limited government and coordinate powers. The idea, more than once utilized as the basis of the explanation of Article II of the Constitution, that the jealousy of kingship was a controlling force in the federal convention, is far, very far, from the truth. The majority of the delegates brought with them no far-reaching distrust of executive power, but rather a sobering consciousness that, if their new plan should succeed, it was necessary for them to put forth their best efforts to secure a strong, albeit safe, national executive.

Madison but expressed the general conservative view when he declared on the convention floor:

Experience had proved a tendency in our governments to throw all power into the legislative vortex. The Executives of the States are in general little more than cyphers; the legislatures omnipotent. If no effective check be devised for restraining the instability and encroachment of the latter, a revolution of some kind or the other would be inevitable. The preservation of Republican Government therefore required some expedient for the purpose, but required evidently that in devising it the genuine principles of that form should be kept in view.

With the exception of the New York executive and, with reservations, that of Massachusetts, the state executive was, it is evident, in no sense of the word a model to be followed in the creation of the national executive. A meticulous calculation of the proportion of state constitutions granting this or that presidential power to their chief magistrate does not at all affect the truth of this statement. The conservatives desired something besides a mere cypher for a national executive.

And yet state experience had a definite, positive value. It taught that executive energy and responsibility are inversely proportional to executive size; that, consequently, the one-man executive is best. It taught the value of integration; the necessity of executive appointments, civil and military; the futility of legislative military control. It demonstrated the necessity for the veto as a protective measure. It showed that this power could be utilized as a means of preventing unwise legislation. It even, if we accept the argument of the Essex Result, revealed the desirability of bringing legislative business into a single whole by the executive department. It demonstrated the value of a fixed executive salary which the legislature could not reduce. It discredited choice by the legislature, though without teaching clearly the lesson of popular choice, for, after all, the people chose a Clinton instead of a Schuyler and replaced a Bowdoin by a Hancock. And, above all, it assured the acceptance of, if it did not create, a new concept of constitutional government—the fundamental principles of which were the ruling constitution, the limited legislature, and the three equal and coordinate departments.

There is no need to point out that the New York governorship in large measure fulfilled the requirements of the concept thus attained. The relatively fixed constitutional principles of that state, a result chiefly of the Council of Revision's action, and of its vigorous, dominating executive, known only too well to the leaders of the national party, caused it quite generally to be accepted as the best of the state governments. Here, and here only, was a satisfactory model.

It was in significant language that John Jay, from the midst of the turbulence of Pennsylvania's political life, expressed to the chief executive of his state this approval:

The exceeding high opinion entertained here of your Constitution and the wisdom of your Counsels, has made a deep impression on many People of wealth and Consequence in this State, who are dissatisfied with their own; and unless their opinions should previously be changed, will remove to New York the moment the Enemy leave it. Mr. Gerard (who seems better acquainted with Republics than almost any man I have ever known) has passed many Enconiums on our Constitution & Government, and I am persuaded no Circumstance will conduce more to the Population of our Country by migrations from others, than the Preservation of its vigor and Reputation.

This unhappy city is all Confusion; the Government wants nerves, and the public Peace has for some Days been destroyed by mobs and Riots which seem to defy the authority of the magistrate. This is one of the Fruits of their whimsical Constitution, and of the Countenance given to Committees & let Politicians learn from this, to dread the least Deviation from the Line of Constitutional authority. *Obsta principiis,* is a good maxim, but all have not sufficient Decision in their conduct to observe it. Government once relaxed is not easily braced. And it is far more difficult to reassume Powers than permit them to be taken and executed by those who have no right by the Constitution to hold them.

2. James Madison to Thomas Jefferson*

JAMES MADISON

NEW YORK, OCTOBER 24, 1787

You will herewith receive the result of the Convention, which continued its session till the 17th of September. I take the liberty of making some observations on the subject, which will help to make up a letter, if they should answer no other purpose. . . .

This ground-work being laid, the great objects which presented themselves were:

(1) to unite a proper energy in the Executive, and a proper stability in the Legislative departments, with the essential characters of Republican Government;

(2) to draw a line of demarkation which would give to the General Government every power requisite for general purposes, and leave to the States every power which might be most beneficially administered by them;

(3) to provide for the different interests of different parts of the Union;

(4) to adjust the clashing pretensions of the large and small States.

Each of these objects was pregnant with difficulties. The whole of them together formed a task more difficult than can be well conceived by those who were not concerned in the execution of it. Adding to these considerations the natural diversity of human opinions on all new and complicated subjects, it is impossible to consider the degree of concord which ultimately prevailed as less than a miracle.

The first of these objects, as respects the Executive, was peculiarly embarrassing. On the question whether it should consist of a single person, or a plurality of co-ordinate members, on the mode of appointment, on the duration in office, on the degree of power, on the re-eligibility, tedious and reiterated discussions took place. The plurality of co-ordinate members had finally but few advocates. Governour Randolph was at the head of them. The modes of appointment proposed were various, as by the people at large—by electors chosen by the people—by the Executives of the States—by the Congress, some preferring a joint ballot of the two Houses—some a separate concurrent ballot, allowing to each a negative on the other house—some, a nomination of several candidates by one House, out of whom a choice should be made by the other. Several other modifications were started. The expedient at length adopted seemed to give pretty general satisfaction to the members. As to the duration in office, a few would have preferred a tenure during good behaviour—a considerable number would have done so in case an easy & effectual removal by impeachment could be settled. It was much agitated whether a long term, seven years for example, with a subsequent & perpetual ineligibility, or a short term with a capacity to be re-elected, should be fixed. In favor of the first opinion were urged the danger of a gradual degeneracy of re-elections from time to time, into first a life and then a hereditary tenure, and the favorable effect of an incapacity to be reappointed

*Source: Excerpted from The Records of the Federal Convention of 1787, by Max Ferrand, vol. 3, pp. 131-33, New Haven, Conn.: Yale University Press. Copyright © 1966 by Yale University; © 1911, 1937 by Yale University Press. Reprinted by permission.

on the independent exercise of the Executive authority. On the other side it was contended that the prospect of necessary degradation would discourage the most dignified characters from aspiring to the office, would take away the principal motive to ye faithful discharge of its duties—the hope of being rewarded with a reappointment would stimulate ambition to violent efforts for holding over the Constitutional term—and instead of producing an independent administration, and a firmer defence of the constitutional rights of the department, would render the officer more indifferent to the importance of a place which he would soon be obliged to quit forever, and more ready to yield to the encroachmts. of the Legislature of which he might again be a member. The questions concerning the degree of power turned chiefly on the appointment to offices, and the controul on the Legislature. An *absolute* appointment to all offices—to some offices—to no offices, formed the scale of opinions on the first point. On the second, some contended for an absolute negative, as the only possible mean of reducing to practice the theory of a free Government which forbids a mixture of the Legislative & Executive powers. Others would be content with a revisionary power, to be overruled by three fourths of both Houses. It was warmly urged that the judiciary department should be associated in the revision. The idea of some was that a separate revision should be given to the two departments—that if either objected two thirds, if both, three fourths, should be necessary to overrule.

3. To the Citizens of the State of New York*

GEORGE CLINTON

NOVEMBER 8, 1787

Admitting, however, that the vast extent of America, together with the various other reasons which I offered you in my last number, against the practicability of the just exercise of the new government are insufficient to convince; still it is an undesirable truth, that its several parts are either possessed of principles, which you have heretofore considered as ruinous and that others are omitted which you have established as fundamental to your political security, and must in their operation, I will venture to assert, fetter your tongues and minds, enchain your bodies, and ultimately extinguish all that is great and noble in man.

In pursuance of my plan I shall begin with observations on the executive branch of this new system; and though it is not the first in order, as arranged therein, yet being the *chief*, is perhaps entitled by the rules of rank to the first consideration. The executive power as described in the 2d article, consists of a president and vice-president, who are to hold their offices during the term of four years; the same article has marked the manner and time of their election, and established the qualifications of the president; it also provides against the

---

removal, death, or inability of the president and vice-president—regulates the salary of the president, delineates his duties and powers; and, lastly, declares the causes for which the president and vice-president shall be removed from office.

Notwithstanding the great learning and abilities of the gentlemen who composed the convention, it may be here remarked with deference, that the construction of the first paragraph of the first section of the second article is vague and inexplicit, and leaves the mind in doubt as to the election of a president and vice-president, after the expiration of the election for the first term of four years; in every other case, the election of these great officers is expressly provided for; but there is no explicit provision for their election in case of expiration of their offices, subsequent to the election which is to set this political machine in motion; no certain and express terms as in your state constitution, that *statedly* once in every four years, and as often as these offices shall become vacant, by expiration or otherwise, as is therein expressed, an election shall be held as follows, &c., this inexplicitness perhaps may lead to an establishment for life.

It is remarked by Monesquieu, in treating of republics, that *in all magistracies, the greatness of the power must be compensated by the brevity of the duration, and that a longer time than a year would be dangerous.* It is, therefore, obvious to the least intelligent mind to account why great power in the hands of a magistrate, and that power connected with considerable duration, may be dangerous to the liberties of a republic, the deposit of vast trusts in the hands of a single magistrate, enables him in their exercise to create a numerous train of dependents; this tempts his *ambition,* which in a republican magistrate is also remarked, *to be pernicious,* and the duration of his office for any considerable time favors his views, gives him the means and time to perfect

and execute his designs, *he therefore fancies that he may be great and glorious by oppressing his fellow-citizens, and raising himself to permanent grandeur on the ruins of his country.* And here it may be necessary to compare the vast and important powers of the president, together with his continuance in office, with the foregoing doctrine—his eminent magisterial situation will attach many adherents to him, and he will be surrounded by expectants and courtiers, his power of nomination and influence on all appointments, the strong posts in each state comprised within his superintendence, and garrisoned by troops under his direction, his control over the army, militia, and navy, the unrestrained power of granting pardons for treason, which may be used to screen from punishment those whom he had secretly instigated to commit the crime, and thereby prevent a discovery of his own guilt, his duration in office for four years: these, and various other principles evidently prove the truth of the position, that if the president is possessed of ambition, he has power and time sufficient to ruin his country.

Though the president, during the sitting of the legislature, is assisted by the senate, yet he is without a constitutional council in their recess; he will therefore be unsupported by proper information and advice, and will generally be directed by minions and favorites, or a council of state will grow out of the principal officers of the great departments, the most dangerous council in a free country.

The ten miles square, which is to become the seat of government, will of course be the place of residence for the president and the great officers of state; the same observations of a great man will apply to the court of a president possessing the powers of a monarch, that is observed of that of a monarch— *ambition with idleness—baseness with pride—the thirst of riches without labor—aversion to truth—flattery— treason—perfidy—violation of engage-*

ments—contempt of civil duties—hope from the magistrate's weakness; but above all, the perpetual ridicule of virtue—these, he remarks, are the characteristics by which the courts in all ages have been distinguished.

The language and the manners of this court will be what distinguishes them from the rest of the community, not what assimilates them to it; and in being remarked for a behavior that shows they are not *meanly born,* and in adulation to people of fortune and power.

The establishment of a vice-president is as unnecessary as it is dangerous. This officer, for want of other employment, is made president of the senate, thereby blending the executive and legislative powers, besides always giving to some one state, from which he is to come, an unjust pre-eminence.

It is a maxim in republics that the representative of the people should be of their immediate choice; but by the manner in which the president is chosen, he arrives to this office at the fourth or fifth hand, nor does the highest vote, in the way he is elected, determine the choice, for it is only necessary that he should be taken from the highest of five, who may have a plurality of votes.

Compare your past opinions and sentiments with the present proposed establishment, and you will find, that if you adopt it, that it will lead you into a system which you heretofore reprobated as odious. Every American Whig, not long since, bore his emphatic testimony against a monarchical government, though limited, because of the dangerous inequality that it created among citizens as relative to their rights and property; and wherein does this president, invested with his powers and prerogatives, essentially differ from the king of Great Britain (save as to name, the creation of nobility, and some immaterial incidents, the offspring of absurdity and locality). The direct prerogatives of the president, as springing from his political character, are among the following: It is necessary, in order to distinguish him from the rest of the community, and enable him to keep, and maintain his court, that the compensation for his services, or in other words, his revenue, should be such as to enable him to appear with the splendor of a prince; he has the power of receiving ambassadors from, and a great influence on their appointments to foreign courts; as also to make treaties, leagues, and alliances with foreign states, assisted by the Senate, which when made become the supreme law of land: he is a constituent part of the legislative power, for every bill which shall pass the House of Representatives and Senate is to be presented to him for approbation; if he approves of it he is to sign it, if he disapproves he is to return it with objections, which in many cases will amount to a complete negative; and in this view he will have a great share in the power of making peace, coining money, etc., and all the various objects of legislation, expressed or implied in this Constitution: for though it may be asserted that the king of Great Britain has the express power of making peace or war, yet he never thinks it prudent to do so without the advice of his Parliament, from whom he is to derive his support, and therefore these powers, in both president and king, are substantially the same: he is the generalissimo of the nation, and of course has the command and control of the army, navy and militia; he is the general conservator of the peace of the union—he may pardon all offences, except in cases of impeachment, and the principal fountain of all offices and employments. Will not the exercise of these powers therefore tend either to the establishment of a vile and arbitrary aristocracy or monarchy? The safety of the people in a republic depends on the share or proportion they have in the government; but experience ought to teach you, that when a man is at the head of an elective government invested with great powers, and interested in his re-election, in what circle appointments will be made; by which means an *imperfect aristocracy* bordering on monarchy may be established.

You must, however, my countrymen, beware that the advocates of this new system do not deceive you by a fallacious resemblance between it and your own state government which you so much prize; and, if you examine, you will perceive that the chief magistrate of this state is your immediate choice, controlled and checked by a just and full representation of the people, divested of the prerogative of influencing war and peace, making treaties, receiving and sending embassies, and commanding standing armies and navies, which belong to the power of the confederation, and will be convinced that this government is no more like a true picture of your own than an Angel of Darkness resembles an Angel of Light.

November 22, 1787

In my last number I endeavored to prove that the language of the article relative to the establishment of the executive of this new government was vague and inexplicit; that the great powers of the president, connected with his duration in office, would lead to oppression and ruin; that he would be governed by favorites and flatterers, or that a dangerous council would be collected from the great officers of state; that the ten miles square, if the remarks of one of the wisest men, drawn from the experience of mankind, may be credited, would be the asylum of the base, idle, avaricious and ambitious, and that the court would possess a language and manners different from yours; that a vice-president is as unnecessary as he is dangerous in his influence; that the president cannot represent you because he is not of your own immediate choice; that if you adopt this government you will incline to an arbitrary and odious aristocracy or monarchy; that the president, possessed of the power given him by this frame of government, differs but very immaterially

from the establishment of monarchy in Great Britain; and I warned you to beware of the fallacious resemblance that is held out to you by the advocates of this new system between it and your own state governments.

And here I cannot help remarking that inexplicitness seems to pervade this whole political fabric; certainly in political compacts, which Mr. Coke calls *the mother and nurse of repose and quietness* the want of which induced men to engage in political society, has ever been held by a wise and free people as essential to their security; as on the one hand it fixes barriers which the ambitious and tyrannically disposed magistrate dare not overleap, and on the other, becomes a wall of safety to the community—otherwise stipulations between the governors and governed are nugatory; and you might as well deposit the important powers of legislation and execution in one or a few and permit them to govern according to their disposition and will; but the world is too full of examples, which prove that *to live by one man's will became the cause of all men's misery.* Before the existence of express political compacts it was reasonably implied that the magistrate should govern with wisdom and justice; but mere implication was too feeble to restrain the unbridled ambition of a bad man, or afford security against negligence, cruelty or any other defect of mind. It is alleged that the opinions and manners of the people of America are capable to resist and prevent an extension of prerogative or oppression, but you must recollect that opinion and manners are mutable, and may not always be a permanent obstruction against the encroachments of government; that the progress of a commercial society begets luxury, the parent of inequality, the foe to virtue, and the enemy to restraint; and that ambition and voluptuousness, aided by flattery, will teach magistrates where limits are not explicitly fixed to have separate and distinct interests from the people; besides, it will not be denied that government assimilates the manners and opinions of the community to it. Therefore, a general presumption that rulers will govern well is not a sufficient security. You are then under a sacred obligation to provide for the safety of your posterity, and would you now basely desert their interests, when by a small share of prudence you may transmit to them a beautiful political patrimony, which will prevent the necessity of their travelling through seas of blood to obtain that which your wisdom might have secured? It is a duty you owe likewise to your own reputation, for you have a great name to lose; you are characterized as cautious, prudent and jealous in politics; whence is it therefore that you are about to precipitate yourselves into a sea of uncertainty, and adopt a system so vague, and which has discarded so many of your valuable rights? Is it because you do not believe that an American can be a tyrant? If this be the case, you rest on a weak basis: Americans are like other men in similar situations, when the manners and opinions of the community are changed by the causes I mentioned before; and your political compact inexplicit, your posterity will find that great power connected with ambition, luxury and flattery, will as readily produce a Caesar, Caligula, Nero and Domitain in America, as the same causes did in the Roman Empire.

4. The Federalist, No. 69*

ALEXANDER HAMILTON

I proceed now to trace the real characters of the proposed executive, as they are marked out in the plan of the convention. This will serve to place in a strong light the unfairness of the representations which have been made in regard to it.

The first thing which strikes our attention is that the executive authority, with few exceptions, is to be vested in a single magistrate. This will scarcely, however, be considered as a point upon which any comparison can be grounded; for if, in this particular, there be a resemblance to the king of Great Britain, there is not less a resemblance to the Grand Seignior, to the khan of Tartary, to the Man of the Seven Mountains, or to the governor of New York.

That magistrate is to be elected for *four* years; and is to be re-eligible as often as the people of the United States shall think him worthy of their confidence. In these circumstances there is a total dissimilitude between *him* and a king of Great Britain, who is an *hereditary* monarch, possessing the crown as a patrimony descendible to his heirs forever; but there is a close analogy between *him* and a governor of New York, who is elected for *three* years, and is re-eligible without limitation or intermission. If we consider how much less time would be requisite for establishing a dangerous influence in a single state than for establishing a like influence throughout the United States, we must conclude that a duration of *four* years

*Source: This essay by "Publius" was originally published in the New York Packet, March 14, 1788.

for the chief magistrate of the Union is a degree of permanency far less to be dreaded in that office, than a duration of *three* years for a corresponding office in a single state.

The president of the United States would be liable to be impeached, tried, and, upon conviction of treason, bribery, or other high crimes or misdemeanors, removed from office; and would afterwards be liable to prosecution and punishment in the ordinary course of law. The person of the king of Great Britain is sacred and inviolable; there is no constitutional tribunal to which he is amenable; no punishment to which he can be subjected without involving the crisis of a national revolution. In this delicate and important circumstance of personal responsibility, the president of Confederated America would stand upon no better ground than a governor of New York, and upon worse ground than the governors of Virginia and Delaware.

The president of the United States is to have power to return a bill, which shall have passed the two branches of the legislature, for reconsideration; but the bill so returned is not to become a law unless, upon that reconsideration, it be approved by two thirds of both houses. The king of Great Britain, on his part, has an absolute negative upon the acts of the two houses of Parliament. The disuse of that power for a considerable time past does not affect the reality of its existence and is to be ascribed wholly to the crown's having found the means of substituting influence to authority, or the art of gaining a majority in one or the other of the two houses, to the necessity of exerting a prerogative which could seldom be exerted without hazarding some degree of national agitation. The qualified negative of the president differs widely from this absolute negative of the British sovereign and tallies exactly with the revisionary authority of the council of revision of this state, of which the governor is a constituent part. In this respect the power of the president would exceed that of the governor of New York, because the former would possess, singly, what the latter shares with the chancellor and judges; but it would be precisely the same with that of the governor of Massachusetts, whose constitution, as to this article, seems to have been the original from which the convention have copied.

The president is to be the

commander-in-chief of the army and navy of the United States, and of the militia of the several States, when called into the actual service of the United States. He is to have power to grant reprieves and pardons for offenses against the United States, *except in cases of impeachment;* to recommend to the consideration of Congress such measures as he shall judge necessary and expedient; to convene, on extraordinary occasions, both houses of the legislature, or either of them, and, in case of disagreement between them *with respect to the time of adjournment,* to adjourn them to such time as he shall think proper; to take care that the laws be faithfully executed; and to commission all officers of the United States.

In most of these particulars, the power of the president will resemble equally that of the king of Great Britain and of the governor of New York. The most material points of difference are these:

- *First.* The president will have only the occasional command of such part of the militia of the nation as by legislative provision may be called into the actual service of the Union. The king of Great Britain and the governor of New York have at all times the entire command of all the militia within their several jurisdictions. In this article, therefore, the power of the president would be inferior to that of either the monarch or the governor.

- *Second.* The president is to be commander-in-chief of the army and navy of the United States. In this respect his authority would be nominally the same with that of the king of Great Britain, but in substance much inferior to it. It would amount to nothing more than the supreme command and direction of the military and naval forces, as first general and admiral of the Confederacy; while that of the British king extends to the *declaring* of war and to the *raising* and *regulating* of fleets and armies—all which, by the Constitution under consideration, would appertain to the legislature.[1] The governor of New York, on the other hand, is by the constitution of the state vested only with the command of its militia and navy. But the constitutions of several of the states expressly declare their governors to be commanders-in-chief, as well of the army as navy; and it may well be a question whether those of New Hampshire and Massachusetts, in particular, do not, in this instance, confer larger powers upon their respective governors than could be claimed by a president of the United States.

● *Third.* The power of the president, in respect to pardons, would extend to all cases, *except those of impeachment.* The governor of New York may pardon in all cases, even in those of impeachment, except for treason and murder. Is not the power of the governor, in this article, on a calculation of political consequences, greater than that of the president? All conspiracies and plots against the government which have not been matured into actual treason may be screened from punishment of every kind by the interposition of the prerogative of pardoning. If a governor of New York, therefore, should be at the head of any such conspiracy, until the design had been ripened into actual hostility he could insure his accomplices and adherents an entire impunity. A president of the Union, on the other hand, though he may even pardon treason, when prosecuted in the ordinary course of law, could shelter no offender, in any degree, from the effects of impeachment and conviction. Would not the prospect of a total indemnity for all the preliminary steps be a greater temptation to undertake and persevere in an enterprise against the public liberty, than the mere prospect of an exemption from death and confiscation, if the final execution of the design, upon an actual appeal to arms, should miscarry? Would this last expectation have any influence at all, when the probability was computed that the person who was to afford that exemption might himself be involved in the consequences of the measure, and might be incapacitated by his agency in it from affording the desired impunity? The better to judge of this matter, it will be necessary to recollect

that, by the proposed Constitution, the offense of treason is limited "to levying war upon the United States, and adhering to their enemies, giving them aid and comfort"; and that by the laws of New York it is confined within similar bounds.

● *Fourth.* The president can only adjourn the national legislature in the single case of disagreement about the time of adjournment. The British monarch may prorogue or even dissolve the Parliament. The governor of New York may also prorogue the legislature of this state for a limited time; a power which, in certain situations, may be employed to very important purposes.

The president is to have power, with the advise and consent of the Senate, to make treaties, provided two-thirds of the senators present concur. The king of Great Britain is the sole and absolute representative of the nation in all foreign transactions. He can of his own accord make treaties of peace, commerce, alliance, and of every other description. It has been insinuated that his authority in this respect is not conclusive, and that his conventions with foreign powers are subject to the revision, and stand in need of the ratification, of Parliament. But I believe this doctrine was never heard of until it was broached upon the present occasion. Every jurist[2] of that kingdom, and every other man acquainted with its Constitution knows, as an established fact, that the prerogative of making treaties exists in the crown in its utmost plenitude; and that the compacts entered into by the royal authority have the most complete legal validity and perfection, independent of any other sanction. The Parliament, it is true, is sometimes seen employing itself in altering the existing laws to conform them to the stipulations in a new treaty; and this may have possibly given birth to the imagination that its cooperation was necessary to the obligatory efficacy of the treaty. But this parliamentary interposition proceeds from a different cause: from the necessity of adjusting a most artificial and intricate system of revenue and commercial laws, to the changes made in them by the operation of the treaty; and of adapting new provisions and precautions to the new state of things, to keep the machine from running into disorder. In this respect, therefore, there is no comparison between the intended power of the president and the actual power of the British sovereign. The one can perform alone what the other can only do with the concurrence of a branch of the legislature. It must be admitted that in this instance the power of the federal executive would exceed that of any state executive. But this arises naturally from the exclusive possession by the Union of that part of the sovereign power which relates to treaties. If the Confederacy were to be dissolved, it would become a question whether the executives of the several states were not solely invested with that delicate and important prerogative.

The president is also to be authorized to receive ambassadors and other public ministers. This, though it has been a rich theme of declamation, is more a matter of dignity than of authority. It is a circumstance which will be without consequence in the administration of the government; and it was far more convenient that it should be arranged in this manner than that there should be a necessity of convening the legislature, or one of its branches, upon every arrival of a foreign minister, though it were merely to take the place of a departed predecessor.

The president is to nominate, and, *with the advice and consent of the Senate,* to appoint ambassadors and other public ministers, judges of the Supreme Court, and in general all officers of the United States established by law, and whose appointments are not otherwise provided for by the Constitution. The king of Great Britain is emphatically and truly styled the fountain of honor. He not only appoints to all offices, but can create offices. He can confer titles of nobility at pleasure, and has the disposal of an immense number of church preferments. There is evidently a great inferiority in the power of the president, in this particular, to that of the British king; nor is it equal to that of the governor of New York, if we are to interpret the meaning of the constitution of the state by the practice which has obtained under it. The power of appointment is with us lodged in a council, composed of the governor and four members of the senate, chosen by the assembly. The governor *claims,* and has frequently *exercised,* the right of nomination, and is *entitled* to a casting vote in the appointment. If he really has the right of nominating, his authority is in this respect equal to that of the president, and exceeds it in the article of the casting vote. In the national government, if the Senate should be divided, no appointment could be made; in the government of New York, if the council should be divided, the governor can turn the scale and confirm his own nomination.[3] If we compare the publicity which must necessarily attend the mode of appointment by the president and an entire branch of the national legislature, with the privacy in the mode of appointment by the governor of New York, closeted in a secret apartment with at most four, and frequently with only two persons; and if we at the same time consider how much more easy it must be to influence the small number of which a council of appointment consists than the considerable number of which the national Senate would consist, we cannot hesitate to pronounce that the power of the chief magistrate of this state, in the dispostion of offices, must, in practice, be greatly superior to that of the chief magistrate of the Union.

Hence it appears that, except as to the concurrent authority of the president in the article of treaties, it would be difficult to determine whether that magistrate would, in the aggregate, possess more or less power than the governor of New York. And it appears yet more unequivocally that there is no pretense for the parallel which has been attempted between him and the king of Great Britain. But to render the contrast in this respect still more striking, it may be of use to throw the principal circumstances of dissimilitude into a closer group.

The president of the United States would be an officer elected by the people for *four* years; the king of Great Britain is a perpetual and *hereditary* prince. The one would be amenable to personal punishment and disgrace; the person of the other is sacred and inviolable. The one would have a *qualified* negative upon the acts of the legislative body; the other has an *absolute* negative. The one would have a right to command the military and naval forces of the nation; the other, in addition to this right, possesses that of *declaring* war, and of *raising* and *regulating* fleets and armies by his own authority. The one would have a concurrent power with a branch of the legislature in the formation of treaties; the other is the *sole possessor* of the power of making treaties. The one would have a like concurrent authority in appointing to offices; the other is the sole author of all appointments. The one can confer no privileges whatever; the other can make denizens of aliens, noblemen of commoners; can erect corporations with all the rights incident to corporate bodies. The one can prescribe no rules concerning the commerce or currency of the nation; the other is in several respects the arbiter of commerce, and in this capacity can establish markets and fairs, can regulate weights and measures, can lay embargoes for a limited time, can coin money, can authorize or prohibit the circulation of foreign coin. The one has no particle of spiritual jurisdiction; the other is the supreme head and governor of the national church! What answer shall we give to those who would persuade us that things so unlike resemble each other? The same that ought to be given to those who tell us that a government, the whole power of which would be in the hands of the elective and periodical servants of the people, is an aristocracy, a monarchy, and a despotism.

NOTES

1. A writer in a Pennsylvania paper, under the signature of Tamony, has asserted that the king of Great Britain owes his prerogative as commander-in-chief to an annual mutiny bill. The truth is, on the contrary, that his prerogative in this respect is immemorial, and was only disputed "contrary to all reason and precedent," as Blackstone, vol. i, page 262, expresses it, by the Long Parliament of Charles I; but by the statute the 13th of Charles II, chap. 6, it was declared to be in the king alone, for that the sole supreme government and command of the militia within his Majesty's realms and dominions, and of all forces by sea and land, and of all forts and places of strength, *ever was and is* the undoubted right of his Majesty and his royal predecessors, kings and queens of England, and that both or either house of Parliament cannot nor ought to pretend to the same.

2. *Vide* Blackstone's *Commentaries,* vol. 1, p. 257.

3. Candor, however, demands an acknowledgment that I do not think the claim of the governor to a right of nomination well founded. Yet it is always justifiable to reason from the practice of a government till its propriety has been constitutionally questioned. And independent of this claim, when we take into view the other considerations and pursue them through all their consequences, we shall be inclined to draw much the same conclusion.

5. The Federalist, No. 70*

ALEXANDER HAMILTON

There is an idea, which is not without its advocates, that a vigorous executive is inconsistent with the genius of republican government. The enlightened well-wishers to this species of government must at least hope that the supposition is destitute of foundation; since they can never admit its truth, without at the same time admitting the condemnation of their own principles. Energy in the executive is a leading character in the definition of good government. It is essential to the protection of the community against foreign attacks; it is not less essential to the steady administration of the laws; to the protection of property against those irregular and high-handed combinations which sometimes interrupt the ordinary course of justice; to the security of liberty against the enterprises and assaults of ambition, of faction, and of anarchy. Every man the least conversant in Roman history knows how often that republic was obliged to take refuge in the absolute power of a single man, under the formidable title of dictator, as well against the intrigues of ambitious individuals who aspired to the tyranny, and the seditions of whole classes of the community whose conduct threatened the existence of all government, as against the invasions of external enemies who menaced the conquest and destruction of Rome.

There can be no need, however, to multiply arguments or examples on this head. A feeble executive implies a feeble execution of the government. A feeble execution is but another phrase for a bad execution; and a government ill executed, whatever it may be in theory, must be, in practice, a bad government.

Taking it for granted, therefore, that all men of sense will agree in the necessity of an energetic executive, it will only remain to inquire, what are the ingredients which constitute this energy? How far can they be combined with those other ingredients which constitute safety in the republican sense? And how far does this combination characterize the plan which has been reported by the convention?

The ingredients which constitute energy in the executive are unity; duration; an adequate provision for its support; and competent powers.

The ingredients which constitute safety in the republican sense are a due dependence on the people, and a due responsibility.

Those politicians and statesmen who have been the most celebrated for the soundness of their principles and for the justness of their views have declared in favor of a single executive and a numerous legislature. They have, with great propriety, considered energy as the most necessary qualification of the former, and have regarded this as most applicable to power in a single hand; while they have, with equal propriety, considered the latter as best adapted to deliberation and wisdom, and best calculated to conciliate the confidence of the people and to secure their privileges and interests.

*Source: This essay by "Publius" was originally published in the New York Packet, March 18, 1788.

That unity is conducive to energy will not be disputed. Decision, activity, secrecy, and dispatch will generally characterize the proceedings of one man in a much more eminent degree than the proceedings of any greater number; and in proportion as the number is increased, these qualities will be diminished.

This unity may be destroyed in two ways: either by vesting the power in two or more magistrates of equal dignity and authority, or by vesting it ostensibly in one man, subject in whole or in part to the control and cooperation of others, in the capacity of counselors to him. Of the first, the two consuls of Rome may serve as an example; of the last, we shall find examples in the constitutions of several of the states. New York and New Jersey, if I recollect right, are the only states which have intrusted the executive authority wholly to single men.[1] Both these methods of destroying the unity of the executive have their partisans; but the votaries of an executive council are the most numerous. They are both liable, if not to equal, to similar objections, and may in most lights be examined in conjunction.

The experience of other nations will afford little instruction on this head. As far, however, as it teaches anything, it teaches us not to be enamored of plurality in the executive. We have seen that the Achaens, on an experiment of two Praetors, were induced to abolish one. The Roman history records many instances of mischiefs to the republic from the dissensions between the consuls, and between the military tribunes, who were at times substituted for the consuls. But it gives us no specimens of any peculiar advantages derived to the state from the circumstance of the plurality of those magistrates. That the dissensions between them were not more frequent or more fatal is matter of astonishment, until we advert to the singular position in which the republic was almost continually placed, and to the prudent policy pointed out by the circumstances of the state, and pursued by the consuls, of making a division of the government between them. The patricians engaged in a perpetual struggle with the plebeians for the preservation of their ancient authorities and dignities; the consuls, who were generally chosen out of the former body, were commonly united by the personal interest they had in the defense of the privileges of their order. In addition to this motive of union, after the arms of the republic had considerably expanded the bounds of its empire, it became an established custom with the consuls to divide the administration between themselves by lot—one of them remaining at Rome to govern the city and its environs, the other taking command in the more distant provinces. This expedient must no doubt have had great influence in preventing those collisions and rivalships which might otherwise have embroiled the peace of the republic.

But quitting the dim light of historical research, and attaching ourselves purely to the dictates of reason and good sense, we shall discover much greater cause to reject than to approve the idea of plurality in the executive, under any modification whatever.

Whenever two or more persons are engaged in any common enterprise or pursuit, there is always danger of difference of opinion. If it be a public trust or office in which they are clothed with equal dignity and authority, there is peculiar danger of personal emulation and even animosity. From either, and especially from all these causes, the most bitter dissensions are apt to spring. Whenever these happen, they lessen the respectability, weaken the authority, and distract the plans and operations of those whom they divide. If they should unfortunately assail the supreme executive magistracy of a country, consisting of a plurality of persons, they might impede or frustrate the most important measures of the government in the most critical emergencies of the state. And what is still worse, they might split the community into the most violent and ir-reconcilable factions, adhering dif-ferently to the different individuals who composed the magistracy.

Men often oppose a thing merely be-cause they have had no agency in plan-ning it, or because it may have been planned by those whom they dislike. But if they have been consulted, and have happened to disapprove, opposi-tion then becomes, in their estimation, an indispensable duty of self-love. They seem to think themselves bound in honor, and by all the motives of per-sonal infallibility, to defeat the success of what has been resolved upon con-trary to their sentiments. Men of upright, benevolent tempers have too many op-portunities of remarking, with horror, to what desperate lengths this disposition is sometimes carried, and how often the great interests of society are sacrificed to the vanity, to the conceit, and to the ob-stinacy of individuals, who have credit enough to make their passions and their caprices interesting to mankind. Perhaps the question now before the public may, in its consequences, afford melan-choly proofs of the effects of this despi-cable frailty, or rather detestable vice, in the human character.

Upon the principles of a free govern-ment, inconveniences from the source just mentioned must necessarily be submitted to in the formation of the legislature; but it is unnecessary, and therefore unwise, to introduce them into the constitution of the executive. It is here too that they may be most perni-cious. In the legislature, promptitude of decision is oftener an evil than a bene-fit. The differences of opinion, and the jarring of parties in that department of the government, though they may some-times obstruct salutary plans, yet often promote deliberation and circumspec-tion, and serve to check excesses in the majority. When a resolution too is once taken, the opposition must be at an end. That resolution is a law, and resistance to it punishable. But no favorable cir-cumstances palliate or atone for the dis-advantages of dissension in the execu-tive department. Here they are pure and unmixed. There is no point at which they cease to operate. They serve to embarrass and weaken the execution of the plan or measure to which they re-late, from the first step to the final con-clusion of it. They constantly counteract those qualities in the executive which are the most necessary ingredients in its composition—vigor and expedition, and this without any counterbalancing good. In the conduct of war, in which the energy of the executive is the bulwark of the national security, everything would be to be apprehended from its plurality.

It must be confessed that these obser-vations apply with principal weight to the first case supposed—that is, to a plu-rality of magistrates of equal dignity and authority, a scheme, the advocates for which are not likely to form a numerous sect; but they apply, though not with equal yet with considerable weight to the project of a council, whose con-currence is made constitutionally neces-sary to the operations of the ostensible executive. An artful cabal in that coun-cil would be able to distract and to enervate the whole system of adminis-tration. If no such cabal should exist, the mere diversity of views and opinions would alone be sufficient to tincture the exercise of the executive authority with a spirit of habitual feebleness and di-latoriness.

But one of the weightiest objections to a plurality in the executive, and which lies as much against the last as the first plan is that it tends to conceal faults and destroy responsibility. Re-sponsibility is of two kinds—to censure and to punishment. The first is the more important of the two, especially in an elective office. Men in public trust will much oftener act in such a manner as to render them unworthy of being any longer trusted, than in such a manner as to make them obnoxious to legal punishment. But the multiplication of the executive adds to the difficulty of

detection in either case. It often becomes impossible, amidst mutual accusations, to determine on whom the
blame or the punishment of a pernicious measure, or series of pernicious
measures, ought really to fall. It is
shifted from one to another with so
much dexterity, and under such plausible appearances, that the public opinion
is left in suspense about the real author.
The circumstances which may have led
to any national miscarriage or misfortune are sometimes so complicated that
where there are a number of actors who
may have had different degrees and
kinds of agency, though we may clearly
see upon the whole that there has been
mismanagement, yet it may be imprac-
ticable to pronounce to whose account
the evil which may have been incurred
is truly chargeable.

"I was overruled by my council. The
council were so divided in their opinions that it was impossible to obtain any
better resolution on the point." These
and similar pretexts are constantly at
hand, whether true or false. And who is
there that will either take the trouble or
incur the odium of a strict scrutiny into
the secret springs of the transaction?
Should there be found a citizen zealous
enough to undertake the unpromising
task, if there happened to be a collusion
between the parties concerned, how
easy it is to clothe the circumstances
with so much ambiguity as to render it
uncertain what was the precise conduct
of any of those parties.

In the single instance in which the
governor of this state is coupled with a
council—that is, in the appointment to
offices, we have seen the mischiefs of it
in the view now under consideration.
Scandalous appointments to important
offices have been made. Some cases,
indeed, have been so flagrant that *all
parties* have agreed in the impropriety
of the thing. When inquiry has been
made, the blame has been laid by the
governor on the members of the council, who, on their part, have charged it
upon his nomination; while the people

remain altogether at a loss to determine
by whose influence their interests have
been committed to hands so unqualified
and so manifestly improper. In tender-
ness to individuals, I forbear to descend
to particulars.

It is evident from these considerations
that the plurality of the executive tends
to deprive the people of the two greatest
securities they can have for the faithful
exercise of any delegated power, *first,*
the restraints of public opinion, which
lose their efficacy, as well on account of
the division of the censure attendant on
bad measures among a number as on
account of the uncertainty on whom it
ought to fall; and, *second,* the opportunity of discovering with facility and
clearness the misconduct of the persons
they trust, in order either to their removal from office or to their actual
punishment in cases which admit of it.

In England, the king is a perpetual
magistrate; and it is a maxim which has
obtained for the sake of the public
peace that he is unaccountable for his
administration, and his person sacred.
Nothing, therefore, can be wiser in that
kingdom than to annex to the king a
constitutional council, who may be responsible to the nation for the advice
they give. Without this, there would be
no responsibility whatever in the executive department—an idea inadmissible
in a free government. But even there the
king is not bound by the resolutions of
his council, though they are answerable
for the advice they give. He is the absolute master of his own conduct in the
exercise of his office and may observe
or disregard the counsel given to him at
his sole discretion.

But in a republic where every magistrate ought to be personally responsible
for his behavior in office, the reason
which in the British Constitution dictates the propriety of a council not only
ceases to apply, but turns against the
institution. In the monarchy of Great
Britain, it furnishes a substitute for the
prohibited responsibility of the chief
magistrate, which serves in some degree

as a hostage to the national justice for his good behavior. In the American republic, it would serve to destroy, or would greatly diminish, the intended and necessary responsibility of the chief magistrate himself.

The idea of a council to the executive, which has so generally obtained in the state constitutions, has been derived from that maxim of republican jealousy which considers power as safer in the hands of a number of men than of a single man. If the maxim should be admitted to be applicable to the case, I should contend that the advantage on that side would not counterbalance the numerous disadvantages on the opposite side. But I do not think the rule at all applicable to the executive power. I clearly concur in opinion, in this particular, with a writer whom the celebrated Junius pronounces to be "deep, solid, and ingenious," that "the executive power is more easily confined when it is one";[2] that it is far more safe there should be a single object for the jealousy and watchfulness of the people; and, in a word, that all multiplication of the executive is rather dangerous than friendly to liberty.

A little consideration will satisfy us that the species of security sought for in the multiplication of the executive is unattainable. Numbers must be so great as to render combination difficult, or they are rather a source of danger than of security. The united credit and influence of several individuals must be more formidable to liberty than the credit and influence of either of them separately. When power, therefore, is placed in the hands of so small a number of men as to admit of their interests and views being easily combined in a common enterprise, by an artful leader, it becomes more liable to abuse, and more dangerous when abused, than if it be lodged in the hands of one man, who, from the very circumstance of his being alone, will be more narrowly watched and more readily suspected, and who cannot

unite so great a mass of influence as when he is associated with others. The decemvirs of Rome, whose name denotes their number,[3] were more to be dreaded in their usurpation than any one of them would have been. No person would think of proposing an executive much more numerous than that body; from six to a dozen have been suggested for the number of the council. The extreme of these numbers is not too great for an easy combination; and from such a combination America would have more to fear than from the ambition of any single individual. A council to a magistrate, who is himself responsible for what he does, are generally nothing better than a clog upon his good intentions, are often the instruments and accomplices of his bad, and are almost always a cloak to his faults.

I forbear to dwell upon the subject of expense; though it be evident that if the council should be numerous enough to answer the principal end aimed at by the institution, the salaries of the members, who must be drawn from their homes to reside at the seat of government, would form an item in the catalogue of public expenditures too serious to be incurred for an object of equivocal utility.

I will only add that, prior to the appearance of the Constitution, I rarely met with an intelligent man from any of the states who did not admit, as the result of experience, that the *unity* of the executive of this state was one of the best of the distinguishing features of our Constitution.

NOTES

1. New York has no council except for the single purpose of appointing to offices; New Jersey has a council whom the governor may consult. But I think, from the terms of the Constitution, their resolutions do not bind him.
2. De Lolme.
3. Ten.

II

Presidential Views of the Office

Introduction. In the history of the presidency, three presidential views of the office have competed for ascendancy at one time or another. The first is called the executive prerogative view of the presidency; the second, the stewardship view; the third, the restricted view.

The executive prerogative view of the president's powers has its origin in John Locke's *Second Treatise of Government.* Locke wrote that

> Where the legislative and executive powers are in distinct hands, as they are in all moderated monarchies and well-formed governments, there the good of the society requires that several things should be left to the discretion of him that has the executive power. For the legislators not being able to foresee and provide by laws for all that may be useful to the community, the executor of the laws having the power in his hands, has by the common law of nature a right to make use of it for the good of the society, in many cases where the municipal law has given no direction, till the legislative can conveniently be assembled to provide for it. Many things there are which the law can by no means provide for; and those must necessarily be left to the discretion of him that has the executive power in his hands, to be ordered by him as the public good and advantage shall require; nay, it is fit that the laws themselves should in some cases give way to the executive power, or rather to the fundamental law of nature and government, to wit, that as much as may be, all the members of society are to be preserved.

Abraham Lincoln, the sixteenth president of the United States, is said to have subscribed to the prerogative view of presidential powers. To be sure, Lincoln's presidency presided over the greatest internal crisis in American history, but Lincoln's conception of executive power went far beyond that held by any president before or since, albeit both Franklin Roosevelt and Richard Nixon came close to asserting similar views. Lincoln's view is summarized in his essay, "The Prerogative Theory of the Presidency," which is actually a letter he sent to a newspaper editor in 1864.

Two later presidents were to contribute significantly to the conceptualization of the powers of the presidency. They were Theodore Roosevelt and William Howard Taft. Theodore Roosevelt, the twenty-sixth president of the United States, coming to office on the eve of an era of demand for reform, came to hold a less grandiose notion of presidential powers than Abraham Lincoln, but did feel that the Constitution contained an undefined residuum of power upon which the president could call in the national interest. Theodore Roosevelt's essay on the subject is reprinted here as "The Stewardship Doctrine." It is an interesting footnote, however, to point out that Roosevelt was careful not to articulate such a doctrine while he was in the White House, but stated it in his autobiography several years after his tenure of office was completed. Interestingly enough, Theodore Roosevelt often associated his own view with that of Abraham Lincoln, which, as we have seen earlier, went far beyond the stewardship view.[1]

William Howard Taft, the twenty-seventh president of the United States and later the tenth chief justice of the United States, held a strictly limitationist view of the power of the presidency. Taft's views were in direct contrast to that of his predecessor, although it was his predecessor who picked Taft to succeed him. For Taft, there is no undefined residuum of presidential power, as he explained in "A Restricted View of the Office."

Precisely what view of the office the framers envisioned for the president is and must remain a matter of speculation. Nearly two centuries of academic and non-academic debate has yielded no definitive answer.

NOTE

1. For a careful comparison and contrast between executive prerogative and stewardship views of presidential power, see Harry A. Bailey, Jr., "Controlling the Runaway Presidency," *Public Administration Review* 35 (September/October 1955): 547-54.

6. The Prerogative Theory of the Presidency*

ABRAHAM LINCOLN

EXECUTIVE MANSION, APRIL 4, 1864

My dear Sir: You ask me to put in writing the substance of what I verbally said the other day in your presence, to Governor Bramlette and Senator Dixon. It was about as follows:

"I am naturally antislavery. If slavery is not wrong, nothing is wrong. I cannot remember when I did not so think and feel, and yet I have never understood that the presidency conferred upon me an unrestricted right to act officially upon this judgment and feeling. It was in the oath I took that I would, to the best of my ability, preserve, protect, and defend the Constitution of the United States. I could not take the office with-

*Source: From *The Complete Works of Abraham Lincoln*, vol. X, John Nicolay and John Hays, eds., pp. 65-68, New York: Francis D. Tandy Co., 1894. This letter to Albert G. Hodges, editor of the Frankfort, Kentucky, *Commonwealth*, was used as a campaign document in the election of 1864.

out taking the oath. Nor was it my view that I might take an oath to get power, and break the oath in using the power. I understood, too, that in ordinary civil administration this oath even forbade me to practically indulge my primary abstract judgment on the moral question of slavery. I had publicly declared this many times, and in many ways. And I aver that, to this day, I have done no official act in mere deference to my abstract judgment and feeling on slavery. I did understand, however, that my oath to preserve the Constitution to the best of my ability imposed upon me the duty of preserving, by every indispensable means, that government—that nation, of which that Constitution was the organic law. Was it possible to lose the nation and yet preserve the Constitution? By general law, life and limb must be protected, yet often a limb must be amputated to save a life; but a life is never wisely given to save a limb. I felt that measures otherwise unconstitutional might become lawful by becoming indispensable to the preservation of the Constitution through the preservation of the nation. Right or wrong, I assume this ground, and now avow it. I could not feel that, to the best of my ability, I had even tried to preserve the Constitution, if, to save slavery or any minor matter, I should permit the wreck of government, country, and Constitution all together. When, early in the war, General Fremont attempted military emancipation, I forbade it, because I did not then think it an indispensable necessity. When, a little later, General Cameron, then Secretary of War, suggested the arming of the blacks, I objected because I did not yet think it an indispensable necessity. When, still later, General Hunter attempted military emancipation, I again forbade it, because I did not yet think the indispensable necessity had come. When in March and May and July, 1862, I made earnest and successive appeals to the border states to favor compensated emancipa-

tion, I believed the indispensable necessity for military emancipation and arming the blacks would come unless averted by that measure. They declined the proposition, and I was, in my best judgment, driven to the alternative of either surrendering the Union, and with it the Constitution, or of laying strong hand upon the colored element. I chose the latter. In choosing it, I hoped for greater gain than loss; but of this, I was not entirely confident. More than a year of trial now shows no loss by it in our foreign relations, none in our home popular sentiment, none in our white military force—no loss by it anyhow or anywhere. On the contrary it shows a gain of quite a hundred and thirty thousand soldiers, seamen, and laborers. These are palpable facts, about which, as facts, there can be no caviling. We have the men; and we could not have had them without the measure.

"And now let any Union man who complains of the measure test himself by writing down in one line that he is for subduing the rebellion by force of arms; and in the next, that he is for taking these hundred and thirty thousand men from the Union side, and placing them where they would be but for the measure he condemns. If he cannot face his case so stated, it is only because he cannot face the truth."

I add a word which was not in the verbal conversation. In telling this tale I attempt no compliment to my own sagacity. I claim not to have controlled events, but confess plainly that events have controlled me. Now, at the end of three years' struggle, the nation's condition is not what either party, or any man, devised or expected. God alone can claim it. Whither it is tending seems plain. If God now wills the removal of a great wrong, and wills also that we of the North, as well as you of the South, shall pay fairly for our complicity in that wrong, impartial history will find therein new cause to attest and revere the justice and goodness of God.

7. The Stewardship Doctrine*

THEODORE ROOSEVELT

My view was that every executive officer, and above all every executive officer in high position, was a steward of the people bound actively and affirmatively to do all he could for the people, and not to content himself with the negative merit of keeping his talents undamaged in a napkin. I declined to adopt the view that what was imperatively necessary for the nation could not be done by the president unless he could find some specific authorization to do it. My belief was that it was not only his right but his duty to do anything that the needs of the nation demanded unless such action was forbidden by the Constitution or by the laws. Under this interpretation of executive power I did and caused to be done many things not previously done by the president and the heads of the departments. I did not usurp power, but I did greatly broaden the use of executive power. In other words, I acted for the public welfare, I acted for the common well-being of all our people, whenever and in whatever manner was necessary, unless prevented by direct constitutional or legislative prohibition. . . .

The course I followed, of regarding the executive as subject only to the people, and, under the Constitution, bound to serve the people affirmatively in cases where the Constitution does not explicitly forbid him to render the service, was substantially the course followed by both Andrew Jackson and Abraham Lincoln. Other honorable and well-meaning presidents, such as James Buchanan, took the opposite and, as it seems to me, narrowly legalistic view that the president is the servant of Congress rather than of the people, and can do nothing, no matter how necessary it be to act, unless the Constitution explicitly commands the action. Most able lawyers who are past middle age take this view, and so do large numbers of well-meaning, respectable citizens. My successor in office took this, the Buchanan, view of the president's powers and duties.

For example, under my administration we found that one of the favorite methods adopted by the men desirous of stealing the public domain was to carry the decision of the secretary of the interior into court. By vigorously opposing such action, and only by so doing, we were able to carry out the policy of properly protecting the public domain. My successor not only took the opposite view, but recommended to Congress the passage of a bill which would have given the courts direct appellate power over the secretary of the interior in these land matters. . . . Fortunately, Congress declined to pass the bill. Its passage would have been a veritable calamity.

I acted on the theory that the president could at any time in his discretion withdraw from entry any of the public lands of the United States and reserve the same for forestry, for water-power sites, for irrigation, and other public purposes. Without such action it would have been impossible to stop the activity of the land-thieves. No one ventured to test its legality by lawsuit. My successor, however, himself questioned it, and referred the matter to Congress. Again Congress showed its wisdom by passing a law which gave the president the power which he had long exercised, and of which my successor had shorn himself.

Perhaps the sharp difference between what may be called the Lincoln–Jackson and the Buchanan–Taft schools, in their views of the power and duties of the president, may be best illustrated by comparing the attitude of my successor toward his secretary of the interior, Mr. Ballinger, when the latter was accused of gross misconduct in office, with my attitude toward my chiefs of department and other subordinate officers. More than once while I was president my officials were attacked by Congress, generally because these officials did their duty well and fearlessly. In every such case I stood by the official and refused to recognize the right of Congress to interfere with me excepting by impeachment or in other constitutional manner. On the other hand, wherever I found the officer unfit for his position, I promptly removed him, even although the most influential men in Congress fought for his retention. The Jackson–Lincoln view is that a president who is fit to do good work should be able to form his own judgment as to his own subordinates, and, above all, of the subordinates standing highest and in

closest and most intimate touch with him. My secretaries and their subordinates were responsible to me, and I accepted the responsibility for all their deeds. As long as they were satisfactory to me I stood by them against every critic or assailant, within or without Congress; and as for getting Congress to make up my mind for me about them, the thought would have been inconceivable to me. My successor took the opposite, or Buchanan, view when he permitted and requested Congress to pass judgment on the charges made against Mr. Ballinger as an executive officer. These charges were made to the president; the president had the facts before him and could get at them at any time, and he alone had power to act if the charges were true. However, he permitted and requested Congress to investigate Mr. Ballinger. The party minority of the committee that investigated him, and one member of the majority, declared that the charges were well-founded and that Mr. Ballinger should be removed. The other members of the majority declared the charges ill-founded. The president abode by the view of the majority. Of course believers in the Jackson–Lincoln theory of the presidency would not be content with this town-meeting majority and minority method of determining by another branch of the government what it seems the especial duty of the president himself to determine for himself in dealing with his own subordinate in his own department.

8. A Restricted View of the Office*

WILLIAM HOWARD TAFT

While it is important to mark out the exclusive field of jurisdiction of each branch of the government, legislative, executive and judicial, it should be said that in the proper working of the government there must be cooperation of all branches, and without a willingness of each branch to perform its function, there will follow a hopeless obstruction to the progress of the whole government. Neither branch can compel the other to affirmative action, and each branch can greatly hinder the other in the attainment of the object of its activities and the exercise of its discretion. . . .

The true view of the executive functions is, as I conceive it, that the president can exercise no power which cannot be fairly and reasonably traced to some specific grant of power or justly implied and included within such express grant as proper and necessary to its exercise. Such specific grant must be either in the federal Constitution or in an act of Congress passed in pursuance thereof. There is no undefined residuum of power which he can exercise because it seems to him to be in the public interest, and there is nothing in the *Neagle* case and its definition of a law of the United States, or in other precedents, warranting such an inference. The grants of executive power are necessarily in general terms in order not to embarrass the executive within the field of action plainly marked for him, but his jurisdiction must be justified and vindicated by affirmative constitutional or statutory provision, or it does not exist. There have not been wanting, however, eminent men in high public office holding a different view and who have insisted upon the necessity for an undefined residuum of executive power in the public interest. They have not been confined to the present generation. We may learn this from the complaint of a Virginia statesman, Abel P. Upshur, a strict constructionist of the old school, who succeeded Daniel Webster as secretary of state under President Tyler. He was aroused by Story's commentaries on the Constitution to write a monograph answering and criticizing them, and in the course of this he comments as follows on the executive power under the Constitution:

The most defective part of the Constitution beyond all question, is that which related to the Executive Department. It is impossible to read that instrument, without being struck with the loose and unguarded terms in which the powers and duties of the President are pointed out. So far as the legislature is concerned, the limitations of the Constitution, are, perhaps, as precise and strict as they could safely have been made; but in regard to the Executive, the Convention appears to have studiously selected such loose and general expressions, as would enable the President, by implication and construction either to neglect his duties or to enlarge his powers. *We have heard it gravely asserted in Congress that whatever power is neither legislative nor judiciary, is of course executive, and, as such, belongs to the President under the Constitution.* How far a majority of that body would have sustained a doctrine so monstrous, and so utterly at war with the whole genius of our government, it is impossible to say, but this, at least, we know, that it met with no rebuke from those who supported the particular act of Executive power, in defense of which it was urged. Be this as it may, it is a reproach to the Constitution that the Executive trust is so ill-defined, as to leave any plausible pretense even to the insane zeal of party devotion, for attributing to the President of the United States the powers of a despot; powers which are wholly unknown in any limited monarchy in the world.

The view that he takes as a result of the loose language defining the executive powers seems exaggerated. But one must agree with him in his condemnation of the view of the executive power which he says was advanced in Congress. In recent years there has been put forward a similar view by executive officials and to some extent acted on. Men who are not such strict constructionists of the Constitution as Mr. Upshur may well feel real concern if such views are to receive the general acquiescence. Mr. Garfield, when secretary of the interior, under Mr. Roosevelt, in his final report to Congress in reference to the power of the executive over the public domain, said:

Full power under the Constitution was vested in the Executive Branch of the Government and the extent to which that power may be exercised is governed wholly by the discretion of the Executive unless any specific act has been prohibited either by the Constitution or by legislation.

In pursuance of this principle, Mr. Garfield, under an act for the reclamation of arid land by irrigation, which authorized him to make contracts for irrigation works and incur liability equal to the amount on deposit in the Reclamation Fund, made contracts with associations of settlers by which it was agreed that if these settlers would advance money and work, they might receive certificates from the government engineers of the labor and money furnished by them, and that such certificates might be received in the future in the discharge of their legal obligations to the government for water rent and other things under the statute. It became necessary for the succeeding administration to pass on the validity of these government certificates. They were held by Attorney General Wickersham to be illegal, on the ground that no authority existed for their issuance. He relied on the Floyd acceptances in 7th Wallace, in which recovery was sought in the court of claims on commercial paper in the form of acceptances signed by Mr. Floyd when secretary of war and delivered to certain contractors. The court held that they were void because the secretary of war had no statutory authority to issue them. Mr. Justice Miller, in deciding the case, said:

The answer which at once suggests itself to one familiar with the structure of our government, in which all power is delegated, and is defined by law, constitutional or statutory, is, that to one or both of these sources we must resort in every instance. We have no officers in this government, from the President down to the most subordinate agent, who does not hold office under the law, with prescribed duties and limited authority. And while some of these, as the President, the Legislature, and the Judiciary, exercise powers in some sense left to the more general definitions necessarily incident to fundamental law found in the Constitution, the larger portion of them are the creation of statutory law, with duties and powers prescribed and limited by that law.

[Three paragraphs of text omitted at this point.]

My judgment is that the view of Mr. Garfield and Mr. Roosevelt, ascribing an undefined residuum of power to the president is an unsafe doctrine and that it might lead under emergencies to results of an arbitrary character, doing irremediable injustice to private right. The mainspring of such a view is that the executive is charged with responsibility for the welfare of all the people in a general way, that he is to play the part of a Universal Providence and set all things right, and that anything that in his judgment will help the people he ought to do, unless he is expressly forbidden not to do it. The wide field of action that this would give to the executive one can hardly limit.

III

The Presidential Personality

Introduction. What kind of person do we need in the presidency? Can presidential behavior be predicted? To both questions, political scientist James David Barber believes there is an answer. In the best of Barber's worlds, the nation could do well with an Active-Positive President. And yes, presidential behavior can be predicted.

Barber believes that presidential behavior can be predicted if one studies and has knowledge of the early psychological development of persons who seek the presidency. Barber argues that although political circumstances often create opportunities for presidential leadership, it is the president's personality that determines how a president may be expected to use the power of his office.

Barber's study, based upon psychobiographies of presidents from Woodrow Wilson to Richard Nixon, resulted in the development of a quadripartite typology of the presidential personality based on two dichotomized dimensions. His essay, "The Presidential Character," illustrates how much of the guesswork can be removed in assessing a president's personality.

James Barber's effort to determine the role of personality in presidential behavior is a pioneering one. No other student of the presidency has produced a satisfactory alternative explanation, but political scientist Erwin C. Hargrove presents an interesting critique of a good deal of the presidential personality literature, including Barber's, in his essay, "Presidential Personality and Revisionist Views of the Presidency." Hargrove's study concludes with an interesting set of propositions that can guide the study of personalities of presidents.

9. The Presidential Character*

JAMES DAVID BARBER

When a citizen votes for a presidential candidate he makes, in effect, a prediction. He chooses from among the contenders the one he thinks (or feels, or guesses) would be the best president. He operates in a situation of immense uncertainty. If he has a long voting history, he can recall time and time again when he guessed wrong. He listens to the commentators, the politicians, and his friends, then adds it all up in some rough way to produce his prediction and his vote. Earlier in the game, his anticipations have been taken into account, either directly in the polls and primaries or indirectly in the minds of politicians who want to nominate someone he will like. But he must choose in the midst of a cloud of confusion, a rain of phony advertising, a storm of sermons, a hail of complex issues, a fog of charisma and boredom, and a thunder of accusation and defense. In the face of this chaos, a great many citizens fall back on the past, vote their old allegiances, and let it go at that. Nevertheless, the citizen's vote says that on balance he expects Mr. X would outshine Mr. Y in the presidency.

This [work] is meant to help citizens and those who advise them cut through the confusion and get at some clear criteria for choosing presidents. To understand what actual presidents do and what potential presidents might do, the first need is to see the man whole—not as some abstract embodiment of civic virtue, some scorecard of issue stands, or some reflection of a faction, but as a human being like the rest of us, a person trying to cope with a difficult environment. To that task he brings his own character, his own view of the world, his own political style. None of that is new for him. If we can see the pattern he has set for his political life we can, I contend, estimate much better his pattern as he confronts the stresses and chances of the presidency.

The presidency is a peculiar office. The Founding Fathers left it extraordinarily loose in definition, partly because they trusted George Washington to invent a tradition as he went along. It is an institution made a piece at a time by successive men in the White House. Jefferson reached out to Congress to put together the beginnings of political parties; Jackson's dramatic force extended electoral partisanship to its mass base; Lincoln vastly expanded the administrative reach of the office; Wilson and the Roosevelts showed its rhetorical possibilities—in fact every president's mind and demeanor has left its mark on a heritage still in lively development.

But the presidency is much more than an institution. It is a focus of feelings. In general, popular feelings about politics are low-key, shallow, casual. For example, the vast majority of Americans knows virtually nothing of what Congress is doing and cares less. The presidency is different. The presidency is the

---

focus for the most intense and persistent emotions in the American polity. The president is a symbolic leader, the one figure who draws together the people's hopes and fears for the political future. On top of all his routine duties, he has to carry that off—or fail.

Our emotional attachment to presidents shows up when one dies in office. People were not just disappointed or worried when President Kennedy was killed; people wept at the loss of a man most had never even met. Kennedy was young and charismatic—but history shows that whenever a president dies in office, heroic Lincoln or debased Harding, McKinley or Garfield, the same wave of deep emotion sweeps across the country. On the other hand, the death of an ex-president brings forth no such intense emotional reaction.

The president is the first political figure children are aware of (later they add Congress, the court, and others, as "helpers" of the president). With some exceptions among children in deprived circumstances, the president is seen as a "benevolent leader," one who nurtures, sustains, and inspires the citizenry. Presidents regularly show up among "most admired" contemporaries and forebears, and the president is the "best known" (in the sense of sheer name recognition) person in the country. At inauguration time, even presidents elected by close margins are supported by much larger majorities than the election returns show, for people rally round as he actually assumes office. There is a similar reaction when the people see their president threatened by crisis: if he takes action, there is a favorable spurt in the Gallup Poll whether he succeeds or fails.

Obviously the president gets more attention in schoolbooks, press, and television than any other politician. He is one of very few who can make news by doing good things. *His* emotional state is a matter of continual public commentary, as is the manner in which his personal and official families conduct themselves. The media bring across the president not as some neutral administrator or corporate executive to be assessed by his production, but as a special being with mysterious dimensions.

We have no king. The sentiments English children—and adults—direct to the queen have no place to go in our system but to the president. Whatever his talents—Coolidge-type or Roosevelt-type—the president is the only available object for such national-religious-monarchical sentiments as Americans possess.

The president helps people make sense of politics. Congress is a tangle of committees, the bureaucracy is a maze of agencies. The president is one man trying to do a job—a picture much more understandable to the mass of people who find themselves in the same boat. Furthermore, he is the top man. He ought to know what is going on and set it right. So when the economy goes sour, or war drags on, or domestic violence erupts, the president is available to take the blame. Then when things go right, it seems the president must have had a hand in it. Indeed, the flow of political life is marked off by presidents: the "Eisenhower Era," the "Kennedy Years."

What all this means is that the president's *main* responsibilities reach far beyond administering the executive branch or commanding the armed forces. The White House is first and foremost a place of public leadership. That inevitably brings to bear on the president intense moral, sentimental, and quasi-religious pressures which can, if he lets them, distort his own thinking and feeling. If there is such a thing as extraordinary sanity, it is needed nowhere so much as in the White House.

Who the president is at a given time can make a profound difference in the whole thrust and direction of national politics. Since we have only one president at a time, we can never prove this by comparison, but even the most superficial speculation confirms the commonsense view that the man himself weighs heavily among other historical factors. A Wilson re-elected in 1920, a Hoover in 1932, a John F. Kennedy in 1964 would, it seems very likely, have guided the body politic along rather different paths from those their actual successors chose. Or try to imagine a Theodore Roosevelt ensconced behind today's "bully pulpit" of a presidency, or Lyndon Johnson as president in the age of McKinley. Only someone mesmerized by the lures of historical inevitability can suppose that it would have made little or no difference to government policy had Alf Landon replaced FDR in 1936, had Dewey beaten Truman in 1948, or Adlai Stevenson reigned through the 1950s. Not only would these alternative presidents have advocated different policies—they would have approached the office from very different psychological angles. It stretches credibility to think that Eugene McCarthy would have run the institution the way Lyndon Johnson did.

The burden of this [work] is that the crucial differences can be anticipated by an understanding of a potential president's character, his world view, and his style.[1] This kind of prediction is not easy; well-informed observers often have guessed wrong as they watched a man step toward the White House. One thinks of Woodrow Wilson, the scholar who would bring reason to politics; of Herbert Hoover, the Great Engineer who would organize chaos into progress; of Franklin D. Roosevelt, that champion of the balanced budget; of Harry Truman, whom the office would surely overwhelm; of Dwight D. Eisenhower, militant crusader; of John F. Kennedy, who would lead beyond moralisms to achievements; of Lyndon B. Johnson, the Southern conservative; and of Richard M. Nixon, conciliator. Spotting the errors is easy. Predicting with even approximate accuracy is going to require some sharp tools and close attention in their use. But the ex-

periment is worth it because the question is critical and because it lends itself to correction by evidence.

My argument comes in layers.

First, a president's personality is an important shaper of his presidential behavior on nontrivial matters.

Second, presidential personality is patterned. His character, world view, and style fit together in a dynamic package understandable in psychological terms.

Third, a president's personality interacts with the power situation he faces and the national "climate of expectations" dominant at the time he serves. The tuning, the resonance—or lack of it—between these external factors and his personality sets in motion the dynamic of his presidency.

Fourth, the best way to predict a president's character, world view, and style is to see how they were put together in the first place. That happened in his early life, culminating in his first independent political success.

But the core of the argument (which organizes the structure of the [work]) is that presidential character—the basic stance a man takes toward his presidential experience—comes in four varieties. The most important thing to know about a president or candidate is where he fits among these types, defined according to (a) how active he is and (b) whether or not he gives the impression he enjoys his political life.

Let me spell out these concepts briefly before getting down to cases.

PERSONALITY SHAPES PERFORMANCE

I am not about to argue that once you know a president's personality you know everything. But as the cases will demonstrate, the degree and quality of a president's emotional involvement in an issue are powerful influences on how he defines the issue itself, how much attention he pays to it, which facts and persons he sees as relevant to its resolution, and, finally, what principles and purposes he associates with the issue. Every story of presidential decision-making is really two stories: an outer one in which a rational man calculates and an inner one in which an emotional man feels. The two are forever connected. Any real president is one whole man and his deeds reflect his wholeness.

As for personality, it is a matter of tendencies. It is not that one president "has" some basic characteristic that another president does not "have." That old way of treating a trait as a possession, like a rock in a basket, ignores the universality of aggressiveness, compliancy, detachment, and other human drives. We all have all of them, but in different amounts and in different combinations.

THE PATTERN OF CHARACTER, WORLD VIEW, AND STYLE

The most visible part of the pattern is style. *Style is the president's habitual way of performing his three political roles: rhetoric, personal relations, and homework.* Not to be confused with "stylishness," charisma, or appearance, style is how the president goes about doing what the office requires him to do—to speak, directly or through media, to large audiences; to deal face to face with other politicians, individually and in small, relatively private groups; and to read, write, and calculate by himself in order to manage the endless flow of details that stream onto his desk. No president can escape doing at least some of each. But there are marked differences in stylistic emphasis from president to president. The *balance* among the three style elements varies; one president may put most of himself into rhetoric, another may stress close, informal dealing, while still another may devote his energies mainly to study and cogitation. Beyond the balance, we want to see each president's peculiar habits of style, his mode of coping with

and adapting to these presidential demands. For example, I think both Calvin Coolidge and John F. Kennedy were primarily rhetoricians, but they went about it in contrasting ways.

A president's *world view consists of his primary, politically relevant beliefs, particularly his conceptions of social causality, human nature, and the central moral conflicts of the time.* This is how he sees the world and his lasting opinions about what he sees. Style is his way of acting; world view is his way of seeing. Like the rest of us, a president develops over a lifetime certain conceptions of reality—how things work in politics, what people are like, what the main purposes are. These assumptions or conceptions help him make sense of his world, give some semblance of order to the chaos of existence. Perhaps most important: a man's world view affects what he pays attention to, and a great deal of politics is about paying attention. The name of the game for many politicians is not so much "Do this, do that" as it is "Look here!"

"Character" comes from the Greek word for engraving; in one sense it is what life has marked into a man's being. As used here, *character is the way the president orients himself toward life*—not for the moment, but enduringly. Character is the person's stance as he confronts experience. And at the core of character, a man confronts himself. The president's fundamental self-esteem is his prime personal resource; to defend and advance that, he will sacrifice much else he values. Down there in the privacy of his heart, does he find himself superb, or ordinary, or debased, or in some intermediate range? No president has been utterly paralyzed by self-doubt and none has been utterly free of midnight self-mockery. In between, the real presidents move out on life from positions of relative strength or weakness. Equally important are the criteria by which they judge themselves. A president who rates himself by the standard of achievement, for instance, may be little affected by losses of affection.

Character, world view, and style are abstractions from the reality of the whole individual. In every case they form an integrated pattern: the man develops a combination which makes psychological sense for him, a dynamic arrangement of motives, beliefs, and habits in the service of his need for self-esteem.

THE POWER SITUATION AND "CLIMATE OF EXPECTATIONS"

Presidential character resonates with the political situation the president faces. It adapts him as he tries to adapt it. The support he has from the public and interest groups, the party balance in Congress, the thrust of Supreme Court opinion together set the basic power situation he must deal with. An activist president may run smack into a brick wall of resistance, then pull back and wait for a better moment. On the other hand, a president who sees himself as a quiet caretaker may not try to exploit even the most favorable power situation. So it is the relationship between president and the political configuration that makes the system tick.

Even before public opinion polls, the president's real or supposed popularity was a large factor in his performance. Besides the power mix in Washington, the president has to deal with a national climate of expectations, the predominant needs thrust up to him by the people. There are at least three recurrent themes around which these needs are focused.

People look to the president for *reassurance*, a feeling that things will be all right, that the president will take care of his people. The psychological request is for a surcease of anxiety. Obviously, modern life in America involves considerable doses of fear, tension, anxiety, worry; from time to time, the public mood calls for a rest, a time of peace, a breathing space, a "return to normalcy."

Another theme is the demand for a *sense of progress and action*. The president ought to do something to direct the nation's course—or at least be in there pitching for the people. The president is looked to as a take-charge man, a doer, a turner of the wheels, a producer of progress—even if that means some sacrifice of serenity.

A third type of climate of expectations is the public need for a sense of *legitimacy* from, and in, the presidency. The president should be a master politician who is above politics. He should have a right to his place and a rightful way of acting in it. The respectability—even religiosity—of the office has to be protected by a man who presents himself as defender of the faith. There is more to this than dignity, more than propriety. The president is expected to personify our betterness in an inspiring way, to express in what he does and is (not just in what he says) a moral idealism which, in much of the public mind, is the very opposite of "politics."

Over time the climate of expectations shifts and changes. Wars, depressions, and other national events contribute to that change, but there also is a rough cycle, from an emphasis on action (which begins to look too "political") to an emphasis on legitimacy (the moral uplift of which creates its own strains) to an emphasis on reassurance and rest (which comes to seem like drift) and back to action again. One need not be astrological about it. The point is that the climate of expectations at any given time is the political air the president has to breathe. Relating to this climate is a large part of his task.

PREDICTING PRESIDENTS

The best way to predict a president's character, world view, and style is to see how he constructed them in the first place. Especially in the early stages, life is experimental; consciously or not, a person tries out various ways of defining and maintaining and raising self-esteem. He looks to his environment for clues as to who he is and how well he is doing. These lessons of life slowly sink in: certain self-images and evaluations, certain ways of looking at the world, certain styles of action get confirmed by his experience and he gradually adopts them as his own. If we can see that process of development, we can understand the product. The features to note are those bearing on presidential performance.

Experimental development continues all the way to death; we will not blind ourselves to midlife changes, particularly in the full-scale prediction case, that of Richard Nixon. But it is often much easier to see the basic patterns in early life histories. Later on a whole host of distractions—especially the image-making all politicians learn to practice—clouds the picture.

In general, character has its *main* development in childhood, world view in adolescence, style in early adulthood. The stance toward life I call character grows out of the child's experiments in relating to parents, brothers and sisters, and peers at play and in school, as well as to his own body and the objects around it. Slowly the child defines an orientation toward experience; once established, that tends to last despite much subsequent contradiction. By adolescence, the child has been hearing and seeing how people make their worlds meaningful, and now he is moved to relate himself—his own meanings—to those around him. His focus of attention shifts toward the future; he senses that decisions about his fate are coming and he looks into the premises for those decisions. Thoughts about the way the world works and how one might work in it, about what people are like and how one might be like them or not, and about the values people share and how one might share in them too—these are typical concerns

for the post-child, pre-adult mind of the adolescent.

These themes come together strongly in early adulthood, when the person moves from contemplation to responsible action and adopts a style. In most biographical accounts this period stands out in stark clarity—the time of emergence, the time the young man found himself. I call it his first independent political success. It was then he moved beyond the detailed guidance of his family; then his self-esteem was dramatically boosted; then he came forth as a person to be reckoned with by other people. The *way* he did that is profoundly important to him. Typically he grasps that style and hangs onto it. Much later, coming into the presidency, something in him remembers this earlier victory and re-emphasizes the style that made it happen.

Character provides the main thrust and broad direction—but it does not *determine,* in any fixed sense, world view and style. The story of development does not end with the end of childhood. Thereafter, the culture one grows in and the ways that culture is translated by parents and peers shapes the meanings one makes of his character. The going world view gets learned and that learning helps channel character forces. Thus it will not necessarily be true that compulsive characters have reactionary beliefs, or that compliant characters believe in compromise. Similarly for style: historical accidents play a large part in furnishing special opportunities for action—and in blocking off alternatives. For example, however much anger a young man may feel, that anger will not be expressed in rhetoric unless and until his life situation provides a platform and an audience. Style thus has a stature and independence of its own. Those who would reduce all explanation to character neglect these highly significant later channelings. For beyond the root is the branch, above the foundation the superstructure, and starts do not prescribe finishes.

FOUR TYPES OF PRESIDENTIAL CHARACTER

The five concepts—character, world view, style, power situation, and climate of expectations—run through the accounts of presidents . . . , which cluster the presidents since Theodore Roosevelt into four types. This is the fundamental scheme of the study. It offers a way to move past the complexities to the main contrasts and comparisons.

The first baseline in defining presidential types is *activity-passivity*. How much energy does the man invest in his presidency? Lyndon Johnson went at his day like a human cyclone, coming to rest long after the sun went down. Calvin Coolidge often slept eleven hours a night and still needed a nap in the middle of the day. In between the presidents array themselves on the high or low side of the activity line.

The second baseline is *positive-negative affect* toward one's activity—that is, how he feels about what he does. Relatively speaking, does he seem to experience his political life as happy or sad, enjoyable or discouraging, positive or negative in its main effect. The feeling I am after here is not grim satisfaction in a job well done, not some philosophical conclusion. The idea is this: is he someone who, on the surfaces we can see, gives forth the feeling that he has *fun* in political life? Franklin Roosevelt's secretary of war, Henry L. Stimson wrote that the Roosevelts "not only understood the *use* of power, they knew the *enjoyment* of power, too. . . . Whether a man is burdened by power or enjoys power; whether he is trapped by responsibility or made free by it; whether he is moved by other people and outer forces or moves them—that is the essence of leadership."

The positive-negative baseline, then, is a general symptom of the fit between the man and his experience, a kind of register of *felt* satisfaction.

Why might we expect these two simple dimensions to outline the main character types? Because they stand for two central features of anyone's orientation toward life. In nearly every study of personality, some form of the active-passive contrast is critical; the general tendency to act or be acted upon is evident in such concepts as dominance-submission, extraversion-introversion, aggression-timidity, attack-defense, fight-flight, engagement-withdrawal, approach-avoidance. In everyday life we sense quickly the general energy output of the people we deal with. Similarly we catch on fairly quickly to the affect dimension—whether the person seems to be optimistic or pessimistic, hopeful or skeptical, happy or sad. The two baselines are clear and they are also independent of one another: all of us know people who are very active but seem discouraged, others who are quite passive but seem happy, and so forth. The activity baseline refers to what one does, the affect baseline to how one feels about what he does.

Both are crude clues to character. They are leads into four basic character patterns long familiar in psychological research. In summary form, these are the main configurations:

Active-positive: There is a congruence, a consistency, between much activity and the enjoyment of it, indicating relatively high self-esteem and relative success in relating to the environment. The man shows an orientation toward productiveness as a value and an ability to use his styles flexibly, adaptively, suiting the dance to the music. He sees himself as developing over time toward relatively well defined personal goals—growing toward his image of himself as he might yet be. There is an emphasis on rational mastery, on using the brain to move the feet. This may get him into trouble; he may fail to take account of the irrational in politics. Not everyone he deals with sees things his way and he may find it hard to understand why.

Active-negative: The contradiction here is between relatively intense effort and relatively low emotional reward for that effort. The activity has a compulsive quality, as if the man were trying to make up for something or to escape from anxiety into hard work. He seems ambitious, striving upward, power-seeking. His stance toward the environment is aggressive and he has a persistent problem in managing his aggressive feelings. His self-image is vague and discontinuous. Life is a hard struggle to achieve and hold power, hampered by the condemnations of a perfectionistic conscience. Active-negative types pour energy into the political system, but it is an energy distorted from within.

Passive-positive: This is the receptive, compliant, other-directed character whose life is a search for affection as a reward for being agreeable and cooperative rather than personally assertive. The contradiction is between low self-esteem (on grounds of being unlovable, unattractive) and a superficial optimism. A hopeful attitude helps dispel doubt and elicits encouragement from others. Passive-positive types help soften the harsh edges of politics. But their dependence and the fragility of their hopes and enjoyments make disappointment in politics likely.

Passive-negative: The factors are consistent—but how are we to account for the man's *political* role-taking? Why is someone who does little in politics and enjoys it less there at all? The answer lies in the passive-negative's character-rooted orientation toward doing dutiful service; this compensates for low self-esteem based on a sense of uselessness. Passive-negative types are in politics because they think they ought to be. They may be well adapted to certain nonpolitical roles, but they lack the experience and flexibility to perform effectively as political leaders. Their tendency is to withdraw, to escape from the conflict and uncertainty of politics by emphasizing vague principles (especially prohibitions) and procedural arrangements. They become guardians of the right and proper way, above the sordid politicking of lesser men.

Active-positive presidents want most to achieve results. Active-negatives aim to get and keep power. Passive-positives are after love. Passive-negatives emphasize their civic virtue. The relation of activity to enjoyment in a president thus tends to outline a cluster of characteristics, to set apart the adapted from the compulsive, compliant, and withdrawn types.

The first four presidents of the United States, conveniently, ran through this gamut of character types. (Remember, we are talking about tendencies, broad directions; no individual man exactly fits a category.) George Washington— clearly the most important president in the pantheon—established the fundamental legitimacy of an American government at a time when this was a matter in considerable question. Washington's dignity, judiciousness, his aloof air of reserve and dedication to duty fit the passive-negative or withdrawing type best. Washington did not seek innovation, he sought stability. He longed to retire to Mount Vernon, but fortunately was persuaded to stay on through a second term, in which, by rising above the political conflict between Hamilton and Jefferson and inspiring confidence in his own integrity, he gave the nation time to develop the organized means for peaceful change.

John Adams followed, a dour New England Puritan, much given to work and worry, an impatient and irascible man—an active-negative president, a compulsive type. Adams was far more partisan than Washington; the survival of the system through his presidency demonstrated that the nation could tolerate, for a time, domination by one of its nascent political parties. As president, an angry Adams brought the United States to the brink of war with France, and presided over the new nation's first experiment in political repression: the Alien and Sedition Acts, forbidding, among other things, unlawful combinations "with intent to oppose any measure or measures of the government of the United States," or "any false, scandalous, and malicious writing or writings against the United States, or the president of the United States, with intent to defame . . . or to bring them or either of them, into contempt or disrepute."

Then came Jefferson. He too had his troubles and failures—in the design of national defense, for example. As for his presidential character (only one element in success or failure), Jefferson was clearly active-positive. A child of the Enlightenment; he applied his reason to organizing connections with Congress aimed at strengthening the more popular forces. A man of catholic interests and delightful humor, Jefferson combined a clear and open vision of what the country could be with a profound political sense, expressed in his famous phrase, "Every difference of opinion is not a difference of principle."

The fourth president was James Madison, "Little Jemmy," the constitutional philosopher thrown into the White House at a time of great international turmoil. Madison comes closest to the passive-positive, or compliant, type; he suffered from irresolution, tried to compromise his way out, and gave in too readily to the "warhawks" urging combat with Britain. The nation drifted into war, and Madison wound up ineptly commanding his collection of amateur generals in the streets of Washington. General Jackson's victory at New Orleans saved the Madison administration's historical reputation; but he left the presidency with the United States close to bankruptcy and secession.

These four presidents—like all presidents—were persons trying to cope with the roles they had won by using the equipment they had built over a lifetime. The president is not some shapeless organism in a flood of novelties, but a man with a memory in a system with a history. Like all of us, he draws on his past to shape his future. The pathetic hope that the White House will turn a Caligula into a Marcus Aurelius is as naive as the fear that ultimate power inevitably corrupts. The problem is to understand—and to state understandably—what in the personal past foreshadows the presidential future.

NOTE

1. The book's central concepts have grown on me through a series of previous studies. See: *The Lawmakers: Recruitment and Adaptation to Legislative Life* (New Haven, Yale University Press, 1965); "Peer Group Discussion and Recovery from the Kennedy Assassination," in Bradley A. Greenberg and Edwin B. Parker, eds., *The Kennedy Assassination and the American Public* (Stanford, Stanford University Press, 1965); *Power in Committees: An Experiment in the Governmental Process* (Chicago, Rand-McNally, 1966); "Leadership Strategies for Legislative Party Cohesion," *Journal of Politics*, Vol. 28, 1966; "Adult Identity and Presidential Style: The Rhetorical Emphasis," *Daedalus*, Summer 1968; "Classifying and Predicting Presidential Styles: Two 'Weak' Presidents," *Journal of Social Issues*, Vol. 24, 1968; *Citizen Politics* (Chicago, Markham, 1969); "The Interplay of Presidential Character and Style: A Paradigm and Five Illustrations," in Fred I. Greenstein and Michael Lerner, eds., *A Source Book for the Study of Personality and Politics* (Chicago, Markham, 1971); "The Presidency: What Americans Want," *The Center Magazine*, Vol. 4, 1971.

10. Presidential Personality and Revisionist Views of the Presidency*

ERWIN C. HARGROVE

Our evaluation of presidents is greatly influenced not only by how we study them, but when we do so. Political scientists seem to have to learn anew what historians take for granted, that our pictures of reality, past and present, change as we change. The battle between the orthodox and revisionists among scholars is inevitable and neither side should be taken to have the whole truth. We reflect our times even when we do not know it. We are selective in what we see according to our values and implicit models of man; and new adjustments we make in response to flaws in models may, in turn, be selectively distorted.

We are entering a period of revisionist writing about the presidency. The FDR halo effect on the office has finally been dispelled by Vietnam, the failures of the Great Society, the negative characteristics of the personalities of Lyndon Johnson and Richard Nixon, an awareness of the relatively unchecked and unaccountable faceless men in the institutionalized presidency of which Watergate is the denouement, and a growing concern about the impotence of both Congress and the bureaucracy in the face of arrogant executive authority. There is dismay among liberals that their beliefs about the benevolence of power have been shattered by experience. The older literature on the presidency is filled with litanies to heroic leadership, to the skills of power-maximizing, to the importance of presidential autonomy in foreign affairs,

and to the sure success of presidential leadership for social change provided sufficient political power could be amassed in the White House. We are now unhappy because a conservative president has acted as we have said only a liberal should act. Our conservative presidents, as depicted in the literature, were supposed to be restrained, and ultimately failures at achievement, in order that the political way might be paved for heroic liberal presidents. But our disenchantment is also with ourselves. Vietnam was a liberal's war. The failures of the Great Society were, in part, failures of liberal ideology. Lyndon Johnson should have been a great heroic president in the tradition of Roosevelt. The quiet crisis in our beliefs about the presidency may be one manifestation of the larger dilemma of American liberalism. We have believed in the goodness of the American mission abroad and in our capacity, through the use of reason, to solve our social problems. We have looked on the presidency as the chief agency for this end. We may have been naive. Reinhold Niebuhr writes of the element of "irony" in history in which a hidden relationship is discovered through experience. Virtue becomes vice through some hidden defect in the virtue. Strength becomes weakness because of the vanity in strength. Wisdom becomes folly because we do not know its limits. The ironic situation is distinguished from the pathetic or the tragic because

*Source: From American Journal of Political Science, vol. 17, no. 11 (November 1973), pp. 819-835. Copyright © 1973 by the University of Texas Press. Reprinted by permission.

the individual bears some responsibility for it.[1] Niebuhr sees American liberal culture as continually overtaken by irony in its pretensions about the relationships of virtue, wisdom, and power. We are blind to the sin of pride in our sense of virtue. Perhaps our innocence has been both our greatest hope and chief flaw. This is a fundamental dilemma for American liberals in their beliefs about power and progress.

Revisionist thought about the presidency in political science may, therefore, have something of a conservative flavor which will seek to diminish the heroic conception of the presidency. There are signs of that. Sundquist tells us that Congress has always been more important in the development of liberal legislation than we had admitted. Cronin asks us to expect less of the office in the way of programs until we know more about how to solve problems and find ways to manage the bureaucracy. De Grazia calls us to a strict model of checks and balances as the beginning of wisdom.[2] Thus, we can expect the path of institutional reform to be one kind of revisionism.

Another revisionist approach will be to look very carefully at the psychological and cultural dimensions of presidential power in terms of the original assumptions of liberal ideology about the office which we find in our literature. In order to do this we must not only understand individual presidents in psychological terms, but also compare presidents according to the cultural values they carry and act upon. In studying the presidency in this way we necessarily study ourselves and our own beliefs about power and purpose.

This kind of revisionist writing will surely carry limitations inherent in the intent. In our praise for checks and balances, we may overlook the deadlock and malaise they often cause. Our search for psychologically healthy and ideologically pure leaders may lead us into new forms of idealizations of heroic leaders without our being aware of it.

Therefore, every piece of political science can be read as a document for the future intellectual historian, a datum illustrating the relativity of historical perspectives and judgment. This relativity of perspective applies to method of research as well. A new awareness of the importance of a factor which had received insufficient attention may lead to the development of new research methods, or a new emphasis in method, in order to better explore that neglected factor.

James David Barber's *The Presidential Character* is a revisionist study in regard to both message and method. It challenges a commonly held assumption that a power-maximizing president will be a "good" president, so long as he is a liberal. He shows that politicians of very similar values and highly developed skills of political leadership can have very different careers and behave quite differently, depending upon the existence of inner self-confidence and self-esteem. And he insists that we take "character," meaning the system of the inner self, seriously when we study and assess presidents and the presidency. Too often we look at potential presidents in political terms and do not ask what the effects of "character" might be. Barber thinks it is the most important factor.

Message and method come together in his comparison of the men whom we have considered "great" presidents in the twentieth century. A political classification would put Wilson, Roosevelt, Truman, Kennedy, and Johnson in the same category as progressive presidents. Barber separates them into two types, "active-positives" (Roosevelt, Truman, and Kennedy) and "active-negatives" (Wilson and Johnson). Hoover and Nixon also are treated as active-negatives. The active-positives are men who have survived the developmental crises of youth with success. They are happy, integrated, self-respecting and expansive, open to people and new experiences. They have a capacity for growth and a willingness to admit mistakes. Their energy is not bound up in defensive mechanisms but directed outward toward achievement. The active-negative is always in pursuit of inner phantoms. His frenetic activity is a compensatory striving for inner feelings of insecurity which, because they are in part unconscious, are insatiable. Political life provides the attention, deference, or power needed to allay anxieties about the self. Such people strive ceaselessly but never achieve satisfaction. They may respond to threats to self-esteem in ego-defensive ways that are personally cued and inappropriate for the objective political situation. We are given the examples of Wilson's refusal to compromise with the Senate over the League of Nations, Hoover's stubborn adherence to ineffective programs against the depression, Johnson's rigidity and defensiveness about a losing Vietnam policy, and Nixon's compulsive need to test himself in time of crisis by aggressive actions. Roosevelt, Truman, and Kennedy, in contrast, are pictured as leaders who were continually learning and growing in office, and who seldom confused private fears with public realities.

These two types are close to Lasswell's "democratic character" and "political man," respectively.[3] The "political man" seeks attention and power in order to overcome low estimates of the self. The "democratic character" has passed through his developmental stages successfully, and has outgrown the political drives. He does not need to dominate men. It is important to draw this parallel between the early Lasswell and Barber's work because Lasswell's distinction between "political man" and "democratic character" may have been forgotten in our idealization of the power-maximizing political leader in political science. Our liberal optimism has lulled us into a belief that a "political man" who serves democratic values is what we need. The experience of Lyndon

Johnson, a thoroughly political man, has caused us to think again; he surely was one source of the sensitivity out of which Barber's book grew, drawing attention anew to the original Lasswellian distinction.

Barber is, however, still the liberal, searching for the ideal type of liberal leader. All of his active-positives are liberals and they are presented in idealized form. He holds out the hope that a "good" man can be our salvation. We must learn to tell active-positives from active-negatives and choose accordingly. However, I can see some problems. These are ideal types and, as such, seldom fit individuals in their richness. Since we are all creatures of mixed feelings and uneven development, it is likely that many of us, including politicians, are some combination of positive and negative attitudes toward the self. Many talented and successful political leaders in the past seem to have been mixes of active-positive and active-negative characteristics. Theodore Roosevelt, whom Barber does not treat, loved life and politics but all his life was driven by a demon of insecurity which drove him to outbursts of aggression under stress.[4] The same is true of Fiorello La Guardia, and among Englishmen of superior talent, one could cite both Churchill and Lloyd George.[5] In fact, FDR may be unique among greatly talented political men in being a pure active-positive type. Robert Sherwood called him "the most spiritually healthy man I ever met." But this is not a common attribute of great politicians.

This existence of a mix of positive and negative tendencies in a political man is not necessarily bad. It depends upon which tendency predominates. However, it does suggest that it may be hard to tell whether a leader is an active-positive or active-negative. Both Wilson and Johnson had strong active-positive sides to their characters. It also suggests that there may be a relation between a high degree of political skill and active-negative tendencies.

Lasswell's "political man" was characterized by compensatory striving. He developed skills of attention-getting—usually through oratory and self-dramatizing—and power maximizing in order to overcome low estimates of the self. One might ask, "Does 'democratic man' have the incentives to develop such skills?" In fact, highly healthy and well-integrated personalities like Truman, Kennedy, and Eisenhower clearly were "democratic characters," and in my view active-positives, but the component missing from the character of each was an inner spur of insecurity linked to the development of extraordinary political skills. None were "natural" political men, but each taught himself the political arts. Franklin Roosevelt stands alone as a "natural" political man whose needs and skills combined in a high degree of political talent, and who was also a fairly pure active-positive.

There may be three types rather than two: (1) an active-positive who is a "democratic character" and not a "political man"; (2) a mix of active-positive and negative who is a "democratic character" and "political man"; and (3) the pure active-negative who is also a "politial man," but not a "democratic character." On the one hand, if this corresponds to reality in any way we may find it very difficult to find a pure active-positive type—Barber's ideal leader—who is also a highly skilled politician. On the other hand, we may have overemphasized the importance of political skill in the form of the capacity to manipulate and bargain, and underemphasized the importance of moral character and inner security as bases for the authority and influence of political leaders. Dwight Eisenhower was criticized for his lack of manipulative skills, but in retrospect his ability to draw men together, to dampen conflict, and to inspire public confidence because of his manifest integrity, appear as valuable skills of leadership in their own right.

Barber grasps this link between inner character and the ability to inspire external confidence. He has tapped a very real problem of the contemporary presidency, and given us an original insight into the importance of a leader's self-esteem to his capacity for creating moral authority as a basis for support from others. An earlier literature on presidential style assumed that bargaining and manipulative skills were the chief means to presidential power.[6] Critics of this model of leadership have shown that it was too limited in its enumeration of the bases of power.[7] Ideological agreement, the legitimacy of the office, rational persuasion, and the moral authority of a leader are all important bases of presidential influence in and out of government. Barber links this argument to character by showing that a lack of self-esteem in a president can lead to a style of authority in interpersonal relations which becomes so closed, constricted, and ego-defensive that that president undermines his own moral authority and runs the risk of losing both his capacity to lead and be followed.

Moral authority is a base of power which is analytically independent of approval of presidential policy and respect for the legitimacy of the office, although in practice all three dimensions get intertwined. Lyndon Johnson virtually had to resign from politics in the Spring of 1968 not only because of a failing policy, but also because he had lost moral authority, in terms of his own style of leading, within his own political coalition both inside and outside of government. His overbearing, closed, secretive style of leadership had created not only a credibility problem, but also a separation of the president from reality. It took a series of shocks to bring Johnson back to an awareness of his position. This self-destructive style seems to have been rooted in basic insecurities of personality, and Barber brings this out clearly. We really are not talking about Lyndon Johnson as a crisis leader under pressure, something to which Barber gives great attention, but about Johnson's everyday style—a compound of both insecurity and the highly developed political skill which served that insecurity.

The case of Richard Nixon and the Watergate is even more revealing. At this writing (May 1973) Nixon's everyday style seems to have been one of the root causes of Watergate in three ways: (1) his compulsion for isolation and reliance upon tough surrogates to protect him from the outside world permitted them extraordinary latitude in how they served him; (2) his demand for total loyalty and often-expressed harsh criticism, of both opponents and friendly critics from within his own administration and political camp, encouraged excessive partisanship in his associates; and (3) his chronic inability to see any mote in his own eye because of his view of himself as constantly beleaguered by enemies caused him to deny that anything was wrong about Watergate until it was too late. All of these traits of leadership are rooted in insecurity, and they have proved to be self-destructive.

Therefore, while we need not deny the value of Neustadt's prescriptions about the importance of a president having a great sensitivity to power relationships, and being able to guard his stakes and resources in this regard through bargaining skill, we must broaden the range of personality characteristics and skills required for a full gamut of influence relationships. Sensitivity to personal power is not enough. Such sensitivity may at times lead a president astray if it becomes confused in his mind with his institutional position as president. He may guard his personal power stakes and neglect his responsibility to the institutionalized presidency.[8] This is perhaps what happened to both Johnson and Nixon. Insecurity caused them to personalize the office too much.

Barber is very persuasive about the active-negatives; he strikes a responsive chord in the light of current history. But one must ask some questions about his depiction of the active-positives. Truman is particularly well-handled by Barber. We not only see him as a combination of positive and negative estimates of the self, which accounts for much of his erratic behavior, but also we see that he did have a happy optimism about himself and life, which permitted growth and a continuous touch with reality. However, Roosevelt and Kennedy are presented in too idealized a form. We need to see more warts. This may be due to the liberal idealism of the book, the search for a new model of the democratic hero, which is hard to fault since it is deeply rooted in American culture and thus in us. But it may also be due to the method of biography. At the outset Barber incorporated "culture," meaning values and ideology, into his model of political personality. Culture must be made to operate as a motive along with other impulses in the purposive striving of an individual. He clearly sees this but in fact his depiction of Roosevelt, Truman, and Kennedy is almost cultureless in the sense that he stresses "character" and gives little attention to their actual beliefs as a motive force in their actions. We are left with the conclusion that a happy, healthy president is sufficient for the country. In fact, Barber has not so much ignored culture as taken it for granted. The liberal ideological impulses that animated these three presidents are assumed to be good ones and are not questioned. An approach to the study of presidents which was critical of that cultural and ideological continuity might draw very different conclusions.

We can test this by looking at John F. Kennedy, whom Barber accurately depicts as a secure and happy person with a great capacity for magnanimity, affection, and growth. But when we are told that Kennedy's ability to learn from his mistakes at the Bay of Pigs is seen in his mastery of command and control mechanisms at the time of the Cuban missile crisis, we must ask if this was progress? It has become fashionable among political scientists to praise Kennedy's handling of the missile crisis as a pure example of the virtues of "multiple advocacy" in government. What is often forgotten is that he precluded diplomatic and non-military responses at the outset, actually considering a very narrow set of military options. In fact, he came very close to adopting the proposal for an air strike. This suggests that a political ideology, and perhaps a concern about domestic politics, can limit "multiple advocacy" even in the most open of presidents. We may become even more credulous when we learn that many of those who survived Kennedy in government believed that the missile crisis was the appropriate model for our ability to control the tempo of escalation in Vietnam in 1964 and 1965.[9] The point is that a president can be a healthy personality and yet have a deficient view of the world and set of values.

This is the value of Henry Fairlie's revisionist book about Kennedy. It is written from the vantage point of an English conservative who reacts against the militant, activist tone of the Kennedy rhetoric and world view. Fairlie, coming from a more Burkean political culture, sees that Vietnam was in fact a war of the liberal activists, men obsessed with the American mission in the world. He demonstrates this clearly by quoting the Kennedy rhetoric, including the call of the nation to arms in the inaugural address. He sees Kennedy's tough-minded celebration of crisis and confrontation as mock heroic, and essentially unpolitical. The very things for which Kennedy and his supporting cadre have been most praised—such as drive, vitality, activism, and tough-minded realism—are seen in retrospect to have caused many of our problems. The *Pentagon Papers* are filled with such rhetoric.[10]

Barber relates that Kennedy became convinced while living in England before World War II and through the writing of *Why England Slept* that the central problem of leadership in a democracy was mobilization of publics to do the right thing.[11] His public rhetorical style, so different from the private man, was developed to call the people to sacrifice and support for action. This seems to be FDR all over again, something a liberal should admire. But Fairlie suggests that Kennedy was the Cold Warrior who sought to govern by crisis, confrontation, and appeals for popular support in the face of crisis. According to Fairlie, Kennedy lacked a world view of how tensions might be reduced. He encouraged his associates to think in terms of pragmatic options and short-run situations. Therefore, his foreign policies reflected a kind of pragmatic bouncing from crisis to crisis, a defensive response to perceived Soviet acts, in which the American government became the prisoner of events, with the tragic denouement occurring in Vietnam.

We see here a fusion of ideology common to most political elites, a style of tough-minded, pragmatic activism shared by Kennedy and his contemporaries, and a personal commitment to activism which probably was deeply rooted in character. For Fairlie, this style of leadership ignored the necessities of "politics," which require slow and studied cultivation of possibilities and a respect for inaction at times if the only alternative is rashness. Neustadt implicitly takes the Kennedy team to task in this way in his study of the fiasco of Skybolt.[12] There was a fragile and fallacious optimism in the American handling of the situation, particularly in the offer of Polaris to de Gaulle, which assumed that we could get other governments to do our bidding. Neustadt calls for more cautious goals in our dealings with other nations because of the limits of our knowledge about them and potential influence over them.

Of course Fairlie overdoes it because he has a single theme, relying primarily upon the public rhetoric and failing to look sufficiently at the man himself. He gives us very little of the private man's curiosity, skepticism, and dislike of pomposity. Kennedy did not have the arrogance of many of his aides who survived him in government. Nor does Fairlie solve the riddle of why a man with so much private skepticism about vainglory should have put so much vainglory into his public rhetoric. This is a major task for Kennedy biographers. Fairlie fails to show us how Kennedy grew until at the end of his life he had made an open-ended emotional commitment to three policy adventures, regardless of the political cost: civil rights, the test ban treaty, and a tax cut and deficit financing. This returns us to Barber's basically valid insight about Kennedy, that he was a strong, secure man who could and did grow, and who seldom was carried away by the foolish enthusiasms of lesser men. This is the key point to be made about the value of active-positive political leaders. We want leaders who care about objective achievement, not about proving something to themselves as a result of some old hurt.

However, we must inevitably ask if Kennedy's view of the world was adequate; increasingly the contemporary answer is that it was not. This suggests that the study of presidents which emphasizes psychological and cultural variables will inevitably be time-bound. Our judgments of the goodness of a man for the time and the office will be colored by the implicit political ideology, or perhaps one should say cultural ideology, which underlies it. Psychological health is not ideologically neutral. Concentration upon the basic personality of an individual may fail to catch the dimension of culture which he incorporates in his personality. And concentration upon a single president, even in this dual sense, may fail to capture the themes of cultural and ideological continuity which join successive presidents over time.

When we introduce this cultural and ideological dimension into the study of presidential personality we are not only studying them but also looking at the values of our society which they personify.

Bruce Mazlish understands this very well, and his study of Nixon is a combined culture and personality approach. We are given a very full picture of the psychological roots of Nixon's political skills and style. We see how in college he began to turn weaknesses into strengths. The development of skills of oratory, calculated caution, and planning were all compensation for deep inner uncertainties. He overcompensated for an inner lack of integration and spontaneity by exaggerating skills of order and control. Add to this a distrust of people, a preference for going it alone, a belief in his own virtue, and you get a pattern indicating a political style which emphasized control, order, privacy, and rhetoric-at-a-distance. The basic need indicated is for deference to shore up low self-esteem.

A number of Nixon patterns make sense in these terms. He is not comfortable with individuals and small groups but feels at home with crowds. Such an insecure man, uncertain about his own identity, finds identity in the many roles he plays. Thus, what often is taken to be a lack of conviction is rather an absorption in varied roles of the moment, which causes contradictory statements. He derives the sense of strength that he craves by surrounding himself with tough men who will protect him and strengthen his own resolve. He sees life and political events as a recurring series of personal crises because he really doubts his ability to cope. Every key event in his life is thus seen as a time of testing. He is a dirty fighter in politics, but actually sees himself as virtuous and projects his aggression onto his opponents. He has a great amount of self-pity, justifying his attacks on others by depicting himself as constantly beleaguered by enemies. This is the Uriah

Heap part of his character which so annoys people and which appears in every major speech from Checkers, to Cambodia, to Watergate.

Mazlish arrives at this model of Nixon's political personality by piecing together bits of evidence from his entire life in terms of a psychoanalytic theory. He concludes that the essential Nixon displays three traits known to psychoanalysts as absorption of self in role, ambivalence, and denial. However, the actual description of Nixon does not really seem to need specific psychoanalytic theory about mechanisms. It is Mazlish's sensitivity that builds up the picture, not a reliance on theory. A great deal of the baggage brought to the discussion detracts from the convincingness of the analysis, and one suspects that Mazlish did not need to rely on it at all for his conclusions. For example, he speculates how Nixon must have felt when his mother "deserted" him to tend a sick brother. A death wish is deduced from the likely reaction to the deaths of two brothers. Nixon's opposition to abortion is attributed to childish death fears. The submissive posture toward Eisenhower is seen as a duplication of his passivity with his father. Finally, we are told that Nixon is an uneasy truce between his father's aggressiveness and his mother's quietism. None of this psychologizing is necessary, and it detracts from a perceptive analysis of the adult. What Mazlish actually did was to trace the development of the young adult to the point at which feelings and beliefs had jelled into a mature personal and political style. We see insecurity worn on his sleeve. No great speculation about inner mechanisms is required to see it. Barber is much better here. He draws the picture of an emotional and materially barren early life, concluding that from a number of harsh experiences Nixon "brought a persistent bent toward life as painful, difficult and perhaps as significant, uncertain."[13] We do not need to know the actual links between child-

hood experiences and adult patterns in order to see the emotional connotations of those patterns which emerged from a turbulent childhood. The important picture is that of the adult patterns and the emotions in which they are rooted.

Mazlish is much better on the fusion between the psychological and cultural in Nixon's personality. He cites the existence of "corresponding processes" in personality for the explanation of action, meaning that several levels of motivation operate simultaneously in tandem. Nixon's drive for success may be in part an unconscious redeeming of his father's failure, and thus a private thing, but it is also the experience, fed by the American fear of failure, of millions of men of his and other generations. His ambivalence about the East, and resentments against liberal intellectuals whom he identifies with the East, are deeply grounded in his insecurities, much as they were with Lyndon Johnson. But again, it is hard to separate the person and the sub-culture. His speech to the 1968 Republican National Convention, in which he gave his own boyhood dream to succeed in life as the hope of America, is a perfect fusion of his own striving, the Horatio Alger myth of the society, and a popular political appeal. Mazlish shows how Nixon has been able to achieve a congruence of personal themes, including the cultural values he carries, into wide political appeals. He agrees with Gary Wills that Nixon is the "last liberal" who has transcended Whittier by an act of super-Whittierism.[14] He has invested his own weaknesses and drives into a gospel of Americanism.

Mazlish indulges in a good bit of foolishness trying to explain the actions of Nixon the president in terms of orality and anality. Such ideas add little to an analysis based upon Nixon's overt behavior. When Nixon attacks the Senate after his defeat on Carswell or appeals to ideas of national honor in the speech on Cambodia, we see the fusion of a time of personal testing, the brandishing of a set of values of strong fundamentalist impulses against college "bums" and political "liberals," and a conscious political strategy. All three motives probably were operative at once. We are given a believable picture of a man who is not so much cold and calculating at a time of crisis but disturbed, depressed and very human. Nixon appears in this book to be much like Willy Loman in *Death of a Salesman,* the lonely American trying to succeed in a barren society.

The similarity of the quite independently drawn pictures of Nixon by Barber and Mazlish give encouragement that sensitive biographers who use personality theory carefully can add to our understanding of a person. This is best done without psychoanalyzing. Rather, the biographer must keep personality theories handy as one possible source of explanation for motivation. To be plausible, personality theory must provide the most reasonable explanation for the given facts. Enough good work of this kind has now been done to show its feasibility and desirability.

But political scientists who study the presidency wish to do more than write biographies. They would like to have a theory of political personality which could be applied to individual presidents—past, present and future. This would be the purpose of a typology and predictive propositions drawn from it.

Barber gives us the best typology to date, but its very virtues raise questions about the usefulness of typology. It is clear and plausible, and it can be used by scholars who are not psychologists, but these may be debits as well as strengths. The typology admits of four "nuclear types" on two dimensions: (1) degree of activity, and (2) enjoyment of political life. The active-positives and negatives are contrasted with passive-positives and negatives. The passive-positive is a man in search of affection and respect as a reward for being agreeable and cooperative. His low self-

esteem is qualified by optimistic hope that he will be loved. William Howard Taft and Warren Harding are placed here. The passive-negative does little and enjoys it less, and is in politics out of a sense of duty. In power he avoids conflict and invokes high principles as a protective cover. Coolidge and Eisenhower are said to be here.

The typology as such is comprehensive and seems to exhaust the logical possibilities. It is useful as a sensitizing device with which to scan political leaders. The difficult methodological and conceptual problems come with fitting individuals into the boxes. Taft and Harding are believably classified, seeming to conform to the general characteristics of the passive-positive type. Another twentieth century example might be Stanley Baldwin, a British Conservative prime minister in the 1920s and 1930s whose passivity and manipulative cleverness in office evidently was rooted in a continuous need for affection and respect. The consequence was that he played the role of cautious party and parliamentary manager in the face of the menace of Hitlerism. He was a little man in a hard time. This suggests that the passive-positive may no longer be with us as a dominant type of national political leader, although this type certainly may be found in lesser posts, particularly legislative ones. Passive-positives are not likely to seek or be chosen for the high pressure jobs of president and prime minister. The years before and after World War I may have thrown up a number of men of this type in an atmosphere of "politics as usual."

The passive-negative is a much less believable type when one thinks in terms of national leadership. In my judgment neither Coolidge nor Eisenhower belongs here. Both were much more politically ambitious and skilled than Barber admits. Coolidge in particular was possessed by political ambition. His passivity seems to have been a deliberate style of leadership designed to draw support. Eisenhower actually seems very close to an active-positive. His personality was much freer of kinks than that of Truman; one can find in him no lack of self-esteem and very few, if any, instances of ego-defensive behavior. Ike was certainly not as active and energetic a political leader as the active-positive presidents described by Barber, but this may have been due to Eisenhower's conception of the office, a role requiring restraint, rather than to basic personality. Barber frankly admits that Eisenhower is the most difficult of presidents to classify, but we are left with his feet dangling over several boxes in the typology.

Perhaps the point is that "ideal types" must never be confused with individuals. We must pick and choose from the theory implicit in a typology as we seek to explain an individual, but he must be explained ultimately in his own unique terms. This is not to say that the propositions derived from an abstract typology and grouping of individuals are not helpful. They permit us to see common threads in different persons. For example, a sensitivity to the active-negative syndrome of compulsive activity laced with stubbornness joins together Wilson, Hoover, and perhaps Neville Chamberlain in common explanations for particularly rigid, hard-driving styles of leadership. This is a use of typology and personality theory for explanation of common patterns in diverse political personalities.

The great risk in a typology is that we will be lazy, relying on the type to explain the individual, thereby distorting individuality. This could be a problem if the language of a typology gets into common usage among scholars, journalists and members of the public. In fact, a typology is no substitute for the very hard task of trying to understand an individual and in the process trying to explain historical causation. For example, Barber hinges much of his argument about the danger of active-negatives in power on examination of

Wilson, Hoover, Johnson, and Nixon in crisis situations. This type of leader is said to be likely to develop ego-defensive and therefore rigid behavior during a crisis situation if the inner sense of insecurity is heightened. The prototype explanation here is that of Alexander and Juliette George, who have analyzed Wilson's stubbornness during times of testing, including the fight with the Senate over the League of Nations.[15] Other explanations are plausible but not complete because none of the three presidents—Hoover, Johnson, or Nixon—has yet been the subject of a definitive biographical study. Hoover's rigidity about programs in the face of the Depression may have stemmed as much from ideological as from personality factors. Johnson's refusal to face alternatives on Vietnam could very well have reflected ego-defensive behavior. But it could also have been interpreted as a self-styled consensus leader seeking to keep his opponents off balance and manipulate support from disparate sources much as he had in the Senate.[16] In the new setting and problem the old style was inappropriate. This style was rooted in personality, but it may have not been ego-defensive testing. Nixon exploding with fury over Carswell and making references on television to the Cambodian crisis as a time of testing for his political career is more plausibly understood in ego-defensive terms. This is because Barber supplies a wealth of evidence about Nixon's inner uncertainties and compulsion to test himself. However, one suspects that Nixon has acted aggressively in regard to North Vietnam on several occasions not only for reasons of personal testing reasons, but also because he seems to believe deeply in the ideology of American national power and honor, and could not permit a surface American "defeat." He and his adviser, Henry Kissinger, seem to have made conscious calculations that future detente with China and the USSR requires a strong American posture in Southeast Asia. In short, as Mazlish shows, there is often a congruence of the psychological, cultural and political in the actions of leaders. But it is difficult to fit such multi-causal explanations into typologies based upon psychological variables. And if one tries to develop a typology which encompasses the psychological, cultural and political, one is faced with the uncomfortable fact that individuals can be joined on one dimension but not another and that no one fits nearly into any box.

Although Barber has constructed the most useful typology for the analysis of presidential character, it is not clear to me that much will be done with the typology by political scientists. Most of them lack the knowledge of personality theory or the intuitive ability to work well with psychological variables in a biographical sense. One can hope that graduate training for students of the presidency, and of political leadership in general, will in the future include rigorous training in personality theory and biographical methods, for both historians and political scientists. There is no reason why this should not be part of the standard methodological kit. But there are more serious obstacles. Our knowledge of personality is far too limited to permit very many causal political style and actions. And it is not clear if the psychologists are going to be much help in their own research in exploring the lives of politicians.

Therefore, lacking a comprehensive typology and lacking a general empirical theory of political personality, my preference would be for marginal comparisons of presidents and other leaders in a historical context using an inductive method of generalization. The efforts of Barber and others to develop deductive theory can of course contribute to such marginal comparisons. At its least general level, this kind of research can permit us to compare how different presidents played a similar role differently. Of course we have always done this but usually without the assistance of personality theory. Such marginal comparisons can lead to general propositions which will guide the study of all presidents. These propositions will not be derived directly from a typology, although a typology may be one source of origin. Let me suggest a number of such propositions which are derived from the literature. They are intended to apply only to presidents and are drawn from comparisons of presidents.

(1) There is a relationship between personal needs and the development of skills of political leadership such that: (a) the need for attention is related to dramatizing skills and style; (b) the need for dominance is related to skills of leadership which emphasize a sensitivity to power relationships and an ability to move and manipulate others; (c) the need for order is related to a highly organized style of administrative leadership and the preference for a highly structured decision system; and (d) the need for achievement is related to an open, catalytic style of administrative leadership.

(2) High self-esteem is related to an open, learning style of leadership, although ideology intervenes, so that progressives prefer open, fragmented, fluid decision systems, and conservatives prefer ordered, hierarchical decision systems.

(3) Low self-esteem is related to a preference for a closed, centralized, structured decision system for both progressives and conservatives, although conservatives of low self-esteem prefer a closed, hierarchical decision system more than conservatives of high self-esteem.

(4) High self-esteem is related to the ability of presidents to inspire support from others.

(5) Similar skills of political leadership, such as dramatizing and manipulative skills, can be rooted in need structures of either high or low self-esteem; but the uses to which the skills are put are correspondingly different.

(6) The skills of political leadership are more commonly related to low rather than high self-esteem, and in this sense many political leaders are acting out a compensatory striving.

(7) Low self-esteem and high political ambition may lead to ego-defensive actions under situations of personal stress.

(8) The themes of ideology usually are congruent with personality needs and political skills. In this sense political personality is usually a unity. Therefore, most political acts of leaders are caused by more than one factor and level of explanation.

These propositions are only first beginnings. We must begin to formulate such propositions not only because of the imperatives of political science, but also because of the needs and values of American democracy. An understanding of the importance of the character of elites is as old as Plato. Our present crisis of liberal democracy is in part reflected in questioning about our deeply rooted optimistic assumptions about power and progress. We have seen fundamental flaws in the personalities of men in our highest office, and are concerned about the implicit ideology they have carried into power, which is our own ideology. Therefore, when we study our presidents in these ways we study not only our society but ourselves.

NOTES

1. Reinhold Niebuhr, The Irony of American History (New York: Charles Scribner's Sons, 1952).

2. James Sundquist, Politics and Policy: The Eisenhower, Kennedy and Johnson Years (Washington: Brookings, 1968); Thomas Cronin, "The Textbook Presidency and Political Science," reprinted in 116 Congressional Record S17, 102-15 (daily ed., 1970); Alfred De Grazia, Republic in Crisis (New York: Federal Legal Publications, 1965), chap. 5.

3. Harold Lasswell, Power and Personality (New York: William Norton, 1948). Also, see Harold Lasswell, "Democratic Character" in The Political Writings of Harold Lasswell (Glencoe, Ill.: Free Press, 1951), pp. 465-525; and Fred Greenstein and Michael Lerner, eds., A Source Book for the Study of Personality and Politics (Chicago: Markham Publishing Co., 1971).

4. John Morton Blum, The Republican Roosevelt (Cambridge: Harvard University Press, 1954).

5. Dennis Kavanaugh, "Crisis, Charisma and British Political Leadership: The Case of Churchill." Unpublished ms.

6. Richard Neustadt, Presidential Power (New York: John Wiley and Sons, 1960).

7. Peter W. Sperlich, "Bargaining and Overload: An Essay on Presidential Power" in Aaron Wildavsky, ed., The Presidency (Boston: Little, Brown and Co., 1969), pp. 168-92.

8. Alexander George, "The Case for Multiple Advocacy in Making Foreign Policy," American Political Science Review 66 (September 1972), 751-85.

9. David Halberstam, The Best and the Brightest (New York: Random House, 1972).

10. The Pentagon Papers, as published by The New York Times (New York: Bantam Books, Inc., 1971).

11. John F. Kennedy, Why England Slept (New York: Funk, 1961).

12. Richard Neustadt, Alliance Politics (New York: Columbia University Press, 1970).

13. James David Barber, The Presidential Character (Englewood Cliffs, New Jersey: Prentice-Hall, Inc., 1972), p. 401.

14. Gary Wills, Nixon Agonistes (New York: New American Library, 1969).

15. Alexander L. and Juliette L. George, Woodrow Wilson and Colonel George (New York: John Day, 1956). See also the essay by Alexander George, "Some Uses of Dynamic Psychology in Political Biography: Case Materials on Woodrow Wilson" in Greenstein and Lerner, op. cit., pp. 78-98. George deals with the difficulty of relating an individual to a conception of the "compulsive" personality type. It should be pointed out that Barber has been experimenting with a typology for some time, so this surely is not his last word. The typology for presidents was originally developed from the study of Connecticut legislators. See James D. Barber, The Lawmakers (New Haven: Yale University Press, 1965).

16. Philip B. Geyelin, Lyndon B. Johnson and the World (New York: Frederick A. Praeger, 1966).

IV

The Presidency: Focus of Political Leadership

Introduction. In this last quarter of the twentieth century, the beginning of the third century of the American Republic, the increasing complexities of our national and international political life have pressed greater responsibilities and burdens upon the president, far beyond those anticipated by the Founding Fathers. The Founding Fathers, after all, lived under a laissez faire economy and in a pre-automobile, pre-jet aircraft, pre-nuclear, pre-guided missile age. These greater responsibilities and burdens have resulted in the presidency becoming the nerve center of our domestic political life and, to a considerable extent, the western world. In short, the presidency has become the focus of political leadership.

How much power is granted to the presidency to meet the demands thrust upon him? The answer is, I believe, problematic. But political scientist James MacGregor Burns has articulated three models of leadership, each of which are said to grant certain amounts of power and to withhold certain amounts of power. Obviously, a president adopting one of these models and, in turn, having his "publics" accept his choice is, perhaps, a clue to whether the presidency can exercise the necessary political leadership for the nation at any one time or another. Burns' essay, "Three Approaches to Presidential Leadership," spells out each of the models and indicates the necessary political conditions for each to work.

Just what powers are available to the presidency regardless of the approach to leadership he adopts? Political scientist Clinton Rossiter sees the presidency as an office which encompasses a diversity of functional roles and exercises a variety of powers to include constitutional, statutory, and legal (judicially sanctioned) ones. In the next essay, "The Powers of the Presidency," Rossiter outlines those roles and powers. His study emphasizes the institutional nature of the American presidency.

Although the formal authority of the presidency, as Rossiter points out, may be considerable, implementing the authority is quite another matter according to political scientist Richard Neustadt. More importantly, Neustadt argues, the formal powers of the presidency are not all that formidable. Indeed, the presidency is in many ways institutionally weak, and because this is so, each president, in order to lead, must develop his own power resources. The president accomplishes this in large measure, says Neustadt, through persuasion. In the next essay, "The Power to Persuade," Neustadt spells out what a president must do to convince other great power holders in the government that they ought to do what the president wants done.

Some observers of the presidency are not so sure that persuasion is, alone, the key to presidential leadership. A president, it is argued, needs "sticks" as well as "carrots" to lead. As political scientist Richard Pious says, "presidents must rely on their constitutional prerogatives because they cannot obtain an electoral mandate, do not gain control of party machinery, fail to lead their legislative parties and cannot obtain expertise from the advisory systems that would permit them to lead Congress and the nation by force of argument."[1] Historian R. Gordon Hoxie certainly agrees with this assessment, particularly in the area of the president's commander-in-chief and foreign policy powers. The viewpoint represented in Hoxie's essay is certainly not the conventional wisdom that presidential power is merely the power to persuade. Hoxie points out, in his essay, "The Power to Command," that the command decision power of the presidency makes it possible for presidents to deal decisively with foreign affairs and military policy. Moreover, this power to command has more times than not been functional for the well-being of the Republic.

If the president is the focal point of leadership in both the United States and most of the western world, how certain are his hands on the levers of government upon which he must exercise authority, both in terms of persuasion and command? Are the linking mechanisms between the White House and the operating departments of government adequate for the program direction necessary for accomplishment of the presidential purpose? Political scientist Hugh Heclo makes clear that the president is not "all powerful" in the executive branch, that power is dispersed among a number of "temporary government" officials (who in many cases have few ties to each other and thus are a "government of strangers"), and between the temporary government and the top civil servants of the "permanent government." In the political universe, the temporary government gravitates toward the presidential planet, whereas the permanent government gravitates toward the congressional planet. Heclo in the next essay, "Political Executives: A Government of Strangers," provides a most insightful look into how the fragmentation of power between the government of strangers and the careerists can prove a raft of problems for the presidency.

In the final selection of this chapter, attention is paid to some of the problems that get in the way of the presidency as a focus of political leadership. One of the problems is, as political scientist Erwin Hargrove has put it: "We no longer possess a coherent picture of presidential power and purpose that can be invoked to justify leadership in the White House."[2] The absence of a coherent picture of presidential power is due in large measure to the many ambivalences and reservations we Americans have about the presidency. Political scientist Thomas Cronin discusses many of these political leadership contradictions and problems in his essay, "The Presidency and Its Paradoxes." Clearly, if the presidency is to exercise the central leadership role, care must be taken to avoid imposing on the president a "Catch-22" dilemma or forcing him into a political cul-de-sac.

NOTES

1. Richard Pious, *The American Presidency* (New York: Basic Books, Inc., 1979), p. 17.
2. Erwin Hargrove, *The Power of the Modern Presidency* (New York: Alfred A. Knopf, Inc., 1974), p. 3.

11. Three Approaches to Presidential Leadership*

JAMES MACGREGOR BURNS

THREE MODELS

It is a measure of both the genius and the flexibility of the Constitution that the first three presidencies provided three different models of government under the great charter. The first was the Hamiltonian model of a vigorous executive working within the system of checks and balances. After his earlier doubts that executive power and good republicanism were compatible, Hamilton succeeded in "tuning Government high"—so high that Washington's administration stands as one of the truly creative presidencies in American history.

The second great experiment I have labeled the Madisonian model after the "father of the Constitution," who mainly established it in theory and in law, but it was first tried out in practice by John Adams.[1] While not himself a member of the Constitutional convention, Adams had long preached the need of governments with countervailing powers and had fashioned for Massachusetts a marvelously contrived instrument that balanced powers within the executive and legislative branches as well as between them. A believer in prudent, orderly, and stable governments and in an ordered set of individual liberties and responsibilites, Pres-

*Source: Reprinted from *Presidential Government* by James MacGregor Burns, pp. 28-31, 108-17. Copyright © 1965 by James MacGregor Burns. Used by permission of the publisher, Houghton Mifflin Company. Footnotes combined and renumbered; selection title and some subheadings added.

ident Adams dissolved many of the Hamiltonian arrangements and tried to carry out a model of government quite close to the hopes and expectations of most of the Framers.

The third model was the Jeffersonian. Within fifteen years of the framing of the Constitution the first Republican president was presiding over a strong national party, dominating the legislature, and even trying to subdue a Federalist-controlled judiciary. If the Hamiltonian model implied a federal government revolving around the presidency, and depending on energy, resourcefulness, inventiveness, and a ruthless pragmatism in the executive office, and if the Madisonian model implied a prudent, less daring and active government, one that was balanced between the legislative and executive forces and powers, the Jeffersonian model was almost revolutionary, implying government by majority rule, under strong presidential leadership, with a highly competitive two-party system and with a more popular, democratic, and egalitarian impetus than the Madisonian. The Hamiltonian model was perhaps a more resourceful and flexible kind of government, the Madisonian more stable and prudent, and the Jeffersonian more democratic and potentially more powerful.

During the next fifty years American presidents governed in the light of these models or variations of them. They did not, of course, consciously try to adhere to a set general design, but they were influenced by memories of the early great administrations, by precedents, by institutional arrangements, by popular expectations, and by speeches and dicta that ran back to the first three presidencies.

Madison himself tried to shape and administer his government in the true spirit of the checks and balances. Since he lacked Washington's prestige, Hamilton's ability to manipulate people and Jefferson's strength as national party leader, he soon discovered that centrifugal forces in the government were frustrating his plans; that if he did not exert force through the political circuits, his opponents would exert pressure through the same circuits against him; that political structure could never be neutral; that even carefully designed checks and balances favored some interests and policies against others. The cabinet, supposedly an instrument of executive power, was turned against President Madison by congressional forces that blocked him from appointing the secretary of the treasury he wanted. The vice-president acted virtually as he wished against the president. The speakership, the caucus, the committee system were also turned against him.

We need not here review the tortuous history of the presidency between Madison's time and Abraham Lincoln's. Nor is it necessary to squeeze the various administrations into any one of our three models in order to find pattern or continuity. Some administrations—most notably Andrew Jackson's—had a sharply Jeffersonian cast; buttressed by a strong Democratic party, by a rising tide of votes and local party politicians, and by his own demagogic appeal, Jackson even more than Jefferson made the presidency the Tribune of the People. Here was a president that would really have horrified Hamilton and vindicated his worst fears. Other presidencies had more of a Hamiltonian cast, as the chief executives opportunistically sought to keep or expand their power as political conditions made it possible. Most of the presidencies were closer to the Madisonian model. It was not, in general, a time of executive leadership or creativity.

The vital question is not how well various administrations fit various models, but the implications for us today of the Hamiltonian, Jeffersonian, and Madisonian approaches to government. Each of these models was a way of granting and withholding power to the president, which meant granting and withholding power to the party and group interests represented by the president. Each model was subject to distortion and caricature. The Democratic party use of patronage under Jackson and other presidents was party government carried to extremes. Calhoun's theory of concurrent majority rule was virtually a caricature of the Madisonian model and its checks and balances; Calhoun would give a veto not simply to an institution representing (in some form) the whole nation, but to any substantial region or interest even if in the minority.

What about the Hamiltonian model—the model that lent itself most easily to opportunism, experimenting, manipulation, pressuring, and perhaps endless expansion? Since the essence of Hamilton's political tactics, especially in enacting his fiscal measures, had been the exertion of influence regardless of constitutional theory and principle, what were the natural limitations on the exercise of this power? Or were there none? Was there no limit to expediency? Hamilton in office had been limited less by constitutional niceties or principle than by counterpressure and counterorganization. What if the Hamiltonian impulse should be projected in a time when the natural counterforces to political pressure were enfeebled? Partial answers to these questions would not come until the latter years of the first century of the American Republic. . . .

At the close of the eighteenth century the Washington-Hamilton administration had been followed by a Madisonian type of president in John Adams and a Jeffersonian type in Thomas Jefferson. Doubtless by pure chance the same sequence occurred at the start of the twentieth century in Theodore Roosevelt, William Howard Taft, and Woodrow Wilson. This sequence under more recent political conditions makes possible a closer view of the three types of presidency in action. Happily for our purposes, these three men had more coherent and articulate theories of presidential power and its limitations than any other presidents in this century.

MADISONIAN MODEL

The *Madisonian* model, in this century, has embraced these concepts:

1. *Checks and balances.* Each branch of the federal government possesses some kind of veto power over the two other branches. At a minimum each branch must protect its own independence arising from its unique constitutional powers and bolstered by its special constituency and method of recruitment. Even the so-called weak presidents of the latter nineteenth century made gallant, and eventually successful, efforts to protect their powers as chief executives, notably their appointive powers. The widest power and the broadest duty of the president, Taft once observed, was the constitutional provision that "he shall take care that the laws be faithfully executed."[2]

2. *Minority rights.* The chief purpose of checks and balances is the protection of minority rights. Because, as Madison noted so brilliantly in the 51st Federalist Paper, ambition must be made to counteract ambition and the "interest of the man must be connected with the constitutional rights of the place," each major constituency in the nation—each major interest or region or ideology—had its "own" branch or sector of government that would protect its interests. Note, however, that this was the expression of minority rights *against* federal power; this theory did not grapple with the question of the achievement of minority rights *through* government.

3. *Anti-majoritarianism.* By the same token, the Madisonian formula quite deliberately aimed at thwarting popular majorities from getting control of government and turning it toward its own ends—usually seen as "tyrannical" or "despotic" ends. The great fear was that a majority would get control of all the branches of government, for the accumulation of powers in the same hands—even hands as numerous as majority control would imply—was considered the "very definition of tyranny." So various barricades were erected against majority rule through the mechanisms of automatic stabilizing devices, such as the presidential veto and (implicitly) judicial review, powered by separate and mutually conflicting sources of political energy in the various constituencies supporting the House, Senate, and president.

4. *Prudent, limited government.* The major inarticulate premise of the Madisonians was a belief in deliberate, circumscribed government, at the national level especially. They feared rash governmental action; they feared above all that government might succumb to the mob. They did not propose that government be deadlocked indefinitely—after all, they saw the need *to be governed*—but they preferred that government wait until such a popular consensus was built up in favor of some action that all the separate interests and constituencies would have been brought into agreement.

The Madisonian model required that each branch of government observe constitutional limitations and proprieties. Nobody has expressed this point of view better than Taft in a passage from his *Our Chief Magistrate and His Powers* that was clearly designed as an answer to Theodore Roosevelt's Stewardship theory: "The true view of the Executive functions is, as I conceive it," said Taft,

> that the President can exercise no power which cannot be fairly and reasonably traced to some specific grant of power or justly implied and included within such express grant as proper and necessary to its exercise. Such specific grant must be either in the Federal Constitution or in an act of Congress passed in pursuance thereof. There is no undefined residuum of power which he can exercise because it seems to him to be in the public interest. . . . The grants of Executive power are necessarily in general terms in order not to embarrass the Executive within the field of action plainly marked for him, but his jurisdiction must be justified and vindicated by affirmative constitutional or statutory provision, or it does not exist. There have not been wanting, however, eminent men in high public office holding a different view and who have insisted upon the necessity for an undefined residuum of Executive power in the public interest. . . .[3]

JEFFERSONIAN MODEL

The *Jeffersonian* model embraces somewhat antithetical concepts:[4]

1. *Unified political system.* A united group of political leaders and government officials overcome the checks and balances (while leaving the constitutional provisions intact) through party control of the machinery of government. This party control depends on the existence of a coherent and disciplined party that won office at the last election on a meaningful and principled party platform and hence can claim a popular mandate. The leaders act as a team—usually through some such body as a cabinet.

2. *Collegial leadership.* The party leader becomes president and governs through his party. His main responsibility in policy and programs is to the party and majority that elected him. He is a "team man" in office as well as out of office: that is, he governs with at least the passive consent of his fellow party leaders, who have some independent power. While the president as party leader can operate within fairly wide limits, ultimately he is governed by party purpose and limited, as well as supported, by the other national party leaders. In practice, his leadership cuts across all sectors of government and politics, except perhaps the judiciary, but in style he may be much more the undramatic corporate leader, like Baldwin, Attlee, or Macmillan in Britain, than the heroic type.

3. *Majority rule.* Government can act on the basis of a mandate endorsed by a majority of the voters, who have judged the competing platforms and candidates. Once granted power on this basis, the party leaders can govern subject to only two basic limitations: free criticism protected by the Bill of Rights and other constitutional safeguards; and free elections within a limited span of time. Otherwise the leaders can override traditional institutional and political restraints on action, even to the point of changing machinery (such as congressional procedure or administrative organization). According to theorists believing in majority rule, majoritarianism would not be tyrannical or despotic because any candidate who must win the support of the majority of people in a pluralistic and socially stable nation must hew to the center of the political spectrum, and so many of the various interests of the nation would be represented in any majority, that minority rights would be protected. The system, moreover, can positively protect minorities who wish to defend or expand their rights through government, rather than against

government. While majority rule could operate on behalf of a laissez-faire majority, the thrust of the doctrine is toward a more energetic and productive government.

4. *Minority opposition.* The Jeffersonian model assumes that the opposition party will maintain a vigorous and vocal opposition to the party in power. The opposition party can declare certain issues, such as "bipartisan" foreign policy, outside the arena of party rivalry, but this is the right of the opposition, not the government. The opposition party is compelled to criticize the government responsibly, and with some moderation, however, because as the alternative party it is always on the brink of gaining office and governing and hence would imperil its own tenure in office if it had made reckless and vainglorious promises.

HAMILTONIAN MODEL

The *Hamiltonian* model is much harder to define than either of the above models, because at its core there lies a large element of opportunism and expediency. Indeed, this kind of presidency can be and has been justified on the ground that it is flexible and resourceful enough to meet a variety of political situations. At its most limited, the Hamiltonian model could be described simply as Madisonianism plus a vigorous and versatile president; at the other extreme a Hamiltonian might use party machinery and serve as a national party leader, at least for a time, in much the same style as a Jeffersonian. Still, key elements can be found in it:

1. *Heroic leadership.* The president must be more than administrative chief or party leader. He must exert great leadership in behalf of the whole nation. He must not be unduly restricted by his party; when necessary (as he sees necessity) he can ignore it or even desert it. In practice he both uses party and "rises above" it. Heroic presidents have some of the qualities of the hero in modern setting: they cut an impressive figure on the hustings and before the television camera; they have style; they speak movingly and even passionately; they seem to establish a direct connection with the mass public. And they

are invested by the press and the people with even magical qualities: they are physically inexhaustible, it is said; they can read with lightning speed; they have total recall; and so on.

2. *Personal organization.* The president depends less—and is committed less—to the party as a whole than to his personal organization built up over the years. This personal organization is far more centralized, disciplined, and efficient than the general party organization. It is bound directly to the leader by ties of intense personal loyalty and hope of reward. Its relation to the regular party is ambiguous and changeable; the personal organization is ascendant during the presidential campaign, especially in the convention fight for the nomination, but cannot control the vast and diffused regular party that has its roots in scores of state and local organizations. Both Hamilton and Theodore Roosevelt maintained personal organizations; under Lincoln the Republican party was transmuted into the Union party, which served as a vehicle for mobilizing support for Lincoln and the war effort.

3. *Expedient use of power.* It is in this respect that the Hamiltonian model differs most sharply from the Jeffersonian. A president with the backing of a strong party enjoys a relatively assured basis of power; he may still have to marshal influence, but the building of the party and the success of the party in winning executive and congressional office at the preceding election provides the president with a reservoir of power that he can draw on from day to day. The Hamiltonian president has no such reservoir; he must employ every weapon that he has—his own reputation, his prestige, his patronage power, his political friendships—to achieve the results he wants. He must constantly fill, draw on, and replenish his own store of political credits. He depends more on personal influence than on party influence. He deals with opposition party leaders, as Theodore Roosevelt did with Senator Benjamin R. "Pitchford Ben" Tillman in winning railroad legislation, to muster support for his policies. Because he is not obligated to a great political party, he can "rise above" party when he wishes and pose as leader of all the nation. Although the power arrangements within which he operates are somewhat institutionalized, he has far

more leverage in manipulating personal and presidential power than if he were the responsible leader of a unified and disciplined party.

4. *Disorganized opposition.* The freedom of the president from party obligation and control gives him a latitude of political tactics and governmental decision making that in turn complicates the role of the opposition party leadership. The "out" party needs a clear target to shoot at, but it sees only a constantly moving one. The president may even make off with some of the opposition's leadership, as in 1940, when Franklin Roosevelt enlisted Henry Stimson and Frank Knox to his cause on the eve of the Republican nominating convention. By flirting with the opposition the president can seem to lift certain issues above partisanship. The opposition party is tempted to become opportunistic too, to attack the president from opposite and conflicting positions, but in doing so it loses face as a party cohesive and clear-minded enough to govern.

LEADERSHIP MODELS AND SUCCESSIVE PRESIDENTS

Woodrow Wilson and Franklin D. Roosevelt are tangible examples of the latter two presidential models. Brought up in the belief that the best politics was a mighty forensic battle between two organized and principled parties over meaningful differences in platform and policy, Wilson acted as a strong party leader both as governor of New Jersey in 1911-1912 and in his early years as president. Despite the grave weaknesses in the national Democracy of 1913, he used his party expertly to marshal opinion behind his program, and to put it through Congress. He worked closely with party and committee leaders; used the caucus to unify the congressional party behind his proposals for tariff reduction and a federal reserve system; and borrowed the influence of his fellow partisan and secretary of state, William Jennings Bryan, to push his program through. He acted, in his own term, as "the responsible leader of the party in power." But Wilson knew that party leadership meant more than cleaving to the dead center of the party; it

must be a leadership that moved with changing circumstances and popular attitudes. In 1916, with the Progressive party of 1912 crumbling, and with much of the old Democratic party agenda enacted or irrelevant, Wilson reoriented his party toward urban needs and claims. In that year, Link says, Wilson became "almost a new political creature, and under his leadership a Democratic Congress enacted the most sweeping and significant progressive legislation in the history of the country up to that time."[5] He led his party to victory in 1916, tried (and failed) to win a Democratic congressional majority in 1918, and made the League of Nations fight mainly a party struggle.

Contrast the political leadership of Franklin D. Roosevelt, a liberal Democrat who also had to re-orient his party toward urban economic needs, internationalism, and war. Taking office during economic crisis, he assumed the role of nonpartisan leader as he urged the nation to attack depression as though it were a foreign foe. As the election of 1936 neared, he assumed the posture of party leader and conducted, at least in the final stages, one of the most militant party campaigns the nation had seen. In 1938 he took his party leadership so seriously that he tried to purge conservative members of Congress from the party. As the European crisis grew he reverted to his nonpartisan role, which he adhered to through much of the war. He had to fight the campaign of 1944 as a Democrat, however, and in the last year of his life he was apparently contemplating the possibilities of party realignment that would shift liberal Republicans into the Democratic party and bring about "two real parties—one liberal and the other conservative."[6]

Roosevelt was a Hamiltonian in more than his party leadership. He was the gay, ebullient president who overcame economic and military crisis. He seemed to have magical personal and political gifts. He was flexible, resourceful, versatile, manipulative—even Machiavellian—in his employment of power. He developed and managed a highly personal political organization. He disorganized the opposition. And he had a clear and self-conscious desire to govern in the tradition of Hamilton, Lincoln, and Roosevelt—though often for Jeffersonian and Wilsonian goals.

But Franklin Roosevelt more than any other president exemplifies the central problem of this [work]. He made the presidency essentially his personal instrument and he used it brilliantly to experiment, innovate, and establish important reforms. But he failed during his first two terms to realize the main goal for which he had been elected—overcoming depression. He greatly enhanced the power and reach of the presidential office, but failed to develop a political base that could have provided sustained and dependable support for long-run programs. Partly for reasons outside his control, he was unable in the end to bring into productive relation his ultimate goals, his instrumental ends, and his means; on the other hand,

by his dexterous employment of presidential power he helped set the stage for the more purposeful action to come.

NOTES

1. James MacGregor Burns, *The Deadlock of Democracy* (Engledwood Cliffs, N.J.: Prentice-Hall, Inc., 1963), chap. 1.
2. William Howard Taft, *Our Chief Magistrate and His Powers* (New York: Columbia University Press, 1916), p. 78.
3. *Ibid.*, p. 138.
4. For further development of the Madisonian and Jeffersonian concepts and practices see Robert A. Dahl, *A Preface to Democratic Theory* (Chicago: The University of Chicago Press, 1956), especially chap. 1, "Madisonian Democracy"; and James M. Burns, *The Deadlock of Democracy* (Englewood Cliffs, N.J.: Prentice-Hall, Inc., 1963), esp. chaps. 1 and 2.
5. Arthur S. Link, *Woodrow Wilson and the Progressive Era* (New York: Harper & Row, 1954), p. 225.
6. Samuel I. Rosenman, *Working with Roosevelt* (New York: Harper & Row, 1952), chap. 24.

12. The Powers of the Presidency*

CLINTON ROSSITER

Sometimes the stranger outside the gates has a clearer vision of an American institution than we who have lived with it all our lives. John Bright, best friend in all England of the embattled Union, paid this tribute to the presidency in 1861:

We know what an election is in the United States for President of the Republic. . . . Every four years there springs from

the vote created by the whole people a President over that great nation. I think the whole world offers no finer spectacle than this; it offers no higher dignity; and there is no greater object of ambition on the political stage on which men are permitted to move. You may point, if you will, to hereditary rulers, to crowns coming down through successive generations of the same family, to thrones based on prescription or on conquest, to sceptres wielded over veteran legions and subject realms,—but to

*Source: From *The American Presidency*, Revised Edition, Copyright © 1956, 1960 by Clinton Rossiter. Reprinted by permission of Harcourt Brace Jovanovich, Inc. Subheadings added.

my mind there is nothing more worthy of reverence and obedience, and nothing more sacred, than the authority of the freely chosen magistrate of a great and free people; and if there be on earth and amongst men any right divine to govern, surely it rests with a ruler so chosen and so appointed.

My purpose is to make good Bright's splendid judgment by examining coolly at a hot time the powers and limits, the strengths and weaknesses, the past and present and future of the American presidency. This [work] is very far from a detailed or definitive portrait of the office. It is at best an impressionistic rendering of the main dimensions, and I beg early forgiveness for all the things I cannot possibly find room to say about it. My hope is simply that those who read these [pages] may come to a sharper understanding of the position the presidency occupies in the annals of our past and the hopes of our future.

This cool examinatiom must begin with a careful accounting of those tasks the president performs in our system of government, for if there is any one thing about our highest office that strikes the eye immediately, it is the staggering number of duties we have laid upon its incumbent. Those who cherish Gilbert and Sullivan will remember Pooh-Bah, the "particularly haughty and exclusive person" in The Mikado, who filled the offices of "First Lord of the Treasury, Lord Chief Justice, Commander-in-Chief, Lord High Admiral, Master of the Buckhounds, Groom of the Back Stairs, Archbishop of Titipu, and Lord Mayor, both acting and elect." We chuckle at the fictitious Pooh-Bah; we can only wonder at the real one that history had made of the American president. He has at least three jobs for every one of Pooh-Bah's, and they are not performed with the flick of a lacquered fan. At the risk of being perhaps too analytical, let me review the functions of the modern president. These, as I interpret them, are the major roles he plays in the sprawling drama of American government:

MAJOR PRESIDENTIAL FUNCTIONS

CHIEF OF STATE

First, the president is chief of state. He remains today, as he has always been, the ceremonial head of the government of the United States, and he must take part with real or apparent enthusiasm in a range of activities that would keep him running and posing from sunrise to bedtime if he were not protected by a cold-blooded staff. Some of these activities are solemn or even priestly in nature; others, through no fault of his own, are flirtations with vulgarity. The long catalogue of public duties that the queen discharges in England, the president of the Republic in France, and the governor-general in Canada is the president's responsibility in this country, and the catalogue is even longer because he is not a king, or even the agent of one, and is therefore expected to go through some rather undignified paces by a people who think of him as a combination of scoutmaster, Delphic oracle, hero of the silver screen, and father of the multitudes.

As figurehead rather than working head of our government, he greets distinguished visitors from all parts of the world, lays wreaths on the tomb of the Unknown Soldier and before the statue of Lincoln, makes proclamations of thanksgiving and commemoration, bestows the Medal of Honor on flustered pilots, holds state dinners for the diplomatic corps and the Supreme Court, lights the nation's Christmas tree, buys the first poppy from the Veterans of Foreign Wars, gives the first crisp banknote to the Red Cross, throws out the first ball for the Senators (the nine, not the ninety-six), rolls the first egg for the Easter Bunny, and in the course of any month greets a fantastic procession of firemen, athletes, veterans, Boy Scouts, Campfire Girls, boosters, hog callers, exchange students, and heroic school children. The March of Dimes or the Community Chest Drive could not possibly get under way without a five-minute telecast from the White House; Sunday isn't Sunday if the president and his lady skip church; a public works project isn't public until the president presses a silver key in Washington and explodes a charge of dynamite in Fort Peck or Hanford or the Tennessee Valley.

The president is not permitted to confine this sort of activity to the White House and the city around it. The people expect him to come to them from time to time, and the presidential grand tour, a precedent set conspicuously by George Washington, is an important aspect of the ceremonial function. Nor is this function, for obvious political and cultural reasons, untainted with commercialism. If it isn't one "Week" for him to proclaim or salute it's another, and what president, especially in an election year, would turn away the Maid of Cotton or the Railroad Man of the Year, or, to keep everybody happy, the Truck Driver of the Year from the White House door?

The president, in short, is the one-man distillation of the American people just as surely as the queen is of the British people; he is, in President Taft's words, "the personal embodiment and representative of their dignity and majesty." (Mr. Taft, it will be remembered, was uniquely shaped by nature's lavish hand to be a personal embodiment of dignity and majesty.) The role of chief of state may often seem trivial, yet it cannot be neglected by a president who proposes to stay in favor and, more to the point, in touch with the people, the ultimate source of all his power. It is a conspicuous thief of his precious time, yet more than one president has played it in such a way as to gain genuine release from the routine tasks and hard decisions that fill the rest of his day.

And whether or not he enjoys this role, no president can fail to realize that all his powers are invigorated, indeed are given a new dimension of authority, because he is the symbol of our sovereignty, continuity, and grandeur. When he asks a senator to lunch in order to enlist his support for a pet project, when he thumps his desk and reminds the antagonists in a labor dispute of the larger interests of the American people, when he orders a general to cease cavilling or else be removed from his command, the senator and the disputants and the general are well aware—especially if the scene is laid in the White House—that they are dealing with no ordinary head of government. The framers of the Constitution took a momentous step when they fused the dignity of a king and the power of a prime minister in one elective office.

CHIEF EXECUTIVE

The second of the president's roles is that of chief executive. He reigns, but he also rules; he symbolizes the people, but he also runs their government. "The true test of a good government is its aptitude and tendency to produce a good administration," Hamilton wrote in *The Federalist,* at the same time making clear that it would be the first duty of the proposed president to produce this "good administration." For reasons that I shall touch upon later, the president—and I mean any president, no matter how happily he may wallow in the details of administration—has more trouble playing this role successfully than he does any of the others. It is, in fact, the one major area of presidential activity in which his powers are simply not equal to his responsibilities. Yet the role is an important one, and we cannot savor the fullness of the president's duties unless we recall that he is held primarily and often exclusively accountable for the ethics, loyalty, efficiency, frugality, and responsiveness to the public's wishes of the two and a third million Americans in the national administration.

Both the Constitution and Congress have recognized his power to supervise the day-to-day activities of the executive branch, strained and restrained though it may often be in practice. From the Constitution, explicitly or implicitly, he receives the twin powers of appointment and removal, as well as the primary duty, which no law or plan or circumstance can ever take away from him, to "take care that the laws be faithfully executed." He alone may appoint, with the advice and consent of the Senate, the several thousand top officials who run the government; he alone may remove, with varying degrees of abruptness, those who are not executing the laws faithfully. The power of removal—the "gun behind the door"—is the symbol and final sanction of his position as chief executive. I doubt that there has ever been a more dramatic vindication of the president's authority "to produce a good administration" that Mr. Roosevelt's cashiering of Dr. A. E. Morgan from the chairmanship of the Tennessee Valley Authority in 1938. Frustrated in his attempts to secure Dr. Morgan's co-operation in clearing up a nasty clash of personalities that had brought the activities of T.V.A.'s governing board to a standstill, the president removed him peremptorily, made a new appointment to the position, and sent T.V.A. about its business. There were screams of anguish and prophecies of dictatorship, but there was no effective challenge to the president's contention that, although he could not construe Morgan's duties for him nor substitute his own judgment for that of a board rendered independent by statute, he could and must act to keep T.V.A. in operation.

From Congress, through such legislative mandates as the Budget and Accounting Act of 1921 and the succession of Reorganization Acts, the president has received further acknowledgment of his administrative leadership. Although independent agencies such as the Interstate Commerce Commission and the National Labor Relations Board operate by design outside his immediate area of responsibility, most of the government's administrative tasks are still carried on within the fuzzy-edged pyramid that has the president at its lonely peak; the laws that are executed daily in his name and under his general supervision are numbered in the hundreds. One task illustrates the scope of the president's administrative responsibility: the preparation and execution of the federal budget. One program attests the power he wields over the public's servants: the loyalty standards instituted by President Truman's Executive Order 9835 of March 21, 1947 and tightened by President Eisenhower's Executive Order 10450 of April 29, 1953. One passage from the *United States Code* makes clear that Congress itself expects much of him:

> The president is authorized to prescribe such regulations for the admission of persons into the civil service of the United States as may best promote the efficiency thereof, and ascertain the fitness of each candidate in respect to age, health, character, knowledge, and ability for the branch of service into which he seeks to enter; and for this purpose he may employ suitable persons to conduct such inquiries, and may prescribe their duties, and establish regulations for the conduct of persons who may receive appointment in the civil service.

It might be useful to hear the most recent opinion of the experts in this field. I take these paragraphs from the report of the sixth American Assembly, which met at Arden House in October 1954 to consider the "character, prestige, and problems" of the public service:

> *The President* has the responsibility for leadership of the Executive Branch of the Federal government service. Constitutional principles, the necessities of our national life and the example of successful corporate enterprise all underscore the indispensability of executive responsibility for the personnel policies and the personnel management of the Federal Government.
>
> This leadership must be acknowledged and supported by the heads and employees of executive departments, by the party leaders and by the members of the Congress. This leadership must be accepted

and exercised by the President, if the business of the National Government is to be efficiently performed.

Whether it is his letters or his taxes that the ordinary citizen wants more efficiently collected, he looks first of all to the president as business manager of the administration. There was a time when presidents could and did pay strict attention to matters such as these, and about a hundred million people still do not seem to realize that the time has passed.

CHIEF DIPLOMAT

Next, the president is chief diplomat. Although authority in the field of foreign relations is shared constitutionally among three organs—president, Congress, and, for two special purposes, the Senate—his position is paramount, if not indeed dominant. In 1799 John Marshall, no particular friend of executive power, spoke of the president as "the sole organ of the nation in its external relations, and its sole representative with foreign nations." In 1936 Justice Sutherland, no particular friend of executive power and even less of Franklin D. Roosevelt, put the Court's stamp of approval on "the very delicate, plenary and exclusive power of the President as the sole organ of the government in the field of international relations."

The primacy of the executive comes under vigorous attack from time to time, chiefly those who object to a specific policy even more strongly than to a president's pursuit of it, and it is true that he acts more arbitrarily and independently than the framers of the Constitution ever intended him to act. Yet the growth of presidential authority in this area seems to have been almost inevitable, and hardly the outcome of a shameful conspiracy by the three Democratic presidents of the twentieth century. Constitution, laws, custom, the practice of other nations, and the logic of history have combined to place the president in a dominant position. Secre-

cy, dispatch, unity, continuity, and access to information—the ingredients of successful diplomacy—are properties of his office, and Congress, I need hardly add, possesses none of them.

This field can be conveniently if somewhat inexactly divided into two sectors: the formulation of policy and the conduct of affairs. The first of these is a joint undertaking in which the president proposes, Congress disposes, and the wishes of the people prevail in the end. The president's leadership is usually vindicated. Our most ancient and honored policy is significantly known as the *Monroe* Doctrine; our leading policy of the past ten years has been the *Truman* Doctrine. From Washington's Proclamation of Neutrality in 1793 to Eisenhower's decision to go to the Summit in 1955, the president has repeatedly committed the nation to decisive attitudes and actions abroad, more than once to war itself. Occasionally Congress has compelled him to abandon a policy already put forward, as it did in the case of Grant's plans for Santo Domingo, or has forced distasteful policies upon him, as it did upon Madison in 1812 and McKinley in 1898. Nevertheless, a stubborn president is hard to budge, a crusading president hard to thwart. The diplomatic lives of the two Roosevelts are proof enough of these assertions. Mr. Truman was not exaggerating much when he told an informal gathering of the Jewish War Veterans in 1948: "I make American foreign policy."

The transaction of business with foreign nations is, as Jefferson once wrote, "executive altogether," and Congress finds it difficult to exercise effective control or to deliver constructive criticism—not that Congress can be accused of lack of trying. The State Department carries on its many activities in the name of the president, and he is or ought to be in command of every procedure through which our foreign relations are carried on from one day to the next: negotiation of treaties and executive agreements, recognition of new governments and nations, selection and supervision of diplomatic personnel, adjustment of tariff barriers within statutory limits, direction of our delegation to the United Nations, and communications with foreign powers. As commander in chief he deploys our armed forces abroad and occasionally supports our policies with what is known as "presidential warmaking." The conduct of foreign relations as a short-range proposition is a presidential prerogative, and short-range actions—the recognition of a revolutionary regime in Argentina, the reception of a Burmese prime minister, the raising of the duty on Swiss watches—can have long-range consequences.

In recent years, the role of chief diplomat has become the most important and exacting of all those we call on the president to play. . . .

COMMANDER IN CHIEF

The President's fourth major function is one he could not escape if he wished, and several presidents have wished it mightily. The Constitution designates him specifically as "Commander-in-Chief of the Army and Navy of the United States, and of the militia of the several States when called into the actual service of the United States." In peace and war he is the supreme commander of the armed forces, the living guarantee of the American belief in "the supremacy of the civil over military authority."

In time of peace he raises, trains, supervises, and deploys the forces that Congress is willing to maintain. With the aid of the secretary of defense, the Joint Chiefs of Staff, and the National Security Council—all of whom are his personal choices—he looks constantly to the state of the nation's defenses. He is never for one day allowed to forget that he will be held accountable by people, Congress, and history for the nation's readiness to meet an enemy assault. There is no more striking indica-

tion of the present latitude of the president's military power than these matter-of-fact words in the Atomic Energy Act of 1946:

Sec. 6(a) *Authority.* The commission is authorized to—

(1) conduct experiments and do research and development work in the military application of atomic energy; and

(2) engage in the production of atomic bombs, atomic bomb parts, or other military weapons utilizing fissionable materials; except that such activities shall be carried on only to the extent that the express consent and direction of the President of the United States has been obtained, which consent and direction shall be obtained at least once each year.

The President from time to time may direct the Commission (1) to deliver such quantities of fissionable materials or weapons to the armed forces for such use as he deems necessary in the interest of the national defense or (2) to authorize the armed forces to manufacture, produce, or acquire any equipment or device utilizing fissionable material or atomic energy as a military weapon.

It should be added that, despite the wounded protests of Senator Bricker, most citizens agreed with Mr. Truman's brisk assertion in 1950 that it was for the president to decide whether the H-bomb should be built. And, as the same man demonstrated in 1945, it is for the president to decide in time of war when and where and whether it should be dropped.

In such time, "when the blast of war blows in our ears," the president's power to command the forces swells out of all proportion to his other powers. All major decisions of strategy, and many of tactics as well, are his alone to make or to approve. Lincoln and Franklin Roosevelt, each in his own way and time, showed how far the power of military command can be driven by a president anxious to have his generals and admirals get on with the war. No small part of his time, as we know from Lincoln's experience, can be spent searching for the right generals and admirals.

But this, the power of command, is only a fraction of the vast responsibility the modern president draws from the commander-in-chief clause. The framers of the Constitution, to be sure, took a narrow view of the authority granted in this clause. "It would amount," Hamilton wrote offhandedly in *The Federalist,* "to nothing more than the supreme command and direction of the military and naval forces, as first General and Admiral of the Confederacy." This view of presidential power as something purely military foundered on the hard facts of the first of our modern wars. Faced by an overriding necessity for harsh, even dictatorial action, Lincoln used the commander-in-chief clause—at first gingerly, in the end boldly—to justify an unprecedented series of measures that cut deeply into the accepted liberties of the people and the routine pattern of government. Wilson added another cubit to the stature of the wartime presidency by demanding that Congress give him those powers over the economy about which there was any constitutional doubt, and Franklin Roosevelt, who had read about Lincoln and lived with Wilson, carried the wartime presidency to breath-taking heights of authority over the American economy and social order. The creation and staffing of a whole array of emergency boards and offices, the seizure and operation of more than sixty strike-bound or strike-threatened plants and industries, and the forced evacuation of 70,000 American citizens of Japanese descent from the West Coast are three massive examples of what a President can do as commander in chief to stiffen the home front in support of the fighting forces. It is important to recall that Congress came to Roosevelt's aid in each of these series of actions by passing laws empowering him to do what he had done already or by fixing penalties for violating the orders of his subordinates. Congress, too, likes to win wars, and Congressmen are more likely to needle the president for inactivity and timidity than to accuse him of acting too swiftly and arbitrarily.

Now that total war, which ignores the old line between battlefield and home front, has been compounded by the absolute weapon, which ignores every rule we have ever tried to honor, we may expect the president to be nothing short of a "constitutional dictator" in the event of war. The next wartime president, who may well be our last, will have the right, of which Lincoln spoke with feeling, to take "any measure which may best subdue the enemy."

CHIEF LEGISLATOR

The president's duties are not all purely executive in nature. He is also intimately associated, by Constitution and custom, with the legislative process, and we may therefore consider him to be the chief legislator. Congress still has its strong men, but the complexity of the problems it is asked to solve by a people who assume that all problems are solvable has made *external* leadership a requisite of effective operation. The president alone is in a political, constitutional, and practical position to provide such leadership, and he is therefore expected, within the limits of constitutional and political propriety, to guide Congress in much of its lawmaking activity. Indeed, since Congress is no longer minded or organized to guide itself, the refusal or inability of the president to serve as leader results in weak and disorganized government.

Success in the delicate area of executive-legislative relations depends on several variables: the political complexion of president and Congress, the state of the Union and of the world around us, the vigor and tact of the president's leadership, and the mood of Congress, which is generally friendly near the beginning of a president's term and rebellious near the end. Yet even the president whose announced policy is to "restore our hallowed system of the separation of powers" and leave Congress strictly alone—Coolidge is a capital example, one not likely to be repeated—must exercise his constitutional option to veto or not to veto about a thousand times each session, must discourse once a year on the state of the Union and occasionally recommend "such measures as he shall judge necessary and expedient," must present the annual budget, and must make some effort to realize at least the less controversial promises in his party's platform. In the hands of a Wilson or a Roosevelt, and now in the hands of an Eisenhower, the presidency becomes a sort of prime ministership or "third House of Congress," and the chief concern of the president is to push for the enactment of his own or his party's legislative desires.

Upon many of our most celebrated laws the presidential imprint is clearly stamped. Each of these was drafted in the president's offices, introduced and supported by his friends, defended in committee by his aides, voted through by a party over which every form of discipline and persuasion was exerted, and then made law by his signature. The signature, of course, was affixed with several dozen fountain pens, which were then passed out among the beaming friends and aides. Among the "ploys and gambits" the president may have used in the process were the White House breakfast with his chief lieutenants, or perhaps with his chief obstructionists; the fireside chat with his constituents, some of whom were also constituents of the obstructionists; the press conference, in which he proclaimed his astonishment at the way Congress was dragging its feet; the dangled patronage or favor, which brought a wavering or even hostile senator to his side; and the threat of a veto, which he brandished like the Gorgon's head to frighten the mavericks into removing objectionable amendments to the bill he had first sent over.

Even the president who lacks a congressional majority must go through the motions of leadership; and if, like President Eisenhower, his majority position in the country overmatches his minority position in Congress, he will be expected by the country, and therefore by Congress, to turn his policies into law. The Republicans always waited politely for Mr. Truman's proposals on labor, taxes, inflation, civil rights, and education, however scant the regard they intended to pay them. The Democrats, if we may believe Speaker Rayburn and Senator Johnson, have been impatient to hear President Eisenhower's proposals and to feel the lash of his leadership. In any case, the chief responsibility for bridging the constitutional gulf between executive and legislature now rests irrevocably with the president. His tasks as leader of Congress are difficult and delicate, yet he must bend to them steadily or be judged a failure. The president who will not give his best thoughts to guiding Congress, more so the President who is temperamentally or politically unfitted to "get along with Congress," is now rightly considered a national liability.

ADDITIONAL PRESIDENTIAL FUNCTIONS

Chief of state, chief executive, chief diplomat, commander in chief, chief legislator—these functions make up the strictly constitutional burden of the president. As Mr. Truman himself allowed in several of his folksy sermons on the presidency, they form an aggregate of power that would have made Caesar or Genghis Khan or Napoleon bite his nails with envy. Yet even these do not fill out the whole range of presidential responsibility. I count at least five additional limbs that have been grafted onto the original trunk.

CHIEF OF PARTY

The first of these is the president's role as chief of party, one that he has played by popular demand and to a mixed reception ever since the administration of Thomas Jefferson. However sincere Washington's abhorrence of "factions" may have been, his own administration and policies spawned our first two parties, and their arrival upon the scene altered the character of the presidency radically. No matter how fondly or how often we may long for a president who is above the heat of party strife, we must acknowledge resolutely his right and duty to be the leader of his party. He is at once the least political and most political of all heads of government.

The value of this function has been attested by all our first-rate presidents. Jackson, Lincoln, Wilson and the two Roosevelts were especially skillful party leaders. By playing the politician with unashamed zest the first of these gave his epic administration a unique sense of cohesion, the second rallied doubting Republican leaders and their followings to the cause of the Union, and the other three achieved genuine triumphs as catalysts of congressional action. That gifted amateur, Dwight D. Eisenhower, has also played the role for every drop of drama and power in it. It would have astonished George Washington, but it cannot even ruffle us, to learn that the president devoted breakfast and most of the morning of June 20, 1955—a day otherwise given over to solemn celebration of the tenth birthday of the United Nations—to mending a few fences with Republican leaders of California. He was demonstrating only what close observers of the presidency know well: that its incumbent must devote an hour or two of every working day to the profession of chief Democrat or chief Republican. The president dictates the selection of the national chairman and other top party officials, reminds his partisans in Congress that the legislative record must be bright if victory is to crown their joint efforts, delivers "fight talks" to the endless procession of professionals who call upon him, and, through the careful distribution of the loaves and fishes of federal patronage, keeps the party a going concern. The loaves and fishes are not so plentiful as they were in the days of Jackson and Lincoln, but he is still a wholesale distributor of "jobs for the boys."

It troubles many good people, not entirely without reason, to watch their dignified chief of state dabbling in politics, smiling on party hacks, and endorsing candidates he knows to be unfit for anything but immediate delivery to the county jail. Yet if he is to persuade Congress, if he is to achieve a loyal and cohesive administration, if he is to be elected in the first place (and re-elected in the second), he must put his hand firmly to the plow of politics. The working head of government in a constitutional democracy must be the nation's number-one boss, and most presidents have had no trouble swallowing this truth.

Yet he is, at the same time if not in the same breath, the Voice of the People, the leading formulator and expounder of public opinion in the United States. While he acts as political leader of some, he serves as moral spokesman for all. Well before Woodrow Wilson had come to the presidency, but not before he had begun to dream of it, he expressed the essence of this role:

> His is the only national voice in affairs. Let him once win the admiration and confidence of the country, and no other single force can withstand him, no combination of forces will easily overpower him. His position takes the imagination of the country. He is the representative of no constituency, but of the whole people. When he speaks in his true character, he speaks for no special interest. If he rightly interpret the national thought and boldly insist upon it, he is irresistible; and the country never feels the zest for action so much as when its President is of such insight and calibre.

Throughout our history there have been moments of triumph or dedication or frustration or even shame when the will of the people—the General Will, I suppose we could call it—demanded to be heard clearly and unmistakably. It took the line of presidents some time to grasp the meaning of this function, but since the day when Andrew Jackson thundered against the Nullifiers of South

Carolina no effective president has doubted his prerogative to speak the people's mind on the great issues of his time, to act, again in Wilson's words, as "the spokesman for the real sentiment and purpose of the country." The coming of the radio, and now of television, has added immeasurably to the range and power of his voice. Neither Jackie Gleason nor Ed Sullivan, neither George Gobel nor Edward R. Murrow—not even, I would insist, the peddlers of Revlon lipstick—can gain access to so many millions of American homes. Indeed, the president must be especially on his guard not to pervert these mighty channels and debase representative government. It is one thing for a huckster to appeal to the people to buy a mouthwash, quite another for a president to appeal to them to stampede the Senate.

Sometimes, of course, it is no easy thing, even for the most sensitive and large-minded of presidents, to know the real sentiment of the people or to be bold enough to state it in defiance of loudly voiced contrary opinion. Yet the president who senses the popular mood and spots new tides even before they start to run, who practices shrewd economy in his appearances as spokesman for the nation, who is conscious of his unique power to compel discussion on his own terms, and who talks the language of Christian morality and the American tradition, can shout down any other voice or chorus of voices in the land. There have been times, to be sure, when we seemed as willing to listen to an antagonist as to the president—to Senator Taft in 1950, General MacArthur in 1951, Clarence Randall of Inland Steel in June 1952— but in the end, we knew, and the antagonist knew, too, that the battle was no Armageddon, that it was being fought between grossly ill-matched forces.

The president is the American people's one authentic trumpet, and he has no higher duty than to give a clear and certain sound. "Words at great moments of history are deeds," Clement Attlee said of Winston Churchill on the day the latter stepped down in 1945. The strong and imaginative president can make with his own words the kind of history that Churchill made in 1940 and 1941. When the events of 1933 are all but forgotten, we shall still recall Roosevelt's words, "The only thing we have to fear is fear itself."

PROTECTOR OF PEACE

In the memorable case of *In re Neagle* (1890), which still makes good reading for those who like a touch of horse opera in their constitutional law, Justice Samuel Miller spoke with feeling of the "peace of the United States"—a happy condition, it would appear, of domestic tranquility and national prosperity that is often broken by violent men and forces and just as often restored by the president. Perhaps the least known of his functions is the mandate he holds— from the Constitution and the laws, but even more positively from the people of the United States—to act as protector of the peace. The emergencies that can disturb the peace of the United States seem to grow thicker and more vexing every year, and hardly a week now goes by that the president is not called upon to take forceful steps in behalf of a section or city or group or enterprise that has been hit hard and suddenly by disaster. Generally, it is for state and local authorities to deal with social and natural calamities, but in the face of a riot in Detroit or floods in New England or a railroad strike in Chicago or a panic in Wall Street the people turn almost instinctively to the White House and its occupant for aid and comfort.

And he, certainly, is the person to give it. No man or combination of men in the United States can muster up so quickly and authoritatively the troops, experts, food, money, loans, equipment, medical supplies, and moral support that may be needed in a disaster. Are thousands of homes flooded in the

Missouri and Ohio Valleys?—then the president will order Coast Guardsmen and their boats to be flown to the scene for rescue and patrol work, and he will go himself to bring cheer to the homeless. Are cattle starving on the snowbound western plains?—then the president will order the Air Force to engage in Operation Haylift. Are the farmers of Rhode Island and Massachusetts facing ruin in the wake of a September hurricane?—then the president will designate these states as disaster areas and order the secretary of agriculture to release surplus foods and make emergency loans on easy terms. Or are we having a March 1933 all over again, and are we caught up in the first dreadful moments of a financial panic?—then the president will issue the necessary orders on the authority of two laws that have been waiting quietly on the books since the first year of the New Deal:

Section 4 of the Emergency Banking Act of 1933:

> In order to provide for the safer and more effective operation of the National Banking System ... during such emergency period as the President of the United States by proclamation may prescribe, no member bank of the Federal Reserve System shall transact any banking business except to such extent and subject to such regulations, limitations and restrictions as may be prescribed by the Secretary of the Treasury, with the approval of the President.

Section 19(a) of the Securities Exchange Act of 1934:

> The Commission is authorized ... if in its opinion the public interest so requires, summarily to suspend trading in any registered security on any national securities exchange for a period not exceeding ten days, or with the approval of the President, summarily to suspend all trading on any national securities exchange for a period not exceeding ninety days.

In short, the president has been statutorily empowered in the event of any future panic like that of March 1933 to declare what amounts to financial martial law. At the same time, he remains constitutionally, even extra-constitutionally empowered in the event of an atomic attack to declare straight-out martial law through all the land. This, it will be remembered, is exactly what President Eisenhower pretended to do in the simulated hydrogen bomb attack of June 1955. One of the remarkable events of that three-day test of our readiness for atomic war was the startled discovery by Mr. Eisenhower and his staff that "the inherent powers of the presidency," something about which Republicans usually maintain uneasy silence, would be the nation's chief crutch in the aftermath of the ultimate disaster. This fact, and thus his status as protector of the peace, had already been recognized by a group of senators who called on Mr. Eisenhower to "assume personal responsibility" for creating an adequate program of civil defense.

MANAGER OF PROSPERITY

In one area of American life, the economy in whose health most of the world now has a stake, the people of this country are no longer content to let disaster fall upon them unopposed. They now expect their government, and especially their president, to prevent a depression or panic and not simply to wait until one has developed before putting it to rout. Thus the president has a new function, which is still taking shape, that of manager of prosperity.

The origin of this function can be fixed with unusual exactness. The Employment Act of 1946 was the first clear acknowledgment by the federal government of a general responsibility for maintaining a stable and prosperous economy:

> Sec. 2. The Congress hereby declares that it is the continuing policy and responsibility of the Federal Government to use all practicable means consistent with its needs and obligations and other essential considerations of national policy, with the assistance and cooperation of industry, agriculture, labor, and State and local governments, to coordinate and utilize all its plans, functions, and resources for the purpose of creating and maintaining, in a

manner calculated to foster and promote free competitive enterprise and the general welfare, conditions under which there will be afforded useful employment opportunities, including self-employment, for those able, willing, and seeking to work, and to promote maximum employment, production, and purchasing power.

The significant feature of this law from our point of view is the deliberate manner in which, in section after section, the president is singled out as the official who is "to foster and promote free competitive enterprise, to avoid economic fluctuations or to diminish the effects thereof, and to maintain employment, production, and purchasing power." He is granted the splendid gift of the Council of Economic Advisers; he is requested to make the annual Economic Report and such supplementary reports as may be advisable; he is expected to propose "a program for carrying out the policy declared in section 2, together with such recommendations for legislation as he may deem necessary or desirable." There is apparently no doubt in Congress's collective mind that one of the President's prime duties is to watch like a mother hen over all the eggs in all our baskets. As for the American people, it is a notorious fact that we give our president small credit for prosperity and full blame for hard times.

Yet even if the Employment Act had never been passed, he would have this duty and most of the powers that go with it. We have built some remarkable stabilizing devices into our political economy since 1929, and the men who control them—in the Federal Reserve System, the Securities and Exchange Commission, the Federal Security Agency, the countless credit organizations of which former President Hoover has complained so bitterly, the Federal Deposit Insurance Corporation—are wide open to suggestions from the White House. And there is always the presidency itself for men to rush to in the face of impending economic disaster.

There are limits, both strategic and physical, to what can be done in the White House, but certainly the alert president stands always ready to invite the managers of a sick industry or the leading citizens of a city plagued by chronic unemployment to come together and take counsel under his leadership. Of course, it is not his counsel but a well-placed government contract or a hike in the tariff or a dramatic recommendation to Congress that they have come for. Fortunately for the president, his position as overseer of the entire economy is obvious to even the most embittered spokesman for special interests, and he can take refuge from their pleas for relief by insisting that he must consider the whole picture before deciding on action in their behalf.

The very notion of the president as manager of prosperity is, for many people, an economic and political heresy. The tattered doctrine of the self-healing economy still claims the allegiance of several million Americans, who are especially vocal in the months before an election. Most of us, however, now accept the idea of a federal government openly engaged in preventing runaway booms and plunging busts. We need only think of Mr. Eisenhower's creditable performance in the slack days of 1954 to recognize the central position of the presidency in this new kind of government. Lest there be any doubt how the president himself—this Republican president dedicated to the cause of free enterprise—feels about the new dimension of government responsibility, let me quote from his message to Congress accompanying the Economic Report for 1953:

> The demands of modern life and the unsettled status of the world require a more important role for government than it played in earlier and quieter times. . . .
>
> Government must use its vast power to help maintain employment and purchasing power as well as to maintain reasonably stable prices.
>
> Government must be alert and sensitive to economic developments, including its

own myriad activities. It must be prepared to take preventive as well as remedial action; and it must be ready to cope with new situations that may arise. This is not a start-and-stop responsibility, but a continuous one.

The arsenal of weapons at the disposal of Government for maintaining economic stability is formidable. It includes credit controls administered by the Federal Reserve System; the debt-management policies of the Treasury; authority of the President to vary the terms of mortgages carrying Federal insurance; flexibility in administration of the budget; agricultural supports; modification of the tax structure; and public works. We shall not hesitate to use any or all of these weapons as the situation may require.

LEADER OF A COALITION OF FREE NATIONS

In order to grasp the full import of the last of the president's roles, we must take him as chief diplomat, commander in chief, and chief of state, then thrust him onto a far wider stage, there to perform before a much more numerous but no less critical audience. For the modern president is, whether we or our friends abroad like it or not, marked out for duty as the leader of a coalition of free nations, or at least as permanent presiding officer of various committees of his peers, the leaders of those nations united in the face of Soviet pressure. The president has a much larger constituency than the American electorate, for his words and deeds in behalf of our own survival as a free nation have a direct bearing upon the freedom and stability of at least a dozen, perhaps even two dozen other countries.

The reasons why he, rather than the British prime minister or French premier or an outstanding figure from one of the smaller countries, should be singled out for supranational leadership are too clear to require extended mention. Not only are we the richest and most powerful member of any coalition we may enter, not only are we the chief target of the enemy and thus the most truculent of the powers arrayed against him, but

the presidency, for the very reasons I have dwelled upon, unites power, drama, and prestige as does no other office in the world. Its incumbent sits, wherever he sits, at the head of the table. Winston Churchill, an A-plus student of our system of government, recognized this great truth with unerring eye when he insisted that not he, the elder statesman, but Mr. Eisenhower, the American president, take the chair in the middle at the Big Three conference in Bermuda in 1953. No British prime minister would ever be likely to forget that the president with whom he must deal every week of the year is a head of state as well as a head of government, a king and a prime minister rolled into one.

This role is not much more than a decade old, although there was a short rehearsal of it in late 1918 and the first few months of 1919. Whether it will continue to grow in the years of tension ahead depends, of course, on just how taut the tension remains. It does seem probable that the president will have no choice but to act consciously for and speak openly to the nations with whom we are associated in defense of freedom—to act as Mr. Truman did in the North Korean aggression of June 1950, to speak as Mr. Eisenhower did in his proposal for an international atomic energy pool delivered to the Assembly of the United Nations in December 1953.

UNIFICATION OF THE FUNCTIONS

Having engaged in this piecemeal analysis of the presidency, I hasten to fit the pieces back together into a seamless unity. For that, after all, is what the presidency is, and I hope this exercise in political taxonomy has not obscured the paramount fact that it is a single office filled by a single man. I feel something like a professor of nutritional science who has just ticked off the ingredients of a wonderful stew. The members of the audience may be clear in their minds about the items in the pot, but they haven't the slightest notion of what the final product looks like or tastes like or will feel like in their stomachs. The presidency, too, is a wonderful stew whose unique flavor cannot be accounted for simply by making a list of its ingredients. It is a whole greater than and different from the sum of its parts, an office whose power and prestige are something more than the arithmetical total of these ten functions. The president is not one kind of official one part of the day, another kind in another part—king in the morning, legislator at lunch, administrator in the afternoon, commander before dinner, and politician at odd moments that come his weary way. He is all these things all the time, and any one of his functions feeds upon and into all the others. He is a more exalted chief of state because he is also voice of the people, a more forceful chief diplomat because he commands the armed forces personally, a more effective chief legislator because the political system forces him to be chief of party, a more artful manager of prosperity because he is chief executive.

At the same time, several of these functions are plainly in competition, even in conflict, with one another, and not just in terms of their demands on the president's time and energy. The roles of voice of the people and chief of party cannot both be played with equal fervor, as Mr. Truman proved on several occasions that had best be forgotten, while to act as chief diplomat but to think as chief of party, as Mr. Truman did in the Palestine crisis of 1948, can throw our foreign relations into indelicate confusion. Mr. Eisenhower certainly has had his periods in which, despite perfect health, he reigned too much and thus ruled too little, and one can think of several competent presidents—Cleveland and Hoover, for example—who tried much too hard to be faithful chief executives.

There is no easy formula for solving this problem inherent in the nature of the office. If the presidency is a chamber orchestra of ten pieces, all played by the leader, he must learn for himself by hard practice how to blend them together, remembering always that perfect harmony is unattainable, remembering, too, with Whitman, to "resist anything better than my own diversity." The only thing he can know for certain before he begins to make presidential music is that there are several parts—notably those of chief of party and chief administrator—that he must not play too long and loud lest he drown out the others.

The burden of these ten functions is colossal, and the president carries it as well as he does only because a remarkable array of administrative machinery has been invented to help him in his daily tasks. . . .

Yet the activities of this train of experts, the Executive Office and the cabinet and all their offshoots and auxiliaries, must not draw our final attention away from the man all alone at the head. The presidency . . . has been converted into an institution during the past quarter-century, and we can never again talk about it sensibly without accounting for "the men around the president." Yet if it has become a twelve-hundred-man job in the budget and in the minds of students of public administration, it remains a one-man job in the Constitution and in the minds of the people—a truth of which we were dramatically reminded when the president fell ill in September 1955. Since it is a one-man job, the one man who holds it can never escape making the final decisions in each of the many areas in which the American people and their Constitution hold him responsible.

Mr. Truman, so it is said, used to keep a sign on his desk that read: "The buck stops here." That, in the end, is the essence of the presidency. It is the one office in all the land whose occupant is forbidden to pass the buck.

13. The Power to Persuade*

RICHARD E. NEUSTADT

The limits on command suggest the structure of our government. The constitutional convention of 1787 is supposed to have created a government of "separated powers." It did nothing of the sort. Rather, it created a government of separated institutions *sharing* powers.[1] "I am part of the legislative process," Eisenhower often said in 1959 as a reminder of his veto.[2] Congress, the dispenser of authority and funds, is no less part of the administrative process. Federalism adds another set of separated institutions. The Bill of Rights adds others. Many public purposes can only be achieved by voluntary acts of private institutions; the press, for one, in Douglass Cater's phrase, is a "fourth branch of government."[3] And with the coming of alliances abroad, the separate institutions of a London, or a Bonn, share in the making of American public policy.

What the Constitution separates our political parties do not combine. The parties are themselves composed of separated organizations sharing public authority. The authority consists of nominating powers. Our national parties are confederations of state and local party institutions, with a headquarters that represents the White House, more or less, if the party has a president in office. These confederacies manage presidential nominations. All other public offices depend upon electorates confined within the states.[4] All other nominations are controlled within the states. The president and congressmen who bear one party's label are divided by dependence upon different sets of voters. The differences are sharpest at the stage of nomination. The White House has too small a share in nominating congressmen, and Congress has too little weight in nominating presidents for party to erase their constitutional separation. Party links are stronger than is frequently supposed, but nominating processes assure the separation.[5]

The separateness of institutions and the sharing of authority prescribe the terms on which a president persuades. When one man shares authority with another, but does not gain or lose his job upon the other's whim, his willingness to act upon the urging of the other turns on whether he conceives the action right for him. The essence of a president's persuasive task is to convince such men that what the White House wants of them is what they ought to do for their sake and on their authority.

Persuasive power, thus defined, amounts to more than charm or reasoned argument. These have their uses for a president, but these are not the whole of his resources. For the men he would induce to do what he wants done on their own responsibility will need or fear some acts by him on his responsibility. If they share his authority, he has some share in theirs. Presidential "powers" may be inconclusive when a president commands, but always remain relevant as he persuades. The status and authority inherent in his office reinforce his logic and his charm.

Status adds something to persuasive-

*Source: From *Presidential Power: The Politics of Leadership with Reflections on Johnson and Nixon* by Richard E. Neustadt, pp. 101-110 and 114. Copyright © 1960 and 1976 by John Wiley & Sons, Inc. Reprinted by permission of John Wiley & Sons, Inc.

ness; authority adds still more. When Truman urged wage changes on his secretary of commerce while the latter was administering the steel mills, he and Secretary Sawyer were not just two men reasoning with one another. Had they been so, Sawyer probably would never have agreed to act. Truman's status gave him special claims to Sawyer's loyalty, or at least attention. In Walter Bagehot's charming phrase "no man can *argue* on his knees." Although there is no kneeling in this country, few men—and exceedingly few cabinet officers—are immune to the impulse to say "yes" to the president of the United States. It grows harder to say "no" when they are seated in his oval office at the White House, or in his study on the second floor, where almost tangibly he partakes of the aura of his physical surroundings. In Sawyer's case, moreover, the president possessed formal authority to intervene in many matters of concern to the secretary of commerce. These matters ranged from jurisdictional disputes among the defense agencies to legislation pending before Congress and, ultimately, to the tenure of the secretary, himself. There is nothing in the record to suggest that Truman voiced specific threats when they negotiated over wage increases. But given his *formal* powers and their relevance to Sawyer's other interests, it is safe to assume that Truman's very advocacy of wage action conveyed an implicit threat.

A president's authority and status give him great advantages in dealing with the men he would persuade. Each "power" is a vantage point for him in the degree that other men have use for his authority. From the veto to appointments, from publicity to budgeting, and so down a long list, the White House now controls the most encompassing array of vantage points in the American political system. With hardly an exception, the men who share in governing this country are aware that at some time, in some degree, the doing of *their* jobs, the furthering of *their* ambitions, may depend upon the president of the United States. Their need for presidential action, or their fear of it, is bound to be recurrent if not actually continuous. Their need or fear is his advantage.

A president's advantages are greater than mere listing of his "powers" might suggest. The men with whom he deals must deal with him until the last day of his term. Because they have continuing relationships with him, his future, while it lasts, supports his present influence. Even though there is no need or fear of him today, what he could do tomorrow may supply today's advantage. Continuing relationships may convert any "power," any aspect of his status, into vantage points in almost any case. When he induces other men to do what he wants done, a president can trade on their dependence now *and* later.

The president's advantages are checked by the advantages of others. Continuing relationships will pull in both directions. These are relationships of mutual dependence. A president depends upon the men he would persuade; he has to reckon with his need or fear of them. They too will possess status, or authority, or both, else they would be of little use to him. Their vantage points confront his own; their power tempers his.

Persuasion is a two-way street. Sawyer, it will be recalled, did not respond at once to Truman's plan for wage increases at the steel mills. On the contrary, the secretary hesitated and delayed and only acquiesced when he was satisfied that publicly he would not bear the onus of decision. Sawyer had some points of vantage all his own from which to resist presidential pressure. If he had to reckon with coercive implications in the president's "situations of strength," so had Truman to be mindful of the implications underlying Sawyer's place as a department head, as steel administrator, and as a cabinet spokesman for business. Loyalty is reciprocal. Having taken on a dirty job in the steel crisis, Sawyer had strong claims to loyal support. Besides, he had authority to do some things that the White House could ill afford. Emulating Wilson, he might have resigned in a huff (the removal power also works two ways). Or emulating Ellis Arnall, he might have declined to sign necessary orders. Or, he might have let it be known publicly that he deplored what he was told to do and protested its doing. By following any of these courses Sawyer almost surely would have strengthened the position of management, weakened the position of the White House, and embittered the union. But the whole purpose of a wage increase was to enhance White House persuasiveness in urging settlement upon union and companies alike. Although Sawyer's status and authority did not give him the power to prevent an increase outright, they gave him capability to undermine its purpose. If his authority over wage rates had veen vested by a statute, not by revocable presidential order, his power of prevention might have been complete. So Harold Ickes demonstrated in the famous case of helium sales to Germany before the Second World War.[6]

The power to persuade is the power to bargain. Status and authority yield bargaining advantages. But in a government of "separated institutions sharing powers," they yield them to all sides. With the array of vantage points at his disposal, a president may be far more persuasive than his logic or his charm could make him. But outcomes are not guaranteed by his advantages. There remain the counter pressures those whom he would influence can bring to bear on him from vantage points at their disposal. Command has limited utility; persuasion becomes give-and-take. It is well that the White House holds the vantage points it does. In such a business any president may need them all—and more.

This view of power as akin to bargaining is one we commonly accept in the sphere of congressional relations. Every

textbook states and every legislative session demonstrates that save in times like the extraordinary Hundred Days of 1933—times virtually ruled out by definition at mid-century—a president will often be unable to obtain congressional action on his terms or even to halt action he opposes. The reverse is equally accepted: Congress often is frustrated by the president. Their formal powers are so intertwined that neither will accomplish very much, for very long, without the acquiescence of the other. By the same token, though, what one demands, the other can resist. The stage is set for that great game, much like collective bargaining, in which each seeks to profit from the other's needs and fears. It is a game played catch-as-catch-can, case by case. And everybody knows the game, observers and participants alike.

The concept of real power as a give-and-take is equally familiar when applied to presidential influence outside the formal structure of the federal government. The Little Rock affair may be extreme, but Eisenhower's dealings with the governor—and with the citizens—become a case in point. Less extreme but no less pertinent is the steel seizure case with respect to union leaders, and to workers, and to company executives as well. When he deals with such people a president draws bargaining advantage from his status or authority. By virtue of their public places or their private rights they have some capability to reply in kind.

In spheres of party politics the same thing follows, necessarily, from the confederal nature of our party organizations. Even in the case of national nominations a president's advantages are checked by those of others. In 1944 it is by no means clear that Roosevelt got his first choice as his running mate. In 1948 Truman, then the president, faced serious revolts against his nomination. In 1952 his intervention from the White House helped assure the choice of Adlai Stevenson, but it is far from clear that Truman could have done as much for any other candidate acceptable to him.[7] In 1956 when Eisenhower was president, the record leaves obscure just who backed Harold Stassen's effort to block Richard Nixon's renomination as vice-president. But evidently everything did not go quite as Eisenhower wanted, whatever his intentions may have been.[8] The outcomes in these instances bear all the marks of limits on command and of power checked by power that characterize congressional relations. Both in and out of politics these checks and limits seem to be quite widely understood.

Influence becomes still more a matter of give-and-take when presidents attempt to deal with allied governments. A classic illustration is the long unhappy wrangle over Suez policy in 1956. In dealing with the British and the French before their military intervention, Eisenhower had his share of bargaining advantages but no effective power of command. His allies had their share of counter pressures, and they finally tried the most extreme of all: action despite him. His pressure then was instrumental in reversing them. But had the British government been on safe ground *at home,* Eisenhower's wishes might have made as little difference after intervention as before. Behind the decorum of diplomacy—which was not very decorous in the Suez affair—relationships among allies are not unlike relationships among state delegations at a national convention. Power is persuasion and persuasion becomes bargaining. The concept is familiar to everyone who watches foreign policy.

In only one sphere is the concept unfamiliar: the sphere of executive relations. Perhaps because of civics textbooks and teaching in our schools, Americans instinctively resist the view that power in this sphere resembles power in all others. Even Washington reporters, White House aides, and congressmen are not immune to the illusion that administrative agencies comprise a single structure, "the" executive branch, where presidential word is law, or ought to be. Yet we have seen . . . that when a president seeks something from executive officials his persuasiveness is subject to the same sorts of limitations as in the case of congressmen, or governors, or national committeemen, or private citizens, or foreign governments. There are no generic differences, no differences in kind and only sometimes in degree. The incidents preceding the dismissal of MacArthur and the incidents surrounding seizure of the steel mills make it plain that here as elsewhere influence derives from bargaining advantages; power is a give-and-take.

Like our governmental structure as a whole, the executive establishment consists of separated institutions sharing powers. The president heads one of these; cabinet officers, agency administrators, and military commanders head others. Below the departmental level, virtually independent bureau chiefs head many more. Under mid-century conditions, federal operations spill across dividing lines on organization charts; almost every policy entangles many agencies; almost every program calls for interagency collaboration. Everything somehow involves the president. But operating agencies owe their existence least of all to one another—and only in some part to him. Each has a separate statutory base; each has its statutes to administer; each deals with a different set of subcommittees at the Capitol. Each has its own peculiar set of clients, friends, and enemies outside the formal government. Each has a different set of specialized careerists inside its own bailiwick. Our Constitution gives the president the "take-care" clause and the appointive power. Our statutes give him central budgeting and a degree of personnel control. All agency administrators are responsible to him. But they *also* are responsible to Congress, to their clients, to their staffs, and to themselves. In short, they have five masters. Only after all of those do they owe any loyalty to each other.

"The members of the cabinet," Charles G. Dawes used to remark, "are a president's natural enemies." Dawes had been Harding's budget director, Coolidge's vice-president, and Hoover's ambassador to London; he also had been General Pershing's chief assistant for supply in the First World War. The words are highly colored, but Dawes knew whereof he spoke. The men who have to serve so many masters cannot help but be somewhat the "enemy" of any one of them. By the same token, any master wanting service is in some degree the "enemy" of such a servant. A president is likely to want loyal support but not to relish trouble on his doorstep. Yet the more his cabinet members cleave to him, the more they may need help from him in fending off the wrath of rival masters. Help, though, is synonymous with trouble. Many a cabinet officer, with loyalty ill-rewarded by his lights and help withheld, has come to view the White House as innately hostile to department heads. Dawe's dictum can be turned around.

A senior presidential aide remarked to me in Eisenhower's time: "If some of these cabinet members would just take time out to stop and ask themselves 'What would I want if I were president?', they wouldn't give him all the trouble he's been having." But even if they asked themselves the question, such officials often could not act upon the answer. Their personal attachment to the president is all too often overwhelmed by duty to their other masters.

Executive officials are not equally advantaged in their dealings with a president. Nor are the same officials equally advantaged all the time. Not every officeholder can resist like a MacArthur, or like Arnall, Sawyer, Wilson, in a rough descending order of effective counter pressure. The vantage points conferred upon officials by their own authority and status vary enormously. The variance is heightened by particulars of time and circumstance. In mid-October 1950, Truman, at a press conference, remarked of the man he had considered firing in August and would fire the next April for intolerable insubordination:

> Let me tell you something that will be good for your souls. It's a pity that you . . . can't understand the ideas of two intellectually honest men when they meet. General MacArthur . . . is a member of the Government of the United States. He is loyal to that Government. He is loyal to the President. He is loyal to the President in his foreign policy. . . . There is no disagreement between General MacArthur and myself. . . .[9]

MacArthur's status in and out of government was never higher than when Truman spoke those words. The words, once spoken, added to the general's credibility thereafter when he sought to use the press in his campaign against the president. And what had happened between August and October? Near-victory had happened, together with that premature conference on *post*-war plans, the meeting at Wake Island.

If the bargaining advantages of a MacArthur fluctuate with changing circumstances, this is bound to be so with subordinates who have at their disposal fewer "powers," lesser status, to fall back on. And when officials have no "powers" in their own right, or depend upon the president for status, their counter pressure may be limited indeed. White House aides, who fit both categories, are among the most responsive men of all, and for good reason. As a director of the budget once remarked to me,

> Thank God I'm here and not across the street. If the president doesn't call me, I've got plenty I can do right here and plenty coming up to me, by rights, to justify my calling him. But those poor fellows over there, if the boss doesn't call them, doesn't ask them to do something, what *can* they do but sit?

Authority and status so conditional are frail reliances in resisting a president's own wants. Within the White House precincts, lifted eyebrows may suffice to set an aide in motion; command, coercion, even charm aside. But even in the White House a president does not monopolize effective power. Even there persuasion is akin to bargaining. A former Roosevelt aide once wrote of cabinet officers:

> Half of a President's suggestions, which theoretically carry the weight of orders, can be safely forgotten by a Cabinet member. And if the President asks about a suggestion a second time, he can be told that it is being investigated. If he asks a third time, a wise Cabinet officer will give him at least part of what he suggests. But only occasionally, except about the most important matters, do Presidents ever get around to asking three times.[10]

The rule applies to staff as well as to the cabinet, and certainly has been applied by staff in Truman's time and Eisenhower's.

Some aides will have more vantage points than a selective memory. Sherman Adams, for example, as the assistant to the president under Eisenhower, scarcely deserved · the appelation "White House aide" in the meaning of the term before his time or as applied to other members of the Eisenhower entourage. Although Adams was by no means "chief of staff" in any sense so sweeping—or so simple—as press commentaries often took for granted, he apparently became no more dependent on the president than Eisenhower on him. "I need him," said the president when Adams turned out to have been remarkably imprudent in the Goldfine case, and delegated to him even the decision on his own departure.[11] This instance is extreme, but the tendency it illustrates is common enough. Any aide who demonstrates to others that he has the president's consistent confidence and a consistent part in presidential business will acquire so much business on his own account that he becomes in

some sense independent of his chief. Nothing in the Constitution keeps a well-placed aide from converting status into power of his own, usable in some degree even against the president—an outcome not unknown in Truman's regime or, by all accounts, in Eisenhower's.

The more an officeholder's status and his "powers" stem from sources independent of the president, the stronger will be his potential pressure on the president. Department heads in general have more bargaining power than do most members of the White House staff; but bureau chiefs may have still more, and specialists at upper levels of established career services may have almost unlimited reserves of the enormous power which consists of sitting still. As Franklin Roosevelt once remarked:

> The Treasury is so large and far-flung and ingrained in its practices that I find it is almost impossible to get the action and results I want—even with Henry [Morgenthau] there. But the Treasury is not to be compared with the State Department. You should go through the experience of trying to get any changes in the thinking, policy, and action of the career diplomats and then you'd know what a real problem was. But the Treasury and the State Department put together are nothing compared with the Na-a-vy. The admirals are really something to cope with—and I should know. To change anything in the Na-a-vy is like punching a feather bed. You punch it with your right and you punch it with your left until you are finally exhausted, and then you find the damn bed just as it was before you started punching.[12]

[Three pages of original text omitted at this point.]

The essence of a president's persuasive task with congressmen and everybody else, *is to induce them to believe that what he wants of them is what their own appraisal of their own responsibilities requires them to do in their interest, not his.* Because men may differ in their views on public policy, because differences in outlook stem from differences in duty—duty to one's office, one's constituents, oneself—that task is bound to be more like collective bargaining than like a reasoned argument among philosopher kings. Overtly or implicitly, hard bargaining has characterized all illustrations offered up to now. This is the reason why: persuasion deals in the coin of self-interest with men who have some freedom to reject what they find counterfeit.

NOTES

1. The reader will want to keep in mind the distinction between two senses in which the word *power* is employed. When I have used the word (or its plural) to refer to formal constitutional, statutory, or customary authority, it is either qualified by the adjective "formal" or placed in quotation marks as "power(s)." Where I have used it in the sense of effective influence upon the conduct of others, it appears without quotation marks (and always in the singular). Where clarity and convenience permit, *authority* is substituted for "power" in the first sense and *influence* for power in the second sense.

2. See, for example, his press conference of July 22, 1959, as reported in the *New York Times* for July 23, 1959.

3. See Douglass Cater, *The Fourth Branch of Government* (Boston: Houghton-Mifflin, 1959).

4. With the exception of the vice-presidency, of course.

5. See David B. Truman's illuminating study of party relationships in the 81st Congress, *The Congressional Party* (New York: Wiley, 1959), especially chaps. 4, 6, and 8.

6. As secretary of the interior in 1939, Harold Ickes refused to approve the sale of helium to Germany despite the insistence of the State Department and the urging of President Roosevelt. Without the secretary's approval, such sales were forbidden by statute. See *The Secret Diaries of Harold L. Ickes*, vol. 2 (New York: Simon and Schuster, 1954), especially pp. 391-393, 396-399. See also Michael J. Reagan, "The Helium Controversy" in the forthcoming case book on civil-military relations prepared for the Twentieth Century Fund under the editorial direction of Harold Stein.

In this instance the statutory authority ran to the secretary as a matter of *his* discretion. A president is unlikely to fire cabinet officers for the conscientious exercise of such authority. If the president did so, their successors might well be embarrassed both publicly and at the Capitol were they to reverse decisions previously taken. As for a president's authority to set aside discretionary determinations of this sort, it rests, if it exists at all, on shaky legal ground not likely to be trod save in the gravest of situations.

7. Truman's *Memoirs* indicate that having tried and failed to make Stevenson an avowed candidate in the spring of 1952, the president decided to support the candidacy of Vice President Barkley. But Barkley withdrew early in the convention for lack of key northern support. Though Truman is silent on the matter, Barkley's active candidacy nearly was revived during the balloting, but the forces then aligning to revive it were led by opponents of Truman's Fair Deal, principally southerners. As a practical matter, the president could not have lent his weight to *their* endeavors and could back no one but Stevenson to counter them. The latter's strength could not be shifted, then, to Harriman or Kefauver. Instead the other northerners had to be withdrawn. Truman helped withdraw them. But he had no other option. See Memoirs by Harry S. Truman, vol. 2, *Years of Trial and Hope* (Garden City: Doubleday, 1956, copr. 1956 Time Inc.), pp. 495-496.

8. The reference is to Stassen's public statement of July 23, 1956, calling for Nixon's replacement on the Republican ticket by Governor Herter of Massachusetts, the later secretary of state. Stassen's statement was issued after a conference with the president. Eisenhower's public statements on the vice-presidential nomination, both before and after Stassen's call, permit of alternative inferences: either that the president would have preferred another candidate, provided this could be arranged without a showing of White House dictation, or that he wanted Nixon on condition that the latter could show popular appeal. In the event, neither result was achieved. Eisenhower's own remarks lent strength to rapid party moves which smothered Stassen's effort. Nixon's nomination thus was guaranteed too quickly to appear the consequence of popular demand. For the public record on this matter see reported statements by Eisenhower, Nixon, Stassen, Herter, and Leonard Hall (the

National Republic Chairman) in the *New York Times* for March 1, 8, 15, 16; April 27; July 15, 16, 25-31; August 3, 4, 17, 23, 1956. See also the account from private sources by Earl Mazo in *Richard Nixon: A Personal and Political Portrait* (New York: Harper, 1959), pp. 158-187.

9. Stenographic transcript of presidential press conference, October 19, 1950, on file in the Truman Library at Independence, Missouri.

10. Jonathan Daniels, *Frontier on the Potomac* (New York: Macmillan, 1946), pp. 31-32.

11. Transcript of presidential press conference, June 18, 1958, in *Public Papers of the Presidents: Dwight D. Eisenhower, 1958* (Washington: The National Archives, 1959), p. 479. In the summer of 1958, a congressional investigation into the affairs of a New England textile manufacturer, Bernard Goldfine, revealed that Sherman Adams had accepted various gifts and favors from him (the most notoriety attached to a vicuña coat). Adams also had made inquiries about the status of a Federal Communications Commission proceeding in which Goldfine was involved. In September 1958, Adams was allowed to resign. The episode was highly publicized and much discussed in that year's congressional campaigns.

12. As reported in Marriner S. Eccles, *Beckoning Frontiers* (New York: Knopf, 1951), p. 336.

14. The Power to Command*

R. GORDON HOXIE

. . . Discounting all the rhetoric, the pessimism of the recent past appears to have been replaced by a rededication and an increased optimism. Moreover, as Herman Kahn has written, "the world seems [now] to be steadily moving into a much more confident and self-assured mood." Indeed, perhaps it is too self-assured in the light of (1) the perilous state of the strategic balance; (2) the enormous Soviet arms and civil defense buildup; (3) the restiveness both in the Soviet Union and its satellites over the human rights issue; and (4) the world's continuing tinderbox areas, including the Korean peninsula, the Middle East, and southern Africa.

With these mounting perils there is no substitute for strength—economic, military, moral, and spiritual—as the nation, with a new president, charts its course in a competitive, demanding world. As chief diplomat, as commander in chief, he must be able to conduct American foreign policy and make his command decisions with the confidence and support of the Congress and the American people.

In his first seven months in office, Jimmy Carter, a president in a hurry, made more than his quota of command decisions, ranging from an announced United States troop withdrawal on the Korean peninsula to two Panama Canal treaties, which would require either congressional or senatorial approval for their fulfillment. Only time would tell, for example, whether his controversial decision of June 30, 1977, opposing present production of the B-1 bomber, which surprised the congressional leadership of his own party, had enhanced

*Source: Excerpted from *Command Decision and the Presidency: A Study of National Security Policy and Organization*, pp. xiii-xiv, and 311-323, by R. Gordon Hoxie. Copyright © 1977 by R. Gordon Hoxie. Used with permission of McGraw-Hill Book Company. Selection has been retitled and originally appeared as the Preface and Chapter XII, "Command Decision, Continuity, and Crisis Management."

or impaired this "confidence and support," the sine qua non for national security. . . .

CONTINUITY

From the declaration of the founders of the nation, who pledged "our lives, our fortunes, and our sacred honor," to President Carter's definition of a foreign policy that will "make you proud to be an American," there is a continuity of idealism. So also from the time Washington took the oath of office of president through Carter's having done so there is a continuity of principles of leadership. Immediately after the Constitution's adoption, in urging Washington's candidacy for the presidency, Hamilton emphasized, "It is of little purpose to have introduced a system, if the weightiest influence is not given to its firm establishment in the outset."[1]

By the end of the first Washington administration, aided by both Hamilton and Jefferson, Washington had established presidential primacy in national security policy. This then has been no Cold War aberration or conceit. It is only that the nuclear age has underscored the principle of command decision, again and again confirmed in crisis management.

KENNEDY

Many of the most persuasive critics of the so-called imperial presidency were witness to the most crucial command decision of the nuclear age, the Kennedy execution of the Cuban missile crisis. In his quest for the presidential nomination Kennedy contended, "Our task is to devise a national strategy." He promised he would not have a strategy predicated upon "eleventh hour responses to Soviet created crises. . . ."[2] Ironically, of the Kennedy thousand days, the most masterful thirteen were "eleventh hour responses." The Kennedy of the October 1962 missile crisis

had grown considerably beyond the Kennedy of June 1961, who, in his meeting with Khrushchev in Vienna, had given the wily Soviet prime minister the impression of a muted schoolboy.

Concerning that Vienna meeting, diplomat-scholar George Kennan observed that Kennedy "had not acquitted himself well on that occasion . . ." and that "it definitely misled Khrushchev."[3] This, then, taken with pressures on Khrushchev by his own military elite, prompted Khrushchev to direct the placement of Soviet missiles in Cuba. Much in the tradition of Cato the Elder, who repeatedly warned in the ancient Roman Senate that "Carthage must be destroyed," Senator Kenneth B. Keating finally alerted the Kennedy administration to the menace only ninety miles from the Florida coast.

In the ensuing thirteen critical days of Soviet–United States confrontation, as James T. Crown has pointed out, "the missile crisis set a far reaching precedent of turning the White House into a battle command post. . . ."[4] Former Under Secretary of State U. Alexis Johnson amplified that fact, based upon his own participation:

> I remember Admiral Anderson and other admirals of the Navy were not at all pleased at having their destroyers controlled from the White House. However, it was only by such fine selective and detailed control that we were able to bring about the result that we did.

Johnson concluded,

> I am convinced that any other control could have resulted in the situation getting quickly out of hand, not because of lack of confidence on the part of anybody, but simply because the president is at the only point at which all aspects of a situation like that can be seen and the point from which all aspects must have control.[5]

United States demands that the missiles be removed was countered by a Soviet threat on beleaguered West Berlin. Kennedy kept his cool, asserting in a telecast on October 22, 1962: "Any hostile move anywhere in the world against the safety and freedom of people to whom we are committed—including in particular the brave people of West Berlin—will be met by whatever action is needed."[6] "Whatever action," as in Truman's pronouncement after the Chinese entry into the Korean War, was regarded as including "going nuclear." In a communication four days later, Khrushchev offered to remove the missiles if the United States did likewise with its missile emplacement in Turkey. Standing tough, Kennedy refused to do so, thereby earning the criticism of doveish critics. However, Kennedy was so conciliatory as to promise, beyond the Cuban missile crisis, to review the whole issue of NATO and Warsaw Pact forces and, indeed, general disarmament.

Throughout the thirteen days, aided by his brother Robert, the president, receiving multiple advice from his immediate staff and from the Defense and State departments, was clearly in command of the situation. Preferred strategies ranged from air strikes to a blockade. As Bobby Kennedy said of the president, "It was now up to one single man. No committee was going to make this decision."[7] As commander in chief he ordered a blockade of any ships equipping or supplying the missile installations. In the face of such persuasion, despite the invasion on October 28 of the Soviet airspace by an American reconnaissance plane, Khruschchev that day directed the dismantling and withdrawal of the missiles.

Secretary of State Rusk avowed, "We looked into the mouth of the cannon; the Russians flinched."[8] Perhaps it was not quite so simple as that," British Prime Minister Harold Macmillan estimated. "Nevertheless, the president's will prevailed. . . . He was ready to carry the burden of responsibility himself."[9]

This shining hour was followed by Kennedy's efforts at rapprochement with the Soviets, including the establishment of the "hot line" for Soviet–United States dialogue and the nuclear test ban treaty, both signaling the beginnings of détente.

The new national strategy which Kennedy had promised, "a comprehensive set of carefully prepared long term policies designed to increase the strength of the non-Communist world,"[10] brought forth the Peace Corps, through which volunteers served in projects ranging from agriculture to education to medicine in the Third World; also the Alliance for Progress, building upon Eisenhower's Latin American programs. Limited war and graduated response comprised the new Kennedy military strategy. The second-youngest commander in chief created all kinds of limited war forces, headed by his personally sponsored elite, the Green Berets. A new Strike Command was created, with forces which would be transported to all parts of the world at a moment's notice to put out fires.

Kennedy first involved the Americans more directly in combat operations in Vietnam, commencing in December 1961 with U.S. crews flying armed helicopters. (It was not, however, until June 1965 that Johnson directed the first U.S. combat ground operations.) Although the Cuban missile crisis under Kennedy represented the upper reaches in the employment of force and Vietnam under Johnson the lower, both were consonant with the gradual response theories advanced by General Maxwell Taylor and, among others, Harvard professor Henry Kissinger. Since 1954 Kissinger had headed a study group mandated to "explore all factors in making and implementing foreign policy in the nuclear age." By 1957 he was writing of "a twentieth century equivalent of 'showing the flag.'"[11] McGeorge Bundy, then Harvard dean of the arts and sciences faculty (he became Kennedy's special assistant for national security affairs in 1961 and was to continue in that post under Johnson until 1966) was much impressed by this work of his former student.

Despite the brilliance of Camelot, the president's relationships with the Congress so deteriorated during his last year in office as to create a legislative stalemate. Surveying this in October 1963, Walter Lippmann wrote, "This is one of those moments when there is reason to wonder whether the congressional system as it now operates is not a grave danger to the Republic."[12] Such was the political climate when President Kennedy the following month journeyed to Texas to seek to rebuild his political support. As George Reedy observed, "President Kennedy . . . was definitely losing his political force at the time he made his tragic trip to Dallas. . . ."[13] On the day the brave, inspiring president was struck down, he was holding the torch of freedom high. That fateful morning, November 22, 1963, he avowed, "We are still the keystone in the arch of freedom, and I think we will continue to do as we have in the past, our duty."[14]

It was and is poignantly difficult to assess the martyred president. He had a magnetism coupled with a rapierlike wit. When a reporter once asked him whether McGeorge Bundy and the National Security Council staff were not getting a bit too powerful, he responded, "I shall continue to exercise some *residual* function."[15] In fact, although he had with Bundy created his own cadre of security advisers at the White House, he had dismantled the Eisenhower NSC structure. As former Under Secretary of State Casey observed, Kennedy as a senator had been accustomed to "a small free-rolling staff."[16] This had been his style, as it was to become that of his successor, Lyndon Johnson, who was likewise inspired by senatorial experience. By training, experience, and instinct, Eisenhower had a much stronger administrative sense of command than either of them.

Such seasoned observers as General Lucius Clay and Alexis Johnson recognized Kennedy's administrative difficul-

ties.[17] Nonetheless, Kennedy, particularly in the thirteen days of the Cuban missile crisis, best exemplified to Alexis Johnson the vital importance of the presidential command decision: "In the world of nuclear weapons today," Johnson concluded,

the president of the United States has control of virtually unlimited power, and correspondingly having unlimited power, he requires virtually unlimited control. The day that a commander in the field could be given a mission and permitted to go off to carry out the mission only with broad guidance is gone. The world is entirely too dangerous for that.[18]

JOHNSON

Former presidents have provided valuable bridges in times of crisis. It is perhaps useless to speculate whether Richard Nixon would have conducted himself differently if there had been a living former president in whom he might have confided and received counsel at the time he first was confronted with the Watergate break-in. Certainly Eisenhower, who sent his own chief of staff, Adams, packing over a vicuña coat, would have counseled a different course of action than that which Nixon pursued. Eisenhower was available when Lyndon Johnson, following the Kennedy assassination, was confronted for the first time with presidential responsibilities. At Johnson's request, the day after the assassination, Eisenhower drove down from Gettysburg to meet with the new president. After this meeting, at Johnson's further request, Eisenhower prepared a confidential memorandum setting forth principles and policies for action and suggesting persons who would be helpful. The former president reminded the new president, "You are sworn to defend the Constitution and execute the laws. In doing so you will follow the instincts, principles and convictions that have become part of you during many years of public service."[19]

Johnson as president and commander

in chief did follow those "instincts, principles and convictions" which had served him so well as Senate majority leader in working with President Eisenhower. But as president he lacked the ability of a Roosevelt or an Eisenhower to make of the presidency a "bully pulpit" or a "crusade." Still, if he had not bogged down in the swamps around the Mekong, he might have been viewed as a remarkable president and commander in chief. He sought consciously to carry through the Kennedy programs at home and overseas. In domestic policy he pledged in his first address before a joint session of Congress on November 27, 1963: "This nation will keep its commitments from South Vietnam to West Berlin."[20] He also sought to carry forward the Kennedy beginnings in détente. As Senate majority leader he had supported Eisenhower's 1955 "open skies" proposal to ensure meaningful inspection of disarmament agreements. He also sought what he termed "building bridges" to eastern Europe through trade, travel, and humanitarian aid.

Johnson sought to restore policymaking primacy to the Department of State through the formation of the Senior Interdepartmental Group (SIG), which consisted of the deputy secretary of defense, the administrator of AID, the director of CIA, the chairman of the Joint Chiefs of Staff, the director of the USIA, and the special assistant for international security affairs. With State's under secretary as chairman of SIG, it was anticipated that State would be restored to primacy in national security policy. However, policy increasingly gravitated about the president and his White House staff, a tendency which was even more characteristic of the succeeding administration. Johnson was increasingly occupied in his commander in chief role. As a result, the Department of Defense's International Security Agency, which Kennedy had fostered as a "little State Department," continued to exert considerable influence. How-

ever, the National Security Council as such under Johnson, as under Kennedy and Truman, never played the full institutional role it had under Eisenhower.

Just as Eisenhower's efforts for a final summit with the Soviets were aborted by the U-2 incident, Johnson's for a final summit were negated by the 1968 invasion of Czechoslovakia. Yet he did complete the Nuclear Nonproliferation Treaty with the Soviets, although its Senate confirmation in March 1969 would be credited to the Nixon administration. Also, at Glassboro and beyond, Johnson laid the foundations for the SALT talks which were finally to get under way in Helsinki in November 1969. Johnson was deeply troubled that he had not secured an armistice in Vietnam or a lessening of tensions in the Middle East, which had erupted in the swift Israeli victory of the Seven-Day War of 1967. So also he was remorseful that he had not slowed down the nuclear arms race. Yet, as he concluded, "Five years and more of crisis, of meetings and memos, of agonizing decisions and midnight phone calls, had taught me that the work of peace is an endless struggle to tip the balance in the right direction."[21]

Johnson's last futile command decision, the bombing pause in Vietnam, was greeted with contempt by the implacable North Vietnamese enemy. Secretary of State Rusk correctly analyzed: "It boils down to a question of will." Rusk added,

I realize that I am branded as a "hawk" and that this has been an embarrassment to the administration in some quarters. But looking at all of our experiences in the management of crisis in the past three decades, I cannot for the life of me see how we can achieve any peace unless some elementary notions of reciprocity, fairness, and equity are maintained.[22]

NIXON

And so it remained for Nixon, with his command decisions—mining the harbor at Haiphong and the December 1972 bombing attacks on North Vietnamese military targets, plus overtures to the People's Republic of China—to bring the January 27, 1973, signing by his representatives in Paris of "The Agreement on Ending the War and Returning Peace to Vietnam." This was followed by the summer 1973 Brezhnev-Nixon final summit visit. Crisis management was much on the mind of the troubled president. He reached an agreement with Brezhnev for "urgent consultations" should relations between the Soviets and the United States or between one and another country" appear to involve the risk of nuclear conflict."[23]

Shortly thereafter, when the Egyptian-Israeli so-called Yom Kippur War erupted in October 1973, in the light of the threatening intervention of the Soviets, a United States command decision was swiftly exercised, placing the nation's armed forces on alert. By that time rumors were spread that the president, enmeshed in Watergate inquiries, was not clearly in command. This was vigorously denied by both Admiral Thomas S. Moorer, chairman of the Joint Chiefs of Staff, and Secretary of Defense James R. Schlesinger. Although Schlesinger asserted that Nixon was "in command at all times. . . ." a student of crisis management, Louis Koenig, has suggested that "a remote president cannot fulfill his commander in chief role in a nuclear age."[24] Rumors were even floated during Nixon's last days in office in August 1974 that Secretary of Defense Schlesinger and Chairman of the Joint Chiefs of Staff Brown had conferred on steps to be taken should the commander in chief pull an irrational act. Such rumors have been unequivocally denied by both men.[25]

Although disgraced by Watergate, Nixon exhibited strength in making command decisions. While the Congress had forced the War Powers Act upon the wounded president, the courts, for their part, had refused to interpose. In Congresswoman Elizabeth Holtzman's 1973 effort on that subject (on the war in Cambodia), which went all the way to the Supreme Court, only two justices perceived a possible case.[26] This underscored Archibald Cox's conclusion that "the task of formulating a workable principle for delimiting the president's power to engage in military activities overseas is far from easy."[27]

Who is to decide the constitutionality of such operations? The Court has never accepted an invitation to do so. However, Justice William H. Rehnquist of the Supreme Court, who learned much of his law under Justice Jackson, did, while serving as Assistant Attorney General, term Nixon's Cambodian incursion a "valid exercise of his constitutional authority as commander in chief. . . . The president's authority to do what he did," Rehnquist concluded, "must be conceded by those who read executive authority narrowly."[28]

FORD

For an understanding of President Ford's views as commander in chief it is well to recall the conceptions of his mentor, Senator Arthur Vandenberg, regarding the congressional role in national security policy. Vandenberg viewed the congressional role as at best consultative and jointly formulative with the presidency on major policy issues. There should be no congressional interference in presidential command decisions, and congressional advice should be given sparingly in strategic matters. Indeed, as Vandenberg expressed it in 1948,

> . . . only in those instances in which the Senate can be sure of a complete command of all the essential information prerequisite to an intelligent decision, should it take the terrific chance of muddying the international waters by some sort of premature and ill-advised expression of its advice to the Executive.[29]

Ford also shared his mentor's concern as to how the Congress could perform even an intelligent consultative role in crisis management. As Vandenberg lamented, "The trouble is that these 'crises' never reach Congress until they have developed to a point where Congressional discretion is pathetically restricted."[30] Vandenberg's answer, like Congressman John B. Anderson's a quarter-century later, was to gear up the Congress with better information gathering for a more intelligent consultative role. This had also been the view of Senator Fulbright as late as 1967, as he surveyed what he termed "an entire era of crises in which decisions have been required again and again, decisions of a kind that the Congress is ill-equipped to make. . . ."[31]

Although as a junior congressman Ford had been witness to the 1951 foreign policy debate regarding the commander in chief's conduct of the Korean War and his movement of troops to NATO without congressional consultation, for the next fifteen years he had witnessed considerable congressional consensus with the presidency on foreign policy, including that in Southeast Asia. He recalled how in 1955, for example, the SEATO treaty had been approved by the Senate 82 to 1 and how the Gulf of Tonkin Resolution in 1964 had been passed in the Senate 88 to 2 and in the House 414 to 0. By the latter the Congress had avowed that it "approves and supports the determination of the president as commander in chief, to take all necessary measures to repel any armed attack against the forces of the United States and to prevent further aggression."[32] But by 1967, as the frustrating Vietnam War deepened, Ford recalled, "Our national unity was shattered, and with it the essential foreign policy coordination between president and Congress."[33] And so the move culminating in the War Powers Resolution of 1973 got underway. Ford, who was in a small minority that opposed the resolution, held with Senator George Aiken of Vermont that it was "largely a political

effort . . ., an attempt to amend the Constitution by congressional resolution."[34] He also held with former Under Secretary of State George Ball, who perceived the resolution as a means of trying to do what the constitutional framers "felt they were not wise enough to do."[35]

As president, Ford was particularly troubled as to how to make meaningful the War Powers Resolution's mandate of presidential consultation with the Congress in times of crisis. He inquired, "Can the president satisfy the law by having breakfast with three or four or a dozen leaders he decides are the key people?"[36] He was troubled by the implication of continuing consultation during the execution of policy. How can command decisions be shared in fast-moving operations?

Ford contended that "when the president as commander in chief undertakes . . . military operations . . .," he should "take the Congress into his confidence in order to receive its advice and, if possible, ensure its support." But he found this kind of consultation vastly different "from the detailed information and time limits imposed by the War Powers Resolution." He believed the crisis management role of the president was succinctly clear: "as commander in chief and chairman of the National Security Council . . . to concentrate on resolving the crisis as expeditiously and as successfully as possible."[37]

In accordance with the War Powers Resolution, Ford consulted and reported to the Congress in six crisis situations during his presidency: the evacuation of United States citizens and refugees from Da Nang, Phnom Penh, and Saigon in the spring of 1975, the rescue of *Mayaguez* in May of 1975, and the two evacuation operations in Lebanon in June 1976. He did not, in candor, believe that the War Powers Resolution was applicable to these kinds of operations, and he found some congressional sentiment agreeing with him. He recognized that a president in a more urgent crisis situation could by his failure to consult and report open himself up to impeachment. But, he mused, in a swiftly moving scenario, if the president waited for congressional consultation "the consequences to the nation" might be irreparable.[38]

The Congress might well ponder whether Truman could have taken the incisive action he did to salvage South Korea in the first weeks of the Korean War if he had had to operate through the War Powers Resolution. Could Kennedy have successfully consummated the Cuban missile crisis if he had been inhibited in his commander in chief role by the War Powers Resolution? Such ill-conceived measures as the Jackson-Vanik Amendment to the Trade Act of 1972 and congressional restrictions on military assistance to Turkey point to the wisdom of Vandenberg's warning about "muddying the international waters." If such a climate is to continue, as Eugene Rostow has observed, it "would tend to convert every crisis of foreign policy into a crisis of will, of pride and of precedence between Congress and the president."[39]

The decade 1966-1976 has then witnessed the partnership of the Congress and the presidency in foreign policy formulation replaced by a relationship of conflict, distrust, and suspicion. On that foundation the Congress has sought to erect a new and permanent legalistic structure by such measures as the War Powers Resolution, the National Emergencies Act, and the Impoundment Control Act. Within this climate the presidency has sought means to circumvent legislation. In the case of the Impoundment Act, so seasoned a hand as Ford contested the legislation by sending back to the Congress a barrage of proposed budget recisions and deferrals. Such maneuvering and mutual suspicion leads, as Ford pointed out, to division at home and danger abroad. Ford believed that both the National Emergencies Act, with its provision for congressional termination of presidential declarations by a concurrent resolu-

tion, and the War Powers Resolution were unconstitutional encroachments on presidential authority.

An imperative and a crucial opportunity for the Congress and the presidency is to restore a working partnership in the building of a new American foreign policy. In this there must be recognition of presidential responsibility in crisis management, in which the ultimate decision must reside with the president. In such decisionmaking there is through the NSC machinery provision for advisory inputs. There is also the counselor role of the Congress. There is the vital sense of public opinion. But in the system conceived by the framers of the Constitution and set in motion by the first Washington administration, command decision is inherent in the commander in chief office. There has been continuity in the exercise of this principle from Washington and Lincoln to the present. As Herbert Feis expressed it, "When peace or war is at issue, the president cannot leave the decision to others without forfeiting the responsibility of his office."[40]

NOTES

1. Richard B. Morris, *Alexander Hamilton and the Founding of the Nation* (New York: Dial Press, 1957), p. 500.

2. Joseph A. Bognall, *A Grand and Glorious Alliance* (Minneapolis: Burgess Publishing Company, 1968), pp. 11-12.

3. Transcription of oral tapes in the Center for the Study of the Presidency.

4. J. T. Crown, "Fresh Views of John Kennedy's Life and Work," manuscript in the Center for the Study of the Presidency.

5. Transcription of oral tapes in the Center for the Study of the Presidency.

6. Robert F. Kennedy, *Thirteen Days: A Memoir of the Cuban Missile Crisis* (New York: W. W. Norton & Company, 1969), p. 170.

7. *Ibid.*, p. 47.

8. *Ibid.*, pp. 18-20.

9. *Ibid.*

10. R. Gordon Hoxie, "The Office of

Commander in Chief: An Historical and Projective View," *Presidential Studies Quarterly* 6 (Fall 1976): 22-23.

11. James A. Nathan and James K. Oliver, *United States Foreign Policy* (Boston: Little Brown and Co., 1976), p. 252.

12. Lyndon B. Johnson, *The Vantage Point: Perspective of the Presidency 1963-1969* (New York: Holt, Rinehart and Winston, 1971), p. 34.

13. R. Gordon Hoxie (ed.), *The Presidency of the 1970's* (New York: Center for the Study of the Presidency, 1973), p. 12.

14. Johnson, *op. cit.,* p. 42.

15. R. Gordon Hoxie (ed.), *The White House: Organization and Operations* (New York: Center for the Study of the Presidency, 1971), p. 194.

16. *Ibid.,* p. 115.

17. Transcription of oral tapes in the Center for the Study of the Presidency.

18. *Ibid.*

19. Johnson, *op. cit.,* p. 32.

20. *Ibid.,* p. xi.

21. *Ibid.,* p. 492.

22. *Ibid.,* p. 509.

23. Louis W. Koenig, *The Chief Executive* (New York: Harcourt, Brace, Jovanovich, Inc., 3rd ed., 1975), p. 258.

24. *Ibid.,* p. 257.

25. Letter from Major Robert N. Ginsburgh to R. Gordon Hoxie, Feb. 20, 1976, Center for the Study of the Presidency.

26. *Holtzman et al.* v. *Schlesinger et al.,* 414 U.S. 1304 (1973).

27. Archibald Cox, "The Role of Congress in Constitutional Determination," *University of Cincinnati Law Review* 11 (1971): 199, 204.

28. Arthur M. Schlesinger, Jr., "Congress and the Making of Foreign Policy," in Rexford G. Tugwell and Thomas E. Cronin (eds.), *The Presidency Reappraised* (New York: Praeger Publishers, 1974), pp. 104-105.

29. Nathan and Oliver, *op. cit.,* p. 488.

30. *Ibid.,* p. 520.

31. *Ibid.*

32. Arthur M. Schlesinger, Jr., *The Imperial Presidency* (Boston: Houghton Mifflin Company, 1973), p. 179.

33. *Congressional Record, Senate,* April 21, 1977, p. S6177.

34. *Ibid.*

35. *Ibid.*

36. *Ibid.*

37. *Ibid.*

38. *Ibid.*

39. *Ibid.*

40. Herbert Feis, *Trust to Terror: The Onset of the Cold War, 1945-1950* (New York: W. W. Norton & Company, 1970), p. 6.

15. Political Executives: A Government of Strangers*

HUGH HECLO

To speak of political appointees in Washington is obviously to embrace a wide variety of people and situations. Political appointments cover everything from the temporary file clerk recouping a campaign obligation to the cabinet secretary heading a department organization larger than many state governments or the national administrations of some foreign countries. [Table 1] shows the number and types of what are considered to be the most clearly political appointments in the executive branch.

My focus in this [essay] is on the political executives at or near the top of government agencies. Volumes could

*Source: From *A Government of Strangers: Executive Politics in Washington* by Hugh Heclo, pp. 84-88 and 100-112. Copyright © 1977 by The Brookings Institution. Reprinted by permission. Footnotes combined and renumbered.

Table 1

FULL-TIME POLITICAL APPOINTMENTS IN THE
EXECUTIVE BRANCH, JUNE 1976

		Political Officials			
Schedule	Presidential appointments with Senate confirmation	Presidential appointments without Senate confirmation	Schedule C appointments	Noncareer executive assignments	Miscellaneous[a]
Executive schedule					
I	12	—	—	—	—
II	61	10	—	—	—
III	109	4	1	—	1
IV	311	12	27	—	3
V	113	3	66	—	12
General schedule supergrades					
18	30	13	6	178	20
17	36	1	6	184	19
16	49	4	14	171	38
(16-18)[b]	—	18	—	—	24
General schedule lower grades					
15	10	2	282	—	15
14	36	—	98	—	16
13	54	—	63	—	20
12	1	—	75	—	14
11 and below	1	—	500	—	126
Total[c]	823	67	1,138	533	308

Source: Compiled from official estimates and sources.
a. Includes certificated White House staff, some Veterans Administration personnel, and others.
b. The grade level is administratively determined within this range and in a few cases can include executive schedule V.
c. Excludes a number of positions that are exempted from civil service examinations (although insiders argue about whether they are or are not "political" jobs). Thus the table does not include schedules A and B mentioned in chapter 2 or 162 noncareer positions that fall under the Foreign Assistance Act.

be devoted to describing the maze of special circumstances in which these roughly 700 men and women find themselves. Here, however, attention will be given to some important points of common reference—the political executives' recruitment problems, inexperience, transience, disunity, and—not least—their strategically vulnerable position. Despite the large variety of government agencies and types of appointment, the most interesting thing is how much U.S. political executives actually have in common.

THE POLITICAL EXECUTIVE SYSTEM

From the outset political executives share one broad feature: all hold an ambivalent leadership position in what might loosely be termed the American "system" of public executives. To appreciate the peculiarity of their political situation, one must return to the basic rationale for having a number of nonelected political appointees in the executive branch in the first place. According to the Founding Fathers' design, power for the legislative functions of government was spread among the various representatives from states and congressional districts; for the executive function, power was deliberately unified in one elected chief executive. A single president to nominate and supervise the principal officers of the executive branch would promote the unity and vigor of executive operations, while requiring the Senate's consent to make appointments final would safeguard against any presidential abuse of the appointment power and would stabilize administration.[1] Theorists of party government later elaborated on what some of the founders only hinted at—that competition in the electoral marketplace would result in choices between alternative political teams and policies.[2]

The idea of a single chief executive entering office to promote his measures through a band of loyal political supporters in the executive branch is an easily understood model. It fits well with the media's desire to focus on the central presidential personality, and the notion of undertaking public service at the call of the president attracts many new political appointees to Washington. Astute scholars have pointed out that in reality the president's formal power as the single chief executive is often illusory, that even within his own executive branch he must persuade others and calculate his power stakes rather than cudgel his minions. This revisionist view, however, has not altered the customary concentration on the president and, like the standard constitutional or party government models, it relegates the bulk of political executives to a secondary, derivative role in the executive branch.

As noted earlier, the problem with relying on such president-centered models of executive politics is that they all depend on a tenuous political chain of events. The links of this chain are unlikely to hold from a preelection formulation of intentions, through an election contest giving a clear mandate to a particular president and his measures, to the installation of his team of executives in positions of control over government actions, to faithful administrative implementation of the promised policies. Nevertheless, there is an underlying psychological validity to the president-centered models. In good times and bad the president *is* the focus of national political attention. His popular following and public stature give him resources for bargaining and leadership that no political executive in the departments can hope to match.

Hence, even if one disregarded all the policy challenges and personnel trends . . . , U.S. federal executives would still find themselves in an extraordinarily difficult political situation. In theory political executives are supposed to provide departmental leadership and to work together under the president. But there are no "natural" political forces bolstering such expectations. Where, after all, does the political strength of these executives lie?

In elections? Departmental appointees are supposed to be helping the president make and carry out public policies affecting millions of lives, but no one has elected them. Typically, in fact, they will have played little part in the election responsible for their presence in Washington. Can ties to the president supply political strength? The president's closest companions are those who have followed him—not necessarily the party—and they will often have done so throughout the long march to the White House. Knowing the source of their power, they usually prefer proximity as White House aides rather than isolation as executive appointees somewhere "out" in the departments. And in any event a president who calculates his own power stakes is unlikely to let department executives borrow heavily on his political resources. Might political executives look for strength in their managerial authority? Hardly. Their second-hand mandate from the president competes with the mandates of elected congressmen who call the hearings, pass the enabling legislation, and appropriate the money. What about interest groups and clienteles? Obviously they have power, and many new political appointees do arrive in office closely tied to one or another such group.[3] But if this is the executive's exclusive source of political backing, any leadership role will be severely constrained. A public executive's responsibility is supposed to entail something more than advocacy for private groups.

Since these are "political" appointees, can strength perhaps be derived from political parties? As this [essay] will show, new political executives may be outsiders, but they are not outsiders who have been linked together politically during periods of opposition. Whatever central campaign machinery there is belongs largely to the individual president rather than to a set of national party leaders. At the vital state and local party level, those ambitious for their own elective careers know they must prepare their true political bases back home rather than in the Washington bureaucracy. Political parties are in no position to reward appointed executives for their successes or punish them for their failures.

On all of these counts, Washington's political executives have as few incentives to pull together as they have resources to stand alone as political leaders. Like the president, they must persuade rather than command others, but they lack the president's preeminent position to improve their bargaining power. The glare of White House attention may occasionally sweep across their agencies' activity, but for most political executives the president's traditional handshake and photograph will be his way of saying both hello and goodbye. In the constitutional structure and in the public eye, they are distinctly secondary figures to the single chief executive, yet the president's limited time, interests, and fighting power will make him utterly dependent on them for

most of what is done by the executive branch. That they exist in such a twilight zone of political leadership is the first and primary fact of life shared by political appointees. . . .

CHARACTERISTICS OF POLITICAL EXECUTIVES

Although reliable information about political executives' behavior is lacking, a surfeit of data exists concerning their biographical characteristics. These data add up to a description of a statistical elite—statistical because there is little evidence of a self-conscious group seeking agreed upon goals and screening out other entrants; elite because political appointees in the federal government are consistently drawn from the most socially and economically advantaged portions of the population. With a degree of certainty rare in social science, political executives can be predicted to be disproportionately white, male, urban, affuent, middle-aged, well educated at prestige schools, and pursuers of high-status white-collar careers. They are unlikely to be female, nonwhite, wage-earning, from a small town, or possessors of average educational and social credentials.[4]

WORK EXPERIENCE

These socioeconomic data, however, reveal little about the kind of experience political executives gain on the job. For this type of information, researchers have examined job tenure and mobility in hopes of describing the government executives' opportunities to learn about their working environments. Such information does not entirely support several commonly held assumptions about the characteristics of political appointees. One is that the top political layers are filled with newcomers to government—politically imported outsiders credited by defenders with introducing a fresh view of government operations and labeled by detractors as ignorant intruders. Another common view (and one of the chief justifications for the extensive use of political appointments in government) is that those in the top strata resemble the Founding Fathers, in that they are "in-and-outers," that is, people who periodically interrupt their private careers to move in and out of the public service. Qualifying, if not entirely dispelling, each of these assumptions leaves behind a more realistic picture of the public careers of political executives.

Compared with the government experience of civil servants, that of the men and women coming to top political positions naturally seems meager. [Table 2] shows that in 1970 the highest political executives (presidential appointees) had the least experience in the federal government, the next echelon of political appointees (noncareerists in the supergrade range of GS 16-18) had somewhat more, and higher civil servants had the longest experience of all.[5]

It is worth emphasizing the general point evident in such data: unlike the situation in most private organizations, in the U.S. executive branch those in the top positions of formal authority are likely to be substantially less familiar with their working environment than both their civil service and political subordinates.

But ... this relative inexperience at the top does not mean that political executives are complete novices to government. One bureaucratic-type feature of the layers of political executives is the tendency (particularly after the early days of a new administration) for recruitment to occur from subordinate to superordinate political positions. Studies of top political executives from the Roosevelt to Johnson administrations have shown that the large majority had some previous experience in the federal government. During those years 29 percent of the senior appointees (cabinet secretaries, undersecretaries, assistant secretaries, general counsels, administrators, deputy administrators, and commissioners) had previously held high political positions in the same agency and 11 percent in other agencies; 24 percent had held lower-echelon political appointments (special assistants, personal aides, etc.) in the same agency and 37 percent in other agencies. All together about two-thirds of the top political executives had federal administrative service before their

Table 2

POLITICAL EXECUTIVES' YEARS OF EXPERIENCE IN THE FEDERAL GOVERNMENT, 1970[a] (Percent)

Years of government experience	Presidential appointees	Noncareer supergrades	Career supergrades
Less than 2	69	40	3
2–5	19	7	11
6–10	6	14	9
Over 10	6	39	77
Total	100	100	100

Source: Reproduced with the permission of Joel D. Aberbach and the Comparative Elite Project at the University of Michigan. The project is a comparative study of the attitudes of high-level administrators and elected officials in Western Europe and the United States. More information on the American portion of the study can be found in Joel D. Aberbach, James D. Chesney, and Bert A. Rockman, "Exploring Elite Political Attitudes," Political Methodology 2 (1975): 1-28.

a Figures refer to years of continuous or noncontinuous experience at the time of the survey (1970) and therefore overstate the amount of experience in government enjoyed by these officials (17 presidential appointees, 43 noncareer supergrades, and 64 career supergrades) at the time of their appointment to executive positions.

appointment by the President.[6] Lower-level political appointees, *i.e.*, noncareer executives in the supergrades, also are often recruited from among people with narrow experience inside government. During 1974, for example, over three-quarters of noncareer vacancies were filled from within the same agency, 11 percent from other agencies, and only 13 percent from outside government.[7]

These statistics, however, should not summon up images of a top government layer peopled with men of public affairs who, like modern counterparts of Cincinnatus or George Washington, repeatedly exchange private lives for public offices. While prominent examples of such men do exist (Nelson Rockefeller, Clark Clifford, Averell Harriman, etc.), true in-and-out careers are much less common than usually thought. Such careers would presumably show a periodic interchange of public service and private employment, possibly with several appointments in different administrations. In fact, these characteristics are uncommon. Between 1933 and 1965 nine out of ten top political executives had no more than two government appointments. Four-fifths served only one president and while most appointees reported their principal occupations to be in the private sector, seven out of ten held government rather than private positions immediately before their presidential appointment. Since nine out of ten of these top political executives served in only one agency, it is also difficult to see how the in-and-outers can be thought to supply anything like a general, government-wide capability for political leadership in the bureaucracy. Similar tendencies are evident in the lower-level political appointments, *i.e.*, the noncareer executive assignments in the supergrade range. Very few of these noncareer executives have repeated spells of government service and rarely have they worked in more than one agency. In 1975, noncareer supergrades actually had somewhat less experience outside their agency than did the relatively immobile career bureaucrats at the same grade level.[8]

In sum, political appointees are generally people who will move in and sometimes up. They will cope as best they can and move out without returning. The few top executives with continual government experience may be extraordinarily valuable, but as a former civil servant said, "What most people don't realize is that an in-and-outer usually ends up staying an outer." The conventional image of Washington in-and-outers erroneously suggests a political team of utility players, when what actually exists is a one-time sequence of pinch hitters.

BIRDS OF PASSAGE

The single most obvious characteristic of Washington's political appointees is their transience. While most take up their appointments with somewhat more government experience and have a more terminal government career than is usually assumed, political executives are not likely to be in any one position for very long. The standard figure quoted is that the average undersecretary or assistant secretary remains in his job for about twenty-two months. More detailed breakdowns show this average to contain a large number of very short tenures; about half the top political executives can expect to stay in their jobs less than two years. (*See Table 3.*) The Nixon administration provided an extreme example of the general tendency when its personnel office in 1970 (*before* large-scale purges by the White House) found there was already an annual turnover rate of 27-30 percent in presidential and executive-level appointments to the departments and agencies. The tenure of cabinet secretaries declined from a previous average of forty months to eighteen months during the Nixon administration.

Again, those in the lower rather than in the higher political echelons have a better chance to acquire job experience.

Table 3

TENURE OF POLITICAL EXECUTIVES, 1960-72 (Percent)

Type of executive	Months on the job		
	Less than 12	12–24	Over 24
Cabinet secretaries	16	25	59
Undersecretaries	16	35	49
Assistant secretaries	22	32	46

Source: Arch Patton, "Government's Revolving Door," Business Week (September 22, 1973): 12.

Unlike the high political executives just mentioned, noncareer supergrade appointees have an average tenure of fifteen years in the federal service. But . . . up to one-half of these "political appointees" are in effect former career officials. One year after the Johnson–Nixon transition about 90 percent of these civil-servant-type appointees were still in their jobs, and the turnover rate was in line with what could be expected of comparable civil servants. As for the other half (the 300 or so younger outsiders), two-thirds were no longer in their jobs a year after the Johnson–Nixon transition.[9]

Much more important than the experience or inexperience of political appointees as individuals is their transience as a group. Cabinet secretaries may bring with them a cadre of personal acquaintances to fill some of their subordinate political positions, but in general public executives will be strangers with only a fleeting chance to learn how to work together. This characteristic is worth examining in a little more detail.

One of the most persistent themes in comments from political executives of all recent administrations is the absence of teamwork characterizing the layers of appointees. This absence of unifying ties is foreordained, given the fractionalized, changing, and job-specific sets of forces that make up the selection process. But it is not only methods of selection that put mutually reinforcing loyalties at a premium. Rapid turnover intensifies all the other problems of political teamwork.

In many ways what matters most is not so much an individual's job tenure as the duration of his executive relationships. Those in superior positions need to assess the capacities of their subordinates; subordinates need to learn what is expected of them. Political appointees at the same hierarchical level need to learn each other's strengths, weaknesses, priorities, and ways of communicating. Normally the opportunity to develop these working relationships is even shorter than the time span for learning a particular job. As the following percentages show, during the Kennedy, Johnson, and Nixon administrations, almost two-thirds of the undersecretaries and four-fifths of the assistant secretaries worked two years or less for the same immediate political superiors:[10]

	Under 12 months (percent)	12-24 months (percent)	Over 2 years (percent)
Same undersecretary-cabinet secretary relationship	29	34	37
Same assistant secretary-undersecretary relationship	39	38	23

The effects of this group instability are reflected incountless ways, all expressive of the fundamental point that a political executive in Washington must operate amid kaleidoscopic sets of interpersonal relations. These situations are predictable only in the sense that they are likely to arise in unexpected ways to affect the chances for political leadership in the bureaucracy. For example, with one set of personalities and circumstances, a cabinet officer dealing with an assistant secretary may bypass an undersecretary but create little difficulty. An undersecretary who found himself in this position said, "It was something I knew [the cabinet secretary] was interested in. I was made to feel welcome if I wanted to get into it, so why should I be upset?" Later, with other people and in other circumstances: "There was [the undersecretary] from the California crowd. [The cabinet secretary] had no trouble with that because he simply outflanked him by bringing in his own man as assistant secretary. So there was poor old [the undersecretary] between the hammer and the anvil." But within another two years turnover in the assistant secretary's slot brought a new constellation of forces. "[The new man] made it clear he wasn't going to perform the same sort of hatchet job on the undersecretary. He was going to be strictly nonpartisan, and you could see things becoming more politically sanitized." One political appointee found that the cabinet secretary regularly used meetings to alert him that he "was being torpedoed by [a political colleague] who was always cutting deals on his own." Another man formally in the same position found himself "going to meetings, and people would want to know why I was there."

THE LARGER PICTURE

The unstable teams within departments are positively collegial when compared with the attenuated relations of political appointees across departments. At least within departments there may be the shared need to protect and promote a common set of agency programs. Weighed against this territorial imperative, political appointees elsewhere can seem like alien tribes.

Few political appointees are likely to be united by bonds of party loyalty, the academics' favorite prescription for overcoming political incoherence in Washington. Though they may be in broad agreement with the president's general approach, political executives usually will not have been active members of his party and only a small minority will have struggled together against common opponents in electoral campaigns. Civil servants are identifying a fundamental characteristic of executive leadership in Washington when they report that they have worked for many political appointees but rarely for a politician.[11] Most would probably agree with the assistant secretary who said, "As far as I can tell, in this town a political appointee is simply someone whose career isn't in this department."

None of this inexperience necessarily means a lack of partisanship in "nonpolitical" political appointees. Quite the opposite. Many of those eventually known as the most partisan of Nixon's appointees came from backgrounds with a minimum of party-political experience. "I came to Washington with absolutely no party or political background," one of them said. "I had a naive idea of managing as in private enterprise but quickly learned political factors are all pervasive."

The record of the Nixon White House demonstrated in a number of cases how those least politically experienced can be susceptible to developing more extreme personal partisanship than those accustomed to regular political interaction and its inevitable compromises. Often the zealousness of the new convert to Washington politics can make effective political teamwork that much more difficult. One official summed up his experience in four administrations by observing: "Inexperienced people tend to lack the political instinct. . . . Sometimes the political instinct means the best politics is no politics. And it knows where that's true, it's not pure partisanship."

Lacking any larger political forces to help unify political executives, the lines of mutual interdependence normally run vertically down the departments and their loosely related programs—not horizontally across the layers of political leadership in various departments. Insofar as top political executives need each other (as opposed to needing the president's support or endorsement) the needs are temporary and issue-specific, not enduring. Even at the height of public criticism concerning the placement of Nixon loyalists in the departments, many of those placed recognized the lack of any workable horizontal contacts. As one appointee said:

For all the talk about teams, I have no contact that amounts to anything with other appointees outside the department. The few lunches we have aren't of much use for getting business done. There is no strong mechanism for getting political appointees together. As a group there's no trust.

It would be a mistake, however, to conclude that political executives are averse to creating alliances. At any given moment, informal communications and networks do exist throughout the political levels and across the departments in Washington. But as participants and issues change frequently, so do the nature and location of these relationships. Some political appointees will have enough common objectives and mutual knowledge to create fairly close informal groups. "There are me and six other assistant secretaries from other departments," said one such man. "We've got some management techniques we want to move on." A year later two of these executives were left in government. Another appointee was trying to draw his counterparts into monthly meetings but recognized "the

problem is how to get continuity and institutionalize this sort of thing to keep it going." A year later, he too was gone and his group largely dismantled.

Equally revealing of the flux confronting any outsider is the fact that the last man quoted was like many resigning political appointees. He did not depart for reasons bearing any relation to the substance of what he was doing in government but because his own political patrons were leaving. While resignation for reasons of conscience or policy are relatively rare,[12] the chancy circumstances that create political executives in the first place can just as easily lead to their departure. Political executives and their particular sets of relationships with each other not only fade, but fade fortuitously. Even a close observer of these political comings and goings is likely to pick up confusing signals about whether an executive personnel change is a case of tactics, accident, or grand political strategy.

In recent years greater efforts have been made to formalize cross-departmental ties, with the hope of institutionalizing more permanent and general-purpose relationships than those that usually prevail. The Undersecretaries' Group, begun informally toward the end of the Johnson administration, is a good example. Formal organization occurred in 1968-69 at the urging of Bureau of the Budget officials and mainly, as one of the founders described it, "to get more political weight behind some procedural reforms we were pushing."[13] Nixon's advisers attempted later to broaden the scope of the Undersecretaries' Group and to establish regular meetings of a governmentwide team identified with the administration as a whole. According to one of the plan's promoters:

It was something we should have done a lot earlier in the administration. We started monthly meetings, even had an executive order. We had a weekend session at Camp David with the wives along. The undersecretaries got to know each other. We talked about where we should be going and had some very thought-provoking sessions. . . . I think these people at this level are interested in things bigger than the department. I think they realize their success is measured by the success of the president.

Unfortunately, sociability and big thinking could not provide a foundation for serious working relationships. After one year, another presidential aide more closely connected with the activities of the group concluded:

I didn't get the feeling they were acting like prima donnas, [but] it's just generally hard to get their attention, even concerning the federal regional councils, if they don't feel it's important to their departmental operations. . . . They just weren't interested in talking about these broader issues. Where they'd had a problem, they'd already met to settle it informally.

Undoubtedly every administration could help itself by doing more to exchange information and create understanding across political levels. But governmentwide teamwork is another question. One undersecretary, generally recognized as a leading member of the group, went to the heart of the matter:

You can't build a government-wide executive team through artificial structures like the Undersecretaries' Group. It's a group in search of a mission. You can't build an executive team by pressing issues that aren't particularly relevant to people just for the sake of having everybody in on them. You can't do it by bypassing people to get to another layer. [Insofar as there is going to be a team] it has to begin at the top and use the cabinet secretaries.

Yet if there were to be such a serious effort at decisionmaking by enduring teams of political leaders across the top of departments, the U.S. presidency would look far different than it does today or ever has. In such a system cabinet secretaries would need each other as a group more than they would need their departmental identifications and more than they would need any individual member, including the president. Presidents may be advised that

they need more collegial help and reactivated cabinets, and they may with good reason even take such advice, at least for a while. But barring any profound institutional and structural changes, no modern president can be expected to be like a foreign prime minister, merely the first among equals. He needs the particular colleagues in his cabinet too little; his colleagues need him too much and each other too little for that to happen. No public executive short of the president has a vested interest in coordinating political leadership in the executive branch as a whole. Political appointees out in the departments and agencies can expect to remain in their twilight zone.

Because the executive branch has a single head, its political leadership is inherently noncollegial—except for a sharing of some executive powers with Congress. That is the way the founders designed it. That is the way it functions. But "single" does not mean unitary. The political executives' very lack of coequality—no one is the president's peer—means that their successes are likely to be expropriated by the president, their failures left behind in the departments with little effect on the appointees' real vocations outside government. Since there is only one chief executive but many sources of political support and inspiration, top political appointees do not necessarily hang separately if they fail to hang together. *E unibus plurum.*

A SUMMARY AND LOOK FORWARD

Any commitment to democratic values necessarily means accepting a measure of instability in the top governing levels. Democratic elections are, after all, "a political invention to assure uncertainty of leadership, in what are deemed to be optimum amounts and periods of time."[14] But to the inherent electoral changes, the American executive political system adds a considerably greater range of nonelectoral uncertainty to political leadership. This system produces top executives who are both expendable over time and in a relatively weak, uncertain position at any one time.

The number of political executives is small vis-à-vis the bureaucracy but large and fragmented in relation to any notion of a trim top-management structure. To the normal confusions of pluralistic institutions and powers in Washington, the selection process contributes its own complexities. White House personnel efforts have rarely been effectively organized. Political forces intervene from many quarters, and their interests in political appointments often bear little relation to presidential needs or to qualifications required for effective performance by public executives. White House efforts at political recruitment can be effective, but the organizational requirements are difficult to master. A White House operation that veers too far in the direction of centralized control can easily become self-defeating by overlooking the need for political executives to balance their responsiveness to the president with their usefulness to the departments.

While political appointees are more experienced in government than might be assumed, their government service does not usually provide continuity of experience, either through periodic spells of officeholding or long tenure in particular jobs. This is especially true at the higher political levels. Hence without a very steep learning curve, political appointees are likely to find that their capacities for effective action have matured at just about the time they are leaving office. As one assistant secretary said, "You're given this particular situation for one moment in time . . . you've got to get on your feet quickly." The entire process does not produce long-suffering policymakers who realize their major changes will come gradually through persistence. Most political appointees are more impatient. Any civil servant who offers the standard and often sensible bureaucratic advice to watch, wait, and be careful can expect to arouse more than a little suspicion.

All these tendencies are vastly intensified by the instability and uncertainty of working relationships among political appointees as a group. Over time, changes in the Washington community, particularly the declining role of parties, have provided even fewer points of political reference to help orient leadership in the executive branch. Despite the conventional models, political interaction is less like regularly scheduled matches between competing teams of partisans (president versus Congress, Republicans versus Democrats) and more like a sandlot pick-up game, with a variety of strangers, strategies, and misunderstandings. Such working relationships as exist are created and re-created sporadically as the political players come and go. Each largely picks up his lore anew—how to make his way, look for support, and deal with officialdom. It is circumstances such as these that lead many civil servants and experienced political executives to echo the words of one presidential appointee (in fact a Nixon placement in the supposedly enemy territory of the Department of Health, Education, and Welfare): "In my time I've come to the conclusion you can't say it's the damn bureaucrats. With some exceptions, that's not the problem. What's lacking is the political leadership." Political executives have no common culture for dealing with the problems of governing, and it is seldom that they are around long enough or trust one another enough to acquire one.

Weaknesses among political executives lead inevitably to White House complaints about their "going native" in the bureaucracy. The image is apt. To a large extent the particular agencies and bureaus are the native villages of executive politics. Even the most presidentially minded political executive will discover that his own agency provides the one relatively secure reference point amid all the other uncertainties of Washington. In their own agencies, appointees usually have at least some knowledge of each other and a common identity with particular programs. Outside the agency it is more like life in the big city among large numbers of anonymous people who have unknown lineages. Any common kinship in the political party or a shared political vocation is improbable, and in the background are always the suspicions of the president's "true" family of supporters in the White House. Political appointees in the larger Washington environment may deal frequently with each other, but these are likely to be the kind of ad hoc, instrumental relations of the city, where people interact without truly knowing each other.

Yet the political appointee's situation is not so simple that he can act as if he is surrounded by a random collection of strangers outside the confines of his agency village. Everywhere extensive networks of village folk in the bureaucracy, Congress, and lobby organizations share experiences, problems, and readings on people and events. An appointee may or may not be in touch with people in these networks, but they are certain to be in touch with each other independently of him. In sociological terms his networks are thin, transient, and single-stranded; theirs are dense, multiple, and enduring. Among public executives themselves there is little need to worry about any joint action to enforce community norms, because there is no community. In dealing with outside villagers who know each other, however, appointees can find that reprisals for any misdeeds are extraordinarily oblique and powerful. The political executive system may be a government of strangers, but its members cannot act as if everyone else is.

Now one can begin to see the real challenge to the political executives' statecraft in Washington. They must be able to move in two worlds—the tight,

ingrown village life of the bureaucratic community and the open, disjointed world of political strangers. A public executive in Washington needs the social sensitivity of a villager and the political toughness of a city streetfighter. It is an increasingly unlikely combination. Despite all the resources devoted to more topside staff, new management initiatives, more elaborate analytic techniques, and so on, there remain few—probably fewer than ever—places where political executives can look for reliable political support in any efforts at leadership in the bureaucracy. Political appointees in Washington are substantially on their own and vulnerable to bureaucratic power.

NOTES

1. For the political appointment process and the decision against a plural executive, see Arthur Taylor Prescott, *Drafting the Federal Constitution* (Louisiana State University Press, 1941), pp. 544-646; and Alexander Hamilton, James Madison, and John Jay, *The Federalist*, ed. Max Beloff (Oxford: Basil Blackwell, 1948), nos. 70, 72, and 76. There is some question about how far the founders actually intended the president to function alone or with the cabinet and Senate as a semicollegial group.

2. Alexander Hamilton contended that after an election,

the person substituted is warranted in supposing that the dismission of his predecessor has proceeded from a dislike to his measures, and that the less he resembles him, the more he will recommend himself to the favor of his constituents. These considerations, and the influence of personal confidences and attachments, would be likely to induce every new president to promote a change of men to fill the subordinate stations. . . . (*Ibid.*, no. 72, p. 370)

3. See for example, U.S., Congress, Senate, Committee on Commerce, *Appointments to the Regulatory Agencies*, 94th Cong. 2nd sess. (Washington, D.C.: U.S. Government Printing Office, 1976); and Common Cause,

Serving Two Masters: A Common Cause Study of Conflicts of Interest in the Executive Branch (Washington: Common Cause, 1976; processed).

4. See David T. Stanley, Dean E. Mann, and Jameson W. Doig, *Men Who Govern* (Brookings Institution, 1967), pp. 9-36; and Thomas R. Dye and John W. Pickering, "Governmental and Corporate Elites," *Journal of Politics* 37 (1974): 913-15.

5. Nixon political executives in 1970, however, had somewhat less government experience than those in previous administrations, including Eisenhower's.

6. Stanley, Mann, and Doig, *op. cit,* table 3-5, p. 45, and table E-5, p. 137.

7. U.S. Civil Service Commission, *Executive Manpower in the Federal Service* (Washington, D.C.: U.S. Government Printing Office, 1975), table 15, p. 19.

8. Information on presidential appointees between 1933 and 1965 is from Stanley, Mann, and Doig, *op.cit.,* pp. 6, 8, 34, 50. Data on noncareer supergrades in 1975 is in unpublished tables prepared by the U.S. Civil Service Commission, Bureau of Executive Manpower.

9. U.S. Civil Service Commission, Bureau of Executive Manpower, "Non-Career Executive Assignments" (July 1975; processed).

10. See Arch Patton, "Government's Revolving Door," *Business Week* (September 22, 1973): 13.

11. Although data are not entirely comparable, certainly less than half the political executives in all recent administrations had any record of political party activity, if by that is meant experience as campaign or party officials, convention delegates, elected officials, or political candidates or their staff members. See Stanley, Mann, and Doig, *op. cit.,* table E-1, p. 132; and Dean E. Mann, *The Assistant Secretaries* (Brookings Institution, 1965), table A-9, p. 295.

12. See Edward Weisband and Thomas Franck, *Resignation and Protest* (Penguin, 1976), especially pp. 121-63 and fig. 1, app. B, p. 201.

13. These procedural reforms are described in Joint Administrative Task Force, *Reducing Federal Grant-in-Aid Processing Time: Final Report,* An Interagency Report to the President (Washington, D.C.: U.S. Government Printing Office, March 1968).

14. Dwight Waldo, *Perspectives on Administration* (University of Alabama Press, 1956), p. 14.

16. The Presidency and Its Paradoxes*

THOMAS E. CRONIN

Why is the presidency such a bewildering office? Why do presidents so often look like losers? Why is the general public so disapproving of recent presidential performances, and so predictably less supportive the longer a president stays in office?

The search for explanations leads in several directions. Vietnam and the Watergate scandals must be considered. Then, too, the personalities of Lyndon B. Johnson and Richard M. Nixon

doubtless were factors that soured many people on the office. Observers also claim that the institution is structurally defective—that it encourages isolation, palace guards, "groupthink" and arrogance.

Yet something else seems at work. Our expectations of, and demands on, the office are frequently so paradoxical as to invite two-faced behavior by our presidents. We seem to want so much so fast that a president, whose powers are often simply not as great as many of us believe, gets condemned as ineffectual. Or a president often will overreach or resort to unfair play while trying to live up to our demands. Either way, presidents seem to become locked into a rather high number of no-win situations.

The Constitution is of little help in explaining any of this. The Founding Fathers purposely were vague and left the presidency imprecisely defined. They knew well that the presidency would have to provide the capability for swift and competent executive action; yet they went to considerable lengths to avoid enumerating specific powers and duties, so as to calm the then persuasive popular fear of monarchy.

In any event, the informal and symbolic powers of the presidency today account for as much as the formal ones. Further, presidential powers expand and contract in response to varying situational and technological changes. Thus, the powers of the presidency are interpreted in ways so markedly different as to seem to describe different offices. In some ways the modern presidency has virtually unlimited authority for nearly anything its occupant chooses to do with it. In other ways, however, our beliefs and hopes about the presidency very much shape the character and quality of the presidential performances we get.

The modern (post-Roosevelt II) presidency is bounded and constrained by various expectations that are decidedly paradoxical. Presidents and presidential candidates must constantly balance themselves between conflicting demands. It has been suggested by more than one observer that it is a characteristic of the American mind to hold contradictory ideas simultaneously without bothering to resolve the potential conflicts between them. Perhaps some paradoxes are best left unresolved. But we should, at least, better appreciate what it is we expect of our presidents and would-be presidents. For it could

well be that our paradoxical expectations and the imperatives of the job make for schizophrenic presidential performances.

We may not be able to resolve the inherent contradictions and dilemmas these paradoxes point up. Still, a more rigorous understanding of these conflicts and no-win or near no-win situations should make possible a more refined sensitivity to the limits of what a president can achieve. Exaggerated or hopelessly contradictory public expectations tend to encourage presidents to attempt more than they can accomplish and to overpromise and overextend themselves.

Perhaps, too, an assessment of the paradoxed presidency may impel us anew to revise some of our unrealistic expectations concerning presidential performance and the institution of the presidency and encourage, in turn, the nurturing of alternative sources or centers for national leadership.

A more realistic appreciation of presidential paradoxes might help presidents concentrate on the practicable among their priorities. A more sophisticated and tolerant consideration of the modern presidency and its paradoxes might relieve the load so that a president can better lead and administer in those critical realms in which the nation has little choice but to turn to him. Whether we like it or not, the vitality of our democracy still depends in large measure on the sensitive interaction of presidential leadership with an understanding public willing to listen and willing to provide support when a president can persuade. Carefully planned innovation is nearly impossible without the kind of leadership a competent and fair-minded president can provide.

Each of the ten paradoxes following is based on apparent logical contradictions. Each has important implications for presidential performance and public evaluation of presidential behavior. A better understanding may lead to the removal, reconciliation, or more enlightened toleration of the contradictions to which they give rise.

1
THE GENTLE AND DECENT BUT FORCEFUL AND DECISIVE PRESIDENT PARADOX

Opinion polls time and again indicate that people want a just, decent, humane "man of good faith" in the White House. Honesty and trustworthiness repeatedly top the list of qualities the public values most highly in a president these days. However, the public just as strongly demands the qualities of toughness, decisiveness, even a touch of ruthlessness.

Adlai Stevenson, George McGovern, and Gerald Ford were all criticized for being "too nice," "too decent." (Ford's decisive action in the Mayaguez affair was an exception, and perhaps predictably, his most significant gain in the Gallup Poll—eleven points—came during and immediately after this episode.) Being a "Mr. Nice Guy" is too easily equated with being too soft. The public dislikes the idea of a weak, spineless, or sentimental person in the White House.

Morris Udall, who was widely viewed as a decidedly decent candidate in the 1976 race for the Democratic nomination, had to advertise himself as a man of strength. He used a quotation from House Majority Leader Thomas P. O'Neill in full-page newspaper ads that read, "We need a Democratic president who's tough enough to take on big business. Mo Udall is tough." The image sought was unquestionably that of toughness of character.

Perhaps, too, this paradox may explain the extraordinary public fondness for President Dwight D. Eisenhower. For at one and the same time he was blessed with a benign smile and reserved, calming disposition and yet also was the disciplined, strong, no-nonsense five-star general with all the medals and victories to go along with it. His ultimate resource as president was

this reconciliation of decency and decisiveness, likability alongside demonstrated valor.

During the 1976 presidential campaign, Jimmy Carter appeared to appreciate one of the significant by-products of this paradox. He pointed out that the American male is handicapped in his expressions of religious faith by those requisite "macho" qualities of overt strength, toughness, and firmness. Carter's personal reconciliation of this paradox is noteworthy:

> But a truer demonstration of strength would be concern, compassion, love, devotion, sensitivity, humility—exactly the things Christ talked about—and I believe that if we can demonstrate this kind of personal awareness of our own faith we can provide that core of strength and commitment and underlying character that our nation searches for.

Thus this paradox highlights one of the distinctive frustrations for presidents and would-be presidents. Plainly, we demand a double-edged personality. We, in effect, demand the sinister as well as the sincere, President Mean and President Nice—tough and hard enough to stand up to a Khrushchev or to press the nuclear button; compassionate enough to care for the ill-fed, ill-clad, ill-housed. The public in this case "seems to want a softhearted son of a bitch," as a friend of mine, Alan Otten, aptly put it. It's a hard role to cast, a harder role to perform for eight years.

2
THE PROGRAMMATIC BUT PRAGMATIC LEADER PARADOX

We want both a programmatic (committed on the issues and with a detailed program) and a pragmatic (flexible and open, even changeable) person in the White House. We want a moral leader; yet the job forces the president to become a constant compromiser.

On the one hand, Franklin D. Roosevelt proclaimed that the presidency is pre-eminently a place for moral leadership. On the other hand,

Governor Jerry Brown aptly notes that "a little vagueness goes a long way in this business."

A president who becomes too committed risks being called rigid; a president who becomes too pragmatic risks being called wishy-washy. The secret, of course, is to stay the course by stressing character, competence, rectitude, and experience, and by avoiding strong stands that offend important segments of the population.

Jimmy Carter was especially criticized by the press and others for avoiding commitments and stressing his "flexibility" on the issues. This prompted a major discussion of what came to be called the "fuzziness issue." Jokes spread the complaint. One went as follows: "When you eat peanut butter all your life, your tongue sticks to the roof of your mouth, and you have to talk out of both sides." Still, his "maybe I will and maybe I won't" strategy proved very effective in overcoming critics and opponents who early on claimed he didn't have a chance. Carter talked quietly about the issues and carried a big smile. In fact, of course, he took stands on almost all the issues, but being those of a centrist or a pragmatic moderate, his stands were either not liked or dismissed as nonstands by most liberals and conservatives—especially purists.

What strikes one person as fuzziness or even duplicity appeals to another person as remarkable political skill, the very capacity for compromise and negotiation that is required if a president is to maneuver through the political minefields that come with the job.

Most candidates view a campaign as a fight to win office, not an opportunity for adult education. Barry Goldwater in 1964 may have run with the slogan "We offer a choice not an echo," referring to his unusually thematic strategy, but Republican party regulars who, more pragmatically, aspired to win the election preferred "a chance not a choice." Once in office, presidents often operate the same way; the electoral connection looms large as an issue-avoiding, controversy-ducking political incentive. Most presidents also strive to maximize their options, and hence leave matters up in the air or delay choices. JFK mastered this strategy, whereas on Vietnam LBJ permitted himself to be trapped into his tragically irreparable corner because his options had so swiftly dissolved. Indeed, this yearning to maximize their options may well be the core element of the pragmatism we so often see when we prefer moral leadership.

3
THE INNOVATIVE AND INVENTIVE YET MAJORITARIAN AND RESPONSIVE PRESIDENCY PARADOX

One of the most compelling paradoxes at the very heart of our democratic system arises from the fact that we expect our presidents to provide bold, innovative leadership and yet respond faithfully to public-opinion majorities.

Walter Lippmann warned against letting public opinion become the chief guide for leadership in America, but he just as forcefully warned democratic leaders: Don't be right too soon, for public opinion will lacerate you! Hence, most presidents fear being in advance of their times. They must lead us, but also listen to us.

Put simply, we want our presidents to offer leadership, to be architects of the future and providers of visions, plans, and goals, and at the same time we want them to stay in close touch with the sentiments of the people. To talk about high ideals, New Deals, Big Deals, and the like is one thing. But the public resists being led too far in any one direction.

Most of our presidents have been conservatives or at best "pragmatic liberals." They have seldom ventured much beyond the crowd. John F. Kennedy, the author of the much acclaimed *Profiles in Courage,* was often criticized for presenting more profile than courage; if political risks could be avoided, he shrewdly avoided them. Kennedy was fond of pointing out that he had barely won election in 1960 and that great innovations should not be forced upon a leader with such a slender mandate. Ironically, Kennedy is credited with encouraging widespread public participation in politics. But he repeatedly reminded Americans that caution was needed, that the important issues are complicated, technical, and best left to the administrative and political experts. As Bruce Miroff writes in *Pragmatic Illusions,* Kennedy seldom attempted to change the political context in which he operated:

> More significantly, he resisted the new form of politics emerging with the civil rights movement: mass action, argument on social fundamentals, appeals to considerations of justice and morality. Moving the American political system in such a direction would necessarily have been long range, requiring arduous educational work and promising substantial political risk. The pragmatic Kennedy wanted no part of such an unpragmatic undertaking.

Presidents can get caught whether they are coming or going. The public wants them to be both *leaders* of the country and *representatives* of the people. We want them to be decisive and rely mainly on their own judgment; yet we want them to be very responsive to public opinion, especially to the "common sense" of our own opinions. It was perhaps with this in mind that an English essayist once defined the ideal democratic leader as an "uncommon man of common opinions."

4
THE INSPIRATIONAL BUT "DON'T PROMISE MORE THAN YOU CAN DELIVER" LEADER PARADOX

We ask our presidents to raise hopes, to educate, to inspire. But too much inspiration will invariably lead to dashed hopes, disillusionment, and cynicism. The best of leaders often suffer from one of their chief virtues—an instinctive tendency to raise aspirations, to summon us to transcend personal needs and subordinate ourselves to dreaming dreams of a bolder, more majestic America.

We enjoy the upbeat rhetoric and promises of a brighter tomorrow. We genuinely want to hear about New Nationalism, New Deals, New Frontiers, Great Societies, and New American Revolutions; we want our fears to be assuaged during a "fireside chat" or a "conversation with the president"; we want to be told that "the torch has been passed to a new generation of Americans . . . and the glow from that fire can truly light the world."

We want our fearless leaders to tell us that "peace is at hand," that the "only fear we have to fear is fear itself," that "we are Number One," that a recession has "bottomed out," and that "we are a great people." So much do we want the "drive of a lifting dream," to use Nixon's awkward phrase, that the American people are easily duped by presidential promises.

Do presidents overpromise because they are congenital optimists or because they are pushed into it by the demanding public? Surely the answer is an admixture of both. But whatever the source, few presidents in recent times have been able to keep their promises and fulfill their intentions. Poverty was not ended; a Great Society was not realized. Vietnam dragged on and on. Watergate outraged a public that had been promised an open presidency. Energy independence remains an illusion just as crime in the streets continues to rise.

A president who does not raise hopes is criticized for letting events shape his presidency rather than making things happen. A president who eschewed inspiration of any kind would be rejected as un-American. For as a poet once wrote, "America is promises." For people everywhere, cherishing the dream of individual liberty and self-fulfillment, American has been the land of promises, of possibilities, of dreams. No president can stand in the way of this truth, no matter how much the current dissatisfaction about the size of big government in Washington and its incapacity to deliver the services it promises.

William Allen White, the conservative columnist, went to the heart of this paradox when he wrote of Herbert Hoover. President Hoover, he noted, is a great executive, a splendid desk man. "But he cannot dramatize his leadership. A democracy cannot follow a leader unless he is dramatized."

5
THE OPEN AND SHARING BUT COURAGEOUS AND INDEPENDENT PRESIDENCY PARADOX

We unquestionably cherish our three-branched system with its checks and balances and its theories of dispersed and separated powers. We want our presidents not only to be sincere but to share their powers with their cabinets, Congress, and other "responsible" national leaders. In theory, we oppose the concentration of power, we dislike secrecy, and we resent depending on any one person to provide all of our leadership. In recent years (the 1970s in particular), there have been repeated calls for a more open, accountable, and deroyalized presidency.

On the other hand, we reject a too secularized presidency. We reject, as well, the idea that complete openness is a solution; indeed, it has been suggested, instead, that the great presidents have been the strong presidents, who stretched their legal authority, who occasionally relied on the convenience of secrecy, and who dominated the other branches of government. This point of view argues that the country, in fact, often yearns for a hero in the White

House, that the human heart ceaselessly reinvents royalty, and that Roosevelts and Camelots, participatory democracy notwithstanding, are vital to the success of America.

If some people feel we are getting to the point where all of us would like to see a demythologized presidency, others claim we need myth, we need symbol. As a friend of mine put it, "I don't think we could live without the myth of a glorified presidency, even if we wanted to. We just aren't that rational. Happily, we're too human for that. We will either live by the myth that has served us fairly well for almost two hundred years or we will probably find a much worse one."

The clamor for a truly open or collegial presidency was opposed on other grounds by the late Harold Laski when he concluded that Americans, in practice, want to rally round a president who can demonstrate his independence and vigor:

A president who is believed not to make up his own mind rapidly loses the power to maintain the hold. The need to dramatize his position by insistence upon his undoubted supremacy is inherent in the office as history has shaped it. A masterful man in the White House will, under all circumstances, be more to the liking of the multitude than one who is thought to be swayed by his colleagues.

Thus we want our president not only to be both a lion and a fox, but more than a lion, more than a fox. We want simultaneously a secular leader and a civil religious mentor; we praise our three-branched system, but we place capacious hopes upon and thus elevate the presidential branch. Only the president can give us heroic leadership, or so most people feel. Only a president can dramatize and symbolize our highest expectations of ourselves as almost a chosen people with a unique mission. Note too that only the president is regularly honored with a musical anthem of his own: "Hail to the Chief." If it seems a little hypocritical for a semisovereign people deferentially to delegate so much hierarchical stature and semiautocratic power to their president, this is nonetheless precisely what we continually do.

We want an open presidency, and we oppose the concentration of vast power in any one position. Still, we want forceful, courageous displays of leadership from our presidents. Anything less than that is condemned as aimlessness or loss of nerve. Further, we praise those who leave the presidency stronger than it was when they entered.

6
THE TAKING THE PRESIDENCY OUT OF POLITICS PARADOX

The public yearns for a statesman in the White House, for a George Washington or a second "era of good feelings"—anything that might prevent partisanship or politics-as-usual in the White House. In fact, however, the job of a president demands that he be a gifted political broker, ever attentive to changing political moods and coalitions.

Franklin Roosevelt illustrates this paradox well. Appearing so remarkably nonpartisan while addressing the nation, he was in practice one of the craftiest political coalition-builders to occupy the White House. He mastered the art of politics—the art of making the difficult and desirable possible.

A president is expected to be above politics in some respects and highly political in others. A president is never supposed to act with his eye on the next election; he's not supposed to favor any particular group or party. Nor is he supposed to wheel and deal or to twist too many arms. That's politics and that's bad! No, a president, or so most people are inclined to believe, is supposed to be "president of all the people." On the other hand, he is asked to be the head of his party, to help friendly members of Congress get elected or re-elected, to deal firmly with party barons and con-

gressional political brokers. Too, he must build political coalitions around what he feels needs to be done.

To take the president out of politics is to assume, incorrectly, that a president will be so generally right and the general public so generally wrong that a president must be protected from the push and shove of political pressures. But what president has always been right? Over the years, public opinion has been usually as sober a guide as anyone else on the political waterfront. Anyway, having a president constrained and informed by public opinion is what a democracy is all about.

In his re-election campaign of 1972, Richard Nixon in vain sought to display himself as too busy to be a politician: He wanted the American people to believe he was too preoccupied with the Vietnam War to have any personal concern about his election. In one sense, Nixon may have destroyed this paradox for at least a while. Have not the American people learned that we *cannot* have a president *above* politics?

If past is prologue, presidents in the future will go to considerable lengths to portray themselves as unconcerned with their own political future. They will do so in large part because the public applauds the divorce between the presidency and politics. People naively think that we can somehow turn the job of president into that of a managerial or strictly executive post. (The six-year, single-term proposal reflects this paradox.) Not so. The presidency is a highly political office, and it cannot be otherwise. Moreover, its political character is for the most part desirable. A president separated from, or somehow above, politics might easily become a president who doesn't listen to the people, doesn't respond to majority sentiment or pay attention to views that may be diverse, intense, and at variance with his own. A president immunized to politics would be a president who would too easily become isolated from the processes of government and removed from the thoughts and aspirations of his people.

In all probability, this paradox will endure. The standard diagnosis of what's gone wrong in an administration will be that the presidency has become too politicized. But it will be futile to try to take the president out of politics. A more helpful approach is to realize that certain presidents try too hard to hold themselves above politics—or at least to give that appearance—rather than engage in it deeply, openly, and creatively enough. A president in a democracy has to act politically in regard to controversial issues if we are to have any semblance of government by the consent of the governed.

7
THE COMMON MAN WHO GIVES AN UNCOMMON PERFORMANCE PARADOX

We like to think that America is the land where the common sense of the common man reigns. We prize the common touch, the "man of the people." Yet few of us settle for anything but an uncommon performance from our presidents.

This paradox is splendidly summed up by some findings of a survey conducted by the Field Research Corporation, a California public-opinion organization. Field asked a cross-section of Californians in 1975 to describe in their own words the qualities a presidential candidate should have. Honesty and trustworthiness topped the list. But one of the organization's more intriguing findings was that "while most (72 percent) prefer someone with plain and simple tastes, there is also a strong preference (66 percent) for someone who can give exciting speeches and inspire the public."

It has been said that the American people crave to be governed by men who are both Everyman and yet better than Everyman. The Lincoln and Kennedy presidencies are illustrative. We cherish the myth that anyone can grow up to be president—that there are no barriers, no elite qualifications—but we don't want a person who is too ordinary. Would-be presidents have to prove their special qualifications—their excellence, their stamina, their capacity for uncommon leadership.

The Harry Truman reputation, at least as it flourished in the mid-1970s, demonstrates the apparent reconciliation of this paradox. Fellow commoner Truman rose to the demands of the job and became an apparent gifted decision-maker, or so his admirers would have us believe.

Candidate Carter in 1976 nicely fitted this paradox as well. Local, down-home farm boy next door makes good! The image of the peanut farmer turned gifted governor and talented campaigner contributed greatly to Carter's success as a national candidate, and he used it with consummate skill. Early on in his presidential bid, Carter enjoyed introducing himself as a peanut farmer *and* a nuclear physicist—yet another way of suggesting he was down-to-earth but cerebral as well.

A president or would-be president must be bright, but not too bright; warm and accessible, but not too folksy; down-to-earth, but not pedestrian. Adlai Stevenson was witty and clever, but these are talents that seldom pay in politics. Voters prefer plainness and solemn platitudes, but these too can be overdone. For instance, Ford's talks, no matter what the occasion, dulled our senses with the banal. Both suffered because of this paradox. The "catch 22" here, of course, is that the very fact of an uncommon performance puts distance between a president and the truly common man. We persist, however, in wanting both at the same time.

8
THE NATIONAL UNIFIER—NATIONAL DIVIDER PARADOX

One of the paradoxes most difficult to alleviate arises from our longing for a president who will pull us together again and yet be a forceful priority-setter, budget-manager, and executive leader. The two tasks are near opposites.

Ours remains one of the few nations in the world that call upon their chief executives to serve also as their symbolic, ceremonial heads of state. Elsewhere, these tasks are spread around. In some nations there is a monarch *and* a prime minister; in other nations there are three visible national leaders—the head of state, a premier, and a powerful party head.

In the absence of an alternative, we demand that our presidents and our presidency act as a unifying force in our lives. Perhaps it all began with George Washington, who so artfully performed this function. At least for a while, he truly was above politics and a near unique symbol of our new nation. He was a healer, a unifier, and an extraordinary man for all seasons. Today we ask no less of our presidents than that they should do as Washington did.

However, we have designed a presidential job description that impels our contemporary presidents to act as national dividers. They necessarily divide when they act as the leaders of their political parties, when they set priorities that advantage certain goals and groups at the expense of others, when they forge and lead political coalitions, when they move out ahead of public opinion and assume the role of national educators, and when they choose one set of advisers over another. A president, as a creative executive leader, cannot help but offend certain interests. When Franklin Roosevelt was running for a second term, some garment workers unfolded a great sign that said, "We love him for the enemies he has made." Such is the fate of a president on an everyday basis; if he chooses to use power he usually will lose the goodwill of those who preferred inaction over action. The opposite is, of course, true if he chooses not to act.

Look at it from another angle. The nation is torn between the view that a president should primarily preside over the nation and merely serve as a referee among the various powerful interests that actually control who gets what, when, and how and a second position, which holds that a president should gain control of government processes and powers so as to use them for the purpose of furthering public, as opposed to private, interests. Obviously the position that one takes on this question is relevant to how you value the presidency and the kind of person you'd like to see in the job.

Harry S. Truman said it very simply. He noted that 14 million or 15 million Americans had the resources to have representatives in Washington to protect their interests, and that the interests of the great mass of other people, the 160 million or so others, were the responsibility of the president of the United States.

The president is sometimes seen as the great defender of the people, the ombudsman or advocate-general of "public interests." Yet he is sometimes (and sometimes at the same time) viewed as hostile to the people, isolated from them, wary of them, antagonistic to them, inherently their enemy.

This debate notwithstanding, Americans prize the presidency as a grand American invention. As a nation we do not want to change it. Proposals to weaken it are dismissed. Proposals to reform or restructure it are paid little respect. If we sour on a president, the conventional solution has been to find and elect someone we hope will be better.

9
THE "THE LONGER HE IS THERE, THE LESS WE LIKE HIM" PARADOX

Every four years we pick a president, and for the next four years we pick on him and at him, and sometimes pick him entirely apart. There is no adequate prepresidential job experience, so much of the first term is an on-the-job learning experience. But we resent this. It is too important a job for on-the-job learning, or at least that's how most of us feel.

Too, we expect presidents to grow in office and to become better acclimated to their powers and responsibilities. But the longer they are in office, the more they find themselves involved in crises with less and less public support. There is an apocryphal presidential lament that goes as follows: "Every time I seem to grow into the job, it gets bigger."

Simply stated, the more we know of a president, or the more we observe his presidency, the less we approve of him. Familiarity breeds discontent. Research on public support of presidents indicates that approval peaks soon after a president takes office and then slides downward at a declining rate over time until it reaches a point in the latter half of the four-year term when it bottoms out. Thereafter it rises a bit but never attains its original levels. Why this pattern of declining support afflicts presidents is a subject of debate among social scientists. Unrealistic early expectations are, of course, a major factor. These unrealistic expectations ensure a period of disenchantment.

Peace and prosperity can help stem the unpleasant tide of ingratitude, and Eisenhower's popularity remained reasonably high in large part because of his (or the nation's) achievements in these respects. For other presidents, however, their eventual downsliding popularity was due nearly as much to the public's inflated expectations as to the presidents' actions. It was often as if the downslide in popularity would occur no matter what the president did. If this seems unfair, even cruel, it is, nonetheless, what happens to those skilled and lucky enough to win election to the "highest office in the land."

And all this occurs despite our conventional wisdom that the *office makes the man*—"that the presidency with its

built-in educational processes, its spacious view of the world, its command of talent, and above all its self-conscious historic role, does work its way on the man in the Oval Office," as James MacGregor Burns puts it. If we concede that the office in part does make the man, we must admit also that time in office often unmakes the man.

10
THE "WHAT IT TAKES TO BECOME PRESIDENT MAY NOT BE WHAT IS NEEDED TO GOVERN THE NATION" PARADOX

To win a presidential election takes ambition, ambiguity, luck, and masterful public-relations strategies. To govern the nation plainly requires all of these, but far more as well. It may well be that too much ambition, too much ambiguity, and too heavy a reliance on phony public-relations tricks actually undermine the integrity and legitimacy of the presidency.

Columnist David Broder offered an apt example:

> People who win primaries may become good presidents—but "it ain't necessarily so." Organizing well is important in governing just as it is in winning primaries. But the Nixon years should teach us that good advance men do not necessarily make trustworthy White House aides. Establishing a government is a little more complicated than having the motorcade run on time.

Likewise, ambition (in very heavy doses) is essential for a presidential candidate, but too much hunger for the office or for "success-at-any-price" is a danger to be avoided. He must have boldness and energy, but carried too far these can make him cold and frenetic. To win the presidency obviously requires a single-mindedness, and yet we want our presidents to be well rounded, to have a sense of humor, to be able to take a joke, to have hobbies and interests outside the realm of politics—in short, to have a sense of proportion.

Another aspect of this paradox can be

seen in the way candidates take ambiguous positions on issues in order to increase their appeal to the large bulk of centrist and independent voters. Not only does such equivocation discourage rational choices by the voters, but it also may alienate people who learn later, after the candidate has won, that his views and policies are otherwise. LBJ's "We will not send American boys to fight the war that Asian boys should be fighting" and Richard Nixon's "open presidency" pledges come readily to mind. Their prepresidential stands were later violated or ignored.

Political scientist Samuel Huntington calls attention to yet another way this paradox works. To be a winning candidate, he notes, the would-be president must put together an *electoral coalition* involving a majority of voters advantageously distributed across the country. To do this, he must appeal to all regions and interest groups and cultivate the appearance of honesty, sincerity, and experience. But once elected, the electoral coalition has served its purpose and a *governing coalition* is the order of the day. This all may sound rather elitist, but Harvard Professor Huntington insists that this is what has to be:

> The day after his election the size of his majority is almost—if not entirely—irrelevant to his ability to govern the country. What counts then is his ability to mobilize support from the leaders of the key institutions in society and government. He has to constitute a broad governing coalition of strategically located supporters who can furnish him with the information, talent, expertise, manpower, publicity, arguments, and political support which he needs to develop a program, to embody it in legislation, and to see it effectively implemented. This coalition must include key people in Congress, the executive branch, and the private-sector "Establishment." The governing coalition need have little relation to the electoral coalition. The fact that the president as a candidate put together a successful electoral coalition does not insure that he will have a viable governing coalition.

Presidential candidate Adlai Steven-son had another way of saying it in 1956. He said he had "learned that the hardest thing about any political campaign is how to win without proving that you are unworthy of winning." The process of becoming president is an extraordinarily taxing one that defies description. It involves, among other things, an unflagging salesmanship job on television.

Candidates plainly depend upon television to transform candidacy into incumbency. Research findings point out that candidates spend well over half their funds on radio and television broadcasting. Moreover, this is how the people "learn" about the candidates. Approximately two-thirds of the American public report that television is the best way for them to follow candidates, and about half of the public acknowledge that they got their best understanding of the candidates and issues from television coverage.

Thus, television is obviously the key. But the candidate has to travel to every state and hundreds of cities for at least a four-year period to capture the exposure and the local headlines before earning the visibility and stature of a "serious candidate." For the most part, it becomes a grueling ordeal, as well as a major learning experience. In quest of the Democratic nomination for president, Walter F. Mondale of Minnesota spent most of 1974 traveling some 200,000 miles, delivering hundreds of speeches, appearing on countless radio and television talk shows, and sleeping in Holiday Inn after Holiday Inn all across the country. He admits that he enjoyed much of it, but says, too, that he seldom had time to read or to reflect, not to mention having time for a sane family life. Eventually he withdrew on the grounds that he simply had neither the overwhelming desire nor the time, as an activist United States senator, to do what was necessary in order to win the nomination.

Mondale would later—in 1976—show that he is an extremely effective national campaigner, but his frustrations about his 1974 presidential bid are worth remembering:

> I love to ponder ideas, to reflect on them and discuss them with experts and friends over a period of time, but this was no longer possible. It struck me as being unfortunate and even tragic that the process of seeking the Presidency too often prevents one from focusing on the issues and insights and one's ability to express them, which are crucially important. I believe this fact explains many of the second-rate statements and much of the irrational posturing that are frequently associated with Presidential campaigns. In any case, after eighteen months I decided this wasn't for me. It wasn't my style and I wasn't going to pretend that it was. Instead of controlling events in my life, I was more and more controlled by them. Others have had an easier time adapting to this process than I did, and I admire them for it. But one former candidate told me, three years after his campaign had ended, that he *still* hadn't fully recovered emotionally or physically from the ordeal.

What it takes to *become* president may differ from what it takes to *be* president. It takes a near megalomaniac who is also glib, dynamic, charming on television, and hazy on the issues. Yet we want our presidents to be well rounded, careful in their reasoning, clear and specific in their communications, and not excessively ambitious. It may well be that our existing primary-and-convention system adds up to an effective obstacle course for testing would-be presidents. Certainly they have to travel to all sections of the country, meet the people, deal with interest-group elites, and learn about the challenging issues of the day. But with the Johnson and Nixon experiences in our not too distant past, we have reason for asking whether our system of producing presidents is adequately reconciled with what is required to produce a president who is competent, fair-minded, and emotionally healthy.

CONCLUSIONS

Perhaps the ultimate paradox of the modern presidency is that it is always too powerful and yet it is always inadequate. Always too powerful because it is contrary to our ideals of a government by the people and always too powerful, as well, because it must now possess the capacity to wage nuclear war (a capacity that unfortunately doesn't permit much in the way of checks and balances and deliberative, participatory government). Yet always inadequate because it seldom achieves our highest hopes for it, not to mention its own stated intentions.

The presidency is always too strong when we dislike the incumbent. On the other hand, its limitations are bemoaned when we believe the incumbent is striving valiantly to serve the public interest as we define it. For many people, the Johnson presidency captured this paradox vividly: Many who felt that he was too strong in Vietnam also felt that he was too weakly equipped to wage his War on Poverty (and vice versa).

The dilemma for the attentive public is that curbing the powers of a president who abuses the public trust will usually undermine the capacity of a fair-minded president to serve the public interest. In the nearly two centuries since Washington took office, we have multiplied the requirements for presidential leadership and made it increasingly difficult to lead. Certainly this is no time for mindless retribution against the already fragile institution of the presidency. Neither presidents nor the public should be relieved of their respective responsibilities of trying to fashion a more effective and fair-minded leadership system simply because these paradoxes are pointed out and even widely agreed upon. It is also not enough to throw up our hands and say, "Well, no one makes a person run for that crazy job in the first place.". . .

While the presidency will surely remain one of our nation's best vehicles for creative policy change, it will also continue to be a hardpressed office, laden with the cumulative weight of these paradoxes. We urgently need to probe the origins and to assess the consequences of these paradoxes and to learn how presidents and the public can better coexist with them, for it is apparent that these paradoxes serve to isolate a president from the public. Whether we like it or not, the growing importance of the presidency and our growing dependence on presidents seem to ensure that presidents will be less popular, and more often handy scapegoats when anything goes wrong.

V

The Presidential Advisory System

Introduction. To develop and monitor his programs and policies, the president must rely on his own advisory mechanisms as well as the advice and program proposals from his departments. It is his own advisory mechanisms that are capable of presenting the presidentialist as against the otherwise essentially departmentalist view.

The development of the presidential advisory system is of rather recent origin. It began during the administration of Franklin D. Roosevelt, the thirty-second president of the United States. To be sure, Woodrow Wilson, the twenty-eighth president of the United States, initially asked for additional budgetary staff, but the Budget and Accounting Act of 1921, signed into law by Warren Harding, the twenty-ninth president of the United States, must be considered the early starting point for the institutionalized presidency.[1]

In any event, President Roosevelt, on March 20, 1936, appointed a small group of men—Louis Brownlow, Charles Merriam and Luther Gulick—and assigned them the job to diagnose the manpower support needs of the presidency and to make appropriate recommendations for the reorganization of the executive branch.

The President's Committee on Administrative Management or the Brownlow Committee, as it was popularly known, made its report to the president in January 1937. The proposals of the committee were simple enough. Essentially they combined to say, "The president needs help," and proposed a major reorganization of the executive branch to permit such help. Legislation was prepared and submitted to Congress in 1938, but Congress killed the bill, fearing too much power to the presidency, especially in the wake of FDR's attempts to "pack" the Supreme Court.

Roosevelt resubmitted the legislation in 1939 at which time Congress passed a considerably modified reorganization law. The 1939 law authorized the president, subject to congressional veto, to redistribute and restructure executive branch agencies. Under the Reorganization Act, President Roosevelt created the Executive Office of the President. The rationale for the president needing help, indeed, an advisory system, is clearly seen in the first selection, "Report of the President's Committee on Administrative Management."

Although nothing in the Constitution ever said the president had to share power with his cabinet, myth has it that the cabinet is to be the major source of advice to the president. Historically, however, a "collective cabinet" has been little used by the presidency. Former President William Howard Taft put the collective cabinet in proper perspective when he wrote:

> ... while the Constitution refers to the head of a department and authorizes the President to make him an adviser as to matters in his own department, it contains no suggestion of a meeting of all the departments, in consultation over general governmental matters. The cabinet is a mere creation of the President's will. It is an extra-statutory and extra-constitutional body. It exists only by custom. If the President desired to dispense with it, he could do so.[2]

Thus, although every president has a cabinet, presidents do not usually turn to their cabinets for their collective advice. This is so because many presidents have found considerable barriers between themselves and their cabinet members. Why this is so, is pointed out by political scientist Richard F. Fenno in the next selection, "The President's Cabinet and Advisory Politics."

Although a collective cabinet may be of little use to the president for good political reasons, some cabinet members are perceived as outright enemies of the president. President Calvin Coolidge's vice president, Charles Dawes, is reported to have said that "the members of the cabinet are a president's natural enemies." Paradoxically, each president has appointed cabinet heads who are loyal to him and will usually look to him for guides to action—thus the use of the cabinet on an individual basis. Indeed, the reliance of the president on individual cabinet members differs considerably from their collective use, as British political scientist Graham K. Wilson illustrates in his novel study, "Are Department Secretaries Really a President's Natural Enemies?"

The "institutionalized presidency," as the presidential advisory system has become popularly known, especially the White House Office and other Executive Office of the President agencies (not the cabinet), has increased considerably since the Budget and Accounting Act of 1921. This trend in the growth of the White House staff is not likely to easily be reversed. It is the president who can assure the effective coordination of the executive branch. Since the president cannot do it alone, it is the president's men and women who facilitate this presidential function.

Nevertheless, the growth of presidential establishment is said to have had at least two important negative consequences on the presidency. First, the president is more isolated from reality, because the large staff he has tends to cut him off from his critics. Secondly, the presence of a large staff has resulted in the White House injecting itself more deeply into departmental jurisdictions. Political scientist Thomas Cronin's essay, "The

Swelling of the Presidency" documents the growth of the presidential establishment and grapples with some of the questions that this growth raises.

NOTES

1. See, for example, Francis H. Heller, *The Presidency: A Modern Perspective* (New York: Random House, 1960), p. 26.
2. William Howard Taft, *Our Chief Magistrate and His Powers* (New York: Columbia University Press, 1925), pp. 29-30.

17. Report of the President's Committee on Administrative Management*

LOUIS BROWNLOW
CHARLES E. MERRIAM
LUTHER GULICK

THE AMERICAN EXECUTIVE

The need for action in realizing democracy was as great in 1789 as it is today. It was thus not by accident but by deliberate design that the Founding Fathers set the American executive in the Constitution on a solid foundation. Sad experience under the Articles of Confederation, with an almost headless government and committee management, had brought the American Republic to the edge of ruin. Our forefathers had broken away from hereditary government and pinned their faith on democratic rule, but they had not found a way to equip the new democracy for action. Consequently, there was grim purpose in resolutely providing for a presidency which was to be a national office. The president is indeed the one and only national officer representative of the entire nation. There was hesitation on the part of some timid souls in providing the president with an election independent of the Congress; with a longer term than most governors of that day; with the duty of informing the Congress as to the state of the Union and of recommending to its consideration "such Measures as he shall judge necessary and expedient"; with a two-thirds veto; with a wide power of appointment; and with military and diplomatic authority. But this reluctance was overcome in the face of need and a democratic executive established.

Equipped with these broad constitutional powers, reenforced by statute, by custom, by general consent, the American executive must be regarded as one of the very greatest contributions made by our nation to the development of modern democracy—a unique institution the value of which is as evident in times of stress and strain as in periods of quiet.

*Source: President's Committee on Administrative Management, *Administrative Management in the Government of the United States, January 8, 1937* (Washington, D.C.: United States Government Printing Office, 1937), pp. 1-6.

As an instrument for carrying out the judgment and will of the people of a nation, the American executive occupies an enviable position among the executives of the states of the world, combining as it does the elements of popular control and the means for vigorous action and leadership—uniting stability and flexibility. The American executive as an institution stands across the path of those who mistakenly assert that democracy must fail because it can neither decide promptly nor act vigorously.

Our presidency unites at least three important functions. From one point of view the president is a political leader—leader of a party, leader of the Congress, leader of a people. From another point of view he is head of the nation in the ceremonial sense of the term, the symbol of our American national solidarity. From still another point of view the president is the chief executive and administrator within the federal system and service. In many types of government these duties are divided or only in part combined, but in the United States they have always been united in one and the same person whose duty it is to perform all of these tasks.

Your Committee on Administrative Management has been asked to investigate and report particularly upon the last function; namely, that of administrative management—the organization for the performance of the duties imposed upon the president in exercising the executive power vested in him by the Constitution of the United States.

IMPROVING THE MACHINERY OF GOVERNMENT

Throughout our history we have paused now and then to see how well the spirit and purpose of our nation is working out in the machinery of every-day government with a view to making such modifications and improvements as prudence and the spirit of progress might suggest. Our government was the first to set up in its formal Constitution a method of amendment, and the spirit of America has been from the beginning of our history the spirit of progressive changes to meet conditions shifting perhaps more rapidly here than elsewhere in the world.

Since the Civil War, as the tasks and responsibilities of our government have grown with the growth of the nation in sweep and power, some notable attempts have been made to keep our administrative system abreast of the new times. The assassination of President Garfield by a disappointed office seeker aroused the nation against the spoils system and led to the enactment of the civil-service law of 1883. We have struggled to make the principle of this law effective for half a century. The confusion in fiscal management led to the establishment of the Bureau of the Budget and the budgetary system in 1921. We still strive to realize the goal set for the nation at that time. And, indeed, many other important forward steps have been taken.

Now we face again the problem of governmental readjustment, in part as the result of the activities of the nation during the desperate years of the industrial depression, in part because of the very growth of the nation, and in part because of the vexing social problems of our times. There is room for vast increase in our national productivity and there is much bitter wrong to set right in neglected ways of human life. There is need for improvement of our governmental machinery to meet new conditions and to make us ready for the problems just ahead.

Facing one of the most troubled periods in all the troubled history of mankind, we wish to set our affairs in the very best possible order to make the best use of all of our national resources and to make good our democratic claims. If America fails, the hopes and dreams of democracy over all the world go down. We shall not fail in our task and our responsibility, but we cannot live upon our laurels alone.

We seek modern types of management in national government best fitted for the stern situations we are bound to meet, both at home and elsewhere. As to ways and means of improvement, there are naturally sincere differences of judgment and opinion, but only a treasonable design could oppose careful attention to the best and soundest practices of government available for the American nation in the conduct of its heavy responsibilities.

THE FOUNDATIONS OF GOVERNMENTAL EFFICIENCY

The efficiency of government rests upon two factors: the consent of the governed and good management. In a democracy consent may be achieved readily, though not without some effort, as it is the cornerstone of the Constitution. Efficient management in a democracy is a factor of peculiar significance.

Administrative efficiency is not merely a matter of paper clips, time clocks, and standardized economies of motion. These are but minor gadgets. Real efficiency goes much deeper down. It must be built into the structure of a government just as it is built into a piece of machinery.

Fortunately the foundations of effective management in public affairs, no less than in private, are well known. They have emerged universally wherever men have worked together for some common purpose, whether through the state, the church, the private association, or the commercial enterprise. They have been written into constitutions, charters, and articles of incorporation, and exist as habits of work in the daily life of all organized peoples. Stated in simple terms these canons of efficiency require the establishment of a responsible and effective chief executive as the center of energy, direction, and administrative management; the systematic organization of all activities in the hands of a qualified personnel under the direction of the chief executive; and to aid him in this, the establishment of appropriate managerial and staff agencies. There must also be provision for planning, a complete fiscal system, and means for holding the executive accountable for his program.

Taken together, these principles, drawn from the experience of mankind in carrying on large-scale enterprises, may be considered as the first requirement of good management. They comprehend the subject matter of administrative management as it is dealt with in this report. Administrative management concerns itself in a democracy with the executive and his duties, with managerial and staff aides, with organization, with personnel, and with the fiscal system because these are the indispensable means of making good the popular will in a people's government.

MODERNIZING OUR GOVERNMENTAL MANAGEMENT

In the light of these canons of efficiency, what must be said of the government of the United States today? Speaking in the broadest terms at this point, and in detail later on, we find in the American government at the present time that the effectiveness of the chief executive is limited and restricted, in spite of the clear intent of the Constitution to the contrary; that the work of the executive branch is badly organized; that the managerial agencies are weak and out of date; that the public service does not include its share of men and women of outstanding capacity and character; and that the fiscal and auditing systems are inadequate. These weaknesses are found at the center of our government and involve the office of the chief executive itself.

While in general principle our organization of the presidency challenges the admiration of the world, yet in equipment for administrative management our Executive Office is not fully abreast of the trend of our American times, either in business or in government. Where, for example, can there be found an executive in any way comparable upon whom so much petty work is thrown? Or who is forced to see so many persons on unrelated matters and to make so many decisions on the basis of what may be, because of the very press of work, incomplete information? How is it humanly possible to know fully the affairs and problems of over 100 separate major agencies, to say nothing of being responsible for their general direction and coordination?

These facts have been known for many years and are so well appreciated that it is not necessary for us to prove again that the president's administrative equipment is far less developed than his responsibilities, and that a major task before the American government is to remedy this dangerous situation. What we need is not a new principle, but a modernizing of our managerial equipment.

This is not a difficult problem in itself. In fact, we have already dealt with it successfully in state governments, in city governments, and in large-scale private industry. Gov. Frank O. Lowden in Illinois, Gov. Alfred E. Smith in New York, Gov. Harry F. Byrd in Virginia, and Gov. William Tudor Gardiner in Maine, among others, have all shown how similar problems can be dealt with in large governmental units. The federal government is more extensive and more complicated, but the principles of reorganization are the same. On the basis of this experience and our examination of the executive branch we conclude that the following steps should now be taken:

1. To deal with the greatly increased duties of executive management falling upon the president the White House staff should be expanded.
2. The managerial agencies of the government, particularly those dealing with the budget, efficiency research, personnel, and planning, should be greatly

strengthened and developed as arms of the chief executive.

3. The merit system should be extended upward, outward, and downward to cover all non-policy-determining posts, and the civil service system should be reorganized and opportunities established for a career system attractive to the best talent of the nation.

4. The whole executive branch of the government should be overhauled and the present 100 agencies reorganized under a few large departments in which every executive activity would find its place.

5. The fiscal system should be extensively revised in the light of the best governmental and private practice, particularly with reference to financial records, audit, and accountability of the executive to the Congress.

These recommendations are explained and discussed in the following sections of this report.

THE PURPOSE OF REORGANIZATION

In proceeding to the reorganization of the government it is important to keep prominently before us the ends of reorganization. Too close a view of machinery must not cut off from sight the true purpose of efficient management. Economy is not the only objective, though reorganization is the first step to savings; the elimination of duplication and contradictory policies is not the only objective, though this will follow; a simple and symmetrical organization is not the only objective, though the new organization will be simple and symmetrical; higher salaries and better jobs are not the only objectives, though these are necessary; better business methods and fiscal controls are not the only objectives, though these too are demanded. There is but one grand purpose, namely, to make democracy work today in our national government; that is, to make our government an up-to-date, efficient, and effective instrument for carrying out the will of the nation. It is for this purpose that the government needs thoroughly modern tools of management.

As a people we congratulate ourselves justly on our skill as managers— in the home, on the farm, in business big and little—and we properly expect that management in government shall be of the best American model. We do not always get these results, and we must modestly say "we count not ourselves to have attained," but there is a steady purpose in America to press forward until the practices of our governmental administration are as high as the purpose and standards of our people. We know that bad management may spoil good purposes, and that without good management democracy itself cannot achieve its highest goals.

THE WHITE HOUSE STAFF

In this broad program of administrative reorganization the White House itself is involved. The president needs help. His immediate staff assistance is entirely inadequate. He should be given a small number of executive assistants who would be his direct aides in dealing with the managerial agencies and administrative departments of the government. These assistants, probably not exceeding six in number, would be in addition to his present secretaries, who deal with the public, with the Congress, and with the press and the radio. These aides would have no power to make decisions or issue instructions in their own right. They would not be interposed between the president and the heads of his departments. They would not be assistant presidents in any sense. Their function would be, when any matter was presented to the president for action affecting any part of the administrative work of the government, to assist him in obtaining quickly and without delay all pertinent information possessed by any of the executive departments so as to guide him in making his responsible decisions; and then when decisions have been made, to assist him

in seeing to it that every administrative department and agency affected is promptly informed. Their effectiveness in assisting the president will, we think, be directly proportional to their ability to discharge their functions with restraint. They would remain in the background, issue no orders, make no decisions, emit no public statements. Men for these positions should be carefully chosen by the president from within and without the government. They should be men in whom the president has personal confidence and whose character and attitude is such that they would not attempt to exercise power on their own account. They should be possessed of high competence, great physical vigor, and a passion for anonymity. They should be installed in the White House itself, directly accessible to the president. In the selection of these aides the president should be free to call on departments from time to time for the assignment of persons who, after a tour of duty as his aides, might be restored to their old positions.

This recommendation arises from the growing complexity and magnitude of the work of the president's office. Special assistance is needed to insure that all matters coming to the attention of the president have been examined from the over-all managerial point of view, as well as from all standpoints that would bear on policy and operation. It also would facilitate the flow upward to the president of information upon which he is to base his decisions and the flow downward from the president of the decisions once taken for execution by the department or departments affected. Thus such a staff would not only aid the president but would also be of great assistance to the several executive departments and to the managerial agencies in simplifying executive contacts, clearance, and guidance.

The president should also have at his command a contingent fund to enable him to bring in from time to time particular persons possessed of particular competency for a particular purpose and whose services he might usefully employ for short periods of time.

The president in his regular office staff should be given a greater number of positions so that he will not be compelled, as he has been compelled in the past, to use for his own necessary work persons carried on the pay rolls of other departments.

If the president be thus equipped he will have but the ordinary assistance that any executive of a large establishment is afforded as a matter of course.

In addition to this assistance in his own office the president must be given direct control over and be charged with immediate responsibility for the great managerial functions of the government which affect all of the administrative departments. . . . These functions are personnel management, fiscal and organizational management, and planning management. Within these three groups may be comprehended all of the essential elements of business management.

The development of administrative management in the federal government requires the improvement of the administration of these managerial activities, not only by the central agencies in charge, but also by the departments and bureaus. The cental agencies need to be strengthened and developed as managerial arms of the chief executive, better equipped to perform their central responsibilities and to provide the necessary leadership in bringing about improved practices throughout the government.

The three managerial agencies, the Civil Service Administration, the Bureau of the Budget, and the National Resources Board should be a part and parcel of the Executive Office. Thus the president would have reporting to him directly the three managerial institutions whose work and activities would affect all of the administrative departments.

The budgets for the managerial agencies should be submitted to the Congress by the president as a part of the budget for the Executive Office. This would distinguish these agencies from the operating administrative departments of the government, which should report to the president through the heads of departments who collectively compose his cabinet. Such an arrangement would materially aid the president in his work of supervising the administrative agencies and would enable the Congress and the people to hold him to strict accountability for their conduct.

18. The President's Cabinet and Advisory Politics*

RICHARD F. FENNO, JR.

THE CABINET MEETING

President Truman once described the cabinet as "a body whose combined judgment the president uses to formulate the fundamental policies of the administration . . . a group which is designed to develop teamwork wisdom on all subjects that affect the political life of

*Source: From The President's Cabinet by Richard F. Fenno, Jr., pp. 154-56, 247-49, Cambridge, Mass.: Harvard University Press. Copyright © 1959 by the President and Fellows of Harvard College. Reprinted by permission.

the country."[1] The historians of the cabinet concluded, similarly though earlier, that, "The rule may be laid down that the president ordinarily consults the cabinet on matters of grave public importance."[2] The cabinet has been described by observers and participants as "the board of directors of the nation," as "a combination of qualified experts that have stood behind every president," and as producers of "committee government."[3] Pictures have been painted of the family circle thrashing out the great issues of the day under conditions of closest intimacy. "In fact, it is assumed today simply as a matter of course that the secretary of a new department will become as such an intimate adviser and associate of the president."[4] Since it is impossible to obtain conclusive data on cabinet proceedings, dogmatic conclusions are not in order, but on the available evidence of the last forty-five years, at least, these versions of cabinet activity do not square with the facts. It is, perhaps, significant that President Truman's comment was made in December 1945, at a time when he had been in office less than a year. With respect to all of its possible functions, the group's performance has been haphazard and its success has been sporadic. This is not to say that the cabinet should be classified as an ornamental antique. It is not. But neither does it correspond to the over-idealized discussions of its activity which have acquired, from time to time, substantial currency.

Instead of exaggerating its importance or relegating it to the dust bin, it is of more purpose to examine its activity in order to distinguish its areas of greatest strength and those of greatest weakness. It is weakest in performing the function of interdepartmental coordination and in making direct contributions to decisions through a well-informed, well-organized discussion of policy alternatives. It is most useful as a presidential adviser, in the sense of a political sounding board equipped to provide clues as to likely public or group reactions, and as a forum in which some overall administrative coherence can be secured. Neither of the latter two functions requires a high degree of institutionalization. The first can be carried on in the face of departmentalism; the second operates to combat it. With regard to administrative coherence, the importance of the cabinet meeting may well be measured by the extent to which it prevents the degree of cabinet-level disunity from becoming any greater than it is.

What is perhaps the most striking part of the overall picture is the number of factors which operate to *prevent* the cabinet from fulfilling its potential functions. They are factors, however, which cannot be eliminated at the level of the cabinet meeting. Insofar as the president's behavior, e.g., his differentiation among members, constitutes a limitation on the effectiveness of the meeting, that behavior is grounded in the American conception of executive leadership. The limiting behavior of the department heads, e.g., departmentalism, stems from the basic pluralism of the American political system. The low degree of institutionality characteristic of the cabinet meeting is not an independent limiting factor, but a political derivative determined by the interaction of president and cabinet members.

The problem of greater or lesser institutionalization must be put in perspective as one possible method for capitalizing on assets or minimizing liabilities, but *not* as a fundamental solution to cabinet weakness. Thus, one can find changes such as the Eisenhower ones to be helpful under the existing circumstances; but they should not be looked upon as permanent cure-alls. This is so because the president-cabinet nexus will always be an unstable accomodation rather than a fixed relationship. What seems necessary for a successful accommodation is a degree of institutionality sufficient to hold the group together, coupled with a degree of resiliency sufficient to convince the president that he can use it. Insofar as this kind of relationship can be maintained, the successes of the cabinet meeting are likely to underwrite its continuance, while its limitations are likely to guarantee the coexistence of other avenues of presidential assistance. . . .

THE CABINET AND POLITICS

The investigations which we have made into cabinet-member activity in the areas of public prestige, party, Congress, and departmental administration lead to a few conclusions about the cabinet and the political system in which it operates. One striking circumstance is the extent to which the cabinet concept breaks down in the course of the members' activities outside the cabinet meeting. In matters of prestige, partisan politics, and legislative relations alike, the cabinet as a collectivity has only a symbolic value, a value which readily disappears when the need for action supersedes the need for a show window. In the day-to-day work of the cabinet member, each man fends for himself without much consideration for cabinet unity. His survival, his support, and his success do not depend on his fellow members. His performance is judged separately from theirs. This condition is but another result of the combination of the centrifugal tendencies in our political system with the low degree of institutionalization which characterizes the cabinet.

The political help which the president receives comes not from the group but from individual cabinet members, who can and do augment the president's effectiveness in his leadership roles. It would be a serious mistake not to emphasize the possibilities for crucial assistance by individuals. But probably most striking is the fact that the possibilities for such assistance are very frequently negated by the number of limitations which surround them. There are pervasive limitations of a personal or a situational nature, and there are limitations inherent in the political system—all of which make it neither easy for a cabinet member to help the president nor axiomatic that he should do so. In the final reckoning, the president receives much less assistance of a positive, non-preventive type from his individual cabinet members than one might expect. This fact serves to accent the high degree of success which is represented by preventive assistance. It also helps to underline the tremendous gap which separates the presidential level of responsibility from that of his subordinates. It demonstrates, too, the extent to which the two levels are subject to the pulls of different political forces.

The president-cabinet power-responsibility relationship is, according to the analysis of this [essay], inadequate as a total explanation for the extra-cabinet performance of the individual member. As a group the cabinet draws its life breath from the President, but as individuals the cabinet members are by no means so dependent on him. In many instances, we are presented with the paradox that in order for the cabinet member to be of real help to the president in one of his leadership roles, the member must have non-presidential "public" prestige, party following, legislative support, or roots of influence in his department. And in any case, the problems of his own success and survival will encourage him to consolidate his own nexus of power and will compel him to operate with some degree of independence from the president. For his part, the president's influence over the cabinet member becomes splintered and eroded as the member responds to political forces not presidential in origin or direction. From the beginnings of his involvement in the appointment process, the president's power is subject to the pervasive limitations of the pluralistic system in which he seeks to furnish political leadership.

One final conclusion takes the form

of a restatement of the pluralism of American politics. In every area we have noted the diffusion, the decentralization, and the volatility of political power. The same kaleidoscopic variety which characterized the factors influential in the appointment process is evident in the political processes which engulf the cabinet member. Each member interacts with a great variety of political units, interest groups, party groups, and legislative groups, and each has his own pattern of action and his own constellation of power. The feudal analogy is an apt one. It frequently makes more sense to describe the cabinet member as part of a "feudal pattern of fiefs, baronies, and dukedoms than . . . an orderly and symmetrical pyramid of authority."[5]

Here, then, is an underlying explanation for cabinet-meeting behavior. Departmentalism is a condition whose roots are grounded in the basic diversity of forces which play upon the individual member. By the same token, this pluralism generates centrifugal influences which help to keep the cabinet in its relatively non-institutionalized state. The greatest problems for cabinet and president, like the greatest problems in American politics, are those which center around the persistent dilemmas of unity and diversity.

NOTES

1. Louis W. Koenig, ed., *The Truman Administration* (New York, 1956), p. 360.

2. Mary Hinsdale, *A History of the President's Cabinet* (Ann Arbor, Mich., 1911), p. 326.

3. James A. Farley, *Jim Farley's Story: The Roosevelt Years* (New York, 1948), p. 39; Henry B. Learned, *The President's Cabinet* (New Haven, 1912), pp. 4-7.

4. Learned, *op. cit.*, p. 6.

5. Pendleton Herring, "Executive-Legislative Responsibilities," *American Political Science Review* (December 1944): 1160.

19. Are Department Secretaries Really a President's Natural Enemies?*

GRAHAM K. WILSON

It is widely believed that there exists in the United States a phenomenon called "clientelism": that most federal government departments in the USA do not really control the interests with whom they do business but rather are controlled by them; that the interests and the departments between them typically have great influence over the department secretaries appointed by the president; and that in consequence a department secretary is, in reality, more likely to act as the interests' spokesman, or as his department's, than as the spokesman of the president. Thus it is often asserted that "cabinet officers are a president's natural enemies." My aim in this article is to show that this belief,

---

Source: Excerpted from "Are Department Secretaries Really a President's Natural Enemies?" by Graham K. Wilson, *British Journal of Political Science*, vol. 7 (July, 1977), pp. 273-282, 285-289, 291-293, 294-299. Copyright © 1977 by Cambridge University Press. Reprinted by permission. Footnotes combined and renumbered.

as it relates to the relationship between department secretaries and presidents, is widely held, plausible, but mistaken.

A WIDELY HELD BELIEF

When someone seeks to show that a piece of conventional wisdom is mistaken, a typical response is, "But no one ever really believed *that*." We need to begin, therefore, by showing that the belief in clientelism, as it affects the relations between department secretaries and presidents, is almost universally held amongst political scientists, and is widely held amongst political leaders. Indeed, so common is the belief that it becomes almost invidious to cite individuals. The quotations that follow have been chosen either because of the prestige of the author—a prestige that has lent credence to the clientelism idea—or more or less at random from the political-science literature. Other quotations could have been chosen; but these should serve to make the point.

David Truman in *The Governmental Process* argued that "expediencies . . . turn department heads in varying degrees into political opponents [of the president]."[1] Richard Fenno, whose study of the presidental cabinet remained for many years the sole major study of relations between the president and his secretaries, likewise maintained that "the President's influence over a cabinet member becomes splintered and eroded as the member responds to political forces not presidential in origin and direction."[2] Nor have more recent studies suggested that the conventional wisdom established by Truman and Fenno was mistaken. The British political scientist Maurice Vile, argues that department secretaries

must look to important figures in Congress and they must also look to their "clientele." Each of the great Departments, even the Department of State, has a clientele . . . Sometimes the identification with a section of the community can become so strong as in the case of the Departments of Agriculture, Commerce and Labor for example

that their aim seems to be to promote a particular interest to the government rather than to represent the government itself.[3]

One of the most recent textbooks on American politics published in Britain similarly maintains: "Some government Departments, of course, exist primarily to promote the interests of private industry. The Departments of Agriculture, Commerce and Labor try to discover what their clientele want done so that the government may do it for them."[4] The author, R. V. Denenberg, makes no distinction between the department and its secretary, and goes on to cite the United States Department of Agriculture as a prime example. Clinton Rossiter shared this belief, explicitly stating that the heads of departments were susceptible to clientelism:

Were the Presidents of the last fifty years to be polled . . . several would doubtless . . . insist that the President's hardest job is not to persuade Congress to support a policy dear to his political heart but to persuade the pertinent bureau or agency or mission, *even when headed by men of his own choosing* to follow his direction faithfully and transform the shadow of the policy into the substance of a program.[5]

Clientelism, he says, is the major reason.

Nor is this belief that clientelism overwhelms the loyalty to the president of departments and even their secretaries confined to pluralists and the writers of textbooks. Most, if not all, authorities on the presidency take the same view. Richard Neustadt noted in *Presidential Power,*

A senior presidential aide remarked to me in Eisenhower's time: "If some of those Cabinet members would just take time out to stop and ask themselves 'What would I want if I were President?' they wouldn't give him all the trouble he's been having." But, even if they asked themselves the question, such officials often could not act on the answer. Their personal attachment to the President is all too often overwhelmed by their duty to other masters.[6]

Neustadt had in mind the clienteles of the departments and their representatives in Congress. James MacGregor Burns, writing more than a decade later, agreed: "The "clientele" departments such as Commerce, Agriculture, Labor and Interior continue to speak for their interest groups *through their department heads.*"[7] Erwin Hargrove drew out the implication:

> Thus the President cannot rely upon the department heads he has appointed to serve his point of view completely. They must live with and speak for their departments' constituents and must answer to Congress. This often leads to relationships of tension with Presidents. . .[8]

Cronin introduced a refinement into the argument by exempting from clientelism an "inner cabinet" covering vital national interests and including such departments as the Department of State. But, of the rest, he noted:

> The explicitly domestic policy departments, with the exception of justice, have made up the outer cabinet. By custom, if not designation, *these cabinet officers* assume a relatively straightforward advocacy orientation that overshadows their counseling role.[9]

Richard Nathan similarly argued that cabinet secretaries were likely to be affected by clientelism:

> Besides agency pressures which draw the newly appointed Cabinet Secretary towards the agency viewpoint . . . there are strong outside pressures which have the same effect. The most notable are those of congressional committees and various interest groups.[10]

Some writers, in the pluralist tradition, have seen the clientelism of cabinet secretaries not as a problem but as an advantage. Thus Seidman suggested: "It may be doubted that either the national interest or, in the final analysis, those of the President himself would be best served if departments were headed by agnostics who did not believe in the goals and values of the institutions they administered."[11] Many political practitioners have been less enthusiastic about the tendency for cabinet secretaries to be captured by their clientele, but they have noted its strength. President Truman, for example, wrote that: "a skillful department head who maintains strong support among the interest groups affected by his agency and among members of Congress can be virtually free to ignore the preferences of the Chief Executive."[12] Truman's *caveats,* however, are, as we shall see, important. Theodore Sorensen, who saw the executive branch from the heart of the presidency took a stronger view: "each department has its own clientele and point of view, its own experts and bureaucratic interests, its own relations with Congress and certain subcommittees, its own statutory authority, objectives and standards of success. *No Cabinet member is free to ignore all this. . .*"[13]

It is worth repeating that the quotations above were chosen because of the prestige of the author or more or less at random. They merely serve to illustrate how common the belief is that most departments, and their secretaries, are captured by their clientele.

THE ORTHODOX VIEW OF CLIENTELE–DEPARTMENT RELATIONS IN THE USA

Clientelism exists in many countries outside the United States. It has long been associated with multi-party systems such as that of the French Fourth Republic[14] or contemporary Italy.[15] Recent research has found many of the symptoms in British government, which had long been thought to be immune because of the British constitution and Britain's ideologically-differentiated class-based parties.[16] Yet, if clientelism is omnipresent, its strength varies from country to country. In some, clientelism rests merely on factors such as close social and professional links between civil servants and interest group officials, or on the belief of civil servants that one of their duties is representing the interests and attitudes of their clients in the policy-making process. Civil servants, in

turn, may influence ministers or secretaries. Yet such pressures are contingent; they may be withstood by a strong
man or woman. In other countries,
clientelism is a stronger force because
interest groups and their members have
the ability to inflict real political sanctions on politicians or officials in "their"
department who offend them. In such
countries clientelism is a political imperative. The reason why it is plausible
to argue that even department secretaries in the United States are victims
of clientelism is that the United States
can be, and often is, regarded as just
such a country.

Clientelism is widely believed to be a
political imperative in the USA because
interest groups are unusually powerful
in the United States and because the
centrifugal tendencies in American government appear to be much stronger
than the centripetal. Ever since the
Federalist Papers and (later) the work of
Tocqueville, it has been customary to
stress the importance of interest groups
in American politics. In more recent
times, pluralists such as Key, Dahl and
David Truman have presented a picture
of American politics in which groups
rather than classes are important, and in
which the groups pursue their interests
rather than ideological goals or
dreams.[17] It is almost equally commonplace to follow David Truman in
arguing (as he did in The Governmental
Process) that Congress, as well as the
president, claims to have the right to
control departmental policies. The balance of influence between Congress
and the presidency fluctuates.[18] The
president is the chief executive with
powers to nominate and dismiss top officials, but Congress and its committees
approve or reject nominations, and
Congress has the power to approve or
deny requests for funds and legislation.
In the post-Watergate era, Congress is
expanding its control over departments
by requiring affirmative votes in both
chambers before certain courses of action (such as supplying nuclear arms to

a foreign country) can be undertaken.
This sharing of control over departments
between Congress and the White House
means that departments can be very
largely controlled by the White House,
or by Congress and its Committees, or
in certain circumstances can even come
under the control of those it is supposed
to administer, i.e. can come to constitute an example of clientelism.

The main conditions for a department
coming under the control of its clientele
are that its clientele are reasonably
numerous, politically significant and
sufficiently concentrated geographically
to be of outstanding importance to a
number of congressmen and senators. If
these conditions obtain, the congressional committees from which a department must obtain legislation and
appropriations will be composed of
legislators who are elected to a significant degree on the votes of that department's clients. Congressmen and
senators are usually allocated to committees where they can serve their district or state.[19] Thus interior committees
are dominated by westerners, labour
committees by legislators representing
blue-collar workers, agriculture committees by representatives of rural
America[20] and defence committees by
representatives of areas in which military contracts are a major source of
employment.[21] Such legislators, given
the importance of interest groups in
American politics, are bound to press
the department concerned to fall in with
the wishes of interest groups that represent his constituents. If the legislator
fails to exert such pressure or to act in a
way that advances the interests of his
constituents and the department's clientele, he endangers his chances of re-
election. However, since the department can be presumed to yield to these
pressures, the interest groups and the
legislators representing its clientele can,
in turn, be expected to help the department in any disputes it may have with
the White House or other legislators and
interest groups. There develops inexor-

ably, therefore, what Truman calls "the institutionalized relationships between an established agency and its attendant interest groups and legislators."[22] In this iron triangle, all parties must necessarily support each other, for their interests coincide. A secretary's desire to defend his department, a legislator's desire for re-election and an interest group's desire for benefits for its members will create a permanent alliance that the White House will find difficult to overcome.

The orthodox view would not assert that the weaker causes of clientelism are absent in the United States. On the contrary, American civil servants are likely to be particularly affected by such universal phenomena as the tendency of civil servants to absorb the attitudes of the pressure groups with which they deal, because transfers between departments are less common in the United States than in many other civil services. Even if they are not, however—even if civil servants and politicians in the USA manage to withstand the psychological pressures in the direction of clientelism—they will still be confronted by permanent structural features of the American political system which will oblige them to accommodate themselves to the wishes of their clientele.

The "countervailing pressures" from the White House to adhere to the general policies of the administration and to resist pressures from a department's clientele can be surprisingly weak. This is partly because no president has fully succeeded in creating machinery to control departments. Reliance on an expanded and tightly structured White House staff has been shown in fact to insulate presidents from reality while avowedly keeping them in touch with it. The attempts by presidents, culminating with Eisenhower, to exercise authority over departments by building up the Bureau of the Budget (now the Office of Management and the Budget) also met with limited success. Most authorities agree that the influence of the Office has been declining during the last fifteen years;[23] even at the height of its powers, it was never able to impose the president's attitudes on departments but merely tried (not always successfully) to prevent them from taking public stands on issues that were incompatible "with the program of the President."[24] The problem has never, however, been wholly administrative; it is also political. Presidents, too, compete for the favours of blocks of voters such as farmers, union members and businessmen. They are thus likely to appoint people to head departments who will help them establish good relations with these sectors of the community. Thus secretaries of the interior and their assistants tend to come from the West, those of agriculture from the countryside and secretaries of labor and their assistants from the ranks of the unions. Ultimately and appropriately, a pluralist society is reflected in a pluralist executive branch; in Fenno's words: "The greatest problems for Cabinet and President like the greatest problems in American politics are those which center around the persistent dilemmas of unity and diversity."[25]

In short, it is generally thought that the pressures on departments to overfavour their clients are particularly great in the USA, while the restraints are weak.

THE AIMS OF THIS PAPER

This paper attempts to test the proposition that clientelism is so strong in the United States that even the secretaries appointed to head departments must concern themselves more with the interests of their clients than with the programme of the president. In attempting to test this view, it is desirable that we should meet it at its strongest. Obviously the strength of clientelism varies from department to department in the USA, and it is important to avoid picking an example where clientelism is unlikely to be strong. For example, it would be absurd to test clientelist theories by looking to see if the Justice Department had been captured by criminals or the State Department by foreign governments. It is also useful to bear in mind that the interest taken by the president in departments varies and that the strength of clientelism may be expected to increase as the president's interest decreases, leaving client pressures unopposed. The distinction to bear in mind here is the one that Cronin makes between the inner cabinet of departments in which most presidents take a close interest (including State and Defense) and the outer cabinet in which presidential interest is weak and intermittent. Clientelism should be at its strongest where a department is confronted by legitimate, strong and geographically-concentrated interest groups and is part of the "outer" rather than the "inner" cabinet.[26] The most obvious examples of such departments are Agriculture and Labor. This paper concentrates on the United States Department of Agriculture, long regarded as an extreme example of a department captured by its clientele, but argues later that the conclusions to be drawn are also applicable to other departments.

THE DEPARTMENT OF AGRICULTURE'S POLICIES AND POLITICS

The United States Department of Agriculture (USDA) was founded in 1862 with the explicit purpose of serving the farmer and advancing his interests. The department was thus one of a series (with Labor and Commerce) created in the late nineteenth century with a particular clientele in mind. To this day, it is traditional to appoint secretaries and assistant secretaries of agriculture who have had prior links with the industry. The department is easily fitted into the orthodox picture of clientelism. It has to obtain legislation and funds from the ag-

riculture committees, which have become cherished examples of the ways in which congressmen and senators seek committee assignments that enable them to further their constituents' interests; it is rare for more than one member of each of the two agriculture committees to represent an area in which farmers do not constitute a significant proportion of the electorate. Moreover, farmers support some of the longest established and best known of America's pressure groups, ready to correct any congressman or secretary of agriculture acting contrary to farmers' best interests.

Not surprisingly, agricultural policy seems at first sight to show many signs of clientelism. Secretaries of agriculture who have appeared to attach greater importance to the interests of consumers than of producers have been subjected to great pressure. Above all, the Department of Agriculture has, since the New Deal, administered farm subsidy laws which have seemed one of the most blatant concessions to a sectional interest in all of American public policy.[27] The department subsidizes farmers by more than $6 billion each year.[28] A very large slice of these subsidies (40.3 percent) has gone to the wealthiest 7.1 percent of America's farmers.[29] As subsidies have been created by raising prices (irrespective of the ability of the consumer to pay them), the farm subsidy laws have had a regressive effect on the distribution of income in the United States. Yet, if the farm subsidy policies implemented by the USDA have been of dubious social value, they have been economically totally indefensible. The effect of farm subsidies has been not only to keep men, capital and machinery unnecessarily employed in agriculture but to foster a maldistribution of the factors of production within the industry. Farmers have been encouraged by artificially high prices to produce products already in oversupply, and thereby discouraged from producing products of which there was a shortage. The farm policies of the USA have been so open to criticism that they have seemed the final proof that the USDA has been captured by the interests that it governs. Such major American political scientists as Theodore Lowi have used agriculture as a vivid example of a mutually supporting "subgovernment," consisting of farm interest groups, congressional agriculture committees and the USDA, operating autonomously and contrary to the public interest. The interest groups support legislators who support agencies which benefit their members. The agencies work to support helpful legislators and interest groups. The boundaries between the legislature, executive agencies and interest groups break down.[30]

It is striking that many social scientists are more Marxist than the Marxists in that they attach overwhelming explanatory power to the material interests of political actors. Thus political scientists tend to proceed from the observation that a department has to generate political support amongst client interest groups, and amongst legislators whose constituencies have an important stake in the department's work, to the conclusion that this will have a stable and predictable influence on policy. That influence will lead departments to benefit their clients materially, even at the expense of the public interest. Though such beliefs are popular, they are too simplistic. The striking feature of the politics of special interests in the United States is that, unlike in Britain, there is little consensus on what constitutes a group's best interests. This absence of consensus exists not merely because of disagreements over the best practical way to help a group; there is often no agreement, even among its members, about what a group should aim at. Agricultural policy provides a vivid illustration of such a dispute about both the ends and the means of policies designed to benefit a special interest, in this case farmers.

From the earliest stages of the New Deal to the advent of food shortages in the early 1970s, American agricultural policy sought to raise farmers' incomes by raising the price of agricultural products above the free-market level. When prices rose above the free-market level, two predictable consequences followed. The first was that farmers found it profitable to produce more; the second was that consumption tended to fall. The result was that the government, which often acted as buyer of last resort was frequently left with large surpluses which could not be sold at the prices the government had set. In an attempt (usually vain) to keep these surpluses within manageable levels, the government was forced to impose ever more severe restrictions on the amount that farmers could produce. Farmers who exceeded their quota were subjected to penalties, usually deprivation of entitlement to subsidies, but sometimes actually fines. Yet, though the basic direction of policy remained unchanged for a generation, it provoked a vigorous debate. Many economists, believing in the efficacy of market forces, argued that the farm subsidy laws were both futile and wasteful.[31] The prices set by the government for agricultural produce (known as "parity," because it was supposed to keep farmers' prices and incomes in line with those of the rest of the community) became further and further out of line with free-market prices as technological change increased output and lowered real production costs. The result was waste—waste most vividly demonstrated by surpluses which the government lacked the space to store, but waste less visibly reflected in the fact that too many farmers remained on the land, wasting talents, energy and capital that could have been better used in other ways and in the retention of the production of commodities such as cotton in traditional areas when they could have been produced more cheaply elsewhere. The free-market economists argued that most farm subsidies should be phased out so that market forces could reduce the number of farmers to the point where only the most efficient were left earning salaries comparable to those in the city. An equally distinguished group of economists, taking a position first formulated by John Kenneth Galbraith,[32] argued that the market would not work as smoothly as the *laissez faire* economists pretended. Farmers were too attached to their land to leave the farm; if the government withdrew farm subsidies, the countryside would lapse into a permanent recession which could ultimately have an adverse effect on the economy as a whole. The homeostatic model of the *laissez faire* school, they said, worked only in the textbooks, to which it should be confined.

Whatever policies they favoured, economists agreed that agricultural subsidies were immensely valuable to the farmer, raising farm incomes, according to the studies I have cited, from about $6 billion to $12 billion. We might suppose, therefore, the farmers' interest groups would be united in their defence. In fact, however, such a supposition would be false. Indeed, the largest of the American farm pressure groups, the Farm Bureau Federation, has fiercely advocated the phasing out of farm subsidies. Government price guarantees should be set well below the natural market price so that they come into effect only in extraordinary circumstances; in return, government controls over production should be ended. The federation argues that it believes in high farm incomes but argues that these should be earned in a free market; the only farm subsidy policies it would accept would be those designed to ease the transition to a free market and which would be phased out within a few years. The federation has, however, been vigorously opposed by the smaller National Farmers' Union (NFU). The NFU argues that farm subsidies are merely compensation for the fact that, unlike industry, farmers operate in an almost perfect market. Farmers cannot

"administer" prices in the same way that large corporations are said to. In exchange for subsidies, the NFU has accepted extensive government intervention in the industry, even arguing that farmers should be given licenses specifying how much they can produce. A large number of pressure groups limited to producers of a single commodity, the Grange and the National Farmers' Organization (NFO), have tended to support the position of the NFU.

Many attempts have been made to explain the conflict between the agricultural interest groups in a way compatible with traditional accounts of American interest-group politics. These explanations attempt to establish that policy differences reflect class or economic differences. Thus critics of the Farm Bureau Federation contend that it represents "agribusiness" rather than the family farmer. Surveys show, however, that federation's members are on average slightly less affluent than the members of such radical farm groups as the NFO. Others have argued that the opposition to farm subsidies has rested on farmers who produce livestock using grains to feed them. Thus, it is argued, higher prices for feed grains merely increase their costs. Yet the evidence is that, in areas where the federation and the NFU coincide, their members produce the same commodities while their representatives take opposing positions.[33] Moreover, the response of less ideological pressure groups like the British NFU to such a conflict of interest would be to seek a higher subsidy for livestock producers too, rather than trying to phase out the subsidies enjoyed by grain producers. Perhaps, following Olson,[34] we should assume that most farmers, having joined the Farm Bureau because of an immediate personal interest (for example in cheap insurance), participate little in its affairs and have allowed it to be captured by a dogmatic, highly politicized but unrepresentative elite. Whatever the cause, American farm pressure groups are sharply divided. Unlike their British counterparts, American rural politicians and USDA are not confronted by a united clientele. Instead they are offered sharply conflicting advice. The American politician, unlike the British, has to choose which interest group to listen to. . . .

It is clear that the standard theory of departmental clientelism in the USA is in some trouble when applied to the USDA. The standard theory would suggest that the department, faced by a coalition of interest groups and congressmen representing rural interests, would be obliged to compromise with them, irrespective of the president's wishes or the public interest. The reality, however, is that the department is faced not by concerted pressure in the farmers' interest but by pressure groups and legislators bitterly divided about what constitutes the farmers' interest and how it is best advanced. This division, based on a matter of principle rather than on regional or commodity rivalries, is not easily compromised; the department is faced not with a united but sharply divided clientele. What pattern of executive politics does this produce?

TWO SECRETARIES OF AGRICULTURE

The pattern can best be appreciated by considering the careers of the two secretaries of agriculture in the postwar period who have some claim to be considered the most successful, in that they retained their posts during the entire period (1953-61 and 1961-69) that their parties controlled the executive branch. We shall see, too, that the experience of their successors is wholly consistent with the pattern that emerges.

EISENHOWER AND BENSON

Eisenhower disliked the farm subsidy system. The Agriculture Acts seemed to him a prime example of wasteful public expenditure, while the production controls associated with them seemed a dangerous invasion of freedom. (After leaving office, Eisenhower was reported as saying that he would rather face prosecution than implement production controls on his Gettysburg farm.) Yet Eisenhower was no political innocent, particularly in regard to elections. Republicans had frequently, if possibly erroneously, concluded that Dewey's defeat in 1948 was due to his loss of the midwestern farm vote caused by his lack of enthusiasm for farm subsidies. Truman, so the argument went, had, by capturing the farm vote and with it several states that had eluded Roosevelt's grasp in 1944, secured enough votes in the electoral college to win. When, therefore, Eisenhower was asked about farm policy in the 1952 campaign, he obfuscated. His promise to maintain existing laws was widely thought to imply maintaining existing subsidies; but after the election Eisenhower argued that, on the contrary, he was thinking of a little known, and suspended, provision of the Agriculture Acts giving the secretary discretion to reduce subsidies.

Eisenhower's sympathies became much clearer after the 1952 campaign when he appointed Ezra Taft Benson as secretary of agriculture. An elder of the Mormon church, Benson felt to a greater degree than most politicians that his policies were not only correct but the only policies that were morally justifiable. His deep belief in property rights and individualism took him to the far right wing of the Republican party. Benson described himself as a "conservative conservative"; as early as 1960, he felt that Senator Goldwater was the ideal Republican candidate. To Benson, the American way of life was a capitalist way of life. "The blessings of abundance," he argued in his memoirs, "that we now possess have come down to us through an economic system that rest on three pillars—free enterprise, private property, and market economy."[35]

Not surprisingly in the light of his holding such views, Benson waged increasing war on the farm subsidy system established during the New Deal. Benson's policy was, in brief, to reduce subsidies to normal market prices, safeguarding farmers only against major natural disasters. At the same time, controls over production would be removed. Agriculture would once more become a free market, saving the government money but also putting many farmers out of business. There can be little doubt that Benson's policies contributed to a significant drop in farm income in the 1950s; Benson also steadfastly resisted calls for help to offset other, non-political factors that were also tending to reduce farm income. Both Benson's policies and his inflexible personality helped produce extremely bad relations with Congress. His appearances before congressional committees usually degenerated into slanging matches: in 1958 he was unable to complete even his opening statement to the Senate Committee on Agriculture and Forestry. Neither Benson's policies nor his relations with the Agriculture Committee are consistent with the clientelism model.

Indeed. it is surprising that Benson was able to have Congress adopt legislation in 1954 and 1958 that went some way towards his objectives. These triumphs were triumphs, however, not of persuasion but coercion. In 1958, for example, Benson was able to blackmail a Democratic Congress by means of a vigorous use of the presidential veto which the Republicans in Congress could prevent being over-ridden. Congress was forced to adopt legislation acceptable to Benson because, without fresh legislation, policies unfavourable to certain commodities, particularly cotton, automatically took effect. The president would veto any legislation to continue existing policies. Faced with serious dangers to their constituents' interests, many Democrats were obliged to support Benson's legislation against their better judgement. Clearly such a strategy relied on an extremely close relationship with the president. Both Ben-

son's tactics and his strategy militated against the creation of the independent political base that every secretary supposedly needs. Far from winning friends in Congress, Benson made enemies. Far from relying on interest groups and legislators representing his department's clientele, Benson came to rely on the president's willingness to veto legislation that Congress produced. By and large, Eisenhower was willing to provide Benson with whatever help the presidency could muster. On several occasions, however, Eisenhower found himself not pleased but embarrassed by the eagerness with which his secretary pursued the policies of the administration. On one occasion, Eisenhower called Benson in to explain to him that there were more ways to defeat an enemy than frontal attack. In other words, Eisenhower thought his secretary was *too* loyal to his policies. In 1956, with the elections in mind, Eisenhower ordered Benson to reverse his policies and increase the subsidies for feed grains, a move which, because it was not accompanied by production controls, proved to be one of the most expensive "giveaways" of American agricultural policy.

ORVILLE FREEMAN

The secretary of agriculture under both Kennedy and Johnson was Orville Freeman, a former governor of Minnesota who had nominated Kennedy at the 1960 Democratic convention. Freeman was to win great personal popularity in Congress through his patience, humour and willingness to sing the praises of the American farmer. Yet this should not blind us to the fact that, when it came to farm policy, Freeman was every bit as committed to one approach as was Benson. The difference was that Freeman's policies were sharply interventionist and were therefore diametrically opposed to Benson's.

Kennedy had lavished a degree of attention on the farm problem which observers found surprising given the size of the farm population.[36] The reason was that Kennedy's tacticians were hoping that the discontent with Benson's policies that had helped the Democrats in the 1958 midterm elections could bring Kennedy votes too. In the event, Kennedy's religion was to prove too great a handicap in the countryside. Yet, if Kennedy was determined to try to win the farm vote, he was equally determined that the cost of farm subsidies should be kept within bounds. The solution, with which Freeman became associated before the election, seemed to be an approach known as "supply management." Supply management, as the term implies, was a system of imposing limits on production. If the producers of a commodity approved by a majority of at least two-thirds, the department would calculate the amount of, for example, wheat which could be sold at a price that would bring farmers a reasonable income. Registered farmers who had a history of producing wheat would be given permits to produce the amount that had been set. The government would not be faced with any surpluses that it would have to buy; farmers would be sure of higher incomes. Kennedy was emphatic, however, that farmers would have to make a choice. If farmers rejected controls, they would be rejecting subsidies simultaneously. Farmers could not have both subsidies and freedom to produce as they wished. If controls were rejected, and subsidies ended, farm incomes would, of course, drop sharply.

Only after the White House had put considerable pressure on congressmen to vote for his proposals could Freeman secure a very limited version of "demand management." Such important commodities as cotton, feed grains and dairy produce were excluded. In some ways, such exclusions seemed to strengthen the hand of the administration, for its chances of obtaining the two-thirds majority in a referendum of producers (as the law required) were thought to be greater with those that

were still included. No group had been readier to accept extensive government regulation than wheat farmers. Yet after a fiercely contested campaign, far from providing the necessary two-thirds majority, wheat farmers rejected demand management. Under the administration's original policy, there was no doubt that this should have prompted the withdrawal of existing subsidies and the abandoning of farmers to the mercies of a free market. With the same adherence to the policy of his administration that Benson had displayed earlier, Freeman recommended exactly that course of action. The White House, aware that the 1964 election was not far away, reacted differently, and less resolutely. From the viewpoint of the president, it was not realistic to punish farmers in an election year. Shortly after President Johnson took office, he ordered Freeman to prepare fresh legislation providing subsidies for wheat farmers—legislation that was less controversial and could be enacted before the presidential elections.[37] By their obduracy, wheat farmers extracted subsidies without strict controls to limit their cost.

It is in this context of electoral competition that the true relationship between presidents and secretaries becomes obvious. Both Benson and Freeman had strong views on how to solve the "farm problem," which, though consistent with the general economic and social philosophy of the Administrations to which they belonged, got them into trouble. Far from their presidents having to urge them on to fulfill the administration's programme, the problem for Eisenhower, Kennedy and Johnson was to restrain secretaries who were overzealous. There can be little doubt that Benson cost the Republican party support in both congressional and presidential elections.[38] The 1958 midterm elections produced many Democratic gains in what had been considered safe Republican territory in the Midwest. Many commentators, including the influential *Congressional Quarterly*, placed much of the blame on Benson. Farmers were also the only bloc to favour Eisenhower less in 1956 than in 1952.[39] So bad was Benson's image that even Republican congressmen put pressure on Eisenhower to dismiss him. Eisenhower, often thought to be overloyal to subordinates, refused, but could often see the dangers. As we have seen, Eisenhower's personal interventions in agricultural affairs were directed towards *reducing* Benson's adherence to his own administration's policies. It was Eisenhower, not Benson, who was prepared to modify policy in the face of such political pressures as the 1958 midterm elections.

Orville Freeman's relations with Congress were much better than Benson's. As Hadwiger and Talbot note,[40] he was accorded the highly unusual honour of a standing ovation by the House Agriculture Committee. Yet, like Benson, Freeman did not allow mere popularity with Congress to deflect him from his administration's policies. As with the Eisenhower administration, it was not the secretary of agriculture but the president who was unwilling to pay the political costs of getting tough with the farmers. The vulnerability to political pressure lay not in the department but in the White House. It is worth emphasizing that the tendency of secretaries of agriculture to be *plus royaliste que le roi* did not hurt their careers as cabinet officers (though it may have put paid to any other ambitions they nursed). Both Benson and Freeman served out a full eight years, losing office only when their party lost the presidency. . . .

AGRICULTURE AND DEPARTMENTAL CLIENTELISM

It is clear that agricultural politics in the USA does not fit the classical theories of departmental clientelism. Conventional accounts of American politics lead us to expect to find an alliance of agricultural interest groups, legislators from rural areas (particularly on the congressional agriculture committees) and the Department of Agriculture, working to defend farmers' interests, possibly at the expense of the public at large. The real situation has been that interest groups, Congress and secretaries of agriculture have differed sharply over the choice between higher farm incomes and extensive government control over the industry, on the one hand, and greater independence but lower subsidies, on the other.

Quite naturally, stable alliances have emerged. The National Farmers' Union has naturally worked closely with the Democrats, both in Congress and in the USDA, to secure government intervention to raise farm incomes. The NFU has been an obvious source of talent from which Democratic administrations can select appointed officials. More strikingly, the NFU's close lobbying relationship with the Democrats in Congress has drawn it into electoral politics on their behalf. Thus Talbot argues that the NFU played a major role in establishing the Democratic party in North Dakota in the mid-1950s.[41] Equally naturally, the Farm Bureau Federation has found itself at home with the congressional Republicans and aggressively *laissez faire* Republican secretaries of agriculture. Republican secretaries have responded by recruiting assistant secretaries from the Farm Bureau Federation. Two coalitions have faced each other, taking opposite positions. Each has been based on an interest group and on either the Republican or the Democratic party in Congress. Control of the USDA has fluctuated between the coalitions as the presidency has passed from Democrats to Republicans.

Normal "clientele" politics therefore have been impossible. On major issues of agricultural policy, a secretary of agriculture is bound to offend a substantial proportion of the agricultural policy community. If he pleases the NFU, he offends the Farm Bureau Federation. If his proposals are acceptable to the Republicans on the agriculture committees, they will offend most Democrats. In brief, there has been no agreement on what constitutes the interest of farmers in the USA. The USDA has, therefore, been unable to pursue uncontroversially the interests of its clients, because the legislators whom farmers elect and the interest groups that farmers join give radically conflicting advice.

For both Republican and Democratic secretaries of agriculture, the institutions that are supposed to provide them with an independent political base, congressional committees and rural interest groups, have always contained vociferous critics. They have therefore been forced to rely heavily on the White House for support. The importance of the presidential veto to Benson's legislative strategy has been mentioned already. Presidential backing was equally important to Freeman in his attempts to find a majority in Congress in the early 1960s. In 1962, for example, the White House set to work not only its own legislative liaison staff but some rather surprising departments such as the Post Office to work for a farm subsidy bill.[42] Faced with a weak strategic situation outside the executive branch, secretaries of agriculture have been very much presidents' men; the problem for presidents, as we have seen, is their tendency to be *plus royaliste que le roi*.

Why, then, has the Department of Agriculture been so widely regarded as an example of unbridled clientelism? The answer lies in the misfortune that earlier studies of the department focused not on farm subsidies, which account for the bulk of its work and expenditure, but on the less important and controversial work of its more specialized agencies.[43] The politics of soil erosion provide a good example. The department funds a large number of small projects designed to halt soil erosion—more in fact than the Office of Management and the Budget thinks are justified. Yet the

department has usually been able to marshal pressure group and congressional support to overcome such opposition. The reasons why the politics of soil erosion differ from the politics of subsidies are obvious. In the first place, who can be in favour of soil erosion, or against the department's efforts to check it? Secondly, the discrete, divisible work done for conservation is particularly easy to manipulate to gain congressional support. Helpful congressmen can be rewarded with projects in their own districts and even, on occasion, of benefit to their own farms. Such projects are not representative of the general work of the department; it is regrettable that the special politics of special projects such as conservation have coloured the general impression of the department.

WIDER IMPLICATIONS

This article started by arguing that the USDA ought to fit the general model of departmental clientelism particularly well. The USDA had a readily identifiable constituency both in the country at large and in Congress which it could mobilize against the White House. The USDA seemed to meet all the conditions for the control of a department by its clientele. We expected to find, therefore, that even secretaries of agriculture were obliged to accommodate themselves not so much to wishes of the White House but to those of agricultural interest groups and the agriculture committees of Congress. Yet it appears that the USDA does not fit the model particularly well. Secretaries of agriculture have, if anything, been too loyal to the policies approved by their presidents. Confronted by sharp divisions on the central issues of agricultural policy amongst legislators, interest groups and presidential candidates, secretaries of agriculture have tended to antagonize their clientele by their loyalty to the policy of the administration.

Defenders of the orthodox theory of

clientelism may be ready to concede at this point that the USDA does not fit the model to which we are accustomed. Their response, however, may be to argue that the USDA is an exception, that other departments are consistent with the orthodoxy. It is necessary, therefore, to see whether the causes and symptoms of the USDA's incompatibility with the usual model of clientelism appear in the case of other departments. One of the most important reasons why the USDA did not fit the orthodox model was that its clientele was divided. . . .

"CAPTURED" SECRETARIES?

Another surprising feature in the case of the USDA was that its secretaries were on poor terms with many interest groups with which their department was faced. Again, we must ask how typical was the case of the USDA?

It is not the case that obvious "clientele" departments other than Agriculture necessarily have secretaries from the ranks of their clients or controlled by them. The idea that the secretary of labor is picked by or approved by the unions has been challenged. Goulden tells us that George Meany, president of the AFL-CIO, presented President-elect Kennedy with a list of labour leaders suitable for secretary of labor. Kennedy rejected them all, suggesting that the public would not tolerate a labour leader administering acts such as the Landrum Griffin Act designed to regulate unions.[44] Carter has followed Kennedy's example, rejecting AFL-CIO nominees in favour of F. Ray Marshall. Kennedy appointed instead Arthur Goldberg, a man who, though close to the labour movement, was surprisingly unpopular with its leaders. Meany was not even pleased with Nixon's appointment of a leader of a construction union, Peter Brennan, commenting "Who is he? He is not my Secretary of Labor."[45] Brennan, for reasons unconnected with Meany's outburst, did not last long and was replaced by an

academic. Domhoff points out that secretaries of labor are rarely from unions;[46] Truman, Kennedy and Johnson chose lawyers like Willard Wirtz and Arthur Goldberg while Roosevelt appointed "a reform-minded member of the Boston upper class," Frances Perkins. After a short period with the president of the Plumbers Union as secretary of labor, Eisenhower reverted to type and appointed James P. Mitchell, vice president of Bloomingdales, a New York department store. This trend was repeated at the assistant secretary level. Mann and Doig report that

> the *impasse* over one union prospect resulted in mutual agreement that there would be no attempt to provide direct union representation in the high ranks of the Labor Department. As a result from 1954, Eisenhower appointees in the Department of Labor were men with professional or business backgrounds.[47]

It is also the case that the AFL-CIO feels that it is too important to rest content with being represented by the Department of Labor. George Meany prefers to go to the top, to the president himself. As he himself argued "I don't pay too much attention to the Secretary . . . if you have a problem with the landlord, you don't discuss it with the janitor."[48]

Nor have all secretaries of defense become mouthpieces for the defence establishment. Indeed, McNamara, secretary of defense under Kennedy and Johnson was criticized for suppressing, not representing the views of the military establishment.[49] Kennedy gave McNamara substantial backing, as did Johnson, against critics amongst his "clients." Nor, as Adam Yarmolinsky points out, have the military undermined the authority of the White House as advocates of departmental particularism might believe. Truman received immensely valuable support from the military during the controversy after his dismissal of MacArthur. Indeed the crisis might have been worse had the military openly criticized the president. Asked by a Senate committee whether he would speak out publicly if he believed a presidential decision was wrong, General Bradley replied, "No Sir, . . . I was brought up a little differently."[50]

PARTY DIFFERENCES

One factor ignored by the classic account of clientelism which turned out to be enormously important in the case of the USDA was the political party. To know whether a secretary of agriculture was a Republican or a Democrat has been sufficient to predict his policies almost perfectly in the post-New Deal period. Democrats have favoured interventionist policies, Republicans a shift towards a freer market. If we confine our attention to the other two alleged classic examples of clientelism (Commerce and Labor), are there comparable differences in policy apparent between the parties? I have to admit that in the case of Commerce such differences are difficult to perceive. Administrations of both parties have usually appointed a secretary of commerce acceptable to business opinion, Roosevelt's selection of Henry Wallace being the conspicuous exception.

In the case of Labor, however, differences comparable to those in Agriculture are in fact apparent. Post-war Republicans have, as analysts of congressional voting and the labour unions have noted, proved more sympathetic to legislation guaranteeing the rights of management than of labour. At the same time, however, the split between the peace movement and the labour unions within the Democratic party in the late 1960s and early 1970s, gave Republicans anxious to create the "emerging Republican majority" a great incentive to form close ties with the right-wing unions. The appointment of Peter Brennan, A New York construction union leader, as secretary of labor showed President Nixon's awareness of the potential value of such a strategy. Unfortunately Brennan soon demonstrated his unsuitability. His successor was John Dunlop, a Harvard academic known to be sympathetic to the construction unions. Dunlop, however, soon found his position untenable. Having convinced President Ford that he should sign a "sites picketing" bill extending the picketing rights of the construction unions (a decision that was made public), Dunlop had to resign when President Ford vetoed the bill. Ford realized that in a close contest for the Republican nomination with Governor Reagan he could not afford to sign a measure that offended most Republicans. The construction unions, which in 1972 favoured President Nixon, in 1976 joined the other AFL-CIO unions in endorsing Ford's Democratic opponent, Jimmy Carter. In a way reminiscent of agricultural politics, the ideological attitude of the Republican party towards an interest had made traditional clientele politics impossible; party ideology overcame the optimal political strategy. . . .

CONCLUSIONS

This article has suggested that, at least in the case of the Department of Agriculture, traditional notions of departmental clientelism do not fit. Faced with conflicting interest groups and legislators, secretaries have been forced to choose between two approaches to policy: the interventionist and the free market. They have made the choice in a way entirely predictable in terms of their party. Democratic secretaries have chosen interventionist policies; Republicans have moved towards a free market policy. No one is likely to mistake the rhetoric or policies of a Democratic secretary for a Republican secretary of vice versa. Far from being captured by a united farm interest and lured away from administration policy, secretaries of agriculture have been more loyal to party principles than even their presidents. The article has also suggested that many of the factors militating against departmental clientelism in the case of Agriculture have been present in other departments, too. The idea that

the secretary of labour is the mouth-
piece of all the unions or that the secretary of defense is necessarily the
spokesman for the military is at best
simplistic and at worst simply incorrect. . . .

FURTHER IMPLICATIONS

It would be presumptuous for a British
student of politics to seem to offer advice to the American government, but
one implication in my argument is too
obvious to avoid mentioning. Partly because of the belief that secretaries fall a
victim to particularism, the American
cabinet, never a strong institution, has
suffered a steady decline since
Eisenhower. I have argued that secretaries are not necessarily disloyal to
the programme of the president and that
in the case of Agriculture, previously
thought to be a paradigm of particularism, secretaries have been more
loyal to the president's programme than
to the president. It is also the case that
not only Watergate but the more minor
scandals of the Truman, Eisenhower and
Johnson administrations coupled with
the climate of sycophancy so vividly described by George Reedy must raise
doubts about the desirability of government by White House staff.[51] Perhaps
the time is ripe for presidents to put
more faith in their secretaries. Past evidence does not suggest that secretaries
will betray it.

NOTES

1. David B. Truman, *The Governmental
Process* (New York: Knopf, 1951), p. 406.
2. Richard Fenno, Jr., *The President's
Cabinet* (Cambridge, Mass.: Harvard University Press, 1959), p. 249.
3. M. J. C. Vile, *Politics in the USA* (London: Hutchinson, 1976), p. 199.
4. R. V. Denenberg, *Understanding
American Politics* (London: Fontana/Collins,
1976).
5. Clinton Rossiter, *The American Presidency* (London: Rupert Hart-David, 1960), p.
59, emphasis added.
6. Richard E. Neustadt, *Presidential

Power: The Politics of Leadership* (New York:
Wiley, 1960), p. 40.
7. James MacGregor Burns, *Presidential
Government: The Crucible of Leadership*
(Boston, Mass.: Houghton Mifflin, 1973), p.
127, emphasis added.
8. Erwin C. Hargrove, *The Power of the
Modern Presidency* (Philadelphia: Temple
University Press, 1974), p. 238.
9. Thomas E. Cronin, *The State of the
Presidency* (Boston, Mass.: Little, Brown,
1975), p. 191, emphasis added.
10. Richard Nathan, *The Plot that Failed:
Nixon and the Administrative Presidency*
(New York: Wiley, 1975), p. 41.
11. Harold Seidman, *Politics, Position,
and Power: The Dynamics of Federal Organization* (New York: Oxford University Press,
1970), p. 107.
12. Quoted by Truman in *The Governmental Process*, p. 407.
13. Theodore C. Sorensen, *Decision-
making in the White House: The Olive
Branch or the Arrows* (New York: Columbia
University Press, 1963), p. 68, emphasis added.
14. P. M. Williams, *Crisis and Compromise: Politics in the Fourth Republic*
(London: Longmans, Green, 1964), p. 342.
15. Joseph LaPalombara, *Interest Groups
in Italian Politics* (Princeton, N.J.: Princeton
University Press, 1964), esp. chaps. 18 and
19.
16. Hugh Heclo and Aaron Wildavsky,
The Private Government of Public Money
(London: Macmillan, 1973), passim.
17. V. O. Key, *Politics, Parties and Pressure Groups* (New York: Crowell, 1952),
Truman, *op. cit.* Robert A. Dahl, *Who Governs?: Democracy and Power in an American City* (New Haven, Conn.: Yale University Press, 1961).
18. Truman, *op. cit.*, pp. 404-10.
19. Richard Fenno. Jr., *Congressmen in
Committees* (Boston, Mass.: Little, Brown,
1973), p. 5.
20. C. O. Jones, "The Agriculture Committee and the Problem of Representation,"
American Political Science Review 55
(1961): 358-67.
21. Adam Yarmolinsky, *The Military Establishment* (New York: Harper and Row,
1971), p. 38 ff.
22. Truman, *op. cit.*, p. 406.
23. R. S. Gilmour, "Central Clearance: A
Revised Perspective," *Public Administration
Review* 31 (1971): 150-58.
24. U.S. Congress, House of Repre-

150 GRAHAM K. WILSON

sentatives, 89th Congress 2nd Session, Committee on Agriculture, Serial MM, *Legislative Policy of the Bureau of the Budget.*

25. *Fenno, Congressmen . . ., op. cit.,* p. 253.

26. Thomas E. Cronin, "Presidents As Chief Executives," in Rexford G. Tugwell and Thomas E. Cronin (eds.), *The Presidency Reappraised* (New York: Praeger Publishers, 1974), p. 250.

27. A more detailed study by the author of agricultural subsidy politics in Britain and the USA, *Special Interests and Policymaking: Agricultural Policies and Politics in Britain and the United States of America, 1956-70,* is to be published by John Wiley later in 1977.

28. United States Senate, Committee on Agriculture and Forestry, 89th Congress 1st Session, *Farm Programs and Dynamic Forces in Agriculture* (prepared by the Legislative Reference Section of the Library of Congress), Luther Tweeten, Earl G. Heady, and Les U. Mayer. "Farm Program Alternatives, Farm Incomes and Public Costs under Alternative Commodity Programs," *CAED Report 18,* Iowa State University, n.d.

29. Charles Schultze, *The Distribution of Farm Subsidies: Who Gets the Benefits?* (Washington, D.C.: Brookings Institution Staff Paper, 1971).

30. Theodore Lowi, "Agriculture's Subgovernments," *The Reporter* (May 21, 1964), and "How the Farmers Get What They Want," in *The Politics of Economic Policy,* ed. John L. Anderson (Reading, Mass.: Addison-Wesley, 1970).

31. For a compelling statement of this view, *vide* D. Gale Johnson, *World Agriculture in Disarray* (London: Fontana World Economic Issues, 1973).

32. J. K. Galbraith, "Economic Preconceptions and Farm Policy," *American Economic Review* 44 (1954): 40-52.

33. See J. A. Crampton, *The National Farmers' Union: Ideology of a Pressure Group* (Lincoln: University of Nebraska Press, 1965), esp. p. 59; Robert A. Rohwer, "Organized Farmers in Oklahoma," *Rural Sociology* 17 (1952): 30-6; D. E. Morrison and W. Keith Warner "Correlates of Farmers' Attitudes Towards Public and Private Aspects of Agricultural Organizations," *Rural Sociology* 36 (1971): 5-19; Denton E. Morrison and Allan D. Streves, "Deprivation, Discontent and Social Movement Participation: Evidence on a Contemporary Farmers' Movement, the NFO," *Rural Sociology* 32 (1967):

414-34.

34. Mancur Olson, Jr., *The Logic of Collective Action* (Cambridge, Mass.: Harvard University Press, 1965).

35. Ezra Taft Benson, *Cross Fire: The Eight Years with Eisenhower* (New York: Doubleday, 1962), p. 58. See also Ezra Taft Benson, *Freedom to Farm* (New York: Doubleday, 1962).

36. Robert Novak, *Wall Street Journal,* September 29, 1960.

37. *Washington Post,* December 18, 1963; *Wall Street Journal,* January 17, 1964; Don F. Hadwiger and Ross B. Talbot, *Pressures and Protests: The Kennedy Farm Program and the Wheat Referendum of 1963* (San Francisco: Chandler, 1965), p. 216.

38. *Congressional Quarterly Weekly Report,* March 14, 1958.

39. V. O. Key, *The Responsible Electorate* (New York: Vintage Books, 1966), p. 87.

40. Hadwiger and Talbot, *Pressures and Protests,* p. 29.

41. Ross B. Talbot, "The North Dakota Farmers' Union and North Dakota Politics," *Western Political Quarterly* 10 (1957): 875-901.

42. The Republican minority leader, Charles Hallek, read out a letter from the New York Democrat, Otis Pike, to his constituents complaining of threats not to provide a new post office for his district during the debates on the 1962 act. *Congressional Record,* 108, pt. 8, col. 11342.

43. Charles M. Hardin, *The Politics of Agriculture: Soil Conservation and the Struggle for Power in Rural America* (Glencoe, Ill.: Free Press, 1952).

44. Joseph C. Goulden, *Meany* (New York: Atheneum, 1972), p. 303.

45. *New York Times,* November 8, 1974.

46. G. William Domhoff, *Who Rules America?* (Englewood Cliffs, N.J.: Prentice-Hall, 1967).

47. Dean Mann and James W. Doig, *The Assistant Secretaries: Problems and Processes* (Washington, D.C.: The Brookings Institute, 1965), p. 54.

48. Goulden, *op. cit.,* p. 429.

49. Jack Raymond, "The McNamara Monarchy," in *The Military and American Society: Essays and Readings,* eds. Stephen E. Ambrose and James Alden Barber (New York: Free Press, 1972), esp. p. 228.

50. Yarmolinsky, *op. cit.,* p. 36.

51. George Reedy, *The Twilight of the Presidency* (New York: Mentor Books, 1970).

20. The Swelling of the Presidency*

THOMAS E. CRONIN

The advent of Richard Nixon's second term in the White House is marked by an uncommon amount of concern, in Congress and elsewhere, about the expansion of presidential power and manpower. Even the president himself is ostensibly among those who are troubled. Soon after his reelection, Mr. Nixon announced that he was planning to pare back the presidential staff. And in recent days, the president has said he is taking action to cut the presidential workforce in half and to "substantially" reduce the number of organizations that now come under the White House. Mr. Nixon's announcements have no doubt been prompted in part by a desire to add drama and an aura of change to the commencement of his second term. But he also seems genuinely worried that the presidency may have grown so large and top-heavy that it now weakens rather than strengthens his ability to manage the federal government. His fears are justified.

The presidency has, in fact, grown a full 20 percent in the last four years alone in terms of the number of people who are employed directly under the president. It has swelled to the point where it is now only a little short of the State Department's sprawling domestic bureaucracy in size.

This burgeoning growth of the presidency has, in the process, made the traditional civics textbook picture of the executive branch of our government nearly obsolete. According to this view, the executive branch is more or less

neatly divided into cabinet departments and their secretaries, agencies and their heads, and the president. A more contemporary view takes note of a few prominent presidential aides and refers to them as the "White House staff." But neither view adequately recognizes the large and growing coterie that surrounds the president and is made up of dozens of assistants, hundreds of presidential advisers, and thousands of members of an institutional amalgam called the Executive Office of the President. While the men and women in these categories all fall directly under the president in the organizational charts, there is no generally used term for their common terrain. But it has swelled so much in size and scope in recent years, and has become such an important part of the federal government, that it deserves its own designation. Most apt perhaps is the Presidential Establishment. [*Dated organizational chart omitted.*]

The Presidential Establishment today embraces more than twenty support staffs (the White House Office, National Security Council, and Office of Management and Budget, etc.) and advisory offices (Council of Economic Advisers, Office of Science and Technology, and Office of Telecommunications Policy, etc.). It has spawned a vast proliferation of ranks and titles to go with its proliferation of functions (Counsel to the President, Assistant to the President, Special Counselor, Special Assistant, Special Consultant, Director, Staff Director, etc.). "The White House now has

*Source: From *Saturday Review*, Vol. 1 (February 1973), pp. 30-36. Copyright © 1973 by Saturday Review Company. Reprinted by permission.

enough people with fancy titles to popu-late a Gilbert and Sullivan comic op-era," Congressman Morris Udall has reasonably enough observed.

There are no official figures on the size of the Presidential Establishment, and standard body counts vary widely depending on who is and who is not in-cluded in the count, but by one fre-quently used reckoning, between five and six thousand people work for the president of the United States. Payroll and maintenance costs for this staff run between $100 million and $150 million a year. (These figures include the Office of Economic Opportunity (OEO), which is an Executive Office agency and employs two thousand people, but not the roughly fifteen-thousand-man Cen-tral Intelligence Agency, although that, too, is directly responsible to the chief executive.) These "White House" workers have long since outgrown the White House itself and now occupy not only two wings of the executive man-sion but three nearby high-rise office buildings as well.

The expansion of the Presidential Es-tablishment, it should be emphasized, is by no means only a phenomenon of the Nixon years. The number of employees under the president has been growing steadily since the early 1900s when only a few dozen people served in the White House entourage, at a cost of less than a few hundred thousand dollars annually. Congress's research arm, the Congressional Research Service, has compiled a count that underlines in par-ticular the accelerated increase in the last two decades. This compilation shows that between 1954 and 1971 the number of presidential advisers has grown from 25 to 45, the White House staff from 266 to 600, and the Executive Office staff from 1,175 to 5,395.

But if the growth of the Presidential Establishment antedates the current ad-ministration, it is curious at least that one of the largest expansions ever, in both relative and absolute terms, has taken place during the first term of a conservative, management-minded president who has often voiced his ob-jection to any expansion of the federal government and its bureaucracy.

Under President Nixon, in fact, there has been an almost systematic bureau-cratization of the Presidential Establish-ment, in which more new councils and offices have been established, more specialization and division of labor and layers of staffing have been added, than at any time except during World War II. Among the major Nixonian additions are the Council on Environmental Qual-ity, Council on International Economic Policy, Domestic Council, and Office of Consumer Affairs.

The numbers in the White House en-tourage may have decreased somewhat since November when the president announced his intention to make certain staff cuts. They may shrink still more if, as expected, the OEO is shifted from White House supervision to cabinet control, mainly under the Department of Health, Education, and Welfare. Also, in the months ahead, the president will probably offer specific legislative pro-posals, as he has done before, to repro-gram or repackage the upper reaches of the executive.

Even so, any diminution of the Presi-dential Establishment has so far been more apparent than real, or more inci-dental than substantial. Some aides, such as former presidential counselor Robert Finch, who have wanted to leave anyway, have done so. Others, serving as scapegoats on the altar of Watergate, are also departing.

In addition, the president has offi-cially removed a number of trusted domestic-policy staff assistants from the White House rolls and dispersed them to key sub-cabinet posts across the span of government. But this dispersal can be viewed as not so much reducing as creating yet another expansion—a vir-tual setting up of White House outposts (or little White Houses?) throughout the cabinet departments. The aides that are being sent forth are notable for their intimacy with the president, and they will surely maintain direct links to the White House, even though these links do not appear on the official organizational charts.

Then, too, one of the most important of the president's recent shifts of executive branch members involves an unequivocal addition to the Presidential Establishment. This is the formal setting up of a second office—with space and a staff in the White House—for Treasury Secretary George Shultz as chairman of yet another new presidential body, the Council on Economic Policy. This move makes Shultz a member of a White House inner cabinet. He will now be over-secretary of economic affairs alongside Henry Kissinger, over-secretary for national security affairs, and John Ehrlichman, over-secretary for domestic affairs.

In other words, however the names and numbers have changed recently or may be shifted about in the near future, the Presidential Establishment does not seem to be declining in terms of function, power, or prerogative; in fact, it may be continuing to grow as rapidly as ever.

Does it matter? A number of political analysts have argued recently that it does, and I agree with them. Perhaps the most disturbing aspect of the expansion of the Presidential Establishment is that it has become a powerful inner sanctum of government, isolated from traditional, constitutional checks and balances. It is common practice today for anonymous, unelected, and unratified aides to negotiate sensitive international commitments by means of executive agreements that are free from congressional oversight. Other aides in the Presidential Establishment wield fiscal authority over billions of dollars in funds that Congress has appropriated, yet the president refuses to spend, or that Congress has assigned to one purpose and the administration routinely redirects to another—all with no semblance of public scrutiny. Such

exercises of power pose an important, perhaps vital, question of governmental philosophy: Should a political system that has made a virtue of periodic electoral accountability accord an ever-increasing policy-making role to White House counselors who neither are confirmed by the U.S. Senate nor, because of the doctrine of "executive privilege," are subject to questioning by Congress?

Another disquieting aspect of the growth of the Presidential Establishment is that the increase of its powers has been largely at the expense of the traditional sources of executive power and policy-making—the cabinet members and their departments. When I asked a former Kennedy-Johnson cabinet member a while ago what he would like to do if he ever returned to government, he said he would rather be a presidential assistant than a cabinet member. And this is an increasingly familiar assessment of the relative influence of the two levels of the executive branch. The Presidential Establishment has become, in effect, a whole layer of government between the president and the cabinet, and it often stands above the cabinet in terms of influence with the president. In spite of the exalted position that cabinet members hold in textbooks and protocol, a number of cabinet members in recent administrations have complained that they could not even get the president's ear except through an assistant. In his book *Who Owns America?*, former Secretary of the Interior Walter Hickel recounts his combat with a dozen different presidential functionaries and tells how he needed clearance from them before he could get to talk to the president, or how he frequently had to deal with the assistants themselves because the president was "too busy." During an earlier administration, President Eisenhower's chief assistant, Sherman Adams, was said to have told two cabinet members who could not resolve a matter of mutual concern: "Either make up your mind or else tell me and I will do it. We must not bother the president with this. He is trying to keep the world from war." Several of President Kennedy's cabinet members regularly battled with White House aides who blocked them from seeing the president. And McGeorge Bundy, as Kennedy's chief assistant for national security affairs, simply sidestepped the State Department in one major area of department communications. He had all important incoming State Department cables transmitted simultaneously to his office in the White House, part of an absorption of traditional State Department functions that visibly continues to this day with presidential assistant Henry Kissinger. Indeed, we recently witnessed the bizarre and telling spectacle of Secretary of State William Rogers insisting that he *did* have a role in making foreign policy.

In a speech in 1971, Senator Ernest Hollings of South Carolina plaintively noted the lowering of cabinet status. "It used to be," he said,

> that if I had a problem with food stamps, I went to see the secretary of agriculture, whose department had jurisdiction over that problem. Not anymore. Now, if I want to learn the policy, I must go to the White House to consult John Price [a special assistant]. If I want the latest on textiles, I won't get it from the secretary of commerce, who has the authority and responsibility. No, I am forced to go to the White House and see Mr. Peter Flanigan. I shouldn't feel too badly. Secretary Stans [Maurice Stans, then secretary of commerce] has to do the same thing.

If cabinet members individually have been downgraded in influence, the cabinet itself as a council of government has become somewhat of a relic, replaced by more specialized comminglings that as often as not are presided over by White House staffers. The cabinet's decline has taken place over several administrations. John Kennedy started out his term declaring his intentions of using the cabinet as a major policy-making body, but his change of mind was swift, as his postmaster general, J. Edward Day, has noted. "After the first two or three meetings," Day has written,

> one had the distinct impression that the President felt that decisions on major matters were not made—or even influenced—at Cabinet sessions, and that discussion there was a waste of time.... When members spoke up to suggest or to discuss major administration policy, the President would listen with thinly disguised impatience and then postpone or otherwise bypass the question.

Lyndon Johnson was equally disenchanted with the cabinet as a body and characteristically held cabinet sessions only when articles appeared in the press talking about how the cabinet was withering away. Under Nixon, the cabinet is almost never convened at all.

Not only has the Presidential Establishment taken over many policy-making functions from the cabinet and its members, it has also absorbed some of the operational functions. White House aides often feel they should handle any matters that they regard as ineptly administered, and they tend to intervene in internal departmental operations at lower and lower levels. They often feel underemployed, too, and so are inclined to reach out into the departments to find work and exercise authority for themselves.

The result is a continuous undercutting of cabinet departments—and the cost is heavy. These intrusions can cripple the capacity of cabinet officials to present policy alternatives, and they diminish self-confidence, morale, and initiative within the departments. George Ball, a former undersecretary of state, noted the effects on the State Department:

> Able men, with proper pride in their professional skills, will not long tolerate such votes of no-confidence, so it should be no surprise that they are leaving the career service, and making way for mediocrity with the result that, as time goes on, it may be hopelessly difficult to restore the Department.

The irony of this accretion of numbers

and functions to the Presidential Establishment is that the presidency is finding itself increasingly afflicted with the very ills of the traditional departments that the expansions were often intended to remedy. The presidency has become a large, complex bureaucracy itself, rapidly acquiring many dubious characteristics of large bureaucracies in the process: layering, overspecialization, communication gaps, interoffice rivalries, inadequate coordination, and an impulse to become consumed with short-term, urgent operational concerns at the expense of thinking systematically about the consequences of varying sets of policies and priorities and about important long-range problems. It takes so much of the president's time to deal with the members of his own bureaucracy that it is little wonder he has little time to hear counsel from cabinet officials.

Another toll of the burgeoning Presidential Establishment is that White House aides, in assuming more and more responsibility for the management of government programs, inevitably lose the detachment and objectivity that is so essential for evaluating new ideas. Can a lieutenant vigorously engaged in implementing the presidential will admit the possibility that what the president wants is wrong or not working? Yet a president is increasingly dependent on the judgment of these same staff members, since he seldom sees his cabinet members.

Why has the presidency grown bigger and bigger? There is no single villain or systematically organized conspiracy promoting this expansion. A variety of factors is at work. The most significant is the expansion of the role of the presidency itself—an expansion that for the most part has taken place during national emergencies. The reason for this is that the public and Congress in recent decades have both tended to look to the president for the decisive responses that were needed in those emergencies. The Great Depression and World War II in

particular brought sizable increases in presidential staffs. And once in place, many stayed on, even after the emergencies that brought them had faded. Smaller national crises have occasioned expansion in the White House entourage, too. After the Russians successfully orbited *Sputnik* in 1957, President Eisenhower added several science advisers. After the Bay of Pigs, President Kennedy enlarged his national security staff.

Considerable growth in the Presidential Establishment, especially in the post-World War II years, stems directly from the belief that critical societal problems require that wise men be assigned to the White House to alert the President to appropriate solutions and to serve as the agents for implementing these solutions. Congress has frequently acted on the basis of this belief, legislating the creation of the National Security Council, the Council of Economic Advisers, and the Council on Environmental Quality, among others. Congress has also increased the chores of the presidency by making it a statutory responsibility for the president to prepare more and more reports associated with what are regarded as critical social areas—annual economic and manpower reports, a biennial report on national growth, etc.

Most recently, President Nixon responded to a number of troublesome problems that defy easy relegation to any one department—problems like international trade and drug abuse—by setting up special offices in the Executive Office with sweeping authority and sizable staffs. Once established, these units rarely get dislodged. And an era of permanent crisis ensures a continuing accumulation of such bodies.

Another reason for the growth of the Presidential Establishment is that occupants of the White House frequently distrust members of the permanent government. Nixon aides, for example, have viewed most civil servants not only as Democratic but as wholly unsympathetic to such objectives of the Nixon administration as decentralization, revenue sharing, and the curtailment of several Great Society programs. Departmental bureaucracies are viewed from the White House as independent, unresponsive, unfamiliar, and inaccessible. They are suspected again and again of placing their own, congressional, or special-interest priorities ahead of those communicated to them from the White House. Even the president's own cabinet members soon become viewed in the same light; one of the strengths of cabinet members, namely their capacity to make a compelling case for their programs, has proved to be their chief liability with presidents.

Presidents may want this type of advocacy initially, but they soon grow weary and wary of it. Not long ago, one White House aide accused a former labor secretary of trying to "out-Meany Meany." Efforts by former Interior Secretary Hickel to advance certain environmental programs and by departing Housing and Urban Development Secretary George Romney to promote innovative housing construction methods not only were unwelcome but after a while were viewed with considerable displeasure and suspicion at the White House.

Hickel writes poignantly of coming to this recognition during his final meeting with President Nixon, in the course of which the president frequently referred to him as an "adversary." "Initially," writes Hickel,

> I considered that a compliment because, to me, an adversary is a valuable asset. It was only after the President had used the term many times and with a disapproving inflection that I realized he considered an adversary an enemy. I could not understand why he would consider me an enemy.

Not only have recent presidents been suspicious about the depth of the loyalty of those in their cabinets, but they also invariably become concerned about the possibility that sensitive administration secrets may leak out through the departmental bureaucracies, and this is another reason why presidents have come to rely more on their own personal groups, such as task forces and advisory commissions.

Still another reason that more and more portfolios have been given to the presidency is that new federal programs frequently concern more than one federal agency, and it seems reasonable that someone at a higher level is required to fashion a consistent policy and to reconcile conflicts. Attempts by cabinet members themselves to solve sensitive jurisdictional questions frequently result in bitter squabbling. At times, too, cabinet members themselves have recommended that these multidepartmental issues be settled at the White House. Sometimes new presidential appointees insist that new offices for program coordination be assigned directly under the president. Ironically, such was the plea of George McGovern, for example, when President Kennedy offered him the post of director of the Food-for-Peace program in 1961. McGovern attacked the buildup of the Presidential Establishment in his campaign against Nixon, but back in 1961 he wanted visibility (and no doubt celebrity status) and he successfully argued against his being located outside the White House—either in the State of Agriculture departments. President Kennedy and his then campaign manager Robert Kennedy felt indebted to McGovern because of his efforts in assisting the Kennedy presidential campaign in South Dakota. Accordingly, McGovern was granted not only a berth in the Executive Office of the President but also the much-coveted title of special assistant to the president.

The Presidential Establishment has also been enlarged by the representation of interest groups within its fold. Even a partial listing of staff specializations that have been grafted onto the White House in recent years reveals how interest-group brokerage has become added to the more traditional staff activities of counseling and administration. These specializations form a veritable index of American society:

Budget and management, national security, economics, congressional matters, science and technology, drug abuse prevention, telecommunications, consumers, national goals, intergovernmental relations, environment, domestic policy, international economics, military affairs, civil rights, disarmament, labor relations, District of Columbia, cultural affairs, education, foreign trade and tariffs, past Presidents, the aged, health and nutrition, physical fitness, volunteerism, intellectuals, blacks, youth, women, "the Jewish community," Wall Street, governors, mayors, "ethnics," regulatory agencies and related industry, state party chairmen, Mexican-Americans.

It is as if interest groups and professions no longer settle for lobbying Congress, or having one of their number appointed to departmental advisory boards or sub-cabinet positions. It now appears essential to "have your own man right there in the White House." Once this foothold is established, of course, interest groups can play upon the potential political backlash that could arise should their representation be discontinued.

One of the more disturbing elements in the growth of the Presidential Establishment is the development, particularly under the current administration, of a huge public-relations apparatus. More than 100 presidential aides are now engaged in various forms of press-agentry or public relations, busily selling and reselling the president. This activity is devoted to the particular occupant of the White House, but inevitably it affects the presidency itself, by projecting or reinforcing images of the presidency that are almost imperial in their suggestions of omnipotence and omniscience. Thus the public-relations apparatus not only has directly enlarged the presidential workforce but has expanded public expectations about the presidency at the same time.

Last, but by no means least, Congress, which has grown increasingly critical of the burgeoning power of the presidency, must take some blame itself for the expansion of the White House. Divided within itself and illequipped, or simply disinclined to make some of the nation's toughest political decisions in recent decades, Congress has abdicated more and more authority to the presidency. The fact that the recent massive bombing of North Vietnam was ordered by the president without even a pretense of consultation with Congress buried what little was left of the semblance of that body's war-making power. Another recent instance of Congress's tendency to surrender authority to the presidency, an extraordinary instance, was the passage by the House (though not the Senate) of a grant to the president that would give him the right to determine which programs are to be cut whenever the budget goes beyond a $250 billion ceiling limit—a bill which, in effect, would hand over to the president some of Congress's long-cherished "power of the purse."

What can be done to bring the Presidential Establishment back down to size? What can be done to bring it to a size that both lightens the heavy accumulation of functions that it has absorbed and allows the Presidential Establishment to perform its most important functions more effectively and wisely?

First, Congress should curb its own impulse to establish new presidential agencies and to ask for yet additional reports and studies from the president. In the past Congress has been a too willing partner in the enlargement of the presidency. If Congress genuinely wants a leaner presidency, it should ask more of itself. For instance, it could well make better use of its own General Accounting Office and Congressional Research Service for chores that are now often assigned to the president.

Congress should also establish in each of its houses special committees on Executive Office operations. Most congressional committees are organized to deal with areas such as labor, agriculture, armed services, or education, paralleling the organization of the cabinet. What we need now are committees designed explicitly to oversee the White House. No longer can the task of overseeing presidential operations be dispersed among dozens of committees and subcommittees, each of which can look at only small segments of the Presidential Establishment.

Some will complain that adding yet another committee to the already overburdened congressional system is just like adding another council to the overstuffed Presidential Establishment. But the central importance of what the presidency does (and does not do) must rank among the most critical tasks of the contemporary Congress. As things are organized now, the presidency escapes with grievously inadequate scrutiny. Equally important, Congress needs these committees to help protect itself from its own tendency to relinquish to the presidency its diminishing resources and prerogatives. Since Truman, presidents have had staffs to oversee Congress; it is time Congress reciprocated.

Similar efforts to let the salutary light of public attention shine more brightly on the presidency should be inaugurated by the serious journals and newspapers of the nation. For too long, publishers and editors have believed that covering the presidency means assigning a reporter to the White House press corps. Unfortunately, however, those who follow the president around on his travels are rarely in a position to do investigative reporting on what is going on inside the Presidential Establishment. Covering the Executive Office of the President requires more than a president watcher; it needs a specialist who understands the arcane language and highly complex practices that have grown up in the Presidential Establishment.

Finally, it is time to reverse the downgrading of the cabinet. President Nixon ostensibly moved in this direction with his designation several days ago of three cabinet heads—HEW's Caspar W. Weinberger, Agriculture's Earl L. Butz, and HUD's James T. Lynn—as, in effect, super-secretaries of "human resources," "natural resources," and "community development" respectively. The move was expressly made in the name of cabinet consolidation, plans for which Mr. Nixon put forward in 1971 but which Congress has so far spurned.

The three men will hold onto their cabinet posts, but they have been given White House offices as well—as presidential counselors—and so it may be that the most direct effect of the appointments is a further expansion of the Presidential Establishment, rather than a counter-bolstering of the cabinet. But if the move does, in fact, lead to cabinet consolidation under broader divisions, it will be a step in the right direction.

Reducing the present number of departments would strengthen the hand of cabinet members vis-à-vis special interests, and might enable them to serve as advisers, as well as advocates, to the president. Cabinet consolidation would also have another very desirable effect: it would be a move toward reducing the accumulation of power within the Presidential Establishment. For much of the power of budget directors and other senior White House aides comes from their roles as penultimate referees of interdepartmental jurisdictional disputes. Under consolidated departments, a small number of strengthened cabinet officers with closer ties to the president would resolve these conflicts instead. With fewer but broader cabinet departments, there would be less need for many of the interest-group brokers and special councils that now constitute so much of the excessive baggage in the overburdened presidency.

Meantime, the presidency remains sorely overburdened—with both functions and functionaries—and needs very much to be cut back in both. Certainly, the number of presidential workers can and should be reduced. Harry Truman put it best, perhaps, when he said with characteristic succinctness: "I do not like this present trend toward a huge White House staff . . . . Mostly these aides get in each other's way." But while the number of functionaries is the most tangible and dramatic measure of the White House's expansion, its increasing absorption of governmental functions is more profoundly disturbing. The current White House occupant may regard cutting down (or transferring) a number of his staff members as a way of mollifying critics who charge that the American presidency has grown too big and bloated, but it is yet another thing to reduce the president's authority or his accumulated prerogatives. As the nation's number-one critic of the swelling of government, President Nixon will, it is hoped, move—or will continue to move if he has truly already started—to substantially deflate this swelling in one of the areas where it most needs to be deflated—at home, in the White House.

VI

The Public Policy Presidency

Introduction. The public policy presidency is the presidency aimed at achieving a productive output from Congress and the executive bureaucracy in response to domestic and foreign pressures as well as the president's own felt needs about what policies are appropriate for the Republic.

Because the American national political system is so highly decentralized, the presidency is usually perceived as the major initiator and formulator of key policy proposals for our national and international political life. This chapter examines several policy areas in which a president operates and may become immersed. It also evaluates the president's capacity to adequately consummate the public policy function.

In the first selection, "The Two Presidencies," political scientist Aaron Wildavsky argues that the politics of foreign policy are different in degree and kind from the politics of domestic affairs. This is so because the potential for presidential direction is usually greater in the former than the latter. Basically, the reasons are a variety of constitutional, statutory, legal, and behavioral considerations, which make a considerable foreign policy impact possible while the same factors regularly act as constraints to effective domestic policymaking. Moreover, these same factors often result in presidential neglect of many domestic policy questions, whereas the presidency to negotiate with foreign leaders without the constant interference of Congress and significant other political actors, is a happy allurement to the presidency becoming preoccupied with foreign affairs. Some political scientists, notable Donald A. Peppers, believe that the two presidencies are becoming more equal, but one of the paradoxes of the presidency is its continuing weakness in domestic affairs.[1]

Political scientist Morton Halperin looks into the question of the president's relations with the military. Can the President make national security policy? Or is the president simply *primus inter pares* among a large number of powerful military chieftains, including such institutions as the National Security Council and the Pentagon, which share military policymaking with him? Halperin explores these issues in the next essay, "The President and the Military."

Whereas it is clear that the president must do some bargaining for the policies he desires to bring about in the military arena, it is clearer still that bargaining and compromise are the *sine qua non* for domestic policy success. Political scientist Norman Thomas explores some of the problems of policy formulation and adoption in the area of educational policy in his essay, "Policy Formulation for Education: The Johnson Administration."

To be sure, it was in the educational policy arena that Lyndon Johnson enjoyed remarkable legislative success with important consequences for the nation's colleges and schools. Thus, the view that presidents are necessarily weak in domestic policymaking does not always hold up, especially with respect to this one administration and this one domestic policy area.

Since 1946, at least, Congress has gone on record as making the president the leader in national economic policymaking. This was true, to some extent, as early as 1921 when Congress passed the Budgeting and Accounting Act and placed a Bureau of the Budget in the Department of the Treasury for the purpose of preparing an annual executive budget for submission to Congress. Moreover, vast economic controls given to the president during World War II opened up new vistas with respect to presidential power over the budget. The Employment Act of 1946, as well as subsequent amendments and acts, now makes a number of economic policy weapons available to the presidency and thus permits him to pursue a variety of economic policies to deal with the economy, as political scientist William Lammers illustrates in his essay, "The President and Economic Power."

How deeply into the reaches of the bureaucracy can and may a president influence public policy? High policy, the policy with which presidents deal, usually percolates up to the White House, because that is where such policy gets resolved if it can be resolved. Low policy, that policymaking process that is of considerable distance from the White House, is so located because, usually, lower level bureaucrats make the decisions. But what happens when the president decides that a lower level policy question is of some concern to him? Political scientist Robert Sullivan, in his essay, "The Role of the Presidency in Shaping Lower Level Policymaking Processes," spells out the ways and means by which a president may intervene in lower level policy processes and the costs and benefits associated with each approach.

NOTE

1. For the view that the differences between the two presidencies are beginning to equal out, see Donald A. Peppers, "The Two Presidencies: Eight Years Later" in *Perspective on the Presidency,* ed. Aaron Wildavsky (Boston: Little, Brown and Co., 1975), pp. 462-471.

21. The Two Presidencies*

AARON WILDAVSKY

The United States has one president, but it has two presidencies; one presidency is for domestic affairs, and the other is concerned with defense and foreign policy. Since World War II, presidents have had much greater success in controlling the nation's defense and foreign policies than in dominating its domestic policies. Even Lyndon Johnson has seen his early record of victories in domestic legislation diminish as his concern with foreign affairs grows.

What powers does the president have to control defense and foreign policies and so completely overwhelm those who might wish to thwart him?

The president's normal problem with domestic policy is to get congressional support for the programs he prefers. In foreign affairs, in contrast, he can almost always get support for policies that he believes will protect the nation—but his problem is to find a viable policy.

Whoever they are, whether they begin by caring about foreign policy like Eisenhower and Kennedy or about domestic policies like Truman and Johnson, presidents soon discover they have more policy preferences in domestic matters than in foreign policy. The Republican and Democratic parties possess a traditional roster of policies, which can easily be adopted by a new president—for example, he can be either for or against Medicare and aid to education. Since existing domestic policy usually changes in only small steps, presidents find it relatively simple to make minor adjustments. However, although any president knows he supports foreign aid and NATO, the world outside changes much more rapidly than the nation inside—presidents and their parties have no prior policies on Argentina and the Congo. The world has become a highly intractable place with a whirl of forces we cannot or do not know how to alter.

THE RECORD OF PRESIDENTIAL CONTROL

It takes great crises, such as Roosevelt's hundred days in the midst of the Depression, or the extraordinary majorities that Barry Goldwater's candidacy willed to Lyndon Johnson, for presidents to succeed in controlling domestic policy. From the end of the 1930s to the present (what may roughly be called the modern era), presidents have often been frustrated in their domestic programs. From 1938, when conservatives regrouped their forces, to the time of his death, Franklin Roosevelt did not get a single piece of significant domestic legislation passed. Truman lost out on most of his intense domestic preferences, except perhaps for housing. Since Eisenhower did not ask for much domestic legislation, he did not meet consistent defeat, yet he failed in his general policy of curtailing governmental commitments. Kennedy, of course, faced great difficulties with domestic legislation.

In the realm of foreign policy there has not been a single major issue on

*Source: Published by permission of Transaction, Inc., from *Trans-action*, vol. 4, no. 2. Copyright © December 1966 by Transaction, Inc.

which presidents, when they were serious and determined, have failed. The list of their victories is impressive: entry into the United Nations, the Marshall Plan, NATO, the Truman Doctrine, the decisions to stay out of Indochina in 1954 and to intervene in Vietnam in the 1960s, aid to Poland and Yugoslavia, the test-ban treaty, and many more. Serious setbacks to the president in controlling foreign policy are extraordinary and unusual.

Table 1, compiled from the Congressional Quarterly Service tabulation of presidential initiative and congressional response from 1948 through 1964, shows that presidents have significantly better records in foreign and defense matters than in domestic policies. When refugees and immigration—which Congress considers primarily a domestic concern—are removed from the general foreign policy area, it is clear that presidents prevail about 70 percent of the time in defense and foreign policy, compared with 40 percent in the domestic sphere.

WORLD EVENTS AND PRESIDENTIAL RESOURCES

Power in politics is control over governmental decisions. How does the president manage his control of foreign and defense policy? The answer does not reside in the greater constitutional power in foreign affairs that presidents have possessed since the founding of the Republic. The answer lies in the changes that have taken place since 1945.

The number of nations with which the United States has diplomatic relations has increased from 53 in 1939 to 113 in 1966. But sheer numbers do not tell enough; the world has also become a much more dangerous place. However remote it may seem at times, our government must always be aware of the possibility of nuclear war.

Yet the mere existence of great powers with effective thermonuclear weapons would not, in and of itself, vastly increase our rate of interaction with most other nations. We see events in Assam or

Table 1
CONGRESSIONAL ACTION ON PRESIDENTIAL PROPOSALS FROM 1948-1964

Policy Area	Congressional Action % Pass	% Fail	Number of Proposals
Domestic policy (natural resources, labor, agriculture, taxes, etc.)	40.2	59.8	2,499
Defense policy (defense, disarmament, manpower, misc.)	73.3	26.7	90
Foreign policy	58.5	41.5	655
Immigration, refugees	13.2	86.0	129
Treaties, general foreign relations, State Department, foreign aid	70.8	29.2	445

Source: Congressional Quarterly Service, Congress and the Nation, 1945-1964 (Washington, 1965).

Burundi as important because they are also part of a larger worldwide contest, called the cold war, in which great powers are rivals for the control of support of other nations. Moreover, the reaction against the blatant isolationism of the 1930s has led to a concern with foreign policy that is worldwide in scope. We are interested in what happens everywhere because we see these events as connected with larger interests involving, at the worst, the possibility of ultimate destruction.

Given the overriding fact that the world is dangerous and that small causes are perceived to have potentially great effects in an unstable world, it follows that presidents must be interested in relatively "small" matters. So they give Azerbaijan or Lebanon or Vietnam huge amounts of their time. Arthur Schlesinger, Jr. wrote of Kennedy that "in the first two months of his administration he probably spent more time on Laos than on anything else." Few failures in domestic policy, presidents soon realize, could have as disastrous consequences as any one of dozens of mistakes in the international arena.

The result is that foreign policy concerns tend to drive out domestic policy. Except for occasional questions of domestic prosperity and for civil rights, foreign affairs have consistently higher priority for presidents. Once, when trying to talk to President Kennedy about natural resources, Secretary of the Interior Stewart Udall remarked, "He's imprisoned by Berlin."

The importance of foreign affairs to presidents is intensified by the increasing speed of events in the international arena. The event and its consequences follow closely on top of one another. The blunder at the Bay of Pigs is swifly followed by the near catastrophe of the Cuban missile crisis. Presidents can no longer count on passing along their most difficult problems to their successors. They must expect to face the consequences of their actions—or failure to act—while still in office.

Domestic policy-making is usually based on experimental adjustments to an existing situation. Only a few decisions, such as those involving large dams, irretrievably commit future generations. Decisions in foreign affairs, however, are often perceived to be irreversible. This is expressed, for example, in the fear of escalation or the various "spiral" or "domino" theories of international conflict.

If decisions are perceived to be both important and irreversible, there is every reason for presidents to devote a great deal of resources to them. Presidents have to be oriented toward the future in the use of their resources. They serve a fixed term in office, and they cannot automatically count on support from the populace, Congress, or the administrative apparatus. They have to be careful, therefore, to husband their resources for pressing future needs. But because the consequences of events in foreign affairs are potentially more grave, faster to manifest themselves, and less easily reversible than in domestic affairs, presidents are more willing to use up their resources.

THE POWER TO ACT

Their formal powers to commit resources in foreign affairs and defense are vast. Particularly important is their power as commander-in-chief to move troops. Faced with situations like the invasion of South Korea or the emplacement of missiles in Cuba, fast action is required. Presidents possess both the formal power to act and the knowledge that elites and the general public expect them to act. Once they have committed American forces, it is difficult for Congress or anyone else to alter the course of events. The Dominican venture is a recent case in point.

Presidential discretion in foreign affairs also makes it difficult (though not impossible) for Congress to restrict their actions. Presidents can use executive agreements instead of treaties, enter into tacit agreements instead of written ones, and otherwise help create de facto situations not easily reversed. Presidents also have far greater ability than anyone else to obtain information on developments abroad through the Departments of State and Defense. The need for secrecy in some aspects of foreign and defense policy further restricts the ability of others to compete with presidents. These things are all well known. What is not so generally appreciated is the growing presidential ability to use information to achieve goals.

In the past presidents were amateurs in military strategy. They could not even get much useful advice outside of the military. As late as the 1930s the number of people outside the military establishment who were professionally engaged in the study of defense policy could be numbered on the fingers. Today there are hundreds of such men. The rise of the defense intellectuals has given the president of the United States enhanced ability to control defense policy. He is no longer dependent on the military for advice. He can choose among defense intellectuals from the research corporations and the academics for alternative sources of advice. He can install these men in his own office. He can play them off against each other or use them to extend spheres of coordination.

Even with these advisers, however, presidents and secretaries of defense might still be too bewildered by the complexity of nuclear situations to take action—unless they had an understanding of the doctrine and concepts of deterrence. But knowledge of doctrine about deterrence has been widely diffused; it can be picked up by any intelligent person who will read books or listen to enough hours of conversation. Whether or not the doctrine is good is a separate question; the point is that civilians can feel they understand what is going on in defense policy. Perhaps the most extraordinary feature of presidential action during the Cuban missile

crisis was the degree to which the commander-in-chief of the armed forces insisted on controlling even the smallest moves. From the positioning of ships to the methods of boarding, to the precise words and actions to be taken by individual soldiers and sailors, the president and his civilian advisers were in control.

Although presidents have rivals for power in foreign affairs, the rivals do not usually succeed. Presidents prevail not only because they may have superior resources but because their potential opponents are weak, divided, or believe that they should not control foreign policy. Let us consider the potential rivals—the general citizenry, special interest groups, the Congress, the military, the so-called military-industrial complex, and the State Department.

COMPETITORS FOR CONTROL OF POLICY

THE PUBLIC

The general public is much more dependent on presidents in foreign affairs than in domestic matters. While many people know about the impact of social security and Medicare, few know about politics in Malawi. So it is not surprising that people expect the president to act in foreign affairs and reward him with their confidence. Gallup Polls consistently show that presidential popularity rises after he takes action in a crisis—whether the action is disastrous as in the Bay of Pigs or successful as in the Cuban missile crisis. Decisive action, such as the bombing of oil fields near Haiphong, resulted in a sharp (though temporary) increase in Johnson's popularity.

The Vietnam situation illustrates another problem of public opinion in foreign affairs: it is extremely difficult to get operational policy directions from the general public. It took a long time before any sizable public interest in the subject developed. Nothing short of the large scale involvement of American troops under fire probably could have brought about the current high level of concern. Yet this relatively well developed popular opinion is difficult to interpret. While a majority appear to support President Johnson's policy, it appears that they could easily be persuaded to withdraw from Vietnam if the administration changed its line. Although a sizable majority would support various initiatives to end the war, they would seemingly be appalled if this action led to Communist encroachments elsewhere in Southeast Asia. (See "The President, the Polls, and Vietnam" by Seymour Martin Lipset, *Trans-action,* Sept/Oct 1966.)

Although presidents lead opinion in foreign affairs, they know they will be held accountable for the consequences of their actions. President Johnson has maintained a large commitment in Vietnam. His popularity shoots up now and again in the midst of some imposing action. But the fact that a body of citizens do not like the war comes back to damage his overall popularity. We will support your initiatives, the people seem to say, but we will reserve the right to punish you (or your party) if we do not like the results.

SPECIAL INTEREST GROUPS

Opinions are easier to gauge in domestic affairs because, for one thing, there is a stable structure of interest groups that covers virtually all matters of concern. The farm, labor, business, conservation, veteran, civil rights, and other interest groups provide cues when a proposed policy affects them. Thus people who identify with these groups may adopt their views. But in foreign policy matters the interest group structure is weak, unstable, and thin rather than dense. In many matters affecting Africa and Asia, for example, it is hard to think of well-known interest groups. While ephemeral groups arise from time to time to support or protest particular policies, they usually disappear when the immediate problem is resolved. In con-

trast, longer-lasting elite groups like the Foreign Policy Association and Council on Foreign Relations are composed of people of diverse views; refusal to take strong positions on controversial matters is a condition of their continued viability.

The strongest interest groups are probably the ethnic associations whose members have strong ties with a homeland, as in Poland or Cuba, so they are rarely activated simultaneously on any specific issue. They are most effective when most narrowly and intensely focused—as in the fierce pressure from Jews to recognize the state of Israel. But their relatively small numbers limits their significance to presidents in the vastly more important general foreign policy picture—as continued aid to the Arab countries shows. Moreover, some ethnic groups may conflict on significant issues such as American acceptance of the Oder-Neisse line separating Poland from what is now East Germany.

THE CONGRESS

Congressmen also exercise power in foreign affairs. Yet they are ordinarily not serious competitors with the president because they follow a self-denying ordinance. They do not think it is their job to determine the nation's defense policies. Lewis A. Dexter's extensive interviews with members of the Senate Armed Services Committee, who might be expected to want a voice in defense policy, reveal that they do not desire for men like themselves to run the nation's defense establishment. Aside from a few specific conflicts among the armed services which allow both the possibility and desirability of direct intervention, the Armed Services Committee constitutes a sort of real estate committee dealing with the regional economic consequences of the location of military facilities.

The congressional appropriations power is potentially a significant resource, but circumstances since the end of World War II have tended to reduce its effectiveness. The appropriations committees and Congress itself might make their will felt by refusing to allot funds unless basic policies were altered. But this has not happened. While Congress makes its traditional small cuts in the military budget, presidents have mostly found themselves warding off congressional attempts to increase specific items still further.

Most of the time, the administration's refusal to spend has not been seriously challenged. However, there have been occasions when individual legislators or committees have been influential. Senator Henry Jackson in his campaign (with the aid of colleagues on the Joint Committee on Atomic Energy) was able to gain acceptance for the Polaris weapons system and Senator Arthur H. Vandenberg played a part in determining the shape of the Marshall Plan and so on. The few congressmen who are expert in defense policy act, as Samuel P. Huntington says, largely as lobbyists with the executive branch. It is apparently more fruitful for these congressional experts to use their resources in order to get a hearing from the executive than to work on other congressmen.

When an issue involves the actual use or threat of violence, it takes a great deal to convince congressmen not to follow the president's lead. James Robinson's tabulation of foreign and defense policy issues from the late 1930s to 1961 (Table 2) shows dominant influence by Congress in only one case out of seven—the 1954 decision not to intervene with armed force in Indochina. In that instance President Eisenhower deliberately sounded out congressional opinion and, finding it negative, decided not to intervene—against the advice of Admiral Radford, chairman of the Joint Chiefs of Staff. This attempt to abandon responsibility did not succeed, as the years of American involvement demonstrate.

THE MILITARY

The outstanding feature of the military's participation in making defense policy is their amazing weakness. Whether the policy decisions involve the size of the armed forces, the choice of weapons systems, the total defense budget, or its division into components, the military have not prevailed. Let us take budgetary decisions as representative of the key choices to be made in defense policy. Since the end of World War II the military has not been able to achieve significant (billion dollar) increases in appropriations by their own efforts. Under Truman and Eisenhower defense budgets were determined by what Huntington calls the remainder method: the two presidents estimated revenues, decided what they could spend on domestic matters, and the remainder was assigned to defense. The usual controversy was between some military and congressional groups supporting much larger expenditures while the president and his executive allies refused. A typical case, involving the desire of the Air Force to increase the number of groups of planes is described by Huntington in *The Common Defense:*

> The FY [fiscal year] 1949 budget provided 48 groups. After the Czech coup, the Administration yielded and backed an Air Force of 55 groups in its spring rearmament program. Congress added additional funds to aid Air Force expansion to 70 groups. The Administration refused to utilize them, however, and in the gathering economy wave of the summer and fall of 1948, the Air Force goal was cut back again to 48 groups. In 1949 the House of Representatives picked up the challenge and appropriated funds for 58 groups. The President impounded the money. In June, 1950, the Air Force had 48 groups.

The great increases in the defense budget were due far more to Stalin and modern technology than to the military. The Korean War resulted in an increase from 12 to 44 billions and much of the rest followed Sputnik and the huge costs of missile programs. Thus modern technology and international conflict put an end to the one major effort to

Table 2
CONGRESSIONAL INVOLVEMENT IN FOREIGN AND DEFENSE POLICY DECISIONS

Issue	Congressional Involvement (High, Low, None)	Initiator (Congress or Executive)	Predominant Influence (Congress or Executive)	Legislation or Resolution (Yes or No)	Violence at Stake (Yes or No)	Decision Time (Long or Short)
Neutrality Legislation, the 1930s	High	Exec	Cong	Yes	No	Long
Lend-Lease, 1941	High	Exec	Exec	Yes	Yes	Long
Aid to Russia, 1941	Low	Exec	Exec	No	No	Long
Repeal of Chinese Exclusion, 1943	High	Cong	Cong	Yes	No	Long
Fulbright Resolution, 1943	High	Cong	Cong	Yes	No	Long
Building the Atomic Bomb, 1944	Low	Exec	Exec	Yes	Yes	Long
Foreign Services Act of 1946	High	Exec	Exec	Yes	No	Long
Truman Doctrine, 1947	High	Exec	Exec	Yes	No	Long
The Marshall Plan, 1947-48	High	Exec	Exec	Yes	No	Long
Berlin Airlift, 1948	None	Exec	Exec	No	Yes	Long
Vandenberg Resolution, 1948	High	Exec	Cong	Yes	No	Long
North Atlantic Treaty, 1947-49	High	Exec	Exec	Yes	No	Long
Korean Decision, 1950	None	Exec	Exec	No	Yes	Short
Japanese Peace Treaty, 1952	High	Exec	Exec	Yes	No	Long
Bohlen Nomination, 1953	High	Exec	Exec	Yes	No	Long
Indo-China, 1954	High	Exec	Cong	No	Yes	Short
Formosan Resolution, 1955	High	Exec	Exec	Yes	Yes	Long
International Finance Corporation, 1956	Low	Exec	Exec	Yes	No	Long
Foreign Aid, 1957	High	Exec	Exec	Yes	No	Long
Reciprocal Trade Agreements, 1958	High	Exec	Exec	Yes	No	Long
Monroney Resolution, 1958	High	Cong	Cong	Yes	No	Long
Cuban Decision, 1961	Low	Exec	Exec	No	Yes	Long

Source: James A. Robinson, *Congress and Foreign Policy Making* (Homewood, Illinois, 1962).

subordinate foreign affairs to domestic policies through the budget.

It could be argued that the president merely ratifies the decisions made by the military and their allies. If the mili- tary and/or Congress were united and insistent on defense policy, it would cer- tainly be difficult for presidents to resist these forces. But it is precisely the dis- unity of the military that has characterized the entire postwar period. Indeed, the military have not been united on any major matter of defense policy. The apparant unity of the Joint Chiefs of Staff turns out to be illusory. The vast majority of their recommendations appear to be unanimous and are accepted by the secretary of defense and the president. But this facade of unity can only be achieved by methods that vitiate the impact of the recommendations. Genuine disagreements are hidden by vague language that commits no one to anything. Mutually contradictory plans are strung together so everyone appears to get something, but nothing is decided. Since it is impossible to agree on really important matters, all sorts of trivia are brought in to make a record of agreement. While it may be true, as Admiral Denfield, a former chief of naval operations, said, that "On nine-tenths of the matters that come before them the Joint Chiefs of Staff reach agreement themselves," the vastly more important truth is that "normally the *only* disputes are on strategic concepts, the size and composition of forces, and budget matters."

MILITARY-INDUSTRIAL

But what about the fabled military-industrial complex? If the military alone is divided and weak, perhaps the giant industrial firms that are so dependent on defense contracts play a large part in making policy.

First, there is an important distinction between the questions *Who will get a given contract?* and *What will our defense policy be?* It is apparent that different answers may be given to these quite different questions. There are literally tens of thousands of defense contractors. They may compete vigorously for business. In the course of this competition, they may wine and dine military officers, use retired generals, seek intervention by their congressmen, place ads in trade journals, and even contribute to political campaigns. The famous TFX controversy—Should General Dynamics or Boeing get the expensive contract?—is a larger than life example of the pressures brought to bear in search of lucrative contracts.

But neither the TFX case nor the usual vigorous competition for contracts is involved with the making of substantive defense policy. Vital questions like the size of the defense budget, the choice of strategic programs, massive retaliation vs. a counter-city strategy, and the like were far beyond the policy aims of any company. Industrial firms, then, do not control such decisions, nor is there much evidence that they actually try. No doubt a precipitous and drastic rush to disarmament would meet with opposition from industrial firms among other interests. However, there has never been a time when any significant element in the government considered a disarmament policy to be feasible.

It may appear that industrial firms had no special reason to concern themselves with the government's stance on defense because they agree with the national consensus on resisting communism, maintaining a large defense establishment, and rejecting isolationism. However, this hypothesis about the climate of opinion explains everything and nothing. For every policy that is adopted or rejected can be explained away on the grounds that the cold war climate of opinion dictated what happened. Did the United States fail to intervene with armed force in Vietnam in 1954? That must be because the climate of opinion was against it. Did the United States send troops to Vietnam in the 1960s? That must be because the cold war climate demanded it. If the United States builds more missiles, negotiates a test-ban treaty, intervenes in the Dominican Republic, fails to intervene in a dozen other situations, all these actions fit the hypothesis by definition. The argument is reminiscent of those who defined the Soviet Union as permanently hostile and therefore interpreted increases of Soviet troops as menacing and decreases of troop strength as equally sinister.

If the growth of the military establishment is not directly equated with increasing military control of defense policy, the extraordinary weakness of the professional soldier still requires explanation. Huntington has written about how major military leaders were seduced in the Truman and Eisenhower years into believing that they should bow to the judgment of civilians that the economy could not stand much larger military expenditures. Once the size of the military pie was accepted as a fixed constraint, the military services were compelled to put their major energies into quarreling with one another over who should get the larger share. Given the natural rivalries of the military and their traditional acceptance of civilian rule, the president and his advisers—who could claim responsibility for the broader picture of reconciling defense and domestic policies—had the upper hand. There are, however, additional explanations to be considered.

The dominant role of the congressional appropriations committee is to be guardian of the treasury. This is manifested in the pride of its members in cutting the president's budget. Thus it was difficult to get this crucial committee to recommend even a few hundred million increase in defense; it was practically impossible to get them to consider the several billion jump that might really have made a difference. A related budgetary matter concerned the planning, programming, and budgeting system introduced by Secretary of Defense McNamara. For if the defense budget contained major categories that crisscrossed the services, only the secretary of defense could put it together. Whatever the other debatable consequences of program budgeting, its major consequence was to grant power to the secretary and his civilian advisers.

The subordination of the military through program budgeting is just one symptom of a more general weakness of the military. In the past decade the military has suffered a lack of intellectual skills appropriate to the nuclear age. For no one has (and no one wants) direct experience with nuclear war. So the usual military talk about being the only people to have combat experience is not very impressive. Instead, the imaginative creation of possible future wars—in order to avoid them—requires people with a high capacity for abstract thought combined with the ability to manipulate symbols using quantitative methods. West Point has not produced many such men.

THE STATE DEPARTMENT

Modern presidents expect the State Department to carry out their policies. John F. Kennedy felt that State was "in some particular sense 'his' department." If a secretary of state forgets this, as was apparently the case with James Byrnes under Truman, a president may find another man. But the State Department, especially the Foreign Service, is also a highly professional organization with a life and momentum of its own. If a president does not push hard, he may find his preferences somehow dissipated in time. Arthur Schlesinger fills his book on Kennedy with laments about the bureaucratic inertia and recalcitrance of the State Department.

Yet Schlesinger's own account suggests that State could not ordinarily resist the president. At one point, he writes of "the President, himself, increasingly the day-to-day director of American foreign policy." On the next page, we learn that "Kennedy dealt personally with almost every aspect of policy around the globe. He knew more about certain areas than the senior officials at State and probably called as many issues to their attention as they did to his." The president insisted on his way in Laos. He pushed through his policy on the Congo against strong opposition with the State Department. Had Kennedy wanted to get a great deal more initiative out of the State Department, as Schlesinger insists, he could have replaced the Secretary of State, a man who did not command special support in the Democratic party or in Congress. It may be that Kennedy wanted too strongly to run his own foreign policy. Dean Rusk may have known far better than Schlesinger that the one thing Kennedy did not want was a man who might rival him in the field of foreign affairs.

Schlesinger comes closest to the truth when he writes that "the White House could always win any battle it chose over the [Foreign] Service; but the prestige and proficiency of the Service limited the number of battles any White House would find it profitable to fight." When the president knew what he wanted, he got it. When he was doubtful and perplexed, he sought good advice and frequently did not get that. But there is no evidence that the people on his staff came up with better ideas. The real problem may have been a lack of good ideas anywhere. Kennedy undoubtedly encouraged his staff to prod the State Department. But the president was sufficiently cautious not to push so hard that he got his way when he was not certain what that way should be. In this context Kennedy appears to have played his staff off against elements in the State Department.

The growth of a special White House staff to help presidents in foreign affairs expresses their need for assistance, their refusal to rely completely on the regular executive agencies, and their ability to find competent men. The deployment of this staff must remain a presidential prerogative, however, if its members are to serve presidents and not their opponents. Whenever critics do not like existing foreign and defense policies, they are likely to complain that the White House staff is screening out divergent views from the president's attention. Naturally, the critics recommend introducing many more different viewpoints. If the critics could maneuver the president into counting hands all day ("on the one hand and on the other"), they would make it impossible for him to act. Such a viewpoint is also congenial to those who believe that action rather than inaction is the greatest

present danger in foreign policy. But presidents resolutely refuse to become prisoners of their advisers by using them as other people would like. Presidents remain in control of their staff as well as of major foreign policy decisions.

HOW COMPLETE IS THE CONTROL?

Some analysts say that the success of presidents in controlling foreign policy decisions is largely illusory. It is achieved, they say, by anticipating the reactions of others, and eliminating proposals that would run into severe opposition. There is some truth in this objection. In politics, where transactions are based on a high degree of mutual interdependence, what others may do has to be taken into account. But basing presidential success in foreign and defense policy on anticipated reactions suggests a static situation which does not exist. For if presidents propose only those policies that would get support in Congress, and Congress opposes them only when it knows that it can muster overwhelming strength, there would never be any conflict. Indeed, there might never be any action.

How can "anticipated reaction" explain the conflict over policies like the Marshall Plan and the test-ban treaty in which severe opposition was overcome only by strenuous efforts? Furthermore, why doesn't "anticipated reaction" work in domestic affairs? One would have to argue that for some reason presidential perception of what would be successful is consistently confused on domestic issues and most always accurate on major foreign policy issues. But the role of "anticipated reactions" should be greater in the more familiar domestic situations, which provide a backlog of experience for forecasting, than in foreign policy with many novel situations such as the Suez crisis or the Rhodesian affair.

Are there significant historical examples which might refute the thesis of presidential control of foreign policy? Foreign aid may be a case in point. For many years, presidents have struggled to get foreign aid appropriations because of hostility from public and congressional opinion. Yet several billion dollars a year are appropriated regularly despite the evident unpopularity of the program. In the aid programs to Communist countries like Poland and Yugoslavia, the Congress attaches all sorts of restrictions to the aid, but presidents find ways of getting around them.

What about the example of recognition of Communist China? The sentiment of the country always has been against recognizing Red China or admitting it to the United Nations. But have presidents wanted to recognize Red China and been hamstrung by opposition? The answer, I suggest, is a qualified "no." By the time recognition of Red China might have become a serious issue for the Truman administration, the war in Korea effectively precluded its consideration. There is no evidence that President Eisenhower or Secretary Dulles ever thought it wise to recognize Red China or help admit her to the United Nations. The Kennedy administration viewed the matter as not of major importance and, considering the opposition, moved cautiously in suggesting change. Then came the war in Vietnam. If the advantages for foreign policy had been perceived to be much higher, then Kennedy or Johnson might have proposed changing American policy toward recognition of Red China.

One possible exception, in the case of Red China, however, does not seem sufficient to invalidate the general thesis that presidents do considerably better in getting their way in foreign and defense policy than in domestic policies.

THE WORLD INFLUENCE

The forces impelling presidents to be concerned with the widest range of foreign and defense policies also affect the ways in which they calculate their power stakes. As Kennedy used to say, "Domestic policy . . . can only defeat us; foreign policy can kill us."

It no longer makes sense for presidents to "play politics" with foreign and defense policies. In the past, presidents might have thought that they could gain by prolonged delay or by not acting at all. The problem might disappear or be passed on to their successors. Presidents must now expect to pay the high costs themselves if the world situation deteriorates. The advantages of pursuing a policy that is viable in the world, that will not blow up on presidents or their fellow citizens, far outweigh any temporary political disadvantages accrued in supporting an initially unpopular policy. Compared with domestic affairs, presidents engaged in world politics are immensely more concerned with meeting problems on their own terms. Who supports and opposes a policy, though a matter of considerable interest, does not assume the crucial importance that it does in domestic affairs. The best policy presidents can find is also the best politics.

The fact that there are numerous foreign and defense policy situations competing for a president's attention means that it is worthwhile to organize political activity in order to affect his agenda. For if a president pays more attention to certain problems he may develop different preferences; he may seek and receive different advice; his new calculations may lead him to devote greater resources to seeking a solution. Interested congressmen may exert influence not by directly determining a presidential decision, but indirectly by making it costly for a president to avoid reconsidering the basis for his action. For example, citizen groups, such as those concerned with a change in China policy, may have an impact simply by keeping their proposals on the public agenda. A president may be compelled to reconsider a problem even though he could not overtly be forced to alter the prevailing policy.

In foreign affairs we may be approaching the stage where knowledge is power. There is a tremendous receptivity to good ideas in Washington. Most anyone who can present a convincing rationale for dealing with a hard world finds a ready audience. The best way to convince presidents to follow a desired policy is to show that it might work. A man like McNamara thrives because he performs; he comes up with answers he can defend. It is, to be sure, extremely difficult to devise good policies or to predict their consequences accurately. Nor is it easy to convince others that a given policy is superior to other alternatives. But it is the way to influence with presidents. For if they are convinced that the current policy is best, the likelihood of gaining sufficient force to compel a change is quite small. The man who can build better foreign policies will find presidents beating a path to his door.

22. The President and the Military*

MORTON H. HALPERIN

All presidents are dependent on the permanent bureaucracies of government inherited from their predecessors. A president must have the information and analysis of options which the bureaucracies provide in order to anticipate problems and make educated choices. He must, in most cases, also have the cooperation of the bureaucracies to turn his decisions into governmental action. A bureaucracy can effectively defuse a presidential decision by refusing to support it with influential members of Congress or to implement it faithfully.

The president's dependence on the bureaucracy and his limited freedom to maneuver are acute in all areas. The military, however, poses a unique set of problems for him. These arise in part from the limitations upon the president when he is seeking military advice. When the National Security Council or other presidential sessions are convened to discuss high-level foreign and national security matters, the president has a great deal of influence on the selection of all those who will attend, except the chairman of the Joint Chiefs of Staff (JCS), who must be chosen from a small group of senior career military officers. Compare also the president's ability to appoint noncareer people to subcabinet and ambassadorial posts with the limitations on his range of selection for appointments to senior military positions or overseas military commands.

One dilemma for the president is finding alternative sources of military advice. The military, for example, has a virtual monopoly on providing information to the president about the readiness and capabilities of U.S. or even allied forces. Other groups and individuals can provide advice on many "military" questions, but their access to information is limited. The president may call for judgments from his secretary of defense, but the secretary's analysis must rely on the basic factual material and field evaluations provided by the military.

Judgments about the likely effectiveness of American combat operations are also the exclusive province of the mili-

*Source: Reprinted by permission from Foreign Affairs, January 1972. Copyright © 1971 by the Council on Foreign Relations, Inc.

tary. In assessing the potential effects of a diplomatic move, the president can turn not only to career Foreign Service officers, but also to businessmen, academics and intelligence specialists in other agencies. On the other hand, if he wishes to know how many American divisions would be necessary to defend Laos against a Chinese attack, the legitimacy of advice from groups other than the military is distinctly reduced. The military's influence on the information and evaluation of options which reach the president is further enhanced by the important role it plays in the preparation of national intelligence estimates.

Yet another source of leverage for the military is the prestige and influence that military leaders have enjoyed, at least in the past, with leading figures in Congress. Until quite recently, this influence limited presidential effectiveness with Congress and the general public. Even now, military influence continues to be strong with the leaders of the Armed Services Committees and appropriations subcommittees. Legislation clearly gives the military the right to inform congressional committees directly of their differences with administration policy, when asked. Senior military officers frequently exercise that right. In addition, military views on matters of major concern to the services often become known to the press. Thus, presidents have shied away from decisions that they believed the military would take to the Congress and the public, and have frequently felt obliged to negotiate with the military.

For example, both Presidents Truman and Eisenhower carried on extensive negotiations with the military to secure its support for defense reorganization programs which appeared to have little chance of getting through Congress without military acquiescence. Later presidents have shied away from defense reorganizations requiring congressional approval, at least in part because of the difficulty of gaining military concurrence, or congressional action without the concurrence. The backing of the military has also been vital to presidents in other important programs. Truman, for example, relied heavily on the military to endorse his Korean War policies, especially in his disagreement with General Douglas MacArthur over limiting the war. MacArthur, who then commanded the U.N. forces in Korea, wanted to expand the war to China and to use nuclear weapons. The Joint Chiefs were not in favor of the expansion and Omar Bradley, chairman of the Joint Chiefs and a much decorated World War II hero, strengthened Truman's position enormously when he stated publicly that MacArthur's proposal would lead to "the wrong war, in the wrong place, at the wrong time."

The political influence of the military has been substantially reduced in the last few years. The fact that the Joint Chiefs favor a particular proposal is no longer a guarantee of congressional support and may in some cases be counterproductive. For example, the Joint Chiefs were not asked by the Nixon administration to play a major role in defending the Safeguard ABM. Nevertheless, the fact that the Joint Chiefs still wield influence with certain members of Congress and some parts of the public may inhibit the president, particularly if he fears a right-wing attack or needs a two-thirds vote to get a treaty through the Senate.

The implementation of presidential decisions by the military works both for and against the chief executive. The military traditions of discipline, efficiency and a clearly delineated chain of command increases the probability that precise orders will be observed and carried out with dispatch. However, the fact that the military implements decisions according to standard procedures may cause presidential orders to be misconstrued through oversimplification. The Joint Chiefs will defer to the field commander and not monitor his compliance carefully. Moreover, presidents find it difficult to develop alternate means to secure implementation of decisions in the domain of the military. For example, the president may use special envoys in place of career Foreign Service officers to carry out delicate negotiations while he can hardly send a retired businessman to land American forces in Lebanon or to command a nuclear missile-carrying submarine.

Presidents also have great difficulty convincing the military to create new capabilities, which they may need in the future but which might tend to alter the traditional role of a particular branch. The services emphasize the forces which conform to their notion of the essence of their role and resist capabilities which involve interservice cooperation (e.g. airlift), noncombat roles (e.g. advisers), and elite forces (e.g. Green Berets). At least until recently, they have also resisted the maintenance of combat-ready nonnuclear forces.

II

This is not to suggest that the president's problems with the military are greater than, for example, those with the Department of Agriculture or other agencies with strong links to domestic constituencies and congressional committees. Nor is it to suggest that the information and advice given the president by the military has over the years been less valuable than the advice of others. The point is rather that within the foreign policy field the greatest limitations on the president's freedom of action tend to come from the military. None of our presidents has been content with his relations with the military.

In fact, presidents have used a number of devices to overcome limitations on their power, to get the information and advice they want and to find support for implementing their decisions. Presidential strategies have varied, depending on the type of issue and depending on whether they were seeking: (1) information or options, (2) political support or (3) faithful implementation.

Their techniques include the following:

(1) *Reorganizations.* The Nixon National Security Council system and the appointment of the President's Blue Ribbon Panel on Defense Reorganization (Fitzhugh Panel) suggest a return to the emphasis on reorganization which tended to dominate thinking in the early postwar period and, indeed, through 1960. Reorganization efforts within the Pentagon have aimed at securing coordinated military advice, rather than separate advice from each service. Presidents have, in general, pressed the Joint Chiefs to transcend service biases and to come up with agreed positions based on a unified perspective. Eisenhower was particularly adverse to JCS splits. But the success of these efforts has been relatively limited. Most observers conclude that JCS papers still tend to reflect particular service views, either by way of deference or compromise, rather than the unified military judgment of a "true" Joint Staff. Secretaries of defense have not looked upon the Joint Staff as part of their own staff.

The reorganization of the National Security Council system beginning in 1969 appears to have been designed to bring to bear a variety of different views on military problems. The evaluation of alternate military forces is centered in the Council's Verification Panel. This group first considered the Strategic Arms Limitation Talks (SALT) and then the prospects and problems of mutual force reductions in Europe, thereby going beyond traditional military and intelligence channels. The Defense Program Review Committee was designed to apply expertise to a review of budget decisions from the Budget Bureau and the president's economic advisers, as well as the State Department and the Arms Control and Disarmament Agency. The NSC system itself was designed to take into account the views of the State Department and other government agencies about military commitments, bases, overseas departments and military assistance. At the same time, these efforts assured the military of orderly consideration of its views, reflecting the judgment that the military is more willing to participate faithfully in the implementation of a decision where it has been overruled if it feels that military views have been fully taken into account.

(2) *Military adviser in the White House.* President Franklin Roosevelt relied heavily on Admiral William Leahy as the chief of staff to the commander in chief. Truman for a brief period continued to use Leahy and then, on a part-time basis, relied on General Eisenhower for advice on budget issues, while Eisenhower was president of Columbia University. Truman later turned to the chairman of the Joint Chiefs.

Eisenhower, his own military adviser in the White House, had only a junior military officer in the person of Colonel Andrew Goodpaster who functioned in effect as a staff secretary, collecting and summarizing for the president intelligence materials from the State Department and the CIA, as well as the military.

Kennedy, after the Bay of Pigs operation, brought General Maxwell Taylor into the White House as the military representative of the president, and Taylor advised the president on a broad range of issues involving all aspects of national security policy. When Taylor moved over to become chairman of the Joint Chiefs, a JCS liaison office was created in the White House, working primarily with the president's assistant for national security affairs.

President Johnson relied primarily on other mechanisms but did use General Taylor as a White House consultant after his return from Vietnam. Taylor functioned in relation to the Vietnam issue, providing an alternate source of advice and information to the president on options open to him in Vietnam operations and negotiations.

President Nixon recalled General Goodpaster briefly during the transition period and the very early days of his administration, but since then has not

had a senior military adviser in the White House. Henry Kissinger's deputy is an army major-general. He ensures, along with the JCS liaison office, that Kissinger and the president are aware of JCS concerns, but he does not serve as an alternate source of military advice.

(3) *A civilian adviser in the White House.* There has been a growing trend in the postwar period toward presidential reliance on White House staff assistance in both domestic and national security policy. In the national security field, civilian assistance has been used not only as a source of additional information, advice and options, but also as an aid to the president in seeing that his decisions are carried through.

Truman tended to rely on his cabinet officers and the uniformed military, but there were episodic interventions by civilians in the White House. Under Truman, Clark Clifford became heavily involved in the negotiations leading to the Defense Unification Act and the National Security Council system. Later he contributed to the creation of the Atomic Energy Commission and the continued control of atomic weapons by the commission. Averell Harriman, who became Truman's national security adviser just before the Korean War, functioned briefly during the early stages of the war as a spokesman for the president's position: his tasks included a visit to General MacArthur to explain the president's policies to him and seek his compliance.

Eisenhower had no single national security adviser in the White House. His assistants for national security council affairs were involved only in the very limited number of issues that were handled in the rather stylized machinery of the National Security Council system as then constituted. Eisenhower brought in several advisers for specific issues, including Nelson Rockefeller, but these advisers tended to interact and overlap with Secretary of State Dulles rather than with the Department of Defense. They were responsible for some new initiatives, such as Eisenhower's "open skies" proposal in 1954, but the instances are few.

The regularization and institutionalization of a civilian adviser in the White House on national security matters came with President Kennedy's appointment of McGeorge Bundy. Bundy, following the Bay of Pigs fiasco, moved to increase the independence of the White House in securing information by arranging to get a good deal of the raw material directly from the field, including State, Defense, and CIA cable traffic. Bundy also assumed primary responsibility for briefing the president. Despite the expanded role which involved them in many foreign policy matters with military implications, neither Bundy nor Walt Rostow, Johnson's adviser for national security affairs, were heavily engaged in Defense budget matters. Under President Nixon, Henry Kissinger has been as active in Defense Department matters as he is in those for which the State Department has primary responsibility. Nixon appears to rely upon Kissinger as an alternative source of information and options on the broad range of military and national security matters, and as a channel for various kinds of military advice.

(4) *Reliance on the secretary of defense.* Truman and Eisenhower tended to rely on their secretaries of defense primarily to secure the implementation of their decisions, particularly Defense budget decisions. They expected the secretaries to bear the weight of military objections to ceilings on defense spending and to force the services to develop forces within those ceilings. Even in this role the defense secretaries were of limited value to the president since they tended to become spokesmen for the military desire for increased spending.

The appointment of Robert S. McNamara brought to fruition a trend which had been developing gradually and had accelerated during the brief tenure of Secretary Thomas Gates. This called for the secretary of defense to become in ef-

fect the principal military adviser to the president, superseding the Joint Chiefs. Over time Kennedy and Johnson, at least until the Vietnam War accelerated in late 1965, tended to look to the secretary of defense for advice on commitments, bases, overseas deployments and military aid, as well as budget decisions. The secretary's job included absorbing the advice tendered by the military and combining that in his recommendations to the president. Both Kennedy and Johnson did, of course, continue to meet with the Chairman of the Joint Chiefs in formal sessions of the National Security Council and in other meetings, but by and large they received military judgments and advice through the filter of the secretary of defense. As the Vietnam War heated up, JCS chairman General Earle Wheeler was included in Johnson's regular Tuesday lunches and began to act as an independent vehicle for reporting JCS views to the president, at least on the range of issues discussed at those meetings. Defense Secretary Laird has continued the tradition of taking positions on substantive issues of military policy and operations, as well as defense budget issues, although the president seems to regard him simply as a second source of advice on military questions. The secretary and the Joint Chiefs have a co-equal role in the National Security Council and in all of its subordinate institutions.

(5) *Reliance on the secretary of state.* No president has given the secretary of state a dominant role in decisions regarding combat operations or the defense budget. Truman did call on General Marshall—when he was secretary of state—for support in keeping the Defense budget down, and Nixon has brought the secretary's staff into the Defense budget process through the Defense Program Review Committee. However, on issues concerning commitments, bases, overseas deployments and military aid, Truman tended to rely largely on Acheson's judgment, and Eisenhower depended to a large extent on Dulles. Secretary Rusk played a

major role in these issues along with Secretary McNamara.

(6) *Reliance on scientists.* Although scientists have occasionally been used to evaluate combat operations, by and large their role has been limited to issues reflected in the Defense budget. Eisenhower depended, particularly in the later years of his administration, on the chief scientist in the Pentagon (the director of defense research and engineering) and on his science advisers. Kennedy also looked to his science adviser, Jerome Weisner, for alternate advice on the Defense budget, as well as on arms-control matters, particularly relating to the nuclear testing issue. The role of the science advisers seems to have declined precipitously under Johnson and Nixon, with their energies going largely to non-Defense matters.

(7) *Reliance on the Bureau of the Budget.* The role of the Budget Bureau (now Office of Management and Budget) in Defense decisions has been very limited. Truman and Eisenhower relied upon the budget director to help set a ceiling on Defense spending, but the bureau did not get involved in deciding how that money would be spent. Under Eisenhower, Kennedy and Johnson it became a matter of tradition that the budget director would have to appeal secretarial decisions on the Defense budget to the president, the reverse of the situation in all other departments. Press reports suggested that initially Nixon had reversed this process, but he now appears to have returned to this traditional pattern. The budget director sits on the Defense Program Review Committee, but the extent of Budget Bureau influence is difficult to determine.

(8) *Ad hoc techniques.* Presidents have used a number of ad hoc or special techniques to secure information and options on military questions. One technique frequently used during the Truman and Eisenhower periods was the president-appointed commission. Nixon's Fitzhugh Panel may mark a re-

turn to the use of this technique, although it has thus far been limited to organizational rather than substantive questions.

Occasionally, presidents have sent special representatives into the field to investigate military questions. Kennedy, for example, sent an old friend and military officer to the camp preparing the Cuban guerrillas for the Bay of Pigs operations, and Richard Nixon sent British guerrilla war expert Brigadier General Thompson to Vietnam for an independent assessment.

Now and then a president has been fortunate enough to have the concurrence of the military on a particular policy, without having to bargain. That the Joint Chiefs of Staff opposed expansion of the Korean War and felt that General MacArthur had indeed been insubordinate was of critical importance to Truman in securing public acceptance of this policy. However, in most cases, the president has been forced to bargain for the public support of the Joint Chiefs. Truman had to accept the case for German rearmament in order to gain JCS approval to send American forces to Europe. Kennedy and his secretary of defense engaged in long hours of bargaining with the Joint Chiefs before they were able to devise an acceptable safeguard program of standby preparations for nuclear testing that made it possible for the Joint Chiefs to give their reluctant support to the Nuclear Test Ban Treaty. Johnson felt obliged to have the Joint Chiefs of Staff on board before he would order the cessation of the bombing of North Vietnam in 1968.

In some cases, the president has sought to use the prestige and power of his office to accomplish his objectives in the face of military opposition. This tactic has a better chance of success when the decisions involve only executive department action; when the chiefs are split; and particularly when the decisions do not require the use of armed forces in combat operations. But it can be done in other cases. For example, on the matter of civilian control of atomic weapons and the creation of a civilian-dominated Atomic Energy Commission, Truman appealed to the public and Congress over the objections of the military, and was able to win. Eisenhower in the same way (although less successfully) enlisted the support of the American business community in his effort to reorganize the Defense Department against the judgment of the military.

Presidents have had the greatest success in bypassing the military on Defense budget limitations, because military demands are essentially open-ended and always have to be overruled. However, the appeal to fiscal conservatism and alternative demands for resources have also tended to check defense expenditures.

III

Techniques used to improve the information and options reaching the president can also be applied to the implementation of decisions. For example, civilian advisers in the White House have been used to monitor compliance with presidential decisions, and other presidents have tended to rely on the secretary of defense to see that their decisions were carried out.

In addition, presidents have sometimes resorted to selecting military officers who they felt shared their views and therefore would act to implement them properly. The most dramatic case came in 1953 when Eisenhower replaced all of the Joint Chiefs of Staff and appointed Admiral Radford, a known supporter of his policy of massive nuclear retaliation, as the chairman of the Joint Chiefs and chose service chiefs who by and large were prepared to comply. After the Cuban missile crisis, Admiral George Anderson, who had not cooperated fully with the president, was not reappointed to the post of chief of naval operations. However, there are several limits to the value of such actions: General Ridgway and later General Taylor, the Army chiefs of staff

appointed by Eisenhower, resisted the reduction in the size of the Army and the administration's reliance on massive nuclear retaliation. When their views were ignored they resigned and protested publicly. In response to Admiral Anderson's reassignment as ambassador to Portugal, Congress legislated statutory terms for the members of the Joint Chiefs.

Another technique that has been used to increase compliance with presidential decisions is the creation of new organizations which reflect new desires. The most successful such effort was to create within the Navy a Special Projects Office to monitor the Polaris program and to alter promotion procedures so that command of a Polaris submarine would permit promotion to senior grades. The least successful effort was Kennedy's attempt in the early 1960s to give the military a greater flexibility in dealing with counterinsurgency operations by creating the Green Berets.

IV

The decline of the prestige of the military over the past several years has given President Nixon and his successors greater freedom to determine how advice from the military reaches them, and to accept or reject that advice. The experience of the postwar period suggests two basic changes which the president could institute now that would increase his leverage vis-à-vis the military—one involving the channel by which he receives advice from senior military officers and the other concerning the role of civilian advisers.

The experience of the last 25 years suggests that the effort to reorganize the Pentagon and then to demand "unified" military advice from the Joint Chiefs of Staff has been a failure. As noted above, most observers who have had the opportunity to view the product of the Joint Chiefs would argue that unified JCS papers reflect either a compromise among the services, a form of log-rolling in which the proposals of all services are endorsed, or deference to the service or field commander most concerned. As long as the function of the Joint Staff is to come up with a paper that will be endorsed by all of the Chiefs, there does not appear to be any way to alter the situation fundamentally, although some progress has been made in the last several years in increasing the flexibility and independence of the Joint Staff.

More radical changes must be effected if the president is to get good military advice. The key to improving the situation is to separate the chairman of the Joint Chiefs of Staff and the Joint Staff from the service chiefs. The president and the secretary of defense would in this case solicit the separate views of each of the service chiefs and of the chairman of the Joint Chiefs, and where appropriate, the views of the relevant unified and specified commanders (e.g. commanders in Europe and Asia and the head of the Strategic Air Command). These latter views might be channeled to the secretary through the chairman of the Joint Chiefs. The chairman would, in turn, be the officer in the line of command through the president and the secretary of defense to the commanders (bypassing the service chiefs) for carrying out operations in the field. ·

The basic rationale behind this change in procedure is that the service chiefs and the unified and specified commands constitute the highest level at which reliable (first-hand) information and advice are available. The Joint Staff, when it needs information, must solicit either the service staffs in Washington or the field commanders. In fact, JCS information and advice presented to the president and the secretary usually come from the services and the subordinate service commands in the field. For example, most of the positions taken by the Joint Chiefs of Staff on questions relating to Vietnam simply involved a JCS endorsement of the recommendations of General Westmorland or General Abrams, the army commanders in Vietnam, and Admiral Sharp, com-

mander in chief of the Pacific, who had particular responsibility for the bombing operations.

On questions of requirements for overseas bases, to take another example, the Joint Chiefs in most cases simply endorse the position of the service which utilizes the base. On budget issues, the chiefs tend to endorse all of the programs desired by each of the services. When forced to choose on an issue of policy the chiefs compromise among the different service positions rather than attempting to develop a position based on a unified military point of view.

Under the proposed change of procedure the president and the secretary of defense would be made aware of differing positions which might otherwise be compromised. In addition this would leave the chairman of the Joint Chiefs and the Joint Staff free from the job of developing a compromise position and therefore able to present the secretary of defense with a military judgment separate from the interests of the Services. If this process is to succeed the president and the secretary will have to choose a chairman of the Joint Chiefs with whom they can work. Then, if the system is developed properly, the chairman and the Joint Staff would come to be seen as part of the office of the secretary of defense, providing him and the president with military advice which could be weighed against the advice of the operators—the service chiefs and the unified and specified commanders. The influence of the chairman would come from his record of persuasiveness with the president and the secretary of defense. They will take his judgments seriously if his choice is shown to be based on a broader range of considerations than the advice of the service chiefs.

Such a procedure would increase the probability that imaginative and innovative proposals would reach the president. It would also make it more likely that the president would become aware of the wide diversity of military opinions on a question and not act on an erroneous assumption that there was a unified view.

One of the few instances on record in which the president did seek separate opinions from the several chiefs came in 1961 when President Kennedy was contemplating an invasion of Laos. Partly because of the Bay of Pigs episode in which the doubts of individual chiefs about the military feasibility of the landing in Cuba never reached him, Kennedy asked each chief separately for his views in writing and then met with them as a group. He discovered by this process that each one had a slightly different position on what should be done, what troops should be committed, and what the likely outcome of American intervention would be. Receiving this conflicting advice, it was harder for Kennedy to make a decision to intervene but it also meant that he did not make a decision under a mistaken impression that there was a unified military view either for or against the intervention.

The proposed procedure would also increase presidential flexibility in accepting or rejecting military advice because he would no longer be confronted with a unanimous but misleading statement of JCS views. He would be able to choose among service and command viewpoints rather than having to develop a new position which in essence overrules all of the military, in as much as JCS opinions now represent all the services.

In order to increase the president's freedom to choose and the likelihood that he will get faithful implementation and political support for his actions, a procedure should be developed which provides for military access to the president on issues of importance to the military. Access should be provided not only for the chairman of the Joint Chiefs, but also for the service chiefs and the unified commanders most concerned. When he finds it necessary to overrule the military, the president should justify his decision on broad political grounds; he should be seen doing so personally; and he should do so in writing with a clear memorandum stating his position. All of these acts would increase military willingness to go along with presidential decisions and to implement them faithfully.

The military takes seriously the president's role as commander in chief and also recognizes that he has broader responsibility concerned with both domestic and international political situations. They are much more amenable to being overruled on these grounds than to being told that their military judgment is questioned. (For this reason the military resented McNamara's reliance on civilians, particularly in the Office of Systems Analysis, for judgments on what they took to be purely military questions, *i.e.* statements of military requirements.) They also implement decisions faithfully when assured that their position has been heard by the president and it has not been lost in the filter of secretary of defense memoranda.

Securing separate advice from the service chiefs and other military commanders will require that the president, or at least his White House staff, spend more time digesting the separate positions. However, this seems a price worth paying to increase the flow of new ideas or doubts about proposed courses of action to the White House.

Military compliance with presidential decisions would also be enhanced by avoiding the practice of using the military to seek public support for presidential decisions. The value of such action has become considerably reduced in recent years, and such use of the military tends to legitimize and increase the importance of their opposition when they choose to oppose policy.

V

Implicit in the new procedures as suggested is a reduced role for the secretary of defense from that which he assumed in the 1960s. His scope would also be affected by another proposed change—that decision-making on matters concerning Defense budgets and the use of military force be moved outside of the Pentagon and into a broader arena involving officials from the White House and other agencies.

The Nixon administration has moved rather significantly, at least in form and to some extent in substance, to change the locus of decisions. The creation of the Washington Special Action Group (WSAG) brings into existence for the first time a forum in which detailed contingency planning for the actual use of military force is carried out beyond the Pentagon. WSAG is chaired by the president's assistant for national security and includes senior State Department and CIA officials as well as civilian and military representatives of the Pentagon. It provides a forum where the military, diplomatic and intelligence evaluations of likely use of American military forces can be brought together in a systematic way, something which was not done in the past. This institution needs to be strengthened, probably with the addition of some White House staff assigned specifically to this task.

A second institution of significance is the Defense Program Review Committee (DPRC), which is also chaired by the president's assistant for national security and includes representatives not only from State but also from the Arms Control and Disarmament Agency, the Council of Economic Advisers and the Office of Management and Budget. The implications of this institution are enormous. If it is functioning effectively, decisions not only on the total size of

the Defense budget but also on the major Defense programs will be made outside the Pentagon in an interagency forum where White House influence is dominant. The president would be receiving advice on Defense budget issues from several different perspectives. While the institution has been created, it does not appear yet to have either the staff or the necessary top level direction to get into a wide range of Defense issues.

For this purpose and also to make WSAG more effective, the president's assistant for national security probably needs a senior deputy who would take some of the responsibility for White House direction for budget and combat decisions, and who would be explicitly charged with bringing to bear the broader concerns of the president.

The procedures suggested here in no sense imply a downgrading of military advice. Instead they are designed to assure that the president receives the full range of the existing military opinions rather than what filters through a JCS compromise procedure or a secretary of defense responsible for presenting military views to the president. They also aim to give the president critical commentary on military proposals from civilian officials with a different and somewhat broader range of responsibilities. In the end, good decisions will depend on the wisdom and judgment of the president. What he decides, however, is greatly influenced by the information presented to him, as well as by his sense of freedom to choose regardless of strong military and other bureaucratic pressures.

23. Policy Formulation for Education: The Johnson Administration*

NORMAN C. THOMAS

This paper views the formulation of national education policy from a systems perspective. A policy system is a process whereby inputs, *i.e.*, demands and support, from organized interests, concerned individuals, and the mass public are converted into policy outputs and ultimately fed back in the form of new inputs. The conversion process, the making of national policy, is the basic activity of the policy system.

The educational policy system considered here, included individuals located in the United States Office of Education (USOE), the Department of Health, Education and Welfare (HEW), the Executive Office of the President, the legislative and appropriations subcommittees in both houses of Congress having jurisdiction over USOE programs, education interest groups, other lobby groups with an interest in education, and persons in the education profession or the general public with access to the official policymakers. I identified the members of the policy system through a procedure that used position, reputation and activity as criteria.[1] Initially, I compiled a list of potential members including all persons holding formal positions of authority, persons having a reputation among informed observers and other potential members as influential participants in the policy process, and individuals who appeared as contributors of inputs to the policy system through such vehicles as testifying before congressional committees or service on presidential task forces and other major advisory bodies. The list contained 175 persons.

The next step involved interviews with 24 individuals possessing substantial knowledge of USOE and its programs including USOE, HEW, and Bureau of the Budget officials, congressional staff members, prominent educators, lobbyists, and journalists. I asked them to examine the list and indicate those whom they regarded as most important with respect to policy formulation, adoption, and implementation. Their responses, along with information obtained from a more general background investigation, provided the basis for narrowing the list to 77 influentials. The determination of the influentials was, necessarily, a subjective judgment although the ratings of the 24 "knowledgeables" was a major factor in making it. I am confident that the panel is a fairly accurate representation of the national policymaking elite for education as it existed in 1967-68.

At the final stage of data gathering, I interviewed 71 members of the educational policy system. The interview instrument employed primarily open-ended questions regarding the respondents' participation in and perceptions of the policymaking process. Thus, the data are mostly non-quantitative and the

*Source: Norman C. Thomas, "Policy Formulation for Education: The Johnson Administration." Educational Researcher, Vol. 2, No. 5 (May 1973), pp. 4-8, 17-18. Copyright © 1973, American Educational Research Association, Washington, D.C. Reprinted by permission.

analysis is conducted in qualitative terms. The principal foci of the inquiry are the origination of ideas and their movement onto the agenda for action.

POLICY CONCEPTION

The question of where ideas come from is almost impossible to answer with precision. Attempts to trace the exact origin of significant new policy proposals may be fruitless, but it does seem that Yarmolinsky's suggestion of a "theory of simultaneous and seemingly spontaneous invention" applies to education.[2] For instance, seven people including Abraham Ribicoff, Wilbur Cohen, Francis Keppel, Senator Wayne Morse, his aide Charles Lee, Representative John Dent, and Representative Roman Pucinski are credited with or claimed credit for tying aid to elementary and secondary education to the war on poverty in a manner that facilitated circumvention of the church-state issue. A major source of new ideas in education is naturally, the academic community. Academia was the origin of such suggestions as the Educational Opportunity Bank, the voucher system and open schools. Proposals for institutional grants in higher education originated with several unknown university and college presidents and were advanced by most national associations in higher education.

There was no shortage of ideas in the education policy system during the Johnson administration. A major problem confronting the policymakers, however, was that of discriminating between feasible proposals and suggestions which, regardless of their merit, had little or no chance of adoption. As knowledgeable and expert as they were, the policy system participants still required some means of analyzing a vast amount of information and synthesizing it into an ordered agenda for action. In education, as in other national policy systems, the presidency performed this function through the preparation of the presi-

dent's legislative program and the budget. These documents, *i.e.*, presidential messages and the annual budget, and specific authorization and appropriation bills, served as the basis of congressional action. They establish a set of definite, but not inflexible, boundaries within which most serious policy deliberation occurs.

The policy formulation stage is crucial for it is where major innovations are spawned and matured. In all but the most exceptional circumstances, new policy departures and significant changes in existing policy must survive the process of agenda setting in order to receive consideration in Congress. This does not mean that modest, incremental changes are not possible without formal incorporation in the presidential policy agenda. They occur routinely through legislative and bureaucratic initiative. Nor does it deny the probability that presidentially supported proposals may be defeated or substantially modified by subsequent action elsewhere in the policy system. But it is manifest that unless and until major policy innovations, e.g., education vouchers, federally funded open schools, institutional grants to colleges and universities, unrestricted block grants to the states, full expense loans to college students with long term repayment, and similar proposals are accorded a high presidential priority, the chances of their adoption and implementation are very small.

In establishing priorities, or in setting his policy agenda, the president necessarily employs the resources of his staff, the Bureau of the Budget, and other units of the Executive Office. In this respect, it is more accurate to speak of policy formulation by the presidency, with the president as the principal individual participant in that institution. The general pattern of presidential policy formulation was developed under Presidents Roosevelt and Truman and had become a systematic routine by the early years of the Eisenhower administration.[3]

The legislative program emerged from proposals prepared by departments and agencies who based them on administrative experience and suggestions and ideas from their clientele groups. The presidency was dependent on the bureaucracy for information, ideas, and new policy proposals. While the bureaucracy had vast information resources and no end of proposals, its perspective was limited and it tended over time to offer suggestions that were remedial and incremental rather than innovative and imaginative. The limits of bureaucratic initiative are almost an article of faith in the presidency. White House staff members and Budget Bureau officials during the Johnson administration were particularly skeptical of the capacity of HEW and USOE to be effective agents of change in American education. A high ranking Bureau of the Budget official, Philip S. Hughes, summed up this presidential staff perspective:

> The routine way to develop a legislative program has been to ask the departments to generate proposals. Each agency sends its ideas through channels, which means that the ideas are limited by the imagination of the old-line agencies. They tend to be repetitive—the same proposals year after year. When the ideas of the different agencies reach the departmental level, all kinds of objections are raised, especially objections that new notions may somehow infringe on the rights of some other agency in the department. By the time a legislative proposal from a department reaches the President, it's a pretty well-compromised product.[4]

TASK FORCES

The last three presidents have sought to overcome some of the liabilities of their dependence on the bureaucracy in program development through the use of task forces of experts, knowledgeable laymen, and public officials. President Kennedy commissioned 29 and President Nixon 18 task forces to report on a wide range of policy problems prior to their inaugurations. The reports of these preinauguration task forces provided a reservoir of proposals which policymakers used during the ensuing presidential administrations. Neither president continued to use task forces systematically, although each appointed similar groups on an ad hoc basis to deal with a varity of domestic and foreign policy problems.

Shortly after taking office, President Johnson appointed a series of task forces to study specific policy areas.[5] Acting at the suggestion of advisers who were familiar with the Kennedy task forces, President Johnson sought to obtain ideas and suggestions from outside the federal government which would serve as the basis of a legislative program that was distinctively his own. The 1964 experience with task force operations was deemed so successful that it was refined and expanded in the following years. Under the direction of Special Assistant Joseph A. Califano, the White House staff assumed the primary role in setting the framework for legislative and administrative policymaking. President Johnson brought the function of policy planning more effectively under his control through the integration of the task force operation with legislative submissions and budget review and the creation of a small policy staff under one of his key assistants.[6] The impact of the departments and agencies in the development of the presidential legislative program was considerable, but it tended to come more through the participation of their policy-level personnel in White House meetings where task force reports were evaluated. Commissioner Harold Howe II acknowledged that during the Johnson administration "much policy development in education has moved from here (USOE) to the White House." Similarly, a career official in the Bureau of the Budget observed that "at the stage of developing the presidential legislative program, the task force reports play a more significant role than any documents or proposals emanating from the agencies."

The agencies proposed a substantial amount of technical legislation which corrected defects and filled gaps in existing statutes but the most important substantive contributions came from elsewhere. "The task forces presented us with meaty propositions to which we could react," recalled a former Budget Bureau official, "not the nuts and bolts stuff which we usually got from the agencies." Although the agencies made major contributions to public policy by refining and making workable the general ideas of the task forces in the course of drafting bills and implementing programs, their participation in the formulative stages was somewhat reduced during the Johnson administration.

CHARACTERISTICS AND FUNCTIONS

Task forces were of two basic types, those composed of members drawn from people outside or from inside the government. Outside task forces were primarily employed to secure new ideas for the development of policy. Initially, in 1964, President Johnson used them as ad hoc devices to produce proposals which almost immediately were incorporated in his legislative program. By 1966, task forces were a normal aspect of presidential operations and they were also used to take a long-range view of major problem areas.

As compared to outside task forces, inside interagency task forces functioned more to coordinate agency approaches, to obtain some measure of interagency agreement in areas of dispute, and to review, in broad terms, the recommendations of outside task forces. While interagency groups may have generated some new proposals, their major purpose was to provide the president with a coordinated overview of functional problems that cut across departmental and agency lines and to suggest alternative solutions. An important aspect of this coordinating function

of the inside task forces was to conduct a "detailed pricing out of all proposals."

Once the task forces had written their reports, they submitted them to the president and deposited them with the Bureau of the Budget. Then the bureau, HEW and USOE forwarded their comments directly to the White House.

Following the initial evaluation, the White House staff took the lead in winnowing down task force proposals. If it appeared that an outside task force report would be followed by an interagency task force, that decision was made by presidential assistant Califano, the budget director, the chairman of the Council of Economic Advisers, and the appropriate departmental and agency officials. Otherwise, in a series of White House meetings, the department and agency officials and their top assistants, representatives of the Bureau of the Budget's Human Resources Division, representatives of the Council of Economic Advisers, and members of Califano's staff examined the reports. After considerable discussion and bargaining, they developed a proposed legislative program which was presented to the president for final decision.

A total of 12 major task forces concerned with education operated during the Johnson administration. The reports of these task forces were made public in January, 1972. The Gardner Task Force of 1964 was responsible for Title III and contributed to Title IV of ESEA. The International Education Task Force developed the proposal for the International Education Act, which Congress passed in 1966 but refused to fund. The Ink Task Force developed the plan for the 1965 reorganization of USOE. The Interagency Task Forces of 1966 and 1967 proposed amendments to existing legislation which were embodied in presidential messages in the following years and some of them were eventually adopted. The recommendations of the Early Childhood Development Task Force of 1966-67 were the basis for the

"Follow Through" program and Parent and Child Centers in the Johnson administration and for the establishment, during the Nixon administration, of HEW's Office of Child Development. The 1967 Interagency Task Force on Child Development was involved in implementing the outside group's report and in reviewing all HEW programs for children. The Friday Task Force of 1967 contributed several recommendations that appeared in President Johnson's 1968 education message. The four remaining task forces produced substantial reports which are full of recommendations that comprised a lengthy agenda for future action.

Although I have not had the opportunity to examine the task force reports and consequently have not traced the fate of the myriad of recommendations and proposals they generated, it is apparent that the earlier task forces of 1964 and 1965 had greater impact on legislation. As the task forces proliferated and the scope of their inquiry broadened, their uniqueness declined and their proposals became increasingly commonplace. In the last two years of the Johnson administration, interagency task forces were centrally involved in policy formulation and played a more important role than outside groups.

Membership on the task forces was neither carefully balanced nor broadly representative. Because the composition of the task forces was kept secret, the administration could avoid striving for balanced representation in favor of imaginativeness. To the extent, however that quickly saleable proposals were desired, task force membership tended to be more representative.

Usually the president and his top policy advisers selected the members of outside task forces. The criteria for selection tended to vary with the mission of the task force. Many respondents emphasized the importance of independence of viewpoint; however, it was acknowledged that persons holding radical views were unlikely to be included.

A conscious effort was made to avoid formal representation of established clientele groups such as the NEA and the ACE which customarily worked closely with the HEW and USOE in developing policy. As USOE's role in policy initiation began to decline as a consequence of the task force operation, the access of the lobby groups to policy makers who set the agenda for action also began to fall.

The task forces do not appear to have used formal votes to reach decisions. The usual mode of decision was bargaining until a consensus developed. When members raised strong objections, efforts were made to satisfy them. Although the task forces were not broadly representative, their members apparently did represent institutional and professional interests to a considerable degree during deliberations.

The secrecy of the task forces was one of their most important operational characteristics. In the eyes of President Johnson and his staff, secrecy was crucial for it enabled them to ignore proposals that were politically infeasible. Recommendations could be adopted or rejected without having to expend political resources defending the choices made. The range of options was not only maximized, it was kept open longer and at very little cost. Secrecy also prevented opposition to task force proposals from developing until a much later stage in the policy process.

There seems almost unanimous agreement among persons familiar with the task forces that competent staffing was essential to the success of their operations. Most education task forces were staffed with Bureau of the Budget personnel. They tended to prod the task forces to be venturesome. Their activities included preparing or assigning the conduct of background studies, acquiring data, drafting reports, and providing liaison with the White House.

HEW and USOE played a peripheral role in the operation of the outside task forces. Since the manifest intent in using outside task forces was to bypass the bureaucracy, departmental and agency officials tended to distrust task forces and minimize their significance. As Samuel Halperin, deputy assistant secretary of HEW for legislation remarked. "The reports are kept so secret that they don't really pollinate anything." In interagency task forces, however, HEW and USOE dominated the proceedings. For example, Commissioner Howe was the key figure in the work of the 1967 inside task force in education. That group developed the administration's 1968 legislative program on the basis of recommendations of the Friday Task Force and agency submissions.

The evaluation of the reports of outside task forces was a somewhat unstructured process. After being sent to the president and deposited with the Budget Bureau's Office of Legislative Reference, the reports went to the bureau's examining divisions, other units in the presidency, and USOE for comment. The role of the agency was minor, however, compared with that of the Bureau of the Budget and the White House staff. Significantly, the same personnel from the bureau and the White House who served on task force staff and sat with them as liaison men were usually involved in evaluating the reports.

The dual role of the bureau and the White House staff meant that the reports had an Executive Office bias. One HEW official charged that "there is an incestuous relationship between the task forces on the one hand and the Budget Bureau and the White House on the other." The bureau was aware of its dual role and the problems inherent in it. According to the staff director for Gardner and Friday Task Forces, "I leaned over backward to be fair, but I did feel like I was meeting myself coming back." Or, as William Carey the assistant director in charge of the Human Resources Division, observed, "We are involved at the bureau with task forces as participants and as critics." Not sur-

prisingly the bureau's dual role was perplexing and frustrating to those outside the presidency who were affected by its actions.

IMPACT

The flexibility and adaptability of the task forces had begun to decline as their operations became increasingly systematized toward the end of the Johnson administration. They were tending to become elaborate instruments of incremental adjustment rather than catalytic agents of change. A leadership technique designed to produce policy innovation worked so well initially that overuse was rendering it counterproductive. It also appears that the substantive innovations resulting from the task forces may have been less than their advocates claimed. As a Bureau of the Budget official acknowledged, "They tended to pull together existing things instead of coming up with new ideas."

To the extent that task forces were made representative through their membership, tendencies toward innovation may have been mitigated. This appears likely since consensus was the fundamental decision-making rule and final agreement tended to represent compromise rather than creative thinking. However, the fact that task forces may not have been as inventive as their proponents claimed does not mean that essentially the same courses of action would be followed without them. The ideas which they promoted may not have been entirely new, but they were not yet embodied in the presidential policy agenda, nor, in most cases, were they supported by the bureaucracy.

Although the task force device provided a substantial advantage to an innovation-minded president, it also entailed sizeable costs in the form of resentments engendered in the bureaucracy and among powerful clientele groups. But whatever its costs and benefits, the Johnson task force operation helped the president to dominate national policy formulation in education. Its failure to survive in the Nixon administration reflects the different leadership style and policy objectives of Johnson's successor and not the insignificance of the task forces as they functioned between 1964 and 1969.

THE PRESIDENCY AND POLICY CONTROL

Policy formulation in the education policy system centered, then in the presidency. The key participants were the president, the White House staff members, and Budget Bureau officials. Acting in response to explicit presidential directives or in accordance with their interpretations of more general presidential objectives, the central decision-makers set education policy priorities within the parameters imposed by budgetary constraints and other external considerations. Also included among the central decision-makers were the commissioner of education and selected HEW officials. Their involvement, while frequent and often intensive, was regulated by the presidency. They were necessarily included as leaders and representatives of the bureaucracy, and they wielded substantial influence in consequence of their positions. Additional influence and involvement was based on their standing with members of the institutionalized presidency. Both Commissioner Howe and Secretary Gardner were held in high regard and exerted considerable influence on personal rather than positional grounds.

Of equal significance in this analysis of educational policy formulation, were the kinds of participants who were not included. Not surprisingly, in contrast to the direct participation of congressional leaders in policy formulation in 1964 and 1965, there was little involvement during the 90th Congress (1967-1969). Congressional leaders were informed of the content of the legislative program before it was made final, but they were not consulted during its development. The major legislative innovations of the 89th Congress were not repeated in the 90th, although the administration continued the search for new ideas and attempted to give the appearance of creativity in its legislative proposals by authorizing small programs which could later be expanded. There was no need for early or sustained congressional involvement in what was basically a noninnovating period. Loyal administration spokesmen on Capitol Hill could be relied on to push the ESEA, HEA, and Vocational Education extension bills through along with the eye-catching but minor new programs and, most importantly, to ward off opposition attempts to redirect the basic legislation. Congressional considerations under such conditions would be effectively incorporated during the adoption of legislation. The education establishment groups were accorded access to the formulation stage through their White House contact, Douglass Cater. Noneducation groups, including labor, civil rights, and other black organizations, were conspicuous by their absence during the formulative stage.[7]

Although priorities were determined and the policy agenda set by a group of central decision-makers operating in the presidency, there were effective limits to the scope of their action. For example, in spite of a strong preference in the presidency for imaginative programs that would change American education, some highly innovative proposals, such as the Educational Opportunity Bank (EOB), were kept off the policy agenda by strong opposition from certain higher education groups and from key members of Congress. The prospect of conflict with some major supporters of the administration's education policies prevented the EOB from receiving serious consideration. Anticipated reaction accorded strategic interests a veto without a fight. Once the Land Grant College Association attacked it publicly, the EOB was a dead letter.

Much of the decision-making regarding the policy agenda did not take place in public, however. Task force reports and, to a large extent agency submissions, were the subject of debate and negotiation inside the presidency. Direct congressional and interest group input was readily available, but generally it was obtained indirectly through brokers. The principal brokers in the education policy system were HEW's legislative liaison officials, Ralph Huitt and Samuel Halperin. Both were highly regarded by the establishment associations and both had the confidence and support of top HEW officials.

In spite of the constraints imposed through anticipated congressional and interest group reactions and indirect external influence exerted through brokers, the formulation stage of the policy process remained under the effective control of the institutionalized presidency. The effectiveness of the presidency in establishing priorities and setting the agenda for action is reflected in the hostility that several respondents expressed to the Bureau of the Budget and the White House staff. Of 33 responses to a question which asked if the major elements involved in making and implementing education policy ought to be more or less powerful, 12 called for a reduction in the power of the Budget

Bureau or the White House staff. (See Table 1.) Although these data cannot be regarded as accurate reflections of the participants' perception of the conversion process, they do indicate the presence of extensive dissatisfaction with the perceived balance of power in the system. The Bureau of the Budget was the focus of much of that dissatisfaction. Bureaucrats, legislative staff members, and lobbyists particularly tended to regard it as too powerful. Their complaints were directed toward the bureau's role in developing legislative proposals and establishing basic policy goals rather than its budgetary function. A recurring theme was the bureau's lack of expertise in education. Typical of the bureau's negative image among other policy system members were the comments of a bureaucrat:

The Budget Bureau strikes me as moving a bit too far into content questions which they aren't competent to carry through. Here and there, because of the frantic pace, many thoughtful program people are at the mercy of the Budget Bureau people who don't know what is in the black book.

A legislator:

The Budget Bureau is far too powerful. It is much too influential in setting national priorities. More so than any other element in the process. This is especially disturbing since the Budget Bureau people have no

Table 1

PERCEPTIONS OF POWER DISTRIBUTION IN POLICY SYSTEM
BY POLICY ROLE

Role	Generally Satisfied	Generally Dissat.	BOB/W. House Too Powerful	Foundations Too Powerful	Own Group Requires More Power
Bureaucrat	2	2	5	1	3
Legislator			1	1	
Leg. Staff	1		3		1
Lobbyist		3	3	3	1
Expert	2	1			
Total	5	6	12	5	5

N = 33

special competence or expertise in education. They are generalists who have no knowledge of the real needs and problems.

A legislative staff member:

The Budget Bureau is exercising too much control. It plays two roles. Before OE and HEW can come up with legislative proposals, the Budget Bureau must approve. I don't know where they get the competence to do it. . . . Secondly, when appropriation requests are being made I have less quarrel.

And, a lobbyist:

The Bureau of the Budget ought to be deemphasized. They don't know enough about education. They have a transitory staff and the directors are laymen.

Objections to the foundations and expressions of general discontent were much less explicit.

For a significant portion of the members of the education policy system, then, too much control over policy was lodged in the institutionalized presidency. The problem as they perceived it was not so much that the president, with the help of his supportive staff aides and units defined goals, established priorities, and set the agenda, but that access to that critical stage of formulation was limited and tightly controlled. As the NEA's principal lobbyist, Dr. John Lumley, remarked in discussing the Bureau of the Budget, "It is the one place in the system which is closed to us. Other than trouble getting access to the Budget Bureau, we have our day in court everywhere else." Yet, it was that very lack of open access to congressional, clientele, bureaucratic, and other interests that enabled the bureau to serve the president so effectively and which led presidents since Roosevelt to rely so heavily on its judgment. The absence of professional experts in the bureau and on the White House staff was no handicap to a president whose primary goal for federal educational programs was to promote change. Furthermore, the lack of education professionals in the presidency was partially compensated for by the inclusion of

Commissioner Howe among the central decision-makers, the ready availability of input from external interests, and the acquired expertise of Bureau of the Budget personnel. Had President Johnson not been so disposed to promote change through federal programs, the bureau's influence would probably have been considerably less. Even so, if one notes only casually the visible effects or outcomes of the education policy "innovations" of the Johnson administration it is apparent that the bureau's impact was somewhat exaggerated. The education programs of the administration contributed more to the maintenance of existing educational systems than to the promotion of fundamental changes. Programs with potential for breakthrough change, e.g., ESEA Title III, were brought under control of the establishment by the end of 1967 despite the protests of the presidency, the reports of task forces, and the arguments of intellectuals and experts in universities and foundations.

CONCLUSION

One of the hallmarks of President Johnson's Great Society was a strong commitment to education with a heavy emphasis on innovation. He wanted the federal role in education to produce qualitative improvements and he wished to be remembered as a president who accomplished a great deal for education. Even as budgetary pressures forced a reduction of the ambitious funding levels visualized in the legislation of 1964 and 1965, he maintained the aspirations which underlay his commitment to education.

By the start of the 90th Congress in January, 1967, a new equilibrium involving the presidency, USOE, its clientele groups, and the congressional subcommittee with jurisdiction over its authorizing legislations and its appropriations had been established. The dominance of the presidency in policy formulation in that equilibrium cannot

be denied, but it must be noted that the
system lacked resources to sustain additional major policy innovations, and it
needed time to absorb fully and
evaluate the effects of ESEA and the
other breakthroughs of the mid-1960s.
Therefore, too much significance should
not be attached to the Rube Goldberg-
ian process developed in the Johnson
administration to formulate policy.
Much of that machinery has since been
dismantled. The Johnson educational
policies and the programs that implement them, although still in effect, are
under attack by the Nixon administration as it moves to institute the New
Federalism, and the task force reports
peacefully accumulate dust in the LBJ
Library.

However, when and if some future
president decides that the time has arrived for a new round of innovations in
federal education policy, those reports
may have some utility and the Johnson
Administration's policy formulation
procedures may be of value as a
strategy for circumventing, if only temporarily, the federal bureaucracy and its
congressional and clientele group supporters.

NOTES

1. K. J. Gergen, "Assessing the Leverage
Points in the Process of Policy Formation," in
The Study of Policy Formation, eds. R. A.
Bauer and K. J. Gergen (New York: The Free
Press, 1968), pp. 182-203.
2. A. Yarmolinsky, "Ideas into Programs,"
The Public Interest 2 (1966): 70-79.
3. R. E. Neustadt, "The Presidency and
Legislation: The Growth of Central Clearance," American Political Science Review 48
(1954): 641-70. R. E. Neustadt, "The Presidency and Legislation: Planning the President's Program," American Political Science
Review 49 (1955): 980-1018.
4. W. E. Leuchtenberg, "The Genesis of
the Great Society," The Reporter (April 21,
1966): 36-39.
5. N. C. Thomas and H. L. Wolman, "The
Presidency and Policy Formulation: The Task
Force Device," Public Administration Review 29 (1969): 459-71.
6. T. E. Cronin, "The Presidency and
Legislation," Phi Delta Kappan 49 (1968):
295-99.
7. H. L. Wolman and N. C. Thomas,
"Black Interests, Black Groups, and Black Influence in the Federal Policy Process: The
Cases of Housing and Education," Journal of
Politics 32 (1970): 875-97.

24. The President and Economic Policy*

WILLIAM W. LAMMERS

The tumultuous economic events of
recent years have thrust presidents increasingly into an economic management responsibility. Questions of overall
growth, unemployment levels, and rates
of inflation have occupied considerable
attention of both the president and the
electorate. The increase in unemployment concerns as the ranks of the unemployed increased to over 8 million in
1975 simply intensified a growing tendency for economic concerns to assume
major importance in presidential politics.

*Source: Chapter 8 from Presidential Politics: Patterns and Prospects by William W. Lam-
mers. Copyright © 1976 by William W. Lammers. Reprinted by permission of Harper and
Row, Publishers, Inc. Selection has been retitled and originally appeared as "Economic Management."

The public has clearly come to expect economic leadership from the Oval Office. Public support for strong economic leadership has even tended on occasion to precede presidential willingness to take the most far-reaching step, the establishment of wage and price controls. Concern for economic matters seemed by 1974 to impinge on presidential abilities to do other things, as President Ford discovered as he received considerable editorial criticism of his foreign policy activities and partisan campaign activities at a time when the economy was in an increasingly disastrous condition. A president simply cannot escape public awareness of major economic indicators and their direct, personal impact experienced at the grocery checkout stand and the unemployment office. Indeed, the rapidly deteriorating economic condition of the United States by the mid-1970s raised more seriously than in many years the question of whether the electorate would be willing to follow a prospective leader on a white horse who promised to right the economy even at the cost of substantial changes in both the economic and the political organization of the nation.

Presidents do have a substantial range of policy tools for use in the economic management role. Neither general students of the presidency nor, for that matter, presidents, on at least some occasions, are quickly able to sort out the economic theories behind respective policy tools. Without seeking to resolve the policy issues directly, it is essential that we examine the political implications and ramifications of the respective policy tools. At the outset, the nature of the recently deteriorating policy context must be highlighted. Several things have happened to reemphasize reasons why the findings of economists have at points produced references to a "dismal science."

THE WORSENING ECONOMIC CONTEXT

Presidential economic management shifted in the short space of 10 years from a golden age of the "new economics" to the aggravating realities of "stagflation." In the early 1960s, the major issue was how to use policy tools for improving growth and levels of employment. President Kennedy inherited in 1961 an economy which had been performing poorly in terms of both unemployment and sluggish growth. An expansionist policy was fairly quickly settled upon in this context, with a particular emphasis on a tax cut as a means of stimulating the economy. The passage of the tax cut measure in 1964, after earlier failures during the Kennedy years, represented a major victory for those desirous of a strong economic management role for the federal government.

The wisdom of economic policies pursued in the Kennedy and Johnson years has been debated, particularly by those who felt that there was too much emphasis on tax policy.[1] What is undisputable is the performance of the economy during the 1960-1968 period. Economic growth was substantial, as it surpassed the sluggish performances of the Eisenhower period. Unemployment also declined overall between 1960 and 1968, with levels often under 4 percent. Yet the rate of inflation was also low, with increases in the consumer price index over 3 percent occurring only once prior to Nixon's inauguration; the then seemingly high figure of 4.2 percent was reached in 1967-1968.

The economic events under Nixon were a disaster.[2] The nation experienced recessions in both 1970 and 1974, with various debates over the labels which should be applied. Unemployment was also much higher, as it often hovered around the 6 percent figure. Yet simultaneously, the inflation rates produced the infamous "double digit inflation," as figures soared over the 10 percent figure by the end of Nixon's presidency. Were the human impacts not so devastating for millions of Americans, one might smile at the humor produced, such as the references to "Nixonomics" as a situation in which those indicators which should rise, fall, and those which should fall, rise. The economic disarray of the Nixon presidency reached its climax as the president went on national television to announce yet another set of proposals and make confident statements in the midst of the televised hearings of the impeachment proceedings.

It is not easy to sort out the degree of responsibility which should be given to Nixon and his economic advisers. In the eyes of many, they acted very slowly in 1970 and 1971. Somewhat more obvious is the highly expansionary thrust of monetary and fiscal policy as part of the wage and price freeze of 1971. An expansionary economic policy was then followed by a rapid and confused turning on and off of wage and price controls. Some even wondered if the real intent in the use of those controls was to show the country how ineffective controls actually were. It seems likely that Nixon and his managers will seldom receive very high ratings in economics.

Underlying pressures nonetheless were involved, pressures which proved difficult for President Ford and which seem destined to make the economic management roles more difficult in the coming years than during the 1960s. The last pressure on Nixon's economic managers was perhaps the most devastating. Arab oil prices were raised between October 1973 and January 1974, from slightly over $3 per barrel to well over $11. The resulting inflationary pressures on the American economy were substantial. At the same time, balance of payment issues intensified as industrial nations including the United States found oil payments to be a serious drain on their economic position, and Americans found themselves locked into an international monetary system which was both ill-equipped to deal with the sudden shifts and also difficult to readily transform.

Other factors were involved earlier in the Nixon presidency. The inability of the national government to adequately finance the Vietnam War in 1967 produced an unusually large debt and had a destabilizing impact on a variety of economic relationships. The political economy which Richard Nixon inherited was facing the problem of running deficits when they were not appropriate.

Declining world food resources and shrinking American surpluses also complicated economic policy making by the early 1970s. In their search for scarce food resources, the industrialized nations at points tended to promote inflation in each other's economies through increased demand in the international markets. The American situation was exacerbated by the clumsy sale of American wheat to the Russians, but the basic situation was only part of a worldwide shift.

The economic policymakers faced, finally, the grim impact of dilemmas which economic theorists have isolated. Under many conditions, it is impossible to develop policies which both combat inflation and reduce unemployment. The problem may not be figuring out how to correctly maximize all values, but rather having to make difficult forced choices.

By the mid-1970s, the nation seemed ready to explore more substantially a variety of techniques for dealing with the economy. Those tools, in their political context, can now be reviewed.

POLICY TOOLS

Presidents do not want for a variety of potential tools and techniques in their economic management role. These include fiscal policy, monetary policy, structural approaches, enforcement of competition, use of guidelines, and wage and price controls. Each of these steps has important ramifications for presidential politics.

FISCAL POLICY

Fiscal policy involves the impacts of government taxing and spending on overall forces in the economy.[3] In economic terms, there has been a widespread recognition that the budgetary deficit or surplus of the federal government has important consequences for the entire economy. A deficit can stimulate the economy by increasing demand, as both government spending and the untaxed individual and business incomes compete for goods and services. A budgetary surplus, conversely, can play an important role in reducing overall demand in the economy. The notion that the federal budget should be viewed in terms of its overall impact and not simply in terms of analogies to individual household budgets gained substantial acceptance in the 1960s. Yet that acceptance was followed shortly by conditions which made the politically more easily accepted concept less helpful economically.

Fiscal policy presents definite political problems for a president. Fiscal decision making is most attractive when the appropriate step is a tax decrease, and for increases in spending. Even this step was resisted in Congress in the early 1960s, while the tendency to view the federal budget as analogous to a household budget persisted. That view was held by a declining minority by the 1970s.

The difficulties confronting fiscal policy came as the necessary step moves counter to the political instincts and political preferences of the president and/or Congress. There clearly should have been an adjustment of the financing of the Vietnam War in 1966-1967, but there was instead a massive shift to deficit spending. The exact nature of the responsibility has been disputed, with Johnson pointing to his attempt at interesting congressional leaders in a tax increase, and others feeling that Johnson did not push hard enough due to his basic desire to minimize public awareness of the magnitude and costs of the Vietnam War.[4] The hope that both guns and butter could be pursued as policy objectives persisted, rather than acceptance of the less popular steps which wise fiscal policy dictated. Persistently, implications of fiscal policy are more readily accepted if they suggest courses of action which accord with other aspects of a person's political philosophy. Democrats in particular tend to be enthusiastic when the appropriate step is to increase federal programs; Republicans at points like to use the suggested directions of fiscal policy as a rationale for cutting their most hated federal programs. A president may be guided into economically unwise positions because of his own tendency to accept fiscal policy solutions with varying degrees of enthusiasm. He will also most certainly run into resistance in Congress from those whose policy desires make a given fiscal policy step uninviting. As a result, it may be hard to get fiscal policy steps accepted at the time they could be of maximum effectiveness.[5]

MONETARY POLICY

Changes in the available money supply also constitute an important tool in economic management. Questions involving the money supply are labeled monetary to distinguish them from the taxing and spending, or fiscal policy, issues. The basic policy concept is fairly simple. By acting to increase interest rates, policy seeks to lower demand in the economy, as fewer individuals and firms will borrow for new purchases and capital improvements. Conversely, a low interest rate is seen as likely to stimulate the economy as more demand is generated through the borrowing process.

A major debate in recent years has surrounded the extent to which monetary policy should be employed in lieu of an active fiscal policy. Generally, those aligned with the Republican party have been somewhat more apt to promote a monetary policy rather than an active fiscal policy. In the Nixon presidency, his second chairman of the Council of Economic Advisers, Herbert Stein, was a major proponent of the monetary policy approach. Stein was a former student of Milton Friedman, the University of Chicago economist, who has developed considerable prominence in emphasizing the importance of monetary rates to economic performance.

The question of how the federal government is to proceed with monetary policy is intensified by the formal separation of the Federal Reserve Board from the operations of the presidency. The "Feds" are comprised of a group of 12 individuals appointed for no less than 14-year terms. Their responsibilities in regulating the nation's banks include the critical role of influencing interest rates. Chairman Martin was often at odds with President Kennedy on the interst-rate issue. President Nixon sought to achieve a smoother relationship by the appointment of his former aide, Arthur Burns, as head of the Federal Reserve Board. Informal interaction among key policymakers is also often fairly substantial, despite formal separation. The head of the Federal Reserve Board, the secretary of the treasury, and the chairman of the Council of Economic Advisers, along with, at points, the head of the Office of Management and Budget, often meet frequently. At points, such labels as "the quadrad" are applied to this foursome by observers who sense the importance of these meetings. Informal consultation can nonetheless be rather cumbersome for a president interested in aggressively pursing monetary policy objectives.

STRUCTURAL APPROACHES

Economic management has included, especially since the Kennedy period, efforts at achieving economic objectives by directly aiding segments of the economy such as depressed regions and undertrained workers. Kennedy made a major push on both aid to depressed regions and also manpower retraining. The Area Redevelopment Administration was to aid areas such as Appalachia, which Kennedy had mentioned extensively in his campaigns,

and numerous new programs were to help workers gain the skills for better jobs.

In economic terms, structural approaches make little sense where the issue is lack of overall demand in the economy. Kennedy faced this problem, as workers were sometimes trained for jobs which did not exist and attempts at aiding depressed areas found marginal firms shuffling around the country in pursuit of one government incentive after another, rather than sustaining real economic growth. Having a textile plant leave already depressed New England to take advantage of low interest loans and low tax rates in South Carolina might make a few people in South Carolina happy for a time, but would do little to reduce overall unemployment rates.

Direct aid approaches have differing political impacts.[6] They do have the advantage of giving a president something tangible to talk about in terms of what his administration is doing. They also tend to generate specific rewards which a president can distribute with an eye toward gaining support for various legislative thrusts. (In time, however, the resentment of those who are excluded can also be substantial.) A president may also find over time, as did Kennedy and Johnson, that the lack of clearly documented accomplishment makes the structural approaches ready targets for critics of federal programs. There may well be good reasons why the costs in educating a ghetto youth at a Job Corps camp surpass those of sending a youngster to Harvard. Many indirect benefits and supports which the college student receives tend not to be measured. Yet such comparisons can be devastating politically. Such popular magazines as the *Reader's Digest* and *Human Events* can fairly easily find aspects of such programs to criticize.

Specific favors to industry are also structural steps with mixed political impacts. Campaign contributions have been one practical political consequence, as firms contribute with an eye toward possible—or at points rather immediate—benefits. Other impacts can raise problems. Thus, the Nixon effort to help sustain the economy of southern California by providing special government loans to the beleaguered Lockheed Corporation became a ready target for criticism in 1971.[7] Such loans often become, as critics of the Lockheed arrangement argued, unwarranted subsidies to firms which would be better served by major adjustments in their operations. Yet such assistance can also be a more effective means of maintaining jobs than trying to get new industries to move into depressed areas. A president worried about unemployment is often impressed with this argument. Structural approaches thus present key political liabilities as well as assets for a president.

ENFORCING COMPETITION

Enforcement of competition was a rather lightly used policy tool in the period from Kennedy through Nixon. Kennedy became impatient with the zealousness of his first key antitrust enforcer, Lee Lovenger. Johnson was more interested in approaching policy issues by stressing growth, plus programs directly aimed at the poor. The lack of commitment to antitrust policy was abundantly clear in the Nixon presidency. In such specific situations as that involving the proposed merger between ITT and Hartford Insurance, Nixon was very specific in denouncing a stern antitrust approach. Some felt that political ties accounted for this attitude, and others felt that the philosophy of the Nixon administration was primarily involved. In any event, the administration's lack of interest in enforcement was evident.

Americans have long had, in fact, a measure of ambivalence regarding antitrust approaches. Several writers have been impressed with the extent to which both the electorate and corporate leaders have tended to enjoy and at points revere big business. Thurman Arnold's *Folklore of Capitalism* describes his skepticism about the American commitment to controlling big business on the basis in part of his own experiences trying to enforce antitrust measures in the 1930s.[8] John K. Galbraith's *New Industrial State* traces both the growth of economic concentration and also the tendency for corporate leaders to prefer managed markets.[9] Theodore Lowi's *End of Liberalism* reviews what he sees as a shift away from capitalism as the dominant ideology in the 1930s.[10]

The results of American regulatory policies, or lack thereof, have been immense. Concentration in the economy has continued to grow. By 1969, the 200 largest manufacturing corporations controlled about two-thirds of all assets held by corporations engaged primarily in manufacturing. The trend was also clear. The largest 100 corporations had a greater share of all manufacturing assets than the largest 200 did in 1950.

The immensity of economic concentration could be seen in another way also. As of 1968-69, the United States government was at the top of the 10 organizations with the largest total revenues; the next 9 included *only 2 states* (California and New York). Revenues of such corporations as General Motors, American Telephone and Telegraph, Standard Oil (New Jersey), Ford Motors, Sears and Roebuck, General Electric, and IBM *all dwarfed any other state.*[11]

By 1975, the issue of competition as an economic management tool seemed apt to receive renewed interest. With a strong emphasis from the Joint Economic Committee of Congress, the question of lack of competition was reexamined as a possible cause of inflation. Concern over lack of competition came as no surprise to those who were impressed, as was Theodore Lowi, with the tendency for various functional areas of the economy to have little competition either in their markets or in the nature of their relationships to the government. The absence of competition was seen not just as a question of legally defined antitrust issues, but one involving as well a variety of governmental practices. Allowing physicians to prescribe generic labels rather than brand labels for drugs, for example, can substantially increase competition in drug pricing. The actions of the regulatory commissions and the strong position granted to some unions were skeptically reviewed in terms of their impact on economic performance.

There is tremendous pressure on a president not to confront the antitrust area more directly. The specific advantages various firms and industries enjoy through limitations on competition produce intense lobbying pressures if they are threatened. Charles Schultze, a former head of Johnson's budgeting operations, recognized these pressures as he suggested that there might be some opportunities for an assault on the issue if one combined a variety of measures into a package with several simultaneous changes.[12] By 1975, the very impact of the Watergate scandals seemed to be giving new life to the interest in antitrust enforcement, both within governmental circles and in some segments of the electorate. Such major firms as American Telephone and Telegraph, Xerox, Goodyear, and Firestone, found themselves subject to new legal challenges as part of renewed antiturst efforts.

GUIDELINES

The odd term *jawboning* crept into economic discussions in the Kennedy presidency. Both Presidents Kennedy and Johnson sought to influence economic development by exercising "moral suasion" on key segments of business and labor. In addition, consumers were at points encouraged to orient their buying habits in keeping with a need for shifts in overall demand in the economy. In 1974, the Nixon administration, despite its reluctance to use guidelines prior to launching wage and price controls, reverted to aspects of a guideline approach.

Guidelines obviously suffer from the absence of specific sanctions. One should recall, however, that it was Kennedy's sense that the steel industry had not kept its gentleman's agreement on prices in relationship to labor restraint which prompted the major flexing of political muscle in April 1962. Kennedy had been seeking to "jawbone," in the sense of putting pressure on both business and labor to avoid excessive price and wage increases. In response to the initially announced steel price increase, Kennedy took several steps. An unusually angry press conference was held, the threat of antitrust investigation emerged, and there was the assurance that any companies not following U.S. Steel's lead in the price increase would be in a highly advantageous position in relation to government contracting through the Department of Defense. For an intense week, Kennedy was showing (and successfully, as U.S. Steel rescinded the price increase) that there were indeed resources in the presidency which could back up the guideline approach.[13]

Guidelines do tend to promote a measure of discussion and, at points, bargaining without the necessity of establishing a major regulatory unit to police all transactions. A popular president, and one skilled in bargaining processes, can have some impact. Problems can nonetheless occur, as his credibility may be marred by frequent noncompliance. Furthermore, economic pressures can fairly easily destroy the measure of restraint which guideline tactics introduce.

WAGE AND PRICE CONTROLS

The most far-reaching step a president can take is to establish wage and price controls. These have been primarily a wartime phenomena in the United States. Even during the Korean War, the Truman administration embarked only very reluctantly on a partial course of wage and price controls. The frustrations with the World War II regulatory activities, which were substantial by 1945-1946, contributed to Truman's reluctance.[14] The Nixon attempt at wage and price controls between August 1971 and April 1974 (when they ended entirely), some six years after the costs of the Vietnam War had begun to mount, was from an historical perspective a most unusual step. In economic terms, there is no question but that wage and price controls constitute a policy tool with tremendous consequences. Anyone who experienced the cancellation of 1971-1972 raises can well testify to the direct impact! The central economic problem, in turn, is that controls may delay adjustments in economic activity which are needed.

Wage and price controls cause an interesting set of political responses. Controls are often greeted with initial enthusiasm. This was particularly the case in 1971, as the Nixon administration had increasingly been badgered for doing too little to combat inflation and recession. Truman was also under substantial pressure to move to meet inflationary pressures in the wake of the outbreak of the Korean War in June 1950. Over time, controls nonetheless encounter considerable resistance. Initial enthusiasm that difficult conditions will be corrected often gives way to irritations with specific decisions and frustration with the inevitable delays and confusions which the bureaucratic mechanisms create. A president may also find that the political responses to economic adjustments as controls are removed is particularly adverse. Truman in 1946 and in 1952, and Nixon in 1974, both felt the adverse responses to the longer-run impact of wage and price controls.

A president moving to establish wage and price controls is also confronted with major internal problems. New capacities for administration must be quickly developed. In both 1950-1951 and in 1971, there was intense concern with the inadequacies of the policing machinery. Previously existing units tend to be understaffed if not downright incompetent, and there is a rush to create more adequate mechanisms. As these mechanisms evolve, opportunities for creating new patterns of access for bargaining become important to both the president and key interests. Individual interest-group leaders and corporate spokesmen vie for access. This may create some new opportunities for a president. Over time, it can also generate substantial conflict, as manifested for example in the hostility of organized labor toward Nixon's operation of the Cost of Living Council.

President Nixon's implementation of wage and price controls did not serve to enhance public confidence in that policy technique. A detailed economic review is necessary to sort out the extent to which specific decisions made within the period of full and partial controls contributed to the sad results. It certainly does not help to sell off a fourth of the American wheat crop to the Soviet Union and then turn around and realize that the country faces inflationary pressures because of an inadequate supply for internal consumption. Given the short-run political gains which are apt to be associated with wage and price controls, a future president may well again look toward those political advantages. Yet the longer-run consequences both economically and politically, for either the incumbent or his successor, dictate a careful look before this most substantial policy step is implemented. Wage and price controls, just like each of the other major tools, have tremendous political consequences for presidential politics.

It is necessary to point out a certain datedness in the available policy techniques. Policy tools developed in the 1960s were substantially oriented toward problems of growth and unemployment. They were also substantially directed toward the internal dynamics of the American economy. Inflation, recession and sharp alterations in the international economy had not been confronted to a comparable degree for several decades. Uncertainty was felt by the mid-1970s about the adequacy of existing policy tools in confronting changes in the international markets and changes in consumer attitudes.

THE POLICY PROCESS

Major political consequences stem from the president's growing economic management role. Where speed seems necessary, the role of Congress tends to be very peripheral. Congressmen often criticize policy, but are reluctant to face the difficult choices themselves. Presidential power thus often increases. Presidents also may face serious problems of credibility with the electorate. The frequent tendency has been for a president to appear on television and announce that economic conditions are soon going to improve, and the electorate need only have confidence. There are certain conditions of inadequate demand in which efforts at promoting consumer confidence are justified. Yet such efforts can easily reflect an unrealistic presidential hope and serve as a convenient reason for not pursuing other policies. As conditions worsen, the president is then confronted with an economic credibility gap with the electorate.

Power issues are also important in the president's growing economic management role. From the vantage point of the president and his advisers, the economic role can be seen taking place in a highly competitive process. The negotiating which tends to take place on economic policy issues clearly produces a competitive environment. Thus C. Jackson Grayson's description of the pressures confronting the Price Commission he headed for Nixon is a continuing account of conflicting pressures

from industry.[15] A substantial amount of economic management activity involves economic decision makers with either individual firm impacts or concerns for their industry.[16] Individual firms and at points unions and other participants lobby for a specific favorable decision, thus producing competition. Industry-wide activities also produce substantial conflict. Those affected by monetary operations are desirous of policies reducing the difficulties in their operations. Those involved with the airlines have been desirous of policies which would reduce the hardship to their industry. Automobile manufacturers have sought relief from the antipollution constraints which have limited their ability to produce cars as cheaply as they would like. Bargaining roles thus often emerge in the president's efforts at dealing with the major actors involved with these constellations of interests.

There has, at the same time, certainly not been uniform access for various interests. Labor union leaders have often spoken with a very definite and overriding interest in the problems of a particular industry. In interacting with dominant voices within areas of the economy, the president and his economic managers have also often been interacting with individuals identified in elite interpretations of presidential politics.[17] The tendency in these discussions has often been to seek quick decisions and speedy results, thus also tending to emphasize such strategies as changes in investment taxes or quick changes in the available supply of energy. Economic discussions in these conditions have generally avoided the longer-run implications of such general issues as income distribution in American society, and the operation of markets in ways destined to give those with dominant positions an ability to influence prices (and their own profits) as well as the quality of goods available to the average citizen. The ability of corporate interests, collectively, to maintain a relatively stable position in the American economy was not influenced by the shift since the early 1960s to a more active presidential responsibility for economic management.

From a presidential perspective, the question of economic management has nonetheless tended to be one of seeking to devise effective policy in the face of both conflicting advice and various economic forces nationally and internationally which can make the development of effective policy very difficult. An easy reliance upon either past wisdom or existing structures seems, in many perspectives, to be inadequate. From the presidential vantagepoint, economic management responsibilities loom as both increasingly important and increasingly difficult.

NOTES

1. Considerable useful material is contained in the debate between Walter Heller and Milton Friedman, *Monetary vs. Fiscal Policy* (New York: Norton, 1969).

2. Two useful books on Nixon's economic policy from a general perspective are Roger Miller and Raburn Williams, *The New Economics of Richard Nixon* (New York: Harper & Row, 1972); and Leonard Silk, *Nixonomics* (New York: Praeger, 1972).

3. A highly readable discussion of the importance of fiscal policy is found in Robert L. Heilbroner and Peter L. Bernstein, *A Primer on Government Spending* (New York: Vintage, 1963).

4. On this point, see Robert Eyestone, *Political Economy: Politics and Policy Analysis,* (Chicago, Markham, 1972), pp. 60-61.

5. Problems in presidential development of fiscal policy are usefully discussed in Lawrence C. Pierce, *The Politics of Policy Formation* (Pacific Palisades, Calif.: Goodyear, 1971).

6. Some of Kennedy's difficulties are discussed in James L. Sundquist, *Politics and Policy: The Eisenhower, Kennedy, and Johnson Years* (Washington, D.C.:, Brookings, 1968), chap. 3.

7. For a critical legislator's view, see William Proxmire, *Uncle Sam: The Last of the Bigtime Spenders* (New York: Simon & Schuster, 1972), p. 231.

8. Thurmon Arnold, *The Folklore of Capitalism* (New Haven, Conn.: Yale University Press, 1937).

9. John K. Galbraith, *The New Industrial State* (Boston: Houghton Mifflin, 1967).

10. Theodore J. Lowi, *The End of Liberalism* (New York: Norton, 1970), chaps. 2, 3.

11. "The Biggest Corporations by Revenues," *Forbes* 105 (May 1970): 75-76.

12. *Los Angeles Times,* August 4, 1974, p. 18.

13. An interesting case account of this use of presidential power is found in Grant McConnell, *Steel and the Presidency* (New York: Norton, 1963).

14. Truman's use of wage and price controls is discussed in Edward S. Flash, Jr., *Economic Advice and Presidential Leadership: The Council of Economic Advisers* (New York: Columbia University Press, 1965), chap. 3.

15. For an informative discussion of issues confronting the Price Commission, see C. Jackson Grayson, Jr., *Confessions of a Price Controller* (Homewood, Illinois: Dow Jones-Irwin, 1974), esp. chap. 7.

16. The extensive individual firm pressures and pressures from major functional areas of the economy are graphically portrayed in Proxmire, *op. cit.,* pp. 130-62.

17. The presence of individuals from the corporate structure in the making of economic policy decisions is emphasized in G. William Domhoff, *The Higher Circles* (New York: Vintage, 1970), chap. 6. See also Michael Parenti, *Democracy for the Few* (New York: St. Martin, 1973), chap. 3.

25. The Role of the Presidency in Shaping Lower Level Policy-Making Processes*

ROBERT R. SULLIVAN

Studies of the American presidency may be placed along a continuum bounded on the one side by static, descriptive analyses of a political institution which has grown in its manifest functions and enumerable powers as a consequence of the idiosyncracies of selected incumbents and the demands of an ever more complex environment. The impressive works of Edward S. Corwin are illustrative of this institutional approach to the presidency.[1] At the opposite end of the continuum are studies of the presidency as a dynamic, changing, and increasingly fascinating focal point for decision making in the political system. Such analysis tends to be not of established structures but rather of methods whereby the chief executive may attain his political will, and case studies are the main source of information on decision making. Richard Neustadt's penetrating and remarkably prescient analysis of presidential power and Theodore Sorenson's brief but insightful study of decision making in the White House are illustrative of this type of study.[2] Somewhere along the middle of this continuum are the elegant and thorough studies of the presidency by Louis W. Koenig, as well as the less monumental but nonetheless useful analytical and prescriptive works of Tugwell, Burns, Rankin, and Dallmayr.[3] While there is a paucity of great literature on the modern American presidency, there is still a sufficient number of first-rate studies so that one may see the institution and the process of decision making from several revealing perspectives and thereby attain a good understanding of the presidency's powers, prospects, and problems.

In the last few years the analytical center of gravity in analyses of the modern presidency has been shifting consistently away from the static institutional studies of the Corwin type toward the dynamic decision-making studies of the Neustadt type. To the extent that this movement is based upon the assumption that the two types of analysis are in competition with each other, the trend is regrettable, for an understanding of the institutional presidency is a necessary, though not sufficient, condition for an understanding of the presidency as a dynamic process. But to the extent that the shift is a consequence of the path-breaking effort by Neustadt and the subsequent and somewhat startling realization that there were few if any other good analyses of the presidency as a dynamic center of decision making, this movement is invaluable and ought to be encouraged until studies of all aspects and dimensions of the dynamics of presidential decision making have been undertaken.

The aim of this paper is to follow the methodological lead of Neustadt but to apply it to a hitherto unstudied area of political decision making—namely, the influence of the presidency on lower-level decision making. This will be done through a case study, but necessarily

*Source: Reprinted by permission from Polity (Winter 1970). Copyright © 1970 by Polity.

one of a different type. Instead of a relatively short process which peaks in a clearly delineated "decision" (Truman fires MacArthur; Eisenhower fails to censure Humphrey), our case is a process of political decision making that continues unabated through four administrations, and one which because of its remoteness from the White House seldom involves the president directly.

Of necessity, a low-level policy process must be distinguished from a high-level policy process in a somewhat arbitrary fashion. All policy processes—high and low—are essentially the same in that they involve the allocation of public resources to maintain or attain public values. As far as this paper is concerned, the key difference between the two types is the proximity of the White House to the policy-making process: the president is directly and continuously involved in high-level policy-making processes (Vietnam) but only remotely involved in numerous low-level policy processes. Another perspective, but one revealing the same difference, is gained by posing the question: who is actually making the key decisions in low-level policy processes? The answer is career bureaucrats (the administrator of a certain section of A.I.D.) rather than temporary political office holders (the president, the secretary of state, etc.). This lays bare a basic problem underlying this paper. A high-level policy process is almost by definition susceptible to changes which reflect changing political values (Vietnam, poverty), but a low-level process is one with a built-in resistance to political change since the key decision makers are relatively isolated from the dynamics of the political system. Yet a measure of the president's skill is his capacity to shape not merely high-level but also low-level policy processes. How is this done, actually and ideally? That is the question which shapes this paper.

The case study of lower-level policy making from which this paper draws its conclusions is the Food-for-Peace partnership between the United States government and American voluntary relief agencies for the distribution abroad of surplus agricultural commodities.[4] After a brief historical section in which the reader is made aware of the salient facts of the partnership, the paper will continue with an analysis in three parts and conclude with a discussion of the presidency as a factor in lower-level policy making.

I

The partnership was initiated with the passage of the Agricultural Act of 1949, Section 416 of which authorized donation of surplus food commodities to voluntary relief agencies registered with the Department of State.[5] The government's main aim was to take advantage of the voluntary agencies' overseas relief programs as surplus food outlets that would not interfere with the normal market for American agricultural exports. Simultaneously, the government expected the addition of surplus foods to reinforce relief programs already serving as buttresses to United States foreign aid programs, at that time still centered in the Marshall Plan countries of Western Europe. Thus, two sets of political interests were being supported, those of domestic agriculture and those of foreign policy. For the voluntary agencies, the addition of surplus food would better enable them to attain their humanitarian values of caring for one's needy fellow man regardless of national origin. The surplus would also support other less evident organizational interests of the voluntary agencies, such as those of the churches some of them represented.[6] These four categories of interests and values have been dominant in shaping the partnership throughout its history.

The operating partnership began in January of 1950, lasted for precisely one year, and then had to be terminated by the government because the demand generated by the Korean War was rapidly absorbing the agricultural surplus. By the beginning of the Eisenhower administration, however, the war had subsided and the surplus had (consequently) risen to such a great extent that new legislation was needed to cope with it. The old Section 416 authorization was incorporated nearly intact as Section 202 of Title III of the new Agricultural Trade Development and Assistance Act, better known as P.L. 480.[7] The partnership existed under this authorization until the passage of new legislation in 1967 as part of President Johnson's War on Hunger. The most significant and dramatic changes to occur in the period between 1954 and 1967 were (1) the liberalization of the partnership's terms so that more of the surplus could be distributed through voluntary agency channels; (2) the prolonged and often painful transfer of feeding programs from Western Europe to less developed countries of Latin America and Asia; (3) the related reorganization of all P.L. 480 activities under the Food-for-Peace program; and (4) the unbalancing of influence within the partnership due to the Vietnam War and expanding world population.

Since 1949 approximately thirty billion pounds of surplus foods valued at nearly four billion dollars have been distributed through the voluntary agencies. Twelve voluntary agencies have participated in the partnership, but four agencies have distributed nearly ninety percent of the foodstuffs made available. These four are CARE, Catholic Relief Services-NCWC, Church World Service, and Lutheran World Relief. Although significant cut-backs have been made in the past three years, the voluntary agencies still provide food for approximately seventy-five million persons each day.

II

The factors involved in the making of policy in the Food-for-Peace partnership may be described in terms as broad as "executive influence" and "legislative influence," or, to be more specific, as a collection comprising the White House, the Departments of State and Agriculture, the House and Senate Committees on Agriculture, the Senate Committee on Foreign Relations, the congressional farm bloc, and the liberal wing of the Democratic party in Congress. Outside of the governmental framework, each of the voluntary agencies, some of the organizations the voluntary agencies represented, and a coordinating agency called the American Council of Voluntary Agencies played a significant role in the making of policy in the partnership. In addition, the organizations the voluntary agencies represent, mainly churches, often were influential in shaping policy. This list includes all of the major actors and forces.

We shall focus here on one source of influence, the presidency. By presidency we mean two things: the president himself and the executive staff closely associated with the presidency. The central conclusion is that the White House has played a significant role in shaping policy within the partnership in three theoretically related ways. They may be placed upon a continuum called *intervention.*

At one pole of the continuum is *periodic direct intervention* by the president himself in the policy-making process. This is an unusual as well as a risky way for the White House to exert its influence on a relatively low-level process of policy making. It is unusual simply because the president does not have the time or the energy to spare. It is risky because it involves placing the ultimate source of political authority on the line for the sake of a relatively unimportant area of decision making. Nonetheless, each president since Mr. Truman has intervened directly in this partnership.

At the opposite end of the continuum is *continuous indirect intervention* by the president. This type of intervention is the main source of White House influence in the partnership and, by analogy, in other lower-level policy-making processes. It is a clear by-product of the president's political will and skill exerted at higher levels of policy making. In a sense, continuous indirect intervention is a spin-off from the central policy-making process. If the chief executive is intellectually disorganized, weak willed, or politically unskilled, then the spin-off will be correspondingly weakened and the president's influence at lower levels of policy making will be minimal. If, on the other hand, the president is intellectually organized, strong willed, and politically highly skilled in asserting and establishing the main thrust of his policies, then the lower-level policy-making process will be deeply informed with political purpose and consequently stiffened. Continuous indirect intervention is thus a means for maintaining remote control over distant policy-making processes.

Finally, between the two poles on the intervention continuum a third alternative emerges from the experience of the partnership. This is *continuous direct intervention by a special assistant to the president*. It might be argued that this type is *sui generis*, unique to this policy process, or that it should not be placed upon an intervention continuum because it is really nothing more than a special case of direct intervention by the president. There is some truth to each of these points, yet not enough effectively to eliminate the presidential special assistant as an object for special consideration. *Sui generis* he may be, but this is mainly because he represents something of a precedent, and one that might be followed in the future. The second objection fails to perceive the significant distinction between a direct intervention which lays the foundations for continuing presidential intervention through an agent (Nixon's appointment of Daniel Moynihan as special assistant in charge of urban affairs) and a direct intervention that is a one-shot affair (Truman's dismissal of MacArthur). It is a difference in degree too substantial to overlook.

These three means of presidential in-

tervention are brought into perspective and stabilized by being compared and contrasted to more familiar categories developed by Richard Neustadt in his book, *Presidential Power*. Periodic direct presidential intervention is a distant cousin of presidential interventions at high levels by command, but whereas the clearly stated personal decision of the president is the *sine qua non* of high-level policy making, it stands out for its infrequency in lower-level processes. Nonetheless, Neustadt's essential criteria for an effective command in high-level processes are, not surprisingly, applicable to lower-level processes. Certainty in the minds of the actual policy makers that the president has indeed spoken is as important as clarity in their minds regarding the political and administrative meaning of the chief executive's order. Publicity of the decision is an excellent creator of both of these effects. Perhaps even more important, direct intervention should be resorted to only in cases of necessity. For Neustadt the direct intervention of the president is a means of last resort that suggests earlier failures (Truman's dismissal of MacArthur); at lower levels it is not so much a consequence of past presidential failures as it is a consequence of the crystallization of a situation in which there is no alternative. In the absence of necessity, the only time direct presidential intervention in low-level policy processes is justified is when it involves little or no risk of failure and the consequent tarnishing of the president's "professional reputation." All of these points will be amply illustrated from each of the past four administrations.

Continuous indirect intervention is largely a distant consequence of the existence of a strong and forceful president, which implies a great deal of what Neustadt calls "self-help" at high levels of policy making. The president who is forceful in the central tasks of policy making will soon establish a professional reputation that will serve him well at lower levels of policy making. A word of caution must be voiced at this point, however. Neustadt's category "professional reputation" is only partly similar to my category of "continuous indirect intervention." His relates to the will and the skill of the president to reward or punish other persons in the political system for compliance or noncompliance with his political wishes, and this reputation is based upon a perceived pattern of past presidential actions in the eyes of the beholder. Neustadt's category is relevant mainly to high-level decision making, where the president will be interested by definition in direct control of the process. It is applicable to lower-level processes only partly, since here the president is very seldom expressing a policy priority directly related to the lower-level program, not intending to directly control the policy process, and not directly promising rewards or threatening punishments. My category of "continuous indirect intervention" is distinguished mainly by another factor: a sure knowledge on the part of the beholder of the president's priorities in high-level policy making and the use of this knowledge for shaping the lower-level program. Control is thus much more remote in lower than in higher decision-making processes. This of course is the rationale for demanding that the president and his staff be very clear and forceful in regard to high level priorities. If the president's actions betray weakness, indecision, or confusion, then they will have a difficult time shaping the lower-level program. The essential difference between Neustadt's category and my category is to be laid bare by posing the question, who decides? In Neustadt's case it is the president or his immediate aides (high-level policy), whereas in my case it is the career bureaucrat. Therefore, the latter must have a clear knowledge of the former's priorities if the former is to influence the latter's decisions.

Finally, Neustadt talks of two types of presidential special assistants, one being an administrative type who actually performs the chores of the president and the other being a political type who helps the president understand his personal power stake in political problems. Sherman Adams is the best illustration of the first type; Harry Hopkins, Robert F. Kennedy, and Walt W. Rostow are good illustrations of the second type. Neustadt focuses very emphatically on the political type of presidential assistant; my focus is equally emphatically on the administrative type, and even here the comparison with Neustadt's type falls short of being fully accurate, since a presidential assistant placed in charge of a hitherto lower-level policy process is not taking on the established chores of the president (Sherman Adams) but is rather bringing a new field of activity into the purview of the White House (Daniel Moynihan). This is the ground upon which some criticism may be based, for this type of expansion needlessly increases the functions of a political office already overburdened with administrative tasks. The existence of a presidential special assistant in charge of such-and-such a hitherto lower-level program implies that the normal bureaucratic channels will not or cannot do an effective job, or if not, such a creation is bound to be demoralizing to bureaucrats. There is another alternative, which is that the president through the creation of a new special assistantship is in effect elevating the lower-level process to a higher level. All these explanations are applicable to this case study.

Let us now take a detailed look at how these three means of intervention have worked out in practice.

PERIODIC DIRECT PRESIDENTIAL INTERVENTION

Each of the four presidents under consideration has intervened directly at least once in the partnership's policy-making processes. Presidents Truman and Johnson were successful, although in substantially different ways. Presidents Eisenhower and Kennedy were unsuccessful; and although neither man paid too high a price for failure, it did—in President Kennedy's case—tarnish the president's professional reputation and give rise to suspicions about his motives and—in President Eisenhower's case—confirm at an early period in his administration the feeling that the president might not be the final arbiter in foreign policy decision-making.

President Truman's only direct intervention came in September of 1950 and was aimed at dislodging an important bill that had become locked up in committee.[8] The president succeeded by writing a letter on September 14, 1950 to Senator Hugh Thomas (D-Okla) requesting that the bill be released.

The Truman intervention was exemplary for a number of reasons. First, it was unequivocally from the chief executive. There was no doubt in anyone's mind that this was direct presidential intervention, and this clarity lent force to the move. Secondly, the intervention was in Congress and not in the executive branch. The failure of a direct presidential intervention in a constitutionally opposed branch of government is seldom very costly. Only if such interventions persistently fail does the president gain a poor political reputation on Capitol Hill. Successful interventions of this type can only gain for the president the inevitable "arm-twister" reputation, and such a label is a political compliment.

President Johnson's direct interventions in the affairs of the partnership were aimed at the executive branch, and they, too, were successful in achieving their apparently intended effects.[9] In 1965 and 1966 President Johnson acted through a series of related steps to demonstrate his lack of interest in the partnership. The moves resulted in the downgrading of President Kennedy's Food-for-Peace Office from its place and status as an adjunct to the White House to a new and nearly meaningless place and status within the Department of State.

The Johnson interventions were, like President Truman's, exemplary for a number of reasons. Above all, they seemed unavoidable and, consequently, above reproach. The president had little interest in Food-for-Peace and the partnership that was a part of it and he was fully within his rights in demoting it. These direct interventions were thus either without risk or unavoidable. In addition, they were unequivocally from the president, and this gave them added force.

Presidents Eisenhower and Kennedy both exerted their personal influence to change policies within the executive branch and both failed. Mr. Eisenhower acted within the context of an interview with a CARE official in 1954, leaving the impression that the chief executive's personal intervention would soon be forthcoming to facilitate the establishment of numerous CARE feeding programs in the Middle East and Asia.[10] But within a week the hopeful initiative had run aground on the shoals of the Department of State. Soon after reaching the desk of Secretary John Foster Dulles the policy was reversed, Mr. Dulles stating that he did not want nongovernmental aid programs to be initiated at that time in Asia.

President Kennedy's lone personal intervention came in the second year of his tenure, and it involved his personal approval of a new policy that would have established a relationship between the government and religiously affiliated voluntary agencies.[11] This policy and the president's informal approval of it were the result of eighteen months of pressure by Roman Catholic officials. However, publication of the new policy triggered an immediate reaction from the church-state separatists, led by the Southern Baptists. As a consequence of mounting criticism that threatened to involve the partnership in the complexities of the domestic church-state issue, the Department of State in August of 1962—apparently on word from the White House—quietly withdrew the policy. It was a small but stinging defeat for the president.

The conclusions on direct presidential intervention in lower-level policy-making processes are few and simple. Those which at the time seemed unavoidable because of high pressure (Truman) or necessary to implement a changed style in the White House (Johnson) were successful, but would be beyond reproach even if they had failed. The interventions of Presidents Eisenhower and Kennedy, on the other hand, were not only unnecessary but misconceived. Even if they had succeeded they would have brought more trouble than gain to the White House, since they both showed favoritism for the most expansive voluntary agencies at times when there was known opposition within the partnership to this type of expansion. In a sense, both presidents were fortunate that their policy innovations failed. The critical factor, then, is necessity. If the president is compelled to become involved because high political pressure is brought to bear or because a lower-level policy-making process is interfering with his activities elsewhere, then the intervention is beyond reproach. If, however, the intervention is the consequence of presidential idiosyncracies or of a desire to push a pet policy, then the personal intervention may be politically ineffective because unnecessary.

A second conclusion has to do with clarity. Presidents Truman and Johnson both intervened directly in writing. Such a commitment left no doubt of the chief executive's will. But Presidents Eisenhower and Kennedy intervened directly by word of mouth only, and this had as its symbolic by-product the creation of an atmosphere of doubt regarding how serious they were. President Eisenhower may have been doing little more than giving voice to a sentiment. President Kennedy, unsure of his position, may have been anticipating retreat

in his half-hearted verbal endorsement. The conclusion is clear: direct intervention implies an unequivocal command from the chief executive if its chances for success are to be enhanced.

THE HALFWAY HOUSE, THE SPECIAL ASSISTANT TO THE PRESIDENT

On the continuum of means by which the White House may intervene in the policy-making process to bring its influence to bear, the post of special assistant to the president stands halfway between the pole of periodic direct intervention and the pole of continuous indirect intervention. President Kennedy must be deemed most successful in this regard, although credit for its success cannot go entirely to him. President Eisenhower, the only other chief executive who attempted a similar intervention, failed to send even a ripple through the partnership.

From 1961 to 1963 the partnership between the government and the voluntary agencies took on a life and personality of its own that left the impression that surplus food disposals had become one of the most dynamic instruments of President Kennedy's liberal foreign policies.[12] This was a period in which the surplus was high, and one would have expected agricultural interests to prevail. In fact they did. President Kennedy's feat was in changing the public image, not the substance, of P.L. 480. This was the consequence of the creation in December of 1960 of the Food-for-Peace Office and the appointment of former (defeated, 1960) Congressman George McGovern to be its director. What followed from these basic decisions was more than President Kennedy anticipated.

The president-elect's motives in December of 1960 were modest. He wanted to create a Food-for-Peace Office to be placed in the newly reorganized Agency for International Development (AID) and he wanted to give George McGovern a political base that would serve him well in preparation for the 1962 election campaign. McGovern agreed enthusiastically with the latter motive and, perhaps therefore, undermined the plan to put his office in AID. He simply occupied a suite of offices in the executive office building, and President Kennedy failed to remove him. The logical consequence was that McGovern became a special assistant to the president.

McGovern then went on to become a New Frontiersman par excellence, and the effect on the partnership with the voluntary agencies was fully beneficial. The president's special assistant toured Latin American capitals with Arthur Schlesinger, Jr., initiated a small magazine called the *Food-for-Peace Bulletin,* created the advisory Food-for-Peace Council made up of prominent private citizens, arranged a formal White House reception for council members and voluntary agency executives, and fully changed the public image of P.L. 480 from that of a somewhat tired and sluggish surplus dumping mechanism to that of a dynamic instrument of economic development equal in importance to the Peace Corps.[13]

President Eisenhower undertook similar programs in the 1950s when he appointed Clarence Francis and later Don Paarlberg to act as special assistant to the president and charged them with the task of coordinating P.L. 480 activities. In both cases the process was one in which Francis and Paarlberg duplicated activities already going on in the bureaucracy.

The conclusion to be drawn from the experience of the two Eisenhower coordinators and the Kennedy director is that if the White House hopes to influence the shaping of policy in the area for which the presidential assistant is responsible, then every effort should be made to choose a man who is a political leader and a trusted agent of the chief executive as well as an administrative coordinator. In effect, only if a lower-level policy-making process is deemed to be in strong need of stimula-

tion from the White House or is judged to have great potential should a special assistant to the president be placed in charge of it. His task would then be to inform the program with the political interests and values of the White House. Administrative coordination, such as that attempted by President Eisenhower, may or may not be successful, but in either case it is difficult to justify. Not only does it duplicate a job that could just as easily be carried out in the regular bureaucracy, but it also clutters the White House with another official whose job will seldom bring him into contact with the president.

The danger of this mode of intervention should be readily apparent. Any special assistant of the administrative type who can demonstrate that he has the confidence of the president will become a power in his own right and may misuse this power by becoming an influence peddler of sorts. The case that comes most readily to mind is that of Sherman Adams. Fortunately, George McGovern was as trustworthy as he was influential in the Kennedy White House staff. Nonetheless, the danger still exists that great influence, existing by virtue of the fact that one is a known confidant of the president, might be misused. This is a problem with which one is continually confronted with the White House staff.

CONTINUOUS INDIRECT PRESIDENTIAL INTERVENTION

No other political office is as awe inspiring as the presidency, but the awe inspired by the office has little perceptible influence on policy formation at lower levels, if one may judge by the experience of this partnership. The key factor in the partnership, and by the analogy in most lower-level policy-making processes, is the style and general policies of the individual who occupies the office. A mild and politically ineffective president will not influence remote policy-making processes greatly, but a strong and politically determined president will energize even the most obscure policy-making process.

It should not be surprising that the most revealing experiences in regard to this third category are from the Eisenhower and Johnson administrations. The continuous indirect influence of President Eisenhower's policies, especially those related to fiscal responsibility and budget balancing in 1956 and later years, provides a clear illustration of the effects of intellectual confusion and weak will at the distant center of the political system. At the opposite extreme, President Johnson's strong and clear policies in relation to Vietnam and other areas of foreign policy provide a no less lucid illustration.

Let us be clear at the outset of this section about the point to be made. Both presidents had identifiable high-level policies (Eisenhower's toward the budget and Johnson's toward Vietnam) which each president made so dominant that they were bound to affect many if not most low-level policy-making processes. Yet the outcomes were substantially different. The reasons are complex, but they can be reduced to the following: a sure knowledge (or the lack of it) on the part of the key decision makers (career bureaucrats) that the president had spoken, that he meant what he prescribed, and that it was more or less necessary to carry out this policy. While no one doubted that Eisenhower had spoken, there was good reason to be skeptical about whether he meant what he said and whether it was necessary to carry out this policy. The bureaucratic decision makers were thus understandably reluctant throughout the entire second term of the Eisenhower administration to follow the president's lead. On the other hand, no one doubted that President Johnson had spoken on Vietnam, that he meant what he said, and that this overriding policy ought to shape most other low-level policy processes. The consequence was that the bureaucrats who made the key decisions during the Johnson adminis-

tration were strong and effective in reforming the partnership to conform to the president's manifest will. Now let us see how these two contrasting processes worked out in detail.

The way in which the Eisenhower administration influenced the partnership in 1956 was in many respects a preview of the confusion that would overtake the administration in 1957 as a consequence of the conflicting budgetary statements of the president and the secretary of the treasury, George M. Humphrey, and the subsequent backpedaling of Mr. Eisenhower.[14] The stake of the 1956 conflict was the amount of money the voluntary agencies would receive as reimbursement from the government to pay for ocean freight, and the main characteristics of the conflict were the hesitant niggardliness of the executive branch and the subsequent rebellion of the voluntary agencies in cooperation with Senate Democrats.

During the first year of the P.L. 480 donation program, the voluntary agencies received $8.3 million in reimbursement for ocean freight. For fiscal year 1956, the second year of the program, $13 million in Mutual Security Funds was originally requested, but the House balked at this figure and cut it to $10 million. At this point Msgr. Swanstrom of Catholic Relief Services-NCWC reacted by sending a telegram to Senator Hubert Humphrey, urging him to take up the cause of the voluntary agencies. The gambit worked. The voluntary agencies were satisfied only temporarily, however. When the International Cooperation Administration (ICA) requested less for ocean freight reimbursement for fiscal 1957 than the agencies had received in fiscal 1956, the agencies finally rebelled. They had not been consulted on the matter, and this compelled them to question the value of the State Department's "powerless" Advisory Committee on Voluntary Foreign Aid, which had been set up by the Truman administration in 1946 to act as the executive branch's intermediary with the voluntary agencies. There was at this point even question about whether the advisory committee should continue to represent the voluntary agencies in the government, and this questioning later crystallized into opposition. In April, Eileen Egan of Catholic Relief Services-NCWC wrote to John Hollister, the acting director of the ICA, protesting the low $13 million request and informing him that the voluntary agencies would no longer depend upon the advisory committee to represent their interests within the government but would instead testify separately to the House Foreign Affairs Committee that at least $20 to $25 million was needed for transportation. Two weeks later Moses Leavitt of the American Jewish Joint Distribution Committee wrote directly to Charles Taft, the director of the advisory committee, informing him that the voluntary agencies felt they had "no channel to Congress through the advisory committee and therefore [were] resorting directly to the open hearings before congressional committees—the only channel open to them." When the voluntary agencies did testify in May of 1956, they asked Congress to provide $25 to $30 million for ocean freight expenses and reinforced this by asserting that they could use up to $50 million if they were to expand to their full potential.

In response to the protest lodged by Egan and Leavitt, Charles Taft wrote on April 27 that he had asked the ICA to increase its request to $18 or $20 million, and that the ICA had agreed to transmit these amounts to Congress. No explanation was given, but it was evident that the economy policy of the executive branch had caved in under the pressure of the voluntary agencies' opposition. If two strong letters had shattered the policy of the ICA, causing it to shift from a proposed budgetary cut to a proposed increase equalling one-third of the previous year's budget, what might more sustained opposition bring?

The voluntary agencies thus persisted in their opposition, and were rewarded with an even greater return. In June the administration's Farm Bill was passed, and with the aid of Senator Humphrey and the concurrence of Senator Allen Ellender, an amendment was included which authorized the payment of *all* ocean freight costs incurred by the voluntary agencies in the shipment of P.L. 480 commodities. Now the voluntary agencies could expand up to their self-imposed limit of $50 million, or beyond if they had the means and the will to do so. The executive branch put up no significant defense against this breakthrough. The first cause of this substantial policy change was the expanding surplus and the consequent growing cost of the farm program, but this should in no way obscure the fact that the initiative for policy making had clearly passed out of the hands of the executive and into the hands of a coalition made up of the voluntary agencies and opposition Democrats in Congress.

Henceforth, the cooperation of the voluntary agencies and the Democrats would grow in opposition to further attempts by the executive branch to circumscribe the partnership in the name of fiscal responsibility. In 1957 this meant a sustained and eventually successful effort by the voluntary agencies and Senator Humphrey to undermine the ICA's attempts to curtail ocean freight payments to Italy and other Western European countries, and in 1958 the focal point of opposition became the Francis Committee Report, which in essence was an attempt coordinated by a presidential assistant to impose a set of limiting guidelines on the partnership. Here as elsewhere, the coalition of the voluntary agencies and Senator Humphrey wore down the executive branch's policy to the point where it became meaningless. Never before or again would the executive branch manifest such a sustained incapacity for influencing the partnership. Or, to rephrase the same conclusion more precisely, lack of consistent, strong, and clear presidential leadership did indeed influence this low-level policy process, but it did so in such a way that the executive branch (the State Department and the White House Staff) was unable to shape the partnership's policies in the face of strong opposition of the voluntary agencies and the Senate Democrats. This is not unlike the experience of the Eisenhower administration in many other fields of policy in the years 1956-58.

The will of President Johnson was to solve the Vietnam problem on his own terms, and the outcome of this high-level policy process was the very obvious one of the president's failure, in spite of increased efforts, to attain his will.[15] Nonetheless, this powerful presidential will and the consequent reordering of priorities to attain the object willed was the major source of a strong and continuous indirect effort after 1964 to reform the partnership. Environmental changes made it easier for this continuous White House influence to be brought to bear effectively. Crop failures in Europe, the Soviet Union, China, and India occurred in the context of a rising world demand for food that was the consequence of an expanding world population. By 1964-65 nearly everyone in Congress as well as the executive branch recognized that the American agricultural surplus was dwindling and that this was a trend not likely to be reversed.

The first indication that the State Department officials planned to adopt a more aggressive approach to the partnership as a consequence of the factors mentioned above came with the occurrence of a shortage of surplus milk in 1964. Individual commodities had been in short supply before, especially in the 1950s, but the Eisenhower administration had never been as minutely calculating in terms of its foreign interests as was the Johnson administration. Moreover, the challenges thrown up by the international political system had

not been as pressing in 1957 or 1959 as they were in 1964. As a consequence, the Department of State did in 1964 what it had not even contemplated in the 1950s: it imposed a set of geographic priorities on the use of milk in voluntary agency programs, and these priorities corresponded closely to what the White House considered to be the areas in which the greatest challenges were being presented to United States foreign policy interests.

Vietnam was the first of three priority categories. The voluntary agencies could use all the milk they desired in that war-torn country. Second priority was assigned to Alliance for Progress countries. The voluntary agencies would have to ration in these Latin American countries, but reductions in the programs would be small and evenly distributed to reduce adverse repercussions. The third and final category was residual. It took in the countires of the rest of the world, and it was here that the government would expect the voluntary agencies to make the greatest cuts.

The third category was purposely left vague in 1964 because there was still no need to define it further. But as it became apparent in 1965 and 1966 that the milk shortage of 1964 was not a temporary phenomenon but rather an integral part of a more profound transition toward the permanent reduction of the surplus, the Department of State saw fit to refine the residual category by developing categories within it.

India was eventually—in 1966—given the greatest emphasis among third category countries. This came as a by-product of President Johnson's emergency grants of famine relief for India. One aspect of this evolving program was an administration request to Congress to authorize $25 million for large scale famine relief projects to be conducted by CARE. To some extent the request was a result of pressure applied by the voluntary agencies, but more decisively it was a reflection of the administration's policy of doing everything possible to prevent the further political fragmentation of the Indian subcontinent. A politically stable India was desired by the White House as a counterbalance to a supposedly expansive China.

Near the bottom of the third category came countries like Korea and Mexico. Here, administration spokesmen asserted, the voluntary agencies ought to close out their programs because the countries were no longer in dire need of foreign aid. Like Formosa, these countries were nearing the take-off into sustained economic growth and, consequently, United States foreign aid programs ought to be phased out. The rule to be applied increasingly to these countries was that of self-help. For the voluntary agencies this would mean mounting pressure from AID to close out feeding programs which, since they served needy persons and not needy states, could still be justified by the voluntary agencies as long as there were continuing pockets of need amidst the rising national wealth of the countries concerned.

The policy applied to Korea had an added dimension, however. The Korean government and not the United States government had originated the pressures to close out voluntary agency programs, and AID had seen fit to give way to the Korean demands without first securing the concurrence or understanding of the voluntary agencies. The added dimension was that in reality Korea was being upgraded, not downgraded. Voluntary agency programs were not being closed out; they were instead being transferred to the control of the Korean government. This may have been related to the substantial military contribution being made by Korea in Vietnam.

Finally, the Johnson administration placed sub-Saharan African countries associated through the Common Market with European nations at the very bottom of the third category. Indirectly, all sub-Saharan African countries were given low priorities, since AID frowned upon the voluntary agencies opening up any new programs in Africa. Moves such as these were part of a trend in the State Department to recognize not only that Africa was that section of the world in which United States political and economic interests were least involved, but also that the cold war in Europe was drawing to a close and that the European allies of the United States ought to assume responsibilities in Africa commensurate with their continued economic control and political influence over the area. In effect, Africa is at the periphery of world political conflict, and the growing United States involvement in Asia coupled with the dwindling surplus forced the Johnson administration toward an increasingly clear policy of nonintervention and noncommitment in an area traditionally Europe's sphere of influence.

III

We have seen that the White House can influence the making of policy at a relatively low level in three ways. The first is by periodic direct presidential intervention. Such a method is dangerous for precisely the same reason that it is effective: it involves putting the ultimate source of political authority on the line. The risk, no matter how small, can hardly be justified by the gain. Direct presidential intervention ought to be employed only when there is no risk of defeat, as with President Johnson's interventions, or where there is no penalty attached to defeat, as with President Truman's 1950 intervention in Congress. The actions of President Eisenhower and especially of President Kennedy in regard to this first means of intervention are difficult to justify.

The halfway house on the continuum is more or less continuous presidential intervention by means of a White House special assistant. In spite of the thoroughly convincing success of President Kennedy's Food-for-Peace director, George McGovern, such a use of a presidential special assistant raises a number of critical questions. First, where does one draw the line on the number of special assistants of the administrative type in the White House? If a president appoints a special assistant to coordinate P.L. 480 activities, then why not appoint a dozen more to coordinate activities in other equally important areas? At some point the White House will be "cluttered up in a pile of appendages," as Richard Reuter phrased it when he was telling the voluntary agencies that President Johnson was moving the Food-for-Peace Office to the Department of State. Secondly, how does the president maintain control over special assistants and their staffs? The answer should be by face-to-face contacts between two political intimates, but at some point in the proliferation of special assistants of the administrative type the intimacy must diminish. Lyndon Johnson hardly knew Richard Reuter. Finally, what effect will such a special assistant have on involved professional bureaucrats? It must be kept in mind that the job of a special assistant of the administrative type duplicates the work of someone in the bureaucracy and that such duplication can be demoralizing. Why not simply appoint a political confidant of the president to a key post in the relevant bureaucratic structure? The answer: This was precisely what President Kennedy intended, but for his own reasons George McGovern undermined the effort.

In regard to low-level policy formulation, the only means beyond reproach or critical skepticism is the last considered—continuous indirect intervention on the part of the White House by a process of informing, energizing, and controlling the political system from its remote but potentially radiant center. If the center of the political system issues only weak or contradictory signals, if it fails to project the president's will and his political skill, then the low-level policy process will become soft as a consequence of its lack of political purpose. On the other hand, the low-level

policy process will be almost miraculously stiffened if the president can project his political will and political skill.

It should be evident that the continuum employed throughout this paper reflects not only the directness or indirectness of the relationship between the president and the partnership but also a value judgment on the part of the writer. In a simpler age, periodic direct personal intervention by the president in lower-level policy-making processes might have been acceptable, harmless, and uninteresting. But in an age increasingly characterized by massive problems, massive solutions to those problems, and correspondingly complex and far-reaching organizational procedures, the president's skill as a politician will of necessity be judged more and more by his capacity to influence and control men and resources far removed from the White House. In these evolving circumstances, periodic personal intervention by the president is something of a quaint if not a dangerous anachronism. In the modern handbook of political expediency, the president who has the capacity to intervene remotely by means of oblique techniques and mass communications will be judged the skilled, if not great, president.

By taking a slightly different perspective one can gain the same set of conclusions. One of the tools we used at the beginning of this paper to make a distinction between high-level and low-level policy processes was the question: Who makes the key decisions? The answer provides the distinguishing feature of low-level policy processes: career bureaucrats. The underlying problem of this paper was how the president could influence these distant policy processes, thereby making them responsive to values generated in the political system. The first answer, it is now evident, is to usurp the bureaucrat's decision-making role; the president takes it over directly. The second means is partially to usurp the bureaucrat's role by the appointment of a presidential agent to make key decisions. The third and final means is to allow the bureaucrat to retain his key role but to influence his decision indirectly and thereby retain remote control over him. In terms of political cost efficiency, the third means is the only one which yielded (in President Johnson's case) a wide ranging restructuring of the partnership with a minimal outlay of presidential time and energy. The second means yielded a less profound political restructuring, and the outlay of energy was higher—a full-time presidential special assistant. The first means consistently yielded only changes in details, and the cost of this was a direct absorption of the president's time and energy. This inverse relationship between cost and effectiveness returns us to our earlier conclusion—namely, that indirect presidential influence is by all standards the preferred means for shaping distant, low-level policies. It is also the most demanding means in terms of the president's political will and political skill, which is another way of saying—with Corwin, Koenig, and Neustadt—that the White House is no place for a political amateur.

NOTES

1. Edward S. Corwin, *The President, Office and Powers, 1787-1948, History and Analysis of Practice and Opinion,* 4th ed. (New York: New York Univ. Press, 1957).

2. Richard E. Neustadt, *Presidential Power, The Politics of Leadership* (New York: John Wiley and Sons, 1964). Theodore Sorenson, *Decision-Making in the White House,* (New York: Columbia University Press, 1965).

3. Louis W. Koenig, *The Invisible Presidency* (New York: Rinehart and Company, 1960). See also Rexford G. Tugwell, *The Enlargement of the Presidency* (New York: Doubleday, 1960); James MacGregor burns, *Presidential Government, The Crucible of Leadership* (Boston: Houghton Mifflin, 1966); and Robert S. Rankin and Winfried R. Dallmayr, *Freedom and Emergency Powers*

in the Cold War (New York: Appleton-Century-Crofts, 1964).

4. This case is drawn from the author's doctoral dissertation: Robert R. Sullivan, "The Politics of Altruism: A Study of the Partnership Between the United States Government and American Voluntary Relief Agencies for the Donation Abroad of Surplus Agricultural Commodities, 1949-1967" (Ph.D. diss., the John Hopkins University, Baltimore, Maryland, 1968). In order to minimize the number of footnotes, only one clustered footnote per illustration or set of illustrations will be used.

5. 63 *Stat.* 1058.

6. See Robert R. Sullivan, "The Politics of Altruism: The American Church-State Conflict in the Food-for-Peace Program," *A Journal of Church and State* (Winter, 1969).

7. 68 *Stat.* 454-59.

8. Sullivan, *op. cit.* (Ph.D. disss), pp. 244-48. See also the minutes of the Shippers and Purchasers Committee of the American Council of Voluntary Agencies, ACVA files, New York, for the following dates: March 7 and 16, June 13, August 10, September 5 and 15, 1950. See also the *New York Times,* July 27, 1950, and the *Congressional Record,* August 22, 1950, p. 13025.

9. Sullivan, *op. cit.,* (Ph.D. disss), pp. 177-83; See also the minutes of the Surplus Commodities Policy Committee of the American Council of Voluntary Agencies (Hereafter, ACVA/SCPC Minutes) for the following dates: April 21, October 28, 1965. See also the letter from Bishop Swanstrom to Senator Fulbright, June 17, 1966, Catholic Relief Services-NCWC (Hereafter, CRS-NCWC) files, New York; the letter of Frank Goffio to President Johnson, July 14, 1966, CARE files, New York, the *New York Times* of December 2 and 6, 1966. See also the "Voluntary Agency Position Paper on Government Food Resources," ACVA files, New York, and see "Food for Peace and the Voluntary Agencies," Report of the Task Force to the Advisory Committee on Voluntary Foreign Aid (mimeo), 1966.

10. Sullivan, *op. cit.* (Ph.D. disss), pp. 277-78. See also the letter of Paul Comly French to Mrs. Olive Clapper, December 6, 1954, and the letter of Mrs. Clapper to Mr. French, December 15, 1954; CARE files, New York. An additional factor, of which Mr. Eisenhower was apparently unaware, was that there was strong opposition from several other voluntary agencies to CARE's aggressive behavior toward the government.

11. Sullivan, *op. cit.* (Ph.D. diss.), p. 99. See also the letter of Bishop Swanstrom to President Kennedy, June 17, 1961; the letter from Dewey R. Heising to Bishop Swanstrom, August 17, 1962; the letters from Bishop Swanstrom to Cardinal Cicognani of August 23 and September 17, 1962; and the memorandum of July 20, 1962, from Msgr. Gremillion to Bishop Swanstrom all in CRS-NCWC files, New York. See also the *Washington Post,* September 10, 1962. See the Dept of State's Policy Determination No. 10, "Religious Organizations and the United States Aid Programs," July 16, 1962. See also Sen. Hubert Humphrey's support of the Roman Catholic position in *A Report on the Alliance for Progress, 1963, to the Committee on Appropriations and the Committee on Foreign Relations, U.S. Senate* (Wash., D.C: Government Printing Office, April 11, 1963), p. 28.

12. Sullivan, *op. cit.* (Ph.D. diss.), pp. 143-47. See also the ACVA Board Minutes of January 26, April 20, and May 18, 1961; the memorandum from George McGovern to President Kennedy, no date, CARE files, New York; and the *New York Times,* April 8, 1962.

13. Arthur Schlesinger, Jr., *A Thousand Days* (New York: Crest Books, 19—), pp. 168-70, 604-05.

14. Sullivan, *op. cit.* (Ph.D. diss.), pp. 248-51. See also the telegram, no date, of Msgr. Swanstrom to Sen. Humphrey; the letters of Eileen Egan to John Hollister, April 16, 1956; Moses Leavitt to Charles Taft, April 27, 1956; and Charles Taft to Eileen Egan, April 27, 1956; the memo of May 28, 1956—all in CRS-NCWC files, New York. See also the American Council Executive Committee Minutes, ACVA files, New York; and the *Congressional Record* of July 22, 1955.

15. Sullivan *op. cit.* (Ph.D. diss.), pp. 166-77. In regard to the set of categories concerning milk, see the ACVA/SCPC Minutes of June 5, 1964, ACVA files, New York; and the memorandum from E. C. Reiss to the files, July 7, 1964, ACVA files, New York. For the subsequent developments see the ACVA/SCPC Minutes of November 27, 1965, January 20 and 28, and May 12, 1966. See also the *New York Times,* February 21, 1967.

VII

The Legislative Presidency

Introduction. Presidents must lead Congress. Indeed, today executive in-itiative in the legislative process is taken for granted. This is so because Congress is perceived as too large, too fragmented, too unwieldy, or simply unable or unwilling to muster the cooperation necessary to come up with a comprehensive legislative program.

Although the legislative presidency is assumed, the Constitution contains very few specific provisions for presidential legislative initiative. It provides that the president give a State of the Union message from time to time and that he recommend to Congress such measures as he judges necessary and expedient, and it permits him, on extraordinary occasions, to call Congress into special session. However, although the constitutional veto cannot count as "presidential initiative," the president's capacity to use it gives him tremendous legislative leadership clout.

In addition to constitutional provisions for legislative leadership, the Congress itself has given the president large grants of power to facilitate his leadership to include greater control of the budgetary process, the war-making process, and the treaty process, which is now mainly an executive agreements process.

In the first article, "The President as Legislative Leader," political scien-tist Edward Corwin details the early ways in which the presidency came to assume legislative leadership. Mainly, as Corwin shows, the presidency was propelled into leadership of Congress by the advent of the Great De-pression and the arrival of the New Deal. The New Deal buried most of the suspicions of strong executive power.

To assist the president in exercising the legislative initiative, the "institu-tionalized presidency" has systematized some procedures on behalf of the president. The Bureau of Budget (BOB)—created in 1921 and moved to the Executive Office of the President (EOP) in 1939 and known as the Office of Management and Budget (OMB) since 1970—developed what is described as the "central clearance" function. Central clearance includes reviewing departmental recommendations on substantive and fiscal legislation as well as getting departmental views on enrolled bills.

The clearance function enables the president to monitor departmental requests for both fiscal and substantive legislation to make certain that such requests are in keeping with his own broad policy goals. In the next essay, "Presidency and Legislation: The Growth of Central Clearance," political scientist Richard Neustadt chronicles and assesses the forces and factors which created, shaped and developed the process of central clearance.

In Federalist No. 58, James Madison provided an interesting argument on the possibilities of Congress's financial control over the presidency. Congressional power over the purse, Madison wrote, "may, in fact, be regarded as the most complete and effectual weapon with which any constitution can arm the immediate representatives of the people, for obtaining a redress of grievance, and for carrying into effect every just and salutary measure." In view of political scientist Louis Fisher's careful study of presidential spending, it is clear that Madison's optimism was illusory almost from the very beginning of the Republic. Even though Congress has, in recent years, sought to return to itself much of the broad discretionary power in the area of spending that it had ceded to the presidency, presidents still retain considerable authority and power to thwart Congress's constitutional control of public spending as Louis Fisher outlines in the next selection, "The President's Spending Power."

Yet if the president's spending powers appear formidable, political scientists Peri Arnold and L. John Roos suggest that in the long run presidents should not be encouraged to believe that their strength and leadership can and should be exercised independently of Congress. More importantly, Arnold and Roos are pessimistic as to whether the president or Congress, left alone in their struggles, can come up with policies and programs which serve the best ends of the polity.

Arnold and Roos articulate a relationship between the president and Congress that they call the theory of the "reciprocating engine." They cite cases to show that a "mutual reciprocity" model is the only one that can work and has worked. Guerrilla warfare between the two branches can only be disastrous. Their arguments for a balanced presidential–congressional relationship are spelled out in the final selection in this chapter, "Toward a Theory of Congressional–Executive Relations."

26. The President as Legislative Leader*

EDWARD S. CORWIN

The revival of presidential leadership in legislation is one phase of the revival of legislation of national scope. Sir Henry Maine's assertion that "the energy of legislatures is the prime characteristic of modern societies" is now nearly a century old, but it is only within the last seventy years that the activities of Congress have brought it notable confirmation. The Reconstruction Era was marked by an outpouring of legislation volcanic in volume and violence as well as in the suddenness with which it came to an end. The succeeding period was dominated by the gospel of *laissez faire,* that government, except when it has favors to confer, had best refrain from meddling in the economic field—doctrine reinforced for the national government by a rigidly conceptualistic constitutional law.

But gradually a new point of view emerged, the increasing influence of which appears especially in the history of congressional legislation touching interstate commerce. I quote from Professor Ribble's volume on *State and National Power over Commerce:*

> Before 1887 there were but few statutes of material importance regulating the conduct of the inland commerce of the United States. Such statutes as existed dealt chiefly with bridges, the improvement of rivers and harbors, and general admiralty regulations. . . .
>
> This record is in sharp contrast with Congressional activity in succeeding years.

To show an awakened Congress, it is sufficient to recite some of the more important statutes following the Interstate Commerce Act of 1887. Thus mention may be made of the following pieces of federal legislation dealing with commerce; Labor Arbitration Act of 1888; Sherman Anti-Trust Act of 1890; Federal Safety Appliance Acts, beginning with that of 1893; Erdman Act of 1898; Elkins Act of 1903; Federal Employers' Liability Law of 1906; Hepburn Act of 1906; Federal Hours of Labor Law of 1907; Federal Employers' Liability Act of 1908; Mann-Elkins Act of 1910; Panama Canal Act of 1912; Newlands Act of 1913; Cotton Futures Act of 1914; Federal Trade Commission Act of 1914; Clayton Act of 1914; Adamson Act of 1916; the Transportation Act of 1920; Packers and Stockyards Act of 1921; Grain Futures Act of 1922; Air Commerce Act of 1926; Railway Labor Act of 1926; Radio Act of 1927; Longshoremen's and Harbor Workers' Compensation Act of 1927; Hawes-Cooper Act, 1929; Perishable Agricultural Commodities Act of 1930; Emergency Railroad Transportation Act of 1933; Agricultural Adjustment Act of 1933; National Industrial Recovery Act, 1933; Communications Act of 1934; Cotton Marketing Act of 1934; Act of 1934, prohibiting the moving in interstate commerce after the commission of certain specified crimes; National Stolen Property Act of 1934; Securities Exchange Act of 1934; National Labor Relations Act of 1935; Interstate Transportation of Petroleum Act of 1935; the Guffey-Snyder Coal Act of 1935; the Railroad Reorganization Act of 1935.

*Source: From The President: Office and Powers, 1787-1957 by Edward S. Corwin. New York: New York University Press, 1957. Copyright © 1957 by New York University Press, Inc. Reprinted by permission. Selection has been retitled and originally appeared as Chapter 7, "Legislative Leader and 'Institution.'" Footnotes omitted.

This list was compiled in 1937. Today, without sticking too closely to the "commerce" clause, I should wish to add mention to the act establishing TVA in 1933, the Social Security Act of 1935, the Agricultural Adjustment Act of 1938, and the Fair Labor Standards Act of the same year, to say nothing of the host of emergency acts that the great international crises leading to and involving our participation in the two world wars evoked.

The nationalization of American industry, the necessity of curbing monopolistic practices resulting from this development, the conservation movement of the first Roosevelt, the rise and consolidation of the labor movement, the altered outlook on the proper scope of governmental function that the Great Depression produced, and finally two great wars and their aftermath have all conspired to thrust into the foreground of our constitutional system the dual role of the president as catalyst of public opinion and as legislative leader.

THE CONSTITUTIONAL BASIS AND "MODUS OPERANDI" OF PRESIDENTIAL LEADERSHIP—FROM ROOSEVELT I TO ROOSEVELT II

The formal taking-off ground of presidential leadership in legislation is furnished by the opening clause of Article II, section 3, of the Constitution: "He shall from time to time give to the Congress information of the state of the Union, and recommend to their consideration such measures as he shall judge necessary and expedient. . . ." Although this language imposes a *duty* rather than confers a *power*, presidents are apt to be like other people who feel they have a duty to perform: they can make themselves extremely importunate at times. Is there any constitutional reason why they should not do so in the present instance? Many persons, including several presidents, have argued at times that there is an excellent reason; namely,

that the Constitution vests the legislative power in *Congress,* and that therefore performance by the president of the duty named ought to stop well short of invading Congress's "autonomy," an argument usually bolstered by an invocation of the principle of the Separation of Powers.

. . . The present-day role of the president as policy determiner in the legislative field is largely the creation of the two Roosevelts and Woodrow Wilson, each of whom came to the presidency following a notable and successful experience as governor of his home state. Discussing his governorship of New York in his *Autobiography,* the first Roosevelt remarks:

> In theory the Executive has nothing to do with legislation. In practice as things now are, the Executive is or ought to be peculiarly representative of the people as a whole. As often as not the action of the Executive offers the only means by which the people can get the legislation they demand and ought to have. Therefore a good executive under the present conditions of American political life must take a very active interest in getting the right kind of legislation, in addition to performing his executive duties with an eye single to the public welfare.

As these words indicate, Roosevelt I's approach to the problem of executive leadership, while positive, was otherwise Jacksonian rather than Jeffersonian; but he enjoyed advantages not available to his predecessor, certainly not in the same measure. One of these was a quite personal gift. No more convinced preacher of the Eternal Verities, none more adept at translating his preferences into moralistic axioms and attitudes, ever attained the presidency. In his own words, "The White House is a bully pulpit"; and not only the White House, but the country-wide press as well. T.R. had access to the news columns of not only those hundreds of papers that supported him editorially, but also of those other hundreds that opposed him. In part this was the result of clever contriving. The Sunday news release, it was early found, was always sure of making the first page in Monday's otherwise usually drab issue. More largely it was the general result of good all-round showmanship. What T.R. did was always interesting, or at least the correspondents came to think it was.

The difficulties that Roosevelt I encountered in building up the legislative role of the president were nevertheless formidable. Foremost of these was the internal organization of the houses of Congress. The committee system was vastly more extended and more closely knit than in Jackson's time, and its governing principle was that of seniority. Therefore, although Congress was in the hands of Roosevelt's own party, its immediate direction was in the hands of the older and more conservative members, men who on the score of experience alone were disposed to regard the temporary occupant of the White House with a certain condescension. And aggravating this situation were the defects of T.R.'s personal qualities of combative assertiveness, impulsiveness, and habit of drastic criticism of any who opposed his purposes at the moment. Commenting in his *Autobiography* on his relations with the principal congressional leaders of the period—Senators Aldrich and Hale and Speaker Cannon— Roosevelt wrote:

I made a resolute effort to get on with all three and with their followers, and I have no question that they made an equally resolute effort to get on with me. We succeeded in working together, although with increasing friction, for some years, I pushing forward and they hanging back. Gradually, however, I was forced to abandon the effort to persuade them to come my way, and then I achieved results only by appealing over the heads of the Senate and House leaders to the people, who were the masters of both of us.

These words are at once an avowal and a confession. For while resort to Jacksonian methods undoubtedly suited Roosevelt's boisterous temperament, yet

the drawbacks to such methods are serious. As Dr. Small puts it:

Unless an Executive be willing to jeopardize his chances of securing the adoption of his remaining recommendations, it is inadvisable to risk an appeal on a single issue; for though he may be successful in his attempt, his conduct is likely to rekindle even more intensely a spirit of resentment in Congress and to confirm it in its resolve to combat his leadership. Moreover, if the public fail to honor his petition . . . the President has thus by his own hand prematurely terminated his ascendancy. . . . An harmonious cooperation between Executive and Legislature in which the former aspires to the role of an uncompromising leader is usually [usually?] tenuous; and, when congressional leaders subsequently rebel against the abridgment of their freedom of discretion, the President has no alternative other than to revert to certain threats of coercion in order to achieve the acceptance of his program.

These words, though written with Wilson's abortive appeal in October 1918 for a Democratic Congress in mind, are more appropriately applicable to the closing chapter of T.R.'s dealings with Congress. They are also descriptive of certain more recent happenings.

Although destined to be cast somewhat in the shade by subsequent achievements in the same field, the first Roosevelt's legislative performance was notable; and his contributions to the technique of presidential leadership were not only contemporaneously impressive but also durable. Detailing the "arts of management" by which "Roosevelt, Taft and Wilson," Roosevelt leading the way, "pushed their suggestions to a legislative conclusion," Professor Finer writes:

They sent messages to the Houses, and letters to party friends; held conferences and breakfasts in their rooms adjoining the Senate, and invited the Chairmen of Committees and the "floor leaders" to the White House. Their most trusted and astute Cabinet officers were often sent to the Congressional lobbies to whip up support, and to exert the influence of personal representation of the President. Heads of departments attended caucus meetings; information was poured into Congress; party friends were provided with drafts of bills and the vindicating briefs.

It is the last of these devices that is of special interest from the constitutional point of view. Bills were not yet sent openly from the White House to the Capitol in those days, but T.R.'s congressional spokesmen nevertheless admitted the practice occasionally. Said Senator Dolliver of Iowa at the time the Senate was debating the Hepburn bill for amending the Interstate Commerce Act: "There are at least five acts of legislation, all of them referring to this and similar questions, that were put through both Houses of Congress in the last five years practically without changes, as they came from the office of the Attorney General of the United States"; and a few weeks later it was admitted on the floor of the House that the then pending Pure Food and Drug bill was of similar provenience.

One trick T.R. missed, probably to his own considerable chagrin later. He retained the outworn and overgrown "annual message," even greatly distending it. It is true that he made the message a vehicle to Congress and the country of his legislative demands in a way not previously surpassed. Yet interlarded in a scissors-and-paste compilation from departmental reports that ran at times to nearly thirty thousand words, these naturally failed of full effectiveness. Woodrow Wilson was to demonstrate how much better the thing could be done.

Wilson, adding his observation of Roosevelt's successes and failures to his studies of British constitutional practice, had conceived by 1908 the idea that it was possible to remodel the presidency somewhat after the pattern of the British premiership. For the first time in its history the United States had a president who knew something about the functioning of political institutions abroad, and who had the intellect and skill to apply his knowledge to the stimulation and enrichment of the political process

in this country. A Jeffersonian in his acceptance of the legislative power as the supreme directing power in a popular government, Wilson rejected unconditionally Jefferson's conception of the Separation of Powers doctrine and boldly proclaimed his constitutional right and duty as executive to guide the legislative process. The similar pretensions of Roosevelt I were divested of their accidental association with the latter's picturesque traits of personality and endowed with the authority of constitutional principle.

Nor was this the only advantage that "the Schoolmaster President" enjoyed over his more "practical" forerunner. For one thing Wilson's party had been out of power for two decades. Consequently he was not compelled as Roosevelt had been to combat or else come to terms with an experienced and sophisticated leadership in the houses of Congress. On the contrary, Wilson's party associates were almost naively ready to concede his intellectual eminence, just as Jefferson's had been more than a century earlier. Best of all, Wilson had the inspiration to dramatize his conception of legislative leadership in a fashion that henceforth put all potential critics of it on the defensive.

This noteworthy event in the history of American governmental usage occurred on April 8, 1913, when the new president appeared before a special session of the 63rd Congress to demand a new tariff act. A memorable passage of his address on this occasion reads:

> I am very glad indeed to have this opportunity to address the two houses directly, and to verify for myself the impression that the president of the United States is a person, not a mere department of the government hailing Congress from some isolated island of jealous power, sending messages, and not speaking naturally and with his own voice, that he is a human being trying to cooperate with other human beings in a common service. After this first experience I shall feel quite normal in all our dealings with one another.

As Wilson gleefully commented at the

time, his predecessor's chagrin on learning of this performance could well be imagined: why had he never thought that one up?

On June 23 Mr. Wilson appeared a second time before the special session to urge it to attack the problem of currency reform. The closing words of this address too are noteworthy for their statement of Wilson's president-prime minister conception:

> I have come to you as the head of the government and the responsible leader of the party in power to urge action now, while there is time to serve the country deliberately, and as we should, in a clear air of common counsel.

The measure finally passed in response to this call to duty, the Federal Reserve Act of December 23, 1913, was largely drafted in conferences at the White House between the president and representatives of all shades of opinion, some quite sharply antagonistic to Mr. Wilson's views. It was then ratified by the Democratic caucus, and so made an obligatory party measure. Its later progress through Congress was greatly aided by Mr. Bryan, whom Mr. Wilson had made a member of his cabinet with just such services in contemplation.

When the European war loomed on the horizon in the summer of 1914 Mr. Wilson is reported to have remarked that it would be "the irony of fate" if his energies as president were to be diverted to problems of foreign relationship, whereas his training had been intended for a very different purpose. In point of fact, not only did the legislative output of Congress during the ensuing two years continue to testify to his strong guidance of its activities, but our own entrance into war in 1917 enabled him to rivet the principle of presidential leadership to the working Constitution of the United States in a way that the demands of domestic reform could hardly have done at that date.

The clash with the Senate mentioned on an earlier page, shortly before our entrance into the First World War, over the question of arming American merchant vessels afforded the president an opportunity to display to Congress the advantage over that body that would be his during a war emergency. For, having failed to get Congress's consent to the proposed step, he took it anyway, in exercise, as he declared, of his "constitutional powers and duties." At the same time he denounced "the Senate of the United States" as "the only legislative body in the world which cannot act when the majority is ready for action." He continued:

> . . . A little group of willful men, representing no opinion but their own, have rendered the great Government of the United States helpless and contemptible.
>
> The remedy? There is but one remedy. The only remedy is that the rules of the Senate shall be so altered that it can act. The country can be relied upon to draw the moral. I believe that the Senate can be relied on to supply the means of action and save the country from disaster.

I return presently to the subject of the filibuster.

Most, if not all, of the principal war statutes, from the Selective Service Act of June 5, 1917 to the Overman Act, which, after being before the Senate eighty-three days, was finally passed by that body April 29, 1918, were drafted in the first instance—at times none too skillfully—in an executive department, and a head of department was generally told off to facilitate the passage of the bill through the purifying flames of the congressional purgatory. From the very nature of the case, moreover, the houses were compelled to devote a good portion of their working hours and energies to the consideration of "administration measures," as they were termed. The situation was summed up at the time by a writer in *The New Republic* in these words:

> The private individual of Congress is dead, and it is surely important that there is none to sing his requiem. The traditional separation of powers has broken down for the simple reason that it results only in confounding them. Congress may delay

presidential action; but there is evidence enough, even apart from the fact of war, that it is finding it increasingly difficult ultimately to thwart it. For congressional debate has largely ceased to influence the character of public opinion. . . . Nor is the individual member of Congress alone in his eclipse. The congressional committees have become less the moulders of legislation than the recipients who may alter its details. Even on the committees themselves the administration now has its avowed spokesmen. They seem to act very much as a British minister in charge of a measure in the House of Commons. They interpret the executive will; and we have seen recalcitrant members interviewed on policy by the President himself. The key to the whole, in fact, has come to lie in the President's hands. The pathway of decision is his own, influenced above all by his personal cast of mind and by the few who can obtain direct access to him. This is not, it is clear, the government envisaged by the Constitution. Equally certain it is not a government which meets with the approval of Congress. But outside of Washington, the old suspicion of executive power is dead, and popular sentiment has become so entirely uninterested in the processes of politics as to ask for substantial results. In such an aspect, executive action is far more valuably dramatic than the action of Congress.

The picture is somewhat exaggerated; but the thing itself was exaggerated by all previous standards, and the war being ended, some degree of reaction to earlier, conventional views of the relations of president and Congress was to be expected. The really surprising thing is that the reaction was so slight. Candidate Harding announced that while as president he would recommend a program, as the Constitution required him to do, legislation would be the work of Congress; but there is good reason to believe that he later regretted the promise thus implied. His ultimate failure to lead was apparently due much less to lack of willingness than of will. Although to Mr. Coolidge's ingrained conservatism legislation was in itself thoroughly distasteful, he nevertheless asserted it to be "the business of the president as party leader to do the best he can to see that the declared party platform purposes are translated into legislative and administrative action." Mr. Hoover was rather less articulate regarding his views on the subject, but according to Mr. Luce, an excellent authority, "he sent drafts of several important proposals to the Capitol to be introduced by leaders." And thanks to his inaction at the time of framing the Hawley-Smoot Tariff, he had in retrospect the doubtful satisfaction of being responsible for that egregious exemplification of the gospel of hands-off.

ROOSEVELT II AND CONGRESS—THE LAW OF EBB AND FLOW

While President Franklin D. Roosevelt's accomplishment as legislator first and last surpassed all previous records, yet the story of it, so far as it is of interest to us, offers little of novelty. Old techniques were sharpened and improved, sometimes with the aid of modern gadgets—for example, radio. But for the most part, except for the dimensions that the familiar sometimes attains, the pleasure afforded by study of it is that of recognition rather than of surprise.

First of all we perceive again the immense reinforcement that recognized "emergency" is capable of bringing to presidential leadership in this field of power as well as in others. For, confronted with such a condition, Congress feels at once the need for action and its inability to plan the action needed; therefore it turns to the president. Contrariwise, once the pressure for action lessens, congressional docility speedily evaporates. Casting a backward glance in his first annual address to Congress on the remarkable performance of the 73rd Congress in its first session, F.D.R. said:

A final personal word. I know that each of you will appreciate that I am speaking no mere politeness when I assure you how much I value the fine relationship that we have shared during these months of hard and incessant work. Out of these friendly contacts we are, fortunately, building a strong and permanent tie between the legislative and executive branches of the Government. The letter of the Constitution wisely declared a separation, but the impulse of common purpose declares a union. In this spirit we join once more in serving the American people.

In point of fact, the "strong and permanent tie" revealed even then to close observation several signs of fraying, and these rapidly became more generally evident.

Secondly, the late president's experience illustrates once more the aid a president can derive from an active and widespread popular understanding of an announced program and from interest in his political good fortunes, a fact of which from the first he evinced constant awareness both in utterance and in practice. Within a few days of his first election Mr. Roosevelt had taken occasion to formulate his conception of the presidency at some length. He said:

> The Presidency is not merely an administrative office. That is the least of it. It is pre-eminently a place of moral leadership.
>
> All of our great Presidents were leaders of thought at times when certain historic ideas in the life of the nation had to be clarified. Washington personified the idea of Federal Union. Jefferson practically originated the party system as we know it by opposing the democratic theory to the republicanism of Hamilton. This theory was reaffirmed by Jackson.
>
> Two great principles of our government were forever put beyond question by Lincoln. Cleveland, coming into office following an era of great political corruption, typified rugged honesty. Theodore Roosevelt and Wilson were both moral leaders, each in his own way and for his own time, who used the Presidency as a pulpit.
>
> That is what the office is—a superb opportunity for reapplying, applying to new conditions, the simple rules of human conduct to which we always go back. Without leadership alert and sensitive to

change, we are bogged up or lose our way.

Aside from the anachronistic attempt to foist upon Jefferson a preference for the word "democratic" over "republican" as descriptive of his creed, there is little of originality here—indeed, except for the complimentary references to Jefferson and Wilson, one might easily parallel the passage from the writings of Roosevelt I. Roosevelt II's assiduity in reducing his philosophy to practical form has, however, never been surpassed. T.R. traveled widely, but not nearly so widely as his relative, who by the time of his re-election in November 1936 had journeyed nearly 83,000 miles by train, and undetermined thousands by automobile, and had visited all but three states of the Union. T.R.'s relations with the press were excellent, but the press was not yet represented at Washington on its later scale, nor was the newspaper columnist the power in the land he has since become. By his liberal employment of off-the-record remarks F.D.R. flattered the newspaperman's sense of honor, while by handing out background information he guaranteed the semiweekly story that spelt for the latter butter and jam for his daily bread; and by both devices he assured publicity for an intelligent, if not always sympathetic, version of presidential policies. Nor did Mr. Roosevelt's suavity, genial and impenetrable, often desert him in his conferences with the press's representatives until toward the end of his second term, when he suddenly developed considerable sensitiveness to being quizzed as to his intentions about running again; and whereas T.R.'s famous Ananias Club came finally to be the best-covered organization in the country, F.D.R. appears to have found it necessary to resort to the "short and ugly" only once. And in the radio Mr. Roosevelt possessed an instrument that enabled him to bring his views to the immediate attention of millions of voters and to invite their response, which, as registered in the suddenly mounting White House mail, soon became prodigious.

In the third place, however, before the dispersed energies of popular support can generate legislative current they must, of course, be adjusted to the organization and procedures of Congress. In the endeavor to accomplish this Mr. Roosevelt relied on the well-timed special message. To the 73rd Congress nearly thirty such communications went; to the 74th about half that number; to the 75th something like seventy; and during the war years the same tactic was continued. Some of these communications merely drew attention in general terms to the need for legislation on a particular subject; others contained specific recommendations as to the content of the needed legislation; a few were accompanied by draft bills to which Congress's attention was definitely directed; the "economy message" of March 9, 1933, the message of March 16 of the same year that led to the first AAA, the message of May 17 that led to the NRA, and—later—the Court Reform message of February 5, 1937, all belonged to this category, as did also the famous H.R. 1776, which became in due course the Lend-Lease Act. But other important measures, especially during Mr. Roosevelt's first term, were also modeled in the first instance by administration draftsmen—the act establishing TVA, the hard-fought Holding Company Act, and the Social Security Act being outstanding illustrations. And more formal communications were frequently followed by letters to committee chairmen or even to private members.

In the fourth place, Mr. Roosevelt's experience underscores a lesson to be drawn also from that of the first Roosevelt and of Woodrow Wilson, that presidential leadership is subject to a law of ebb and flow, or, as Professor Laski suggests, a "law of honeymoon." The remarkable achievement of the 73rd Congress bespoke almost continuous presidential stimulation and direc-

tion and equally continuous congressional response. The first session of the 74th Congress, on the other hand, convened amid cries of "dictatorship," and some of the most raucous voices were of Mr. Roosevelt's own party. The principal policymaking legislation of the session comprised the Wagner National Labor Relations Act and the Social Security Act. While the former, named for its author, represented legislative initiative and presidential sponsorship, the latter was largely the handiwork of the president's own Committee on Economic Security, consisting of the secretaries of the treasury, agriculture, and labor, the attorney general, and the federal emergency relief administrator. Although there were times in the course of the session when it was predicted that the president's leadership had been broken, the final outcome refuted the Cassandras.

On its face the election of 1936 was a tremendous endorsement of the New Deal and hence of the methods of leadership by which it had been set up. ("Who wishes the end wishes the means.") The opening session of the 75th Congress witnessed nevertheless a definite crisis in the president's relations with that body, one largely of Mr. Roosevelt's own creation. For whatever else may be said of his startling and practically unheralded Court Reform message, it produced at a single stroke a serious cleavage in both his popular and his party support, and in so doing afforded his congressional critics a powerful handle for their accumulated discontents. Although special messages were never showered on Congress more lavishly, the legislative product of the 75th Congress was chiefly by way of repairing the breaches that successive Supreme Court decisions hade made in the New Deal; and final adjournment was followed by an attempt by the president, which proved unrewarding for the most part, to "purge" Congress of certain nonresponsive members of the Democratic party. The 76th Congress, with an increased representation of the Republican opposition, speedily disclosed a renewed independence on its part, evidenced in its first session by the enactment, despite many covert frowns from administration circles, of the first Hatch Act for the political sterilization of federal officeholders, by its drastic curtailment of the president's proposals for administrative reorganization, and by the refusal of the Senate Foreign Relations Committee to report out a presidentially sponsored measure to modify the Neutrality Act.

The first session of the 76th Congress marked, in fact, the low point up to that time of F.D.R.'s hold on Congress. But with Hitler's invasion of Poland the ebb in the president's influence with the legislative branch began to slacken; and following the fall of France, the bombing of London in the summer and autumn of 1940, and the November election, it was sharply reversed. The enactment of Lend-Lease in March 1941 advertised the new situation, which was nine months later brought to culmination by the Japanese attack on Pearl Harbor. But once again there came a recession in presidential influence, even in the midst of war. In April 1943 Congress, against the president's vehement protest, repealed his order setting a $25,000 limit to salaries; in June it enacted over his veto the War Labor Disputes Act; throughout the year it rebuffed repeated attempts by the administration to sequester further legislative powers through a third War Powers Act. Nor did F.D.R.'s perfervid plea early in January 1944 meet any better reception. The climax came a month later when Mr. Roosevelt for the first time in the nation's history vetoed a revenue bill and added insult to injury by the contumelious terms in which he couched his veto message. Thereupon ensued one of the most remarkable scenes ever enacted in the Senate, when administration floor leader Barkley declared, with tears streaming from his eyes, that he "did not propose to take this unjustifiable assault lying down." When the day following Mr. Barkley resigned his post as floor leader to the Democratic caucus and was promptly re-elected by acclamation, it was made plain to all that a serious rift existed between the president and his party support in Congress, one not to be repaired by soothing words from the presidential desk to "Dear Alben." Even the president's re-election for a fourth term in November did not improve matters noticeably. Hardly had the 79th Congress convened for its first session when it became clear that "the law of honeymoon" was no longer in operation. The president's death on April 12 brought to a close a constantly renewed feud of more than two years' duration with Congresses in which his own party was in the majority.

Finally, passing reference must be made to a factor of latterday presidential leadership that, although by no means totally novel when Mr. Roosevelt assumed office, became so in effect in view of the dimensions it attained under him. I mean F.D.R.'s consistent championship of the demands of certain groups, especially agriculture and labor. Congressional legislation meant to promote the general welfare via the welfare of particular groups is as old as Congress itself. The element of novelty presented by the New Deal legislation in this respect is furnished by the *size, permanency, and voting strength of the groups served by it.* One of the principal arguments for representative government has been that it assures the responsibility of the governors of society by imposing on them the constant necessity of obtaining a fresh consensus. But when a powerful pressure group or combination of groups furnishes the core of a legislative majority, their easy maneuverability in respect of issues that do not touch their own central interest renders easy the descent into "government by bloc and by blackmail." Not to give the thought too fine a point, a president with a modicum of horse-trading sense will always be able to buy the support of expectant interest groups for policies as to which they have no policy; and what president ever failed to identify his own and his party's political prosperity with the general welfare? At least, such presidents have been few and far between.

ANCILLARY WEAPONS OF PRESIDENTIAL LEADERSHIP—THE VETO POWER

We recur to the constitutional document, and first of all to Article I, section 7, paragraphs 2 and 3, dealing with the "veto power." They read as follows:

Every bill which shall have passed the House of Representatives and the Senate shall, before it become a law, be presented to the President of the United States; if he approve he shall sign it, but if not he shall return it, with his objections, to that house in which it shall have originated, who shall enter the objections at large on their journal and proceed to reconsider it. If after such reconsideration, two-thirds of that house shall agree to pass the bill, it shall be sent, together with the objections, to the other house, by which it shall likewise be reconsidered, and if approved by two-thirds of that house it shall become a law. But in all such cases the votes of both houses shall be determined by yeas and nays, and the names of the persons voting for and against the bill shall be entered on the journal of each house respectively. If any bill shall not be returned by the President within ten days (Sundays excepted) after it shall have been presented to him, the same shall be a law, in like manner as if he had signed it, unless the Congress by their adjournment prevent its return, in which case it shall not be a law.

Every order, resolution or vote to which the concurrence of the Senate and House of Representatives may be necessary (except on a question of adjournment) shall be presented to the President of the United States; and before the same shall take effect, shall be approved by him, or being disapproved by him, shall be repassed by two-thirds of the Senate and House of Representatives, according to the rules and limitations prescribed in the case of a bill.

This ingredient of presidential prerogative is to be accounted for in part by the mistaken belief, derived from Blackstone, that the king's veto was a still vital element of the British constitution, although in fact in 1787 it had not been employed for almost eighty years. Much more is the president's veto to be ascribed to the general conviction of the framers that without some such defense against the legislature the executive would soon be "sunk into nonexistence." But what form was the veto to assume? Was it to be absolute or qualified? If the latter, by what vote ought the houses of Congress to be enabled to override it? And was the president to exercise it alone or in association with a Council of Revision, comprising also "a convenient number of the national judiciary"? The first question was speedily answered; but the convention vacillated almost to the hour of its adjournment between requiring a two-thirds and a three-quarters vote in both houses for overriding a veto; and only a little less pertinacious were the champions of the Council of Revision proposal. The final rejection of this idea, in leaving the president his own sole master in this field of power, was a decision of first importance.

Naturally the veto power did not escape the early talent of Americans for conjuring up constitutional limitations out of thin air. The veto was solely a self-defensive weapon of the president; it was the means furnished him for carrying out his oath to "preserve, protect and defend the Constitution" and was not validly usable for any other purpose; it did not extend to revenue bills, never having been so employed by the king of England; it did not extend to "insignificant and trivial" matters like private pension bills; it was never intended to give effect merely to presidential desires, but its use must rest on considerations of great weight, and so on and so forth. Although efforts of this sort to forge shackles for the power derived a certain specious plausibility from the rarity of the veto's use in English history, they met with failure from the first. Washington exercised the power twice, once on constitutional grounds, once on grounds of expediency. Neither Adams nor Jefferson exercised it at all. Of Madison's six vetoes four urged constitutional objections to the measure involved, two objections of policy. Summing the matter up for the first century under the Constitution, the leading authority on the subject says:

From Jackson's administration to the Civil War vetoes on grounds of expediency became more frequent, but they were still in a decided minority. Since the [Civil] War constitutional arguments in a veto message have been almost unknown.

The latter statement applies moreover equally to more recent years, if exception be made for one or two vetoes by Presidents Taft and Coolidge, both of whom had a special penchant for constitutional niceties. The notion that revenue bills are not subject to veto was punctured by Mr. Roosevelt's veto of February 22, 1944, mentioned a moment ago, although the veto in question was overridden. The precedent thus set was clinched by President Truman on June 16, 1947, and this time the veto stuck.

Nor have attacks on the veto via the amending process fared any better. In 1818 and once or twice later exasperated congressmen have even proposed that the president be entirely stripped of the power, but their efforts were stalled at the first parliamentary hurdles. Proposals to supersede the requirement of a two-thirds vote in each house for overriding the veto with a simple majority vote have been more numerous but no more successful. On the other hand, several dozen amendments have been offered since 1873 to give the president what is sometimes termed the "selective veto," which would enable him to veto parts of an enactment and approve the rest. A suggested device for obtaining much the same end by ordinary legislation will be mentioned in a moment.

Finally, the Court has within recent years shown itself generally diligent to repel all constitutional sophistries whereby the practical availability of the power might have been curtailed. Bills passed within ten days of the end of a session may be kept from becoming laws by the "pocket veto," that is, by the president's failing to return them till an adjournment of Congress has intervened; nor does it make any difference that the adjournment was not a final one for the Congress that passed the bill, but a merely ad interim one between sessions. Also, the president may return a bill with his objections to the house of its origin via a duly authorized officer thereof while it is in temporary recess in accordance with Article I, section 5, paragraph 4—a holding, however, that still leaves it open to either house to fail to provide the duly authorized officer. It would have been better perhaps to hold, as Justice Stone suggested, that neither house acting separately can adjourn so as to prevent a return by the president of his objections to a measure without thereby decapitating the measure. Again, the Court has held that the president may effectively sign a bill at any time within ten calendar days of its presentation to him, Sundays excepted, even though Congress has meantime adjourned, and whether finally or for the session. But here again a criticism should be noted, for the Court's assertion in the course of its opinion that the ten-day limitation applies to the president's power to approve as well as to his power to disapprove is not borne out by the words of the constitutional clause. The Court seems to be going rather out of its way to supply an omission of the Constitution.

And its further statement in this same opinion that "an incoming president, to whom a bill has not been presented by the Congress, cannot approve it" is more or less of this sort. Let us suppose that a new Congress meets, in accordance with the Twentieth Amendment, on January 3 and that a new president takes office on January 20, and suppose also that Congress passes a bill on, say January 13 and presents it to the outgoing president, who fails to sign it before leaving office. His successor, by the dictum cited, would not be entitled to sign the measure. Yet suppose that he was his own successor, what would be the rule then? Or suppose that a president died while still considering a bill: could the succeeding vice-president sign effectively? I see no reason why the legislative process should be stalled in any of these situations. Formerly, it is true, the death of the British monarch involved the dissolution of Parliament, since Parliament meets on his personal summons; but this usage, which was abolished by statute in 1867, obviously furnishes no guidance for practice under the Constitution.

To turn again to the words of the Constitution: The fact that the president has ten days from *presentation* rather than passage in which to disapprove bills makes it possible for him today to visit the remotest quarters of the globe without relaxing this control over Congress. Furthermore, by withholding their signatures from bills that have passed the houses the presiding officers of those bodies can lengthen the period between the actual passage of a measure and its presentation to an absent president, so that on his return he will not be swamped with such measures. By an extraordinary series of accidents, helped out by some contriving, the late President Roosevelt was enabled, on July 13, 1936 to sign a bill no fewer than twenty-three days after the adjournment of Congress.

In fact, Mr. Roosevelt appears to have broken all records in this field of presidential endeavor as in several others. "The Roosevelt disapprovals," said a writer at the close of F.D.R.'s second term,

> represent over 30 percent of the total measures disapproved since 1792, when the veto was first used (505 out of 1,635).

The messaged vetoes have been nearly 30 percent of the total returned measures inviting congressional action (262 out of 901). The pocketed measures, with or without comment, have been over 33 percent of the total pocket vetoes (243 out of 734). The combined disapprovals of Grover Cleveland and Franklin D. Roosevelt represent two-thirds of the total disapproved measures of all veto presidents. The combined messaged vetoes total over 67 percent of all messaged vetoes; the combined pocket vetoes total over 65 percent of all pocketed measures. These two executives may justly be rated as our outstanding veto presidents.

In contrast to Cleveland, who devoted his unfavorable attention to pension, military, and naval relief measures, the range of subjects drawing the adverse action of Roosevelt has been as wide as the activity of Congress. Nothing too large or too small has escaped the penetrating eye of the President and his advisers. The following indicate that range of vision: agricultural relief, general appropriations, adjusted service compensation for World War veterans, interstate commerce, alien deportation, judicial review of administrative tribunals, flood control, protection of fisheries, homestead administration, Indian relief, tax and tariff policy, national defense, Philippine independence, Memorial Day observance, cemetery approaches, shorthand reporting, homing pigeons, District of Columbia street designations, parking meters, credit for beer wholesalers, control of funerals, and the exemption of religious periodicals.

As to the actual effectiveness of the president's veto as a check on Congress the testimony of statistics is conclusive. Between the first inauguration of George Washington and the second inauguration of Franklin D. Roosevelt 750 measures were vetoed, of which 483 were private bills. Of these 750 vetoes only 49 were overridden, 6 being vetoes of private bills. That is to say, 16 percent of vetoes of public bills were overridden and 1 percent plus of vetoes of private bills. Nor does this take account of the fact that 15 of the 43 overridden vetoes of public bills occurred during the vendetta between Andrew Johnson and Congress; nor yet of pocket vetoes, of which some 330 have been uncovered for the period from 1789 to 1936. Later statistics conform substantially to this pattern. Altogether, it seems just to say that the president's veto is normally effective in nine cases out of ten.

Moreover, the president's veto is not always a mere negative; it is at times a *positive* instrument of his legislative leadership. As Professor Finer has put it:

> It would be no wonder if the veto power were not only discriminatory among bills already passed, but if it became an ever-present, if unuttered, threat to promoters of bills (unless they were quite certain of a two-thirds majority in the ultimate resort), and tended to become an instrument of bargaining for other legislation—an instrument to be propitiated by timely and obvious surrenders. This, indeed, has happened.

On the other hand, it is plain that a certain incompatibility exists at times between the president's possession of the veto power and his duty to "take care that the laws be faithfully executed." This was illustrated recently when President Truman felt it incumbent on him to assure the country that he would "carry out his constitutional duty and administer" the Taft-Hartly Act, his ineffective veto of which he had accompanied with a bitter excoriation of the measure as "unworkable" and likely to "do serious harm to the country." . . . enforcement of the laws, far from being a purely mechanical business, frequently involves the application of broad interpretative powers, which of course may be exercised sympathetically from the point of view of Congress's purpose in enacting a particular statute or quite otherwise.

Likewise, certain recent happenings remind us that the obverse of the President's veto is his power to affix his signature to congressional measures of which he approves. Does such approval have to be unqualified or may it be qualified? The question is raised by President Truman's action in accom-

panying his approval on July 3, 1946 of the so-called Hobbs Anti-Racketeering Act of July 3, 1946 with a message purporting to construe certain of its supposedly ambiguous or doubtful provisions—a performance repeated on May 14, 1947, in approving the Portal-to-Portal Act.

Commenting in his column on this probably unprecedented course of the president, Mr. Krock said:

> Usually, when acts of Congress are disputed in the courts, judgment is based on what the judges interpret from the record as the meaning of Congress. But usually this record consists of hearings before the committees which drafted the laws, reports by these committees and the bi-cameral conferences, and the floor debates. If, however, a court test shall be made of the meaning of the Hobbs and portal-to-portal bills, and their effect on other statutes, the President's interpretation of what he believes he signed will become an essential part of that record.

I strongly demur. There is a vast difference between the assumption that Congress's purpose in passing a bill can be gleaned from a study of reports, etc., that Congress had before it while the measure was under consideration and, on the other hand, the assumption that similar light can be obtained from the study of a presidential message that followed the measure's passage by the houses. Equally obvious is it that an act of Congress gets its intention from the houses, in which the Constitution specifically vests "all legislative powers herein granted." For a court to vary its interpretation of an act of Congress in deference to something said by the president at the time of signing it would be to attribute to the latter the power to foist upon the houses intentions that they never entertained, and thereby to endow him with a legislative power not shared by Congress.

I return for a moment to the item veto. As was mentioned above, proposals to amend the Constitution in this respect have been repeatedly offered in Congress, but have never got far along the legislative delivery belt. It was suggested in 1938 that the desired result could be achieved by the simple device of incorporating in appropriation bills a provision modeled on that which appears today in the Reorganization Act of 1939. Thus the president would be authorized to eliminate or reduce specific items of an appropriation, and his orders to that end would become effective unless the houses disallowed them within a stipulated period by concurrent resolution. Although accepted by the House as an amendment to the Independent Offices Appropriation bill of 1938, the proposal failed in the Senate, and a like proposal met the same fate in 1942. I find persuasive, I own, the argument that this reform would require a constitutional amendment.

Of the two remaining factors of the president's participation in legislation, so far as it has direct constitutional basis, his power in case of disagreement between the houses with respect to adjournment to "adjourn them to such time and place as he shall think proper" and his power to convene either or both houses on "extraordinary occasions" may be dealt with very briefly. The former meager remnant of the British monarch's power to prorogue Parliament has never been used, although Andrew Jackson once thought it worth while to pen a veto in its behalf; and in the event of an atom bomb attack it might even today come in handy as to "place." The latter power, contrariwise, has been used so often that the word "extraordinary" in the constitutional clause has taken on a decidedly Pickwickian flavor. Today in common parlance "extraordinary" sessions are simply "extra" or "special" sessions. Conversely, there have been a few really extraordinary occasions when the president in power has disappointed expectations by not summoning Congress. Lincoln did this at the outset of his administration, to the vast aggrandizement of the presidential office for the time being at least, and Johnson fol-

lowed his example four years later with the exactly opposite result. Under a majority of the state constitutions, when the governor calls the legislature together it may deal only with such matters as are specified in his call. On the other hand, once Congress has been convened by the president it is in full possession of its constitutional powers; and, of course, once in session, the houses are able by continuing so or by adjourning for only brief intervals to render this presidential prerogative altogether nugatory. Indeed, by legislation under Article I, section 4, paragraph 2, Congress could long since have rendered itself a practically perpetual body; and it could still do the same under Amendment XX, section 2.

COLLATERAL FACTORS OF PRESIDENTIAL LEADERSHIP—PATRONAGE, FILIBUSTERS, JUDICIAL REVIEW

While, by Article I, section 6, paragraph 2 it is put out of the president's power to "corrupt" the houses directly, he may still attain the same noxious end indirectly by bestowing offices on the political henchmen of members in return for the latter's votes, or by getting rid of members who are willing to exchange their seats for more desirable posts; nor can there by any doubt that presidents have at times been able in this way to turn the scales in favor of desired legislation, as President Cleveland was conspicuously able to do in 1893 in his fight for the repeal of the discredited Sherman Silver Purchase Act. Indeed, it may be asserted generally that so long as the president possesses patronage to dispense, he will often be compelled to use it in order to obtain, or hold, support that ought to be forthcoming on other grounds—will, in brief, have to submit to political blackmail. Indeed, it is a question whether his possession of the loaves and fishes really strengthens the president in the long run. His greatest weapon is always the power of a favoring public opinion. In the words of Lincoln, than whom no president ever dispensed offices more lavishly, "With public sentiment everything is possible; without public sentiment nothing is possible." Pertinent too is Mr. Taft's considered verdict that every time he made an appointment he created "nine enemies and one ingrate." Furthermore, the elimination of federal patronage would tend to undermine the local party machines and to that extent transform the parties into organs of opinion pure and simple, much to the aggrandizement of the president as party leader. It is more than possible that the anxiety of certain authorities to discover some mode of "compensating" the president for the loss of patronage, which an extension of the merit system to the higher echelons would mean, is misconceived; that the president would gain by the reform in his legislative as well as in his executive capacity.

Another collateral factor of presidential leadership is the power of the houses to shape their own rules of procedure, which may either help or hinder the enactment of measures desired by the president. The Senate's individualistic mode of doing business, which occasionally burgeons in the filibuster, must of course be set down as being of the "hinder" order, although it may pay for itself at times by the protection it affords to "rights" of minorities, or for the maturing of a genuine public opinion on a presidential proposal. "It is a remarkable fact," says Professor Rogers in his excellent volume on the Senate, "that practically every proposal defeated by a filibuster has been unregretted by the country and rarely readvocated by its supporters"; but, he at once adds, "Such minority omniscience ... must be more accidental than wise, and the danger is always present ... that the interests of the country will be adversely affected. Nor is the question simply whether the filibuster has killed good measures, but

also whether it has led to the enactment of bad ones. The indefensible concessions that a small bloc of so-called "Silver Senators" were able to wrest from Congress from time to time for some seventy-five years are conclusive testimony on that point.

And whatever its advantages and disadvantages in the past, this institution—altogether unique among the parliamentary devices of popular governments—has long been losing ground. In March 1917 a filibuster against a presidential proposal led to the Senate's adopting a cloture rule for the first time in its history. Subsequently the Twentieth Amendment, by abolishing the "short session" that used to terminate the life of a Congress, has eliminated the situation in which the threat of a filibuster was the most apt to prove effective in extorting special favors for its authors.

Unfortunately, things have recently taken a decided turn for the worse. I refer to the Senate's adoption of a ruling made by the late Senator Vandenberg in 1948, in his capacity as president pro tem, that a motion to change the rules of the Senate requires a two-thirds vote of the entire Senate membership. Asked on January 5, 1957 for a clarification of the Senate's rules, Vice-President Nixon said that in his opinion Rule XXII, which embodies the Vandenberg ruling, was unconstitutional. "We must first turn," Mr. Nixon continued,

to the Constitution ... [which] ... provides that each house may determine the rules of its proceedings. This constitutional right is lodged in the membership of the Senate and it may be exercised by a majority of the Senate at any time. . . . The Senate should not be bound ... by any ... Rule which denies the membership of the Senate the power to exercise its constitutional right to make its own rules.

But the vice-president emphasized that only the Senate could decide the issue and that his view was personal.

This reasoning seems to me unanswerable. I should like also to appeal to the Senate's sense of humor. Just now it is planning to have a device carved on the pediment of the new Senate Office Building. One of those proposed—one that has a good chance of adoption, I am told—characterizes the Senate as "the Voice of the States in Union." One inevitably recalls the Latin tag, "Vox et praetera nihil."

The manner in which the two houses can, when so disposed, facilitate executive participation in legislation is illustrated on a small scale by the steps they have taken to adjust their procedures in financial legislation to the Budget and Accounting Act of 1921. A provision of the act reads:

> No estimate or request for an appropriation and no request for an increase in an item of any such estimate or request, and no recommendation as to how the revenue needs of the Government should be met, shall be submitted to Congress or any committee thereof by any officer or employee of any department or establishment, unless at the request of either House of Congress.

To match this concentration of responsibility on the part of the executive branch the House has transferred the power of initiating appropriation bills, which had been shared theretofore by eight committees, to a single committee, and the Senate later took similar action. This, however, is only a slight indication of what could be done to the same general end. Administration measures, which today have no status as such before either house, could be given preference over other bills to any extent deemed desirable. Imitating what was done during the Reconstruction Era, the houses could by concurrent resolution create a joint standing committee, or "legislative council," to maintain contact with the president for the purpose of discussing with him his legislative program and translating it into mutual satisfactory proposals. Indeed, a provision of the Administrative Reorganization Act of 1939 suggests that such ar-

rangements may even be given the form of statute. Under this act, it will be recalled, the houses have the right by concurrent resolution to veto any presidential order issued under it, provided the disapproving resolution be passed within sixty days: otherwise the presidential order becomes effective. But suppose a Senate filibuster should develop in *support* of the order? In anticipation of this too obvious possibility the act itself provides that debate on a resolution of disapproval shall be limited in each house to ten hours, which shall be equally divided between opponents and advocates. To be sure, any restriction of this kind on the constitutional power of each house to "determine the rules of its proceedings" has only the force of an agreement between the houses; for that reason perhaps the more solemn form of statute may at times be preferable. I shall return to the idea of a legislative council later.

Yet another collateral factor of presidential leadership is the Supreme Court's power of judicial review as it affects acts of Congress. It is a striking fact that of the presidents who have made the presidency what it is all except two sooner or later crossed swords with the Court. The exceptions were Washington, who appointed the first Bench and, indeed, first and last appointed no fewer than thirteen justices, and Woodrow Wilson. And stemming from this fact are two others: first, the survival in face of the generally adverse opinion of the bar of a potentially formidable challenge to the finality of Supreme Court interpretations of the Constitution affecting national legislative power; and, secondly, a series of measures whereby the Court has been subjected sometimes overtly, more often covertly, to political pressure.

Jefferson, invoking the principle of the Separation of Powers, denied that the president and Congress were bound by the views that the Supreme Court adopted of the Constitution any more than the Court was bound by their views. Jackson took the same position, urging also in its support the oath that every officer gives to uphold the Constitution. Lincoln argued that to identify the Court's version of the Constitution, formulated perhaps for the purpose of deciding a single private lawsuit, with the Constitution itself was incompatible with the idea of popular government. Each of these presidents, moreover, took a hand in legislation that altered the size of the Court. By the Judiciary Act of 1802 the Court, whose membership had been contingently decreased the year before from six justices to five in order to prevent Jefferson from appointing a successor to the aged and ailing Cushing was restored to six justices for the diametrically opposed reason, and in 1807 a seventh justice was added. One of Jackson's last acts was to sign a bill enlarging the Court to nine justices, with the probably intended and certainly realized result of watering down the influence of the departed Marshall with his surviving brethren. During the Civil War the Court was temporarily enlarged to ten justices after it had sustained the blockade of the Southern states by the narrow margin of one vote; and meantime by the Act of March 1, 1863 slavery had been prohibited in the territories, thus setting the Republican platform of 1861 above the *Dred Scott* decision as the effective Constitution of the country.

Nor is this the whole story by any means. Both in 1866 and again in 1869 the size of the Court was changed by Congress of its own initiative. In the former year it was prospectively shrunk to a membership of seven justices in order that Johnson should not be able to make any appointments; in the latter year—Grant now being president—it was restored to its antebellum membership of nine. As we know today, Grant utilized his opportunity to nominate, the same day that *Hepburn* v. *Griswold* was decided, two justices, who, he believed, could be relied on to bring about a reversal of that decision; and fifteen months later his confidence was rewarded by the event.

"The traditional American way," it has been wittily remarked, "of being radical with the Supreme Court" is to alter its personnel rather than its structure and powers. It should be added that the procedure is expected to be accompanied by a certain amount of indirectness and disavowal of political motivation; and the late President Roosevelt's famed proposal of February 5, 1937 was shaped by its authors to comply with the demands of the tradition.

The immediate instigation of the Roosevelt proposal came from the general election of 1936. The huge popular endorsement that this gave Mr. Roosevelt he not unreasonably interpreted as a mandate to establish certain legislation that by theories then dominant on the Court was clearly unconstitutional. The president was thus confronted with a difficult problem of political leadership: was he to postpone his program indefinitely while his political following dissolved, or was he to remove the principal obstacle to success within a comparatively brief time?

In his address to Congress of January 6, 1937 he said:

> With a better understanding of our purposes, and a more intelligent recognition of our needs as a nation, it is not to be assumed that there will be prolonged failure to bring legislative and judicial action into closer harmony. Means must be found to adapt our legal forms and our judicial interpretation to the actual present national needs of the largest progressive democracy in the modern world. . . .
>
> The judicial branch also is asked by the people to do its part in making democracy successful. We do not ask the courts to call nonexistent powers into being, but we have a right to expect that conceded powers or those legitimately implied shall be made effective instruments for the common good.
>
> The process of our democracy must not

be imperiled by the denial of essential powers of free government.

Unfortunately, the proposal of February 5 was not presented as a logical method of carrying out the message of January 6, but—in harmony with the evasive tradition mentioned above— was directed to the largely, although certainly not altogether, irrelevant problem of superannuation on the Bench. It was consequently much more extreme than a measure addressed to the main purpose need have been, and furthermore it supplied only a partial guarantee against the recurrence of the situation most demanding remedy, a haphazard system of recruitment that entirely ignores the place of the Court in the lawmaking process.

While the proposal was defeated, this did not occur until the emergency that had challenged the president's leadership had been to a large extent removed by the Court itself by its decisions sustaining the Wagner Labor Relations Act and the Social Security Act. But that the proposal had some influence, in conjunction with the election of 1936 and the C.I.O. strikes early in 1937, in inducing the Court to restudy certain of its doctrines in the light of modern conditions is not an extreme conjecture. At any rate, the time relationship between the proposal and the decisions just mentioned is something to take into account in estimating the present legislative role of the president. History does not regard very seriously the logician's criticism of the *post hoc ergo propter hoc*—to it the chronological *is* the logical.

27. Presidency and Legislation: The Growth of Central Clearance*

RICHARD E. NEUSTADT

Ten months after President Eisenhower's inaugural, an article in *Fortune* extolled a presidential aide in terms which would have seemed familiar ten months before;[1] the picture of his role in Eisenhower's entourage might easily have been drawn in President Truman's time. The subject of this piece was Roger W. Jones, an assistant director of the Bureau of the Budget and chief of its Office of Legislative Reference. In *Fortune's* terms, here was a confidential, if "non-political," member of the White House circle performing tasks of great importance to the president, trusted, respected, and relied upon by all of his associates. As an analysis of governmental functions and relationships, this testimonial was scarcely definitive, but its mere publication testifies to the continuation of the Budget Bureau's so-called legislative clearance operations, handily surviving the Great Transition of 1953.

What are these clearance operations? Essentially they amount to central coordination and review of stands taken by the various federal agencies at three successive stages of the legislative process.

*Source: Excerpted from *American Political Science Review*, vol. 48 (September 1954), pp. 641-57, 660-62, 665, 668. Copyright © 1954 by the American Political Science Association. Reprinted by permission. Footnotes combined and renumbered; some subheadings renumbered.

Large numbers of the public measures introduced in Congress are formally proposed by agencies of the executive branch; departmental drafts officially en route to Congress first have to clear the Bureau of the Budget for interagency coordination and approval on the president's behalf. Once bills are introduced, regardless of their source, congressional committees ordinarily solicit views from interested agencies; official agency responses—in whatever form, to whomever addressed—first channel through the Budget Bureau for coordination and advice on each bill's relation to the president's program. When enrolled enactments come from Congress to the president for signature or veto, the Budget Bureau, as his agent, obtains, coordinates, and summarizes agency opinion on the merits, preparing in each case a presidential dossier complete with covering recommendation.

These are the components of "legislative clearance" as the term is normally employed.[2] In practice, these operations are much more complex and a good deal less absolute than this simple recital would indicate. But generally speaking, central clearance has proceeded along these lines for many years.

Last year, despite the change of administration, 380 agency drafts, 3,571 agency reports on pending bills, and 525 enrolled enactments were processed by the Budget Bureau.[3] In 1954, the Bureau's Office of Legislative Reference, control center for clearance operations, is handling an even larger volume—with President Eisenhower and Budget Director Hughes earnestly supporting clearance regulations in effect since 1948, signed by a budget director long out of office, issued "by direction" of the president whose term expired January 20, 1953.[4]

Here is presidential machinery to coordinate a vital aspect of executive policy development; machinery to control, in some degree at least, the means by which the diverse elements of the executive express and implement their own designs. In Truman's time this mechanism was, as one observer put it, "the only clearing house that operates regularly between the multitudinous departments and bureaus . . . sometimes the only possible way to get government agencies working together. . . ."[5] In the present administration, it may well be that legislative clearance is losing this particular distinction. Elsewhere in the Executive Office of the President, new life has been breathed into the National Security Council, as an apparatus of policy coordination and control. Even the Council of Economic Advisers, with its revised chairmanship and interdepartmental advisory board, shows signs of institutional advance in these directions. So, indeed, does the cabinet—though history suggests this may not last.

But if legislative clearance is no longer unique, it is by far the oldest, best intrenched, most thoroughly institutionalized of the president's coordinative instruments—always excepting the budget itself—receiving new stability and new significance by virtue of its demonstrated power to adapt and to survive. And this power is not something suddenly achieved and first displayed in 1953. The central clearance system has surmounted every governmental transition since the 1920s, preserving into Eisenhower's term not only the accretions of two Democratic decades, but even the inheritance from Harding, Coolidge, and Hoover.

What is the nature of this mechanism? How has it adapted? Why has it survived? These are the questions to which this paper is addressed.[6]

I. FINANCIAL CLEARANCE IN THE TWENTIES

When President Harding approved the Budget and Accounting Act on June 10, 1921, the federal agencies lost their historic freedom to decide for themselves what appropriations they should ask of Congress; now the president, alone, was to decide and to request, with a new staff agency, the Budget Bureau, to help him do it. Moreover, in accordance with the act's intent, but one committee in each House of Congress was to receive and review appropriation requests.[7] Here, prescribed in law, was a new restrictive way of handling the life-and-death concerns of every agency—and most congressmen. And here were new organizations with a tremendous institutional stake in the successful assertion of that new way: the presidential Bureau of the Budget and the congressional Committees on Appropriations. Furthermore, these organizations had a clear mutuality of interest in closing off, as nearly as might be, all avenues to action on appropriations save their own. Substantive congressional committees, no less than executive agencies, were potential conspirators against the exclusive jurisdictions conferred by the new budget system. Facing common dangers, the system's beneficiaries made common cause. Central legislative clearance was a principal result.

It is significant of this community of interest that the original proposal for some form of central clearance came not from the new Budget Bureau, but from the House Appropriations Committee. In November, 1921, less than a month before the first presidential budget went to Congress, the committee chairman voiced to the budget director his concern about two minor measures—introduced at an agency's request and referred to a substantive committee—which authorized diversion of appropriated funds from the purposes originally specified. In the chairman's view,

> . . . matters of this character should come through the Bureau of the Budget . . . I have called them to your attention in order that you may take . . . steps . . . to include [such] requests . . . in the control which the Bureau has over direct estimates.[8]

It was this congressional observation which precipitated the first presidential effort to assert central control over agency views on proposed and pending legislation, an effort embodied in Budget Circular 49, issued December 19, 1921, "by direction of the president," after clearance with the House committee.

This first approach to legislative clearance was a rather curious affair. The language of the Budget Circular was very sweeping, requiring—in accordance with the "spirit" of the Budget and Accounting Act—that all agency proposals for legislation or expressions of views on pending legislation "the effect of which would be to create a charge upon the public treasury or commit the government to obligations which would later require appropriations," be submitted to the Budget Bureau before presentation to Congress. The bureau was to make recommendations to the president, ascertain the "relationship of the legislation to the president's financial program," and advise the agencies accordingly. Agency proposals for legislation were to go forward only if approved by the president; agency views on pending legislation, when presented to Congress, were to include a statement of the advice received from the Budget Bureau.[9]

Here, at least on paper, was a new assertion of presidential control over the agencies, a new form of continuing staff intervention between president and department heads, conceptually a radical departure in American administration matched only by the new budget process. Yet the official sponsors of Circular 49 avowed no such intent. There is nothing in the record prior to the order's issuance to show that either the budget director or the president grasped these implications in the language they approved.[10] But there is plenty in the record demonstrating that the members of the cabinet did not leave them long in ignorance, once the order had gone out. The subsequent course of legislative clearance in Harding's time is mainly a matter of apologies, concessions, limitations tacitly approved or self-applied, to soften agency reactions against Circular 49.

The agencies were aroused both by the circular's potential coverage—broadly interpreted, its criteria reached virtually all subjects of legislation—and by interposition of the Budget Bureau between them and the president on such a range of measures. In beating his retreat, at the president's behest, Dawes did not try to find fixed subject-matter limits for his procedure; instead he let it be known that matters of importance could be cleared with the president directly. Only on routine affairs would the Budget act as agent.[11] In practice, Dawes went even farther, leaving interpretation and compliance to departmental discretion. The Budget Bureau neither guided nor protested; the agencies proceeded accordingly.

For two years Circular 49 remained in limbo. Then a new administration seized on this empty order and within it built a strong and well enforced, if narrowly defined accessory to central budgeting. The forms of financial clearance are traceable to Harding's time. The actuality begins with Coolidge.

By early 1924, the presidential budget system was a going concern, veteran of three "budget seasons." The Budget Bureau had been staffed and organized, routines established, procedures set. The bureau's leadership had passed from Dawes to his handpicked successor, General Lord, a zealot for the small economy.[12] And the presidency had passed to perhaps the most determined economizer ever to hold the office. "I am for economy and after that I am for more economy," so Coolidge put it, conceiving economy not merely as a matter of politics or economics, but as an exercise in personal morality, an ethical principle, a constitutional requirement, an end in itself.[13] In the Coolidge administration the theme of budget policy was reduction: reduction of expenditures, of taxes, and of the public debt, with presidential budgeting

mainly a means of cutting back on current outlays and avoiding new commitments. It is in this context that legislative clearance was revived.

Early in 1924, the Budget Bureau, with presidential support, began a vigorous campaign to activate Circular 49. For nearly two years, Lord peppered key departments with letters of warning, abjuration, and complaint, backed by a considerable amount of Budget staff investigation and analysis.[14] By 1926, he was able to report that agency compliance had become "practically universal."[15] Of course, the Coolidge clearance system, thus successfully asserted, was carried on within a very narrow frame of reference. Cabinet officers were constrained to accept Budget Bureau placement between them and the president, but only on proposals clearly costing money, and only with respect to cost, not substance. The bureau's task of ascertaining the relationship of agency proposals to presidential program was rendered relatively safe and sure by virtue of the program's identification with recorded budget policies and estimates.

The purpose of the exercise is clear from Budget's rules of thumb for processing what came its way. An adverse agency report on a pending measure was usually taken as conclusive. An affirmative report resulted in careful scrutiny of relationship to the current budget and implications for future years. It was common practice to hold favorable agency reports "in conflict" with the president's financial program. Frequently, legislation was held "in conflict" unless the money authorization were reduced. This negative advice also applied wherever a semblance of prior legislative authority could be found to render the current proposal "unnecessary."[16] When the bureau was confronted with opposing views from two departments, its normal procedure was to endorse the negative position. If this were not feasible, an independent staff analysis was sometimes made the basis for decision. Changes in drafting were sometimes suggested to the agencies, but always as a Budget idea, not as the result of any effort at coordination. Occasionally, the bureau would attempt to mediate major differences of opinion, but it never undertook to seek them out.

The Coolidge clearance system, then, was quite straightforward in its negative endeavor to buttress the president's control over his budget policies and his—or the Budget Bureau's—forward financial plans. In no sense did the system operate as a coordinative or developmental mechanism in areas of substantive policy. And what was true in Coolidge's administration was also true in his successor's term. President Hoover not only inherited and applied this form of central clearance, he even refined its terms of reference, emphasizing more than ever its budgetary association and its negative cast.

Shortly after his inauguration, Hoover suggested that the Budget Bureau take no action on agency requests for clearance unless and until it received a clear intimation of congressional interest. The president intended personally to approve all clearance actions and saw no point in bothering with measures which were not going to receive action.[17] A further refinement followed late in 1929, when Hoover sanctioned a formal amendment to Circular 49 exempting from clearance all agency reports on private bills and all *unfavorable* reports on public bills.[18]

These minor changes simply put finishing touches on the edifice of Coolidge clearance; within these limits, the character of clearance actions remained unchanged through Hoover's term. His budgetary problems became immeasurably more difficult than Coolidge's had been. As the economic decline worsened after 1929 and federal revenues fell steadily, enormous pressures built up for increased federal spending. But the Hoover administration remained unalterably opposed to deliberate deficit financing, and in its clearance operations the Budget Bureau tried harder than ever to ward off all possible legislative authorizations for unbudgeted expenditure.[19] Of course, after the mid-term elections of 1930 the president was unable either to develop a coherent budget policy and make it stick, or to avoid the opposition's criticism for his failure to do so. And in that painful situation, financial clearance became the least of remedies.

II. THE ROOSEVELT REVOLUTION AND POLICY CLEARANCE

President Franklin D. Roosevelt's inaugural in 1933 was accompanied by a clean sweep topside in all the departments, after twelve years of continuity under the Republicans. The procedures for financial clearance had grown up in those years and concern about them, or even understanding of them, seems to have been carried off with the outgoing administration. The succeeding regime was enormously busy and very new.[20] Only the president himself was really familiar with governmental administration. His cabinet members were novices at it.[21] Moreover, they were moving at much too fast a pace to stop for the niceties of an auxiliary budget procedure.

They moved fast; they moved the federal government into unprecedented ventures, into new spheres of action on many different fronts. The first years of the New Deal released a torrent of measures for reform, and these were mingled with a host of shifting, often contradictory improvisations in the fight against depression. Roosevelt had pledged financial stringency in the 1932 campaign, attacking Hoover on home grounds. During the next two years "sound money" and "economy in government" remained on-again-off-again themes, but sounding ever fainter as the New Deal gathered impetus, their principal adherents mostly out of office before the end of 1934.[22]

The motives which led Coolidge's

administration to stress financial clearance were scarcely in the forefront of the new regime's concerns. Not until January, 1934 did the Budget Bureau take any steps to remind department heads of their continuing obligations under the old circulars. And then the bureau's action was muted, almost apologetic. Taken by the staff, not the director, it was a bureaucratic restoration of routines, not in any sense a presidentially-inspired campaign for compliance.[23]

Roosevelt's contribution to central clearance was of quite another order. Nearly a year after this Budget Bureau "restoration" of financial clearance, the president took the initiative in launching a different kind of clearance: clearance of all agency proposals for legislation, "policy" clearance in substantive terms.

Roosevelt brought the matter up on his own motion at a National Emergency Council meeting in December, 1934, shortly before the convening of the 74th Congress. He told the assembled officials he had decided to stop the practice of uncoordinated agency requests for legislation. At the preceding session of Congress he had been "quite horrified—not once but half a dozen times—by reading in the paper that some department or agency was after this, that, or the other without my knowledge."[24] He wanted no more of that. In the future, agency officials should come to him with their proposals before taking them to Congress.

One cabinet officer observed that the departments were already clearing through the Budget Bureau. Roosevelt brushed this aside. "That," he said,

> was for appropriations. What I am talking about is legislation. . . . Coming down to legislation there has never been any clearing house . . . and, I think in the last analysis that has got to be tried in and go through the National Emergency Council . . . and up to me if necessary. In all probability it will come to me.[25]

On December 13, 1934, the secretariat of the Emergency Council followed up the president's remarks with a memorandum to all members, signed by Donald Richberg, then NEC's executive director. This instructed the agencies that at the forthcoming Congress all proposals for appropriations and all bills "carrying appropriations measures" should be cleared with the president through the Bureau of the Budget. All "other proposed legislation" was to be cleared through the council's executive director, or in certain cases with special-purpose NEC committees.

While this directive referred to proposals only and contained a caveat on appropriation matters, its language was far from precise. The result was widespread confusion over the relationship between the new procedure and the old Budget circulars. In April, 1935, the acting budget director, Daniel Bell, protested to Richberg; the problem was raised at an Emergency Council meeting on April 23 and the president decided that clarifying instructions should go out.[26] These took the form of a new Budget Circular 336, issued "by direction of the president" on December 21, 1935.[27]

Circular 336 brought together and superseded outstanding NEC directives, as well as previous Budget circulars. It provided that all agency proposals for legislation and all reports on pending legislation should clear through the Budget Bureau "for consideration by the president," before submission to Congress; as before, private relief bills were exempted. Agency proposals or reports when subsequently sent to Congress were to include a statement as to "whether proposed legislation was or was not in accord with the president's program." This was also to apply to oral testimony before congressional committees.

Procedurally, the circular provided that the Budget Bureau was to check directly with the president on legislation "solely concerning fiscal matters." Legislation "solely concerning policy matters" was to be referred to the president through the Emergency Council staff. The two organizations were to clear with him jointly on legislation involving both "fiscal" and "policy" matters. The council was to inform the bureau of clearances which it obtained from the president independently; the bureau was to inform the agencies in all instances.

In print—and in practice—these procedures had a very clumsy look; for obvious reasons they proved cumbersome and somewhat unrealistic. Two years later they were superseded. But while the mechanics were transitional, the basic requirements have remained in force, without essential change, for nineteen years.

The Roosevelt clearance system, thus established, incorporated its financial precursor but was no mere extension of the budget process.[28] On the contrary, in form and fact and terms of reference this was Roosevelt's creation, intended to protect not just his budget, but his prerogatives, his freedom of action, and his choice of policies, in an era of fast-growing government and of determined presidential leadership.

Roosevelt's statements made it plain that he sought to protect both president from agencies and agencies from one another. In the first place, he wanted the administration's stand made known on agency proposals, not only in his own defense but for the sake of everyone concerned, including the congressional leaders. Of these proposals he remarked:

> They fall into three categories: first, the kind of legislation that, administratively, I could not give approval to—[clearance] will eliminate that; secondly, the type of legislation which we are perfectly willing to have the department or agency press for, but at the same time we do not want to put it in the [third] category of major Administration bills. Obviously I have to confine myself to what the newspapers called last year "the comparatively small list of *must* legislation." If I make every bill that the Government is interested in *must* legis-

lation, it is going to complicate things . . . very much; and where I clear legislation with a notation that says "no objection" that means you are at perfect liberty to try to get the thing through, but I am not going to send a special message for it. It is all your trouble, not mine.[29]

In the second place, it was good business to have ideas and information contributed by all agencies concerned, not just the originating departments. Having bills cleared through a central agency would, in Roosevelt's words, "give somebody else outside the department itself the opportunity to have happy thoughts."[30] Moreover, such exchanges in advance would prevent crossed wires within the administration. The president did not want the agencies "stepping on each others' toes" and he definitely did not want them "stepping on mine. . . :"

> Just the other day a resolution was passed through Congress—a House resolution that did not even have to come to me—asking for a certain report on a very important matter from one of the departments. It was a policy matter. The department was asked to send the report up to the Committee and nobody outside the department knew about it. We happened to catch it. If the report had gone up in the form in which it was prepared, it would have been absolutely contrary to the policy of the Government.[31]

On pending bills which the administration had not sponsored, he wanted the departments to keep out of each others' way:

> In all our testimony before Congress and in all our answers to questions, let us stick to our own last and let us be factual about it. This is one of the most important things that has been said for a long time . . . let us say the Secretary of Agriculture goes up there and he doesn't know much about the bill, but he knows that he is going to be asked about it. It might . . . [relate] . . . not only to Agriculture but to Interior and some other departments as well and he ought to in some way find out what the general attitude is through some kind of clearing house. . . .[32]

Thus Roosevelt expressed the purpose of his new clearance system: by and large a negative purpose, even as Coolidge's had been. An opportunity for "happy thoughts" apart, the system's new coordinative elements, no less than broadened clearances, were seen primarily as means to keep the many-voiced executive from shouting itself down in the legislative process.

Granting Roosevelt's purpose, what, in fact, did he obtain? Initially, not very much:

Clearance as practiced in the 74th Congress [1935-6] was restricted almost entirely to minor departmental bills . . . nearly all of the really important bills and many minor measures originating in the Executive Branch, did not pass through this machinery. . . . Matters discussed with the President in person by a department head were not submitted for clearance, except in a few cases . . . the President's approval, orally given or read into his statements was deemed sufficient . . . nearly all of the measures about which the President sent messages to the Congress [the major administration bills] . . . [were] . . . exempt from clearance . . . many lesser matters also escaped such checking.[33]

This appraisal was based on a study utilizing only Emergency Council records. A later survey of the period, based on Budget Bureau files, concluded that there was "less evidence of deliberate agency failure to comply . . . than of Bureau failure to follow the prescribed procedure in the clearance of policy matters."[34] Perhaps so—but there is nothing in print or on file to controvert the general tenor of the earlier view.

Yet by 1939 the budget director was talking confidently before Congress of the scope and general coverage of central clearance.[35] In 1943, an acute and experienced observer could write that Budget clearance was "frequently commanding," the bureau's influence "very great."[36] For this changed appraisal at least four things were responsible: the demise of NEC, the Budget Bureau's great expansion, the slowing down of New Deal creativity, and the formal marriage of central clearance to the veto power.

The Emergency Council was dying on the vine by 1936, commanding little presidential interest, or agency respect. Its diminished status and potential were accurately reflected in the Brownlow committee's recommendation that the council be abolished, and its staff activities discarded or dispersed.[37] Undoubtedly the council's relative and growing weakness had much to do with the lax attitude of agencies and Budget Bureau toward the executive director's prerogatives under Circular 336. Had he been the sole institutional peg for "policy" clearance, that process might well have gone under also, retrievable with difficulty, if at all. But behind him stood the Budget. When he vanished, it inherited. This happened, actually, as a matter of course, a detail of administrative tidying, a minor item among all the major changes in the bureau's status, role, and outlook envisaged by and following upon the Brownlow committee report of January, 1937.[38]

In the two years after publication of the report, the bureau moved, as never since the twenties, to strengthen and consolidate its clearance operations. In the spring of 1937, Director Bell loosed a stream of correspondence on the agencies, reminiscent of Lord's effort thirteen years before.[39] In December, 1937, Circular 336 was formally reissued—renumbered 344—as a means of removing reference to the Emergency Council in official clearance instructions.[40] Henceforth, the bureau was to be in form and fact the president's sole institutional clearance agent, on matters of substance no less than finance. Internally, also, the bureau acted—Brownlow report in hand—to put new life and strength into the job. In 1938, Bell increased the staff assigned specifically to clearance work, reorganized it as a separate, full-time, undertaking and

gave it status as a major bureau function, autonomously organized in a Division of Coordination, precursor of the
present Office of Legislative Reference.[41]

During 1939, in the first session of the
76th Congress, the Budget Bureau processed agency reports on 2,448 pending
public bills. Four years before, in the
days of financial clearance, only 300
pending measures had been covered by
submissions to the bureau. Again, in
1939 the Bureau handled 438 drafts of
proposed legislation; this compares with
170 proposals sent by the agencies to
NEC under the procedure of 1935, or
162 proposals sent to NEC and Budget
both, under the procedure of 1936.[42]
These figures are illustrative of the rise
in clearance coverage after 1937,
though nothing can be more elusive
than the search for such objective
measurements, nor anything more misleading than raw data of this type.[43] But
there are other evidences also, in
Budget Bureau files of agency and
White House correspondence, and in
transcripts of legislative hearings and
debate to demonstrate that central
clearance was now reaching wider than
before.[44]

The climate of the times, perhaps,
contributed to this no less than did improved organization and procedure. The
main thrust of New Deal innovation
was long past by 1939. The emergency
had lost its cutting edge; emergency
agencies had either disappeared or dug
roots into routine. In Europe and in Asia
world war threatened. In Congress, the
anti-New Deal coalition had become a
formidable fact of life. In the executive,
sails were trimmed accordingly. Real
legislative ambitions for most agencies
were now measured largely by consolidation and amendment—goals much
more easily contained in clearance
channels than the great, unprecedented
ventures once hurried before relatively
complaisant Congresses.

And one thing more: in 1938, the
Budget Bureau gained a new sanction,
and an unassailable rationale, for its
clearance of proposed and pending
measures. That year, the bureau came
into control of agency communications
to the president on signature or veto of
enrolled bills. Henceforth, Roosevelt's
clearance agency was also his chief institutional advisor on the generality of
measures passed by Congress. Within
this combination lay real power, and
the bureau made the most of it.

III. POLICY CLEARANCE AND THE VETO POWER

Traditionally, presidents have sought
advice from their department heads on
disposition of enrolled enactments.
Until the thirties, though, this custom
had some drastic built-in limitations.
When an enrolled bill reached the
White House, the president's secretary
or executive clerk would hazard a quick
guess at the agencies concerned; the
bill itself would then be passed by hand
to each in turn—a document of state,
handled with care—and their replies, fil-
tering back, one by one, would get such
correlation as hard-pressed White
House aides might manage. All this
went on during the ten days within
which the president could veto. Frequently he was but poorly served, receiving very late, for fast decision, an
ill-digested mountain of material.[45]

From its establishment in 1921, the
Budget Bureau had been asked for
views on each enrolled appropriations
bill. In 1934, Roosevelt told his staff to
get bureau reactions on all private relief
bills involving an expenditure of funds.
His aides went one step further,
urging—as a measure for their own
relief—that on such bills the bureau also
seek and summarize the views of other
agencies concerned. This worked, and
presently, without fanfare, the White
House staff began to send across the
street all manner of substantive public
bills as well, asking the bureau to cir-
cularize agencies and correlate views.
By 1938 almost all enrolled bills were

going to the bureau for this handling. That year, the few exceptions followed no clear line of demarcation; after 1939, there were no more exceptions. This process of pragmatic delegation took but five years, from start to finish.

So long as the original enrollments had to be handed around, the Budget Bureau was as helpless as the White House staff had been to make of this anything but a thankless, mainly ministerial performance. In 1938, however, the Public Printer was persuaded to prepare facsimile copies of each enrolled bill; these went directly to the bureau at the same time the original went back to Congress for signature by speaker and vice president. Armed with these copies, the bureau could put an official text before each agency simultaneously, hours or even days before the bill itself could reach the White House and the president's time began to run.

This was a simple, mechanical improvement, but what it gave was time, and time spelled opportunity. On January 19, 1939, the bureau issued "by direction of the president" Circular 346, defining agency obligations under the new procedure. For the first time Budget was identified officially as presidential agent on all enrolled enactments. Bureau requests for agency opinions were to receive an absolute priority; agency replies were to be forthcoming within forty-eight hours, and were to include in each case a specific recommendation, backed by as much factual information as possible. Any recommendation against presidential signature was to be accompanied by a draft veto message or memorandum of disapproval (for use with pocket vetoes). In these terms Circular 346 formalized previous practice, giving it a mandatory application beyond anything remotely possible in absence of facsimile procedure.[46]

Within the Budget Bureau, corresponding steps were taken. The chores of asking agencies for views, pressuring the dilatory, correlating replies, reworking message drafts, were all put on a centralized and systematic basis. Summaries and covering recommendations to the president were now developed uniformly, carefully, and in much greater detail than before. All this took organization, specialization, and somebody's time and effort; by 1939, the bureau had these at hand in its Division of Coordination. There full responsibility for enrolled bills was vested.

This new function quickly became the key element in central clearance. The Budget Bureau's work on agency proposals and reports built up a general, comprehensive record, unmatched elsewhere in government, to buttress its consideration of enrolled bills. At the same time, its mandate on enrolled enactments now lent special point and purpose to clearances of measures in proposed and pending stages.[47]

The veto power's potency in this connection depends, of course, upon its use, and Roosevelt was a constant user. "If the decision is close," he once remarked to his department heads, "I want to veto."[48] In 1939, he chose to veto sixteen bills despite approval by the Budget Bureau, remarking to an aide, "The Budget is getting too soft; tell them to stiffen up."[49] Indeed, he was prone to call occasionally for "something I can veto," as a "reminder" to department heads and congressmen alike.[50] This was not frivolity; to FDR the veto power was among the presidency's greatest attributes, an independent and responsible act of participation in the legislative process, and a means of enforcing congressional and agency respect for presidential preferences or programs.[51]

From the beginning, Roosevelt placed a great deal of reliance on the Budget Bureau's weighing and sifting of bureaucratic opinion. On the generality of measures he inclined to discount cabinet, congressional, and interest group advices which found their joint and several ways directly to the White House. But he took care that there should be, between him and the Budget, some White House staff review to check the institutional approach against the personal, to balance off the presidency with the president. In 1943, that task went to Judge Rosenman, in his new post as special counsel to the president; there, with temporary lapses, it has remained, assumed by each of Rosenman's successors in Truman's time and Eisenhower's.[52]

The Budget Bureau took its staff work on enrolled enactments as seriously as Roosevelt did his veto power. Here, unchallengably in the Budget's hands, was all-important preparation for decisive acts of state, exclusively in presidential jurisdiction. Of course, on the great, controversial measures, the White House could expect appraisals and advice from many other sources and through many other channels. But usually on the general run of bills enrolled at every session, particularly the private bills, the Budget file was the "works." Within the bureau, priorities were set accordingly.

In Roosevelt's later years, no other element of central clearance received half the attention, time, and effort which bureau staff gave to enrolled enactments, especially to lesser issues where its word weighed the most. From 1940 on, coordination of proposed and pending bills was routinized increasingly, with stress on negative, protective aspects only, and great reliance on the written word. Rarely were agencies called in for face-to-face discussion; rarely were efforts made to conform clearance actions with the exigencies of the legislative timetable. If agencies and committees wanted such advantages as clearance offered at the pending stage, they could ask and wait their turn; if not, they took their chances when the bills became enrolled. . . .

IV. THE CHARACTER OF CLEARANCE IN TRUMAN'S TIME

All this involved great changes in the character of clearance at proposed and pending stages. After 1947, the Budget Bureau's war-encouraged passive attitude gave way, perforce, to much activity. A first step was the campaign begun early in 1948 to mesh these clearance actions with congressional requirements, and this despite the opposition character of the then Congress:

> We had found in the immediate postwar years that there were a great many situations in which the . . . clearance process was an annoyance to the Congress and properly so. . . . Consequently . . . [in 1948] . . . Webb . . . specifically charged me with responsibility of talking with the staff directors and clerks of . . . major committees to see if our . . . process could be tied more closely into the committees' desires for the scheduling of items to come before them. On the other side of the coin, I was to acquaint the committees with the issues and items which . . . were being advanced in priority by the President, or . . . major departments. . . .
>
> With the . . . cooperation of the Public Works Committees it was possible for us to work out . . . almost a precise schedule of what [they] wanted . . . and when . . . and . . . then go back and hasten our clearance process.
>
> From the Public Works Committees this same kind of cooperative effort was extended to other . . . committees.[53]

Indeed, this operation steadily expanded; by 1950, the Budget was regularly and informally in touch with both majority and minority staffs of most major legislative committees, having by then a record of successful relations with committee chairmen of both parties.

In 1948, the bureau also embarked on a wholly new approach to the coordinative aspects of its clearance tasks, subordinating negative protection of president and agencies to positive development and drafting of administration measures. Executive Office "working teams" came into being with "leadership" assigned to the White House, Budget, or the Economic Council, as the case might be, while Legislative Reference served as secretariat and stimulator of them all. Each unit of the presidential staff contributed its experts and its points of view; all agencies concerned were called on to confer.[54] A high proportion of the Fair Deal's later measures were worked out in detailed form through this new application of "coordination;" for example, the Housing Act of 1949, and the Social Security Act amendments of 1950.[55] On many lesser proposals, involving fewer agency and private interests, or interests lower in importance to the president, the Budget's Legislative Reference staff led similar excursions on its own, sometimes merely tinkering with agency submissions, sometimes redoing the whole drafting job around the conference table.

This new technique—new, anyway, as an adjunct of central clearance—developed alongside and, in part, grew out of efforts to provide fixed meaning, concrete form, and better advance planning for the president's own legislative program. Toward that end, White House and Budget legislative staffs worked in close combination, after 1947, developing relationships which lent both strength and informality to team play on particulars.

Coinciding with these various endeavors came an external change which gave the clearance system a new dimension and new opportunity. In 1947, congressional committees began to ask Budget for its views on pending bills, at the same time that requests for views were sent to the agencies. These so-called "direct referrals" were an 80th Congress innovation; a means whereby Republican committee chairmen could gauge the intentions of the Democratic administration. Whatever the initial motive, the practice became increasingly popular with the committees in each succeeding Congress, regardless of party coloration. During the 80th Congress there were 370 of these direct referrals; during the 81st, 974; during the 82nd, 1,102. In the 83rd Congress, there were 889 for the first session alone. Of course, this volume has not stemmed equally from all committees of each House in every Congress. For example, since 1947 the Senate Labor and Welfare Committee has referred nearly all bills to the Budget; not so its House counterpart.[56] Variations have their roots in diverse compounds of committee composition, jurisdiction, clientele. But while they keep the practice less than universal, this has not altered one significant result: the Budget's growing opportunity to register a presidential view directly on a high proportion of the bills considered actively by both houses.

Moreover, since 1949 other direct channels have opened to the bureau, further enhancing this opportunity. For example, during Truman's second term the majority leader of the House and the Democratic chairmen of several Senate and House committees—including the House Rules Committee—acquired the habit of checking with White House or Budget staff (sometimes both), by telephone or special note, for the current administration stand on bills nearing the reporting stage.[57] Wherever addressed, these inquiries almost always passed through Budget hands; responses, however conveyed, afforded vital supplements to clearance actions and formal reports. While these particulars and others have altered since Eisenhower's accession, comparable avenues continue to link the clearance system not only with congressional committees but with the leadership as well. . . .

In November, 1952, immediately after Eisenhower's election, Truman took a number of specific steps toward the goal of orderly transition, among them an invitation to the president-elect to have his representative participate as an observer in final preparation of the forthcoming (Truman) budget. During the nine weeks before inauguration, Eisenhower's budget director-designate, Joseph M. Dodge, worked full time in the Budget Bureau, conducting himself with great discretion, watching the staff at work, learning their problems and routines, winning their confidence as they gained his respect.[58]

Once installed in office, Dodge emerged as a strong member of the new inner circle. His influence, the value of his services, and his ability to act were enhanced, no doubt, by his acceptance, hence effective leadership, of the established staff at his disposal. This set the stage for firm and confident assertion of Budget Bureau functions in the new regime, central clearance no less than the rest. Even before Inauguration Day, most of the cabinet members-designate were called into the bureau for Dodge-sponsored indoctrination lectures on its prerogatives and their responsibilities. Clearance regulations received attention at that time. And after the inaugural, Dodge made a point of picking up initial failures to comply, taking a strong line with department heads, reminiscent of Lord's language thirty years before.

The new budget director did one thing more for central clearance: to his hold-over chief of Legislative Reference he gave the backing of his own unqualified endorsement, and a total delegation of authority surpassing anything experienced in Truman's time. Between these two men, Dodge and Jones, evolved a personal relationship of greatest moment for clearance's survival. Dodge used his own prestige unsparingly to break a path for Jones into the Eisenhower White House, overcoming tendencies to treat careerists with extreme reserve. He then cut Legislative Reference entirely loose to seek its lead from presidential staff, thus extending under Eisenhower an innovation Webb had introduced in Truman's first term.

It was one thing to open an acquaintance between White House and Legislative Reference; quite another to establish adequate patterns of staff interaction. The Budget's clearance operations were dependent, now more than ever, on guidance from the president and access to him, by and through his White House aides. . . .

V. THE CIRCUMSTANCES OF SURVIVAL

For more than thirty years now, central clearance has persisted, its history marked by a long series of "accidental," unforeseen accretions. Nothing once absorbed has been wholly displaced; each new element somehow encompasses the old. There have been periods of relative stability, if not stagnation; times of obscurity, even decline. But overall, here is a record of great growth, successful adaptation—this under six successive presidents, through every variation in national and governmental circumstances since Harding's term of office.

NOTES

1. Katherine Hammill, "This is a Bureaucrat," *Fortune* (November 1953): 156ff.

2. Agency proposals for executive orders, proclamations, and certain other formal presidential actions are also coordinated and cleared through the Bureau of the Budget, as are feasibility reports on proposed public works requiring congressional action.

3. Source: Office of Legislative Reference, Bureau of the Budget. In addition, there were 889 "direct referrals" from congressional sources asking Budget for views on pending bills.

4. Budget Circular A-19, Revised, dated October 25, 1948 sets forth coordination and clearance procedures and requirements concerning proposed and pending bills. Budget Circular A-9, Revised, issued at the same time, deals with enrolled enactments. Both circulars codified and brought up to date earlier usage and regulations.

5. Bertram M. Gross, *The Legislative Struggle* (New York, 1953), p. 169.

6. This article deals with legislative coordination and review centering in the Bureau of the Budget. At a later date the author hopes to deal with a related process, planning the president's own legislative program: a process but newly and incompletely institutionalized, centering more nearly in the White House than the Budget Bureau, yet also exhibiting a high degree of continuity from Truman's time to Eisenhower's.

7. As an integral part of the budget reform, the House of Representatives changed its rules in 1920, at the second session of the 66th Congress, to reduce from eight to one the number of committees authorized to deal with appropriations. The Senate followed suit two years later, at the second session of the 67th Congress.

8. Letter from Chairman Madden of the House Appropriations Committee to Budget Director Dawes, November 17, 1921. Budget Bureau central files; 1921-38: *Legislation No. 1*. The measures in question were Senate Joint Resolutions of very limited significance, affecting War Department obligating authority. Madden's concern was clearly not with these specifics, but with their procedural implications.

9. In contrast with the asserted presidential veto over agency proposals volunteered to Congress, this circular and its successors have carefully refrained from claiming any right to stop or alter agency responses to congressional requests for views on pending bills. Formally speaking, the only requirement has been that the president's position, as expressed by Budget, be stated in an agency report along with the agency's own views. Furthermore, by long custom now acknowledged in current regulations, an agency's response to congressional requests for "technical drafting service" is exempt from clearance so long as it carries no official endorsement. Thus has the Budget tried to duck the charge of "interference" with congressional access to agency opinion or expertise. In practice, this means non-interference with agency calculation of the risks involved, if any, in holding to views which do not square with those of the Executive Office.

10. Dawes obtained Harding's approval in advance, sending him the proposed circular on December 3, 1921, with the notation that it "needs no argument," being intended "simply to insure that all estimates and requests for appropriations [are] presented in the manner provided in the Budget and Accounting Act." Dawes may have said less than he believed, but there is no hint of this either in the official files or in his published memoirs, *The First Year of the Budget* (New York, 1923).

11. This modification was suggested by Harding himself at a conference with Dawes in January, 1922. A formal amendment to Circular 49 was actually drafted along these lines but was never issued; an oral clarification in cabinet meeting appears to have been

substituted, supplemented by explicit waivers of jurisdiction in Budget Bureau correspondence with particular departments. Budget Bureau, central files; 1921-38: *Legislation No. 1*. For detailed discussion of this and other aspects of the subject, see Richard E. Neustadt, "Presidential Clearance of Legislation" (Ph.d. diss., Harvard, 1950), pp. 28 ff.

12. Herbert Lord, an army careerist and wartime associate of Dawes, served as budget director from 1922 to 1929. It was his custom, in the search for economy, to inspect his subordinates' desk drawers after office hours, confiscating extra pencils, paper clips, and pads of paper. Note that the total full-time bureau staff numbered less than thirty in 1924. Ten years later the total was still under forty.

13. *Addresses of The President of the United States and the Director of the Bureau of the Budget at the Seventh Regular Meeting of the business Organization of the Government* (Washington, D.C.: Government Printing Office, 1924), p. 6. See also the corresponding releases for the ninth meeting (1925), and the eleventh meeting (1926). The Business Organization of the Government, including all department heads and bureau chiefs, met semi-annually from 1922 to 1929 for purposes of presidential exhortation on, and departmental oaths of fealty to, economy in government. Coolidge's addresses on these occasions are classics of their kind. A Dawes innovation, becoming more ritualistic with each passing year, these meetings were abruptly terminated by Herbert Hoover when he assumed the presidency after years of attendance as secretary of commerce.

14. For a detailed review of these efforts, see Donald A. Hansen, "Legislative Clearance by the Bureau of the Budget" (Staff monograph, Budget Bureau, 1940), pp. 10-19. For Lord's correspondence with departments, see Budget Bureau central files; 1921-38: *Legislation No. 1*.

15. Bureau of the Budget, *Third Annual Report of the Director of the Bureau of the Budget to the President of the United States* (Washington, D.C.: Government Printing Office, 1926), p. 28. Within his limited frame of reference, Lord's claim for compliance appears reasonably accurate. Apparently he was afforded the opportunity to see in advance those legislative reports and proposals that he and the president really wanted. See Hansen, *op. cit.*, pp. 19 ff.

16. Hansen, *op. cit.*, especially pp. 17-20. See also Budget Bureau central files; 1921-

38: *Legislation No. 1* for a variety of typical clearance letters in this period.

17. Budget Bureau central files; 1921-38: *Legislation No. 1*, Budget Director's Memorandum to the files, May 17, 1929. Hoover actually did review and initial virtually every Budget Bureau clearance letter issued during his term of office, an interesting commentary on the presidency of twenty-five years ago. The documentation behind such letters was relatively haphazard in those days, frequently lacking in summaries of the issues, or of agency positions, or even of the bills themselves. The president must often have had to plow through the legislative language to reach an understanding of the subject at hand.

18. Budget Circular 273, issued December 20, 1929. The Budget Bureau shortly found it expedient to issue supplementary instructions requiring that to qualify for the exemption, reports on public bills must be definitely unfavorable, not merely noncommittal. This amplifying note was contained in a "Memorandum to the Heads of all Departments and Establishments," issued April 10, 1930, "by direction of the president." In Coolidge's regime, these types of reports had received almost automatic clearance from the Budget Bureau, usually without referral to the president.

19. This theme appears strongly in Hoover's last three Budget messages. For example:

... we cannot afford to embark on any new or enlarged ventures.... There will be before the Congress many legislative matters involving additions to our estimated expenditures.... The plea of unemployment will be advanced ... but Congress [should] give full due to our financial outlook.... In the absence of further legislation ... we can close [the] year with a balanced budget.

Message of the President of the United States Transmitting the Budget for the Fiscal Year Ending June 30, 1932 (Washington, D.C.: Government Printing Office, 1930), p. XIX.

20. For sidelights on the "newness" of the incoming cabinet see Frances Perkins, *The Roosevelt I Knew* (New York, 1946), pp. 228-30. See also Harold Ickes, *The First Thousand Days* (New York, 1953).

21. Roosevelt's really extraordinary grasp of the tempo and politics of departmental administration comes clear in the meetings of the National Emergency Council, an enlarged cabinet group which met under his chairmanship from 1933 to 1936. The verbatim transcripts of these meetings, available in the National Archives, preserve intact his "lectures" to his department heads on such subjects as how to manage bureau chiefs, congressional committees, and the press.

22. Notably Roosevelt's first budget director, Lewis Douglas, and his first undersecretary of the treasury, Dean Acheson. Both returned to government with the coming of World War II.

23. The bureau's reminder was contained in a memorandum from the budget director's career assistant to the heads of all major agencies, January 22, 1934. It was a gently phrased affair and while most of the agencies replied in kind, the bureau's records indicate that they were slow to take their duties very seriously. See Budget Bureau central files; 1921-38: *Legislation No. 1*. Budget Director Douglas seems to have had no part in this proceeding, nor much interest in the outcome. Two weeks later, when queried by a cabinet member, he expressed himself as unfamiliar with the "old orders," and uncertain of their scope. See National Emergency Council, *Proceedings of the Fourth Meeting* (February 6, 1934), pp. 21 ff.

24. National Emergency Council, *Proceedings of the Nineteenth Meeting* (December 11, 1934), p. 7.

25. *Ibid.*

26. National Emergency Council, *Proceedings of the Twenty-sixth Meeting* (April 23, 1935), p. 8. Bell, at the time a senior career official in the Treasury Department, had taken the budget directorship on an acting basis after Douglas' departure. He held the job in addition to his duties as a special assistant to Secretary Morgenthau and this "temporary" arrangement was continued for nearly five years, until Harold Smith relieved him in 1939.

27. This new order was discussed by the Emergency Council before issuance and the president then went to great lengths to emphasize his personal approval. See National Emergency Council, *Proceedings of the Twenty-eighth Meeting* (December 17, 1935), pp. 14-23.

28. In 1937, when a revision of Circular 336 was under discussion, F. J. Bailey—soon to become the first assistant budget director for legislative reference—wrote an undated memorandum pointing out that

There is no authority whatever in the Budget and Accounting Act for our procedure with respect to reports on legislation. And I would not try to make believe that there is. The authority we have over [these] reports comes from Executive authority and *not* from any act of Congress. Budget Bureau central files; 1921-38: *Legislation No. 2.*

29. National Emergency Council, *Proceedings of the Twenty-second Meeting* (January 22, 1935), p. 2.

30. *Ibid.*, p. 3.

31. National Emergency Council, Proceeding of the *Twenty-eighth Meeting* (December 17, 1935), p. 17.

32. *Ibid.*, pp. 19-21.

33. Edwin E. Witte, "The Preparation of Proposed Legislative Measures by Administrative Departments," *Studies on Administrative Management in the Government of the United States for the President's Committee on Administrative Management* (Washington, D.C.: Government Printing Office, 1937), p. 56.

34. Hansen, *op. cit.*, p. 34.

35. Testimony by Daniel W. Bell, acting director of the budget, before the Treasury Subcommittee of the House Committee on Appropriations, *Hearings on the Treasury Department Appropriation Bill for 1940*, 76th Cong., 1st sess. (Washington, D.C.: Government Printing Office, 1939), p. 936.

36. Roland Young, *This is Congress* (New York, 1943), p. 59.

37. See President's Committee on Administrative Management, *Report with Special Studies* (Washington, D.C.: Government Printing Office, 1937), pp. 15-21.

38. *Ibid.* The report recommended essentially that the Budget Bureau become the president's chief staff agent for "administrative management," enlarged, revitalized, and formally made part of the president's own office. In passing, the report endorsed a staff proposal that NEC clearance functions devolve upon the bureau, with Circular 336 simplified accordingly and then generally enforced. In so urging, the committee simply followed the logic of events, which fitted neatly enough into its major theme: building up the Budget Bureau.

39. See Budget Bureau central files; 1921-38: *Legislation No. 2*, especially entries between March and May, 1937.

40. Circular 344—virtually identical in its terms with 336, save for deletion of NEC's participation—was drafted in May, 1937, but for various reasons, mechanical and other, was not released to the agencies until December 17, 1937. Circular 344 was later renumbered A-19.

41. In 1938, the president obtained from Congress a supplemental appropriation enabling the Budget Bureau to start tooling up for the new or redefined tasks envisaged in the Brownlow report. For details on the ensuing reorganization and restaffing see Bell's testimony, *Hearings . . . op. cit.*, pp. 936-55. This preceded by a year the bureau's formal transfer from the Treasury to the Executive Office of the President (Reorganization Plan I and Executive Order 8,248 of 1939). Before Bell's reorganization, clearance work had been handled almost entirely by the bureau's estimates examiners as an adjunct of their other duties. The new Division of Coordination was conceived, both in the Brownlow studies and by its bureau sponsors, as a small, full-time unit to guide and coordinate, but not supplant, the contribution of all other bureau staff to legislative analysis and review. This has remained the concept, though since World War II not just the bureau but the whole growing Executive Office has become the field from which staff contributions have been sought. By 1939, the Coordination Division's professional staff for legislation numbered five; in the fifteen years since, the comparable figure has never risen above nine. The unit's changes in title have had no substantive purpose or effect.

42. Source of Budget figures: Office of Legislative Reference, Bureau of the Budget. For NEC figures see Witte, *op. cit.*, p. 53.

43. To illustrate: in the 1939 session some 5,000 public bills were introduced in the two Houses of Congress; of these, 452 were passed by both Houses and enrolled that year. But only an item-by-item comparison—which no one has ever made—would show the relationship between the 2,400 odd bills cleared and the 5,000 introduced, or between the 438 drafts cleared and the 452 bills passed. To complicate the issue further, the figures on drafts cleared and on bills enrolled represent separate subjects in virtually all cases; not so the figures on bills introduced, where substantial duplications within or between the two Houses may run as high as 40 percent in the average first session. This is an estimate; firm data are not available.

44. For examples see Hansen, *op. cit.*, pp. 81-84.

45. There were other hazards too:

. . . one enrolled bill was lost and once

when we called up one of the new [New Deal] agencies and asked where the bill was, they said they had put it in the files.
Testimony of Frederick J. Bailey, assistant director for legislative reference, Bureau of the Budget, before the House Committee on the Civil Service, 78th Congress, 1st sess. *Hearings Pursuant to H. Res. 16.*, part 2 (Washington, D.C.: Government Printing Office, 1943), p. 361. The writer is indebted to Bailey; to the late Maurice Latta, former White House executive clerk, whose tenure in subordinate capacities began with McKinley; to William J. Hopkins, Latta's successor as executive clerk; and to James H. Rowe, Jr., a Roosevelt administrative assistant, for data on the evolution of enrolled bill procedure. Information here provided is drawn from their recollections, from Roosevelt's enrolled bill files (now at Hyde Park), and from contemporary Budget Bureau records.

46. "This is a splendid contribution," wrote Rudolph Forster, then White House Executive Clerk, "we could never have got half as far before." Budget Bureau central files; 1921-38: *Enrolled Bills No. 1*, undated memorandum from Forster to F. J. Bailey.

47. In order to build up background files for use on enrollments, private bills were brought back under clearance at the pending stage by Budget Circular 390, June 1, 1942.

48. National Emergency Council, *Proceedings of the Twenty-eighth Meeting* (December 17, 1935), p. 17.

49. Budget Bureau central files; 1921-38: *Enrolled Bills No. 1*, undated memorandum from Rudolph Forster to F. J. Bailey.

50. See note 45.

51. All Roosevelt aides consulted by the writer have been emphatically agreed on his conscious adherence to these views and his consistent application of them.

52. Review of Budget Bureau submissions on enrolled bills first became a distinct White House assignment in 1939, shortly after the bureau's formal assumption of responsibility for their handling. Initially, this assignment went to James H. Rowe, Jr., one of the original administrative assistants to the president appointed under the Reorganization Act of 1939. Rowe had left the White House by the time Samuel I. Rosenman was appointed special counsel in 1943; this work then gravitated naturally to Rosenman, who had performed a similar service for F.D.R. in Albany, a decade earlier. Rosenman was succeeded as special counsel by Clark M. Clifford in 1946; Clifford by Charles S. Murphy

in 1950; Murphy by Bernard Shanley, the present incumbent, who took office with the Eisenhower administration.

53. Testimony of Roger W. Jones before the House Select Committee on Lobbying Activities, 81st Congress, 2nd sess. *Hearings Pursuant to H. Res. 298*, part 10 (Washington, D.C.: Government Printing Office, 1950). Note that the current version of Circular A-19 is printed with Jones' testimony.

54. After 1949, NSRB, ODM, and DMS staff, and occasionally NSC staff, were also drawn into or given leadership of such Executive Office teams.

55. Of course, not all proposals were prepared in this way. For example, the so-called "Brannan Plan" was first set forth informally in the shape of "suggestions for study" put to congressional committees in testimony by the then secretary of agriculture. Truman's health insurance proposals were never translated into administration-approved specifics; nor did the administration ever commit itself to the details of bills introduced in Congress. As for revenue measures, their preparation, for the most part, was—and still is—dominated by the Treasury.

56. Currently, the committees which engage most frequently in direct referrals are: Senate Interior, Labor, Public Works, Finance, Banking, Commerce, Civil Service, Government Operations; House Agriculture, Commerce, Merchant Marine, Public Works, Government Operations, Civil Service. Source: Office of Legislative Reference, Bureau of the Budget. Note that the early adherence of the Senate Labor Committee reflects Senator Taft's own view of the need for a formal channel between president and committees on current measures.

57. Also in 1949, the Senate majority leader arranged to have the Budget report to him the number of each bill cleared and the nature of the clearance given, week by week. These data were then tabulated by his staff for ready reference to administration stands on the general run of pending bills. So routinized a transmittal of so much information proved of limited utility. After 1950, the practice was curtailed.

58. Dodge was not precisely a newcomer to government, having organized War Department renegotiation activities in World War II and having carried out significant overseas assignments for the occupation authorities of both Germany and Japan. His attitude toward his new role was very healthy for the institution he would head, fairly free

of the suspicion and uncertainty which plagued so many Eisenhower appointees and their career subordinates. Dodge resigned as budget director, April 15, 1954, and was succeeded by his deputy, Rowland Hughes.

For information on this and other aspects of the 1953 transition, the writer is indebted to the many officials throughout the Executive Office who have answered his inquiries with candor and good will.

28. The President's Spending Power*

LOUIS FISHER

On the basis of the Constitution and traditional legislative prerogatives, Congress lays claim to exclusive control over the purse. Nevertheless, while it is up to Congress to appropriate funds, it is also true that the president and executive officials enjoy considerable discretion as to how those funds are spent. It is a mistake to regard executive spending discretion as essentially a 20th century phenomenon, originating with the Budget and Accounting Act. Administrative discretion over the expenditure of public funds has been a fact of life since the first administration, as will be evident from the following examples.

LUMP-SUM APPROPRIATIONS

It is commonly believed that the Federalists and the Jeffersonian Republicans divided sharply on the question of lump-sum appropriations. We are told that the Jeffersonians advocated specific appropriations as a means of maintaining legislative control, while the Federalists wanted lump-sum appropriations to permit executive discretion. This belief is not borne out by the facts.

The first appropriation act of 1789 provided lump sums for four general classes of expenditures: $216,000 for the civil list; $137,000 for the Department of War; $190,000 to discharge warrants issued by the previous Board of Treasury; and $96,000 for pensions to disabled veterans. The appropriation acts for 1790 and 1791 also provided lump sums, but the funds were to be spent in accordance with estimates given Congress by the secretary of the treasury. His estimates, of course, had been broken down into specific items.

Beginning with the appropriation act of December 23, 1791, Congress narrowed executive discretion still further by using a "that is to say" clause. For instance, a little over a half million was appropriated for the military establishment—"that is to say," $102,686 for pay of troops, $48,000 for clothing, $4,152 for forage, and so forth. By 1793, appropriation acts were descending to such minutiae as an item of $450 for firewood, stationery, printing, and other contingencies in the treasurer's office. Thus, long before the Jeffersonians had gained control of the presidency, the practice of granting lump sums had been abandoned.

The dispute between the Federalists and the Jeffersonians is grounded more in party rhetoric than in administrative reality. After Jefferson's election as president in 1801, he told Congress that it would be prudent to appropriate

*Source: Reprinted with permission of Macmillan Publishing Co., Inc. from President and Congress: Power and Policy by Louis Fisher, pp. 110-32. Copyright © 1972 by The Free Press, a Division of Macmillan Publishing Company, Inc. Selection has been retitled and originally appeared as a part of Chapter 4, "Spending Powers."

"specific sums to every specific purpose susceptible of definition." Hamilton promptly denounced that recommendation as "preposterous," insisting that nothing was "more wild or of more inconvenient tendency. . . ." The biting quality of Hamilton's attack no doubt reflected his assumption that Jefferson's message to Congress was an indirect criticism of Federalist financial policies. Understandably, Hamilton was quick to take offense. Moreover, Jefferson was in error on two counts: first for implying that lump-sum appropriations had been the practice in the past, and second for suggesting that sums should be appropriated for every purpose susceptible of definition.

Jefferson's secretary of the treasury, Albert Gallatin, knew that it was impossible for Congress to foresee, "in all its details, the necessary application of moneys, and a reasonable discretion should be allowed to the proper executive department." Instead of $1,857,242 being appropriated for the War Department, Gallatin had simply wanted such a sum broken down into smaller categories—$488,076 for officers' pay and subsistence, $400,000 for ammunition and arms, $141,530 for clothing, and so forth. There was nothing at all novel about that suggestion; appropriation acts had been passed with that level of detail since December 23, 1791. Jefferson himself, as president, recognized that "too minute a specification has its evil as well as a too general one," and thought it better for Congress to appropriate in gross while trusting in executive discretion.

Lump-sum appropriations become particularly noticeable during emergency periods of war or national depression. During the Civil War, Congress appropriated $50 million to pay two- and three-year volunteers; $26 million for subsistence; another $14 million for transportation and supplies; and $76 million to cover an assortment of items, to be divided among them "as the exigencies of the service may require. . . ." During World War I, Wilson received $100 million for "national security and defense"—to be spent at his discretion—and $250 million to be applied to construction costs under the Emergency Shipping Fund.

Emergency relief programs during the Great Depression set aside billions to be spent at the president's discretion. Congress appropriated $950 million in 1934 for emergency relief programs and the Civil Works Program, making the money available "for such projects and/or purposes and under such rules and regulations as the president in his discretion may prescribe. . . ." The Emergency Relief Appropriation Act of 1935 appropriated $4 billion for eight general classes of projects, the money to be used "in the discretion and under the direction" of the president. Appropriations for World War II included such lump sums as $6.3 billion for the increase and replacement of naval vessels, and $23.6 billion for the Army Air Corps. A general description accompanied these appropriations, but the figures were not broken down.

The atomic bomb project was financed for several years from funds for "Engineer Service, Army" and "Expediting Production." When larger sums for manufacturing the bomb could no longer be concealed by this method, a few legislative leaders were told of the project and asked to provide funds without letting other legislators know how the money would be spent. Accordingly, the money was tucked away unnoticed in an appropriation bill. Total appropriations for the Manhattan Project came to over $2 billion. Members of the House Appropriations Committee told one writer that about $800 million had been spent on the project before they knew about it.

The public works appropriation act of 1970 makes available a lump sum of $1.9 billion to the Atomic Energy Commission. Instead of breaking down the figure into individual line items, there exists a moral understanding between the commission and the appropriations subcommittees involved. The money is expected to be spent fairly much in accordance with the commission's budget estimates, as amended by congressional actions and directives included in committee reports. This kind of nonstatutory control depends on a "keep the faith" attitude among agency officials, as well as a trust by the subcommittees in the integrity of administrators. If the AEC were to violate that trust and abuse its discretionary power, it would face the prospect the next year of budget cutbacks and line-item appropriations.

CONTINGENCY FUNDS

Congress realizes that future events cannot be anticipated—or anticipated with great precision—and that it must therefore provide special funds to cover contingencies and emergencies. Emergency funds were particularly large during World War II. In statutes from June 13, 1940, to October 26, 1942, Congress appropriated a total of $425 million in funds for "emergencies affecting the national security and defense," plus another $320 million in funds for temporary shelters in areas suffering from housing shortage because of the war.

Contingency funds have been used for purposes not even contemplated by Congress when it appropriated the money. For instance, on March 1, 1961, President Kennedy issued an executive order establishing the Peace Corps. Not until seven months later did Congress appropriate funds for the agency. In the meantime, the president financed the agency by using contingency funds from the Mutual Security Act. Also in 1961, the Foreign Assistance Act provided a contingency fund of $275 million, to be used by the president "when he determines such use to be important to the national interest." The contingency fund

for foreign aid the next year was set at $250 million.

The Department of Defense Appropriations Act of 1965 made available $1.7 billion for an Emergency Fund for Southeast Asia. The executive branch enjoyed complete discretion. Upon determination by the president that such action was necessary in connection with military activities, the secretary of defense could transfer the money to any appropriation available to the Defense Department for military functions.

Other sources of emergency funds are found in statutes providing for disaster relief. The Federal Disaster Act of 1950 and subsequent statutes offer financial assistance to state and local governments whenever the president declares a major disaster. From 1951 through 1970, the president issued 338 declarations and allocated $857 million from the disaster relief fund.

FREE WORLD FORCES

The financing of the Vietnam War illustrates how billions can be spent for purposes known to relatively few legislators. In September 1966, President Johnson expressed his "deep admiration as well as that of the American people for the action recently taken by the Philippines to send a civic action group of 2,000 men to assist the Vietnamese in resisting aggression and rebuilding their country." Other announcements from the White House created the impression that not only had the Philippines volunteered troops, but so had Thailand, South Korea, and other members of the "Free World Forces."

Hearings held by the Symington Subcommittee in 1969 and 1970 revealed that the United States had offered sizable subsidies to these countries. It was learned that the Philippines had received river patrol craft, engineer equipment, a special overseas allowance for their soldiers sent to Vietnam, and additional equipment to strengthen Philippine forces at home. The total cost to the United States for the sending of one Philippine construction battalion to Vietnam came to $38.8 million. Senator Fulbright remarked that it was his own feeling that "all we did was go over and hire their soldiers in order to support our then administration's view that so many people were in sympathy with our war in Vietnam."

The Philippine government denied that U.S. contributions represented a subsidy or a fee in return for sending the construction battalion, but an investigation by the General Accounting Office (GAO) confirmed the fact that "quid pro quo assistance" had indeed been given to the Philippines. Moreover, there was evidence that the Johnson administration had increased other forms of military and economic aid to the Philippines in return for the battalion.

The Symington Subcommittee also uncovered an agreement that the Johnson administration had made with the Royal Thai government, in 1967, to cover any additional costs connected with the sending of Thai soldiers to Vietnam. An interim GAO report estimated that the U.S. government had invested "probably more than $260 million in equipment, allowances, subsistence, construction, military sales concessions, and other support to the Thais for their contribution under the Free World Military Assistance program to Vietnam."

U.S. subsidies were used once again to support the sending of South Korean forces to Vietnam. American assistance included equipment to modernize Korean forces at home; equipment and all additional costs to cover the deployment of Korean forces in Vietnam (including the payment of overseas allowances); additional loans from the Agency of International Development; and increased ammunition and communications facilities in Korea. For the period from fiscal 1965 to fiscal 1970, U.S. costs resulting from the dispatch of Korean forces to Vietnam were estimated at $927.5 million. Until the

Symington subcommittee hearings, few members of Congress were aware of this financial arrangement.

TRANSFERS BETWEEN CLASSES

Transfer authority permits the president to take funds that have been appropriated for one class of appropriations and apply them to another. In 1793, Representative Giles offered a number of resolutions charging Hamilton with improper use of national funds. The first resolution stated that "laws making specific appropriations of money should be strictly observed by the administrator of the finances thereof." Representative Smith of South Carolina proceeded to refute Giles point by point, arguing that the administration ought to be free to depart from congressional appropriations whenever the public safety or credit would thereby be improved. When exercised for the public good, executive spending discretion would "always meet the approbation of the National Legislature." All the Giles resolutions were subsequently voted down by the House.

This appears to be a typical collision between the legislative and executive branches, but the dispute was not so much constitutional as it was partisan and personal. It was Hamilton's colleague in the cabinet, Thomas Jefferson, who had drafted the resolutions for Giles. The author of Smith's effective rebuttal? Why, none other than Hamilton himself.

Jefferson's strictures against transfers were excessively narrow and failed to curb the practice. During his own administration, Representative Bayard explained that it was sometimes necessary to allow expenditures to deviate from appropriations, by transferring funds from one account to another. Such transfers were technically illegal, but "its being the custom palliates it." Proposals to abolish transfers altogether were countered by two arguments. Secretary of the Treasury Crawford told

Congress in 1817 that in receiving reports of transfers, legislators automatically learned where appropriations had been redundant and where deficient, thereby providing a convenient guide for future appropriation bills. Second, removal of transfer authority would compel executive departments to submit inflated estimates as a cushion against unexpected expenses. Crawford warned Congress: "The idea that economy will be enforced by repealing the provision will, I am confident, be found to be wholly illusory. Withdraw the power of transfer, and the departments will increase their estimates."

Statutes over the next few decades permitted transfers under various circumstances. Beginning in 1860, departmental heads were prohibited from using surplus funds to cover deficiencies in other accounts, but that restriction had little impact after the outbreak of the Civil War. General lump-sum appropriations during the war gave departmental heads adequate flexibility. In 1868, Congress repealed all previous acts authorizing transfers, and stipulated that "no money appropriated for one purpose shall hereafter be used for any other purpose than that for which it is appropriated."

Nevertheless, Congress has found it necessary at times to delegate broad transfer authority to the administration. The 1932 Economy Act cut federal spending so hastily and in such indiscriminate fashion that Congress permitted the executive branch to transfer funds from one agency to another to repair the damage. The Lend Lease Act of 1941 appropriated $7 billion for ordnance, aircraft, tanks, and for other categories of defense articles. The president could transfer as much as 20 percent of the appropriations from one category to another, provided that no appropriation would be increased by more than 30 percent. In 1943, the budget director was authorized to transfer 10 percent of military appropriations made available for fiscal 1944, subject to certain conditions. Appropriations in that particular act came to about $59 billion.

AID TO CAMBODIA

Current law provides that "Except as otherwise provided by law, sums appropriated for the various branches of expenditures in the public service shall be applied solely to the objects for which they are respectively made, and for no others." Exceptions to this general rule are fairly common. Appropriations for the Defense Department and for foreign assistance are especially generous in permitting the transfer of funds. It was on the basis of transfer authority that President Nixon was able to extend financial assistance to Cambodia after his intervention there in the spring of 1970. At the end of the year, he appealed to Congress for $255 million in military and economic assistance for Cambodia. Of that amount, $100 million was to restore funds which the president had *already* diverted to Cambodia from other programs.

He was able to do that because under Section 610 of the Foreign Assistance Act, the president may transfer up to 10 percent of the funds of one foreign aid program to another, provided that the second program is not increased by more than 20 percent. Operating under that authority, the Nixon administration borrowed $40 million from aid programs originally scheduled for Greece, Turkey, and Taiwan; took another $50 million from funds that had been assigned largely to Vietnam; and diverted still other funds, until a total of $108.9 million in military assistance had been given—or committed—to Cambodia.

REPROGRAMING

Reprograming is a term used to describe the shifting of funds *within* an appropriation item. Reprograming differs from transfers in two respects. Unlike transfers, funds are not shifted from one account to another. The total amount available in an account remains constant under reprograming, while the purpose to which funds are applied can be changed. Second, reprograming, while it must conform to the general appropriation language, does not require specific statutory authority, as is the case with transfers. Instead, an informal clearance procedure takes place between executive agencies and legislative committees, as a means of providing required flexibility, and of meeting contingencies, emergencies, new requirements, and other urgent developments.

The reprograming technique recognizes that during the interval between an agency's justification of a program and its actual expenditure of funds, new and better applications of the money might come to light. Especially is that true of the Defense Department, where various factors can often dictate that funds be used in a different manner than called for in an appropriations bill. In recent years, military reprograming generally runs over a billion dollars a year. When a new administration takes office, the figure can be considerably higher. For instance, several budget revisions by the Kennedy administration brought the fiscal 1961 reprograming figure for the Defense Department to $3.8 billion. That includes reprograming actions only on major procurement and for research, development, test, and evaluation.

In the past decade and a half, Congress has gradually tightened its control over the reprograming of funds. In 1955 the House Committee on Appropriations insisted that the Defense Department submit semi-annual reports on all reprograming actions. A 1959 report by House Appropriations observed that semi-annual tabulations had been helpful but not sufficiently timely. The committee directed the Defense Department to report periodically—but in no case less than 30 days after departmental approval—the approved reprograming actions involving $1,000,000 or more in the case of operation and maintenance; $1,000,000 or more for research, development, test, and evalua-

tion; and $5,000,000 or more in the case of procurement.

In 1963, in response to the committee's request for an immediate revision of reprograming procedures, the Defense Department called for prior approval by committees, not only by the appropriations committees but by authorizing committees as well. Prior approval of selected items and programs was required of the House and Senate Committees on Armed Services and of the House and Senate Committees on Appropriations. In an effort to bring reprograming under broader legislative review, Senator Chiles introduced a bill in 1971 to require the comptroller general to compile information on reprograming and to furnish such information to all committees and to all members of Congress.

TRANSFERS IN TIME

In addition to being transferred from one class to another, funds may be transferred from one year to the next. Congress enacted a law in 1795 to restrict this practice. With certain exceptions, any unexpended funds remaining in the treasury for more than two years were to be transferred to a surplus fund, at which point the appropriation would lapse. Administrative actions quickly nullified the law's intent. For instance, Congress passed legislation in 1819 to suppress the slave trade and to punish crimes of piracy. In so doing, it neglected to appropriate funds to finance these new responsibilities. President Monroe supplied the necessary vessels by using old balances remaining on the books of the Navy Department. When legislators objected that this violated the two-year limit on appropriations, they were told that the balances were exempt from the law because they had been in the hands of the *treasurer* (who acted as agent for the military departments), rather than being in the treasury itself.

An 1820 statute directed the secretary

of the treasury to place funds that had been left unexpended by the Departments of War and Navy into a surplus fund. Implementation of that statute, however, depended on a statement by the secretary of the department that "the object for which the appropriation was made has been effected." Failure to make that declaration meant that the money still remained available for future use.

A more stringent provision appeared in 1852. Congress directed that any moneys unexpended after two years should be carried immediately to a surplus fund and the appropriation regarded as having ceased. Decisions by the attorney general diluted the force of the statute. In cases of contracted items, personal service, or other claims on the government, appropriations would remain available from year to year until the obligation was fully discharged. In such situations "unexpended" came to mean "unobligated," and the appropriation would not lapse into the surplus fund. In a second decision, the attorney general held that a department could spend any balance on hand from the previous year. According to that rule of construction, it would be impossible for a balance of two or more years to exist "unless the balance of a previous year exceed in amount the whole expenditure of the present year. . . ."

New statutes appeared in 1870 and 1874 to restrict the use of unexpended balances. Specifically excluded from those restrictions were appropriations for projects that usually take more than two years to complete. Current law, for instance, permits appropriations to "remain available until expended" for public works under the Bureau of Yards and Docks and for public buildings. Such appropriations are referred to as no-year money.

No-year money permits the president to release funds when he determines that they can be spent in the most effective manner, depending on the availability of labor, of materials, and on the state of technical developments. In the Department of Defense, appropriations for procurement and for research, development, test, and evaluation (R.D.T.&E.) have generally been made available on a no-year basis. For fiscal 1970, the amount of no-year funds for those categories came to $25.5 billion. The fiscal 1971 appropriation bill for the Defense Department brought carryover balances under closer control. Appropriations for major procurement became available for only three fiscal years (except for shipbuilding, which requires a five-year term), while appropriations for R.D.T.&E. were made available only for a two-year period. In order to "dry up" the large amounts of no-year funds available from prior years, this kind of restriction would have to be enacted for about three straight years.

Despite legislative concern about carryover balances, and the existence of statutory restrictions, a huge volume of funds continues to flow from one year to the next. For fiscal 1972, an estimated $259.5 billion in unspent authority remained available from prior years. Of that amount, only $87.4 billion was expected to be spent in fiscal 1972. The remainder will be carried forward to later years.

SPEEDING UP EXPENDITURES

In addition to stretching out the period for making expenditures, presidents can also speed up expenditures. Accelerated spending was employed in 1958 as an anti-recession measure by the Eisenhower administration. Public works were accelerated, housing and home finance programs speeded up, and government supply levels raised—all in an effort to pump more money into the economy and stimulate recovery. Advance procurement adds to the cost of storage space and inventory checks, however, and also creates administrative complications by forcing agencies to depart from prior schedules and long-term contractual commitments.

Moreover, with a fixed amount appropriated for programs, acceleration must at some point be offset by deceleration, unless new funds are provided. Thus, at the very moment when the recovery phase needs reinforcement, the depletion of allotted funds has a retarding effect. That is especially serious, since the automatic stabilizers, in the recovery phase, reverse direction and have a retarding effect of their own.

In 1961, President Kennedy also relied on accelerated programs to combat recession. He directed the Veterans Administration to speed up the payment of $258 million in life insurance dividends, making the money available in the first quarter instead of over the entire year. A special dividend payment of $218 million was made later, thereby reinforcing the speed-up with new funds and contributing a permanent boost to the economy. Kennedy also directed the heads of each department to accelerate procurement and construction wherever possible; he hastened payments to farmers under the price support program; increased the annual rate of free food distribution to needy families (from about $60 million to more than $200 million); and made immediately available to the states the balance of federal-aid highway funds ($724 million) that had been scheduled for the entire fiscal year.

IMPOUNDMENT

Impoundment of funds is a "transfer in time" that deserves separate treatment. During the past three decades, presidents have withheld funds from such programs as the B-70 bomber, Air Force groups, antimissile systems, flood control projects, highways, supercarriers, urban renewal, and Model Cities. By refusing to spend appropriated funds, the president provokes the charge that he is obligated under the Constitution to execute the laws, not hold them in defiance—obligated to interpret appropriation bills not as mere permission to

spend but rather as a mandate to spend as Congress directs. Otherwise, the argument runs, he encroaches upon the spending prerogatives of Congress, violates the doctrine of separated powers, and assumes unto himself a power of item veto neither sanctioned by the Constitution nor granted by Congress.

A number of law journal articles, in advancing this line of argument, invoke phrases from Supreme Court decisions to bolster their case. I have examined these decisions and find that they have only the most tenuous relationship to the issue of impoundment. The decisive appeal over the years has not been to legal principles and Court decisions. As one writer has put it, the president "can and may withhold expenditure of funds to the extent that the political milieu in which he operates permits him to do so."

Political leverage is maximized, naturally, by claims of constitutional support, and both sides therefore invoke the separation doctrine and "intent of the framers" to their own advantage. Thus, when Congress appropriates and the president refuses to spend, legislators chastise him for encroaching upon their spending prerogatives. And yet if Congress tried to compel the president to spend the funds, he could charge usurpation of executive responsibilities.

Instead of introducing into this discussion pieces of evidence from prior Court decisions, I think it is more instructive to understand the larger political and legal framework within which impoundment takes place. Certain statutes require that funds be withheld under conditions and circumstances spelled out by Congress. Title VI of the 1964 Civil Rights Act empowers the president to withhold funds from federally financed programs in which there is discrimination by race, color, or national origin. Special desegregation grants may be terminated when school districts violate civil rights requirements. A 1968 act requires states to update their welfare payment standards to reflect cost-of-living increases; failure to comply with the act can lead to a cutoff of federal welfare aid. The Revenue and Expenditure Control Act of 1968 required expenditure reductions, most of which were achieved by administrative action. Spending ceilings and debt limit requirements provide other opportunities to withhold funds.

By law, the president is expected to set aside funds for contingencies, or to effect savings whenever they are made possible, "by or through changes in requirements, greater efficiency of operations, or other developments" that take place after funds have been appropriated. The Department of Housing and Urban Development suspended a mortgage subsidy program in January 1971 after the discovery of widespread abuses. President Eisenhower impounded funds for the production of antiballistic missiles, insisting that funds should not be released until developmental tests were satisfactorily completed.

When the president impounds funds to prevent deficiencies or to effect savings, few legislators are likely to challenge him. George H. Mahon, chairman of the House Appropriations Committee, has said that

the weight of experience and practice bears out the general proposition that an appropriation does not constitute a mandate to spend every dollar appropriated. . . . I believe it is fundamentally desirable that the Executive have limited powers of impoundment in the interests of good management and constructive economy in public expenditures.

Cases have arisen in the past, and will arise in the future, where the president withholds funds on the basis of what he considers to be "good management and constructive economy," whereas Congress looks at the issue in an entirely different manner. In 1961, Congress added $180 million to the $200 million requested by the Kennedy administration for the development of the B-70 bomber. Defense Secretary McNamara,

stressing the U.S. advantage over the Soviets in bombers and the deterrent capability of American missile strength, refused to release the unwanted funds. The following year the House Armed Services Committee threatened to "direct" the administration to spend money toward production, but later removed the language at the urging of President Kennedy. Even if Congress had gone through with its threat to mandate expenditures, the president could well have argued that there were too many developmental unknowns, too many technical questions unsolved, and therefore no justification for proceeding beyond the prototype stage.

In such situations it is contended that the president thwarts the will of Congress. It is not always easy, however, to know what that will is. President Truman's impoundment of Air Force funds in 1949 would appear to be a clear denial of legislative intent and yet the situation was not at all that simple. The House had voted to increase Air Force funds, while the Senate sided with the president in opposing the increase. The matter lay deadlocked in conference committee, with adjournment close at hand and the military services in need of funds to meet their payrolls. A Senate motion to vote continuing appropriations was rejected by the House. To break the impasse, the Senate reluctantly accepted the extra Air Force funds, but with the understanding, as Senator Thomas said, that "if the money is appropriated it may not be used" by the president. In light of that legislative history, it is clearly an exaggeration to claim that impoundment in this case was a denial of "the will of Congress."

In the cases cited thus far, funds have been withheld either in response to specific statutory directives or on grounds of prudent use of funds in weapons procurement. An entirely different situation has developed under the Nixon administration, where funds have been withheld from domestic programs because the president considers those programs incompatible with his own set of budget priorities. In the spring of 1971, the Nixon administration announced that it was withholding more than $12 billion, most of which consisted of highway money and funds for various urban programs. When Secretary Romney appeared before a Senate committee in March, he explained that funds were being held back from various urban programs because there was no point in accelerating programs that were "scheduled for termination." He was referring to the fact that Congress had added funds to grant-in-aid programs which the administration wanted to consolidate and convert into its revenue sharing proposal. To impound funds in this prospective sense—holding on to money in anticipation that Congress will enact an administration bill—is a new departure for the impoundment technique. Impoundment is not being used to avoid deficiencies, or to effect savings, or even to fight inflation, but rather to shift the scale of priorities from one administration to the next, prior to congressional action.

Political pressures have sometimes been enough to pry loose impounded funds. After the November 1966 elections, President Johnson announced a $5.3 billion reduction in federal programs. Economic and legal justifications presented by the administration failed to placate the localities affected by the cutbacks. Sensitive to criticism from the states, President Johnson released some of the money in February 1967, and on the eve of a conference the next month with governors he released additional amounts.

In the fall of 1970 it was learned that the Nixon administration planned to withhold some education funds. Criticism began to build up in Congress and in the school districts. Two weeks before the November elections, the administration announced that the money would be released. When the secretary of health, education, and welfare was asked whether the pending elections

had prompted the administration to reverse its position and release the funds, he replied, smiling, that there was "no connection whatsoever." Another example: early in 1971 the Nixon administration decided to impound some Model Cities funds to help finance its revenue sharing proposal. Letters explaining the cutoff of funds were ready to be mailed to the mayors. They learned of the plan, however, issued a strong protest, and the letters were never sent out.

These pressure tactics and confrontations, even when successful, are not satisfactory to the mayors. In the midst of their busy schedules they must come to Congress first to support an authorization bill. They testify a second time in behalf of the appropriation bill. Now they must come to Congress and the administration a third time to see that the money, having already been authorized and appropriated, is actually spent.

In March 1971, the Senate Subcommittee on the Separation of Powers held hearings for the purpose of establishing better legislative control over impounded funds. Senator Sam J. Ervin, Jr., subcommittee chairman, introduced a bill several months later to require the president to notify Congress within 10 days whenever he impounds funds appropriated for a specific purpose or project. The president's message would include the amount of funds impounded, the specific projects or functions affected, and the reasons for impounding the funds. Congress would then have 60 days to pass a joint resolution disapproving the impoundment.

In effect, the Ervin bill gives the president a form of item-veto authority without having to amend the Constitution. It also assumes, in the case of a resolution of disapproval, that Congress has the power to compel expenditures. While it is true that a legal memorandum issued by an official in the Nixon administration affirms the power of Congress to mandate expenditures in the area of formula grants for the impacted areas program, the president could exert his prerogatives elsewhere. In the area of defense procurement, in particular, the president could deny that Congress has the power to deprive him of his judgment and discretion in the administration of programs and in the management of funds.

UNAUTHORIZED COMMITMENTS

The Constitution provides that "No money shall be drawn from the treasury but in consequence of appropriations made by law." Presidents have nevertheless found it expedient at times to enter into financial obligations not authorized by Congress. For instance, Jefferson agreed to accept France's offer to sell the whole of Louisiana for $11,250,000—plus an additional $3,750,000 to cover private claims against France—even though the offer exceeded instructions set forth by Congress. Another example of an unauthorized commitment occurred in 1807. After Congress had recessed, a British vessel fired on the American ship *Chesapeake*. Without statutory authority, Jefferson ordered military purchases for the emergency, disclosing to Congress his action when it convened. "To have awaited a previous and special sanction by law." he said, "would have lost occasions which might not be retrieved."

In 1861, after the firing on Fort Sumter, and while Congress was adjourned. Lincoln directed his secretary of the treasury to advance $2 million to three private citizens, to be used by them for "military and naval measures necessary for the defense and support of the government. . . ." Lincoln acted without statutory authority, but the regular channels could not be trusted, since many Treasury officials were Southern sympathizers.

Theodore Roosevelt was determined to send an American fleet around the world as a show of force, despite the insistence of the chairman of the Senate Committee on Naval Affairs that the fleet could not go because Congress would refuse to appropriate the funds. Roosevelt answered that he had enough money to take the fleet halfway around the world, and that "if Congress did not choose to appropriate enough money to get the fleet back, why, it could stay in the Pacific." There was no further difficulty about the money.

Presidential actions in creating unauthorized commitments did not reach the courts, but the Supreme Court reviewed financial initiatives taken by other executive officials. One case involved an agreement made between a government contractor and Buchanan's secretary of war, John B. Floyd. The contractor, lacking sufficient funds to complete the order, was allowed to draw time-drafts and have them purchased by his suppliers to provide interim assistance. The government subsequently accepted drafts of $5 million, but over a million dollars remained unpaid. Holders of unpaid drafts contended that Secretary Floyd's acceptances were binding on the government. The Court dismissed their claim, denying that Floyd possessed either constitutional or statutory authority to enter into his agreements.

In trying to prevent unauthorized commitments, Congress has had to soften the language of statutes at times in order to allow army and navy supply agencies to sign contracts in advance of appropriations. Otherwise, material would not have been available in time. When Congress prohibited unauthorized commitments in 1820, an exception was allowed for contracts for subsistence and clothing for the army and navy, as well as for contracts by the Quartermaster's Department. Legislative delays in passing appropriation bills (enacted after one-fourth to a third of the year had elapsed) forced departments to make expenditures not legally authorized. Legislative instructions for the new appropriations were also delayed. The Secretary of the Navy reported to Congress in 1825 that his department, for nearly half the year, acted in "perfect ignorance of the law under which it is bound to act." As a result, "The law is, necessarily, not complied with, because it is passed after the act is performed."

Administrative discretion in the handling of funds regularly provoked the ire of Congress. The Gilmer committee reported in 1842:

> Under color of what are termed *regulations,* large amounts of money are often applied to purposes never contemplated by the appropriating power, and numerous offices are sometimes actually created in the same way. . . . It is hoped that in future this code of Executive legislation may cease to be known in our history.

CAMBODIA AND THE C-5 A

Contemporary regulations on unauthorized commitments are far more explicit than the Constitution. The U.S. Code contains the following admonition:

> No officer or employee of the United States shall make or authorize an expenditure from or create or authorize an obligation under any appropriation or fund in excess of the amount available therein; nor shall any such officer or employee involve the Government in any contract or other obligation, for the payment of money for any purpose, in advance of appropriations made for such purpose, unless such contract or obligation is authorized by law.

President Nixon's intervention in Cambodia, followed by his request for $255 million in assistance for Cambodia, was made entirely at his own initiative. Here is a clear case where the executive branch involved the government in an obligation—at least a moral obligation—in advance of appropriations. Not only did the intervention lead to a financial obligation in this case, but future requests in addition to the $255 million are expected. As Secretary of State Rogers explained on December 10, l970: "I think it is true that when we ask for military assistance and economic assistance for Cambodia we do certainly take on some obligation for some continuity."

The cost overrun problem with the C-5A cargo plane is another example where the administration can, in effect, commit Congress to hundreds of millions in additional expenditures. The Air Force selected the Lockheed Aircraft Corporation as the airframe prime contractor in 1965. During hearings in November 1968, the Joint Economic Committee learned that the original estimate of $3.4 billion had climbed to $5.3 billion—that is, a cost overrun of almost $2 billion. Problems with other Lockheed contracts, including the Cheyenne helicopter, put the company near bankruptcy. The Pentagon presented a plan to rescue the company with federal funds, at a cost of several hundred million dollars. Critics called this "bailout money," while the Pentagon contended that the collapse of Lockheed would trigger a chain of events injurious to the national defense effort. As was the case with the Cambodian intervention, and the expenditures which that entailed, Congress faced the prospect of funding an executive *fait accompli.*

If a 1958 statute is interpreted broadly enough, the Pentagon has sufficient authority to cover any of its cost overruns. That statute authorized the president to modify any defense contract "whenever he deems that such action would facilitate the national defense." The sole restriction is that the act remains in effect during a national emergency declared by Congress or by the president. The United States is currently in a state of national emergency, not because of Vietnam, but because of a proclamation issued by President Truman on December 16, 1950, after China had intervened in Korea. Two decades later that proclamation has yet to be terminated.

Existing studies tell us how the president formulates the budget and how Congress acts on his budget requests. Surprisingly, we know relatively little about how the money, once appropriated, is actually spent.

For a number of good reasons, expenditures must deviate from appropriations. Appropriations are made many months, and sometimes years, in advance of expenditures. Congress acts with imperfect knowledge in trying to legislate in fields which are themselves highly technical and undergoing constant change. New circumstances will develop to make obsolete and mistaken the decisions reached by Congress at the appropriation stage. It is not practicable for Congress to adjust to these new developments by passing large numbers of supplemental appropriation bills. Were Congress to control expenditures by confining administrators to narrow statutory details, it would perhaps protect its power of the purse but it would not protect the purse itself. Discretion is needed for the sound management of public funds.

While there no doubt exists a need for executive flexibility, that is an abstract term capable of hiding much mischief. It is evident that in a number of areas, including covert financing, impoundment, and unauthorized commitments, Congress has yet to discover a satisfactory means for controlling expenditures. Public policy is then decided by administrators rather than by the elected officials and the budgets they adopt. The results are often incongruous. Congress goes through the motions of authorizing and appropriating funds but the money is never spent. On the other hand, Congress can find itself locked in to paying for administrative commitments it never authorized. New statutory and nonstatutory controls are needed. The objective must be an expenditure process in which administrators enjoy substantial discretion in exercising judgment and taking responsibility for their actions, but those actions will have to be directed toward executing congressional, not administrative, policy.

29. Toward a Theory of Congressional–Executive Relations*

PERI E. ARNOLD
L. JOHN ROOS

The theme of the second Nixon administration appears to be "Save the Presidency." It is clear that Mr. Nixon views his best defense against critics to be the claim of a constitutional imperative to defend his office. And, he continually reminds us, it is an obligation to defend not only the presidency, but the strong presidency.[1]

Mr. Nixon's attachment to the strong presidency is more than a protective strategy. It grows out of American practice and recent theory. His language and themes are predictable within our political system. In American national politics, substantive issues and questions of institutional roles are continually entangled.

Ours is a "made" political system, fashioned through a document at a

*Source: From Review of Politics, vol. 36 (July 1974), pp. 410-29. Copyright © 1974 University of Notre Dame. Reprinted by permission.

specific historical moment. We Americans venerate the framers of the Constitution rather than tradition. But the Constitution could not firmly settle the question of how power was to be exercised by the Congress or president. Rather, the Constitution created a framework within which roles were flexible, even protean. As a result, substantive political issues are likely to escalate into debate over formal powers. Our relation to the Constitution is Talmudic. For us, it only provides questions, not answers.

Our models or theories of the relationship between Congress and the presidency are founded on assertions of the powers one or the other branch ought to exercise. And vice versa, to say that the president ought to have certain prerogatives is to imply a theory about the relationship between his office and Congress.

Our purpose in this essay is to consider the consequences of alternate theories of congressional–presidential relations. These theories are, initially, normative in that they are prescriptions for the political system and potential solutions to the muteness of the Constitution. But these are not simply the mere opinions of academics. Our theories of congressional–presidential relations have real political consequences as they serve to inform, guide and justify political action. Theories frame our alternatives and limit our actions. Hence we must inform ourselves of alternate choices and actions by considering alternate theories.

The method of this essay will be to examine the central premise of the theory which underlies the ongoing debate between the Congress and the president. This premise is that the relationship is of a balance scale or zero-sum character, and assumes that a strong president must mean a weak Congress and vice versa. We will argue that this assumption is not a norm and can lead to a dangerous, unstable politics. We will suggest that a model of concurrent strength for both institutions is a preferable vision and likely to produce a more stable politics.

I. THE MODERN THEORY OF THE PRESIDENCY

The model of the president as democratic monarch is not original with Mr. Nixon. His is only the most recent expression of a common and current view of the office. Ironically, his view is also the liberal one. Liberals, both in academia and public life, dramatized presidential power as the major democratic force in our political system. We came to celebrate this power and decry the conservatism and incapacities of Congress.

This view of the presidency was devised, in a manner of speaking, to institutionalize Franklin Roosevelt. In the past, strong presidents had staked unusual, even radical, claims to power. Lincoln tends to be our favorite example of such cases, but as he claimed a right to use the war power in grave emergency, he stated: "It is with the deepest regret that the executive found the duty of executing the war power . . . forced upon him."[2] Lincoln's claim was of the necessity of radical action to save the Union. The action was justified by the emergency and the justification was given directly to Congress.

In the past, other presidents acted similarly in what they saw as dire emergency. Yet their claims were understood to be temporary and limited. Times of trial did not define what the presidency ought to be. The ability of the presidency to expand to meet crises reflected one of its virtues. The system itself was flexible.[3] We could justify a Lincoln and still not demand that each president be Lincoln.

The new theory is founded on new assumptions concerning the political system and its environment. First, it was argued that the institutions of American government could no longer represent or serve an increasingly complex and differentiated society, and that only the presidency could expand to represent and serve the new groups and claims. Second, we viewed the world as in a state of permanent threat, thus justifying the perpetually strong president. The modern view thus profoundly amended the traditional perspective. Now all the presidents were to be Lincolns, or more precisely, Franklin Roosevelts.

II. THE MAKERS OF THE THEORY

The full intellectual articulation of this modern view of the presidency comes in American political science. The vision of the presidency Mr. Nixon offers his critics is familiar to political scientists: we wrote it. Seminal work of the 1950s and 1960s offered a rationale for powerful leadership as well as an argument for the redistribution of power within the framework of national government. Political science offered a normative model and politicians acted on it. We can best see the substance and values of this model by examining the work of several of its leading exponents.

It began in historical writing. The Franklin Roosevelt pictured by his biographers became the very model of the democratic monarch.[4] Some historians, notably Wilfred Binkley[5] and Walter Johnson,[6] moved to a general approval of presidential power. The conceptualization followed. Clinton Rossiter's The American Presidency,[7] first published in 1956, set out to both examine the character of the office and present an argument for Presidential strength. Rossiter's values were eminently clear:

> We need no special gift of prophecy to predict a long and exciting future for the American Presidency. . . . All the great political and social forces that brought the Presidency to its present state of power and glory will continue to work in the future.[8]

His argument was simple. A terrifyingly complex world necessitated one-man rule and forced us all to rely more and more on that man.

What does this mean for the design of the federal system? Rossiter was too sensible to push schemes to amend the separation of powers. But he saw a necessity for strengthening the president against Congress. Rossiter asks: "Is there nothing, then, that we can do to achieve a more stable relationship between the two great political branches?" He offers no concrete solutions, but rather trusts that "we will continue to make progress. . . . Term by term, crisis by crisis, men in and out of Congress have been educated to accept the necessity of Presidential leadership."[9]

Rossiter's work, then, represents a step forward from the Rooseveltian image of the presidency to a model of what the office ought to be. And, as Rossiter attempted to shape a theory of the office, he was forced to speak of the distribution of power in the national political system. In arguing for the strong president, he clearly envisioned the relationship between the president and Congress as a balance scale. An increase of the power of the president would necessarily be accompanied by a decrease in the power of Congress. If the president leads, then Congress must follow. The relation was a zero-sum game.

With Rossiter we are at the threshold of the full, modern model of the presidency. The outlines and values of the model emerge, but we still do not see its basic logic. Rossiter retains a traditional view of the institutional setting of the presidency. He brushes aside the possibility of enhancing presidential power through systemic reform. He thinks the president has to learn to live with a "coordinate" political system and he simply lectures Congress on the necessity of following the president.

The full-blown modern view goes on to suspend the separation of powers and to focus not on the structural and institutional characteristics of the office but on the dynamic process of leadership. The explicit interest of this view was the maximization of leadership possibilities.

Richard Neustadt's *Presidential Power*[10] and James M. Burns' *Deadlock of Democracy*[11] are two significant works in rounding off the modern view. Neustadt's book, first published in 1960, adopted a novel, dynamic view of the presidency. He set out to understand the presidency as a problem in decision theory. Neustadt inquires into the character of presidential power and decides it as the power to influence. Political and institutional limitations hedge the office. But, and here he takes a critical turn, Neustadt is not concerned with the nature of these limitations. Rather, he attempts to teach the president how to work with those limits so as to have the best chance of overcoming them.[12]

The bare sense of Neustadt's argument is that the president's power is the power to persuade. By conserving his influence and understanding his position the president can overcome the limitations imposed by his environment. In fact, his task must be defined as overcoming the barriers created by the separation of powers:

> The separation of institutions and the sharing of authority prescribe the terms on which a President persuades. When one man shares authority with another, but does not gain or lose his job upon the other's whim, his willingness to act upon the urging of the other turns on whether he conceives the action right for him. The essence of the President's persuasive task is to convince such men that what the White House wants of them is what they ought to do for their sake and on their authority.[13]

To the degree that the president can persuade, he can overcome the frustrations of the separation of powers. Neustadt offers the president a decision theory to aid him in his quest to impose his will over others. He must inquire of each potential decision: "What will this do for my power?" Each action bears on his present and future power to persuade and the president who can maximize his power will be most effective at "leadership." Thus, a president's

capacity to lead, Neustadt argues, is a result of his expertness at persuasion: "In the sphere of viability our system can supply no better expert than a President intent on husbanding his influence—provided that he understands what influence is made of."[14]

James M. Burns' *Deadlock of Democracy*, published in 1963, represents the next logical step in fleshing out the model of the modern presidency. Burns moves back from the view of leadership dynamics we see in Neustadt to a conception of the president within the structure of national government. But Burns carries with him the essence of Neustadt's view. For him as well, there is a need for, and virtue to, expanded presidential power. He states:

> The Presidential leader must ... be a constructive innovator who can re-shape to some degree the constellation of political forces in which he operates. To reach the acme of leadership he must achieve a creative union of intellectual comprehension, strategic planning, and tactical skill, to a degree perhaps not paralleled since Jefferson.[15]

Burns turns to the institutional and party foundations of American national politics and asks whether they support or hamper energetic presidential leadership. His analysis cuts to the heart of the separation of powers which works to negate executive power and independence.

Burns runs his analysis at the level of the political parties. There are four parties. Each of the major national parties has, according to Burns, a presidential and congressional wing. Each wing reflects a distinct tradition, Madisonian or Jeffersonian. This four-party system is a symptom of the pathology of American politics, according to Burns. The separation of powers has created a schizoid political system. The presidency and Congress each rests on different constituencies, manifests different interests and involves different political processes. One checks rather than supports the other. Thus the Madisonian tradition of balance rather than leadership is victorious. The possibilities of dynamic leadership are blunted on the system of checks and balances.

Burns' analysis of the party system is thus an analysis of the implications of the separation of powers. He argues that the American political system negates leadership, the only source for which is the presidency. But:

> The consequences of the four-party system are that American political leaders, in order to govern, must manage multi-party coalitions. . . . But the task of governing is harder in the United States, for the leader . . . must bring together the right combination of presidential party and congressional party.[16]

The resolution of this dilemma lies in majority politics and party realignment. In effect, Burns argues that we must overcome our fractured politics by stable, majority support for a presidential leader. Otherwise:

> We can choose bold and creative national leaders without giving them the means to make their leadership effective. Hence we diminish a democracy's most essential and priceless commodity—the leadership of men who are willing to move ahead to meet emerging problems.[17]

The primacy of leadership and its possibilities, which we find in Rossiter, and fully developed in Neustadt, is taken to its logical conclusion by Burns. He speaks, implicitly, for the repeal of the separation of powers.

This strong-president model of the American political system is shared by a large number of scholars in political science and history. There is a certain irony in the fact that members of Congress, such as Joseph Clark[18] and Richard Bolling,[19] joined in this cry for a strengthened executive and a more docile Congress. Together, such scholars and politicians form an imposing base for the doctrine of inevitable and beneficent presidential domination.

Concomitant with the rise of the strong president literature and perhaps in political reaction, was a minority,

anti-presidential literature. This has been referred to as "the literary theory" of congressional–presidential relations. Roger Davidson, David Kovenock and Michael O'Leary state the theory thus:

> According to the advocates of the literary theory, Congress must assert its right to exercise "all legislative powers." Policies should be initiated by Congress at least as often as by the executive. . . . Executive officials would be consulted on technical aspects of policy making, but when the executive, by necessity, initiates legislative proposals, it should be in an advisory capacity, fully respectful of congressional supremacy in lawmaking. The ultimate authority of elected laymen to set priorities on complicated and technical matters is an indispensable feature of democratic government.[20]

Writers such as Willmoore Kendall,[21] Ernest Griffith,[22] James Burnham[23] and Alfred de Grazia[24] are leading figures among those who see congressional parity or dominance as the precondition of the revival of the good political order.

This brief sketch oversimplifies these writers. Even within the two schools (pro and anti-presidency), allies differ as to how closely the contemporary presidency approximates their ideal of strength or weakness. Table 1 attempts to order the position of these scholars according to both their ideal and their assessment of the actual condition of the presidency.

What is crucial about all these scholars is that while arguing to different conclusions about the balance of power between the president and Congress, they all appear to share one fundamental assumption: one must necessarily *choose* between congressional and presidential strength. Put another way, they view the relationship between the two branches as a zero-sum relationship in which an increase in the power of one branch necessarily involves the loss of power in the other.

III. WHAT IS "STRENGTH"?

We can find, in the authors cited above, five distinct notions of the way

TABLE I

President
OUGHT to be

	strong	weak
strong	**I** Rossiter Johnson Binkley	**II** de Grazia Burnham Griffith
weak	**III** Burns Neustadt Clark Bolling	**IV** Kendall

President IS

Cell I represents those who think the President is and should be dominant.

Cell II represents those who think the President is [strong] and ought to be weak.

Cell III represents those who think the President ought to be strong and is not.

Cell IV represents those who think the President is weak and ought to be.

presidential strength might be manifested:

A. President presents legislation, dominating agenda and maximizing his potential for gathering information (de Grazia).

B. President secures passage by direct pressure—presidential lobby (Kendall).

C. President secures passage by indirect pressure—mandate and appeal to public (Binkley).

D. President acts independently of legislature, with its general consent through a supportive presidential party (Burns).

E. President acts independently of legislature without specific consent requirement (Neustadt).

It is our contention that:

1. The first three aspects of strength are separable from the last two.

2. The first three need not imply the final two.

3. The relationship with Congress in the first three does not imply a zero-sum relationship, whereas it tends toward this in the last two.

Those critics who argue that the president has become too strong often give examples which belong to the last two (D&E) categories of strength. They conclude *generally* that a strengthened president implies a weakened Congress. However, this argument does not infer that the president's exercise of the first three types of strength (A, B & C) implies a weakened Congress. We will forward the proposition that the reverse is true, that in the first three categories a strengthened presidential role also tends to strengthen Congress.

We do not claim novelty for our case. In fact, we can see its origins by turning to the framers and inquiring after their model of relations between the legislature and the executive. James Madison's paper no. 51 of the *Federalist* offers the principle which we most frequently and inadequately identify with the founding: "Ambition must be made to counteract ambition."[25] The framers were concerned with establishing a safe, republican government—limited government. Unfortunately, we too often close our view of the founding principles with this sparse perspective. Thus, we miss the purposes which motivated the establishment of the new government. The other crucial principle of the founding is that government must have the capacity to rule effectively. When we view the separation of powers as a static, protective device we overlook this principle. To properly grasp the framers' model we must add Hamilton to Madison. In *Federalist* no. 70, Hamilton states that: "Energy in the executive is the leading character in the definition of good government." He continues:

A feeble executive implies a feeble execution of government. A feeble execution is but another phrase for a bad execution; and a government ill executed, whatever it may be in theory, must be, in practice, a bad government.[26]

Does Hamilton simply provide a historical precedent for our modern view of the presidency? Did he mean to reject Madison's concerns in no. 51? We do know that Hamilton was given to asserting an unusually strong position on executive power. On June 18, in the Philadelphia convention, Hamilton proposed that the executive office be a monarch.[27] Is the Hamilton of the *Federalist* then to be seen as a closet monarchist, simply making the strongest pro executive argument he could given the possibilities of the situation? We cannot settle this dispute here, but any answer must take into consideration arguments Hamilton makes concerning the provisions for impeachment and trial of the executive.

Hamilton takes up this issue in papers nos. 65 and 66 of the *Federalist*. His concept of an impeachable offense is broad. The executive ought to be responsible to Congress for a wide range of actions and misdeeds. Is not, he asks, the impeachment process "a method of NATIONAL INQUEST into the conduct of public man"?[28] This must be so because the impeachable offense is "POLITICAL" in that it is an injury done "immediately to the society itself."[29] (These are Hamilton's stresses.) Furthermore, this is no simple criminal-like process. In no. 66, Hamilton compares the impeachment powers to the executive veto:

An absolute or qualified negative in the executive upon the acts of the legislative body is admitted, by the ablest adepts in political science, to be an indispensable barrier against the encroachments of the latter upon the former. And it may, perhaps, with no less reason, be contended that the powers relating to impeachments are, as before intimated, an essential check in the hands of that body upon the encroachments of the executive.[30]

Clearly, Hamilton's vision of the executive role is not shaped merely by executive dominance. He seems to begin with a greater value placed on energy in governance than Madison, who appears to fix on a theory of structural limitations and counterbalances. But, by beginning at a different place, Hamilton provides us with a theory of governance for the Madisonian system. Their work is complementary. Madison provided the rationale for the institutional arrangement of the new government, and Hamilton offered the doctrine for the process of governance. For the framers, the virtue of the Constitution was that it not only created institutions that would deter corruption and tyranny: it created institutions which rendered good rule more likely. The vision of the framers is not captured by the metaphor of the balance scale; the metaphor needs a more complex machine, a reciprocating engine. The framers engaged in no talk of the president as chief-this or chief-that. There is less concern with the power of the single parts and a dominant concern with the interrelationships within the system.

There are limits to the practicality of inquiring after the framers' intentions. We are limited by the texts themselves and by our ultimate ability to divine the intentions behind the texts. Yet we can identify their dominant concerns and perceptions in the design of this system of government. More importantly, this inquiry leads to fruitful reconsideration of the relationship between Congress and the president. The framers offer a paradigm for the understanding of the governmental system which overcomes the static view implicit in the modern model of the presidency.

IV. THE RECIPROCATING ENGINE

The modern view of the presidency is based upon twin illusions of omniscience and omnipotence. Increasingly, the office was viewed as promising expansive knowledge, singular energy and rational decision-making. According to our mythology, the president would understand, be sensitive to, and act upon, the real needs of our society. This faith rests on a faulty assumption. The modern view of the presidency is based on the characteristics and functions of the bureaucratic state. The bureaucratic state itself is a reflection of the enlarged scope of public functions over the last half century. As the corpus of government became more bureaucratic the tasks of government seemed more organizational; thus the president must need most of all to be a manager.

But is the president a manager? Does he control the executive branch of government? Alfred de Grazia has spoken to the "myth" of the all-competent and managerial executive:

In part the President is an office, the presidency, whose head knows what is going on in government and has something to say about it. Secondly the President is an office whose head knows what is going on but has nothing to say about it. Thirdly, the President is an office whose head does not know what is going on and has nothing to say about it. There is little of the first in the presidency, a good deal of the second, and a great amount of the third.[31]

Within the executive branch, information, power, and responsibility are all too dispersed to support viable, presidential autonomy. A glance at the administrative processes within the executive branch highlights its fragmentation. The federal budget, for example, is built piecemeal from the incremental demands of hundreds of agencies, each with its own goals, interests and political supports. The rise and fall of planning-programming-budgeting during the 1960s, as an attempt to provide more control for the president, demonstrate the incapacity of the president to manage "his branch."[32] Presidential attempts to direct the activities of administrative agencies provide another lesson in the disorder of the executive establishment. Franklin Roosevelt, in well-documented instances, failed to control the U.S. Army Corps of Engineers in water resource policy and proved incapable of protecting "liberal" farm policy in the care of the Farm Security Administration from the challenge of the Department of Agriculture.[33] Thirty years later, as the president made war in Asia, was he the manager or captive of a complex security bureaucracy?[34] Since the turn of the century, presidents have attempted to overcome their organizational weakness through executive reorganization of the government. But the reforms instituted have not kept up with the fragmented growth of the bureaucracy. Ultimately, the president has not had enough power to create the administrative reforms necessary for greater administrative control.[35]

Clearly, the president is not competent to "run" government. This is not an argument for dismissing the office and its possibilities. The strength of the presidency lies in its singularity as a point of focus and in its visibility. The president cannot manage, but he can dramatize and initiate. He cannot control politics, but can provide focus. . . . Presidential initiation is most often presidential borrowing. He does not create; he adapts from the multiplicity of demands in his political environment.

Is Congress alone more capable of effective rule? No, left to itself, Congress cannot make sound policy. But this is not a dismissal of Congress. Congress is heterogeneous and was meant to be. It is representative and it represents best when it works at its most open, diverse and visible level.

Congress is a complex system composed of members, committees, leadership, and the whole (or floor). This system is capable of several different legislative processes. For example, Professor Ripley's work . . . has shown that the behavior of the legislative system varies in accordance with the loci and distribution of power within the system.[36] It also appears that we can expect certain kinds of substantive legislative proposals to cause specific kinds of legislative processes.[37] For example, "pork-barrel" legislation such as the Rivers and Harbors bill or tariff legislation is characterized by a highly individualistic legislative process in which legislators engage in vote trading for concrete and immediate benefits with no reference to principle. Theodore Lowi calls this the distributive policy arena and distinguishes it from regulatory policy which results in a more conflictive bargaining process, largely confined to the committees of Congress. Here the major actors are the committees and interested pressure groups. Lowi identifies a third kind of policy, that of redistribution. Redistributive policies are highly conflictive and have a broad impact on society. Redistributive legislation, such as social welfare bills or the graduated income tax, create class-like conflict between the extensive groups which are likely to benefit from, or suffer from, the threatened redistribution. The resulting conflict forces the issue to occupy the whole of the institutional processes of the Congress. The issue dominates floor debate and becomes the medium for distinctly visible and accountable processes in Congress.

Congress, working within the arena of redistributive politics, presents an image of democratic strength. Issues of this kind open up Congress and force it into its most visible, formulative and representational role. It is only in this kind of politics that the floor of the legislative body becomes the center of its legislative process. It is here that we approach the democratic legislature. At the same time, it is here that we see the greatest opportunity for the body, as an interacting collective, to shape and reshape public policy.

Presidential strength, in the sense of policy commitment and support, is the factor most likely to result in a Congress dealing with redistributive issues. The presidency alone is incapable of making good public policy. But the visibility of the president is the single most critical factor in framing the political debate over priorities and policy. The president provides focus and Congress provides heterogeneous representation. Ultimately, good public policy can be made only in the presence of both qualities, in the presence of what Professor Rieselbach refers to as "majoritarian democracy."[38]

A theory of legislative-executive relations founded on presidential autonomy must result in tragic consequences. Such a theory flies in the face of our political reality. We must, rather, prescribe those norms and expectations which will lead to the balanced and stable functioning of the political system. The model of the democratic monarch has led to stalemate. What historical evidence might we marshal to suggest the virtues of the theory of the reciprocating engine?

Franklin Roosevelt's Hundred Days is perhaps the best case for those who view the congressional–presidential relationship in zero-sum terms. Here is a president who brutally dominated Congress. Crisis led to an incredibly submissive Congress. The zero-sum model works for this extraordinary period, but we often forget that twelve years followed that Hundred Days and demonstrated how lively a Congress can be vis-à-vis a strong president. Roosevelt, of course, was eventually parried from the right, but far earlier, he was parried from the left. The Wagner Act was forced upon Roosevelt by aggressive Congressional liberals.[39] The administration's Agricultural Adjustment Act was seriously threatened as liberals and a rural revolt almost upset Roosevelt's alliance with the farm bloc.[40] Roosevelt, by creating the agenda, also created a debate which provided access for a variety of interests. The president could not control the process or necessarily define the outcome.

Dwight Eisenhower, especially in his later years, provides an interesting study of the weak president's relation to Congress. Conventional wisdom has it that the late 1950s Congress, under Rayburn and Johnson, provides an exemplar of legislative strength. After the Democratic victory in 1958, Sherman Adams, and recession, Eisenhower initiated little major policy. Did Congress tip the scale and become dynamic? It was not Congress that became strong, but, rather, individuals and interests working within Congress. Without presidential strength, the Congress followed its own inertial forces back to the committees and the bargaining of special interests which flourish there. Professor Ripley, in his Power in the Senate, characterizes the period 1958 to 1961 as one of transition from decentralization to individualism in the Senate. How does this fit with the image of Lyndon Johnson's strong leadership in the Senate? Simply, it may be a false image. Both Johnson and Rayburn were masters at the art of building and managing logrolling coalitions. But skillful manipulations of distributive policy and its self-interested coalitions are not the same as strong leadership. In such an atmosphere the central mode of congressional agreement is "horse trading." And, whole herds were traded in this period. Consider the string of pork-barrel legislation which emerged from that Congress. In 1959 it passed, almost without debate, the $80-billion Highway Trust Fund. Airport subsidies were greatly expanded, again with little deliberation or conflict. Major steps were being taken in national transportation policy without any consideration of the relationship between them. Each step was simply another log to be rolled, with little planning in the distributive policy arena.

Other periods also suggest the utility of our model. Between 1865 and 1885 we find a period of undistinguished and weak presidents. By the conventional wisdom we would expect to find strong Congresses. Indeed, this period would seem to be the apex of congressional strength. But what kind of strength did Congress exhibit? One-tenth of the Senate was indicted at one time or another during this period. Special interests and patronage issues dominated the concerns of the legislature. What kind of representation do we find in this period? What was the role of the floor? It is instructive to note that this period formed the backdrop for Woodrow Wilson's Congressional Government.[41] Government by committee, with the decentralized logrolling it implies, was the dominant modus operandi of the period. Conflict and decisive action came on patronage matters such as the Tenure of Office Act and the appointments to the New York Customs Office. Wilfred Binkley describes the House of Representatives during this period:

The culmination of this vast assumption

of power by Congress in the 1880s coincided almost exactly with the decline of the lower house to almost the nadir of incompetence. Despite its assumption of sovereign power in the government, it lay floundering in a confusion of warring committees.[42]

We find interesting cases in the midst of the strong, independent presidency literature. In his classic *Congress Makes a Law* Stephen Bailey provides a rich account of the legislative history and eventual passage of the Employment Act of 1946.[43] The Employment Act was a significant issue concerning a major symbol of new governmental functions. With it, Congress faced the fundamental question of the government's responsibility to buffer the work force against unemployment and the even larger question of government's role in a free economy. Bailey himself admits that

a few, and as time went on, a growing number of people, felt that whatever the hopes and fears of those responsible for the final act, S. 380 as passed was an important step in the direction of coordinated and responsible economic planning in the federal government.[44]

Yet Bailey was dissatisfied with the lack of unity in the legislative process and called for stronger presidential leadership. He seems to have shared the illusion of the wholly efficient, independent executive. But what is the process he describes? He shows strong presidential involvement, extensive publicity, executive lobbying, campaigns by national and peak associational groups. The bill was debated extensively, and the locus of decision was the floor of Congress. Congress was the ideal place for the reconciliation of diverse interests. And the legislative process Bailey described, while heterogeneous, was strong and creative. This is the best role for a legislature in a democratic society.

Finally, of course, we cannot prove by selected example that our model of the congressional–presidential relationship is an effective descriptive theory. But it is worth noting a possible research strategy and the kinds of data to which our discussion points. Table 2 specifies the relationship we would expect to find between presidential strength and characteristics in legislative behavior.

TABLE II

	Visibility of Issue	Public Knowledge	Role of Individual Congressman	Committee Strength
Strong President	HIGH	HIGH	WEAK	LOW
Weak President	LOW	LOW	MODER-ATE	HIGH
	Role of Floor	Mode of Decision	Congressional Power Structure	Visibility of Action
Strong President	STRONG-CREATIVE	CONFLICT	CENTRAL-IZED	HIGH
Weak President	WEAK-ACCEPT-ING	LOG-ROLLING	DECEN-TRALIZED	LOW

First let us look at the mode of decision and visibility of issues. The incidence of roll-call votes under different presidents might provide a useful measure. We might expect that under strong presidents, decision-making will be more visible and more floor-centered with more evident conflict. Hence we would predict Eisenhower, of the post-World War II presidents, to have the fewest roll-call votes. Table 3, in fact, indicates this.

TABLE III([44])

	Average # of roll calls per year
Truman (50-51)	305
Eisenhower	234
Kennedy	334
Johnson	475
Nixon (69)	422

Another indicator is the role of the floor vis-à-vis the committees. Does a strong president retard or stimulate the role of the floor? Our theory would predict that in lieu of an energetic president Congress tends to decentralize, with the committees and logrolling coalitions being the focus of decisions. Conversely we would predict that a legitimately energetic president, working *through* Congress, would force the decision to the most representative part of Congress, the floor. One measure of floor creativity is the degree of amending activity on the floor. Greater amending activity would indicate a more important and creative function for the floor.[45] Table 4 shows the average number of amendments per bill in one house for selected years.

TABLE IV([44])

	average # of amendments	N
1947	7.5	(11)
1950	19.8	(3)
1953	8.3	(10)
1955	3.8	(5)
1958	4.0	(2)
1959	4.3	(14)
1961-62	6.5	(47)
1966	4.9	(8)

Here again, the results are sketchy but suggestive. With the exception of 1953, all of the Eisenhower years showed markedly less amending activity than under the stronger, more active presidencies of Truman, Kennedy and Johnson. If fully corroborated this would lead us to revise substantially our image of strong presidents simply dominating Congress.

Part of the tragedy of the strong, independent president literature has been that it encouraged presidents to believe that their strength can and should be exercised independently of Congress. Already we have a revisionist mood developing, after Watergate, telling us that Congress should assert its independence against the executive. We have tried to show how both views share the same, zero-sum fallacy. A president without Congress ends up in the Bourbon tendencies of Johnson and Nixon. Hence we cannot again accept the myth of solitary presidential power. But Congress, without the legitimate energies of a forceful and probing executive, will give us an aimless domination by local and special interests.

The notion of the democratic monarch is not likely to regain our affection in the near future. We are driven by recent events to rethink the separation of powers and our theories of the presidency. Two hundred years ago the framers began delving into the fundamental character of good government. Watergate has provided an appropriate way to celebrate the bicentennial of their struggle and success. We can best honor them by reconsidering their accomplishments and purposes.

NOTES

1. Mr. Nixon's question-and-answer session at the Executive Club of Chicago on March 15, l974, provides an excellent example of the motif of presidential strength in his recent statements.

2. President Abraham Lincoln, "Message to Special Session of Congress," July 4, 1861.

3. See Arthur M. Schlesinger, Jr., The Imperial Presidency (Boston, 1973), pp. 64-67, 105-109. Schlesinger stresses informal comity and political understanding as linking the president and Congress at these moments of expansive claims of presidential power.

4. The major political biographies of Roosevelt are: Frank Freidel, Franklin D. Roosevelt, 4 vols. (Boston, 1952-1973); Arthur M. Schlesinger, Jr., The Age of Roosevelt, 3 vols. (Boston, 1957); James M. Burns, Roosevelt, 2 vols. (New York, 1956 & 1971).

5. Wilfred Binkley, The President and Congress (New York, 1947).

6. Walter Johnson, 1600 Pennsylvania Avenue (Boston, 1960).

7. Clinton Rossiter, The American Presidency, 2nd ed. (New York, 1960).

8. Ibid., p. 237.

9. Ibid., pp. 250-251.

10. Richard Neustadt, Presidential Power (New York, 1964).

11. James M. Burns, The Deadlock of Democracy (Englewood Cliffs, N.J., 1963).

12. Neustadt's little book is troublesome and, perhaps, deceptive. We want to tread a fine line between oversimplification and all the rich implications we see in Neustadt's analysis. We admit that there are statements here which can be drawn out of the whole context and used to support the alternate theory of the presidency and Congress we offer below. But we attempt to deal with this book as a whole conception and reconstruct the argument which characterizes the whole work.

13. Neustadt, op. cit., p. 43.

14. Ibid., p. 174.

15. Burns, op. cit., p. 338.

16. Ibid., p. 260.

17. Ibid., p. 325.

18. Joseph Clark, Congress: The Sapless Branch (New York, 1964).

19. Richard Bolling, House Out of Order (New York, 1965).

20. Roger Davidson, David M. Kovenock, and Michael K. O'Leary, "Theories of Congress," in Congress and the President ed. Ronald C. Moe (Pacific Palisades, California, 1971), p. 139.

21. Willmoore Kendall, The Conservative Affirmation (Chicago, 1959). Also see Kendall, "The Two Majorities," Midwest Journal of Political Science 4 (November 1960): 317-45.

22. Ernest Griffith, Congress: Its Contemporary Role (New York, 1951).

23. James Burnham, Congress and the American Tradition (Chicago, 1959).

24. Alfred de Grazia, Republic in Crisis (New York, 1965).

25. Hamilton, Jay and Madison, The Federalist (New York, n.d.), p. 337.

26. Ibid., p. 445.

27. James Madison, Debates of the Fed-

eral Convention, in Records of the Federal Convention, vol. I, rev. ed., ed. Max Farrand (New Haven, 1937), pp. 282-293.

28. Federalist, p. 424.

29. Ibid., p. 423.

30. Ibid., p. 429.

31. de Grazia, op. cit., p. 75.

32. On the politics and practice of PPB see: Allan Schick, "The Road to PPB: The Stages of Budget Reform," Public Administration Review 26 (Dec 1966): 243-58; Leonard Merewitz and Stephen Sosnick, The Budget's New Clothes (Chicago, 1971); Aaron Wildavsky, "The Political Economy of Efficiency," Public Administration Review 26 (Dec 1966): 292-310.

33. On the Army Corps of Engineers, see Arthur Maass, Muddy Waters (Cambridge, 1951). On the Farm Security Administration, see Grant McConnell, The Decline of Agrarian Democracy (Berkeley, 1953).

34. On the "captive" president and Vietnam, see: David Halberstam, The Best and the Brightest (Greenwich, Conn., 1972). A consistent, but different, analysis is offered by Irving Janis, Victims of Groupthink (Boston, 1972), pp. 101-135.

35. On executive reorganization, see: Harold Seidman, Politics, Position and Power (New York, 1970); Peri E. Arnold, "Reorganization and Politics," Public Administration Review 34 (May/June 1974): 205-11.

36. Randall Ripley, Power in the Senate (New York, 1969).

37. Theodore J. Lowi, "American Business, Public Policy, Case Studies, and Political Theory," World Politics 16 (July 1964): 677-715.

38. Leroy N. Rieselbach, "In the Wake of Watergate: Congressional Reform?" Review of Politics 36 (July 1974): 371-393.

39. Arthur M. Schlesinger, Jr., The Coming of the New Deal, vol. II, The Age of Roosevelt (Boston, 1957), pp. 150, 398-406.

40. Ibid., chapter 3 and John L. Shover, "Populism in the Nineteen-Thirties: The Battle for AAA," Agricultural History 39 (January 1965): 17-24.

41. Woodrow Wilson, Congressional Government (Boston, 1885).

42. Binkley, op. cit., p. 178.

43. Stephen Bailey, Congress Makes a Law (New York, 1964), p. 234.

44. Congressional Quarterly Almanac, 1950-1969. Figures for Truman before 1950 were not compiled by CQ. After 1969, rules for recording votes in the House were changed, making totals noncomparable. For 1963 the whole year was attributed to Kennedy.

45. This data is drawn from an examination of the Congressional Record. It is presented in L. John Roos' unpublished master's thesis, University of Chicago, 1969, and Stephen Witham's ongoing master's research at the University of Notre Dame. Our gratitude to Mr. Witham. The bills in 1961-62 were all those receiving a roll call in both houses. In 1947, 1953, 1959, 1962 and 1966, bills were selected at random by Mr. Witham. The other bills come from Roos' thesis.

VIII

The Press and the Presidency

Introduction. Political scientist and attorney Max Kampelman has written: "Freedom of the press is essential to political liberty. A society of self-governing people is possible only if the people are informed, hence the right to exchange and print words."[1] Yet, "throughout the history of the republic," as political scientist Elmer Cornwell has said, "the White House and the press have been living under, at best, an armed truce."[2] Why do two such vital institutions to the nation experience such hostility toward each other? The answers are not easy, but certainly the relationship between the president and the press is complex, symbiotic, and paradoxical. The relationship is complex because a good deal of the president's standing with the public is influenced by what the media says about the president—how it interprets the president to the people. The press, in short, is the president's magnifying glass to the people. It can diminish his warts or enlarge them, especially those he does not want seen.

The relationship is symbiotic because the president provides information for the press and the press, in turn, provides the president access to the people. In this case, the press is the president's link to the people.

The relationship is paradoxical, because the more a president attempts to accomplish in office, the greater the likelihood he will be more closely watched by the press. Thus the "do something" president finds himself checked and balanced by an increasingly attentive press. In a nutshell, presidential prestige is not determined solely by the president himself.

Complicating the relationship between the president and the press is the fact that each has different roles to play in our national political life. The president's role is usually that of an "advocate" of policy positions and programs. To be effective, a president must manage and mold the news, if he can, in support of his positions and programs. News, in short, from the presidential perspective, must enhance the presidency.

On the other hand, the role of the press is to inform the public. This means placing facts before the public in some meaningful perspective. Thus the burden of the press is to objectively report the news. The duty to report reality may not coincide with the president's need to enhance the presidency.

279

Because the burdens of the president and the press are different, the two are often in sharp conflict and, accordingly, the overriding relationship is one of tension.

Should the relationship between the president and the press be an adversary one? Is an adversary relation harmful to the presidency and to the Republic? The presidential view of the press is stated forcefully by former Harvard professor and now United States Senator, Daniel Moynihan, in his essay, "The Presidency and the Press." Moynihan sees much of the conflict between the president and the press resulting from what Lionel Trilling has called the "adversary culture." Essentially, this means that the press is made up increasingly of people whose social values are at variance with the prevailing culture, and, by extension, with the president who represents that culture. Moynihan lists carefully the circumstances which he believes are giving the press a deadly edge over the president in the contemporary tug-of-war between the two. He makes a strong plea for the redress of that imbalance by calling for, among other things, a more "responsible" press.

United States Labor Department program development specialist and a student of journalism, Harry Kranz, argues a view counter to that of Senator Moynihan. Kranz contends that the president, far from knuckling under to the press, continues to maintain ascendancy over the press to include presidential domination of the medium of television. Moreover, argues Kranz, it is the press's fears of the presidency that are well grounded.

To document his position, Kranz chronicles a number of presidential activities that indicate presidents have aggressively tried to manage the news to suit their own political needs. In the next selection, "The Presidency versus the Press—Who is Right?," Kranz argues cogently that an adversary relationship between the president and the press is necessary for the health of the democratic process.

In view of the continuing debate over whether the government should adopt either the view that the press is entitled to a special privilege to serve as the eyes and ears of the polity on the ground that people are an organic whole and have a right to know what government is doing, or the view that each citizen must serve as his own news gatherer and act as his own watchdog over government, the likelihood is that the tension, hostility, and conflict between the presidency and the press will continue. However, the general attitude of the president toward the press is vital. It is he who can set the quality of presidential–press relations, the tone of public discussion, and in all likelihood even the behavior of the courts toward press freedom.

NOTES

1. See his "The Power of the Press: A Problem for Our Democracy," *Policy Review* (Fall 1978): 7.

2. See his *The Presidency and the Press* (Morristown, N.J.: General Learning Press, 1974), p. 3.

30. The Presidency and the Press*

DANIEL P. MOYNIHAN

As his years in Washington came to an end, Harry S. Truman wrote a friend:

I really look with commiseration over the great body of my fellow citizens, who, reading newspapers, live and die in the belief that they have known something of what has been passing in the world in their time.

A familiar presidential plaint, sounded often in the early years of the Republic and rarely unheard thereafter. Of late, however, a change has developed in the perception of what is at issue. In the past what was thought to be involved was the reputation of a particular president. In the present what is seen to be at stake, and by the presidents themselves, is the reputation of government— especially, of course, presidential government. These are different matters, and summon a different order of concern.

There are two points anyone would wish to make at the outset of an effort to explore this problem. First, it is to be acknowledged that in most essential encounters between the presidency and the press, the advantage is with the former. The president has a near limitless capacity to "make" news which must be reported, if only by reason of competition between one journal, or one medium, and another. (If anything, radio and television news is more readily subject to such dominance. Their format permits of many fewer "stories." The president-in-action al-

most always takes precedence.) The president also has considerable capacity to reward friends and punish enemies in the press corps, whether they be individual journalists or the papers, television networks, news weeklies, or whatever these individuals work for. And for quite a long while, finally, a president who wishes can carry off formidable deceptions. (One need only recall the barefaced lying that went with the formal opinion of Roosevelt's attorney general that the destroyer-naval-base deal of 1940 was legal.

With more than sufficient reason, then, publishers and reporters alike have sustained over the generations a lively sense of their vulnerability to governmental coercion or control. For the most part, their worries have been exaggerated. But, like certain virtues, there are some worries that are best carried to excess.

The second point is that American journalism is almost certainly the best in the world. This judgment will be disputed by some. There are good newspapers in other countries. The *best* European journalists are more intellectual than their American counterparts, and some will think this a decisive consideration. But there is no enterprise anywhere the like of the *New York Times*. Few capitals are covered with the insight and access of the *Washington Post* or the *Washington Evening Star*. As with so many American

*Source: Reprinted from Coping: On the Practice of Government by Daniel P. Moynihan, pp. 314-29, 337-42, by permission of Random House, Inc. Copyright © 1971 by Random House, Inc. This selection was first published in Commentary, March 1971. Some footnotes omitted.

institutions, American newspapers tend to be older and more stable than their counterparts abroad. The Hartford *Courant* was born in 1764, twenty-one years before *The Times* of London. The New York *Post* began publication in 1801, twenty years before the *Guardian* of Manchester. What in most other countries is known as the "provincial" press—that is to say journals published elsewhere than in the capital—in America is made up of a wealth of comprehensive and dependable daily newspapers of unusually high quality.

The journalists are in some ways more important than their journals—at least to anyone who has lived much in government. A relationship grows up with the reporters covering one's particular sector that has no counterpart in other professions or activities. The relationship is one of simultaneous trust and distrust, friendship and enmity, dependence and independence. But it is the men of government, especially in Washington, who are the more dependent. The journalists are their benefactors, their conscience, at times almost their reason for being. For the journalists are above all others their audience, again especially in Washington, which has neither an intellectual community nor an electorate, and where there is no force outside government able to judge events, much less to help shape them, save the press.

That there is something wondrous and terrible in the intensities of this relationship between the press and the government is perhaps best seen at the annual theatricals put on by such groups of journalists at the Legislative Correspondents Association in Albany or the Gridiron in Washington. To my knowledge nothing comparable takes place anywhere else in the world. These gatherings are a kind of ritual truthtelling, of which the closest psychological approximation would be the Calabrian insult ritual described by Roger Vailland in his novel *The Law*, or possibly the group-therapy practices of more recent origin. The politicians come as guests of the journalists. The occasion is first of all a feast: the best of everything. Then as dinner progresses the songs begin. The quality varies, of course, but at moments startling levels of deadly accurate commentary of great cruelty are achieved. The politicians sit and smile and applaud. Then some of them speak. Each one wins or loses to the degree that he can respond in kind; stay funny and be brutal. (At the Gridiron John F. Kennedy was a master of the style, but the piano duet performed by Nixon and Agnew in 1970 was thought by many to have surpassed anything yet done.) A few lyrics appear in the next day's papers, but what the newspapermen really said to the politicians remains privileged—as does so much of what the politicians say to them. The relationship is special.

How is it then that this relationship has lately grown so troubled? The immediate answer is, of course, the war in Vietnam. An undeclared war, unwanted, misunderstood, or not understood at all, it entailed a massive deception of the American people by their government. Surely a large area of the experience of the 1960s is best evoked in the story of the man who says: "They told me that if I voted for Goldwater there would be 500,000 troops in Vietnam within a year. I voted for him, and by God, they were right." The story has many versions. If he voted for Goldwater we would be defoliating the countryside of Vietnam; the army would be sending spies to the 1968 party conventions; Dr. Spock would be indicted on conspiracy charges; and so on. By 1968 Richard Rovere described the capital as "awash" with lies.

The essential fact was that of deceit. How else to carry out a full-scale war, that became steadily more unpopular, with none of the legally sanctioned constraints on the free flow of information which even the most democratic societies find necessary in such circumstances? This situation did not spring full-blown from the involvement in Southeast Asia. It was endemic to the cold war. At the close of World War II official press censorship was removed, but the kinds of circumstance in which any responsible government might feel that events have to be concealed from the public did not go away. The result was a contradiction impossible to resolve. The public interest was at once served and disserved by secrecy; at once disserved and served by openness. Whatever the case, distrust of government grew. At the outset of the U-2 affair in 1960, the United States government asserted that a weather plane on a routine mission had been shot down. The *New York Times* (May 6, 1960) reported just that. *Not* that the U.S. government *claimed* it was a weather plane, but simply that it was. Well, it wasn't. Things have not been the same since.

But there are problems between the presidency and the press which have little to do with the cold war or with Vietnam and which—if this analysis is correct—will persist or even intensify should those conditions recede, or even dissolve, as a prime source of public concern. The problems flow from five basic circumstances which together have been working to reverse the old balance of power between them. It is the thesis here that if this balance should tip too far in the direction of the press, our capacity for effective democratic government will be seriously and dangerously weakened.

I

The first of these circumstances has to do with the tradition of "muckraking"—the exposure of corruption in government or the collusion of government with private interests—which the American press has seen as a primary mission since the period 1880-1914. It is, in Irving Kristol's words, "a journalistic phenomenon that is indigenous to democracy, with its instinctive suspi-

cion and distrust of all authority in general, and of concentrated political and economic power especially." Few would want to be without the tradition, and it is a young journalist of poor spirit who does not set out to uncover the machinations of some malefactor of great wealth and his political collaborators. Yet there is a cost, as Roger Starr suggests in his wistful wish that Lincoln Steffens's *The Shame of the Cities* might be placed on the restricted shelves of the schools of journalism. Steffens has indeed, as Starr declares, continued "to haunt the city rooms of the country's major newspapers." The question to be asked is whether, in the aftermath of Steffens, the cities were better, or merely more ashamed of themselves. Looking back, one is impressed by the energy and capacity for governance of some of the old city machines. Whatever else, it was popular government, of and by men of the people. One wonders: did the middle- and upper-class reformers destroy the capacity of working-class urban government without replacing it with anything better so that half-a-century later each and all bewail the cities as ungovernable? One next wonders whether something not dissimilar will occur now that the focus of press attention has shifted from City Hall to the White House. (And yet a miracle of American national government is the almost complete absence of monetary corruption at all levels, and most especially at the top.)

The muckraking tradition is well established. Newer, and likely to have far more serious consequences, is the advent of what Lionel Trilling has called the "adversary culture" as a conspicuous element in journalistic practice. The appearance in large numbers of journalists shaped by the attitudes of this culture is the result of a process whereby the profession thought to improve itself by recruiting more and more persons from middle- and upper-class backgrounds and trained at the universities associated with such groups. This is a change but little noted as yet. The stereotype of American newspapers is that of publishers ranging from conservative to reactionary in their political views balanced by reporters ranging from liberal to radical in theirs. One is not certain how accurate the stereotype ever was. One's impression is that twenty years and more ago the preponderance of the "working press" (as it liked to call itself) was surprisingly close in origins and attitudes to working people generally. They were not Ivy Leaguers. They now are or soon will be. Journalism has become, if not an elite profession, a profession attractive to elites. This is noticeably so in Washington, where the upper reaches of journalism constitute one of the most important and enduring *social* elites of the city, with all the accouterments one associates with a leisured class. (The Washington press corps is not leisured at all, but the style is that of men and women who *choose* to work.)

The political consequence of the rising social status of journalism is that the press grows more and more influenced by attitudes genuinely hostile to American society and American government. This trend seems bound to continue into the future. On the record of what they have been writing while in college, the young people now leaving the Harvard *Crimson* and the Columbia *Spectator* for journalistic jobs in Washington will resort to the Steffens style at ever-escalating levels of moral implication. They bring with them the moral absolutism of George Wald's vastly popular address, "A Generation in Search of a Future," that describes the Vietnam War as "the most shameful episode in the whole of American history." Not tragic, not heartbreaking, not vastly misconceived, but *shameful*. From the shame of the cities to the shame of the nation. But nobody ever called Boss Croker any name equivalent in condemnatory weight to the epithet "war criminal."

II

An ironical accompaniment of the onset of the muckraking style directed toward the presidency has been the rise of a notion of the near-omnipotency of the office itself. This notion Thomas E. Cronin describes as the "textbook president." Cronin persuasively argues that in the aftermath of Franklin Roosevelt a view of the presidency, specifically incorporated in the textbooks of recent decades, was developed which presented seriously "inflated and unrealistic interpretations of presidential competence and beneficence," and which grievously "overemphasized the policy change and policy accomplishment capabilities" of the office. Cronin cites Anthony Howard, a watchful British commentator:

> For what the nation has been beguiled into believing ever since 1960 is surely the politics of evangelism: the faith that individual men are cast to be messiahs, the conviction that Presidential incantations can be substituted for concrete programs, the belief that what matters is not so much the state of the nation as the inspiration-quotient of its people.

In his own researches among advisers of Kennedy and Johnson, Cronin finds the majority to hold "tempered assessments of presidential determination of 'public policy.'" Indeed, only 10 percent would describe the president as having "very great impact" over such matters.

Working in the White House is a chastening experience. But it is the experience of very few persons. Watching the White House, on the other hand, is a mass occupation, concentrated especially among the better-educated, better-off groups. For many the experience is one of infatuation followed much too promptly by disillusion. First, the honeymoon—in Cronin's terms, the "predictable ritual of euphoric inflation." But then "the Camelot of the first few hundred days of all presidencies fades away. . . . Predictably, by the second year, reports are spread that the president has become isolated from criticism." If this is so, he has only himself to blame when things go wrong. And things do go wrong.

If the muckraking tradition implies a distrust of government, it is nonetheless curiously validated by the overly trusting tradition of the "textbook presidency" which recurrently sets up situations in which the presidency will be judged as having somehow broken faith. This is not just the experience of a Johnson or a Nixon. Anyone who was in the Kennedy administration in the summer and fall of 1963 would, or ought to, report a pervasive sense that our initiative had been lost, that we would have to get reelected to get going again.

Here, too, there is a curious link between the presidency and the press. The two most important *presidential* newspapers are the *New York Times* and the *Washington Post* (though the *Star* would be judged by many to have the best reporting). Both papers reflect a tradition of liberalism that has latterly been shaped and reinforced by the very special type of person who *buys* the paper. (It is well to keep in mind that newspapers are capitalist enterprises which survive by persuading people to buy them.) Theirs is a "disproportionately" well-educated and economically prosperous audience. The geographical areas in which the two papers circulate almost certainly have higher per-capita incomes and higher levels of education than any of comparable size in the nation or the world. More of the buyers of these two papers are likely to come from "liberal" Protestant or Jewish backgrounds than would be turned up by a random sample of the population; they comprise, in fact, what James Q. Wilson calls "the Liberal Audience." Both the working-class Democrats and the conservative Republicans, with exceptions, obviously, have been pretty much driven from office among the constituencies where the *Times* and the

Post flourish. It would be wrong to ascribe this to the influence of the papers. Causality almost certainly moves both ways. Max Frankel of the *Times,* who may have peers but certainly no betters as a working journalist, argues that a newspaper is surely as much influenced by those who read it as vice versa.

The readers of the *New York Times* and the *Washington Post,* then, are a special type of citizen: not only more affluent and more liberal than the rest of the nation, but inclined also to impose heavy expectations on the presidency, and not to be amused when those expectations fail to be met. Attached by their own internal traditions to the "textbook presidency," papers like the *Times* and the *Post* are reinforced in this attachment by the temperamental predilections of the readership whose character they inevitably reflect. Thus they help to set a tone of pervasive dissatisfaction with the performance of the national government, whoever the presidential incumbent may be and whatever the substance of his policies.

III

A third circumstance working to upset the old balance of power between the presidency and the press is the fact that Washington reporters depend heavily on more or less clandestine information from federal bureaucracies which are frequently, and in some cases routinely, antagonistic to presidential interests.

There is a view of the career civil service as a more or less passive executor of policies made on high. This is quite mistaken. A very great portion of policy ideas "bubble up" from the bureaucracy, and, just as importantly, a very considerable portion of the "policy decisions" that go down never come to anything, either because the bureaucrats cannot or will not follow through. (The instances of simple inability are probably much greater than those of outright hostility.) Few modern presidents have made any impact on the federal bureaucracies save by creating new ones. The bureaucracies are unfamiliar and inaccessible. They are quasi-independent, maintaining, among other things, fairly open relationships with the congressional committees that enact their statutes and provide their funds. They are usually willing to work with the president, but rarely to the point where their perceived interests are threatened. Typically, these are rather simple territorial interests: not to lose any jurisdiction, and if possible to gain some. But recurrently, issues of genuine political substance are also involved.

At the point where they perceive a threat to those interests, the bureaucracies just as recurrently go to the press. They know the press; the press knows them. Both stay in town as presidential governments come and go. Both cooperate in bringing to bear the most powerful weapon the bureaucracies wield in their own defense, that of revealing presidential plans in advance of their execution. Presidents and their plans are helpless against this technique. I have seen a senior aide to a president, sitting over an early morning cup of coffee, rise and literally punch the front page of the *New York Times*. A major initiative was being carefully mounted. Success depended, to a considerable degree, on surprise. Someone in one of the agencies whose policies were to be reversed got hold of the relevant document and passed it on to the *Times*. Now everyone would know. The mission was aborted. There was *nothing* for the presidential government to do. No possibility of finding, much less of disciplining, the bureaucrat responsible. For a time, or rather from time to time, President Johnson tried the technique of *not* going ahead with any policy or appointment that was leaked in advance to the press. Soon, however, his aides began to suspect that this was giving the bureaucracy the most powerful weapon of all, namely the power to veto a presidential decision by learning of it early

enough and rushing to the *Times* or the *Post*. (Or, if the issue could be described in thirty seconds, any of the major television networks.)

What we have here is disloyalty to the presidency. Much of the time what is involved is no more than the self-regard of lower-echelon bureaucrats who are simply flattered into letting the reporter know how much *they* know, or who are just trying to look after their agency. But just as often, to repeat, serious issues of principle are involved. Senator Joseph McCarthy made contact with what he termed "the loyal American underground"—State Department officials, and other such, who reputedly passed on information to him about Communist infiltration of the nation's foreign-policy and security systems. President Johnson made it clear that he did not trust the Department of State to maintain "security" in foreign policy. Under President Nixon the phenomenon has been most evident in domestic areas as OEO warriors struggle among themselves to be the first to disclose the imminent demise of VISTA, or HEW functionaries reluctantly interpret a move to close some fever hospital built to accommodate an eighteenth-century seaport as the first step in a master plan to dismantle public medicine and decimate the ranks of the elderly and disadvantaged.

It is difficult to say whether the absolute level of such disloyalty to the presidency is rising. One has the impression that it is. No one knows much about the process of "leaking" except in those instances where he himself has been involved. (*Everyone* is sooner or later involved. That should be understood.) The process has not been studied and little is known of it. But few would argue that the amount of clandestine disclosure is decreasing. Such disclosure is now part of the way we run our affairs. It means, among other things, that the press is fairly continuously involved in an activity that is something less than honorable. Repeatedly it benefits from the self-serving acts of government officials who are essentially hostile to the presidency. This does the presidency no good, and if an outsider may comment, it does the press no good either. Too much do they traffic in stolen goods, and they know it.

This point must be emphasized. The leaks which appear in the *Post* and the *Times*—other papers get them, but if one wants to influence decisions in Washington these are clearly thought to be the most effective channels—are ostensibly published in the interest of adding to public knowledge of what is going on. This budget is to be cut; that man is to be fired; this bill is to be proposed. However, in the nature of the transaction the press can only publish half the story—that is to say the information that the "leaker" wants to become "public knowledge." What the press *never* does is say who the leaker is and why he wants the story leaked. Yet, more often than not, this is the more important story: that is to say, what policy wins if the one being disclosed loses, what individual, what bureau, and so on.

There really are ethical questions involved here that have not been examined. There are also serious practical questions. It is my impression that the distress occasioned by leaks has used up too much presidential energy, at least from the time of Roosevelt. (Old-time brain-trusters would assure the Johnson staff that nothing could compare with FDR's distractions on the subject.) The primary fault lies within government itself, and one is at a loss to think of anything that might be done about it. But it is a problem for journalism as well, and an unattended one.

IV

The fourth of the five conditions making for an altered relation between the presidency and the press is the concept of objectivity with respect to the reporting of events and especially the statements of public figures. Almost the first canon of the great newspapers, and by extension of the television news networks which by and large have taken as their standards those of the best newspapers, is that "the news" will be reported whether or not the reporter or the editor or the publisher likes the news. There is nothing finer in the American newspaper tradition. There is, however, a rub and it comes when a decision has to be made as to whether an event really is news, or simply a happening, a nonevent staged for the purpose of getting into the papers or onto the screen.

The record of our best papers is not reassuring here, as a glance at the experience of the Korean and the Vietnam wars will suggest. Beginning a bit before the Korean hostilities broke out, but in the general political period we associate with that war, there was a rise of right-wing extremism, a conspiracy-oriented politics symbolized by the name of Senator Joseph McCarthy, and directed primarily at the institution of the presidency. There was, to be sure, a populist streak to this movement: Yale and Harvard and the "striped-pants boys" in the State Department were targets too. But to the question, "Who promoted Peress?" there was only one constitutional or—for all practical purposes—political answer, namely that the president did. McCarthy went on asking such questions, or rather making such charges, and the national press, which detested and disbelieved him throughout, went on printing them. The American style of objective journalism made McCarthy. He would not, I think, have gotten anywhere in Great Britain, where, because it would have been judged he was lying, the stories would simply not have been printed.

Something not dissimilar has occurred in the course of the Vietnam War, only this time the extremist, conspiracy-oriented politics of protest has been putatively left-wing. Actually both movements are utterly confusing if one depends on European analogues. McCarthy was nominally searching out Communists, but his preferred targets were Eastern patricians, while his supporters were, to an alarming degree, members of the Catholic working class. The Students for a Democratic Society if that organization may be used as an exemplar, was (at least in its later stages) nominally revolutionist, dedicated to the overthrow of the capitalist-imperialist-fascist regime of the United States. Yet, as Seymour Martin Lipset, Nathan Glazer, and others have shown, its leadership, and perhaps also its constituency, were disproportionately made up of upper-class Jewish and Protestant youth. By report of Steven Kelman, who lived as a contemporary among them at Harvard, the SDS radicals were "undemocratic, manipulative, and self-righteous to the point of snobbery and elitism." Peter Berger, a sociologist active in the peace movement, has demonstrated quite persuasively—what others, particularly persons of European origin like himself have frequently seemed to sense—that despite the leftist ring of the slogans of SDS and kindred groups, their ethos and tactics are classically fascist: the cult of youth, the mystique of the street, the contempt for liberal democracy, and the "totalization of friend and foe [with] the concomitant dehumanization of the latter," as in the Nazi use of *"Saujuden"* ("Jewish pigs").

In any case, the accusations which have filled the American air during the period of Vietnam have been no more credible or responsible than those of McCarthy during the Korean period, and the tactics of provocation and physical intimidation have if anything been more disconcerting. Yet the national press, and especially television, have assumed a neutral posture, even at times a sympathetic one, enabling the neofascists of the Left to occupy center stage throughout the latter half of the sixties with consequences to American politics that have by no means yet worked themselves out. (It took Sam Brown to point out that one consequence was to make the work of the antiwar movement, of which he has been a principal leader, vastly more difficult.)

Would anyone have it otherwise? Well, yes. Irving Kristol raised this question in an article that appeared before the New Left had made its presence strongly felt on the national scene, but his views are doubtless even more emphatic by now. He wrote of the "peculiar mindlessness which pervades the practice of journalism in the United States," asserting that the ideal of objectivity too readily becomes an excuse for avoiding judgment. If McCarthy was lying, why print what he said? Or why print it on the front page? If the SDS stages a confrontation over a trumped-up issue, why oblige it by taking the whole episode at face value? Here, let it be said, the editorials of the *Times* and the *Post* have consistently served as a thoughtful corrective to the impressions inescapably conveyed by the news columns. But the blunt fact is that just as the news columns were open to astonishingly false assertions about the nature of the American national government during the McCarthy period, they have been open to equally false assertions—mirror images of McCarthyism indeed—during the period of Vietnam. And although it is impossible to prove, one gets the feeling that the slanderous irresponsibilities now being reported so dutifully are treated with far more respect than the old.

The matter of a policy of "genocide" pursued by the national government against the Black Panthers is a good example. By late 1969, preparing a preface to a second edition of *Beyond the Melting Pot*, Nathan Glazer and I could insist that the charge that twenty-eight Panthers had been murdered by the police was on the face of it simply untrue. Yet in that mindless way of which Kristol writes, the *Times* kept reprinting it. Edward Jay Epstein has brilliantly explained the matter in a recent article in *The New Yorker.* What he finds is an immense fraud. No such policy existed. There was no conspiracy between the Department of Justice, the FBI, and various local police forces to wipe out the Panthers. Yet that fraudulent charge has so profoundly affected the thinking of the academic and liberal communities that they will probably not even now be able to see the extent to which they were deceived. The hurt that has been done to blacks is probably in its way even greater. None of it could have happened without the particular mind-set of the national press.

If the press is to deserve our good opinion, it must do better in such matters. And it should keep in mind that the motivation of editors and reporters is not always simply and purely shaped by a devotion to objectivity. In the course of the McCarthy era James Reston recalled the ancient adage which translated from the Erse proposes that "If you want an audience, start a fight." This is true of anyone who would find an audience for his views, or simply for himself. It is true also of anyone who would find customers for the late city edition. T. S. Matthews, sometime editor of *Time,* retired to England to ponder the meaning of it all. In the end, all he could conclude was that the function of journalism was entertainment. If it is to be more—and that surely is what the Rosenthals and Bradlees and Grunwalds and Elliotts want—it will have to be willing on occasion to forego the entertainment value of a fascinating but untruthful charge. It will, in short, have to help limit the rewards which attend this posture in American politics.

V

The final, and by far the most important, circumstance of American journalism relevant to this discussion is the absence of a professional tradition of self-correction. The mark of any developed profession is the practice of correcting mistakes, by whomsoever they

are made. This practice is of course the great invention of Western science. Ideally, it requires an epistemology which is shared by all respected members of the profession, so that when a mistake is discovered it can be established as a mistake to the satisfaction of the entire professional community. Ideally, also, no discredit is involved: to the contrary, honest mistakes are integral to the process of advancing the field. Journalism will never attain to any such condition. Nevertheless, there is a range of subject matter about which reasonable men can and will agree, and within this range American journalism, even of the higher order, is often seriously wide of the mark. Again Irving Kristol:

> It is a staple of conversation among those who have ever been involved in a public activity that when they read the *Times* the next morning, they will discover that it has almost never got the story quite right and has only too frequently got it quite wrong.

Similar testimony has come from an editor of the *New York Times itself.* In an article published some years ago in the *Times Magazine,* A. H. Raskin had this to say:

> No week passes without someone prominent in politics, industry, labor, or civic affairs complaining to me, always in virtually identical terms: "Whenever I read a story about something in which I really know what is going on, I'm astonished at how little of what is important gets into the papers—and how often even that little is wrong." The most upsetting thing about these complaints is the frequency with which they come from scientists, economists, and other academicians temporarily involved in government policy but without any proprietary concern about who runs the White House or City Hall.[1]

This is so, and in part it is unavoidable. Too much happens too quickly: that the *Times* or the *Post* or the *Star* should appear once a day is a miracle. (Actually they appear three or four times a day in different editions.) But surely when mistakes are made they ought to be corrected. Sometimes they are, but

not nearly enough. It is in this respect
that Kristol is right in calling, journalism
"the underdeveloped profession. . . ."

VI

In the wake of so lengthy an analysis,
what is there to prescribe? Little. Indeed,
to prescribe much would be to miss the
intent of the analysis. I have been hoping to make two points—the first
explicitly, the second largely by implication. The first is that a convergence of
journalistic tradition with evolving cultural patterns has placed the national
government at a kind of operating disadvantage. It is hard for government to
succeed: this theme echoes from every
capital of the democratic world. In the
United States it is hard for government
to succeed and just as hard for government to appear to have succeeded
when indeed it has done so. This situation can be said to have begun in the
muckraking era with respect to urban
government; it is now very much the
case with respect to national government, as reflected in the "national
press" which primarily includes the
New York Times, the *Washington Post,*
Time, Newsweek, and a number of
other journals.

There is nothing the matter with investigative reporting; there ought to be
more. The press can be maddeningly
complacent about real social problems
for which actual countermeasures, even
solutions, exist. (I spent a decade,
1955-65, trying to obtain some press
coverage of the problem of motor-
vehicle design, utterly without avail.
The press, from the most prestigious
journals on down, would print nothing
but the pap handed out by the automobile companies and wholly owned
subsidiaries such as the National Safety
Council.) The issue is not one of serious
inquiry, but of an almost feckless hostility to power.

The second point is that this may not
be good for us. American government
will only rarely and intermittently be

run by persons drawn from the circles of
those who own and edit and write for
the national press; no government will
ever have this circle as its political base.
Hence the conditions are present for a
protracted conflict in which the national
government keeps losing. This might
once have been a matter of little consequence or interest. It is, I believe, no
longer such, for it now takes place
within the context of what Nathan
Glazer recently described as an "assault
on the reputation of America . . . which
has already succeeded in reducing this
country, in the eyes of many American
intellectuals, to outlaw status. . . ." In
other words, it is no longer a matter of
this or that administration; it is becoming a matter of national morale, of a
"loss of confidence and nerve," some of
whose possible consequences, as
Glazer indicates, are not pleasant to
contemplate.

Some will argue that in the absence
of a parliamentary question-time only
the press can keep the presidency honest. Here we get much talk about presidential press conferences and such. This
is a serious point, but I would argue that
the analogy does not hold. Questions
are put in Parliament primarily by
members of an opposition party hoping
to replace the one in office. Incompetent questions damage those chances;
irresponsible questions damage the office. Indeed, British politicians have
been known to compare the press lords
to ladies of the street, seeking "power
without responsibility." It would, of
course, be better all around if Congress
were more alert. Thus the *Times* has reported that the GNP estimate in the
1971 Budget Message was not that of
the Council of Economic Advisors, but
rather a higher figure dictated by the
White House for political purposes. This
is a profoundly serious charge. Someone has a lot to explain. It could be the
administration; it could be the *Times.*
Congress should find out.

Obviously the press of a free country
is never going to be and never should

be celebratory. Obviously government at all levels needs and will continue to get criticism and some of it will inevitably be harsh or destructive, often enough justifiably so. Obviously we will get more bad news than good. Indeed the content of the newspapers is far and away the best quick test of the political structure of a society. Take a morning plane from Delhi to Karachi. One leaves with a sheaf of poorly printed Indian papers filled with bad news; one arrives to find a small number of nicely printed Pakistani papers filled with good news. One has left a democracy, and has entered a country that is something less than a democracy.

Nonetheless there remains the question of balance. Does not an imbalance arise when the press becomes a too-willing outlet for mindless paranoia of the Joseph McCarthy or New Left variety? Does it not arise when the press becomes too self-satisfied to report its own mistakes with as much enterprise as it reports the mistakes of others?

Norman E. Isaacs, a working journalist, has written thoughtfully about the possibility of establishing a "national press council." This, in effect, was proposed by Robert M. Hutchins's Commission on Freedom of the Press in 1947: "A new and independent agency to appraise and report annually upon the performance of the press." There are press councils in other democratic countries which hear complaints, hand down verdicts, and even, as in Sweden, impose symbolic fines. There is a case to be made here, but I would argue that to set up such a council in this country at this time would be just the wrong thing to do. There is a statist quality about many of the press councils abroad: often as not they appear to have been set up to ward off direct government regulation. Freedom of the press is a constitutional guarantee in the United States: how that freedom is exercised should remain a matter for the professional standards of those who exercise it. Here, however, there really is room

for improvement. First in the simple matter of competence. The very responsibility of the national press in seeking to deal with complex issues produces a kind of irresponsibility. The reporters aren't up to it. They get it wrong. It would be astonishing were it otherwise.

Further, there needs to be much more awareness of the quite narrow social and intellectual perspective within which the national press so often moves. There are no absolutes here; hardly any facts. But there is a condition that grows more not less pronounced. The national press is hardly a "value-free" institution. It very much reflects the judgment of owners and editors and reporters as to what is good and bad about the country and what can be done to make things better. It might be hoped that such persons would give more thought to just how much elitist criticism is good for a democracy. Is this a shocking idea? I think not. I would imagine that anyone who has read Peter Gay or Walter Laqueur on the history of the Weimar Republic would agree that there are dangers to democracy in an excess of elitist attack. A variant of the Jacksonian principle of democratic government is involved here. Whether or not ordinary men are capable of carrying out any governmental task whatsoever, ordinary men are going to be given such tasks. That is what it means to be a democracy. We had best not get our expectations too far out of line with what is likely to happen, and we had best not fall into the habit of measuring all performance by the often quite special tastes, preferences, and interests of a particular intellectual and social elite. (Perhaps most importantly, we must be supersensitive to the idea that if things are not working out well it is because this particular elite is not in charge. Consider the course of events that led to the war in Indochina.)

As to the press itself, one thing seems clear. It should become much more open about acknowledging mistakes. The *Times* should have printed Dr.

Henderson's letter. Doubtless the bane of any editor is the howling of politicians and other public figures claiming to have been misquoted. But often they *are* misquoted. At the very least, should not more space be allotted to rebuttals and exchanges in which the issue at hand is how the press performed?

Another possibility is for each newspaper to keep a critical eye on itself. In the article previously cited which he did for the *New York Times Magazine,* A. H. Raskin called for "a Department of Internal Criticism" in every paper "to put all its standards under reexamination and to serve as a public protection in its day-to-day operations." The *Times* itself has yet to establish such a department but the *Washington Post* has recently set a welcome example here by inaugurating a regular editorial-page feature by Richard Harwood entitled "The News Business." Harwood's business is to check up on what his paper runs, and he is finding a good deal to check up on. (To all editors: *Please* understand there is nothing wrong with this. It is a routine experience of even the most advanced sciences. Perhaps especially of such.) Harwood has made a useful distinction between mistakes of detail—the ordinary garbles and slips of a fast-moving enterprise—and mistakes of judgment about the nature of events:

> The mistakes that are more difficult to fix are those that arise out of our selection and definition of the news. Often we are unaware of error until much time has passed and much damage has been done.
>
> In retrospect, it seems obvious that the destructive phenomenon called "McCarthyism"—the search in the 1950s for witches, scapegoats, traitors—was a product of this kind of error. Joseph McCarthy, an obscure and mediocre senator from Wisconsin, was transformed into the Grand Inquisitor by publicity. And there was no way later for the newspapers of America to repair that damage, to say on the morning after: "We regret the error."

Which will turn out "in retrospect" to seem the obvious errors of the 1960s? There were many, but they are past. The question now is what might be the errors of the 1970s, and whether some can be avoided. One Richard Harwood does not a professional upheaval make, but he marks a profoundly important beginning. All major journals should have such a man in a senior post, and very likely he should have a staff of reporters to help him cover "the news business."

As for government itself, there is not much to be done, but there is something. It is perfectly clear that the press will not be intimidated. Specific efforts like President Kennedy's to get David Halberstam removed as a *Times* correspondent in Vietnam almost always fail, as they deserve to do. Nonspecific charges such as those leveled by Vice President Agnew, get nowhere either. They come down to an avowal of dislike, which is returned in more than ample measure, with the added charge that in criticizing the press the government may be trying to intimidate it, which is unconstitutional.

What government can do and should do is respond in specific terms to what it believes to be misstatements or mistaken emphases; it should address these responses to specific stories in specific papers and it should expect that these will be printed (with whatever retort the journal concerned wishes to make). Misrepresentations of government performance must never be allowed to go unchallenged. The notion of a "one-day story," and the consoling idea that yesterday's papers are used to wrap fish, are pernicious and wrong. Misinformation gets into the bloodstream and has consequences. The *Times* ought by now to have had a letter from the chairman of the Civil Service Commission pointing out the mistakes in the November 15 story on minority employment, and the even more important omissions. If the first letter was ignored, he should have sent another. Similarly the *Times* ought long since have had a letter from an HEW official exposing the errors of its coverage of federal aid to black colleges. Failing that, someone should have called in the education writers of the *Times* and asked why they let other men misreport their beat. Etc. Hamilton's formulation has not been bettered: the measure of effective government is energy in the executive.

In the end, however, the issue is not one of politics but of culture. The culture of disparagement that has been so much in evidence of late, that has attained such an astonishing grip on the children of the rich and the mighty, and that has exerted an increasing influence on the tone of the national press in its dealings with the national government, is bad news for democracy. Some while ago the late Richard Hofstadter foresaw what has been happening:

> Perhaps we are really confronted with two cultures (not Snow's), whose spheres are increasingly independent and more likely to be conflicting than to be benignly convergent: a massive adversary culture on the one side, and the realm of socially responsible criticism on the other.

But given what has been happening to the press in recent years and what is likely to go on being the case if current trends should continue on their present path, where is such "socially responsible criticism" to come from? Or rather, where is it to appear in a manner that will inform and influence the course of public decision-making?

NOTE

1. It should not, of course, be supposed that people inside government "know" what happens. The *Rashomon* effect is universal. It is, moreover, not uncommon for men in government to be doing something quite different from what they think or intend. In such cases, the more accurate the press reporting, the more baffled or enraged the officials will be. Still, the judgment Raskin reports is near universal.

31. The Presidency Versus the Press—Who Is Right?*

HARRY KRANZ

During the somewhat placid summer of 1971, the media apparently won two battles with the President. In the first, the Supreme Court, by a vote of 6 to 3, blocked the administration's attempt to suppress publication in the *New York Times* and the *Washington Post* of the secret Pentagon history of the Vietnam War.[1] In the second, the House of Representatives refused, by a vote of 181 to 226, to cite the Columbia Broadcasting System for refusing to turn over to a congressional committee the unused portions of material gathered for a documentary television show[2] ("The Selling of the Pentagon") which had been bitterly attacked by the vice-president.

In the 200-year-old cold war between the presidency and the press, which flares up periodically and is likely to be blazing again throughout the coming months as the 1972 election campaign gets underway, these two media vic-

*Source: From *Human Rights*, vol. 2 (March 1972), pp. 27-47. Copyright © 1972 American Bar Association. Reprinted by permission.

tories have been hailed as historic reaffirmations of freedom of the press,[3] particularly by critics who charge that the two cases involving the Pentagon epitomize the Nixon administration's blatant and unprecedented attempts to "manage" the news, intimidate or discredit the media, and propagandize the public.[4]

On the other hand, the decisions are decried by administration defenders[5] who feel that the media have grown too powerful and imperiled the president's capacity to govern. In a lengthy article in Commentary in March 1971 on "The Presidency & The Press," written several months before the Pentagon Papers case broke, and widely reprinted by newspapers throughout the United States, former White House counselor Daniel P. Moynihan argued that the balance between the presidency and the press had tipped in favor of the latter, and that this "is bad news for democracy."[6]

Both sides of the presidency versus the press controversy insist that the other's ascendency is not only bad for the public interest, but endangers democratic government. Who is right? Is the president or the press ahead now—and have the two recent media victories affected the balance much? What can we do about it?

My contention will be that the White House continues to maintain ascendency over the media, that the two recent battles, far from improving the media's position, actually are a setback for the press; that presidential dominance is bad for the nation; and that specific actions can and must be taken to counter presidential power.

In determining where truth lies, and where truth and lies diverge, my judgment is influenced not only by the Ivory Tower neutrality of a lawyer, teacher and student of public administration but by firsthand participation in both press management and presidential government. As a reporter, city editor and editor of daily newspapers early in my career, I have observed press cynicism

and distortions. During my work with the federal government over the past decade, I have served on presidential task forces and study groups, and witnessed governmental attempts to mislead the press.

Critical to an evaluation of the conflict between the contemporary president and the mass media, is a realization that the two sides are not just battling against each other; what they are fighting for is public opinion. Popular government rests on the assumption that the people are capable of passing a verdict for or against the administration in power; the accuracy of that verdict depends upon the public's knowledge of what the government has done or failed to do. Hence, the information received by the people from government and from the media will affect their democratic choices of candidates and policies.

Accordingly, it is both ironic and significant that Mr. Moynihan, in opening his article in Commentary, quoted Thomas Jefferson's dictum (which Moynihan erroneously attributed to Harry Truman) that he pities his "fellow citizens, who; reading newspapers, live and die in the belief, that they have known something of what has been passing in the world in their time"[7] without either noting that Jefferson was talking about the partisan political press of his day (which censored and distorted statements of its political opponents) or quoting Jefferson's more famous press comment, which gets at the heart of the controversy:

The basis of our governments being the opinion of the people, the very first object should be to keep that right; and were it left to me to decide whether we should have a government without newspapers or newspapers without a government, I should not hestitate a moment to prefer the latter.[8]

Dr. Moynihan's error and omission in presidential quotation is, unfortunately, fairly typical of the ingenuous and ingenious arguments he offers to buttress his claims of press ascendency and presidential powerlessness. Even when he concedes that, over the years, the president has clearly had the advantage over the press, he maintains that press fears of "their vulnerability to governmental coercion or control" have been "exaggerated."

Certainly, every student will agree that presidential news management has been an American dilemma since the birth of the Republic. Ever since the U.S. Constitution set the parameters for their tension and conflict by creating both the presidency and a free press, these two institutions have competed avidly for public opinion. The techniques, the media and the presidency itself have changed over nearly two centuries, but presidential attempts to "manage" the news—to restrict it, to distort it, to interpret it, to leak it, to delay or expedite it, to suppress it, and to punish or reward its purveyors—have not varied. Press fears of government control have been well grounded.

Attempts at presidential news management were rather crude at first. During the ascendancy of the political press, when every paper was either the slave of a great politician or the outright organ of a party, owing its very life to political subsidy or governmental advertising, President John Adams and his Federalist supporters whipped through Congress in July 1798, the Alien and Sedition Acts, one of which was designed to silence all editorial criticism of the president or Congress. During the "reign of terror" which followed, 25 people were arrested, 11 tried and 10 found guilty and sentenced, including at least 3 newspaper editors. Campaigning against these repressive measures, Thomas Jefferson won election as president in 1800. The law expired when Jefferson took office in March 1801, and he promptly pardoned all those convicted under it.

Although always a stout defender of the abstract right of freedom of the press, Jefferson himself, after he became president, was exasperated by the attacks of the Federalist newspapers and thought that "the press ought to be restored to its credibility if possible, by a few prosecutions of the most prominent offenders" in state libel actions. "Not a general prosecution, for that would look like persecution: but a selected one," he wrote.[9]

(Ironically, Jefferson's archenemy, Alexander Hamilton, is credited with establishing the freedom of the press to criticize public officials while defending a client against one of Jefferson's "selected prosecution." In the famous Croswell case, in 1804,[10] Hamilton's formula was adopted: "The liberty of the press is the right to publish with impunity, truth, with good motives, for justifiable ends though reflecting on government, magistracy, or individuals.")

When President Andrew Jackson proposed in December 1835, a law to give Congress the right to determine what newspapers were "incendiary," Senator Calhoun opposed it with his own bill to give that power to postmasters, not because Calhoun opposed censorship, but because he was afraid Jackson's bill would "clothe Congress with the power to abolish slavery."

New media attracted new presidential messages. After the Civil war, the development of fast, inexpensive presses created a mass newspaper market. Ousting the political party organs, the new type of journal got its livelihood from commercial advertising, sought mass circulation and was unwilling to offend whole sections of the public by extreme political bias. The public was increasingly demanding factual news. Political parties, as well as presidential assistants, "found that they could get their propaganda into newspaper columns by dressing it up in interesting clothes."[11]

Congress attempted to restrict the number of "publicity experts" in the federal government in 1913, providing in an appropriation bill: "No money appropriated by this or any other act shall be used for the compensation of any publicity expert unless specifically appropriated for that purpose."[12] The act was easily circumvented by calling them something else. Federal publicists blossomed in every department.

The press conference, like radio and television, was a twentieth century boon to activist presidents. When newsmen began interviewing presidential visitors as they left the White House, President Theodore Roosevelt ordered that an anteroom be set aside for the use of the newspaper men. President Taft was the first president to establish formal but irregular group meetings with the press. President Wilson tried twice-weekly conferences until World War I broke out and he wanted to restrict news. Warren Harding and Calvin Coolidge continued small press conferences but required questions to be submitted in advance. Herbert Hoover virtually abandoned press conferences after the stock market crash of 1929. Franklin Roosevelt refined to a high art the use of presidential press conferences as a management tool and also mastered the medium of radio. John F. Kennedy was the first president to utilize television effectively.

In wartime, of course, presidential powers to manage news have reached their zenith. During the Civil War, President Abraham Lincoln suppressed the Chicago Tribune and New York World & Journal of Commerce and imprisoned 13,000 war critics, including many editors.[13] During World War I, President Woodrow Wilson suppressed more than 100 newspapers, books and magazines, and operated a gigantic internal propaganda machine.[14] During World War II, President Franklin D. Roosevelt controlled virtually all war information through the Office of Censorship, but government propaganda was directed mainly overseas.[15] Our "peacetime" war in Indochina has embroiled three administrations in attempts to suppress war news.

Modern presidents, particularly during the long cold war, have been notorious for their attempts to "manage" news. President Eisenhower authorized lies about the U-2 spy plane crisis with the Soviet Union in 1960; President Kennedy, about American involvement in the invasion of Cuba in 1961; and President Johnson, about U.S. intervention in the Dominican Republic in 1965.[16] In a huff at what he considered biased reportage, Kennedy once cancelled the White House subscription to the late New York Herald-Tribune.[17] And it was Kennedy's Defense Department information chief who publicly defended "the inherent right of the government to lie ... to save itself when faced with nuclear disaster."[18]

While insisting that press fears of presidential power, particularly in peacetime, have been "exaggerated," Moynihan concedes that presidential "deceit" in the cold war and in Vietnam created tensions with the press and public. Although press censorhip was removed after World War II, Moynihan notes, "the kinds of circumstance in which any responsible government might feel that events have to be concealed from the public did not go away. The result was a contradition impossible to resolve." Hence, Vietnam, "an undeclared war, unwanted, misunderstood or not understood at all ... entailed a massive deception of the American people by their government." How else, but with lies, "to carry out a full-scale war that became steadily more unpopular with none of the legally sanctioned constraints on the free flow of information, which even the most democratic societies find necessary in such circumstances?" asks Moynihan.

Ignoring the simple fact that a president who deceives the American public about an undeclared and unpopular war is neither "democratic" nor "responsible," Moynihan blithely implies that presidential involvement in undeclared wars and lies about the war are essential to American democracy, while press exposure of the lies is evil. The possibility of presidential error in unrestricted bombing, in the Tonkin Gulf confusion, in the invasion of Cambodia and Laos is not even considered.

Having condoned wartime lies in the name of effective democratic government, Moynihan disposes of the charges of mammoth news management against the Nixon administration with a two-sentence comment that

> non-specific charges such as those leveled by Vice-President Agnew get nowhere. They come down to an avowal of dislike, which is returned in more than ample measure, with the added charge that in criticizing the press the government may be trying to intimidate it, which is unconstitutional.

As Federal Communications Commission member Nicholas Johnson, a critic of both the Nixon administration and television, pointed out,

> the Agnew-induced cowardice in the networks has produced some of the "chilling effect" on free expression that the administration was out to encourage—and that the Supreme Court has used as a standard for governmental actions violative of the First Amendment.[19]

The unconstitutional intimidation which Johnson says the administration "has produced," Moynihan notes only as a "charge."

Clearly, much of what the Nixon administration has done in managing the news may be both blatant and sophisticated, but it is not unprecedented. Releasing good news prematurely and delaying bad news until after the election, rewarding friendly editors and columnists with exclusive interviews and government transportation, while restricting critical correspondents from easy presidential access, are not original with Mr. Nixon. Similarly, he is not the first twentieth century president to attempt to improve his public relations—by appointing press secretaries, varying the format of his press conferences and occasionally bypassing the White House press corps to talk directly to the people (and editors) outside Washington and via radio and television.

What is novel, perhaps, in the Nixon administration is the overweening concern with public relations techniques: the appointment of advertising agency executives as key presidential assistants; the establishment of a "Director of Communications" to orchestrate the attack on the media, a position which FCC Commissioner Johnson points out is unique outside of communist and fascist countries; and the continuing criticism of media coverage in an attempt to influence (some say "intimidate") journalists.

This last charge, of course, is the most serious, since, if the president is successful in swaying the media, it would clearly violate the First Amendment and his oath to support the Constitution. There is some evidence of administration "success" in the critical area of television:

- On the eve of a crucial Senate vote on the SST, a call from the director of communications' office induced Dick Cavett to interview only an administration proponent, canceling plans to include an SST foe in the television discussion.
- A few days after Vice-President Agnew launched his attack on the media on November 13, 1969, at Des Moines, the television networks provided only "spotty coverage," of the largest march on the White House in American history, when 500,000 angry Americans flooded Washington to protest the Indochina war; but eight months later the networks gave "lavish coverage" to Bob Hope's Honor America Day, when far fewer people gathered in D.C. to support the president.
- Equally intimidated, ABC Sports banned half-time coverage of the Buffalo-Holy Cross football game because it dealt with the controversial subject of "peace," but provided a nationwide audience for the chairman of the Joint Chiefs of Staff to speak on behalf of war at the half-time of the Army-Navy game.
- In the 1970 congressional elections, Mr. Nixon waged the most intensive congressional campaign ever conducted by a U.S. president, covering 23 states in a matter of days. Despite the fact that television was "abused and exploited" as never before, most of the candidates Mr. Nixon sup-

ported lost, partly as a result of what Edward P. Morgan has called the "incredible election eve mistake" of using the 15-minute edited replay on all three television networks of the president's airport hangar speech in Phoenix "attempting to make fear and violence—over a faulty sound track on black and white film—the main national issue."[20]

For a while, the administration retreated to lick its wounds. Not only was Mr. Agnew silenced, but three days after the 1970 elections, Mr. Nixon announced he had directed federal agencies to curtail "inappropriate promotional activities" which, he said,

affront many of our citizens with public relations promotions, fancy publications and exhibits aimed at a limited audience, and similar extravagances that are not in keeping with this administration's often stated policy of frugal management of the public's resources.

The respite was not long, however. On March 18, 1971, Mr. Agnew launched his new attack in Boston on CBS News (over the television documentary "Selling of the Pentagon") and the other networks and media. Commented FCC member Johnson:

Now that the elections backlash has subsided, the old Nixon has the old Agnew back at the same old stand: Clobber the commentators, needle the newsmen and edit the editors just as soon as the Fourth Estate shows signs of refusing to dole out the administration line on this or that Nixon/Agnew policy. This tactic is well recognized. We used to call it "managed news." Nowadays, managed news appears to be shading into a far more nefarious strategy: patent propaganda.

While it is "not surprising" that the administration is trying to blame Mr. Nixon's "slipping public image and growing credibility gap" on the failure of the networks to tell the news as he sees it, Mr. Johnson declared, "what is frightening is the open, brazen effort to affect ideological content." If the press and television refuse to be cowed, then the administration will attempt to discredit them, "because what Nixon-Agnew are really up to is to try to convince the American people that they cannot believe their media," Johnson contends.

Nor should the refusal of the House of Representatives to cite CBS and its president, Frank Stanton, for contempt be viewed as an unmitigated triumph for the media. Not only did the congressional committee involved vote for such a citation—on the grounds that freedom of the press was not at stake in dealing with television and that Congress had a right to investigate the news documentaries of television networks—but 181 members of the House voted to support such a citation, an ominous warning to television executives. This House vote, plus the attacks by the vice-president, are bound to have a chilling effect on both network procedures and substance.

Similarly, the U.S. Supreme Court decision permitting delayed publication of the secret Pentagon history of the Vietnam War, may have been a Pyrrhic press victory. The case set no new legal precedent, both because the justices wrote nine separate opinions and none spoke for the majority and also because the basic rule against "prior restraint" of any publication had been settled law in the United States for more than two centuries.[21] What the press gave up to win its 6 to 3 Court affirmation may, in the long-run, be more costly than what it won.

For the first time in American history, not only was prior restraint imposed on the press by five different federal courts, delaying publication,[22] but secret proceedings, secret testimony and even secret law office work[23] were sanctioned by the federal courts, including the Supreme Court. Only two justices upheld the First Amendment's ban on press censorship, while a majority of the Supreme Court conceded there might be future occasions for prior restraint. Both government and press counsel argued the Frankfurter "balancing" theory—weighing the claimed threat to national security against the First Amendment—and four justices followed this line in holding the government hadn't proven its case.

Moreover, at least four and possibly five of the justices encouraged the government to believe that the Supreme Court would uphold prosecution and conviction of the press for violation of criminal statutes if the press were prosecuted after official secrets were published. Not only has Daniel Ellsberg, who admitted turning the documents over to the newspapers, already been indicted and faced with the possibility of ten years in prison and a $10,000 fine, but Attorney General John Mitchell has announced he would prosecute "all those who have violated federal criminal law in connection with this matter," presumably including reporters, editors and publishers. Sensitive to these pressures, the New York Times and the Washington Post not only refrained from publication of their stories while the restraining orders were pending (unlike early colonial editors who defied government bans and were prosecuted for printing unauthorized criticisms), but they voluntarily withheld publication of parts of the materials which Ellsberg felt did not jeopardize security in any way.

Thus, it is clear that the last has not been heard yet of either the Pentagon Papers case, or of presidential–press conflict. As I. F. Stone commented:

It will be a miracle if this Administration, which is almost paranoid in its attitude toward the media, is not encouraged to include editors and reporters among the "all those who have violated federal criminal laws" the Attorney General now says he will prosecute.[24]

To avoid dealing with the charge that the Nixon administration's news management attempts have surpassed tolerable limits, Dr. Moynihan contended that the issue is not "the reputation of a particular president," but "what is seen to be at stake, and by the presidents themselves, is the reputation of government, especially, of course, presidential government. These are different matters, and summon a different order of concern."

How convenient to have what is at stake defined for the press and the public "by the presidents themselves." One need not examine the news management attempts of a Nixon or a Johnson; one must only look at the struggle of all presidents to get an occasional word in the press!

Even on the higher ground he has thus chosen to defend—presidential government—Moynihan is, nevertheless, shaky. Of Moynihan's five "basic circumstances" which he claims now give the press the upper hand, two attempt to exaggerate press power by deflating the power of the president, while two others argue contradictory positions by chiding the press for both "subjectivity" and "objectivity."

Attempting to show that the press is mightier than the president, Moynihan contends that the modern president is frequently disabled from acting because Washington reporters write news "leaked" from federal bureaucrats "antagonistic to presidential interests." He is wrong on several counts.

As a federal bureaucrat who has yet to leak anything to my friends in the press, my experience is that the Washington press depends too heavily on official press releases, briefings and deliberate "leaks" from the administration in power and seldom seeks out sub-surface news. The occasional unauthorized "leak" drops gently in the bucket of administration snake-oil. The system rewards bureaucrats who "don't rock the boat," not the rare maverick who "blows the whistle" on illegal or unwise administration actions or proposals. (The Ellsberg "leak" came long after he had left the federal government, not while he was a bureaucrat).

Moreover, "leaks," as Moynihan concedes, are primarily of interest to a few national newspapers, not to the 30-second television newscast. The revolutionary development of the media of communication has increased, not diluted, presidential dominance.

The number of daily newspapers has shrunk from 2,600 in 1910, when our population was 92 million, down to 1,750 today, when our population exceeds 200 million.

In the past decade, television has become the primary means of political communication in America. It is not only looked upon by twice as many people as newspapers as the source for news of national election issues and candidates,[25] but 68 percent of Americans consider it their prime source of *all* news.[26] Not only has television helped nominate and elect little known candidates with wealth,[27] but the president commands prime time at will—and once in office, a politician who knows television can use it to keep the mass public behind him. Today's presidential press conference has been called "a T.V. spectacular, a ritual of showmanship dominated by the president."[28]

Minimizing not only the revolution in the mass media, but also the evolution of the presidency itself, Moynihan argues that the power of the modern president has been overstated in the textbooks written since F. D. R. Hence, he says, the over-expectant press and its fellow textbook-readers set "a tone of pervasive dissatisfaction with the performance of the national government, whoever the presidential incumbent may be and whatever the substance of his policies."

The "textbook" president is real, not fictional. He can wipe out life on this planet by a single command, and he can direct men walking on the moon or in outer space. As historian Henry Steele Commager has testified,[29] the president can commit up to 3,000,000 troops to war anywhere on this globe without prior consultation with Congress, without an attack on the U.S. and without an emergency requiring immediate action. He can reach secret agreements with foreign nations without Senate concurrence. He has vast discre-

tion in executing the nation's laws, and he has a retinue and palaces throughout the land, surpassing that of any prior ruler. He is the most powerful chief executive any nation has ever known.

If he chooses to crack down on the broadcasting industry, the president has available the "full panoply of governmental power—including the vice-president, the Justice Department and its subpoenas, the Federal Trade Commission, the FCC, the Pentagon, the Subversive Activities Control Board, the Internal Revenue Service and other agencies" as Commissioner Johnson points out.

Moreover, his constitutional and customary roles make the contemporary president the greatest newsmaker in the land. As leader of his party, as head of state, as commander-in-chief, as foreign policymaker and executor, as chief of the bureaucracy and law administrator, the president is news, and the success of his policies will frequently depend on how successfully he conveys to the public his own view of his acts, words, and thoughts. By the nature of his office, he must seek to "manage" the news.

It is true, of course, that his power is not unlimited. He is subject to occasional checks by Congress, the courts, the people, the press and his wife. But if he makes promises he does not fulfull, if he does not act bravely or wisely in the public interest—it is not usually because he lacks the power to act or to persuade. The president may not be omnipotent—after all, he can't chop off the heads of bearers of bad tidings, as in the old days—but neither is he an impotent straw man created by the press as a target for public ridicule, as Moynihan implies.

Apart from his attempts to distort the power of the presidency in relation to the press, two of Dr. Moynihan's five "basic points" contain an obvious glaring inconsistency. On the one hand, he condemns the young journalists now entering the profession for practicing the Lincoln Steffens muckraking style of subjective personal journalism directed at the presidency, while at the same time, he condemns older journalists for hiding behind "objectivity," avoiding judgment, and printing straight-facedly the charges of presidential opponents. There is a conflict today between those (particularly in the underground press) who advocate more personal judgments by reporters, and those who cling to objectivity in news reporting. But Dr. Moynihan cannot logically attack both schools as equally endangering the presidency.

Arguing that the working press is now "or soon will be" made up of Ivy Leaguers, that it has become a profession attractive to "elites," and is influenced by attitudes "genuinely hostile to American society and American government," Moynihan sees these attitudes reinforced by the "disproportionately well-educated and economically prosperous" readers of Washington and New York newspapers.

Moynihan is wrong on both his facts and his fears. Most of the journalists who have attacked presidents are from non-Ivy League schools.[30] What he overlooks is that our entire society, not just the press, has become more educated in recent years. Virtually every presidential appointee and the top ranks of the federal Civil Service have acquired college degrees, and a "disproportionate" number possess advanced master's and Ph. D. degrees. The U.S. Foreign Service is more Ivy League than the press.[31] And who does Moynihan think reads the Washington Post and the New York Times in the Washington area, if not the highly-educated and economically prosperous government employees who live there? If education is a threat to American society and government, as Moynihan seems to believe, then surely we need to fear the federal bureaucracy as much as the press.

"Far from deserving condemnation for their courageous reporting," commented Justice Black in the Pentagon Papers case,

the New York Times, the Washington Post, and other newspapers should be commended for serving the purpose that the Founding Fathers saw so clearly. In revealing the workings of the government that led to the Vietnam War, the newspapers nobly did precisely that which the Founders hoped and trusted they would do.[32]

Most dangerous of all, however, is Moynihan's adjuration of the press to reject "objectivity." "If McCarthy was lying, why print what he said?" The press has "been open to equally false assertions—mirror images of McCarthyism, indeed—during the period of Vietnam," says Moynihan.

Presumably, the press should decide who is lying—McCarthy, SDS, Secretary Laird, etc.—and not print anything they say—or bury it inside the paper where it won't be read. This is equivalent to the Nazi-Communist-New Left tactic of condemning the man (McCarthy, Nixon, etc.) and thereafter discrediting or ignoring everything he says—even if he happens to be right occasionally.[33] If the press made a habit of not printing what it thought were lies about Vietnam, as Moynihan suggests, much of what the administration has released would be suppressed. (Moynihan concedes government lies and deceit about Indochina.) Such a return to the partisan political press of the early American nation would destroy a free press, endanger the people's right to make up their own minds about who is lying, and truly threaten our democratic government.

The danger of a "little" press censorship is that the American people may become so accustomed to presidential news management or press distortions that they will unwittingly accept even more serious attempts at news control. A Gallup Poll of a few months ago disclosed that 70 percent of the American people believe that Mr. Nixon is attempting to manage the news, but only 17 percent of them feel he is doing any more along these lines than his predecessors; as many people feel that the news from Washington is slanted against the administration as in favor of it.[34] Although the Nixon administration has denied that it intends "censorship" or "intimidation" of the media, it has classified as secret and refused to discuss reports that Theodore D. Koop, a CBS vice-president and deputy U.S. censor in World War II, has been designated as standby censor in case of a national emergency.[35]

Since distorted news is a threat to the people's right to know, whether it comes from the president or the press, Moynihan is on sounder ground in arguing that when the press makes mistakes, they ought to be corrected. "Misrepresentations of government performance must never be allowed to go unchallenged," he says. Admitting that the press "sometimes" corrects its mistakes, Moynihan nevertheless does not prescribe any federal ombudsman or internal critic who will be allowed to challenge the "misrepresentation of government performance" by the president and his administration. It was a "rare admission of error" when Mr. Nixon conceded at his December, 1970 press conference that his pretrial prejudgments of guilt in the My Lai "massacre," and the Charles Manson and Angela Davis cases were "mistakes" and "probably unjustified."[36]

Clearly, the key to counterbalancing omnipresent presidential news management is strengthening and expanding diverse sources of news and power to the people. We may not be able effectively to roll back the powers of the modern president, but we need to guard against their further enhancement, and at the same time unleash countervailing power. Improving our purveyors of news would be an initial step forward.

If they are to survive and help save a free society, the existing media, particularly newspapers, must be made more readable and more believable. To keep up with the mammoth horde of specialists available to the president, newspapermen, particularly Washington correspondents, will have to be better trained and more experienced practitioners. Publishers and editors must encourage not only factual and interpretative news reporting, but also crusading columnists like Jack Anderson and I. F. Stone. Presidential press conferences will need to be revised to become "monthly, one-hour, on-the-record, sitdown, non-televised news conferences with no more than twenty reporters," as urged by the Freedom of Information Committee of Sigma Delta Chi, the professional journalism society.[37] And "underground" newspapers must be encouraged to shift their colorful columns from sex, drugs and revolution to realistic exposes of the wrong doings of the Establishment, including the federal government.

As the dominant medium today, both for general news and for political campaigning, television must be reformed to insure fair exposure to all viewpoints. Congress should enact legislation similar to the bill President Nixon vetoed last fall that would have lowered and tended to equalize the cost of political radio and television broadcasting. Spokesmen for the opposition party should be guaranteed equal time to answer all major presidential telecasts. And the public interest must be ensured in the imminent "wired city" of cable television, where 40 picture channels, several digital display screens, a facsimile newspaper or daily news magazine will be entering each home by 1980.[38]

In addition to improving the media, we can check further expansion of presidential power by strengthening competing governmental institutions. If Congress, the federal courts, governors and mayors engage in meaningful action in behalf of the public interest, they will win the attention of the press and the increasing respect of the American people. Congress can eliminate filibusters, seniority, and secrecy from its procedures and speed up passage of constructive legislation. The courts can move closer and faster toward the goal of equal justice under law for all, including the poor. And state and local governments need to act on social problems without awaiting federal initiative, direction and funds.

Congress can play a particularly significant role in halting executive expansion by a broad, systematic approach to strengthening democracy. It was successful in curtailing federal publicity agents, but it could more effectively attain the same goal by three larger steps.

First, the level of public interest, involvement, and understanding in public affairs must be greatly increased. When Jefferson indicated he would choose newspapers over government, he added "every man should receive those papers, and be capable of reading them." Congress can help wipe out illiteracy and poverty to ensure that every adult American can read, write and afford the media of information and the time to absorb them. We must remove remaining impediments to registration and voting; and shorten the ballot, reducing the number of elective offices at the state and local level.

Second, we must encourage and support a network of public interest law firms, such as Ralph Nader's Center for Study of Responsive Law and Public Interest Research Group, to conduct in-depth studies and publicize and take legal action against federal agencies. In fact, Congress should create and subsidize an independent office of Federal Ombudsman (on a par with G.A.O.) to constantly probe, expose, and correct agency shortcomings—both on behalf of citizens and congressmen, and on its own initiative.

Third, to encourage dissent, civil servants within the federal bureaucracy must be protected against adverse consequences resulting from their exposure of internal wrongdoing. Rather than being fired or condemned for "blowing the whistle" on executive mismanagement, such employees should be promoted and commended. Moreover,

Congress can hasten the de-classification of millions of documents now labeled "secret" and hidden from the public.[39]

Recognizing that our nation's strength rests on diversity, not only in government, but in the private sphere as well, we must enhance the power and effectiveness of diverse non-government civic groups. The American Civil Liberties Union, the League of Women Voters, the A.F.L.-C.I.O. Committee on Political Education, The N.A.A.C.P., and American Bar Association, universities, anti-war groups, and professional associations like the American Society for Public Administration—all have stood against presidents at crucial times in the past, and all have a role to play in diversifying the public media, countering presidential news management and helping keep our nation free.

Thus, while presidential news management has always been with us and likely will be in the future, we can never grow complacent. Since newspapers have been published, every tyrant has sought to control the press. Despite the two apparent victories this summer by the media, the president clearly has the upper hand today. To protect the people's right to know, we must cultivate diversity and guard against excesses in presidential news management. Eternal vigilance is still the price of liberty. It doesn't come cheap.

NOTES

1. *New York Times Co.* v. *United States,* 403 U.S. 713 (1971).

2. "CBS Action Killed by House, 226-181," *Washington Evening Star,* July 14, 1971. Actually the House voted by that margin on July 13 to send back to the Commerce Committee—and thereby kill—a contempt of Congress resolution against CBS and its president, Frank Stanton. Commerce Committee Chairman Harley O. Staggers (D.–W. Va.),

whose committee had voted 25 to 13 to send the contempt resolution to the House floor, admitted the citation was now a dead issue.

3. "Victory for the Press," *Newsweek,* July 12, 1971.

4. Nicholas Johnson, "A Defense of T.V. vs. White House," *Washington Post,* March 28, 1971. Mr. Johnson has been a courageous critic of both the Nixon administration and television networks. Quotations attributed to him hereafter are from this *Washington Post* article.

5. See, *e.g.,* "Victory for the Press," *supra,* note 3.

6. Daniel P. Moynihan, "The Presidency and the Press," *Commentary* (March 1971). Moynihan quotations hereafter are from his *Commentary* article, which was reprinted by the *Washington Post,* the *Christian Science Moniter* and other newspapers.

7. 9 The Writings of Thomas Jefferson 73 (P. L. Ford ed. 1892-1899).

8. 14 The Writings of Thomas Jefferson 359 (P. L. Ford ed. 1892-1899).

9. 8 The Writings of Thomas Jefferson 57 (P. L. Ford ed. 1892-1899).

10. *People* v. *Croswell,* 3 Johns. 337 (N.Y. 1804).

11. Ralph D. Casey, "Party Campaign Propaganda," 179 *Annals of the American Academy of Political and Social Science,* 100, 101 (1935).

12. Cedric Lawson, "How Much Federal Publicity Is There?" 2 *Public Opinion Quarterly,* 636, 644 (1938).

13. F. Bancroft, The Life of William H. Seward 276 (1900).

14. Conklin & Milner, "Wartime Censorship in the United States," 180 *Harpers* 187, 189 (Jan. 1940).

15. E. K. Lindsey, "A Report on the Growing Pains of Censorship," *Newsweek,* Feb. 16, 1942, at 29. See also, *Public Opinion Quarterly* (Spring 1943).

16. Max Frankel, "Nixon and His Press Relations," *New York Times,* Nov. 29, 1968.

17. A. Schlesinger, Jr., *A Thousand Days: John F. Kennedy in the White House* 718 (1965).

18. *Id.* See also, Evans & Novak, Lyndon B. Johnson: The Exercise of Power 355, 410-412 (1966), for a variety of presidential attempts to manage the news.

19. N. Johnson, *supra* note 4.

20. Edward P. Morgan, "The President's Incredible Election Eve Mistake," *Washington Post,* Nov. 14, 1970.

21. In *Near* v. *Minnesota,* 283 U.S. 697 (1931), in which the Supreme Court struck down a state statute which attempted to impose a prior restraint on a newspaper, the court traced the history against prior restraints back to Blackstone and Madison.

22. The district courts involved and the courts of appeals for the Second Circuit and the District of Columbia Circuit, as well as the Supreme Court, had issued temporary restraining orders against publication of the Pentagon Papers by the two newspapers and others. "I believe that every moment's continuance of the injunctions against these newspapers amounts to a flagrant, indefensible and continuing violation of the First Amendment," said Justice Black's opinion in the case.

23. In the first *in camera* proceeding of its kind ever held in the United States, the government was allowed to present much of its evidence in secret. Of the 27 federal judges who passed on the government's pleadings, not a single one thought the evidence impressive enough to warrant a preliminary injunction. (Only temporary restraining orders pending trial and appeal were issued.) Moreover, "the plaintiff in the case was able to dictate what individual defendants, and what counsel, were entitled to participate in determination of the issue. Such procedure can hardly be recommended in a democratic society." Brief of 27 members of Congress, as *amici curiae,* filed by Rep. Bob Eckhardt and Thomas I. Emerson of the Yale Law School in the Supreme Court. And

in preparing their briefs, the *Post's* lawyers encountered some of the anomalies created by the use of secret material in the judicial process. Government security guards kept watch outside the door as they drew up their secret responses to the government's secret affidavits, then swept up both sets of documents to take to court; the paper's lawyers were not even allowed to keep a copy of the secret briefs they had themselves written. "Victory for the Press," *supra* note 3, at 19.

24. I. F. Stone's Bi-Weekly, July 12, 1971, at 1.

25. Herbert Brucker, "Can Printed News Save a Free Society?," *Saturday Review,* Oct. 10, 1970, at 52.

26. A. Stern, Book Review, *Trans-action,* Oct., 1970, at 59.

27. Fred W. Friendly, "Asleep at the Switch of the Wired City," *Saturday Review,* Oct. 10, 1970, at 60.

28. Brucker, *supra* note 25, at 54-55.

29. In testimony before the Senate Foreign Relations Committee March 8, 1971. Commager pointed out that as late as 1915, the armed forces of the U.S. were less than 175,000.

Now we have a wholly new situation. Not only do we keep some 3,000,000 men under arms at all times—since 1951 the number has rarely fallen below that—but we have the greatest and most formidable armaments that any nation ever commanded. What this means is quite simply that while the past presidents could not involve the nation, or the world, very deeply in war without congressional approval, now they can—and do. I. F. Stone's Bi-Weekly, March 22, 1971.

30. Richard Harwood, "Is the Press Corps an 'Adversary Culture' of Elitists?," Washington Post, April 12, 1971, at 18.

31. F. C. Mosher, Democracy and The Public Service 156 (1968).

32. "The Nuances of a Great Case," Newsweek, July 12, 1971, at 18.

33. Brucker, supra note 25, at 55-64.

34. "The People and the Press," Newsweek, Nov. 9, 1970, at 23.

35. "Ziegler Refuses to Comment on Censor Report," Washington Post, Nov. 2, 1970, at 2.

36. "Thank You, Mr. President," Newsweek, Dec. 21, 1970, at 22.

37. "Sigma Delta Chi Hits One-Way News Conference," Washington Post, Nov. 8, 1970.

38. Friendly, supra note 27, at 60.

39. A recently retired Air Force security officer told a House Government Information Subcommittee, June 24, 1971: "I would guess that there are at least 20 million classified documents, including reproduced copies, in existence," adding: "I sincerely believe that less than one-half of one percent of the different documents actually contain information qualifying even for the lowest defense classification." I. F. Stone's Bi-Weekly, July 12, 1971, at 3. Legislation has been introduced to give Congress a role in determining which materials would be declassified and when. "Victory for the Press," supra note 3, at 17. When the author handled classified State Department cables coming through the Peace Corps in 1961-62, most were over-classified. Even news of an overseas Peace Corps volunteer's pregnancy was classified.

IX

Perspectives on the Limits of Presidential Power

Introduction. In the aftermath of the quagmire of Vietnam and the folly and tragedy of Watergate, many observers have begun to raise questions about the vigorous presidential leadership style. Many academics and journalists argue that the once acceptable theory of the "strong" presidency led to an excess of presidential power that could and did threaten American democracy. Moreover, many American citizens who were once sure that strong presidential leadership was necessarily good leadership no longer take the belief as axiomatic. The result has been the argument of many for a more Whiggish view of the presidency. Bluntly put, the effort in some academic and journalist circles, as well as the Congress, has been to "cut the presidency down to size" so that it does not dwarf the other branches and elements of the government. The articles and government decisions in this section are designed to illustrate some of the limits on presidential power, whether or not the system or events require or even justify it.

Students of the American political system have generally approved of a strong presidency, at least since the Brownlow Report of 1937. While many academics, until recently, have supported strong presidential power and even felt that the presidency had adequate power available to it, political scientist Louis Koenig believes otherwise. In his essay, "More Power to the President, Not Less," Koenig argues that there are many political and legislative obstacles which hamstring the president and stand in the way of sustained leadership. Indeed, the strength of the presidency is in reality far less than the image would imply. The president wears far too many chains. Instead of curbing the presidency, Koenig says, we ought to strengthen it and to this end he makes a number of specific recommendations that he believes would enable the presidency to cope with increasingly complex problems faced by it in this last quarter of the twentieth century.

Historian Arthur M. Schlesinger, Jr., a longtime proponent of the strong presidency, unlike Koenig, believes that presidential power had expanded and been so misused by 1972 that it threatened the constitutional system.

The too powerful presidency, Prometheus unbound, Schlesinger suggests, was due to the president's power to make war with only a passing nod to the Congress, his use of executive privilege to keep the activities of the White House secret, and his use of executive agreements rather than treaties to circumvent the necessity of Senate approval for many of his foreign policy initiatives. In his essay, "The Runaway Presidency," Schlesinger calls for a revitalization of the other branches and elements of the political system. He argues that "politics" not "law" must save the Republic from the "runaway" or "imperial" presidency. Only if politics fails, should the presidency be curtailed by other means, this being the heavy artillery of congressional impeachment.

Congress has not always followed Arthur Schlesinger, Jr.'s advice, but rather has counted on "law" not "politics" to rein in the powerful presidency. The president's power to make war, one of the reasons Schlesinger cites for the runaway presidency, has been the subject of congressional action through a public law.

At the outset three points should be made. The first point is this: the Constitution gave Congress alone the power to *declare* war. Over time, however, presidents have come to involve the nation in shooting wars without congressional action.

A second point: opponents of presidential warmaking have argued that the authority to initiate war was not divided between the president and Congress, but was vested exclusively in Congress. Presidents may use the war power only to repel sudden attacks, other emergencies, and other purposes as defined by Congress.

A final point is necessary. In recent years, presidents have extended what was mere practice into constitutional theory. With respect to the war in Vietnam, for example, the State Department's legal adviser said:

> Under the Constitution, the President in addition to being Chief Executive, is Commander-in-Chief of the Army and Navy. He holds prime responsibility for the conduct of United States foreign relations. These duties carry very broad powers, including the power to deploy American forces abroad and commit them to military operations when the President deems such action necessary to maintain the security and defense of the United States.[1]

Hence, the recent dispute with regard to the president's war powers and Congress' role therein.

To provide manageable standards for presidential use of the war power, Congress on November 7, 1973 took an unprecedented step and enacted the War Powers Resolution over the president's veto. The law sets the conditions under which presidents can carry the nation into war. More importantly the law attempted to spell out the dividing line between the constitutional power of Congress to declare war and the constitutional power of the president to conduct war. Thus the president's war power is said to be circumscribed or limited. Since the Constitution provides for Congress to declare war, many of its members as well as other commentators wondered whether or not the 1973 law actually increased the president's war-making power and gave him what amounts to unlimited discretion to conduct a war anywhere for ninety days. Although the debate over who is right is likely to rage on and ultimately may be decided by Schlesinger's "politics," the law does represent the most forceful congressional effort to curb the president's use of the armed forces. The full text of the law is provided in the next selection, "The War Powers Act of 1973: The Limits of the President's War Powers."

Just as Congress has not relied on "politics" to curtail the presidency, neither has the Supreme Court on the question of executive privilege. The term "executive privilege" is nowhere mentioned in the Constitution. However, for many years, certainly since President Dwight Eisenhower's efforts to keep Senator Joseph McCarthy out of executive branch business, the president has asserted a constitutional basis or privilege to refuse information to other branches of the government. This presidential claim was not seriously challenged until the Nixon presidency sought to use the "executive privilege" to sustain immunity from the judicial process. In the next selection, "United States vs. Nixon: The Limits of Executive Privilege," the Supreme Court spells out the conditions under which a president has a constitutional base for a "qualified" executive privilege as well as the circumstances under which no privilege can obtain.

Over the years, Congress has overtly or tacitly permitted much of its control over the pursestrings to slip away to the executive branch of government (see, again, for example, number 28, chapter 7). Whereas the imperial presidency has usually been attributed to the expansion of presidential powers in the military and foreign policy areas, congressional loss of control over the spending power certainly contributed to the overly powerful presidency in the domestic as well as foreign policy areas.

Until 1974, the president's role in the spending process after Congress had appropriated funds was very ambiguous. Presidents, for example, claimed both constitutional and statutory authority to impound appropriated funds.

With the enactment of the budget act of 1974, Congress now has a budget committee in each house. These committees coordinate the taxing and spending policies of Congress. The budget act of 1974 also provided Congress its own budget office (Congressional Budget Office) to evaluate presidential budget proposals (submitted by Office of Management and Budget) and indeed, to help Congress prepare its own budget alternatives.

The Impoundment Control Act of 1974, in particular, acknowledges the right of the president to impound funds subject, however, to congressional approval. With the enactment of the law, the reasons for presidential impoundment can no longer remain vague to suit the president's private political and programmatic goals. In short, the next selection, "Impoundment Control Act of 1974: The Limits of Presidential Impoundment," institutionalizes congressional review of impoundments and, thus, indicates the president may not do anything he wishes with funds after they have been appropriated.

In the final selection, "The Bureaucracy as a Check upon the President," political scientist Peter Woll and his colleague Rochelle Jones provide a novel view of how limits can be—and often are—placed on the power of the president through other than the Constitution, the Congress, and the courts. Woll and Jones see a fourth branch of government, namely, the federal bureaucracy, as placing important checks on presidential power. (For a close approximation of this view see number 15, in chapter 4.) The executive branch bureaucracies have this limiting effect on presidential leadership because of their symbiotic relationship with congressional committees or subcommittees and with various domestic constituencies. Political scientist J. Leiper Freeman has termed this phenomena the "iron triangles."

Woll and Jones make very clear that although the president is chief executive under the Constitution, this does not mean that he has either the complete legal authority or ability to galvanize the necessary political power to control the bureaucracy.[2] Woll and Jones detail the factors which make this so and point out why, in their view, this all redounds to the good of the Republic.

NOTES

1. See "The Legality of United States Participation in the Defense of Vietnam," *Department of State Bulletin* 54 (1966): 474.

2. For the view that, at the very least, bureaucracy should curb the president's capacity to use public power for private purposes, see Harry A. Bailey, Jr., "An Administrative Process Approach to Constraining the American Presidency," *Presidential Studies Quarterly* 7 (Summer 1978): 268-75.

32. More Power to the President (Not Less)*

LOUIS W. KOENIG

I

When Lyndon Baines Johnson is sworn in as president on January 20, attention will again be focused upon this most important office in the land. Although the office is one of great strength, it also has serious weaknesses. In his major roles as party chief, legislative leader, administrative chief and others, the President's capacity to act is bounded with limitations. It is important that in the exhilaration of the coming inaugural, and in the bright glow of Mr. Johnson's remarkable electoral victory, these limitations are not overlooked.

Their seriousness must also be appreciated against the background of hope and concern with which millions will view the new presidential term—those who face unemployment or are short-changed in their rights, or have little access to the banquet tables of the affluent society, or fear for mankind's future in the spread of nuclear competence among the nations—all these and countless others. Upon the American president, more than upon any other figure in the world, are centered man's hopes and fears for survival, freedom and the good life.

By no means do all Americans view the power of the executive with equal expectation and trust. A suspicion is firmly woven into American tradition, an apprehension that the president either has already appropriated, or someday will appropriate, too much authority and responsibility. In our society the legislature has been viewed—and

rightly so—as a champion of liberty, the province of the state governments is substantial, and the economy is chiefly one of private enterprise.

That the presidency already possesses excessive power was a major contention in the 1964 electoral campaign. In an address to the American Political Science Association on September 11 in Chicago, Senator Goldwater deplored the expansion of executive power at the expense of the other branches of government. He took to task those who hailed the concept of the "strong" presidents as having a "totalitarian philosophy that the end justifies the means." "We do not want oppressive powers in the hands of the executive branch," he said at Charlotte, N.C., later in the campaign. "We do want the proper balance between all branches and all levels."

Senator Goldwater, who in a real sense was running against the presidency rather than for it, was articulating a historic sentiment. The Twenty-second Amendment was added to the Constitution in 1951, to cries that it was imperative to limit the president to two terms in order to prevent him from becoming a dictator. All this notwithstanding the fact that no dictator has appeared in the long experience of the American presidency. In actuality, as public discussion made clear, the amendment was a posthumous attack upon Franklin D. Roosevelt.

The Twenty-second Amendment is a tragedy whose full dimensions are yet to be known. It is clear enough already that it inhibits presidential power in the second term and shifts the balance to Congress. Dwight Eisenhower has been the first and only victim, as yet, of the amendment's provisions, and he was made very conscious of its impact. In 1957, the first year of his second term, there was a noticeable weakening of his grip on Republican legislators and a softening of his hitherto strong support from the press and business, though he had been returned to power with a fresh and overwhelming mandate.

There have been other serious attempts to limit presidential power. The Bricker Amendment, also of the 1950s and pushed for years by tireless promoters, would in effect have prevented the chief executive from making treaties and executive agreements with foreign governments. It would have largely shut off the presidency from foreign affairs.

Not a few presidents, in using their powers, have engaged in conscious acts of self-denial. President Eisenhower came into office in 1953 imbued with a sense of duty to restore to Congress power which he believed had gravitated unduly from that body to the president in the era of Franklin Roosevelt. Many a nineteenth century president shared the view of James Buchanan, who said, "My duty is to execute the laws . . . and not my individual opinions." When Congress did little in the face of gathering rebellion, Buchanan too did little.

II

When the realities of presidential power are examined more closely, they reveal an office far less strong than those who attack it would lead us to suppose. A considerable chasm stretches between the presidency that its critics speak of—or imagine—and the presidency of reality.

That the presidency should be a limited office was part of the original conception. Distrustful of power in human hands, the Founding Fathers wrote the principles of checks and balances and separation of powers into the Constitution. Neither Congress nor the excutive was to become dominant, but each shared powers of the other, whether making laws, appointments or treaties, and each therefore could check the other and the Supreme Court could check both.

The president cannot long maintain important policies, domestic or foreign, without congressional support in the form of laws or money. But whereas a British prime minister, with an absolute majority in the House of Commons operating under an altogether different political arrangement can count on legislative enactment of 100 percent of his proposals, the president does well (except in time of crisis, when he does far better) to average between 50 and 60 percent.

He will sustain defeats on key measures, as Lyndon Johnson did in 1964 on health care for the aged under Social Security and aid for the depressed Appalachian region. John Kennedy, at the time of his death, still was deprived of legislation he deemed of highest importance—public school aid, civil rights, Medicare, a cabinet-level urban affairs department and standby authority to lower income taxes. Even with a slender majority of four votes, Harold Wilson launched in the first week of his prime ministership an ambitious and controversial foreign and domestic program, while simultaneously surviving votes of confidence.

The president has no dependable way, as the British prime minister does, to command the legislature's support. A complex of forces prompts Congress to resist or oppose the president much of the time. Because the method of electing the president differs from the method of electing congressmen, their constituencies and therefore their concerns and viewpoints differ.

The president and vice president alone are chosen by the nation. Senators and congressmen are essentially local officers responsible to the voters of a single state or congressional district. Congress neither chooses the president nor is chosen by him, and is therefore not beholden to him, and cannot be bullied by him.

Only once in four years are the president and members of the House of Representatives elected simultaneously, and even then only one-third of the Senate is elected. At the president's midterm, the House and another one-third of the Senate are chosen, usually with local issues predominating. The outcome more often than not worsens the president's own party support in both congressional houses. At no point in any four-year term does the president face a Senate wholly elected during his tenure, owing to the Senate's six-year term and staggered elections. Presidents come and go, but the most powerful legislators—the chairmen of the standing committees—stay on, often for a third of a century and more.

III

The likelihood is that a president who seeks important—and therefore controversial—social and economic legislation will face a hard wall of opposition from legislative leaders of his own party. These are the committee chairmen who have great seniority because they come from "safe" districts, situated chiefly in Southern and in rural and small-town areas.

The House Rules Committee chairman in 1964, Howard W. Smith, a small-town Virginian, has, over three decades, compiled an imposing record of thwarting presidential legislation. He helped bottle up Franklin Roosevelt's wage and hour bill, fought off most of Truman's Fair Deal program, and throttled education and welfare measures of both the Eisenhower and Kennedy administrations.

Mr. Smith's fellow Southerners dominated the committee chairmanships in

1964. Of 20 standing committees in the House, 12 were led by Southerners and Southwesterners. The disproportion was even greater in the Senate, where legislators from the same regions ran 12 out of 16 committees. It has been aptly said that although the South lost the Civil War, it has never lost the U.S. Senate.

The 1964 Democratic landslide had no particular impact on the roster of congressional committee chairmen. All the House chairmen in the 88th Congress who were renominated were reelected. The same is true in the Senate. The 89th Congress, commencing tomorrow, will find Howard Smith back at his old stand on the House Rules Committee, Harry Byrd of Virginia on the Senate Finance Committee, James Eastland of Mississippi on the Senate Judiciary Committee, and so on.

IV

Although the Founding Fathers did not foresee political parties, their rise has not hampered in any significant way the intended effect of checks and balances. President Eisenhower once perceptively observed, "Now let's remember there are no national parties in the United States. There are . . . state parties."

Our parties function effectively as national organizations only when control of the White House is at stake. Otherwise, a party is a loose confederation of state and local organizations, with sectional cleavages and factional differences commonplace. The president and the legislators, although they wear the same party label, are nominated by different party organizations and are chosen by different electorates, an arrangement that hardly works for unity.

There is no common standard of party loyalty, and no party caucus, as in Great Britain, which joins the executive with the legislators of his party in common support of a program. Even in the crisis of an election, which presumably would bring the party and its members into closest unity, differences between the president and his congressional party colleagues may rush to the surface.

The lengths to which the maladies may go is suggested by an episode midway in Eisenhower's second term, during the congressional elections of 1958. Richard M. Simpson of Pennsylvania, then chairman of the Republican Congressional Campaign Committee, went so far as to counsel Republican candidates for the House of Representatives to forget about Eisenhower's favor and support and "make known" to voters any "disagreement with the president's policies." Simpson, a conservative Republican, often opposed the President's "modern Republicanism."

V

Checks and balances and the president's legislative and party weaknesses affect his other functions. Although political science textbooks like to refer to him as "administrative chief," Congress too has powers over administration which it can use with the same independence that it exercises over legislation.

It can vest authority in subordinate officials to act independently of higher leadership, stratify a department's internal organization and require Senate confirmation of bureau chiefs. It can create independent regulatory commissions, such as the Interstate Commerce Commission and the Federal Reserve Board, rather far-removed from the president's control. Congress establishes the missions of departments, authorizes and amends their programs and provides money in such amounts and with such strings attached as it chooses.

Even where his authority is presumably great, in foreign affairs and as commander-in-chief, the president depends on congressional support. He often encounters resistance; George F. Kennan, surveying his tenure as ambassador to Yugoslavia, was driven to remonstrate that "without the support of Congress, it was impossible to carry out an effective policy here."

The requirement that two-thirds of the Senate approve treaties makes the president vulnerable to concessions and reservations and puts him to the difficult test of winning support from the opposition party. Significantly, it was at the request of the Senate Republican leader, Everett Dirksen, that President Kennedy sent a letter to the Senate, when the test ban treaty was in its hands, giving a series of "assurances" to win over uncertain votes.

VI

That the presidency, for all the chains it wears, has served us well is not in question. It has waged and won wars, checked depressions, spread social justice and spurred the nation's growth. But the great crises in the nation's past have tended to come singly and intermittently, and fortunately have been of limited duration.

Our future promises to be quite another matter. It does not require a crystal ball to see that the United States will be engrossed over the next several decades in a simultaneous confrontation of at least three kinds of revolutions: the human rights revolution, the automation revolution and the weapons revolution. None will be short-term. All are enduring phenomena, capable of spawning innumerable subrevolutions: all are apt to be sources of pervasive change for the world, the nation and the lives of each of us.

The human rights revolution is only beginning. President Johnson's announced dedication to equal opportunity for all Americans, regardless of race, will require deep transformations of long prevailing realities in fields such as employment, health, education, housing and recreation. Merely one clue to the magnitude of this task is the

314 LOUIS W. KOENIG

fact that nearly 45 percent of the nation's Negro citizens live in poverty—that is, they have yearly incomes of under $2,000.

We must be prepared to face the possibility that the automation revolution, whose marvels are already well apparent, may, as it gains momentum, increase unemployment to such a degree that the traditional link between jobs and income will be broken. The electronic computer and the automated, self-regulating machine may largely invalidate the general mechanism that undergirds our rights as consumers. Social attitudes toward work and leisure and the basis of individual compensation will need to undergo fundamental revisions.

No less initiative will be required in foreign affairs to make reason prevail over the horrendous alternative of nuclear war. The severity of the problem is already emerging in clear outline with Secretary of Defense McNamara's prediction of a steadily increasing spread of nuclear weapons capability among the nations in coming decades. The clear likelihood is that the adequacy of alliances and the United Nations, and the utility of national sovereignty in such a world, will be brought into serious question.

In the face of these and other possible revolutions, the task of future American leadership is clear. Peoples must be aroused, Congress moved, the bureaucracy stirred and alliances redirected. Only the president can do it.

VII

To enable the presidency to stay with the race, and to provide the nation, the world and mankind creative and forceful responses for the towering problems of the 1960s and beyond, several things might well be done to strengthen the office.

(1) The present uneven terms of the president, Senate and House might be replaced by the simultaneous election of all three for an identical term of four years. Past elections suggest than an election so conducted might produce a president and two houses of Congress in better harmony on party and policy outlook than the present fragmented elections permit.

(2) The president should be given the item veto for appropriation bills. The item veto would equip him with powerful new bargaining strength which he could employ widely to advance his policies on Capital Hill. He could conceivably engage in a kind of "log-rolling," exchanging his acceptance of appropriation items, for support of his own measures by legislators individually and in blocs. The item veto might give the president a truly commanding influence in legislative affairs.

(3) The seniority principle of choosing committee chairmen, which almost assures that a preponderance of those eminences will oppose much of the president's program, urgently needs to be modified. Chairmen might well be chosen by secret ballot of a majority of the entire committee at the beginning of each new Congress. The Speaker might have restored his former power to appoint the chairman and members of the House Rules Committee. A time limit might be placed on the number of weeks or months committees might consider and "bottle up" bills.

(4) If the treaty power were revised to require the approval of only a majority of senators present, rather than two-thirds, the president would be less vulnerable to pressures for concessions and reservations in the treaty's development and approval.

(5) The Twenty-second, or two-term, Amendment should be repealed.

(6) More frequent national party conventions, a national party council or cabinet, the stimulation of regional rather than local organizations, steps toward greater national party financing, all would capitalize on several trends afoot toward stronger national party organizations.

(7) Future presidents might continue what Kennedy began in subordinating party and congressional politics to urban politics. Kennedy pitched his policies, such as civil rights, education, housing and the like, to urban, racial, national and economic groups. Thereupon he could confidently cultivate state and local party leaders who determine the selection of and the support given to congressional candidates. Local leaders, whose business it is to

win elections, presumably would choose congressional candidates responsive to the policy needs of urban groups. Kennedy, had he lived to follow his formula through, doubtless would have lighted bonfires under congressmen and senators, finding his fuel in the urban groups and local party chieftains.

These proposals will require constitutional amendments, creative presiden-tial maneuver and serious congressional reform and party reorganization, all of which admittedly is a very large order. We can console ourselves that other American generations have mastered great problems with bold measures; and we can take a long stride forward and ease the remainder of our task if we disabuse ourselves of the notion that the president has too much power.

33. The Runaway Presidency*

ARTHUR M. SCHLESINGER, JR.

"The tyranny of the legislature is really the danger most to be feared, and will continue to be so for many years to come," Jefferson wrote Madison six weeks before Washington's first inauguration. "The tyranny of the executive power will come in its turn, but at a more distant period."[1] On the eve of the second centennial of independence Jefferson's prophecy appeared on the verge of fulfillment. The imperial presidency, created by wars abroad, was making a bold bid for power at home. The belief of the Nixon administration in its own mandate and in its own virtue, compounded by its conviction that the republic was in mortal danger from internal enemies, had produced an unprecedented concentration of power in the White House and an unprecedented attempt to transform the presidency of the Constitution into a plebiscitary presidency. If this transformation were carried through, the president, instead of being accountable every day to Congress and public opinion, would be accountable every four years to the electorate. Between elections, the president would be accountable only through impeachment and would govern, as much as he could, by decree. The expansion and abuse of presidential power constituted the underlying issue, the issue that, as we have seen, Watergate raised to the surface, dramatized and made politically accessible. Watergate was the by-product of a larger revolutionary purpose. At the same time, it was the fatal mistake that provoked and legitimized resistance to the revolutionary presidency.

I

In giving great power to presidents, Americans had declared their faith in the winnowing processes of politics. They assumed that these processes, whether operating through the electoral college or later through the congressional caucus or still later through the party conventions, would eliminate aspirants to the presidency who rejected the written restraints of the Constitution and the unwritten restraints of the republican ethos.

*Source: From *The Imperial Presidency* by Arthur M. Schlesinger, Jr. Copyright © 1973 by Arthur M. Schlesinger, Jr. Reprinted by permission of Houghton Mifflin Company. Selection has been retitled and originally appeared as Chapter 11, "The Future of the Presidency."

Through most of American history that assumption had been justified. "Not many presidents have been brilliant," Bryce observed in 1921, "some have not risen to the full moral height of the position. But none has been base or unfaithful to his trust, none has tarnished the honour of the nation."[2] Even as Bryce wrote, however, his observation was falling out of date—Warren G. Harding had just been inaugurated—and half a century later his optimism appeared as much the function of luck as of any necessity in the constitutional order. At this point the pessimism of the Supreme Court in ex parte Milligan seemed a good deal more prescient. The nation, as Justice Davis had written for the Court, had

> no right to expect that it will always have wise and humane rulers, sincerely attached to the principles of the Constitution. Wicked men, ambitious of power, with hatred of liberty and contempt of law, may fill the place once occupied by Washington and Lincoln.[3]

The presidency had been in crisis before; but the constitutional offense that led to the impeachment of Andrew Johnson was trivial compared to the charges now accumulating around the Nixon administration. There were, indeed, constitutional offenses here too— the abuse of impoundment and executive privilege, for example; or the secret air war against Cambodia in 1969-1970, unauthorized by and unknown to Congress; or the prosecution of the war in Vietnam after the repeal of the Tonkin Gulf Resolution; or the air war against Cambodia after the total withdrawal of American troops from Vietnam. But these, like Johnson's defiance of the Tenure of Office Act, were questions that a president might contend— till the Supreme Court decided otherwise—lay within a range of executive discretion. The Johnson case had discredited impeachment as a means of resolving arguable disagreements over the interpretation of the Constitution.

What was unique in the history of the presidency was the long list of potential criminal charges against the Nixon administration. Even before the various investigations were concluded, it seemed probable that Nixon's appointees had engaged in a multitude of indictable activities: at the very least, in burglary; in forgery; in illegal wiretapping; in illegal electronic surveillance; in perjury; in subornation of perjury; in obstruction of justice; in destruction of evidence; in tampering with witnesses; in misprision of felony; in bribery (of the Watergate defendants); in acceptance of bribes (from Vesco and the ITT); in conspiracy to involve government agencies (the FBI, the CIA, the Secret Service, the Internal Revenue Service, the Securities and Exchange Commission) in illegal action.

As for the president himself, he consistently denied that he had known either about the warfare of espionage and sabotage waged by his agents against his opponents or about the subsequent cover-up. If Nixon had known about these things, he had himself conspired against the basic processes of democracy. If he really had not known and for nine months had not bothered to find out, he was evidently an irresponsible and incompetent executive. For, if he did not know, it could only have been because he did not want to know. He had all the facilities in the world for discovering the facts. The courts and posterity would have to decide whether the Spectator of London was right in its harsh judgment that in two centuries American history had come full circle "from George Washington, who could not tell a lie, to Richard Nixon, who cannot tell the truth."[4]

Whether Nixon himself was witting or unwitting, what was clearly beyond dispute was his responsibility for the moral atmosphere within his official family. White House aides do not often do things they know their principal would not wish them to do—a proposition to which I and dozens of other former White House aides can attest from experience. It is the president who both sets the example and picks the men. What standards did Nixon establish for his White House? He himself admitted that in 1970, till J. Edgar Hoover forced him to change his mind, he authorized a series of criminal actions in knowing violation of the laws and the Constitution—authorization that would appear to be in transgression both of his presidential oath to preserve the Constitution and of his constitutional duty to see that the laws were faithfully executed. In 1971, as he also admitted, he commissioned the White House plumbers, who set out so soon thereafter on their career of burglary, wiretapping and forgery. "From the time when the break-in occurred," he said of the Watergate affair in August 1973, "I pressed repeatedly to know the facts, and particularly whether there was any involvement of anyone in the White House";[5] but two obvious authorities—John Mitchell, his intimate friend, former law partner, former attorney general, head of the Committee for the Re-election of the President, and Patrick Gray, acting director of the FBI itself—both testified under oath that he never got around to pressing them. He even, through John Ehrlichman, asked the Ellsberg judge in the midst of the trial whether he would not like to be head of the FBI. And he continued to hold up Ehrlichman and Haldeman as models to the nation—"two of the finest public servants it has been my privilege to know."[6]

Nixon, in short, created the Nixon White House. "There was no independent sense of morality there," said Hugh Sloan, who served in the Nixon White House for two years. "If you worked for someone, he was God, and whatever the orders were, you did it. . . . It was all so narrow, so closed. . . . There emerged some kind of separate morality

about things."[7] "Because of a certain atmosphere that had developed in my working at the White House," said Jeb Stuart Magruder, "I was not as concerned about its illegality as I should have been." And again: "You are living in an unreal world when you work there."[8] "The White House is another world," said John Dean. "Expediency is everything."[9] "No one who had been in the White House," said Tom Charles Huston, "could help but feel he was in a state of siege."[10] "On my first or second day in the White House," said Herbert Porter, "Dwight Chapin [the president's appointments secretary] said to me, 'One thing you should realize early on, we are practically an island here.' That was the way the world was viewed." The highest calling, said Porter, was to "protect the president" from the hostile forces surrounding that "island." The "original sin," Porter felt, was the "misuse" of young people "through the whole White House system. They were not criminals by birth or design. Left to their own devices, they wouldn't engage in this sort of thing. Someone had to be telling them to do it."[11] Gordon Strachan told of his excitement at "being 27 years old and walking into the White House and seeing the president"; but, when asked what word he had for young men or women who wanted to come to Washington and enter the public service, he said grimly, "My advice would be to stay away."[12]

This was not the White House we had known—those of us, Democrats or Republicans, who had served other presidents in other years. An appointment to the White House of Roosevelt or Truman or Eisenhower or Kennedy or Johnson seemed the highest responsibility one could expect and called for the highest standards of behavior. And most of us looked back at our White House experience, not with shame and incredulity, as the Nixon young men did, not as the "White House horrors," but as the most splendid time in one's life. Government, as Clark Clifford said, was a chameleon, taking its color from the character and personality of the president.

Nixon's responsibility for the White House ethos went beyond strictly moral considerations. In the First Congress Madison, arguing that the power to remove government officials must belong to the president, had added, "We have in him the security for the good behavior of the officer." This made "the president responsible to the public for the conduct of the person he has nominated and appointed." If the president suffered executive officials to perpetrate crimes or neglected to superintend their conduct so as to check excesses, he himself, Madison said, would be subject to "the decisive engine of impeachment."[13]

II

The crisis of the presidency led some critics to advocate a reconstruction of the institution itself. For a long time people had felt that the job was becoming too much for one man to handle. "Men of ordinary physique and discretion," Woodrow Wilson wrote as long ago as 1908, "cannot be president and live, if the strain be not somehow relieved. We shall be obliged always to be picking our chief magistrate from among wise and prudent athletes,—a small class."[14]

But what had been seen until the late 1950s as too exhausting physically was now seen, after Vietnam and Watergate, as too dizzying psychologically. In 1968 Eugene McCarthy, the first liberal presidential aspirant in the century to run against the presidency, called for the depersonalization and decentralization of the office. The White House, he thought, should be turned into a museum. Instead of trying to lead the nation, the president should become "a kind of channel" for popular desires and aspirations.[15] Watergate made the

point irresistible. "The office has become too complex and its reach too extended," wrote Barbara Tuchman, "to be trusted to the fallible judgment of any one individual." "A man with poor judgment, an impetuous man, a sick man, a power-mad man," wrote Max Lerner, "each would be dangerous in the post. Even an able, sensitive man needs stronger safeguards around him than exist today."[16]

The result was a new wave of proposals to transform the Presidency into a collegial institution. Mrs. Tuchman suggested a six-man directorate with a rotating chairman, each member to serve for a year, as in Switzerland. Lerner wanted to give the president a Council of State, a body that he would be bound by law to consult and that, because half its members would be from Congress and some from the opposite party, would presumably give him independent advice. Both proposals had, in fact, been considered and rejected in the constitutional convention.[17] That was no argument against considering them again.

Still, the reasons why the Founding Fathers turned them down were worth noting. When James Wilson first moved in the convention that the executive consist of a single person, there ensued, as Madison put it in his notes, "a considerable pause." Finally Benjamin Franklin observed that this was an important point and he would like to hear some discussion. Wilson said that a single magistrate would impart "most energy, dispatch and responsibility" to the office. Edmund Randolph of Virginia then strenuously opposed the idea as "the foetus of monarchy," proposing instead a three-man magistracy. Eventually the convention agreed with Wilson, though not before it gave serious thought to surrounding the president with a Council of State, which might include the chief justice, the president of the Senate and the Speaker of the House as well as the heads of the executive departments. George Mason of Virginia said that, if the convention did not establish a Council of State, the new republic would embark on "an experiment on which the most despotic governments had never ventured. The Grand Signor himself had his Divan." Franklin thought a council "would not only be a check on a bad president but be a relief to a good one." But the convention rejected the idea, not, it should be noted, because it considered such a council in violation of the separation of powers, but because, as Charles Pinckney of South Carolina put it, the president ought to be authorized to call for advice or not as he might choose. "Give him an able council and it will thwart him; a weak one and he will shelter himself under their sanction."[18]

Hamilton and Jefferson disagreed on many things, but they agreed that the convention had been right in deciding on a one-man presidency. A plural executive, Hamilton contended, if divided within itself, would lead the country into factionalism and anarchy and, if united, could lead it into tyranny. When power was placed in the hands of a group small enough to admit "of their interests and views being easily combined in a common enterprise, by an artful leader," Hamilton thought,

> it becomes more liable to abuse, and more dangerous when abused, than if it be lodged in the hands of one man, who, from the very circumstances of his being alone, will be more narrowly watched and more readily suspected. . . . From such a combination America would have more to fear, than from the ambition of any single individual.

With a single executive it was possible to fix accountability. But a directorate "would serve to destroy, or would greatly diminish, the intended and necessary responsibility of the chief magistrate himself."[19]

Jefferson had favored a plural executive under the Articles of Confederation, and, as an American in Paris, he had watched with sympathy the *Directoire* of the French Revolution. But these experiments left him no doubt that plurality was a mistake. As he later observed, if Washington's cabinet, in which he had served with Hamilton, had been a directorate, "the opposing wills would have balanced each other and produced a state of absolute inaction." But Washington, after listening to both sides, acted on his own, providing the "regulating power which would keep the machine in steady movement." History, moreover, furnished "as many examples of a single usurper arising out of a government by a plurality, as of temporary trusts of power in a single hand rendered permanent by usurpation."[20]

The question remained whether the world had changed enough in two centuries to make these objections obsolete. There was, of course, the burden-of-the-presidency argument. But had the presidential burden become so much heavier than ever before? The scope of the national government had expanded beyond imagination, but so too had the facilities for presidential management. The only president who clearly died of overwork was Polk, and that was a long time ago. Hoover, who worked intensely and humorlessly as president, lived for more than thirty years after the White House; Truman, who worked intensely and gaily, lived for twenty. The contemporary president was really not all that overworked. Eisenhower managed more golf than most corporation officials or college presidents; Kennedy always seemed unhurried and relaxed; Nixon spent almost as much time in Florida and California as in Washington, or so it appeared. Johnson's former press secretary, Goerge Reedy, dealt with the myth of the presidential workload in terms that rejoiced anyone who had ever served in the White House. "There is far less to the presidency, in terms of essential activity," Reedy correctly said, "than meets the eye." The president could fill his hours with as much motion as he desired; but he also could delegate as much "work" as he desired. "A president moves through his days surrounded by literally hundreds of people whose relationship to him is that of a doting mother to a spoiled child. Whatever he wants is brought to him immediately—food, drink, helicopters, airplanes, people, in fact, everything but relief from his political problems."[21]

As for the moral and psychological weight of these political problems, this was real enough. All major presidential decisions were taken in conditions of what General Marshall, speaking of battle, used to call "chronic obscurity"— that is, on the basis of incomplete and probably inaccurate intelligence, with no sure knowledge where the enemy was or even where one's own men were. This could be profoundly anguishing for reasonably sensitive presidents, especially when decisions determined people's livelihoods or ended their lives. It was this, and not the workload, that did in Wilson and the second Roosevelt. But was the sheer moral weight of decision greater today than ever before? greater for Johnson and Nixon than for Washington and Lincoln or Wilson or FDR? One doubted it very much.

If there was an argument for a plural executive, it was not the alleged burden of the presidency. The serious argument was simply to keep one man from wielding too much power. But here the points of Hamilton and Jefferson still had validity. The Council of Ten in Venice was surely as cruel as any doge. One wonders whether a six-man presidency would have prevented the war in Vietnam. It might well, however, have prevented the New Deal. The single-man presidency, with the right man as president, had its uses; and historically Americans had as often as not chosen the right man.

The idea of a Council of State had more plausibility. But it would work better for foreign than for domestic policy. A prudent president would be well advised to convoke ad hoc Councils of State on issues of war and peace. Ken-

nedy added outsiders to his Executive Committee during the Cuban missile crisis; and it was an ad hoc Council of State in March 1968 that persuaded Johnson to cease and desist in Vietnam. But, as an institutionalized body, with membership the ex officio perquisite of the senior leadership of House and Senate—that is, of the men in Congress who in the past had always been more inclined to go along with presidents—it could easily become simply one more weapon for a strong president. As Gouverneur Morris said at the convention, the president "by persuading his Council . . . to concur in his wrong measures would acquire their protection for them."[22]

Above all, both the plural executive and the Council of State were open to the objection that most concerned the Founding Fathers—the problem of fixing accountability. In the case of high crimes and misdemeanors, who, to put it bluntly, was to be impeached? James Wilson once compared the situations in this regard of England and the United States. There the king's counselors interposed an "impenetrable barrier" between power and responsibility. But

> in the United States, our first executive magistrate is not onubilated behind the mysterious obscurity of counsellors. Power is communicated to him with liberality, though with ascertained limitations. To him [alone] the provident or improvident use of it is to be ascribed.[23]

The more convincing solution surely lay not in diffusing and blurring responsibility for the actions of the executive but in making that responsibility categorical and in finding ways of holding presidents to it.

III

The other change in the institution of the presidency under discussion in the early 1970s ran in the opposite direction. The idea of a single six-year presidential term was obviously designed not to reduce but to increase the independence of the presidency. This idea naturally appealed to the imperial ethos. Lyndon Johnson advocated it; Nixon commended it to his Commission on Federal Election Reform for particular study. What was more puzzling was that it also had the support of two eminent senators, both unsympathetic to the imperial presidency, Mike Mansfield of Montana and George Aiken of Vermont—support that gave it a hearing it would not otherwise have had.

It was not a new idea. Andrew Jackson had recommended to Congress an amendment limiting presidents to a single term of four or six years; Andrew Johnson had done the same; the Confederate constitution provided for a single six-year term; Hayes proposed a single six-year term and Taft a single term of six or seven years. Mansfield and Aiken now pressed their version on the ground, as Mansfield said, that a six-year term would "place the Office of the Presidency in a position that transcends as much as possible partisan political considerations." The amendment, said Aiken, "would allow a president to devote himself entirely to the problems of the nation and would free him from the millstone of partisan politics."[24]

This argument had a certain old-fashioned good-government plausibility. How nice it would be if presidents could be liberated from politics for six years and set free to do only what was best for the country! But the argument assumed that presidents knew better than anyone else what was best for the country and that the democratic process was an obstacle to wise decisions. It assumed that presidents were so generally right and the people so generally wrong that the president had to be protected against political pressures. It was, in short, a profoundly anti-democratic position. It was also profoundly unrealistic to think that any constitutional amendment could transport a president to some higher and more immaculate realm and still leave the United States a democracy. As Thomas Corcoran told

the Senate Judiciary Committee during hearings on the Mansfield-Aiken amendment, "It is impossible to take politics out of politics."[25]

But, even if it were possible to take the presidency out of politics, was there reason to suppose this desirable? The electorate often knew things that presidents did not know; and the nation had already paid a considerable price for presidential isolation and ignorance. Few things were more likely to make presidents sensitive to public opinion than worries about their own political future. Even if public opinion was at times a baneful influence, what else was democracy all about? The need to persuade the nation of the soundness of a proposed policy was the heart of democracy. "A president immunized from political considerations," Clark Clifford told the Senate Judiciary Committee, "is a president who need not listen to the people, respond to majority sentiment, or pay attention to views that may be diverse, intense and perhaps at variance with his own."[26] To release the president from the discipline of consent would be to create irresponsible presidents. The idea of a president "above politics" was plainly hostile to the genius of democracy.

The six-year concept, moreover, had marked disadvantages. In the eighteenth century, when the pace of change was relatively slow, the country could afford a six-year presidency. Still, Jefferson, who began by favoring a seven-year term, decided that "service for eight years, with a power to remove at the end of the first four" was better.[27] In the nineteenth century, as President Kennedy used to point out, a politician had to know only three or four issues, and these issues dominated political life for a generation. But in the twentieth century, with the enormous acceleration in the rate of change, new problems piled up on government in unprecedented variety and with unprecedented rapidity. Six years in the second half of the twentieth century were equivalent in terms of change to a generation in the first half of the nineteenth century; and, given the onward rush of contemporary life, the nation could hardly afford to place in power for so long a time an administration that might lack the capacity or the will to meet fresh problems with fresh solutions. A four-year term gave both the president and the voters a fair test. If they approved his general course, they could then re-elect him for four years more.

The Mansfield-Aiken amendment expressed distrust of the democratic process in still another way—by its bar against re-eligibility. If anything was of the essence of democracy, it was surely that the voters should have an unconstrained choice of their leaders. "I can see no propriety," George washington wrote the year after the adoption of the Constitution, "in precluding ourselves from the service of any man, who on some great emergency shall be deemed universally most capable of serving the public."[28] Hamilton brilliantly amplified this argument in the 72nd *Federalist*. The ban against indefinite re-eligibility, he said, would result in

the banishing men from stations in which, in certain emergencies of the state, their presence might be of the greatest moment to the public interest or safety . . . perhaps it would not be too strong to say, to the preservation of [the nation's] political existence.

There was a great deal to be said for the two-term principle as a tradition; in all normal circumstances it should be controlling. But it had proved itself sufficiently effective as a tradition. The only time the tradition was violated was in precisely the circumstances envisaged by Washington and Hamilton. And there was nothing to be said for setting the two-term tradition in concrete via the Twenty-second Amendment. Except for the eighteenth and the twenty-second, constitutional amendments had invariably enlarged rather than restricted the rights of the people; and the eighteenth was in due course repealed.

In 1912 when Congress had an equivalent of the Mansfield-Aiken amendment under consideration, Wilson observed that the nation appeared to be going in two opposite directions at the same time: "We are seeking in every way to extend the power of the people, but in the matter of the presidency we fear and distrust the people and seek to bind them hand and foot by rigid constitutional provision. My own mind is not agile enough to be both ways." He concluded,

We singularly belie our own principles by seeking to determine by fixed constitutional provision what the people shall determine for themselves and are perfectly competent to determine for themselves. We cast a doubt upon the whole theory of popular government.[29]

If the Twenty-second Amendment seemed on its face a restraint on the imperial presidency, events had shown it totally ineffective. Though its retention or repeal was not one of the momentous issues of the age, it remained an anomaly in a generally democratic Constitution.

IV

Oddly the crisis of the imperial presidency did not elicit much support for what at other times had been a favored theory of constitutional reform: movement in the direction of the British parliamentary system. This was particularly odd because, whatever the general balance of advantage between the parliamentary and presidential modes, the parliamentary system had one feature the presidential system badly needed in the 1970s—the requirement that the head of government be compelled at regular intervals to explain and defend his policies in face-to-face sessions with the political opposition. Few devices, it would seem, would be better calculated both to break down the real isolation of the latter-day presidency and to dispel the spurious reverence that had come to envelop the office.

In a diminished version, applying only to members of the cabinet, the idea was nearly as old as the republic itself. The proposal that cabinet members should go on to the floor of Congress to answer questions and take part in debate, "far from raising any constitutional difficulties," as E. S. Corwin once observed, "has the countenance of early practice under the Constitution."[30] Justice Story contended for it in his *Commentaries* because it would require the President to appoint strong men to his cabinet and require the cabinet to justify the administration's program before the Congress, thereby making for openness and responsibility in government. The Confederate constitution authorized Congress to grant the head of each executive department "a seat upon the floor of either House, with the privilege of discussing any measures appertaining to his department," and Congressman George H. Pendleton of Ohio, with the support of Congressman James A. Garfield, argued for a similar proposal in the Union Congress in 1864. In 1881 Pendleton, now a senator and the champion of civil service reform, renewed the proposal in a rather impressive report supported, among others, by James G. Blaine. In his last State of the Union message Taft suggested that cabinet members be given access to the floor in order, as he later put it,

> to introduce measures, to advocate their passage, to answer questions, and to enter into debate as if they were members, without of course the right to vote.... The time lost in Congress over useless discussion of issues that might be disposed of by a single statement from the head of a department, no one can appreciate unless he has filled such a place.[31]

In the meantime, the young Woodrow Wilson had carried the idea a good deal further toward the British model, arguing that cabinet members should not just sit voteless in Congress but should be actually chosen "from the ranks of the legislative majority." Instead of the chaotic and irresponsible system of government by congressional committees, the republic would then have cabinet government and ministerial responsibility.[32] Though Wilson did not renew this specific proposal in later years, it very likely lingered in the back of his mind. On the eve of his first inauguration he noted that the position of the presidency was "quite abnormal, and must lead eventually to something very different." "Sooner or later," the president must be made

> answerable to opinion in a somewhat more informal and intimate fashion— answerable, it may be, to the Houses whom he seeks to lead, either personally or through a cabinet, as well as to the people for whom they speak. But that is a matter to be worked out.[33]

Wilson never found time to work it out. Those who followed in his footsteps moved from his concern with the president's personal answerability back to the more general problem of the accountability of the cabinet. Before the Second World War Corwin proposed that the president construct his cabinet from a joint legislative council created by the two houses of Congress.[34] Representative Estes Kefauver of Tennessee soon revived the Story-Pendleton-Taft idea to the applause of Walter Lippmann. After the war Thomas K. Finletter set forth a well-argued and ingenious scheme of collaboration between the two branches in his book *Can Representative Government Do the Job?* Finletter saw a joint executive-legislative cabinet as the keystone of a system in which the president could, if faced by legislative stalemate, dissolve the government and call for new elections. Congress obviously had the power to force dissolution itself by rejecting the proposals of the joint cabinet. Finletter distinguished this process from the parliamentary model because it preserved the direct election of the president, the independence of the executive branch, decentralized parties, the federal system, judicial review and, at least in the form contemplated by the Founding Fathers, the separation of powers.[35]

But in the 1970s there appeared little interest in reforms that squinted at parliamentarianism. This may have been in part because the parliamentary regimes best known in America—the British and French—had themselves moved in the direction of prime-ministerial or presidential government[36] and offered few guarantees against the Vietnam-Watergate effect. Kevin Phillips did not elaborate on his proposal of a "new system" tying Congress and the executive together. In 1973, however, Senator Walter Mondale of Minnesota offered a version of the Story-Pendleton-Taft-Kefauver idea, proposing that heads of executive departments be required to appear before the Senate for a weekly question hour on live television.[37]

If enacted, such a question hour, though it still excluded presidents, hedged more than ever now with divinity, might well force them to appoint stronger and therefore more independent men to their cabinets; and it would certainly increase the flow of information and counsel between the two branches. But it would also threaten the vested prerogatives of congressional committees. As for the president, a question hour could subtly alter the balance of his personal power both as against his cabinet, whose members would have the chance to acquire new visibility and develop their own relationships with Congress and the electorate, and as against Congress, which would have the opportunity of playing off his own cabinet against him. Most of all, the fear of plunging into the unknown operated on both sides as a barrier to a change that might have unforeseen and quite extensive consequences for the traditional system.[38]

V

The problem of reining in the runaway presidency, as it was conceived in the 1970s, centered a good deal more on substantive than on structural solutions. Congress, in other words, decided it could best restrain the presidency by enacting specific legislation in the conspicuous fields of presidential abuse. The main author of this comprehensive congressional attack on presidential supremacy was, well before Watergate, Senator Sam Ervin of North Carolina.

The republic owed a great deal to Sam Ervin. No one for a long time had done so much to educate the American people in the meaning and majesty of the Constitution (though his Constitution seemed to stop with the ten amendments adopted in 1791; at least he never showed the same zeal for the Fourteenth and Fifteenth Amendments). For most Americans the Constitution had become a hazy document, cited like the Bible on ceremonial occasions but forgotten in the daily transactions of life. For Ervin the Constitution of 1787, like the Bible, was superbly alive and fresh. He quoted it as if it had been written the day before; the Founding Fathers seemed his contemporaries; it was almost as if he had ambled over himself from the convention at Philadelphia. He was a true believer who endowed his faith with abundant charm, decency, sagacity and toughness. The old-fashioned Constitution—"the very finest document ever to come from the mind of men"[39]—could have had no more fitting champion in the battle against revolutionary presidency.

But Ervin was concerned with more than the vindication of the Constitution. His larger design was to establish a new balance of constitutional power. Congress itself, Ervin thought, had negligently become "the chief aggrandizer of the executive."[40] The restoration of the Constitution, he believed, required the systematic recovery by Congress of powers appropriated by the presidency. The war powers bills were, in his view, a confused and sloppy application of this strategy; he had little use for them. His own approach, direct and unequivocal, was expressed in the bill in which he proposed to give Congress absolute authority to veto executive agreements within sixty days.[41] Congress had never had, or even seriously sought, such authority before. While the provocation was real enough, the bill if enacted would give Congress unprecedented control over the presidential conduct of foreign affairs.

A leading item on Ervin's domestic agenda was executive privilege. This question, as we have seen, had been historically one of conflicting and unresolved constitutional claims. In the nineteenth century, while insisting on a general congressional right to executive information, Congress had acknowledged a right, or at least a power, of presidential denial in specific areas. It acquiesced in these reservations because they seemed reasonable and because responsible opinion outside Congress saw them as reasonable. But what Congress had seen as an expression of comity the presidency in the later twentieth century came to see as its inherent and unreviewable right. Still both Congress and the presidency had taken care to avoid a constitutional showdown.

The Nixon administration, with its extravagant theory of an absolute privilege covering everything, whether related or not to the performance of official duties, made a showdown almost inevitable. Some legal scholars—Raoul Berger, for example—remembering Madison's injunction in the 49th Federalist that neither branch could "pretend to an exclusive or superior right of settling the boundaries between their respective powers," argued that the question should be bucked over to the courts. Nixon himself said in early 1973 that, if the Senate wanted a court test, "we would welcome it. Perhaps this is the time to have the highest court of the land make a definitive decision with regard to the matter."[42] But the judiciary had traditionally steered clear of this question. "The federal courts," as Justice Douglas said in another connection in 1972, "do not sit as an *ombudsman,*

refereeing the disputes between the other two branches."[43]

But could not courts handle the denial of executive information to Congress as they were coming to handle denial of such information to the courts themselves—that is, by judicial inspection of the documents *in camera* to determine whether the executive had a case for withholding them? In 1953, the Supreme Court had reserved for judges the power to "determine whether circumstances are appropriate for the claim of privilege" and added, "Judicial control over the evidence in a case cannot be subordinated to the caprice of executive officers."[44] In this case, the documents involved national security; and the Court did not order their inspection. But the trend of lower court decisions in the early 1970s was plainly to favor judicial examination of documents, even those allegedly concerned with national security, in order to decide whether or not they were admissible as evidence. "No executive official or agency," the Court of Appeals for the District of Columbia said in 1971,

can be given absolute authority to determine what documents in his possession may be considered by the court. . . . Otherwise the head of any executive department would have the power on his own say so to cover up all evidence of fraud and corruption when a federal court or grand jury was investigating malfeasance in office, and this is not the law.[45]

The lower courts made similar rulings in the case of the Nixon tapes. A district judge proposed the same solution when the Nixon White House, in an even more sweeping claim of privilege, asserted absolute power to withhold documents that it admitted had no bearing on national security. This was a case arising from Nixon's decision to increase government price supports for milk after the dairy industry contributed $422,500 to his re-election campaign.[46]

Still, the willingness of judges to assert control over evidence in trials by no means assured an equivalent willingness to assert control over the communication of information between the presidency and Congress. On the other hand, in other critical controversies like the steel seizure case of 1952, the Court had indeed sat as an *ombudsman* and settled disputes between the other two branches. Should the Court rule on the invocation of executive privilege against Congress, one trusts that the justices will respond in the spirit of Felix Frankfurter, who somewhere said: "Democratic government may indeed be defined as the government which accepts in the fullest sense responsibility to explain itself."

Congress, in any case, was in no mood to wait. The Senate Foreign Relations Committee, for example, felt it had been denied too much information too long and for too little reason. The presidency and the State Department thus had only themselves to blame if, when the Senate, after its years of docility, struck back, it overdestroyed the target. In ultimate frustration, Congress passed a bill in 1973 saying that, if the State Department, the United States Information Agency, the Agency for International Development, the Arms Control and Disarmament Agency and other agencies involved in international affairs did not furnish information requested by Congress within 35 days, their funds would be cut off. This was a draconian solution produced by an hubristic policy. The State Department complained that diplomats could not do their job if every cable was turned over to Congress; but the fear was fanciful, and in any case the Nixon administration should have thought of this before it contemptuously denied committees of Congress—committees to which Franklin Roosevelt and George C. Marshall had confided the most secret intelligence in the midst of a rather more considerable national crisis—such things as the Pentagon's five-year program for foreign military aid and, heaven help us, the country program memoranda from the USIA.[47]

Appropriations provided one handle

on the problem of executive privilege. Another, and the one favored by Sam Ervin, was to meet the problem head-on. The Ervin bill, based on an earlier bill introduced by Senator Fulbright, required members of the executive branch summoned by a committee of Congress to appear in person, even if they were intending to claim executive privilege. Only a personal letter from the president could warrant the claim; and the Fulbright-Ervin bill gave the committee the power to decide whether the presidential plea was justified. As Fulbright said, it placed "the final responsibility for judging the validity of a claim of executive privilege in the Congress, where it belongs."[48]

A presidential thesis in violation of the traditional comity between the two branches thus produced a congressional answer that would itself do away with what had been not only an historic but an healthy ambiguity. For 180 years the arbiter in this question had been neither Congress nor the president nor the courts but the political context and process, with responsible opinion considering each case more or less on merit and turning against whichever side appeared to be overreaching itself. The system was not tidy, but it encouraged a measure of restraint on both sides and avoided the constitutional showdown. Now absolute presidential claims provoked an absolute congressional response. Would this really be an improvement? Would Fulbright and Ervin themselves twenty years earlier have wanted to give Joe McCarthy and his committee "the final responsibility" to judge whether executive testimony could be properly withheld? In the area of executive privilege as well as of executive agreements, Nixon's revolutionary conception of the presidency finally forced Congress into sweeping and dramatic proposals of self-defense.

VI

Next in the Ervin agenda to the achievement of congressional control over executive information stood the restoration of congressional control over something Congress thought peculiarly its own—the power of the purse. This meant a solution of the problem of presidential impoundment. Impoundment had existed before Nixon, but no previous president had used it to overturn statutes and abolish programs against congressional will. For Nixon impoundment had become a means of taking from Congress the determination of national priorities.

The courts were by no means so diffident about impoundment as they had initially been about executive privilege. In decision after decision in 1973, judges declared one aspect after another of the impoundment policy illegal. No judge accepted Nixon's claim that he had a "constitutional right" not to spend money voted by Congress. One judge called his use of impoundment "a fragrant abuse of executive discretion." "It is not within the discretion of the executive," said another, "to refuse to execute laws passed by Congress but with which the executive presently disagrees."[49] The decisions were, however, as they should have been, constructions of specific statutes and stopped short of proposing a general solution to the impoundment controversy.

Though the courts had rallied splendidly, it was not really very satisfactory to have to sue the executive branch in every case in order to make it carry out programs duly enacted by Congress. But Congress itself found it hard to make a stand on the Constitution. For Nixon had changed the issue with some success from a constitutional to a budgetary question. Impoundment, in other words, was alleged as the only answer a fiscally responsible president could make to insensate congressional extravagance. Sam Ervin derided this proposition. "Congress," he said, "is not composed of wild-eyed spenders, nor is the president the embattled crusader against wasteful spending that he would have you believe." The figures bore Ervin out. Congress, for example, had cut more than $20 billion from administration appropriation requests in Nixon's first term. Congress and the presidency roughly agreed on the amount of money government should spend but disagreed, as Ervin put it, "over spending priorities and [the president's] authority to pick and choose what programs he will fund." Impoundment, said Ervin, had to do not with the budget but with the separation of powers.

I have voted against many of the programs for which the president has impounded funds, but I do not believe that we should allow him to nullify acts of Congress by executive fiat. There is not one syllable in the Constitution which authorizes the president to exercise such power.[50]

Many members of Congress, however, accepted the view that Congress could not reclaim the appropriation power granted it by the Constitution until it first established its own system of fiscal discipline. Orderly-minded members of Congress, indeed, had long liked the idea of a congressional budget to serve as a baseline from which to criticize the executive budget. Congress might even, it was thought, regain the role in budget-making it had enjoyed in the early republic. For the presidency had not always been in firm command of the budget. Until the Civil War the Senate Finance Committee and the House Ways and Means Committee had each a comprehensive view of national spending while the presidency was without any sort of central budget control. The United States, as Woodrow Wilson wrote in 1885, had "a financial policy directed by the representative body itself, with only clerical aid from the executive."[51] However, this had already begun to change. The Senate Finance Committee doled out some of its powers to the Appropriations Committee (established in 1867) and the Banking and Currency Committee (1913). The House Ways and Means Committee similarly delegated a share of its powers to the Appropriations Committee (1865) and a diversity of particular committees. As responsibility was thus scattered among committees, Congress increasingly regarded each spending bill as a separate entity and lost any ability it might once have had to decide among competing priorities. Then the presidency obtained a unified budget office through the passage of the Budget and Accounting Act in 1921, and the balance of control shifted decisively toward the executive.

As early as 1939 Roosevelt's secretary of the treasury, Henry Morgenthau, Jr., proposed that the appropriations and tax committees of both houses constitute themselves as a single joint committee on the federal budget.[52] Congress remained indifferent to the idea till 1973 when a Joint Study Committee recommended a somewhat similar process designed to produce a unified congressional budget.[53] This vision, however, really ran against the grain of Congress, a body capable under extreme provocation of uniting against a constitutionally insensitive and aggressive president but normally divided within itself by deeply rooted differences of party, section and ideology. While the Nixon presidency induced a momentary sense of congressional unity, a more skillful president could readily restore the customary situation where members of Congress felt more solidarity with a president of their own party than with colleagues of the opposite party. In that more usual situation, a unified budgetary process would not be likely to produce a unified result. Indeed, it could be argued that Congress should build on its strength, which lay precisely in its responsiveness to a diversity of particular pressures, and try to identify choices rather than to seek an institutional position.

It was a political fact, however, fully recognized by Ervin, that anti-impoundment legislation would have to be accompanied by evidences of congressional self-control in spending. He was personally a budget-balancer anyway. So his impoundment bill included a spending ceiling. The bill, as passed

by the Senate in 1973, also had certain eccentricities for a constitutional fundamentalist. After a clear statement in Section I that impoundment was unconstitutional, subsequent sections said that nevertheless the president was authorized to commit this unconstitutional act for periods up to seventy days. Thereafter impoundments not covered by the anti-deficiency laws must cease unless Congress specifically approved them by concurrent resolution. The House, on the other hand, was quite willing to let impoundments stand unless specifically disapproved by one house of Congress. Both bills legitimized impoundment; but, where the House would place the burden on Congress in each case to stop impoundment, Ervin would place the burden on the president in each case to justify impoundment.

A strong argument could be made for conceding presidents leeway in the spending and transfer of appropriated funds, so long as they were not thwarting the intent of Congress when it made the appropriations. But this assumed presidents whom Congress could trust; it assumed, in short, comity. Here as elsewhere presidential abuse produced extreme counterclaims of congressional authority. The revolutionary presidency had tried to abolish the congressional power of the purse and make spending a matter of executive decree. The congressional reaction was to stop the president by measures that introduced rigidity into a political process which had always prospered by flexibility.

VII

There were other elements in Ervin's design. He had, for example, a bill to prevent presidential abuse of the pocket veto by defining adjournment, as used in the Constitution, to mean adjournment *sine die* and not just over the weekend or the Christmas holidays.[54] (In the meantime, a federal judge pronounced Nixon's pocket veto of the

Family Practice of Medicine Act unconstitutional in response to the suit
brought by Senator Edward Kennedy.) In
one area after another, with the concealed passion and will of a deceptively
relaxed personality, Ervin moved to restore the balance of the Constitution by
cutting the presidency down to constitutional size. But his was the "Constitution not of Abraham Lincoln but of *ex
parte Milligan.* "What the framers intended," he said, "was that the president . . . should be merely the executor
of a power of decision that rests
elsewhere; that is, in the Congress. This
was the balance of power between the
president and Congress intended by the
Constitution." The "ultimate power,"
Ervin said, was "legislative."[55]

The Ervin scheme, in short, was a
scheme of presidential subordination.
Where presidential abuse of particular
powers had harmed the country, those
powers were now to be vested in Congress. The authority and discretion of
the presidency were to be held to their
constitutional minimum. All this was entirely understandable as a response to
the Nixon scheme of presidential
supremacy. It had great value both in
checking a deluded president and in
raising the consciousness of Congress
and the people on constitutional issues.
But, pursued to the end, it could produce a national polity which, if it had
many more roots in the Constitution
than the Nixon scheme, would be almost as overbalanced in the direction of
congressional supremacy as the Nixon
scheme was in the direction of presidential supremacy.

The Ervin counterattack envisaged a
general limitation of the presidency with
all functions reconsidered and all powers diminished. It saw presidential
power as unitary and indivisible, and
therefore to be reduced across the
board. Yet the dilemma of the presidency was surely that presidential
power was not unitary. It could well be
argued that while the presidency had
come to have too much discretion in

foreign affairs, where error was sometimes irreversible, it had too little in
domestic affairs, where error could usually be corrected. As President Kennedy
used to say, "Domestic policy can only
defeat us; foreign policy can kill us."
The revolt against the presidency had
begun in reaction against extravagant
assertions of unilateral presidential
power to go to war. It would be ironic if
it were to end in more binding restraints
on the presidency as an instrument of
the general welfare at home.[56]

In domestic affairs the president could
not claim superior information and wisdom, nor could he easily allege life-
and-death crisis and invoke patriotism
and national unity, nor could he even
cite the *Curtiss-Wright* case. His authority was challenged and harassed by
Congress, by the permanent government
establishment, by state and local governments, by reporters, by disc jockeys,
by every wiseacre down the block.
Where the prime minister in a parliamentary regime could be pretty sure
that anything he proposed would become law in short order, the president
of the United States could not even be
sure that *his* proposals would reach the
floor of Congress for debate and vote
(though there was no reason why this
could not be arranged by agreement
with the congressional leadership).

While the American president possessed vast powers over the pattern and
level of economic activity, no chief
executive in any other democratic state
had so little discretion in economic
management. The president could reasonably be given standby authority to
adjust tax rates in response to economic
fluctuations, cutting taxes against recession and increasing them against inflation. But, when Kennedy asked Congress for this authority, he did not
succeed even in getting a bill onto the
floor. Eisenhower denounced the idea
in 1962 as an example of the "thirst for
more and more power centered in the
federal government . . . one-man government . . . unconscionable grab of

power . . . What is Congress for?''[57] There was a strong argument also for standby spending authority, under which the president, if unemployment increased at a specified rate, would have power to release funds for public works. This was another Kennedy proposal, and it too got nowhere.

Congress resisted these eminently sensible ideas on the ground that they meant a delegation of power to the president. But, since Congress had displayed no capacity for quick action in these fields, and since the standards for delegation could be set in part by the indexes of production and employment, such delegation hardly seemed unreasonable. When, thirty years before, Franklin Roosevelt asked Congress for authority to negotiate reciprocal trade agreements and to revise tariff rates up to 50 percent either way in accordance with such agreements, there was similar congressional complaint. "This proposal," said Arthur Vandenberg, "is Fascist in its philosophy, Fascist in its objective . . . palpably unconstitutional . . . economic dictatorship come to America." "We are," said Warren Austin of Vermont, "at the parting of the ways."[58]

Both Vandenberg and Austin, as their subsequent careers showed, came to know better. But both succumbed to facile constitutional sophistries of the moment. If Congress had been able to handle the tariff question in a rational way, it would have been one thing; but a century of American history had proved that it could not. Forty years later no one regretted this delegation to the presidency. I have no doubt that in time the republic will accept standby presidential authority to vary tax rates and initiate public works, as people now accept reciprocal trade agreements, and wonder why any serious person would ever have objected.

VIII

It was hard to know how literally to take the Ervin scheme. If it sounded at times like an effort to replace presidential government by congressional government, it must be remembered that the proposals were provoked by an unprecedented attempt to alter the political order. Ervin and his colleagues were fighting not to frustrate the leadership of a president who recognized his accountability to Congress and the Constitution but to protect Congress and the Constitution from the revolutionary presidency. Yet, if taken literally, the Ervin scheme ran the risk of creating a generation of weak presidents in an age when the turbulence of race, poverty, inflation, crime and urban decay was straining the delicate bonds of national cohesion and demanding, quite as much as in the 1930s, a strong domestic presidency to hold the country together. For Sam Ervin was of the pure Jeffersonian school, like the old Tertium Quids who felt that Jefferson and Madison, in strengthening the presidency and seeing national government as an instrument of the general welfare, had deserted the true faith. It has been noted that Ervin, the eloquent expositor of the First and Fourth Amendments, rarely mentioned the Fourteenth and Fifteenth, and that the great constitutional champion of civil liberties had also been the great constitutional opponent of civil rights.

The pure Jeffersonian doctrine had been a witness rather than a policy, which is why Jefferson and Madison themselves abandoned it. The pure Jeffersonian idea of decentralized power receded in the course of American history because local government simply did not offer the means to attain Jeffersonian ends. In practice, pure Jeffersonianism meant a system under which the strongest local interests, whether planters, landlords, merchants, bankers or industrialists, consolidated their control and oppressed the rest; it meant all power to the neighborhood oligarchs. Theodore Roosevelt explained at the start of the twentieth century why Hamiltonian means had become necessary to achieve Jeffersonian ends, how national authority was the only effective means of correcting injustice in a national society. "If Jefferson were living in our day," said Wilson in 1912, "he would see what we see: that the individual is caught in a great confused nexus of complicated circumstances, and that . . . without the watchful interference, the resolute interference, of the government there can be no fair play."[59] And, for the first Roosevelt and for Wilson, as for their joint heir, the second Roosevelt, national authority was embodied in the presidency.

This had not been a bad thing for the Republic. It was presidential leadership, after all, that brought the country into the twentieth century, that civilized American industry, secured the rights of labor organization, defended the livelihood of the farmer. It was presidential leadership, spurred on by the Supreme Court, that sought to vindicate racial justice against local bigotry. Congress would have done few of these things on its own; local government even fewer. It would be a mistake to cripple the presidency at home because of presidential excesses abroad. History had shown the presidency to be the most effective instrumentality of government for justice and progress. Even Calvin Coolidge, hardly one of the more assertive of presidents, said, "It is because in their hours of timidity the Congress becomes subservient to the importunities of organized minorities that the president comes more and more to stand as the champion of the rights of the whole country."[60]

The scheme of presidential subordination could easily be pressed to the point of national folly. But it was important to contend, not for a strong presidency in general, but for a strong presidency within the Constitution. The presidency deserved to be defended on serious and not on stupid points. In 1973 Watergate produced flurries of near hysteria about the life expectancy of the institution. Thus Charles L. Black, Jr., Luce Profes-

sor of Jurisprudence at the Yale Law School, argued that, if Nixon turned over his White House tapes to Congress or the courts, it would mean the "danger of degrading or even destroying the presidency" and constitute a betrayal of his "successors for all time to come." The Republic, Professor Black said, could not even risk diluting the "symbolism" of the office lest that disturb "in the most dangerous way the balance of the best government yet devised on earth"; and it almost seemed that he would rather suppress the truth than jeopardize the symbolism.[61]

Executive privilege was not the issue. No presidents cherished the presidency more than, say, Jackson or Polk; but both readily conceded to Congress the right in cases of malversation to penetrate into the most secret recesses of the executive department. Nor, in the longer run, did either Ervin's hope of presidential subordination or Black's fantasy of presidential collapse have real substance. For the presidency, though its wings could be clipped for a time, was an exceedingly tough institution. Its primacy was founded in the necessities of the American political order. It had endured many challenges and survived many vicissitudes. It was nonsense to suppose that its fate as an institution was bound up with the fate of the particular man who happened to be president at any given time. In the end power in the American order was bound to flow back to the presidency.

Congress had a marvelous, if generally unfulfilled, capacity for oversight, for advice, for constraint, for chastening the presidency and informing the people. When it really wanted to say no to a president, it had ample means of doing so; and in due course the president would have no choice but to acquiesce. But its purpose was, as Wilson said,

> watchful criticism, talk that should bring to light the whole intention of the government and apprise those who conducted it of the real feeling and desire of the nation

... in order that nothing which contravened the common understanding should be let pass without comment or structure, in order that measures should be insisted on which the nation needed, and measures resisted which the nation did not need or might take harm from.[62]

It was inherently incapable of conducting government and providing national leadership. Its fragmentation, its chronic fear of responsibility, its habitual dependence on the executive for ideas, information and favors—this was life insurance for the presidency.

Both Nixon and Ervin were wrong in supposing that the matter could be settled by shifting the balance of power in a decisive way to one branch or the other. The answer lay rather in preserving fluidity and re-establishing comity. Indeed, for most people—here Ervin was a distinguished exception—the constitutional and institutional issues were make-believe. It was largely a matter, as Averell Harriman said, "of whose ox is getting gored: who is in or out of power, and what actions either side may want."[63] When Nixon was in the opposition, there had been no more earnest critic of presidential presumption. Each side dressed its arguments in grand constitutional and institutional terms, but their contention was like that of the two drunken men described long ago by Lincoln who got into a fight with their greatcoats on until each fought himself out of his own coat and into the coat of the other.[64] To aficionados of constitutional controversy, this doubtless seemed reductionism; but history, in this case as in the case of the war-making power, sustained the proposition. Neutral principles! Neutral principles!

The supreme neutral principle, as vital in domestic policy as in foreign policy, was that all great decisions of the government must be shared decisions. The subsidiary principle was that, if the presidency tried to transform what the Constitution saw as concurrent into exclusive authority, it must be stopped;

and, if Congress tried to transform concurrent into exclusive authority, it must be stopped too. If either the presidency or Congress turned against the complex balance of constitutional powers that had left room over many generations for mutual accommodation, then the ensuing collision would harm both branches of government and the Republic as well. Even together Congress and the presidency were by no means infallible; but their shared decisions, wise or foolish, at least met the standards of democracy. And, shared, the decisions were more likely to be wise than foolish. "I never came out of a committee meeting or a conference," Wilson once said, "without seeing more of the question that was under discussion than I had seen when I went in. And that to my mind is an image of government." He summed up the essential spirit of the constitutional republic: "The whole purpose of democracy is that we may hold counsel with one another, so as not to depend upon the understanding of one man, but to depend upon the counsel of all."[65]

Easier to say than to do, of course, as Wilson's subsequent career attested. All presidents affected a belief in common counsel, but most after a time preferred to make other arrangements. Still, the idea was right, and the process of accountability had to begin inside the president himself. A constitutional president could do many things, but he had to believe in the discipline of consent. It was not enough that he personally thought the country in trouble and genuinely believed he alone knew how to save it. In all but the most extreme cases, action had to be accompanied by public explanation and tested by public acceptance. A constitutional president had to be aware of what Whitman called "the never-ending audacity of elected persons"[66] and had to understand the legitimacy of challenges to his own judgment and authority. He had to be sensitive directly to the diversity of concern and conviction in the nation, sensitive prospectively to the verdict of history, sensitive always to the decent respect pledged in the Declaration of Independence to the opinions of mankind.

Yet presidents chosen as open and modest men were not sure to remain so amid the intoxications of the office; and the office grew steadily more intoxicating in the later twentieth century. A wise president, having read George Reedy and observed the fates of Johnson and Nixon, would take care to provide himself, while there still was time, with passports to reality. Presidents in the last quarter of the twentieth century might, as a beginning, plan to rehabilitate (I use the word in almost the Soviet sense) the executive branch of government. This does not mean the capitulation of the presidency to the permanent government; nor should anyone forget that it was the unresponsiveness of the permanent government that gave rise to the aggressive White House of the twentieth century. But it does mean a reduction in the size and power of the White House staff and the restoration of the access and prestige of the executive departments. The president will always need a small and alert personal staff to serve as his eyes and ears and one lobe of his brain, but he must avoid a vast and possessive staff ambitious to make all the decisions of government. Above all, he must not make himself the prisoner of a single information system. No sensible president should give one man control of all the channels of communication; any man sufficiently wise to exercise such control properly ought to be president himself.[67]

As for the cabinet, while no president in American history has found it a very satisfactory instrument of government, it has served presidents best when it has contained men strong and independent in their own right, strong enough to make the permanent government responsive to presidential policy and independent enough to carry honest dissents into the Oval Office, even on questions apart from their departmental

jurisdictions. Here again, Franklin Roosevelt, instead of being the cause of it all, was really a model of how a strong president fitted the cabinet into the constitutional order. In his first term he recognized that his reform program needed support from the progressive wings of both parties. Accordingly he brought two progressive Republicans, Wallace and Ickes, into his cabinet and took special care to work with progressive Republicans in Congress. Toward the end of his second term Roosevelt saw that foreign policy posed a different set of political problems. He now reorganized his cabinet to include internationalist Republicans like Stimson and Knox. In this way FDR gained some of the objectives and advantages of cabinet government, using the cabinet both to broaden his base of support and to reassure the people that there was no risk of his taking momentous decisions without the counsel of men in whom the nation reposed trust. His idea of government was to gather round him independent and opinionated men and, up to a point, give them their head.

While no president wants to create the impression that his administration is out of control, FDR showed how a masterful president could maintain the most divergent range of contacts, surround himself with the most articulate and positive colleagues and use debate within the executive branch as a means of clarifying issues and trying out people and policies. Or perhaps FDR was in a way the cause of it all, because he alone had the vitality, flair and cunning to be clearly on top without repressing everything underneath. In a joke Henry Wallace, not usually a humorous man, told in my hearing in 1943, FDR could keep all the balls in the air without losing his own. Some of his successors tried to imitate his mastery without understanding the sources of his strength.[68]

But not every president is an FDR, and FDR himself, though his better instincts generally won out in the end, was a flawed, willful and, with time, increasingly arbitrary man. When presidents begin to succumb to delusions of grandeur, when the checks and balances inside themselves stop operating, external checks and balances may well become necessary to save the Republic. The nature of an activist president in any case, in Sam Lubell's phrase, was to run with the ball until he was tackled.[69] As conditions abroad and at home nourished the imperial presidency, tacklers had to be more than usually sturdy and intrepid.

How to make external checks effective? Congress could tie the presidency down by a thousand small legal strings, but, like Gulliver and the Lilliputians, the president could always break loose. The effective means of controlling the presidency lay less in law than in politics. For the American president ruled by influence; and the withdrawal of consent, by Congress, by the press, by public opinion, could bring any president down. The great presidents understood this. The president, said Andrew Jackson, must be "accountable at the bar of public opinion for every act of his administration."[70] "I have a very definite philosophy about the presidency," said Theodore Roosevelt.

> I think it should be a very powerful office, and I think the president should be a very strong man who uses without hesitation every power that the position yields; but because of this fact I believe that he should be sharply watched by the people [and] held to a strict accountability by them.[71]

Holding a president to strict accountability required, first of all, a new attitude on the part of the American people toward their presidents, or rather a return to the more skeptical attitude of earlier times: it required, specifically, a decline in reverence. An insistent theme in Nixon's public discourse was the necessity of maintaining due respect for the presidency. The possibility that such respect might be achieved simply by being a good president evidently did not reassure him. He was preoccupied with "respect for the office" as an entity in itself. Can one imagine Washington or Lincoln or the Roosevelts or Truman or Kennedy going on in public, as Nixon repeatedly did, about how important it was to do this or that in order to maintain 'respect for the office'? But the age of the imperial presidency had in time produced the idea that run-of-the-mill politicians, brought by fortuity to the White House, must be treated thereafter as if they had become superior and perhaps godlike beings.

The Nixon theoreticians even tried to transform reverence into an ideology, propagating the doctrine, rather novel in the United States, that institutions of authority were entitled to respect *per se*, whether or not they had done anything to earn respect. If authority were denied respect, the syllogism ran, the whole social order would be in danger. "Your task, then, is clear," my friend Pat Moynihan charged his president in 1969: "To restore the authority of American institutions." But should institutions expect obedience they do not, on their record of performance, deserve? To this question the Nixon ideologues apparently answered yes.[72] An older American tradition would say no, incredulous that anyone would see this as a question. In that spirit I would argue that what the country needs today is a little serious disrespect for the office of the presidency; a refusal to give any more weight to a president's words than the intelligence of the utterance, if spoken by anyone else, would command; an understanding of the point made so aptly by Montaigne: "Sit he on never so high a throne, a man still sits on his own bottom."

And what if men not open and modest, even at the start, but from the start ambitious of power and contemptuous of law reached the place once occupied by Washington and Lincoln? What if neither personal character, nor the play of politics, nor the Constitution itself availed to hold a president to strict accountability? In the end, the way to control the presidency might have to be not in many little ways but in one large way. In the end, there remained, as Madison said, the decisive engine of impeachment.

IX

This was, of course, the instrument provided by the Constitution. But it was an exceedingly blunt instrument. Only once had a president been impeached, and there was no great national desire to go through the experience again. Yet, for the first time in a century, Americans in the 1970s had to think hard about impeachment, which meant that, because most of them flinched from the prospect, they began to think hard about alternatives to impeachment.

One alternative was the censure of the president by the Congress. That had been tried in 1834 when the Senate censured Andrew Jackson on the ground that, in removing the government deposits from the Second Bank of the United States, he had assumed illegal and unconstitutional powers.[73] Jackson's protest to the Senate had been eloquent and conclusive. If Congress really meant what the Senate said, Jackson replied, let the House impeach him and the Senate try him. Jackson was plainly right. If a president committed high crimes and misdemeanors, censure was not enough. The slap-on-the-wrist approach to presidential delinquency made little sense, constitutional or otherwise. The continuation of a lawbreaker as chief magistrate would be a strange way to exemplify law and order at home or to demonstrate American probity before the world. This did not mean, of course, that a fainthearted Congress might not censure a lawless president and pretend to have done its duty. But unless the terms of the resolution made it clear why the president was merely censurable and not impeachable, the action would be a cop-out and a betrayal of Congress's constitutional responsibility.

Were there other halfway houses?

Another proposal seemed worth consideration: that is the removal of an offending president by some means short of impeachment. A joint resolution calling on the president to resign and passed by an overwhelming two thirds of each house (and therefore immune to veto) could have a powerful effect on a president who cared about the Constitution and the country. If either the president or the vice president then resigned, the president, old or new, could, under the Twenty-fifth Amendment, nominate a new vice president who would take office upon confirmation by both houses of Congress. This would enable a constitutionally responsible president, as Clark Clifford suggested in 1973, to ask Congress for a list of say, three persons, from which he would select a new vice president; after which the president, knowing that he had lost national confidence, would resign and the vice president would become president.[74] This plan would re-establish relations between Congress and the presidency and, presumably, revive popular confidence in the government.

"Admirable," said Cardinal Fleury after he read the Abbé de St. Pierre's *Projet de Paix Perpetuelle*, "save for one omission: I find no provision for sending missionaries to convert the hearts of princes."[75] Alas, a president who had succeeded in provoking a long-suffering Congress into a resolution calling for his resignation was not likely to be deeply moved by congressional disapproval nor inclined to cooperate in his own liquidation.

If presidents would not resign of their own volition, could they be forced out without the personal and national ordeal of impeachment and conviction? A proposal advanced in various forms by leading members of the House of Representatives in 1973 contemplated giving Congress authority by constitutional amendment to call for a new presidential election when it found that the president had so lost popular confidence he could no longer effectively perform his responsibilities (Jonathan Bingham) or that the president had violated the Constitution (Edith Green and Morris Udall).[76] A new election would clear the slate and restore a mandate to govern, while impeachment would, at best, replace a discredited president by a vice president of the president's own choice, elected under the same auspices and by the same methods and inescapably part of the moral climate that caused the president to be impeached. This consideration acquired particular force with the disclosure in the summer of 1973 that Vice President Agnew was under criminal investigation.

The idea of introducing the power of dissolution was not new. But in its previous incarnations it had generally been conceived as giving the president the power to dissolve the Congress.[77] Now members of Congress proposed to give Congress the power to dissolve the presidency. Each of these proposals was punitive in relation to the other branch and self-serving in relation to itself. Thomas K. Finletter alone advocated simultaneous dissolution of both Congress and the presidency. This plainly was the clean way as well as the best means of getting a genuinely fresh mandate. But it was difficult to work special elections into the staggered terms of senators and representatives. The best solution would be to provide that a congressional term expired at the end of six (or two) years, or at the next presidential election, whichever came first. Finletter's solution—to have presidents, senators and congressmen all serve six-year terms[78]—moved the American polity quite far toward plebiscitary if not parliamentary government.

The possibility of dissolution and new elections at times of hopeless stalemate or blasted confidence had serious appeal. Dissolution would give a rigid electoral system flexibility and responsiveness. It would permit the timely replacement of the pilot of the calm by the pilot of the storm, thereby pleasing the ghost of Bagehot. It would remind intractable Congresses that they could not block presidents with immunity, as it would remind high-flying presidents that there were other ways of being shot down besides impeachment. But one's instinct was somehow against it. A congressman observed of the Green–Udall amendment that it "would, in effect, take one-half of the parliamentary processes and not the entire parliamentary process."[79] This was certainly the direction and logic of dissolution. The result might well be to alter the balance of the Constitution in unforeseeable and perilous ways. It might, in particular, strengthen the movement against the sepation of powers and toward a plebiscitary presidency. "The republican principle," said the 71st Federalist,

> demands that the deliberate sense of the community should govern the conduct of those to whom they intrust the management of their affairs; but it does not require an unqualified complaisance to every sudden breeze of passion, or to every transient impulse which the people may receive from the arts of men, who flatter their prejudices to betray their interests.

I think that the possibility of inserting dissolution into the American system is worth careful examination. But digging into the foundations of the state, as Burke said, is always a dangerous adventure.

X

Impeachment, on the other hand, was part of the original foundation of the American state. The Founding Fathers had placed the blunt instrument in the Constitution with every expectation that it would be used, and used most especially against presidents. "No point is of more importance," George Mason told the convention, "than that the right of impeachment should be continued. Shall any man be above Justice? Above all shall that man be above it, who [as President] can commit the most extensive injustice?" Benjamin Franklin pointed out that, if there were no provision for impeachment, the only recourse would be assassination, in which case a president would be "not only deprived of his life but of the opportunity of vindicating his character." Corruption or loss of capacity in a president, said Madison, was "within the compass of probable events. . . . Either of them might be fatal to the Republic."[80]

The genius of impeachment lay in the fact that it could punish the man without punishing the office. For, in the presidency as elsewhere, power was ambiguous: the power to do good meant also the power to do harm, the power to serve the Republic also the power to demean and defile it. The trick was to preserve presidential power but to deter presidents from abusing that power. Shall any man be above Justice? George Mason had asked. Obviously not; not even a president of the United States. But bringing presidents to justice was not all that simple.

History had turned impeachment into a weapon of last resort—more so probably than the Founding Fathers would have anticipated. Still, it was possible to exaggerate its impact on the country. It had taken less than three months to impeach and try Andrew Johnson, nor was the nation—in a favorite apprehension of 1868 as well as of 1974—torn apart in the process. Three months of surgery might be better than three years of paralysis. Yet impeachment presented legal as well as political problems. There was broad agreement, among scholars at least, on doctrine. Impeachment was a proceeding of a political nature, by no means restricted to indictable crimes. On the other hand, it plainly was not to be applied to cases of honest disagreement over national policy or over constitutional interpretation, especially when a president refused to obey a law that he believed struck directly at the presidential prerogative. Impeachment was to be reserved, in Mason's phrase at the constitutional convention, for "great and dangerous offenses."[81]

The Senate, in trying impeachment

cases, was better equipped to be the judge of the law than of the facts. When Johnson was impeached, there had been no dispute about the fact that he had removed Stanton. When Jackson was censured, there had been no dispute about the fact that he had removed the deposits. The issue was not whether they had done something but whether what they had done constituted a transgression of the laws and the Constitution. But in the Nixon case the facts themselves remained at issue—the facts, that is, of presidential complicity—and the effort of a hundred senators to determine those facts might well lead to chaos. The record here was one of negligence, irresponsibility and even deception, but it had not yet been proven one of knowing violation of the Constitution or of knowing involvement in the obstruction of justice. While impeachment was in the Constitution to be used, there was no point in lowering the threshold so that it would be used casually. All this argued for the determination of facts before the consideration of impeachment. There were two obvious ways to determine the facts. One was through the House of Representatives, which had the sole power to initiate impeachment. The House could, for example, instruct the Judiciary Committee to ascertain whether there were grounds for impeachment, or it could establish a select committee to conduct such an inquiry. The other road was through the courts. If the special prosecutor established incriminating facts, these could serve as the basis for impeachment.

But what if a president himself withheld evidence—as, for example, Nixon's tapes—deemed essential to the ascertainment of facts? If a president said "the time has come to turn Watergate over to the courts, where the questions of guilt and innocence belong,"[82] and then denied the courts the evidence they needed to decide on innocence or guilt, what recourse remained to the Republic except impeachment? Apart from the courts, Polk had said quite explicitly that the House, if it were looking into impeachment, could command testimony and papers, public and private, official or unofficial, of every agent of the government.[83] If a president declined for whatever reason to yield material evidence in his possession, whether to the courts or to the House, this itself might provide clear grounds for impeachment.

All these things were obscure in the early autumn of 1973. It was even possible that Nixon might conclude that the Watergate problems were not after all (as he had told the prime minister of Japan) "murky, small, unimportant, vicious little things"[84] but were rather evidence of a profound and grievous imbalance between the presidency and the Constitution. Perhaps he might by an honest display of candor and contrition regain a measure of popular confidence, re-establish constitutional comity and recover presidential effectiveness. But full recovery seemed unlikely unless the president himself recognized why his presidency had fallen into such difficulties. Nixon's continued invocation, after Watergate, of national security as the excuse for presidential excess, his defense to the end of unreviewable executive privilege, his defiant assertion that, if he had it to do over again, he would still deceive Congress and the people about the secret air war in Cambodia—such unrepentant reactions suggested that he still had no clue as to what his trouble was, still failed to understand that the sickness of his presidency had been caused, not by the overzealousness of his friends nor by the malice of his enemies, but by the expansion and abuse of presidential power itself.

For the issue was more than whether Congress and the people wished to deal with the particular iniquities of the Nixon administration. It was whether they wished to rein in the runaway presidency. Nixon's presidency was not an aberration but a culmination. It carried

to reckless extremes a compulsion toward presidential power rising out of deep-running changes in the foundations of society. In a time of the acceleration of history and the decay of traditional institutions and values, a strong presidency was both a greater necessity than ever before and a greater risk— necessary to hold a spinning and distracted society together, necessary to make the separation of powers work,[85] risky because of the awful temptation held out to override the separation of powers and burst the bonds of the Constitution. The nation required both a strong presidency for leadership and the separation of powers for liberty. It could well be that, if continuing structural compulsions were likely to propel future presidents in the direction of government by decree, the rehabilitation of impeachment would be essential to contain the presidency and preserve the Constitution.

Watergate was potentially the best thing to have happened to the presidency in a long time. If the trails were followed to their end, many, many years would pass before another White House staff would dare take the liberties with the Constitution and the laws the Nixon White House had taken. And if the nation wanted to work its way back to a constitutional presidency, there was only one way to begin. That was by showing presidents that, when their closest associates placed themselves above the law and the Constitution, such transgressions would be, not forgiven or forgotten for the sake of the presidency, but exposed and punished for the sake of the presidency.

If the Nixon White House escaped the legal consequences of its illegal behavior, why would future presidents and their associates not suppose themselves entitled to do what the Nixon White House had done? Only condign punishment would restore popular faith in the presidency and deter future presidents from illegal conduct—so long, at least, as Watergate remained a vivid memory.[86] We have noted that corruption appears to visit the White House in fifty-year cycles. This suggests that exposure and retribution inoculate the presidency against its latent criminal impulses for about half a century. Around the year 2023 the American people would be well advised to go on the alert and start nailing down everything in sight.

A constitutional presidency, as the great presidents had shown, could be a very strong presidency indeed. But what kept a strong president constitutional, in addition to checks and balances incorporated within his own breast, was the vigilance of the nation. Neither impeachment nor repentance would make much difference if the people themselves had come to an unconscious acceptance of the imperial presidency. The Constitution could not hold the nation to ideals it was determined to betray.[87] The reinvigoration of the written checks in the American Constitution depended on the reinvigoration of the unwritten checks in American society. The great institutions—Congress, the courts, the executive establishment, the press, the universities, public opinion—had to reclaim their own dignity and meet their own responsibilities, As Madison said long ago, the country could not trust to "parchment barriers" to halt the encroaching spirit of power.[88] In the end, the Constitution would live only if it embodied the spirit of the American people.

"There is no week nor day nor hour," wrote Walt Whitman, "when tyranny may not enter upon this country, if the people lose their supreme confidence in themselves,—and lose their roughness and spirit of defiance—Tyranny may always enter—there is no charm, no bar against it—the only bar against it is a large resolute breed of men."[89]

NOTES

1. Jefferson to Madison, March 15, 1789, quoted by Alexis de Tocqueville, *Democracy in America,* I, Ch. 15.

2. James Bryce, *Modern Democracies* (New York, 1921), II, 73.

3. *Ex Parte Milligan,* 4 Wall 2, 125 (1866).

4. "A President Unfit to Rule," *Spectator,* June 9, 1973.

5. *New York Times,* August 16, 1973.

6. *New York Times,* May 1, 1973.

7. Interview in *New York Times,* May 18, 1973.

8. *New York Times,* June 15, 1973. Interview with Charles Wheeler, *Listener,* July 26, 1973.

9. Mary McGrory. "A Talk with John Dean," *New York Post,* June 18, 1973.

10. Lou Cannon, "The Siege Psychology and How It Grew," *Washington Post,* July 29, 1973.

11. Interview in *New York Times,* August 5, 1973.

12. *New York Times,* July 24, 1973.

13. C. C. Thach, *The Creation of the Presidency, 1775-1789* (Baltimore, 1969), 147.

14. Woodrow Wilson, *Constitutional Government in the United States* (New York, 1908), 79-80.

15. See, for example, his speech in Milwaukee, March 23, 1968.

16. Barbara Tuchman, "Should We Abolish the Presidency?" *New York Times,* February 13, 1973. Max Lerner, "Presidential Watchmen," *New York Post,* June 11, 1972.

17. They also had been brought up recurrently thereafter—as by August B. Woodward, *Considerations on the Executive Government of the United States* (1809); John C. Calhoun, *Discourse on the Constitution* (1851); Henry C. Lockwood, *The Abolition of the Presidency* (1884); C. Perry Paterson, *Presidential Government in the United States* (1947); Charles S. Hyneman, *Bureaucracy in a Democracy* (1950); Herman Finer, *The Presidency: Crisis and Regeneration* (1960); Rexford G. Tugwell, *The Enlargement of the Presidency* (1960). Two valuable recent books on the presidency—Marcus Cunliffe, *American Presidents and the Presidency* (London, 1969); and James MacGregor Burns, *Presidential Government: The Crucible of Leadership* (Boston, 1966)—contain useful discussions.

18. C. C. Tansill, ed., *Documents Illustrative of the Formation of the Union of the American States* (Washington, 1927), 131-33, 567, 595, 686-87.

19. 70th Federalist.

20. Jefferson to Destutt de Tracy, January 26, 1811, *The Complete Jefferson*, S. K. Padover, ed. (New York, 1943), 310-12.

21. George Reedy, *The Twilight of the Presidency* (New York, 1970), 20-26. He continues:

> Lyndon Johnson looked forward with horror to the long weekends in which there was really nothing to do. The result was usually a Saturday afternoon spent in lengthy conferences with individual newspapermen who would be hastily summoned from their homes and would spend hours with him while he expounded the thesis that his days were so taken up with the nation's business that he had no time to devote to friends.

22. Thach, *op. cit.*, 125.

23. *Ibid.*, 174.

24. House Judiciary Committee, *Single Six-Year Term for President: Hearing*, 92 Cong., I Sess. (1972), 3, 33. The argument advanced by Mansfield and Aiken would appear to be the major source of support for the amendment. It should be noted that Joseph Califano, former Special Assistant to President Johnson, disclaimed the Mansfield-Aiken line but advanced a more sophisticated argument: that the contemporary budget process, by requiring a new president to operate for 18 months under his predecessor's budget, gave him little chance to get things done in so short a time as four years. This would seem to me an argument for shortening the budget process (which need not, in any case, be all that inflexible) rather than for lengthening the presidential term. I have not gone into the question of the lame-duck effect as an argument against the single six-year term because lame-duckery seems to me a very minor element in presidential ineffectiveness.

25. Senate Judiciary Committee, *Single Six-Year Term*, 113.

26. *Ibid.*, 63.

27. *Ibid.*, 16.

28. Washington to Lafayette. April 28, 1788, Washington, *Writings*, P. L. Ford, ed. (New York, 1891), XI, 257-58.

29. Wilson to A. Mitchell Palmer. February 5, 1913. Senate Judiciary Committee, *Six-Year Term*, 240-41.

30. E. S. Corwin, *The President: Office and Powers* (New York, 1957), 296.

31. W. H. Taft, *Our Chief Magistrate and His Powers* (New York, 1916), 31-32.

32. See his articles on "Cabinet Government in the United States," *International Review*, August 1879, and "Committee or Cabinet Government?" *Overland Monthly*, January 1884, reprinted in A.S. Link, ed., *The Papers of Woodrow Wilson* (Princeton, 1966), I, 493 ff.; II, 618 ff.; the quotation is from II, 627. Wilson proposed to overcome the constitutional problem by adding four words to Article I, Section 6, to make it read: "and no Person holding *other than a Cabinet* Office under the United States shall be a Member of either House during his Continuance in Office."

33. Wilson to Palmer, Senate Judiciary Committee, *Six-Year Term*, 240.

34. E. S. Corwin, *The President: Office and Powers* (New York, 1940), 304.

35. Thomas K. Finletter, *Can Representative Government Do the Job?* (New York, 1945); cf. also E. S. Corwin, *The President: Office and Powers, 1787-1957* (New York, 1957), 297-98, 489-90. The adoption of a parliamentary system is discussed in such books as William Macdonald. *A New Constitution for America* (1921) and Henry Hazlitt, *A New Constitution Now* (1942).

36. Cf. Don K. Price's prescient article, "The Parliamentary and Presidential Systems," *Public Administration Review*, autumn 1943; and Richard Crossman's introduction to Walter Bagehot, *The English Constitution* (Fontana Books, 1963), especially 51.

37. *Congressional Record*, June 4, 1973, S10235-S10236.

38. Harold Laski thought that it would "transform the president into a person more akin to the president of the French Republic [he was writing at the time of the Third Republic] than to that of the United States"; cf. his thoughtful critique in *The American Presidency* (New York, 1940), 96-110.

39. *Congressional Record*, May 10, 1973, S8839.

40. *Congressional Record*, March 8, 1973, S4204.

41. See pages 314-15 in Arthur M. Schlesinger, Jr., *The Imperial Presidency* (Boston: Houghton Mifflin Company, 1973).

42. Press conference, March 15, 1973, *New York Times*, March 16, 1973.

43. This was, however, dictum and uttered in dissent; *U.S. v. Gravel*, opinion reprinted in *Congressional Record*, August 16, 1972, at S13630.

44. *U.S. v. Reynolds et al.*, 345 U.S. 1, 8, 9 (1953).

45. *Committee for Nuclear Responsibility, Inc., v. Seaborg*, 436 F. 2d 788, 794 (1971).

46. Ralph Nader had sued the government, charging corruption in connection with the decision to raise milk prices. The judge was William B. Jones.

47. For the Senate debate on this question, with Frank Church's understandable incredulity and ample documentation on both sides, see *Congressional Record*, June 14, 1973, S11183-S11202; the State Department complaints—also understandable but what else did they expect?—are recorded in the *New York Times*, July 29, 1973, and the *Washington Post*, August 7, 1973.

48. *Congressional Record*, February 15, l973, S2527; for Ervin's resolution, *Congressional Record*, March 8, 1973, S4204-S4205.

49. The judges were Robert R. Merhige, Jr., in a case involving the Environmental Protection Agency and Charles Richey in a case involving the Department of Housing and Urban Development; see *Congressional Record*, June 12, 1973, S10935, and July 26, 1973, E5121.

50. *Congressional Record*, May 10, 1973, S8838.

51. Woodrow Wilson, *Congressional Government*, 15th ed. (Boston, 1901), 180.

52. House Ways and Means Committee, *Revenue Revision–1939 . . . Hearings*, 76 Cong., 1 Sess. (1939), 3.

53. Joint Study Committee on Budget Control, Interim Report, *Improving Congressional Control over Budgetary Outlay and Receipt Totals*, House Report 93-17, 93 Cong., 1 Sess. (1973). The report recommended the establishment in each house of a committee of the budget, empowered to collaborate in fixing spending and appropriations ceilings on behalf of Congress as a whole. Two thirds of the members of the new budget committees would be drawn from the appropriations and tax committees, which had become after 1938 the fortress of the conservative coalition of Republicans and southern Democrats. A so-called "rule of consistency"—that is, that the ceilings recommended by the budget committees could not be amended unless the amendment matched an increase in one part of the budget with a cut somewhere else or with an equivalent tax increase—would make it almost impossible for Congress thereafter to alter the priorities determined by the committees. The Joint Study Committee's proposals seemed likely to result in the concentration of power over the budget in a small conservative group, generally hostile to social and urban interests and peculiarly susceptible to presidential persuasion and ma-

nipulation. Senator Ervin had his own version of the bill, which would have made the new budget committee a good deal less unrepresentative.

A better approach, advocated by Senator Humphrey, was simply to establish a well-staffed congressional Office of Budget Analysis under the Joint Economic Committee. In addition, Congress would be well advised to try again to pass the bill, vetoed by Nixon in 1973, requiring senatorial confirmation for the director of the Office of Management and Budget. Since the director of OMB had far more power than most cabinet members, ambassadors and other officers on whose qualifications the Senate regularly passed, it seemed reasonable enough that it should pass on his qualifications too. A law requiring senatorial confirmation for the director of the FBI had fully justified itself during the hearings on J. Edgar Hoover's successor.

54. *Congressional Record*, February 28, 1973, S3539-S3560. In a quite unprecedented expression of no confidence in a president, Congress before its August recess in 1973 empowered the congressional leadership to call Congress back into session; this was designed to intercept any effort by Nixon to pocket-veto bills during the summer adjournment. *Congressional Record*, July 28, 1973, S14941. Judge Joseph C. Waddy's decision in the case of *Kennedy* v. *Sampson and Jones* is reprinted in the *Congressional Record*, September 11, 1973, S16293.

55. Senate Judiciary Committee, *Congressional Oversight of Executive Agreements: Hearing*, 92 Cong., 1 Sess. (1972), 6; report, 93 Cong., 1 Sess. (1973), 9.

56. Authoritative observers argue about the idea of the two presidencies. I note the following in the fascinating appendix "The Presidency As I Have Seen It" in Emmet Hughes's valuable book *The Living Presidency* (New York, 1973), 312-68. On one side: Averell Harriman ("All talk of 'two presidencies'—one foreign and one domestic—is nonsense"); Clark Clifford ("I do not find the distinction valid"); Benjamin V. Cohen ("I do not accept the doctrine that the powers of the president are more limited in domestic affairs than in foreign affairs"). On the other: Abe Fortas ("There is obviously a broad difference between the range of presidential power and initiative in domestic and in foreign affairs"); Theodore Sorensen ("There is a clear difference"); Bryce Harlow ("It is incontestably true"). There may be a confusion in this question between

the constitutional accountability of the president to Congress and the people, which is the same in foreign as in domestic affairs, and the president's operating scope, which for a generation after the Second World War was obviously much greater in foreign affairs. That the years 1941-1966 saw the existence of the two presidencies is effectively demonstrated by Aaron Wildavsky, "The Two Presidencies" in Wildavsky, ed., *The Presidency* (Boston, 1969), 230-48.

57. Louis Fisher, *President and Congress* (New York, 1972), 173.

58. Arthur M. Schlesinger, Jr., *The Coming of the New Deal* (Boston, 1958), 254.

59. Woodrow Wilson, *The New Freedom* (Englewood Cliffs, 1961), 164.

60. Calvin Coolidge, "The President Lives Under a Multitude of Eyes," *American Magazine,* August 1929.

61. Charles L. Black, Jr., to Congressman Bob Eckhardt, *Congressional Record,* August 1, 1973, E5321; also "Mr. Nixon, the Tapes and Common Sense," *New York Times,* August 3, 1971.

62. Wilson, *Constitutional Government,* 11, 12.

63. Harriman, "The Presidency As I Have Seen It," in Hughes, *Living Presidency,* 249.

64. Lincoln to H. L. Pierce *et al.,* April 6, 1859, Lincoln, *Collected Works,* R. P. Basler, ed. (New Brunswick, 1953), III, 375. Lincoln was amused by the fact that the Democrats of his day had stopped mentioning Jefferson while the Republicans constantly invoked him. "If the two leading parties of this day are really identical with the two in the days of Jefferson and Adams, they have performed about the same feat as the two drunken men."

65. Wilson, *New Freedom,* 50, 72.

66. In "Song of the Broad-Axe" *(Leaves of Grass).*

67. In his press conference of August 22, 1973, Nixon said: "The president doesn't pick up the phone and call the attorney general every time something comes up on a matter. He depends on his counsel, or whoever he's done the job to—or given the assignment to—to do the job." This really carries the royal theory of the presidency to extraordinary lengths. One wonders where in the world Nixon got the singular idea that presidents don't make phone calls. Johnson, Kennedy, Truman, Roosevelt never hesitated for an instant to pick up the phone when they wanted to find something out. Even the telephone may serve as a link to reality.

68. Though my testimony on this point may well be suspect, I am sure that among FDR's successors John F. Kennedy had far the clearest understanding of the need to fashion a presidency that would be at once strong and open. He thought FDR went a little far in encouraging dissension within his administration, and he himself went a little far in trying to grab hold of decisions at too early a stage; but he understood the problem. For an illuminating comparison of the administrative methods of FDR and JFK, see the observations of Ben Cohen and Tom Corcoran quoted in Arthur M. Schlesinger, Jr., *A Thousand Days* (Boston, 1965), 686.

69. Samuel Lubell, *The Future While it Happened* (New York, 1973), 42.

70. J. D. Richardson, *Messages and Papers of the Presidents* (New York, 1897), III, 1290.

71. Roosevelt to Lodge, July 19, 1908, *Selections from the Correspondence of Theodore Roosevelt and Henry Cabot Lodge* (New York, 1925), II, 304.

72. The quotation is from a Moynihan memorandum to Nixon, January 3, 1969, *New York Times,* March 11, 1970. The doctrine that authority deserves automatic respect has been expounded by Henry Kissinger, Irving Kristol, Robert Nisbet, Edward Shils and others. In this connection it may be well to recall that on October 15, 1972, nearly four months after Nixon's plumbers organized the Watergate break-in, the following full-page advertisement appeared in the *New York Times:*

Of the two major candidates for the Presidency of the United States, we believe that Richard Nixon has demonstrated the superior capacity for prudent and responsible leadership. Consequently, we intend to vote for President Nixon on November 7th and we urge our fellow citizens to do the same.

Kristol, Nisbet and Shils signed this touching testimonial along with such other eminent if addled scholars as Oscar Handlin, George Homans, W. V. Quine, Edward O. Banfield, Sidney Hook, Milton Friedman, Paul Seabury, Morton Keller, Samuel E. Thorne, Ithiel de Sola Pool, Bertram D. Wolfe and Donald Fleming. The last line explained in type of microscopic size that the advertisement had been "published and paid for by the Finance Committee to Re-elect the President, M. H. Stans, Chairman.

73. See page 36 in Schlesinger, *op. cit.*

74. Clark Clifford, "A Government of Na-

tional Unity," *New York Times,* June 4, 1973.

75. I owe this quotation to Rebecca West, "The Hoover Frame of Mind," *Atlantic Monthly,* June 1943.

76. For Bingham's proposal, *Congressional Record,* May 8, 1973, H3413, and May 21, H3816-H3817; for Mrs. Green's variation, *Congressional Record,* July 17, 1973, H6213.

77. The classic argument was made by William Yandell Elliott in *The Need for Constitutional Reform* (New York, 1935), 234-35.

78. Finletter, *Representative Government,* 110.

79. Bill Archer of Texas, *Congressional Record,* July 17, 1973, H6214.

80. Tansill, ed., *Formation of the Union,* 417-19.

81. *Ibid.,* 691.

82. *New York Times,* August 16, 1973.

83. See page 53 in Schlesinger, *op. cit.*

84. *New York Times,* August 2, 1973.

85. "Indeed, in some respects, the separation of powers requires stronger executive leadership than does the parliamentary and cabinet system," Harry S. Truman, *New York Times,* May 9, 1954.

86. "The only way to attack crime in America is the way crime attacks our people—without pity." Richard M. Nixon in his special message to Congress on crime, *New York Times,* March 11, 1973.

87. I adapt here a phrase of Reed Powell's in his review of Zechariah Chafee's *Freedom of Speech* (1920), quoted in Chafee's introduction to the second edition of his *Freedom of Speech in the United States* (Atheneum paperback, 1969), Ch. 14.

88. 48th Federalist.

89. Walt Whitman, "Notes for Lecturers on Democracy and 'Adhesiveness,'" C. J. Furness, *Walt Whitman's Workshop* (Cambridge, 1928), 58.

34. The War Powers Resolution of 1973*

U.S. CONGRESS

SHORT TITLE

Section 1. This joint resolution may be cited as the "War Powers Resolution."

PURPOSE AND POLICY

Section 2. (a) It is the purpose of this joint resolution to fulfill the intent of the framers of the Constitution of the United States and insure that the collective judgment of both the Congress and the president will apply to the introduction of United States armed forces into hostilities, or into situations where imminent involvement in hostilities is clearly indicated by the circumstances, and to the continued use of such forces in hostilities or in such situations.

(b) Under article I, section 8, of the Constitution, it is specifically provided that the Congress shall have the power to make all laws necessary and proper for carrying into execution, not only its own powers but also all other powers vested by the Constitution in the government of the United States, or in any department or officer thereof.

(c) The constitutional powers of the president as commander-in-chief to introduce United States armed forces into hostilities, or into situations where imminent involvement in hostilities is clearly indicated by the circumstances, are exercised only pursuant to (1) a declaration of war, (2) specific statutory authorization, or (3) a national emergency created by attack upon the United States, its territories or possessions, or its armed forces.

Source: Public Law 93-149, 87 Stat. 555 (November 7, 1973).

CONSULTATION

Section 3. The president in every possible instance shall consult with Congress before introducing United States armed forces into hostilities or into situations where imminent involvement in hostilities is clearly indicated by the circumstances, and after every such introduction shall consult regularly with the Congress until United States armed forces are no longer engaged in hostilities or have been removed from such situations.

REPORTING

Section 4. (a) In the absence of a declaration of war, in any case in which United States armed forces are introduced—

(1) into hostilities or into situations where imminent involvement in hostilities is clearly indicated by the circumstances;

(2) into the territory, airspace or waters of a foreign nation, while equipped for combat, except for deployments which relate solely to supply, replacement, repair, or training of such forces; or

(3) in numbers which substantially enlarge United States armed forces equipped for combat already located in a foreign nation;

the President shall submit within 48 hours to the Speaker of the House of Representatives and to the president pro tempore of the Senate a report, in writing, setting forth—

(A) the circumstances necessitating the introduction of United States armed forces;

(B) the constitutional and legislative authority under which such introduction took place; and

(C) the estimated scope and duration of the hostilities or involvement.

(b) The president shall provide such other information as the Congress may request in the fulfillment of its constitutional responsibilities with respect to committing the nation to war and to the use of United States armed forces abroad.

(c) Whenever United States armed forces are introduced into hostilities or into any situation described in subsection (a) of this section, the president shall, so long as such armed forces continue to be engaged in such hostilities or situation, report to the Congress periodically on the status of such hostilities or situation as well as on the scope and duration of such hostilities or situation, but in no event shall he report to the Congress less often than once every six months.

CONGRESSIONAL ACTION

Section 5. (a) Each report submitted pursuant to section 4(a) (1) shall be transmitted to the Speaker of the House of Representatives and to the president pro tempore of the Senate on the same calendar day. Each report so transmitted shall be referred to the Committee on Foreign Affairs of the House of Representatives and to the Committee on Foreign Relations of the Senate for appropriate action. If, when the report is transmitted, the Congress has adjourned sine die or has adjourned for any period in excess of three calendar days, the Speaker of the House of Representatives and the president pro tempore of the Senate, if they seem it advisable (or if petitioned by at least 30 percent of the membership of their respective houses) shall jointly request the president to convene Congress in order that it may consider the report and take appropriate action pursuant to this section.

(b) Within sixty calendar days after a report is submitted or is required to be submitted pursuant to section 4(a) (1), whichever is earlier, the president shall terminate any use of United States armed forces with respect to which such report was submitted (or required to be submitted), unless the Congress (1) has declared war or has enacted a specific authorization for such use of United States armed forces, (2) has extended by law such sixty-day period, or (3) is physically unable to meet as a result of an armed attack upon the United States. Such sixty-day period shall be extended for not more than an additional thirty days if the president determines and certifies to the Congress in writing that unavoidable military necessity respecting the safety of the United States armed forces requires the continued use of such armed forces in the course of bringing about a prompt removal of such forces.

(c) Notwithstanding subsection (b), at any time that United States armed forces are engaged in hostilities outside the territory of the United States, its possessions and territories without a declaration of war or specific statutory authorization, such forces shall be removed by the president if the Congress so directs by concurrent resolution.

CONGRESSIONAL PRIORITY PROCEDURES FOR JOINT RESOLUTION OR BILL

Section 6. (a) Any joint resolution or bill introduced pursuant to section 5(b) at least thirty calendar days before the expiration of the sixty-day period specified in such section shall be referred to the Committee on Foreign Affairs of the House of Representatives or the Committee on Foreign Relations of the Senate, as the case may be, and such committee shall report one such joint resolution or bill, together with its recommendations, not later than twenty-four calendar days before the expiration of the sixty-day period specified in such section, unless such house shall otherwise determine by the yeas and nays.

(b) Any joint resolution or bill so reported shall become the pending business of the house in question (in the case of the Senate the time for debate shall be equally divided between the proponents and the opponents), and shall be voted on within three calendar days thereafter, unless such house shall otherwise determine by yeas and nays.

(c) Such a joint resolution or bill passed by one house shall be referred to the committee of the other house named in subsection (a) and shall be reported out not later than fourteen calendar days before the expiration of the sixty-day period specified in section 5(b). The joint resolution or bill so reported shall become the pending business of the house in question and shall be voted on within three calendar days after it has been reported, unless such house shall otherwise determine by yeas and nays.

(d) In the case of any disagreement between the two houses of Congress with respect to a joint resolution or bill passed by both houses, conferees shall be promptly appointed and the committee of conference shall make and file a report with respect to such resolution or bill not later than four calendar days before the expiration of the sixty-day period specified in section 5(b). In the event the conferees are unable to agree within forty-eight hours, they shall report back to their respective houses in disagreement. Notwithstanding any rule in either house concerning the printing of conference reports in the Record or concerning any delay in the consideration of such reports, such report shall be acted on by both houses not later than the expiration of such sixty-day period.

CONGRESSIONAL PRIORITY PROCEDURES FOR CONCURRENT RESOLUTION

Section 7. (a) Any concurrent resolution introduced pursuant to section 5(c) shall be referred to the Committee on Foreign Affairs of the House of Representatives or the Committee on Foreign Relations of the Senate, as the case may be, and one such concurrent resolution shall be reported out by such committee together with its recommendations within fifteen calendar days, unless such house shall otherwise determine by the yeas and nays.

(b) Any concurrent resolution so reported shall become the pending business of the house in question (in the case of the Senate the time for debate shall be equally divided between the proponents and the opponents) and shall be voted on within three calendar days thereafter, unless such house shall otherwise determine by yeas and nays.

(c) Such a concurrent resolution passed by one house shall be referred to the committee of the other house named in subsection (a) and shall be reported out by such committee together with its recommendations within fifteen calendar days and shall thereupon become the pending business of such house and shall be voted upon within three calendar days, unless such house shall otherwise determine by yeas and nays.

(d) In the case of any disagreement between the two houses of Congress with respect to a concurrent resolution passed by both houses, conferees shall be promptly appointed and the committee of conference shall make and file a report with respect to such concurrent resolution within six calendar days after the legislation is referred to the committee of conference. Notwithstanding any rule in either house concerning the printing of conference reports in the Record or concerning any delay in the consideration of such reports, such report shall be acted on by both houses not later than six calendar days after the conference report is filed. In the event the conferees are unable to agree within forty-eight hours, they shall report back to their respective houses in disagreement.

INTERPRETATION OF JOINT RESOLUTION

Section 8. (a) Authority to introduce United States armed forces into hostilities or into situations wherein involvement in hostilities is clearly indicated by the circumstances shall not be inferred—

(1) from any provision of law (whether or not in effect before the date of the enactment of this joint resolution), including any provision contained in any appropriation act, unless such provision specifically authorizes the introduction of United States armed forces into hostilities or into such situations and states that it is intended to constitute specific statutory authorization within the meaning of this joint resolution; or

(2) from any treaty heretofore or hereafter ratified unless such treaty is implemented by legislation specifically authorizing the introduction of United States armed forces into hostilities or into such situations and stating that it is intended to constitute specific statutory authorization within the meaning of this joint resolution.

(b) Nothing in this joint resolution shall be construed to require any further specific statutory authorization to permit members of United States armed forces to participate jointly with members of the armed forces of one or more foreign countries in the headquarters operations of high-level military commands which were established prior to the date of enactment of this joint resolution and pursuant to the United Nations Charter or any treaty ratified by the United States prior to such date.

(c) For purposes of this joint resolution, the term "introduction of United States armed forces" includes the assignment of members of such armed forces to command, coordinate, participate in the movement of, or accompany the regular or irregular military forces of any foreign country or government when such military forces are engaged, or there exists an imminent threat that such forces will become engaged, in hostilities.

(d) Nothing in this joint resolution—

(1) is intended to alter the constitutional authority of the Congress or of the president, or the provisions of existing treaties; or

(2) shall be construed as granting any authority to the president with respect to the introduction of United States armed forces into hostilities or into situations wherein involvement in hostilities is clearly indicated by the circumstances which authority he would not have had in the absence of this joint resolution.

SEPARABILITY CLAUSE

Section 9. If any provision of this joint resolution or the application thereof to any person or circumstance is held invalid, the remainder of the joint resolution and the application of such provision to any other person or cir-

cumstance shall not be affected thereby.

EFFECTIVE DATE

Section 10. This joint resolution shall take effect on the date of its enactment.

Passed over presidential veto Nov. 7, 1973.

35. United States v. Nixon*

U.S. SUPREME COURT

JUSTICIABILITY

In the district court, the president's counsel argued that the court lacked jurisdiction to issue the subpoena because the matter was an intra-branch dispute between a subordinate and superior officer of the executive branch and hence not subject to judicial resolution. That argument has been renewed in this Court with emphasis on the contention that the dispute does not present a "case" or "controversy" which can be adjudicated in the federal courts. The president's counsel argues that the federal courts should not intrude into areas committed to the other branches of government. He views the present dispute as essentially a "jurisdictional" dispute within the executive branch which he analogizes to a dispute between two congressional committees. Since the executive branch has exclusive authority and absolute discretion to decide whether to prosecute a case, *Confiscation Cases*, 7 Wall. 454 (1869); *United States* v. *Cox*, 342 F. 2d 167, 171 (CA5), cert. denied *sub nom. Cox* v. *Hauberg*, 381 U.S. 935 (1965), it is contended that a president's decision is final in determining what evidence is to

be used in a given criminal case. Although his counsel concedes that the president has delegated certain specific powers to the special prosecutor, he has not "waived nor delegated to the special prosecutor the president's duty to claim privilege as to all materials . . . which fall within the president's inherent authority to refuse to disclose to any executive officer." Brief for the President 42. The special prosecutor's demand for the items therefore presents, in the view of the president's counsel, a political question under *Baker* v. *Carr*, 369 U.S. 186 (1962), since it involves a "textually demonstrable" grant of power under Art. II.

The mere assertion of a claim of an "intra-branch dispute," without more, has never operated to defeat federal jurisdiction; justiciability does not depend on such a surface inquiry. In *United States* v. *ICC*, 337 U.S. 426 (1949), the Court observed, "courts must look behind names that symbolize the parties to determine whether a justiciable case or controversy is p'esented." *Id.*, at 430. See also *Powell* v. *McCormack*, 395 U.S. 486 (1969); *ICC* v. *Jersey City*, 322 U.S. 503 (1944); *United States ex rel. Chapman* v. *FPC*,

Source: United States v. *Nixon*, 418 U.S. 683 (1974). Some parts of the Supreme Court's decision omitted; footnotes renumbered.

345 U.S. 153 (1953); *Secretary of Agriculture* v. *United States*, 347 U.S. 645 (1954); *FMB* v. *Isbrandtsen Co.*, 356 U.S. 481, 483 n. 2 (1958); *United States* v. *Marine Bancorporation, ante,* p. 602; and *United States* v. *Connecticut National Bank, ante,* p. 656.

Our starting point is the nature of the proceeding for which the evidence is sought—here a pending criminal prosecution. It is a judicial proceeding in a federal court alleging violation of federal laws and is brought in the name of the United States as sovereign. *Berger* v. *United States*, 295 U.S. 78, 88 (1935). Under the authority of Art. II, §2, Congress has vested in the attorney general the power to conduct the criminal litigation of the United States government. 28 U. S. C. § 516. It has also vested in him the power to appoint subordinate officers to assist him in the discharge of his duties. 28 U. S. C. §§ 509, 510, 515, 533. Acting pursuant to those statutes, the attorney general has delegated the authority to represent the United States in these particular matters to a special prosecutor with unique authority and tenure.[1] The regulation gives the special prosecutor explicit power to contest the invocation of executive privilege in the process of seeking evidence deemed relevant to the performance of these specially delegated duties.[2] 38 Fed. Reg. 30739, as amended by 38 Fed. Reg. 32805.

So long as this regulation is extant it has the force of law. In *United States ex rel. Accardi* v. *Shaughnessy*, 347 U.S. 260 (1954), regulations of the attorney general delegated certain of his discretionary powers to the Board of Immigration Appeals and required that board to exercise its own discretion on appeals in deportation cases. The Court held that so long as the attorney general's regulations remained operative, he denied himself the authority to exercise the discretion delegated to the board even though the original authority was his and he could reassert it by amending the regulations. *Service* v. *Dulles*, 354

U.S. 363, 388 (1957), and *Vitarelli* v. *Seaton*, 359 U.S. 535 (1959), reaffirmed the basic holding of *Accardi*.

Here, as in *Accardi*, it is theoretically possible for the attorney general to amend or revoke the regulation defining the special prosecutor's authority. But he has not done so.[3] So long as this regulation remains in force the executive branch is bound by it, and indeed the United States as the sovereign composed of the three branches is bound to respect and to enforce it. Moreover, the delegation of authority to the special prosecutor in this case is not an ordinary delegation by the attorney general to a subordinate officer: with the authorization of the president, the acting attorney general provided in the regulation that the special prosecutor was not to be removed without the "consensus" of eight designated leaders of Congress. N. 8, *supra*.

The demands of and the resistance to the subpoena present an obvious controversy in the ordinary sense, but that alone is not sufficient to meet constitutional standards. In the constitutional sense, controversy means more than disagreement and conflict; rather it means the kind of controversy courts traditionally resolve. Here at issue is the production or nonproduction of specified evidence deemed by the special prosecutor to be relevant and admissible in a pending criminal case. It is sought by one official of the executive branch within the scope of his express authority; it is resisted by the chief executive on the ground of his duty to preserve the confidentiality of the communications of the president. Whatever the correct answer on the merits, these issues are "of a type which are traditionally justiciable." *United States* v. *ICC*, 337 U.S., at 430. The independent special prosecutor with his asserted need for the subpoenaed material in the underlying criminal prosecution is opposed by the president with his steadfast assertion of privilege against disclosure of the material. This setting assures there is "that concrete adverseness which sharpens the presentation of issues upon which the court so largely depends for illumination of difficult constitutional questions." *Baker* v. *Carr*, 369 U.S., at 204. Moreover, since the matter is one arising in the regular course of a federal criminal prosecution, it is within the traditional scope of Art. III power. *Id.*, at 198.

In light of the uniqueness of the setting in which the conflict arises, the fact that both parties are officers of the executive branch cannot be viewed as a barrier to justiciability. It would be inconsistent with the applicable law and regulation, and the unique facts of this case to conclude other than that the special prosecutor has standing to bring this action and that a justiciable controversy is presented for decision.

RULE 17 (c)

The subpoena *duces tecum* is challenged on the ground that the special prosecutor failed to satisfy the requirements of Fed. Rule Crim. Proc. 17 (c), which governs the issuance of subpoenas *duces tecum* in federal criminal proceedings. If we sustained this challenge, there would be no occasion to reach the claim of privilege asserted with respect to the subpoenaed material. Thus we turn to the question whether the requirements of Rule 17 (c) have been satisfied. See *Arkansas Louisiana Gas Co.* v. *Dept. of Public Utilities*, 304 U.S. 61, 64 (1938); *Ashwander* v. *TVA*, 297 U.S. 288, 346-347 (1936) (Brandeis, J., concurring).

Rule 17 (c) provides:

A subpoena may also command the person to whom it is directed to produce the books, papers, documents or other objects designated therein. The court on motion made promptly may quash or modify the subpoena if compliance would be unreasonable or oppressive. The court may direct that books, papers, documents or objects designated in the subpoena be produced before the court at a time prior to the trial or prior to the time when they are to be offered in evidence and may upon their production permit the books, papers, documents or objects or portions thereof to be inspected by the parties and their attorneys.

A subpoena for documents may be quashed if their production would be "unreasonable or oppressive," but not otherwise. The leading case in this Court interpreting this standard is *Bowman Dairy Co.* v. *United States*, 341 U.S. 214 (1951). This case recognized certain fundamental characteristics of the subpoena *duces tecum* in criminal cases: (1) it was not intended to provide a means of discovery for criminal cases, *id.*, at 220; (2) its chief innovation was to expedite the trial by providing a time and place *before* trial for the inspection of subpoenaed materials,[4] *ibid.* As both parties agree, cases decided in the wake of *Bowman* have generally followed Judge Weinfeld's formulation in *United States* v. *Iozia*, 13 F. R. D. 335, 338 (SDNY 1952), as to the required showing. Under this test, in order to require production prior to trial, the moving party must show:

(1) that the documents are evidentiary[5] and relevant;
(2) that they are not otherwise procurable reasonably in advance of trial by exercise of due diligence;
(3) that the party cannot properly prepare for trial without such production and inspection in advance of trial and that the failure to obtain such inspection may tend unreasonably to delay the trial; and
(4) that the application is made in good faith and is not intended as a general "fishing expedition."

Against this background, the special prosecutor, in order to carry his burden, must clear three hurdles: (1) relevancy; (2) admissibility; (3) specificity. Our own review of the record necessarily affords a less comprehensive view of the total situation than was available to the trial judge and we are unwilling to conclude that the district court erred in the evaluation of the special prosecutor's showing under Rule 17 (c). Our conclusion is based on the record before us, much of which is under seal. Of course, the contents of the subpoenaed tapes could not at that stage be described fully by the special prosecutor, but there was a sufficient likelihood that each of the tapes contains conversations relevant to the offenses charged in the indictment. *United States* v. *Gross*, 24 F. R. D. 138 (SDNY 1959). With respect to many of the tapes, the special prosecutor offered the sworn testimony or statements of one or more of the participants in the conversations as to what was said at the time. As for the remainder of the tapes, the identity of the participants and the time and place of the conversations, taken in their total context, permit a rational inference that at least part of the conversations relate to the offenses charged in the indictment.

We also conclude there was a sufficient preliminary showing that each of the subpoenaed tapes contains evidence admissible with respect to the offenses charged in the indictment. The most cogent objection to the admissibility of the taped conversations here at issue is that they are a collection of out-of-court statements by declarants who will not be subject to cross-examination and that the statements are therefore inadmissible heresay. Here, however, most of the tapes apparently contain conversations to which one or more of the defendants named in the indictment were party. The heresay rule does not automatically bar all out-of-court statements by a defendant in a criminal case.[6] Declarations by one defendant may also be admissible against other defendants upon a sufficient showing, by independent evidence,[7] of a conspiracy among one or more other defendants and the declarant and if the declarations at issue were in furtherance of that conspiracy. The same is true of declarations of coconspirators who are not defendants in the case on trial. *Dutton* v. *Evans*, 400 U.S. 74, 81 (1970). Recorded conversations may also be admissible for the limited purpose of impeaching the credibility of any defendant who testifies or any other coconspirator who testifies. Generally, the need for evidence to impeach witnesses is insufficient to require its production in advance of trial. See, e. g., *United States* v. *Carter*, 15 F. R. D. 367, 371 (DC 1954). Here, however, there are other valid potential evidentiary uses for the same material, and the analysis and possible transcription of the tapes may take a significant period of time. Accordingly, we cannot conclude that the district court erred in authorizing the issuance of the subpoena *duces tecum*.

Enforcement of a pretrial subpoena *duces tecum* must necessarily be committed to the sound discretion of the trial court since the necessity for the subpoena most often turns upon a determination of factual issues. Without a determination of arbitrariness or that the trial court finding was without record support, an appellate court will not ordinarily disturb a finding that the applicant for a subpoena complied with Rule 17 (c). See, e. g., *Sue* v. *Chicago Transit Authority*, 279 F. 2d 416, 419 (CA7 1960); *Shotkin* v. *Nelson*, 146 F. 2d 402 (CA10 1944).

In a case such as this, however, where a subpoena is directed to a president of the United States, appellate review, in deference to a coordinate branch of government, should be particularly meticulous to ensure that the standards of Rule 17 (c) have been correctly applied. *United States* v. *Burr*, 25 F. Cas. 30, 34 (No. 14,692d) (CC Va. 1807). From our examination of the materials submitted by the special prosecutor to the district court in support of his motion for the subpoena, we are persuaded that the district court's denial of the president's motion to quash the subpoena was consistent with Rule 17 (c). We also conclude that the special prosecutor has made a sufficient showing to justify a subpoena for production *before* trial. The subpoenaed materials are not available from any other source, and their examination and processing should not await trial in the circumstances shown. *Bowman Dairy Co. v. United States*, 341 U.S. 214 (1951); *United States v. Iozia*, 13 F. R. D. 335 (SDNY 1952).

THE CLAIM OF PRIVILEGE

A

Having determined that the requirements of Rule 17 (c) were satisfied, we turn to the claim that the subpoena should be quashed because it demands "confidential conversations between a president and his close advisors that it would be inconsistent with the public interest to produce." App. 48a. The first contention is a broad claim that the separation of powers doctrine precludes judicial review of a president's claim of privilege. The second contention is that if he does not prevail on the claim of absolute privilege, the court should hold as a matter of constitutional law that the privilege prevails over the subpoena *duces tecum*.

In the performance of assigned constitutional duties each branch of the government must initially interpret the Constitution, and the interpretation of its powers by any branch is due great respect from the others. The president's counsel, as we have noted, reads the Constitution as providing an absolute privilege of confidentiality for all presidential communications. Many decisions of this Court, however, have unequivocally reaffirmed the holding of *Marbury v. Madison*, 1 Cranch 137 (1803), that "[i]t is emphatically the province and duty of the judicial department to say what the law is." *Id.*, at 177.

No holding of the Court has defined the scope of judicial power specifically relating to the enforcement of a subpoena for confidential presidential communications for use in a criminal prosecution, but other exercises of power by the executive branch and the legislative branch have been found invalid as in conflict with the Constitution. *Powell v. McCormack*, 395 U.S.

486 (1969); *Youngstown Sheet & Tube Co. v. Sawyer*, 343 U.S. 579 (1952). In a series of cases, the Court interpreted the explicit immunity conferred by express provisions of the Constitution on members of the House and Senate by the Speech or Debate Clause, U.S. Const. Art. I, § 6. *Doe v. McMillan*, 412 U.S. 306 (1973); *Gravel v. United States*, 408 U.S. 606 (1972); *United States v. Brewster*, 408 U.S. 501 (1972); *United States v. Johnson*, 383 U.S. 169 (1966). Since this Court has consistently exercised the power to construe and delineate claims arising under express powers, it must follow that the Court has authority to interpret claims with respect to powers alleged to derive from enumerated powers.

Our system of government "requires that federal courts on occasion interpret the Constitution in a manner at variance with the construction given the document by another branch." *Powell v. McCormack, supra*, at 549. And in *Baker v. Carr*, 369 U.S., at 211, the Court stated:

> Deciding whether a matter has in any measure been committed by the Constitution to another branch of government, or whether the action of that branch exceeds whatever authority has been committed, is itself a delicate exercise in constitutional interpretation, and is a responsibility of this Court as ultimate interpreter of the Constitution.

Notwithstanding the deference each branch must accord the others, the "judicial Power of the United States" vested in the federal courts by Art. III, § 1, of the Constitution can no more be shared with the executive branch than the chief executive, for example, can share with the judiciary the veto power, or the Congress share with the judiciary the power to override a presidential veto. Any other conclusion would be contrary to the basic concept of separation of powers and the checks and balances that flow from the scheme of a tripartite government. The Federalist, No. 47, p. 313 (S. Mittell ed. 1938). We therefore reaffirm that it is the province and duty of this Court "to say what the law is" with respect to the claim of privilege presented in this case. *Marbury* v. *Madison, supra,* at 177.

B

In support of his claim of absolute privilege, the president's counsel urges two grounds, one of which is common to all governments and one of which is peculiar to our system of separation of powers. The first ground is the valid need for protection of communications between high government officials and those who advise and assist them in the performance of their manifold duties; the importance of this confidentiality is too plain to require further discussion. Human experience teaches that those who expect public dissemination of their remarks may well temper candor with a concern for appearances and for their own interests to the detriment of the decisionmaking process.[8] Whatever the nature of the privilege of confidentiality of presidential communications in the exercise of Art. II powers, the privilege can be said to derive from the supremacy of each branch within its own assigned area of constitutional duties. Certain powers and privileges flow from the nature of enumerated powers;[9] the protection of the confidentiality of presidential communications has similar constitutional underpinnings.

The second ground asserted by the president's counsel in support of the claim of absolute privilege rests on the doctrine of separation of powers. Here it is argued that the independence of the executive branch within its own sphere, *Humphrey's Executor* v. *United States,* 295 U.S. 602, 629-630 (1935); *Kilbourn* v. *Thompson,* 103 U.S. 168, 190-191 (1881), insulates a president from a judicial subpoena in an ongoing criminal prosecution, and thereby protects confidential presidential communications.

However, neither the doctrine of separation of powers, nor the need for confidentiality of high-level communications, without more, can sustain an absolute, unqualified presidential privilege of immunity from judicial process under all circumstances. The president's need for complete candor and objectivity from advisers calls for great deference from the courts. However, when the privilege depends solely on the broad, undifferentiated claim of public interest in the confidentiality of such conversations, a confrontation with other values arises. Absent a claim of need to protect military, diplomatic, or sensitive national security secrets, we find it difficult to accept the argument that even the very important interest in confidentiality of presidential communications is significantly diminished by production of such material for *in camera* inspection with all the protection that a district court will be obliged to provide.

The impediment that an absolute, unqualified privilege would place in the way of the primary constitutional duty of the judicial branch to do justice in criminal prosecutions would plainly conflict with the function of the courts under Art. III. In designing the structure of our government and dividing and allocating the sovereign power among three co-equal branches, the framers of the Constitution sought to provide a comprehensive system, but the separate powers were not intended to operate with absolute independence.

> While the Constitution diffuses power the better to secure liberty, it also contemplates that practice will integrate the dispersed powers into a workable government. It enjoins upon its branches separateness but interdependence, autonomy but reciprocity. *Youngstown Sheet & Tube Co.* v. *Sawyer,* 343 U.S., at 635 (Jackson, J., concurring).

To read the Art. II powers of the president as providing an absolute privilege as against a subpoena essential to enforcement of criminal statutes on no more than a generalized claim of the public interest in confidentiality of nonmilitary and nondiplomatic discussions would upset the constitutional balance of "a workable government" and gravely impair the role of the courts under Art. III.

C

Since we conclude that the legitimate needs of the judicial process may outweigh presidential privilege, it is necessary to resolve those competing interests in a manner that preserves the essential functions of each branch. The right and indeed the duty to resolve that question does not free the judiciary from according high respect to the representations made on behalf of the president. *United States* v. *Burr*, 25 F. Cas. 187, 190, 191-192 (No. 14,694) (CC Va. 1807).

The expectation of a president to the confidentiality of his conversations and correspondence, like the claim of confidentiality of judicial deliberations, for example, has all the values to which we accord deference for the privacy of all citizens and, added to those values, is the necessity for protection of the public interest in candid, objective, and even blunt or harsh opinions in presidential decisionmaking. A president and those who assist him must be free to explore alternatives in the process of shaping policies and making decisions and to do so in a way many would be unwilling to express except privately. These are the considerations justifying a presumptive privilege for presidential communications. The privilege is fundamental to the operation of government and inextricably rooted in the separation of powers under the Constitution.[10] In *Nixon* v. *Sirica*, 159 U.S. App. D. C. 58, 487 F. 2d 700 (1973), the court of appeals held that such presidential communications are "presumptively privileged," *id.*, at 75, 487 F. 2d, at 717, and this position is accepted by both parties in the present litigation. We agree with Mr. Chief Justice Marshall's observation, therefore, that "[i]n no case of this kind would a court be required to proceed against the president as against an ordinary individual." *United States* v. *Burr*, 25 F. Cas., at 192.

But this presumptive privilege must be considered in light of our historic commitment to the rule of law. This is nowhere more profoundly manifest than in our view that "the twofold aim [of criminal justice] is that guilt shall not escape or innocence suffer. *Berger* v. *United States*, 295 U.S., at 88. We have elected to employ an adversary system of criminal justice in which the parties contest all issues before a court of law. The need to develop all relevant facts in the adversary system is both fundamental and comprehensive. The ends of criminal justice would be defeated if judgments were to be founded on a partial or speculative presentation of the facts. The very integrity of the judicial system and public confidence in the system depend on full disclosure of all the facts, within the framework of the rules of evidence. To ensure that justice is done, it is imperative to the function of courts that compulsory process be available for the production of evidence needed either by the prosecution or by the defense.

Only recently the Court restated the ancient proposition of law, albeit in the context of a grand jury inquiry rather than a trial,

> that "the public . . . has a right to every man's evidence," except for those persons protected by a constitutional, common-law, or statutory privilege, *United States* v. *Bryan*, 339 U.S. [323, 331, (1950)]; *Blackmer* v. *United States*, 284, U.S. 421, 438 (1932). . . . *Branzburg* v. *Hayes*, 408 U.S. 665, 688 (1972).

The privileges referred to by the Court are designed to protect weighty and legitimate competing interests. Thus, the Fifth Amendment to the Constitution provides that no man "shall be compelled in any criminal case to be a witness against himself." And, generally, an attorney or a priest may not be required to disclose what has been revealed in professional confidence. These and other interests are recognized in law by privileges against forced disclosure, established in the Constitution, by statute, or at common law. Whatever their origins, these exceptions to the demand for every man's evidence are not lightly created nor expansively construed, for they are in derogation of the search for truth.[11]

In this case the president challenges a subpoena served on him as a third party requiring the production of materials for use in a criminal prosecution; he does so on the claim that he has a privilege against disclosure of confidential communications. He does not place his claim of privilege on the ground they are military or diplomatic secrets. As to these areas of Art. II duties the courts have traditionally shown the utmost deference to presidential responsibilities. In C. & S. Air Lines v. Waterman S. S. Corp., 333 U.S. 103, 111 (1948), dealing with presidential authority involving foreign policy considerations, the Court said:

> The President, both as Commander-in-Chief and as the Nation's organ for foreign affairs, has available intelligence services whose reports are not and ought not to be published to the world. It would be intolerable that courts, without the relevant information, should review and perhaps nullify actions of the Executive taken on information properly held secret.

In United States v. Reynolds, 345 U. S. 1 (1953), dealing with a claimant's demand for evidence in a Tort Claims Act case against the government, the Court said:

> It may be possible to satisfy the court, from all the circumstances of the case, that there is a reasonable danger that compulsion of the evidence will expose military matters which, in the interest of national security, should not be divulged. When this is the case, the occasion for the privilege is appropriate, and the court should not jeopardize the security which the privilege is meant to protect by insisting upon an examination of the evidence, even by the judge alone, in chambers. Id., at 10.

No case of the Court, however, has ex-

tended this high degree of deference to a president's generalized interest in confidentiality. Nowhere in the Constitution, as we have noted earlier, is there any explicit reference to a privilege of confidentiality, yet to the extent this interest relates to the effective discharge of a president's powers, it is constitutionally based.

The right to the production of all evidence at a criminal trial similarly has constitutional dimensions. The Sixth Amendment explicitly confers upon every defendant in a criminal trial the right "to be confronted with the witnesses against him" and "to have compulsory process for obtaining witnesses in his favor." Moreover, the Fifth Amendment also guarantees that no person shall be deprived of liberty without due process of law. It is the manifest duty of the courts to vindicate those guarantees, and to accomplish that it is essential that all relevant and admissible evidence be produced.

In this case we must weigh the importance of the general privilege of confidentiality of presidential communications in performance of the president's responsibilities against the inroads of such a privilege on the fair administration of criminal justice.[12] The interest in preserving confidentiality is weighty indeed and entitled to great respect. However, we cannot conclude that advisers will be moved to temper the candor of their remarks by the infrequent occasions of disclosure because of the possibility that such conversations will be called for in the context of a criminal prosecution.[13]

On the other hand, the allowance of the privilege to withhold evidence that is demonstrably relevant in a criminal trial would cut deeply into the guarantee of due process of law and gravely impair the basic function of the courts. A president's acknowledged need for confidentiality in the communications of his office is general in nature, whereas the constitutional need for production of relevant evidence in a criminal proceeding is specific and central to the fair adjudication of a particular criminal case in the administration of justice. Without access to specific facts a criminal prosecution may be totally frustrated. The president's broad interest in confidentiality of communications will not be vitiated by disclosure of a limited number of conversations preliminarily shown to have some bearing on the pending criminal cases.

We conclude that when the ground for asserting privilege as to subpoenaed materials sought for use in a criminal trial is based only on the generalized interest in confidentiality, it cannot prevail over the fundamental demands of due process of law in the fair administration of criminal justice. The generalized assertion of privilege must yield to the demonstrated, specific need for evidence in a pending criminal trial. . . .

NOTES

1. The regulation issued by the attorney general pursuant to his statutory authority, vests in the special prosecutor plenary authority to control the course of investigations and litigation related to

all offenses arising out of the 1972 Presidential Election for which the Special Prosecutor deems it necessary and appropriate to assume responsibility, allegations involving the President, members of the White House staff, or Presidential appointees, and any other matters which he consents to have assigned to him by the Attorney General." 38 Fed. Reg. 30739, as amended by 38 Fed. Reg. 32805. In particular, the Special Prosecutor was given full authority, *inter alia*, "to contest the assertion of 'Executive Privilege' . . . and handl[e] all aspects of any cases within his jurisdiction." *Id.*, at 30739.

The regulation then goes on to provide:

In exercising this authority, the Special Prosecutor will have the greatest degree of independence that is consistent with the Attorney General's statutory accountability for all matters falling within the jurisdiction of the Department of Justice. The Attorney

General will not countermand or interfere with the Special Prosecutor's decisions or actions. The Special Prosecutor will determine whether and to what extent he will inform or consult with the Attorney General about the conduct of his duties and responsibilities. In accordance with assurances given by the President to the Attorney General that the President will not exercise his Constitutional powers to effect the discharge of the Special Prosecutor or to limit the independence that he is hereby given, the Special Prosecutor will not be removed from his duties except for extraordinary improprieties on his part and without the President's first consulting the Majority and the Minority Leaders and Chairmen and ranking Minority Members of the Judiciary Committees of the Senate and House of Representatives and ascertaining that their consensus is in accord with his proposed action.

2. That this was the understanding of Acting Attorney General Robert Bork, the author of the regulation establishing the independence of the special prosecutor, is shown by his testimony before the Senate Judiciary Committee:

Although it is anticipated that Mr. Jaworski will receive cooperation from the White House in getting any evidence he feels he needs to conduct investigations and prosecutions, it is clear and understood on all sides that he has the power to use judicial processes to pursue evidence if disagreement should develop.

Hearings on the special prosecutor before the Senate Committee on the Judiciary, 93d Cong., 1st Sess., pt. 2, 450 (1973).

Acting Attorney General Bork gave similar assurances to the House Subcommittee on Criminal Justice. Hearings on H. J. Res. 784 and H. R. 10937 before the Subcommittee on Criminal Justice of the House Committee on the Judiciary, 93d Cong., 1st Sess., 266 (1973). At his confirmation hearings, Attorney General William Saxbe testified that he shared Acting Attorney General Bork's views concerning the special prosecutor's authority to test any claim of executive privilege in the courts. Hearings on the Nomination of William B. Saxbe to be Attorney General before the Senate Committee on the Judiciary, 93d Cong., 1st Sess., 9 (1973).

3. At his confirmation hearings, Attorney General William Saxbe testified that he agreed with the regulation adopted by Acting Attorney General Bork and would not remove the Special Prosecutor except for

"gross impropriety." *Id.*, at 5-6, 8-10. There is no contention here that the special prosecutor is guilty of any such impropriety.

4. The Court quoted a statement of a member of the advisory committee that the purpose of the rule was to bring documents into court

> in advance of the time that they are offered in evidence, so that they may then be inspected in advance, for the purpose . . . of enabling the party to see whether he can use [them] or whether he wants to use [them]. 341 U.S., at 220 n. 5.

The *Manual for Complex and Multidistrict Litigation* published by the Federal Judicial Center recommends that use of Rule 17 (c) be encouraged in complex criminal cases in order that each party may be compelled to produce its documentary evidence well in advance of trial and in advance of the time it is to be offered. P. 150.

5. The district court found here that it was faced with "the more unusual situation . . . where the subpoena, rather than being directed to the government by defendants, issues to what, as a practical matter, is a third party." *United States* v. *Mitchell*, 377 F. Supp. 1326, 1330 (DC 1974). The special prosecutor suggests that the evidentiary requirement of *Bowman Dairy Co.* and *Iozia* does not apply in its full vigor when the subpoena *duces tecum* is issued to third parties rather than to government prosecutors. Brief for United States 128-129. We need not decide whether a lower standard exists because we are satisfied that the relevance and evidentiary nature of the subpoenaed tapes were sufficiently shown as a preliminary matter to warrant the district court's refusal to quash the subpoena.

6. Such statements are declarations by a party defendant that "would surmount all objections based on the hearsay rule . . ." and, at least as to the declarant himself, "would be admissible for whatever inferences" might be reasonably drawn. *United States* v. *Matlock*, 415 U.S. 164, 172 (1974). *On Lee* v. *United States*, 343 U.S. 747, 757, (1952). See also C. McCormick, Evidence § 270, pp. 651-652 (2d ed. 1972).

7. As a preliminary matter, there must be substantial, independent evidence of the conspiracy, at least enough to take the question to the jury. *United States* v. *Vaught*, 485 F. 2d 320, 323 (CA4 1973); *United States* v. *Hoffa*, 349 F. 2d 20, 41-42 (CA6 1965), aff'd on other grounds, 385 U.S. 293 (1966); *United States* v. *Santos*, 385 F. 2d 43, 45

(CA7 1967), cert. denied, 390 U.S. 954 (1968); *United States* v. *Morton*, 483 F. 2d 573, 576 (CA8 1973); *United States* v. *Spanos*, 462 F. 2d 1012, 1014 (CA9 1972); *Carbo* v. *United States*, 314 F. 2d 718, 737 (CA9 1963), cert. denied, 377 U.S. 953 (1964). Whether the standard has been satisfied is a question of admissibility of evidence to be decided by the trial judge.

8. There is nothing novel about governmental confidentiality. The meetings of the constitutional convention in 1787 were conducted in complete privacy. 1 M. Farrand, The Records of the Federal Convention of 1787, pp. xi-xxv (1911). Moreover, all records of those meetings were sealed for more than 30 years after the convention. See 3 Stat. 475, 15th Cong., 1st Sess., Res. 8 (1818). Most of the framers acknowledged that without secrecy no constitution of the kind that was developed could have been written. C. Warren, The Making of the Constitution 134-139 (1937).

9. The special prosecutor argues that there is no provision in the Constitution for a presidential privilege as to the president's communications corresponding to the privilege of members of Congress under the Speech or Debate Clause. But the silence of the Constitution on this score is not dispositive.

> The rule of constitutional interpretation announced in *McCulloch* v. *Maryland*, 4 Wheat. 316, that that which was reasonably appropriate and relevant to the exercise of a granted power was to be considered as accompanying the grant, has been so universally applied that it suffices merely to state it. *Marshall* v. *Gordon*, 243 U.S. 521, 537 (1917).

10. Freedom of communication vital to fulfillment of the aims of wholesome relationships is obtained only by removing the spector of compelled disclosure. . . . [G]overnment . . . needs open but protected channels for the kind of plain talk that is essential to the quality of its functioning. *Carl Zeiss Stiftung* v. *V. E. B. Carl Zeiss, Jena*, 40 F. R. D. 318, 325 (DC 1966). See *Nixon* v. *Sirica*, 159 U.S. App. D. C. 58, 71, 487 F. 2d 700, 713 (1973); *Kaiser Aluminum & Chem. Cor'.* v. *United States*, 141 Ct. Cl. 38, 157 F. Supp. 939 (1958) (Reed, J.); The Federalist, No. 64 (S. Mittell ed. 1938).

11. Because of the key role of the testimony of witnesses in the judicial process, courts have historically been cautious about privileges. Mr. Justice Frankfurter, dissenting

in *Elkins* v. *United States*, 364 U.S. 206, 234 (1960), said of this:

Limitations are properly placed upon the operation of this general principle only to the very limited extent that permitting a refusal to testify or excluding relevant evidence has a public good transcending the normally predominant principle of utilizing all rational means for ascertaining truth.

12. We are not here concerned with the balance between the president's generalized interest in confidentiality and the need for relevant evidence in civil litigation, nor with that between the confidentiality interest and congressional demands for information, nor with the president's interest in preserving state secrets. We address only the conflict between the president's assertion of a generalized privilege of confidentiality and the constitutional need for relevant evidence in criminal trials.

13. Mr. Justice Cardozo made this point in an analogous context. Speaking for a unanimous Court in *Clark* v. *United States*, 289

U.S.1 (1933), he emphasized the importance of maintaining the secrecy of the deliberations of a petit jury in a criminal case.

Freedom of debate might be stifled and independence of thought checked if jurors were made to feel that their arguments and ballots were to be freely published to the world. *Id.*, at 13.

Nonetheless, the Court also recognized that isolated inroads on confidentiality designed to serve the paramount need of the criminal law would not vitiate the interests served by secrecy:

A juror of integrity and reasonable firmness will not fear to speak his mind if the confidences of debate are barred to the ears of mere impertinence or malice. He will not expect to be shielded against the disclosure of his conduct in the event that there is evidence reflecting upon his honor. The chance that now and then there may be found some timid soul who will take counsel of his fears and give way to their repressive power is too remote and shadowy to shape the course of justice. *Id.*, at 16.

36. Impoundment Control Act of 1974*

U.S. CONGRESS

TITLE X

IMPOUNDMENT CONTROL

PART A—GENERAL PROVISIONS

DISCLAIMER

Sec. 1001. Nothing contained in this Act, or in any amendments made by this Act, shall be construed as—

(1) asserting or conceding the constitutional powers or limitations of either the Congress or the President;

(2) ratifying or approving any impoundment heretofore or hereafter executed or approved by the President or any other Federal officer or employee, except insofar as pursuant to statutory authorization then in effect;

(3) affecting in any way the claims or

defenses of any party to litigation concerning any impoundment; or

(4) superseding any provision of law which requires the obligation of budget authority or the making of outlays thereunder.

AMENDMENT TO ANTIDEFICIENCY ACT

Sec. 1002. Section 3679 (c) (2) of the Revised Statutes, as amended (31 U.S.C. 665), is amended to read as follows:

(2) In apportioning any appropriation, reserves may be established solely to provide for contingencies, or to effect savings whenever savings are made possible by or through changes in requirements or greater efficiency of operations. Whenever it is determined by an officer designated in subsection (d) of this section to make appor-

Source: Title X of Public Law 93-344 (July 12, 1974).

tionments and reapportionments that any amount so reserved will not be required to carry out the full objectives and scope of the appropriation concerned, he shall recommend the rescission of such amount in the manner provided in the Budget and Accounting Act, 1921, for estimates of appropriations. Except as specifically provided by particular appropriations Acts or other laws, no reserves shall be established other than as authorized by this subsection. Reserves established pursuant to this subsection shall be reported to the Congress in accordance with the Impoundment Control Act of 1974.

REPEAL OF EXISTING IMPOUNDMENT REPORTING PROVISION

Sec. 1003. Section 203 of the Budget and Accounting Procedures Act of 1950 is repealed.

PART B—CONGRESSIONAL CONSIDERATION OF PROPOSED RESCISSIONS, RESERVATIONS, AND DEFERRALS OF BUDGET AUTHORITY

DEFINITIONS

Sec. 1011. For purposes of this part—

(1) "deferral of budget authority" includes—

(A) witholding or delaying the obligation or expenditure of budget authority (whether by establishing reserves or otherwise) provided for projects or activities; or

(B) any other type of Executive action or inaction which effectively precludes the obligation or expenditure of budget authority, including authority to obligate by contract in advance of appropriations as specifically authorized by law;

(2) "Comptroller General" means the Comptroller General of the United States;

(3) "rescission bill" means a bill or joint resolution which only rescinds, in whole or in part, budget authority proposed to be rescinded in a special message transmitted by the President under section 1012, and upon which the Congress completes action before the end of the first period of 45 calendar days of continuous session of the Congress after the date on which the President's message is received by the Congress;

(4) "impoundment resolution" means a resolution of the House of Representatives or the Senate which only expresses its disapproval of a proposed deferral of budget authority set forth in a special message transmitted by the President under section 1013; and

(5) continuity of a session of the Congress shall be considered as broken only by an adjournment of the Congress sine die, and the days on which either House is not in session because of an adjournment of more than 3 days to a day certain shall be excluded in the computation of the 45-day period referred to in paragraph (3) of this section and in section 1012, and the 25-day periods referred to in sections 1016 and 1017 (b) (1). If a special message is transmitted under section 1012 during any Congress and the last session of such Congress adjourns sine die before the expiration of 45 calendar days of continuous session (or a special message is so transmitted after the last session of the Congress adjourns sine die), the message shall be deemed to have been retransmitted on the first day of the succeeding Congress and the 45-day period referred to in paragraph (3) of this section and in section 1012 (with respect to such message) shall commence on the day after such first day.

RESCISSION OF BUDGET AUTHORITY

Sec. 1012. (a) Transmittal of Special Message.—Whenever the President determines that all or part of any budget authority will not be required to carry out the full objectives or scope of programs for which it is provided or that such budget authority should be rescinded for fiscal policy or other reasons (including the termination of authorized projects or activities for which budget authority has been provided), or whenever all or part of budget authority provided for only one fiscal year is to be reserved from obligation for such fiscal year, the President shall transmit to both Houses of Congress a special message specifying—

(1) the amount of budget authority which he proposes to be rescinded or which is to be so reserved;

(2) any account, department, or establishment of the Government to which such budget authority is available for obligation,

and the specific project or governmental functions involved;

(3) the reasons why the budget authority should be rescinded or is to be so reserved;

(4) to the maximum extent practicable, the estimated fiscal, economic, and budgetary effect of the proposed rescission or of the reservation; and

(5) all facts, circumstances, and considerations relating to or bearing upon the proposed rescission or the reservation and the decision to effect the proposed rescission or the reservation, and to the maximum extent practicable, the estimated effect of the proposed rescission or the reservation upon the objects, purposes, and programs for which the budget authority is provided.

(b) Requirement to Make Available for Obligation.—Any amount of budget authority proposed to be rescinded or that is to be reserved as set forth in such special message shall be made available for obligation unless, within the prescribed 45-day period, the Congress has completed action on a rescission bill rescinding all or part of the amount proposed to be rescinded or that is to be reserved.

DISAPPROVAL OF PROPOSED DEFERRALS OF BUDGET AUTHORITY

Sec. 1013. (a) Transmittal of Special Message.—Whenever the President, the Director of the Office of Management and Budget, the head of any department or agency of the United States, or any officer or employee of the United States proposes to defer any budget authority provided for a specific purpose or project, the President shall transmit to the House of Representatives and the Senate a special message specifying—

(1) the amount of the budget authority proposed to be deferred;

(2) any account, department, or establishment of the Government to which such budget authority is available for obligation, and the specific projects or governmental functions involved;

(3) the period of time during which the budget authority is proposed to be deferred;

(4) the reasons for the proposed deferral, including any legal authority invoked by him to justify the proposed deferral;

(5) to the maximum extent practicable, the estimated fiscal, economic, and budgetary effect of the proposed deferral; and

(6) all facts, circumstances, and considerations relating to or bearing upon the proposed deferral and the decision to effect the proposed deferral, including an analysis of such facts, circumstances, and considerations in terms of their application to any legal authority and specific elements of legal authority invoked by him to justify such proposed deferral, and to the maximum extent practicable, the estimated effect of the proposed deferral upon the objects, purposes, and programs for which the budget authority is provided.

A special message may include one or more proposed deferrals of budget authority. A deferral may not be proposed for any period of time extending beyond the end of the fiscal year in which the special message proposing the deferral is transmitted to the House and the Senate.

(b) Requirement to Make Available for Obligation.—Any amount of budget authority proposed to be deferred, as set forth in a special message transmitted under subsection (a), shall be made available for obligation if either House of Congress passes an impoundment resolution disapproving such proposed deferral.

(c) Exception.—The provisions of this section do not apply to any budget authority proposed to be rescinded or that is to be reserved as set forth in a special message required to be transmitted under section 1012.

TRANSMISSION OF MESSAGES; PUBLICATION

Sec. 1014. (a) Delivery to House and Senate.—Each special message transmitted under section 1012 or 1013 shall be transmitted to the House of Representatives and the Senate on the same day, and shall be delivered to the Clerk of the House of Representatives if the House is not in session, and to the Secretary of the Senate if the Senate is not in session. Each special message so transmitted shall be referred to the appropriate committee of the House of Representatives and the Senate. Each such message shall be printed as a document of each House.

(b) Delivery to Comptroller General.—A copy of each special message transmitted under section 1012 or 1013 shall be transmitted to the Comptroller General on the same day it is transmitted to the House of Representatives and the Senate. In order to assist the Congress in the exercise of its functions under sections 1012 and 1013, the Comptroller General shall review each such message and inform the House of Representatives and the Senate as promptly as practicable with respect to—

(1) in the case of a special message transmitted under section 1012, the facts surrounding the proposed rescission or the reservation of budget authority (including the probable effects thereof); and

(2) in the case of a special message transmitted under section 1013, (A) the facts surrounding each proposed deferral of budget authority (including the probable effects thereof) and (B) whether or not (or to what extent), in his judgment, such proposed deferral is in accordance with existing statutory authority.

(c) Transmission of Supplementary Messages.—If any information contained in a special message transmitted under section 1012 or 1013 is subsequently revised, the President shall transmit to both Houses of Congress and the Comptroller General a supplementary message stating and explaining such revision. Any such supplementary message shall be delivered, referred, and printed as provided in subsection (a). The Comptroller General shall promptly notify the House of Representatives and the Senate of any changes in the information submitted by him under subsection (b) which may be necessitated by such revision.

(d) Printing in Federal Register—Any special message transmitted under section 1012 or 1013, and any supplemen-

tary message transmitted under subsection (c), shall be printed in the first issue of the Federal Register published after such transmittal.

(e) Cumulative Reports of Proposed Rescissions, Reservations, and Deferrals of Budget Authority.—

(1) The President shall submit a report to the House of Representatives and the Senate, not later than the 10th day of each month during a fiscal year, listing all budget authority for that fiscal year with respect to which, as of the first day of such month—

(A) he has transmitted a special message under section 1012 with respect to a proposed rescission or a reservation; and

(B) he has transmitted a special message under section 1013 proposing a deferral.

Such report shall also contain, with respect to each such proposed rescission or deferral, or each such reservation, the information required to be submitted in the special message with respect thereto under section 1012 or 1013.

(2) Each report submitted under paragraph (1) shall be printed in the first issue of the Federal Register published after its submission.

REPORTS BY COMPTROLLER GENERAL

Sec. 1015. (a) Failure to Transmit Special Message.—If the Comptroller General finds that the President, the Director of the Office of Management and Budget, the head of any department or agency of the United States, or any other officer or employee of the United States—

(1) is to establish a reserve or proposes to defer budget authority with respect to which the President is required to transmit a special message under section 1012 or 1013; or

(2) has ordered, permitted, or approved the establishment of such a reserve or a deferral of budget authority;

and that the President has failed to transmit a special message with respect to such reserve or deferral, the Comptroller General shall make a report on such reserve or deferral and any available information concerning it to both

Houses of Congress. The provisions of this part shall apply with respect to such reserve or deferral in the same manner and with the same effect as if such report of the Comptroller General were a special message transmitted by the President under section 1012 or 1013, and, for purposes of this part, such report shall be considered a special message transmitted under section 1012 or 1013.

(b) Incorrect Classification of Special Message.—If the President has transmitted a special message to both Houses of Congress in accordance with section 1012 or 1013, and the Comptroller General believes that the President so transmitted the special message in accordance with one of those sections when the special message should have been transmitted in accordance with the other of those sections, the Comptroller General shall make a report to both Houses of the Congress setting forth his reasons.

SUITS BY COMPTROLLER GENERAL

Sec. 1016. If, under section 1012(b) or 1013(b), budget authority is required to be made available for obligation and such budget authority is not made available for obligation, the Comptroller General is hereby expressly empowered, through attorneys of his own selection, to bring a civil action in the United States District Court for the District of Columbia to require such budget authority to be made available for obligation, and such court is hereby expressly empowered to enter in such civil action, against any department, agency, officer, or employee of the United States, any decree, judgement, or order which may be necessary or appropriate to make such budget authority available for obligation. The courts shall give precedence to civil actions brought under this section, and to appeals and writs from decisions in such actions, over all other civil actions, appeals, and writs. No civil action shall be brought by the Comptroller General under this section until the expiration of 25 calen-

dar days of continuous session of the Congress following the date on which an explanatory statement by the Comptroller General of the circumstances giving rise to the action contemplated has been filed with the Speaker of the House of Representatives and the President of the Senate.

PROCEDURE IN HOUSE AND SENATE

Sec. 1017. (a) *Referral*.—Any rescission bill introduced with respect to a special message or impoundment resolution introduced with respect to a proposed deferral of budget authority shall be referred to the appropriate committee of the House of Representatives or the Senate, as the case may be.

(b) *Discharge of Committee.*—

(1) If the committee to which a rescission bill or impoundment resolution has been referred has not reported it at the end of 25 calendar days of continuous session of the Congress after its introduction, it is in order to move either to discharge the committee from further consideration of the bill or resolution or to discharge the committee from further consideration of any other rescission bill with respect to the same special message or impoundment resolution with respect to the same proposed deferral, as the case may be, which has been referred to the committee.

(2) A motion to discharge may be made only by an individual favoring the bill or resolution, may be made only if supported by one-fifth of the Members of the House involved (a quorum being present), and is highly privileged in the House and privileged in the Senate (except that it may not be made after the committee has reported a bill or resolution with respect to the same special message or the same proposed deferral, as the case may be); and debate thereon shall be limited to not more than 1 hour, the time to be divided in the House equally between those favoring and those opposing the bill or resolution, and to be divided in the Senate equally between, and controlled by, the majority leader and the minority leader and their designees. An amendment to the motion is not in order, and it is not in order to move to reconsider the vote by which the motion is agreed to or disagreed to.

(c) *Floor Consideration in the House.—*

(1) When the committee of the House of Representatives has reported, or has been discharged from further consideration of, a rescission bill or impoundment resolution, it shall at any time thereafter be in order (even though a previous motion to the same effect has been disagreed to) to move to proceed to the consideration of the bill or resolution. The motion shall be highly privileged and not debatable. An amendment to the motion shall not be in order, nor shall it be in order to move to reconsider the vote by which the motion is agreed to or disagreed to.

(2) Debate on a rescission bill or impoundment resolution shall be limited to not more than 2 hours, which shall be divided equally between those favoring and those opposing the bill or resolution. A motion further to limit debate shall not be debatable. In the case of an impoundment resolution, no amendment to, or motion to recommit, the resolution shall be in order. It shall not be in order to move to reconsider the vote by which a rescission bill or impoundment resolution is agreed to or disagreed to.

(3) Motions to postpone, made with respect to the consideration of a rescission bill or impoundment resolution, and motions to proceed to the consideration of other business, shall be decided without debate.

(4) All appeals from the decisions of the Chair relating to the application of the Rules of the House of Representatives to the procedure relating to any rescission bill or impoundment resolution shall be decided without debate.

(5) Except to the extent specifically provided in the preceding provisions of this subsection, consideration of any rescission bill or impoundment resolution and amendments thereto (or any conference report thereon) shall be governed by the Rules of the House of Representatives applicable to other bills and resolutions, amendments, and conference reports in similar circumstances.

(d) *Floor Consideration in the Senate.—*

(1) Debate in the Senate on any rescission bill or impoundment resolution, and all amendments thereto (in the case of a rescission bill) and debatable motions and appeals in connection therewith, shall be limited to not more than 10 hours. The time shall be equally divided between, and controlled by, the majority leader and the minority leader or their designees.

(2) Debate in the Senate on any amendment to a rescission bill shall be limited to 2 hours, to be equally divided between, and controlled by, the mover and the manager of the bill. Debate on any amendment to an amendment, to such a bill, and debate on any debatable motion or appeal in connection with such a bill or an impoundment resolution shall be limited to 1 hour, to be equally divided between, and controlled by, the mover and the manager of the bill or resolution, except that in the event the manager of the bill or resolution is in favor of any such amendment, motion, or appeal, the time in opposition thereto, shall be controlled by the minority leader or his designee. No amendment that is not germane to the provisions of a rescission bill shall be received. Such leaders, or either of them, may, from the time under their control on the passage of a rescission bill or impoundment resolution, allot additional time to any Senator during the consideration of any amendment, debatable motion, or appeal.

(3) A motion to further limit debate is not debatable. In the case of a rescission bill, a motion to recommit (except a motion to recommit with instructions to report back within a specified number of days, not to exceed 3, not counting any day on which the Senate is not in session) is not in order. Debate on any such motion to recommit shall be limited to one hour, to be equally divided between, and controlled by, the mover and the manager of the concurrent resolution. In the case of an impoundment resolution, no amendment or motion to recommit is in order.

(4) The conference report or any rescission bill shall be in order in the Senate at any time after the third day (excluding Saturdays, Sundays, and legal holidays) following the day on which such a conference report is reported and is available to Members of the Senate. A motion to proceed to the consideration of the conference report may be made even though a previous motion to the same effect has been disagreed to.

(5) During the consideration in the Sen-

ate of the conference report on any rescission bill, debate shall be limited to 2 hours, to be equally divided between, and controlled by, the majority leader and minority leader or their designees. Debate on any debatable motion or appeal related to the conference report shall be limited to 30 minutes, to be equally divided between, and controlled by, the mover and the manager of the conference report.

(6) Should the conference report be defeated, debate on any request for a new conference and the appointment of conferees shall be limited to one hour, to be equally divided between, and controlled by, the manager of the conference report and the minority leader or his designee, and should any motion be made to instruct the conferees before the conferees are named, debate on such motion shall be limited to 30 minutes, to be equally divided between, and controlled by, the

mover and the manager of the conference report. Debate on any amendment to any such instructions shall be limited to 20 minutes, to be equally divided between, and controlled by, the mover and the manager of the conference report. In all cases when the manager of the conference report is in favor of any motion, appeal, or amendment, the time in opposition shall be under the control of the minority leader or his designee.

(7) In any case in which there are amendments in disagreement, time on each amendment shall be limited to 30 minutes, to be equally divided between, and controlled by, the manager of the conference report and the minority leader or his designee. No amendment that is not germane to the provisions of such amendments shall be received.

Approved July 12, 1974.

37. The Bureaucracy as a Check upon the President*

PETER WOLL
ROCHELLE JONES

Watergate has highlighted the dangers of the "imperial presidency." The growing power of the executive branch vis-à-vis Congress is an echo of past concerns. Franklin Roosevelt and the New Deal heralded the growth of the "executive" along modern lines, and it was generally thought then as now by critics of the policies of the president that the executive branch possessed entirely too much power to shape and implement public policies according to the wishes of the White House.

President Nixon is following closely in the path of Democratic presidents of

this century when he assumes—as he has—an active posture in facing the bureaucracy. He accepts the conclusions of the best theories of "scientific management" that the president must hold the reins on the bureaucracy, not only to check any exercise of independent bureaucratic power but also to point the vast array of agencies in the right policy directions. Only in this way can the bureaucracy operate efficiently. In line with these aspirations, the president has vastly expanded the Executive Office to coordinate administrative action in policymaking. Since FDR, similar at-

*Source: The Bureaucrat, vol. 3 (April 1974), pp. 8-20. Copyright © 1974 by the Bureaucrat, Inc. Reprinted by permission.

tempts have been made to coordinate bureaucratic activity under the control of the president.

Is the executive branch a monolithic organization headed by the president? If so, at least the organization of our system reflects the classical separation of powers model given reality in the Constitution, with only three branches of the government existing, checking and balancing each other. Those who view the executive branch as one are deeply concerned about its increasing dominance over the legislature, because of its superior resources, expertise, staying power, and the ability to seize the initiative in any power struggle with Congress. Certainly since the New Deal, a widespread school of thought has held that Congress functions within the shadow of the executive, exercising at best a veto power over recommendations of the executive branch. The struggle over impoundment of funds is but an extension of the script in the play about president versus Congress.

PRESIDENT AS "CHIEF ADMINISTRATOR"

Putting aside, for the moment, the question of whether or not the executive branch *is* a monolith under presidential control, *should it be* directly supervised by the White House? From the early scientific management school of this century to modern day management theory (so much a part of the business-management orientation of Nixon's top echelon), the answer is a resounding yes! A classic statement of this position is that of W. F. Willoughby, an early scientific management theorist:

It can be stated without any hesitation that a prime requisite of any proper administrative system is that . . . the chief executive shall be given all the duties and powers of a general manager and be made in fact, as well as in theory, the head of the administration.[1]

Why does it go without saying that the president is to be, to use Clinton Rossiter's term, "chief administrator"?

Because, to go back to Willoughby, certain advantages flow from this arrangement:

Fundamentally these advantages consist in making of the administrative branch, both as regards its organization and its practical operations, a single, integrated piece of administrative machinery, one in which its several parts, instead of being disjointed and unrelated, will be brought into adjustment with each other and together make a harmonious whole; one that possesses the capacity of formulating a general program and of subsequently seeing that such program as is formulated is properly carried out; one in which means are provided by which duplication of organization, plant personnel, or operations may be eliminated, conflicts of jurisdiction avoided or promptly settled, and standardization of methods of procedure secured; and finally, one in which responsibility is definitely located and means for enforcing this responsibility provided.[2]

These lines from Willoughby are quoted at length not because of their antiquarian value but because they express the premises of the original scientific management school, which have not been altered by most management theorists today as they analyze what is needed in the organization of the executive branch.

Apart from the reasons advanced by scientific management for centralization of control over the bureaucracy in presidential hands, many social scientists have been enamored of presidential power to overcome the influence of vested interests and to provide a focal point for nationwide democratic responsibility in the White House. The president, elected by all the people, must be able to carry out his programs. To do this, he must control the bureaucracy, as well as Congress. He must be chief administrator. The bureaucracy must be an extension of his power, not a limit upon it.

The need for increased presidential power in all areas was emphasized by liberal intellectuals during the New Deal. Franklin Roosevelt needed such power to implement his programs and bring the country out of the depression. He represented the voice of the people. His supporters were impatient, to say the least, with congressional and Supreme Court opposition. And it was during the Roosevelt era that the Executive Office of the President was created, with the Bureau of the Budget (now the Office of Management and Budget) as its central component, to assist the president in the management of the bureaucracy as well as in carrying out his other responsibilities. The bureaucracy came into its own under Roosevelt, expanding to meet the new responsibilities undertaken by government as a result of the New Deal. The president was to coordinate and direct the activities of the executive branch, "to make democracy work," in the words of the President's Committee on Administrative Management of 1937, an advisory group set up to make an exhaustive survey of the bureaucracy and recommend ways for efficiently organizing it. That committee, much like the Hoover Commission in 1949, recommended consolidation of administrative functions under presidential control, and the creation of a "chain of command" from "the top to the bottom, and the bottom to the top."

The same liberal supporters of the New Deal and later Democratic presidents who endlessly sought increased presidential power over the bureaucracy and a general strengthening of the presidency were not overly concerned to see the legacy of their efforts pass to President Eisenhower, whom they considered a responsible if somewhat ineffective president. But when Richard Nixon sought vigorously to carry on the tradition of centralized executive power, suddenly liberal scholars, such as Henry Steele Commager, accused the president of acting unconstitutionally by going far beyond the precedents of his predecessors.[3] They were unable to see the inconsistency in their own position, that if they supported a strong presidency per se they should stick to their position regardless of which party or person occupies the White House. The same holds true for conservatives, some of whom welcomed President Nixon's activist posture but who have criticized active Democratic presidents in the past.

THE BUREAUCRACY AND THE PRESIDENCY

So much for the *theory* of the presidency. *In fact,* what is the nature of the executive branch and its relationship to the presidency? Is the dichotomy between executive branch on the one hand, and Congress on the other accurate? In reality, the executive branch is an important limit upon the presidency that acts independently of presidential wishes far more often than people think. Moreover, the administrative branch is as much attuned to congressional committees and their powerful members as to the White House. The bureaucracy is an arm of Congress as much as it is an extension of presidential power. The president is not and cannot be "chief administrator" in fact—nor should he be.

Richard Neustadt has called the president more of a clerk than king.[4] He is but one component in the constituencies of administrative agencies. Agencies follow the president's lead only insofar as they feel he is useful, in a political sense, to them. He is an important source of political support, but not the only source. All attempts of past presidents to dominate completely the executive branch have failed, and President Nixon's efforts in this direction will not in any permanent way bring the sprawling administrative branch to heel.

The major reasons for lack of presidential control over the bureaucracy are, first, the political support that is given to many agencies by groups outside the presidency. The Departments of Agriculture, Labor, Defense, HEW, and so on, as well as most of the independent regulatory agencies, have pressure group support that is a bulwark against presidential intrusion. For example, presidents from Harry S. Truman to Richard M. Nixon have recommended or at least contemplated abolishing the Interstate Commerce Commission (ICC) by merging its functions into a regular department, such as the Department of Transportation. But railroad support for the ICC, reflected and strongly felt in Congress, has preserved the ICC virtually intact. President Nixon's 1971 proposals for major reorganization of the executive branch that would have caused massive shifts of functions—for example, away from Agriculture to such new umbrella departments as Natural Resources—met with stony silence in Congress because of the political power of these agencies based upon private support, specialized interests that have greater access to congressional committees than to the president.

It is when agencies lack independent political support that they are beholden to the president. Before Henry Kissinger became secretary of state, the department was upstaged by the president and Kissinger, who decided to bring charismatic leadership to the foreign policy arena, leaving the secretary of state and the bureaucrats of the State Department to perform mundane tasks. The State Department is most vulnerable to such domination by the White House because its lack of a domestic constituency results in little support from Congress, which on occasion decides itself to use the department as a political football. When Senator Joseph McCarthy found subversives in government and displayed his famous list, it was no accident that he found them in the State Department. As long as he was taking on State, he was safe. When his imperialism extended to the Department of the Army, his downfall was assured.

The size, complexity, scope of responsibilities, and continuity of the administrative branch are further factors precluding presidential control. Delegation of power within the executive branch is a necessity. Regardless of how large the Executive Office of the President is, the flow of information to it is largely controlled by the agencies. The president's staff cannot know what is going on in every nook of the bureaucracy. The initiative in most policy formulation and implementation is with the agencies, not the president and his immediate advisers. Admittedly, President Nixon made a strong attempt to change this fact, but almost by definition the presidency cannot sustain such an effort over the long run.

No president is in office more than eight years. The first four are spent getting settled, facing a powerful and entrenched bureaucracy, many top officials (below the cabinet level) of which may have been appointed by a prior president of the opposition party. They may remain in office, protected by guaranteed terms of office (the case with independent regulatory commissions) or civil service regulations. By the beginning of the second term, the election out of the way and no prospect of further reelection, the president may decide to make a valiant effort to implement his programs by controlling the bureaucracy and even, as in the case of President Nixon, ignoring the explicit wishes of Congress. If he wants to cut back government programs and reduce spending, as President Nixon did, the president can resort to impoundment of funds and the veto. But if the president is more positively oriented, he must have the cooperation of both Congress and the bureaucracy. In the latter case, the leverage of the bureaucracy over the White House is increased. But regardless of which situation prevails, the central fact remains that the presidency lacks the continuity to control the more permanent bureaucracy.

THE BUREAUCRACY

Although the presidency is an institution, its continuity depends very much upon the president and his staff—upon personal rather than institutional factors. The personal continuity of the presidency is no match for the personal continuity of the bureaucracy. President Nixon's efforts to control the administrative branch depended at first largely upon the style and charisma of the men in the White House (e.g., Henry Kissinger). Nixon has effected no permanent reorganization of the executive branch, nor can he without congressional acquiescence. After Watergate, a new presidential staff, headed by General Haig, continued to try to centralize power in the White House.

Whether more or less dependent upon the agencies, no president has the authority or power to control them in a manner similar to the president of a corporation dealing with lower echelons in his organization. Perhaps President Nixon would like to entitle our government "U.S. Government, Inc.; President: Richard M. Nixon," but the reality this image evokes cannot exist.

The bureaucracy is a fourth branch of the government, and, like the original three, not entirely independent of or dependent upon coordinate branches. Created by Congress, the administrative agencies necessarily must be responsible to congressional inputs. Agencies are the agents of the legislature and are supposed to carry out the mandates set forth in legislation. At the same time, they cannot ignore the president because, in more or less degree, every agency finds presidential support useful. In some cases, without it, an agency cannot exercise power at all. This is true of agencies without powerful constituencies and legislative support, such as the State Department. And, of necessity, Congress has gone along with the gradual increase in the powers of the Executive Office, particularly the Office of Management and Budget (OMB), resulting in greater centralized control over the bureaucracy from the staff of the president if not from the president himself.

Congress has recognized over the years that some centralization of authority is necessary in the executive branch, and that minimum efficiency requires that the president be given management tools, such as increased staff and budgetary clearance power over the agencies. In the budgetary area, clearance has come to mean that OMB determines the limits of agencies' requests to Congress. This does not mean that Congress must adhere to the president's budget, but only that the agencies are not supposed to make end runs to the legislature to avoid the central clearance process. This effectively reduces the power of the agencies, especially since the president can impound funds the legislature appropriates beyond his recommendations.

Although agencies are increasingly being cut off from making direct approaches to Congress in budgetary matters, their interests are represented by outside pressure groups and Congress itself, which is reluctant to see funds for their favorite programs cut off. Should the president, as he threatened, propose legislation to end farm subsidies, Department of Agriculture officials would be forbidden from testifying against presidential plans, but can any congressman doubt the position of Agriculture? Informal contacts between the bureaucracy and Congress continue, whether over the phone or at casual meetings and cocktail parties. And pressure groups that are part of the clientele of the Department of Agriculture vigorously oppose the president's position in this matter. In 1972, the department ended several key agricultural programs at the request of the president and without congressional consultation, only to have an angry Congress overwhelmingly vote to restore the programs. How dare the president interfere with the policies of the Department of Agriculture, an agent of Congress! This incident reflects the fact that the bureaucracy may be considered the special preserve of Congress, and, because of this, it limits the president. Significantly, it is often difficult for the president to use the bureaucracy as a lever against Congress. The Department of Agriculture may pro forma go along with the president, while in fact its sympathies lie in the opposite direction.

The ties existing between Congress and the executive branch deserve closer attention than they have received until now. The headlines, the dramatic actions of President Nixon in impoundment, veto of legislation, and centralization of power (according to the organization chart) in the White House appear to belie any significant legislative power in public administration. But, behind the headlines, the constant interaction that occurs between congressmen and bureaucrats often charts the course of action for the executive branch. A very large sphere of administrative activity is necessarily outside the purview of the president because of his own disinterest, lack of expertise in the Executive Office, or lack of authority. Congressional committees fill the gap, stepping in to assert their power over agencies with which they deal. This can be particularly true in the case of the independent regulatory commissions that are partially isolated from presidential control by their enabling statutes. For example, Representative Moss (D.–Calif.) chairman of the House Subcommittee on Commerce and Finance, and Senator Williams (D.–N.J.), chairman of the Securities Subcommittee of the Senate Banking Committee are known to deal directly, on a continuous basis, with the Securities and Exchange Commission (SEC) to prod it to implement the policy positions they want. With the help of a strong professional staff, these men are directly involved in the regulation of the securities industry. Here the expertise of Congress matches that of the bureaucracy, and through its committees it is controlling the SEC to a far greater extent than is the president.

That bureaucrats are sensitive to the key men on the congressional committees overseeing their operations is un-disputed. There have been instances, admittedly unusual, where important administrative action will not be taken at all without consultation with a committee chairman. More common is the continual informal interchange of ideas and the experssion of congressional intent (actually the intent of a few key committee chairmen) through hearings, committee reports, and floor debates, as well as formal legislation. The nonstatutory expressions of legislative intent are often more important than statutory language, and administrators heed clearly experienced congressional wishes even though they may not be formalized in legislation.

The bureaucracy is responsible to the courts as well as to Congress, and judicial review may produce results that frustrate presidential aspirations to control the executive branch. Virtually all the cases challenging President Nixon's impoundment decisions went against the president. His actions were declared *ultra vires* by federal district and appeals courts—beyond the authority granted the president by law. Moreover, the president's attempt to dismantle Office of Economic Opportunity (OEO) was stymied by the courts, on the grounds that such an action violated congressional intent. These judicial decisions recognize the responsibility of the bureaucracy to Congress by overriding presidential directives that are opposed to legislative intent. The authority of "chief administrator" is shared between the president and Congress. And even though the courts cannot initiate action to control the executive branch, they too exercise a supervisory role. Their decisions can profoundly shape the nature of administrative policy and procedure.

It is evident that the bureaucracy is not solely an agent of the president. It is responsible to all three original governmental branches. It is caught in the middle of the interbranch battles that reflect the separation of powers. Both Congress and the president actively want to control the bureaucracy, while the judiciary, although assuming a passive role, nevertheless influences public administration by deciding cases and controversies concerning administrative actions.

The often conflicting nature of the controls over the bureaucracy may lead to independent bureaucratic decision-making and the playing off of one branch against another by agencies bent on increasing their power and getting their way. The backing of Congress can be used to justify thwarting the Executive Office of the President. Operating in zones of ambiguity, administrators may simply proceed independently or seek explicit congressional statements in reports and hearings to support them in their chosen courses of action. The latter is the safer course. Or, if they are having trouble with Congress, they may use the shield of the president to protect them, provided the president agrees to be on their side.

CONCLUSION

The bureaucracy, as a semi-autonomous fourth branch in our government, adds an important dimension to the political process. As an agent of both Congress and the president, it uniquely exercises all the major functions of government—legislative, executive, and judicial. Its pluralistic responsibilities are matched by its diverse organizational characteristics and lines of accountability. Its ties to Congress fortify the informal spheres of special interests that dominate administrative constituencies. Congressional committees represent these interests and channel their demands to the agencies often with the congressional stamp of approval. Presidential demands reflect a broader, more national constituency; hence, the conflicting nature of presidential and congressional inputs upon the executive branch.

Since, in reality, the executive branch is accountable in different ways to all

three coordinate branches, it is somewhat academic to debate the question of whether or how this should be changed. Nevertheless, attempts are made from time to time to upset the balance of powers existing among the three branches by disproportionately increasing the control of one of them over the administrative branch. President Nixon has attempted this on behalf of the White House. Congress is continually "meddling" in the affairs of the executive branch and, like the president, attempts to gain as much control as possible.

But the real issue is not centralization of control over the bureaucracy in any one part of government, for this is politically impossible, but the independent power and discretion of the bureaucracy itself. The bureaucracy cannot and should not be controlled completely by the president, Congress, or the courts. Is the partial control exercised by these branches sufficient to curtail bureaucratic discretion? Is administrative discretion necessarily bad?

In fact, the bureaucracy is at least as accountable and controlled as the three original branches. It sometimes exercises discretion, but so do the other branches. It is checked by and acts as a check upon the other branches. It is not elected, but is responsive to political constituencies, some of the components of which are elected. It is often rigid and wrong, but these traits are not exclusively those of bureaucrats. Presidents and congressmen too have been known to possess them.

In order to perform properly within our political system, the bureaucracy must maintain at least as much independence as Congress and the president. As an agent of each, it must be able to check both. The separation of powers would be violated if it came under the domination of either. Moreover, the professional character of the administrative branch demands a degree of independence and continuity. Only at the very top levels should it be subject to partisan political influence. The president is a partisan figure, and so is his staff.

The president must respect the professionalism of a large part of the bureaucracy and not attempt to run it along partisan lines. His staff also must not try to assume the major operating responsibilities of the agencies lest professional continuity be destroyed and esprit de corps deteriorated. The bureaucracy must be able to carry on intact from one president to another. This provision of continuity is a major contribution a good bureaucracy can make, but which overcentralization of power in the White House makes unlikely. While recognizing the importance of continuous checks upon bureaucratic power, a respect for the integrity and independence of the bureaucracy will enable it to meet the enormous responsibilities that have been thrust upon it.

NOTES

1. W. F. Willoughby, *Principles of Public Administration* (New York: Harper), p. 36.
2. *Ibid.,* p. 57.
3. *New York Times*, March 4, 1973, p. 1.
4. R. Neustadt, *Presidential Power* (New York: John Wiley, 1960).

X

Evaluating the Presidents

Introduction. Ultimately, evaluating a president's performance and achievements in office is the natural order of things. From the day a president assumes office he is subject to the scrutiny of "president watchers" who want to know whether the president is leading or being led and whether he is, say, a superb, good, or mediocre leader.

Assessments of presidential performance are engaged in by a wide variety of president watchers. They include, among others, Congress, the courts, interest groups, journalists, pollsters, foreign governments and observers to include academics, American academics (see again, for example number 9, in chapter 3) and the public-at-large. The evaluation of individual presidents has led to comparisons of presidential performance.

How do president watchers evaluate presidential achievements? Are evaluations a matter of "watcher" perception? Or are "watcher" conclusions arrived at empirically? How varied are the perceptions of comparisons made of the presidential performance? How are the variations accounted for?

Evaluation of presidential performance is, of course, a difficult process. Men assume the presidency under different sets of circumstances and expectations. Political demands, political supports, and the nature of the times, among other things, influence presidential performance and complicate the evaluative process. Indeed, in the final analysis, it may be that presidential performance cannot and should not be judged apart from the purposes to which a president would employ the presidency. One need only recall (as the readings in chapter 2 illustrate) that presidents themselves do have notions about the purposes to which presidential power ought to be put.

The readings in this chapter cannot answer all of the questions raised here. But the readings are illustrative of the kinds of evaluations of presidential performances made over the years.

British historian and ambassador to the United States from 1907 to 1913, James Bryce visited the United States in the 1880s, published a book, *The American Commonwealth*, and entitled one of its chapters, "Why Great Men Are Not Chosen President." It is the first selection reprinted here.

In his essay, Bryce argued that great men are not chosen president, and thus there are no great presidents. He listed several reasons for the lack of great men in America being chosen president.

Bryce compared the eighteen American Presidents since 1789 with the nineteen English prime ministers who had held office during the same period. He found the parliamentary system to be more suited to bringing great men to office. Bryce explained why he believed this to be so. To better understand Bryce's assessment of the presidential performance, at the time of his study, it would be well to recall that presidents of the nineteenth century functioned within an environment of strong congressional government.

British historian, Harold Laski, in his Indiana University lectures fifty years later took the opposite view of James Bryce and argued that first rate men do become president. Moreover, Laski argued, the opportunities afforded by the office are so great that an ordinary as well as an exceptional man can be stimulated by it to extraordinary performance.

In the next selection, "Why Great Men Are Chosen President," Laski pointed out why he believes as he does. Unlike Bryce, Laski provided no evidence for his views. On the other hand, Laski unlike Bryce, did write from the vantage point of having lived through an era of such presidents as Theodore Roosevelt, Woodrow Wilson, and Franklin D. Roosevelt, each of whom was, respectively, president during a great reform movement, a world war, and a great depression. None of these presidents, under the circumstances of the times, could afford to defer to the prerogatives of congressional government.

The first really empirical efforts to rate presidents were the polls conducted by historian Arthur M. Schlesinger, Sr. in 1948 and 1962. In his 1948 poll, he surveyed fifty-five historians; in 1962 he surveyed seventy-five. These "historians" of the American presidency included journalists, political scientists, and other social scientists, as well as the traditional historians. Schlesinger asked each of them to rate presidents in terms of their greatness. The 1962 poll, because it surveyed a larger group, was chosen for inclusion here.

In the poll, "Our Presidents: A Rating by 75 Historians," Schlesinger found that each of the "greats" was a president at a critical time in history, had been strong leaders, and had expanded and strengthened the powers of the presidency. Each of the "great" presidents was not a "finger in the air" man trying to determine which way the political winds were blowing, but a man who did not hesitate to take the initiative and thereby became a profile in courage. The results of this poll closely followed the findings of Schlesinger's 1948 study.

Schlesinger concluded his study with the observation that James Bryce erred in his assessment of American presidents, and that the nation has, on balance, a good record of executive greatness both in the nineteenth century that Bryce observed, and in the more recent past.

38. Why Great Men Are Not Chosen Presidents*

JAMES BRYCE

Europeans often ask, and Americans do not always explain, how it happens that this great office, the greatest in the world, unless we except the papacy, to which any man can rise by his own merits, is not more frequently filled by great and striking men? In America, which is beyond all other countries the country of a "career open to talents," a country, moreover, in which political life is unusually keen and political ambition widely diffused, it might be expected that the highest place would always be won by a man of brilliant gifts. But since the heroes of the Revolution died out with Jefferson and Adams and Madison some sixty years ago, no person except General Grant has reached the chair whose name would have been remembered had he not been president, and no president except Abraham Lincoln has displayed rare or striking qualities in the chair. Who now knows or cares to know anything about the personality of James K. Polk or Franklin Pierce? The only thing remarkable about them is that being so commonplace they should have climbed so high.

Several reasons may be suggested for the fact, which Americans are themselves the first to admit.

One is that the proportion of first-rate ability drawn into politics is smaller in America than in most European countries. This is a phenomenon whose causes must be elucidated later: in the meantime it is enough to say that in France and Italy, where half-revolutionary conditions have made public life exciting and accessible; in Germany, where an admirably-organized civil service cultivates and develops statecraft with unusual success; in England, where many persons of wealth and leisure seek to enter the political arena, while burning questions touch the interests of all classes and make men eager observers of the combatants, the total quantity of talent devoted to parliamentary or administrative work is far larger, relatively to the population, than in America, where much of the best ability, both for thought and for action, for planning and for executing rushes into a field which is comparatively narrow in Europe, the business of developing the material resources of the country.

Another is that the methods and habits of Congress, and indeed of political life generally, seem to give fewer opportunities for personal distinction, fewer modes in which a man may commend himself to his countrymen by eminent capacity in thought, in speech, or in administration, than is the case in the free countries of Europe.

A third reason is that eminent men

*Source: From James Bryce, The American Commonwealth (New York: G. P. Putnam's Sons, 1959), pp. 27-34; originally published 1888.

make more enemies, and give those enemies more assailable points, than obscure men do. They are therefore in so far less desirable candidates. It is true that the eminent man has also made more friends, that his name is more widely known, and may be greeted with louder cheers. Other things being equal, the famous man is preferable. But other things never are equal. The famous man has probably attacked some leaders in his own party, has supplanted others, has expressed his dislike to the crotchet of some active section, has perhaps committed errors which are capable of being magnified into offences. No man stands long before the public and bears a part in great affairs without giving openings to censorious criticism. Fiercer far than the light which beats upon a throne is the light which beats upon a presidential candidate, searching out all the reasons of his past life. Hence, when the choice lies between a brilliant man and a safe man, the safe man is preferred. Party feeling, strong enough to carry in on its back a man without conspicuous positive merits, is not always strong enough to procure forgiveness for a man with positive faults.

A European finds that this phenomenon needs in its turn to be explained, for in the free countries of Europe brilliancy, be it eloquence in speech, or some striking achievement in war or administration, or the power through whatever means of somehow impressing the popular imagination, is what makes a leader triumphant. Why should it be otherwise in America? Because in America party loyalty and party organization have been hitherto so perfect that any one put forward by the party will get the full party vote if his character is good and his "record," as they call it, unstained. The safe candidate may not draw in quite so many votes from the moderate men of the other side as the brilliant one would, but he will not lose nearly so many from his own ranks. Even those who admit his mediocrity will vote straight when the moment for

voting comes. Besides, the ordinary American voter does not object to mediocrity. He has a lower conception of the qualities requisite to make a statesman than those who direct public opinion in Europe have. He likes his candidate to be sensible, vigorous, and, above all, what he calls "magnetic," and does not value, because he sees no need for, originality or profundity, a fine culture or a wide knowledge. Candidates are selected to be run for nomination by knots of persons who, however expert as party tacticians, are usually commonplace men; and the choice between those selected for nomination is made by a very large body, an assembly of over eight hundred delegates from the local party organizations over the country, who are certainly no better than ordinary citizens. How this process works will be seen more fully when I come to speak of those nominating conventions which are so notable a feature in American politics.

It must also be remembered that the merits of a President are one thing and those of a candidate another thing. An eminent American is reported to have said to friends who wished to put him forward, "Gentlemen, let there be no mistake. I should make a good president, but a very bad candidate." Now to a party it is more important that its nominee should be a good candidate than that he should turn out a good president. A nearer danger is a greater danger. As Saladin says in *The Talisman*, "A wild cat in a chamber is more dangerous than a lion in a distant desert." It will be a misfortune to the party, as well as to the country, if the candidate elected should prove a bad president. But it is a greater misfortune to the party that it should be beaten in the impending election, for the evil of losing national patronage will have come four years sooner. "B" (so reason the leaders), "who is one of our possible candidates, may be an abler man than A, who is the other. But we have a better chance of winning with A than with B, while X, the candidate of our opponents, is anyhow no better than A. We must therefore run A." This reasoning is all the more forcible because the previous career of the possible candidates has generally made it easier to say who will succeed as a candidate than who will succeed as a president; and because the wire-pullers with whom the choice rests are better judges of the former question than of the latter.

After all, too, and this is a point much less obvious to Europeans than to Americans, a president need not be a man of brilliant intellectual gifts. Englishmen, imagining him as something like their prime minister, assume that he ought to be a dazzling orator, able to sway legislatures or multitudes, possessed also of the constructive powers that can devise a great policy or frame a comprehensive piece of legislation. They forget that the president does not sit in Congress, that he ought not to address meetings, except on ornamental and (usually) nonpolitical occasions, that he cannot submit bills nor otherwise influence the action of the legislature. His main duties are to be prompt and firm in securing the due execution of the laws and maintaining the public peace, careful and upright in the choice of the executive officials of the country. Eloquence, whose value is apt to be overrated in all free countries, imagination, profundity of thought or extent of knowledge, are all in so far a gain to him that they make him a bigger man, and help him to gain a greater influence over the nation, an influence which, if he be a true patriot he may use for its good. But they are not necessary for the due discharge in ordinary times of the duties of his post. A man may lack them and yet make an excellent president. Four-fifths of his work is the same in kind as that which devolves on the chairman of a commercial company or the manager of a railway, the work of choosing good subordinates, seeing that they attend to their business, and taking a sound practical view of such administrative questions as require his decision. Firmness, common sense, and most of all, honesty, an honesty above all suspicion of personal interest, are the qualities which the country chiefly needs in its chief magistrate.

So far we have been considering personal merits. But in the selection of a candidate many considerations have to be regarded besides personal merits, whether they be the merits of a candidate, or of a possible president. The chief of these considerations is the amount of support which can be secured from different states or from different regions, or, as the Americans say, "sections," of the Union. State feeling and sectional feeling are powerful factors in a presidential election. The Northwest, including the states from Ohio to Dakota, is now the most populous region of the Union, and therefore counts for most in an election. It naturally conceives that its interests will be best protected by one who knows them from birth and residence. Hence *prima facie* a Northwestern man makes the best candidate. A large state casts a heavier vote in the election; and every state is of course more likely to be carried by one of its own children than by a stranger, because his fellow-citizens, while they feel honoured by the choice, gain also a substantial advantage, having a better prospect of such favours as the administration can bestow. Hence, *coeteris paribus*, a man from a large state is preferable as a candidate. New York casts thirty-six votes in the presidential election, Pennsylvania thirty, Ohio twenty-three, Illinois twenty-two, while Vermont and Rhode Island have but four, Delaware, Nevada, and Oregon only three votes each. It is therefore, parties being usually very evenly balanced, better worth while to have an inferior candidate from one of the larger states, who may carry the whole weight of his state with him, than a somewhat superior candidate from one of the smaller states, who will carry only three or four votes. The problem is further complicated by the fact that some states are already safe for one or other party, while others are doubtful. The Northwestern and New England states are most of them certain to go Republican: the Southern States are (at present) all of them certain to go Democratic. It is more important to gratify a doubtful state than one you have got already; and hence coeteris paribus, a candidate from a doubtful state, such as New York or Indiana, is to be preferred.

Other minor disqualifying circumstances require less explanation. A Roman Catholic, or an avowed disbeliever in Christianity, would be an undesirable candidate. Since the close of the Civil War, any one who fought, especially if he fought with distinction, in the Northern army, has enjoyed great advantages, for the soldiers of that army, still numerous, rally to his name. The two elections of General Grant, who knew nothing of politics, and the fact that his influence survived the faults of his long administration, are evidence of the weight of this consideration. It influenced the selection both of Garfield and of his opponent Hancock. Similarly a person who fought in the Southern army would be a bad candidate, for he might alienate the North.

On a railway journey in the Far West in 1883 I fell in with two newspaper men from the state of Indiana, who were taking their holiday. The conversation turned on the next presidential election. They spoke hopefully of the chances for nomination by their party of an Indiana man, a comparatively obscure person, whose name I had never heard. I expressed some surprise that he should be thought of. They observed that he had done well in state politics, that there was nothing against him, that Indiana would work for him. "But," I rejoined, "ought you not to have a man of more commanding character. There is Senator A. Everybody tells me that he is the shrewdest and most experienced man in your party, and that he has a perfectly clean record. Why not run him?" "Why, yes," they answered, "that is all true. But you see he comes from a small state, and we have got that state already. Besides, he wasn't in the war. Our man was. Indiana's vote is worth having, and if our man is run, we can carry Indiana."

"Surely the race is not to the swift, nor the battle to the strong, neither yet bread to the wise, nor yet riches to men of understanding, nor yet favour to men of skill, but time and chance happeneth to them all."

These secondary considerations do not always prevail. Intellectual ability and force of character must influence the choice of a candidate, and their influence is sometimes decisive. They count for more when times are so critical that the need for a strong man is felt. Reformers declare that their weight will go on increasing as the disgust of good citizens with the methods of professional politicians increases. But for many generations past it is not the greatest men in the Roman Church that have been chosen popes, nor the most brilliant men in the Anglican Church that have been appointed archbishops of Canterbury.

Although several presidents have survived their departure from office by many years, only one, John Quincy Adams, has played a part in politics after quitting the White House. It may be that the ex-president has not been a great leader before his accession to office; it may be that he does not care to exert himself after he has held and dropped the great prize, and found (one may safely add) how little of a prize it is. Something however, must also be ascribed to other features of the political system of the country. It is often hard to find a vacancy in the representation of a given state through which to re-enter Congress; it is disagreeable to recur to the arts by which seats are secured. Past greatness is rather an encumbrance than a help to resuming a political career.

Exalted power, on which the unsleeping eye of hostile critics was fixed, has probably disclosed all a president's weaknesses, and has either forced him to make enemies by disobliging adherents, or exposed him to censure for subservience to party interests. He is regarded as having had his day; he belongs already to the past, and unless, like Grant, he is endeared to the people by the memory of some splendid service, he soon sinks into the crowd or avoids neglect by retirement. Possibly he may deserve to be forgotten; but more frequently he is a man of sufficient ability and character to make the experience he has gained valuable to the country, could it be retained in a place where he might turn it to account. They managed things better at Rome in the days of the republic, gathering into their Senate all the fame and experience, all the wisdom and skill, of those who had ruled and fought as consuls and praetors at home and abroad.

"What shall we do with our ex-presidents?" is a question often put in America, but never yet answered. The position of a past chief magistrate is not a happy one. He has been a species of sovereign at home. He is received— General Grant was—with almost royal honours abroad. His private income may be unsufficient to enable him to live in ease, yet he cannot without loss of dignity, the country's dignity as well as his own, go back to practice at the bar or become partner in a mercantile firm. If he tries to enter the Senate, it may happen that there is no seat vacant for his own state, or that the majority in the state legislature is against him. It has been suggested that he might be given a seat in that chamber as an extra member; but to this plan there is the objection that it would give to the state from which he comes a third senator, and thus put other states at a disadvantage. In any case, however, it would seem only right to bestow such a pension as would relieve him from the necessity of re-entering business or a profession.

We may now answer the question from which we started. Great men are not chosen presidents, firstly, because great men are rare in politics; secondly, because the method of choice does not bring them to the top; thirdly, because they are not, in quiet times, absolutely needed. I may observe that the presidents, regarded historically, fall into three periods, the second inferior to the first, the third rather better than the second.

Down till the election of Andrew Jackson in 1828, all the presidents had been statesmen in the European sense of the word, men of education, of administrative experience, of a certain largeness of view and dignity of character. All except the first two had served in the great office of secretary of state; all were well known to the nation from the part they had played. In the second period, from Jackson till the outbreak of the Civil War in 1861, the presidents were either mere politicians, such as Van Buren, Polk, or Buchanan, or else successful soldiers, such as Harrison or Taylor, whom their party found useful as figureheads. They were intellectual pigmies beside the real leaders of that generation—Clay, Calhoun, and Webster. A new series begins with Lincoln in 1861. He and General Grant his successor, who cover sixteen years between them, belong to the history of the world. The other less distinguished presidents of this period contrast favourably with the Polks and Pierces of the days before the war, but they are not, like the early presidents, the first men of the country. If we compare the eighteen presidents who have been elected to office since 1789 with the nineteen English prime ministers of the same hundred years, there are but six of the latter, and at least eight of the former whom history calls personally insignificant, while only Washington, Jefferson, Lincoln, and Grant can claim to belong to a front rank represented in the English list by seven or possibly eight names. It would seem that the natural selections of the English parliamentary system, even as modified by the aristocratic habits of that country, has more tendency to bring the highest gifts to the highest place than the more artificial selection of America.

39. Why Great Men Are Chosen President*

HAROLD J. LASKI

The big problem that is raised by the American method of nominating presidential candidates is whether it puts a premium, as Lord Bryce argued, against the opportunity of first-rate men to receive consideration. I do not think his case is proved by making a list of first-rate men, Clay and Calhoun and Webster, for example, who missed nomination. The answer to that argument is, first, that many first-rate men have become president by reason of the system; and second, that the reasons which stopped others would have been powerful reasons against their elevation in any representative democracy. It is, I think, at least doubtful whether the elevation of a Roman Catholic to the premiership would be regarded favorably in Great Britain. A great business man, both in England and France, will operate mainly behind the political scene rather than in front of it; of our three business men who have become prime ministers one was, in fact, a rentier, and the others had long retired from active participation therein. Few people could easily explain the nuances that account for the failure of one man to reach the top, and the success of another. And in estimating the meaning of "availability" we must remember, always, that there is a real sense in which the more strong the candidate, supposing that he represents a special point of view, the more strong, also, are likely to be his enemies. Not infrequently, an easy nomination—so long as the renomination of an existing president is not involved—merely means, as it meant with Horace Greely in 1872, with Judge Parker in 1904, with Governor Landon in 1936, that rival candidates do not consider there is much prospect for their party's success, and they are not anxious to be associated with a dismal failure at the polls, with a view of a later nomination.

Granted, this is to say, the greatness of the prize, and the necessity of popular election, it is difficult to see what other method than the nominating convention is available; more, it is true to say that, on balance, it has worked well rather than badly. The criticisms that are brought against it are rather, in their real substance, criticisms of the place of the presidency in the American constitutional scheme than of the method whereby the president is chosen. It is regrettable that an inexperienced man may come to reside in the White House; the answer is that few of those who have reached it have been inexperienced men. If it be said that men like Harding and Coolidge were unfit for the great post they secured, the an-

*Source: From pp. 49-53 from The American Presidency, An Interpretation by Harold J. Laski. Copyright © 1940 by Harper & Row, Publishers, Inc. Reprinted by permission of Harper & Row Publishers, Inc. Selection title added by editor.

swer is that the first had considerable experience both in the Ohio legislature and in the Senate, while the second had been a successful Massachusetts politician, twice occupying the governorship, for twenty years. If we take the presidents of the twentieth century, there is not one who had not been prepared for presidential office by a long experience of politics, and, with the possible exception of the Democratic candidate in 1904, that is true, also, of their defeated rivals. What is lacking in their training is mostly the art of handling Congress; and the rules of that art only partly dependent upon the character of the president for the time.

It must be remembered that, in making the choice, there are two fundamental considerations in the background of which the meaning of "availability" must be set. The first is that the party choosing a candidate wants, if it can, to win; and second, it knows that if it does win, and its nominee becomes president, there is great likelihood of its having to adopt him a second time, since not to do so is to condemn an administration for which it has to bear responsibility. While, therefore, it is quite true that a party convention provides an opportunity for the art of such a dubious wire-puller as Mr. Daugherty, it is also true that the managers of a great party are anxious to avoid, if they can, the consequences of success in that type of manipulation. One has only to read the account of an experience of conventions like that of Senator Hoar of Massachusetts to see that a scrupulous and honorable man will approach the task of selection with all the seriousness that its consequences require.[1]

All in all, I doubt whether the methods of the system are very different from those of other countries. They are, perhaps, more open and crude than in Great Britain. There is no generosity in the fight for power. There is a passionate determination on the part of organized interests to get the "safe" man who can be relied upon to live up to the commitments exacted from him. There is the fierce conflict of rival ambitions. There is the organization of every sort of cabal to win a victory for its man. Press and radio and platform are vigorously manipulated to this end. Immense promises are made, pretty ugly deals are effected. Yet I suggest that anyone who knows the life of a political party from within Great Britain will not feel inclined to cast a stone at the American system. It fits, well enough, the medium in which it has to work. It achieves the results that the needs of the people require.

For there is at least one test of the system that is, I think, decisive. There have been five considerable crises in American history. There was the need to start the new Republic adequately in 1789; it gave the American people its natural leader in George Washington. The crisis of 1800 brought Jefferson to the presidency; that of 1861 brought Abraham Lincoln. The war of 1914 found Woodrow Wilson in office; the Great Depression resulted in the election of Franklin Roosevelt. So far, it is clear, the hour has brought forth the man. It is of course true, as Bagehot said, that "success in a lottery is no argument for lotteries." I agree that no nation can afford a succession of what Theodore Roosevent termed "Buchanan Presidents"—men whose handling of the issues is uncertain and feeble. But the answer is that the nation has never had that succession; an epoch of Hardings and Coolidges produces, by the scale of the problems to which it gives rise, its own regeneration. The weak president, as I have argued, comes from the fact that a strong predecessor has set the feet of the nation on level ground. He is chosen because, after a diet of strong occasions, a nation, like an individual, turns naturally to the chance of a quiet time. "Normalcy" is always certain to be popular after crises. The issue is whether, when a crisis comes, the system can discover the man to handle it. On the evidence, this has so far been very remarkably the case. To urge that it is chance is, I think, a superficial view. It is the outcome of the national recognition that energy and direction are required, and the man chosen is the party response to that recognition. The phenomenon is as natural as the replacement of Mr. Asquith by Mr. Lloyd George in 1917, as instinctive, one may say, as the widespread demand, in the England of 1939, for the strengthening of the personnel of the "National" government. The American scheme involves delay; Mr. Roosevelt did not come to office until the nation had suf-

fered three years of depression. But the essential fact is that he came to office. Nor is there reason to suppose that this is accidental. The more deeply we penetrate the working of the system the more clearly does it emerge that the result is inherent in its nature.

NOTE

1. G. F. Hoar, *Autobiography* (1903), I, pp. 378-421.

40. Our Presidents: A Rating by 74 Historians*

ARTHUR M. SCHLESINGER, SR.

I

How good have America's presidents been? Which ones have left an enduring mark? Who were the failures? Where do the others rank? Seventy-five students of American history, including two in English universities, have undertaken to answer these questions.

Had they been appraising the total careers of the men, the results in some cases might have been quite different. Madison, John Quincy Adams, Grant and Eisenhower, for instance, were great Americans, though not, according to the panel, great presidents. Their title to fame rests on contributions made before and after holding the office.

The present inquiry, however, has to do with a single point—achievement in the executive chair. Omitted from consideration—besides, of course, Mr. Kennedy—are two presidents who were

too briefly at the helm to permit a fair evaluation: William Henry Harrison, who died within a month of his inauguration, and James A. Garfield, who served little more than half a year.

Each participant in the poll applied his measuring rod in accordance with the relative importance he attached to the complex factors that helped make or break the particular Administration. Did the president head the nation in sunny or stormy times? Did he exhibit a creative approach to the problems of statecraft? Was he the master or servant of events? Did he use the prestige and potentialities of the position to advance the public welfare? Did he effectively staff his key government posts? Did he properly safeguard the country's interest in relation to the rest of the world? How significantly did he affect the future destinies of the nation?

Admittedly, the judgment of the histo-

*Source: From *The New York Times Magazine* (July 29, 1962), pp. 12, 40-43. Copyright © 1962 by the New York Times Company. Reprinted by permission.

rians is not necessarily the judgment of history, but it is the best we can have without waiting for the sifting process of time. The members of the panel agreed with little dissent on the great and near-great and, at the opposite extreme, on those who made the poorest records. The principal differences involved the comparative ranking of the presidents regarded as average and of those below average but not failures. Even in these cases, however, the preponderance of opinion was conclusive.

II

Lincoln, Washington, Franklin D. Roosevelt, Wilson and Jefferson receive the accolade of greatness in the order given. The reasons for their pre-eminence will be examined later; but since the inclusion of Roosevelt may surprise persons still smarting from memories of New Deal times, it should be noted now that his place reaffirms the view of fifty-five historians, most of them overlapping on the present panel, whose findings were published in 1948. The longer perspective adds weight to the previous judgment.

After the top group come the half-dozen figures who, while eclipsing the majority of White House residents, yet fail of the foremost rating. Beginning with Jackson and Theodore Roosevelt, the near-great presidents continue with Polk, Truman, John Adams and Cleveland.

Old Hickory marked the advent of the common man to national power and, in particular, distinguished himself by defeating South Carolina's attempt at nullification and by destroying the monopolistic second United States Bank. The 1948 poll, indeed, placed him among the great presidents, but the present one, by a narrow margin, lowers him one degree. Theodore Roosevelt, responding to similar inpulses, taught the electorate the danger to the public weal of consolidated business, and against entrenched opposition he insti-

tuted a program of federal regulation as well as of the conservation of natural resources.

Polk, for his part, extended the national borders until they embraced what is now the great Southwest and all the country lying between the Rocky Mountains and the Pacific Ocean. Added to Jefferson's acquisition of France's Louisiana territory, these accessions from Mexico and England gave the United States its continental breadth. Though Polk's conduct toward Mexico violated international ethics, it is noteworthy that his critics, neither then nor later, have ever proposed that the conquests be returned.

Truman, the only one in the near-great class still with us, discharged impressively the awesome obligations devolving on the United States as the leader of the free world in the cold war with Soviet imperialism. The Truman Doctrine for the protection of Greece and Turkey, the Marshall Plan for the restoration of Western Europe, the Berlin airlift, the Point Four program for backward countries, NATO (our first peacetime military alliance), and the intervention in Korea in support of the United Nations—all these constituted landmarks in an assumption of global responsibilities undreamed of only a few years before.

III

Of the last two in the near-great group, the case for John Adams rests primarily on his successful resistance to his own party's demand for changing a limited conflict with France into an all-out war, while the inclusion of Cleveland recognizes his stubborn championship of tariff reform and of honesty and efficiency in the civil service.

Then follow the presidents—more than a third of the whole number—who fall in the average or mediocre class. By and large these twelve believed in negative government, in self-subordination to the legislative power. They were content to let well enough alone or, when not, were unwilling to fight for their programs or inept at doing so. In descending scale they are Madison, John Quincy Adams, Hayes, McKinley, Taft, Van Buren, Monroe, Hoover, Benjamin Harrison, Arthur, Eisenhower and Johnson.

Johnson was the principal exception to a passive role, but his prolonged contest with Congress over Southern reconstruction brought him the ignominy of impeachment and a narrow escape from dismissal from office. Eisenhower, the most recent and, consequently, the hardest of the presidents to evaluate, received a few votes in the near-great category but many more for beneath the average and failure. A two-thirds majority, however, placed him toward the bottom of the average incumbents.

IV

Of the executives of still less stature, six of the eight qualify as below average: Taylor, Tyler, Fillmore, Coolidge, Pierce and Buchanan in that order. By ill chance, Pierce and Buchanan headed the government in the years of mounting crisis which precipitated the Civil War. Had more statesmanlike hands directed affairs, that tragic failure of the democratic process might have been avoided. A sizable number of the historians, indeed, rated the two as failures.

The verdict of total unfitness, however, was, by the overwhelming majority, reserved alone for Grant and Harding. Both were postwar presidents who, by their moral obtuseness, promoted a low tone in official life, conducting administrations scarred with shame and corruption.

Under Grant the wrongdoing reached as high as his private secretary, the postmaster general and the secretaries of war and the treasury. In Harding's case, three members of the cabinet were, for like reasons, forced out, one of them going to prison along with several other important executive officials.

Harding, who could not plead Grant's political inexperience, worked intimately with the notorious Ohio Gang which had accompanied him to Washington. His belated qualms at betraying the public interest probably helped bring on his death after two and a half years in the White House.

V

A comparison of the findings of the seventy-five historians in 1962 with those of the fifty-five in 1948 shows no significant change except for the reduction of Jackson one notch to the rank of near-great. Otherwise the choices in the five major classes hold good, though the earlier survey, of course, necessarily omitted Truman and Eisenhower. Within each of the intermediate categories—near-great, average and short of average—occurs, however, some rearrangement of the order, notably the lowering somewhat of the positions of Cleveland, Monroe and Coolidge and the upgrading of Polk, Madison and McKinley.

What qualities and achievements elevated five presidents over all their fellows? Was there a pattern of greatness which distinguished these men who otherwise varied so widely in education, personality and political style and who, moreover, faced problems special to their eras? The answer lies in the nature, direction and permanent effect of their accomplishments. A quick review will reveal the common elements.

Each held the stage at a critical moment in American history and by timely action attained timeless results. Washington converted the paper Constitution into a practical and enduring instrument of government. Jefferson expanded the original area of the United States to include the huge region stretching westward from the Mississippi to the Rockies. Lincoln saved the Union from internal destruction. Wilson tightened the restraints on big business and finance and carried the nation successfully through World War I. Franklin Roosevelt preserved the country in the face of its worst depression and marshaled its resources for victory in World War II. Lincoln excepted, all effected profound domestic changes peaceably within the democratic framework— revolutions by popular consent.

By the same token, each took the side of liberalism and the general welfare against the status quo. Washington, to be sure, today seems a staid conservative to persons forgetful of his historical context. In truth, however, this director of a people's war of emancipation from colonialism devoted all his prestige and ability as their civilian head to justifying the daring new "republican model of government," the fate of which, he told his countrymen, was "deeply," yes, "finally, staked on the experiment intrusted to the hands of the American people."

VI

Jefferson, standing on Washington's shoulders, widened the concept of popular rule by word and example, and in acquiring the vast trans-Mississippi domain, he sought, among other things, to check the growing power of the Eastern business interests with an expanding agrarian West. Lincoln, given no choice in the matter, settled on the battlefield the question of "whether, in a free government, the minority have the right to break up the government whenever they choose," and while doing so he advanced the cause of human rights by outlawing the anachronism of slavery.

And in our own century the New Freedom of Wilson and the New Deal of Roosevelt have, in turn, enlarged momentously the government's responsibility for the social and economic well-being of the people.

These towering figures, moreover, acted masterfully and farsightedly in foreign affairs. All cared profoundly about keeping the country out of war, though over the years circumstances beyond American control necessitated differences as to the means. When the Republic was young and craved time to build up its strength, Washington instituted, and Jefferson perfected, the policy of isolationism or neutralism toward the chronic power struggles embroiling Europe; and Lincoln, in the dark days of the Civil War, averted, through consummate diplomacy, the calamity of British intervention on behalf of the South.

But with America's coming fully of age the situation changed. As Washington had foretold in his "Farewell Address," the United States now could take "command of its own fortunes"; and the shrinkage of global distances plus the modern weaponry of destruction obliged a departure from the past. The goal of peace remained unaltered, but the method devised by Wilson and Roosevelt to achieve it was through an international structure for collective security. Under this sign, Wilson pioneered the League of Nations; and Roosevelt, succeeding where Wilson had not in winning senatorial approval, helped reshape that body into the more potent United Nations.

VII

The members of this group were not only constructive statesmen but realistic politicians. Washington apart, none of them waited for the office to seek the man; they pursued it with all their might and main. And upon winning it, they functioned as chiefs of their parties as well as chiefs of state. Washington, it is true, as the first to occupy the position, endeavored to shun political ties; he even appointed the contending party leaders, Jefferson and Hamilton, to his cabinet; but, taught by experience, he presently abandoned his nonpartisanship as "a sort of political suicide." His successors followed this course from the outset.

The arts of the politician were, of course, indispensable to gain the needed congressional support for their policies. With unconvinced members they knew when to reason and to browbeat, to bargain and stand firm, to concede what was relatively unimportant in order to obtain what was essential. If occasion demanded, they used such means as bestowing or withholding federal patronage, employing or threatening to employ the veto and, when all else failed, they appealed over the heads of the lawmakers to the people.

VIII

Every one of these men left the executive branch stronger and more influential than he found it. As a matter of course they magnified the powers expressly granted them by the Constitution and assumed others not expressly denied by it. They acted on the conviction that when the framers of the document provided for a chief magistrate chosen periodically by and responsible to all the people they had intended that he should always be equal to the widening needs of society.

Inevitably, these presidents encountered trouble with the Supreme Court, for its members, enjoying lifetime tenure of office and, moreover, restrained by the tribunal's past decisions, tended to speak for times gone by. Only Washington, the one president to name the entire body, escaped the dilemma.

IX

Jefferson, alarmed lest the judiciary he had inherited from the political opposition would strike down "all the works of republicanism," got Congress to abolish a series of lower judgeships which the outgoing administration had prepared for its adherents, and he induced the House to impeach a grossly partisan member of the Supreme Court. Had the attempt at ouster succeeded, Chief Justice Marshall almost certainly would have been the next quarry.

Over and over again Lincoln, under plea of military necessity, ignored or defied judicial decrees. On one occasion he even disregarded a writ of habeas corpus of Chief Justice Taney himself. Wilson, though managing to avoid open strife, nonetheless viewed the Court's conservative bent as the nation's "most obvious and immediate danger." And Franklin Roosevelt, when thwarted by the high bench in expanding his New Deal program, sought to correct its "horse and buggy" mentality by the addition of younger and more progressive justices. Although Congress did not consent, the tribunal, in alarm, hastily changed its attitude. In all these affairs, moreover, the verdict of time has upheld the presidents' underlying purposes, if not always their methods.

X

Being strong executives, the five also offended vested economic interests and longstanding popular prejudices. Furthermore, their sins of commission and omission, though small in the backward view of history, looked enormous to critical contemporaries. Each, in turn, met with charges of subverting the Constitution, of lusting to be king or dictator, and of knuckling under on occasion to some foreign power.

The "arrows of malevolence" so wounded Washington that he exclaimed to a friend that he "had never repented but once having slipped the moment of resigning his office, and that was every moment since." Jefferson was pelted with such epithets as "Mad Tom," "contemptible hypocrite," "a man without religion" and "a ravening wolf." Lincoln suffered abuse, even from Northerners, as "the baboon in the White House," "a usurper" and "a perjured traitor." He said it was in his heart to pity Satan if "to be head of Hell is as hard as what I have to undergo." Wilson and Roosevelt, as many today will still remember, came off no better, both being reviled for wanton personal ambition and seeking to rule or ruin. In the case of each of the greats, the newspaper press added fuel to the flames when, indeed, it did not start them.

XI

Yet, notwithstanding all the sound and fury, these presidents were more deeply loved than they were hated. The rank and file of Americans re-elected every one of them to a second term and Roosevelt to a third and fourth.

Another factor marking the group was that, but for the self-made Lincoln, they came from an upper level of society (and, indeed, even Lincoln before reaching the White House, had surmounted his humble beginnings to become a leader of the Illinois bar). This willingness of the voter to accept patrician leadership sheds an interesting light on the flexibility of United States democracy. Washington, Jefferson and Roosevelt, alike in being well-to-do, landed proprietors, believed, as a matter of course, in the importance of preserving or recovering for the mass of people the kind of values and human advantages traditional to a rural way of life; and Wilson growing up in a highly cultured but not affluent atmosphere, arrived at pretty much the same outlook on the basis of extensive reading.

XII

But, superior though these personages were, only two, Washington and Wilson, excelled as administrators. The rest either lacked the ability or else believed the ends of public policy more important than the machinery for achieving them. On balance, moreover, their inattention served to unfreeze official routine and inject vitality and a readiness to innovate into the government ranks. Franklin Roosevelt in fact went so far as to declare, "The presidency is not merely an administrative office. That is the least of it." If he overstated the matter, all the others would have heartily endorsed his further view: "It is pre-

eminently a place of moral leadership."

Moral leadership meant a commitment to maintain and transmit to future generations the liberal and humane ideals of the past. It involved the capacity to fit the national purpose to the constantly changing requirements of a dynamic people. In brief, the foremost presidents possessed a profound sense of history, a rooted dedication to time-sanctioned principles which each, in his own day and way, succeeded in reinvigorating and extending. Essential as it was to win approval at the polls, they looked as well to the regard of posterity.

XIII

James Bryce, assessing the United States chief magistrates down to 1900 in his book, "The American Commonwealth," entitled a famous chapter "Why Great Men Are Not Chosen Presidents"; but he erred even for those years. Taking the entire span from Washington to the exit of Eisenhower, the historical consultants find that great men occupied the chair during forty of the 172 years and, if their near-great associates be added, the grand total approaches eighty years, or nearly half the lifetime of the republic. Can any other nation display a better record?

Moreover, even the do-nothing stretches in the White House did not lack value since, as a rule, they provided breathing spells for the country to digest the achievements of the forceful executives.

All in all, the historical picture offers the present-day defenders of democracy against totalitarianism reassuring evidence that Jefferson's—and America's—reliance on the people as "the safest depository of power" is the cure for mankind's ills.

THE SEVENTY-FIVE PARTICIPANTS IN THE POLL

LEWIS E. ATHERTON, University of Missouri
JAMES P. BAXTER, 3d, former president of Williams College

RAY A. BILLINGTON, Northwestern University

WILFRED E. BINKLEY, Ohio Northern University, Ada, Ohio

THEODORE C. BLEGEN, University of Minnesota

JOHN M. BLUM, Yale University

DENIS W. BROGAN, Peterhouse, Cambridge University, England

PAUL H. BUCK, Harvard University

SOLON J. BUCK, former National Archivist, Washington, D.C.

JAMES M. BURNS, Williams College

FRANCIS W. COKER, Yale University

HENRY S. COMMAGER, Amherst College

JAMES B. CONANT, former President of Harvard University

MARCUS CUNLIFFE, University of Manchester, Manchester, England

RICHARD N. CURRENT, University of Wisconsin

MERLE CURTI, University of Wisconsin

VIRGINIUS DABNEY, editor, The Richmond Times Dispatch

CHESTER M. DESTLER, Connecticut College, New London

DAVID DONALD, Princeton University

DWIGHT L. DUMOND, University of Michigan

CLEMENT EATON, University of Kentucky

HAROLD U. FAULKNER, Smith College

GILBERT C. FITE, University of Oklahoma

FELIX FRANKFURTER, United States Supreme Court

JOHN HOPE FRANKLIN, Brooklyn College

FRANK FREIDEL, Harvard University

RALPH H. GABRIEL, American University, Washington, D.C.

PAUL W. GATES, Cornell University

NORMAN A. GRAEBNER, University of Illinois

FLETCHER M. GREEN, University of North Carolina

OSCAR HANDLIN, Harvard University

JAMES B. HEDGES, Brown University

PENDLETON HERRING, President, Social Science Research Council

JOHN D. HICKS, University of California at Berkeley

JOHN HIGHAM, University of Michigan

RICHARD HOFSTADTER, Columbia University

ARTHUR N. HOLCOMBE, Harvard University

SIDNEY HYMAN, Political Analyst, Washington, D.C.

GERALD W. JOHNSON, journalist and historian, Baltimore

WALTER JOHNSON, University of Chicago

ARTHUR S. LINK, Princeton University

DUMAS MALONE, University of Virginia

ASA E. MARTIN, Pennsylvania State University

REGINALD C. McGRANE, University of Cincinnati

FREDERICK MERK, Harvard University

ELTING E. MORISON, Massachusetts Institute of Technology

SAMUEL E. MORISON, Harvard University

GEORGE E. MOWRY, University of California at Los Angeles

CURTIS NETTELS, Cornell University

ROY F. NICHOLS, University of Pennsylvania

RUSSELL B. NYE, Michigan State College

JOHN W. OLIVER, University of Pittsburgh

BRADFORD PERKINS, University of Michigan

DEXTER PERKINS, Cornell University

STOW PERSONS, University of Iowa

EARL POMEROY, University of Oregon

DAVID M. POTTER, Stanford University

EDGAR S. ROBINSON, Stanford University

LINDSAY ROGERS, Columbia University

EUGENE H. ROSEBOOM, Ohio State University

CLINTON ROSSITER, Cornell University

ARTHUR M. SCHLESINGER JR., Harvard University

CHARLES G. SELLERS JR., University of California at Berkeley

FRED A. SHANNON, University of Illinois

JAMES W. SILVER, University of Mississippi

HENRY NASH SMITH, University of California at Berkeley

KENNETH M. STAMPP, University of California at Berkeley

IRVING STONE, biographer and historian

GLYNDON G. VAN DEUSEN, University of Rochester

RICHARD C. WADE, University of Chicago

WALTER P. WEBB, University of Texas

THOMAS J. WERTENBAKER, Princeton University

T. HARRY WILLIAMS, Louisiana State University

HARVEY WISH, Western Reserve University

C. VANN WOODWARD, Yale University

XI

The Future of the Presidency

Introduction. Prognostication is very difficult in a turbulent political environment even with so enduring an institution as the presidency. Yet some assessment of where this very important leadership vehicle is going is appropriate.

What have the "classics" in this volume on the American presidency told us? The "classics" began by showing how so remarkable an institution as the presidency was created, and they continued evaluating the performances of presidents in office. Now the time has come for a summing up.

The goals of this chapter are to recapture the evolution of the "modern" presidency and to assess the political circumstances that are likely to shape its behavior and performance in the future.

In the first selection, political scientist Fred Greenstein reviews and evaluates the different phases in the development of the modern presidency from Franklin Delano Roosevelt to the present, to include what has been described as the "post-imperial presidency." The continuities and discontinuities that Greenstein finds should make clear why so much of the presidential performance is profoundly affected by both the political climate and the president's personality in interaction. While Greenstein detects, as other political scientists and historians have, a recurring cycle of presidential activism and passivism, he concludes with the observation that, "Today's presidency is an institution in search of new role definitions."

In the final selection, "The Past and Future Presidency," political scientist Aaron Wildavsky peers into the future and sees presidents who are capable either of retreating or advancing in the exercise of leadership, depending upon what we the people ask of our presidents. The message that comes through is that though there is no such thing as presidential determinism, the presidency is likely to remain the focus of various citizen expectations and demands.

One final message comes through both selections in this chapter. It is that although political climate (normalcy, crisis, etc.) and followership will influence the choices a president can make, the presidency will remain a very personal office. The individual who occupies it will make a profound difference. And although balance between the president and the Congress is important, the United States cannot afford two governments. The president and the Congress cannot both lead. Thus, the president will still need to be as big a man as he can be, but Congress will always have the right to impeach him, if (to paraphrase Hamilton in Federalist No. 65) "he abuses or violates some public trust."

41. Change and Continuity in the Modern Presidency*

FRED I. GREENSTEIN

Although my main concern here is change in the American presidency since 1960, it is necessary to begin with an extended prefatory account of the evolution of the presidency from Franklin D. Roosevelt's inauguration through the end of the Eisenhower administration. This is because the most striking changes in the institution occurred during the first three modern presidencies, and many of those that have occurred since Kennedy took office appear to have been oscillations in patterns that began under Kennedy's three predecessors.

I am using the phrase "modern presidency" to distinguish the Roosevelt through Carter presidencies from the previous "traditional presidencies."[1] Up to the Hoover administration, there were variations from president to president in how the chief executive conducted his duties. Periodically there were stable shifts in the functioning of the institution itself—for example, the shift to popular election with Jackson and the increased tendency of presidents to interest themselves in legislation beginning around the turn of the century. With Franklin Roosevelt's administration, however, as part of the general increase in the size and impact of American government, the presidency began to undergo not a shift but rather a metamorphosis. The eight post-Hoover presidencies, those I have called modern, have been different from their thirty traditional predecessors in the following respects:

(1) From a state of affairs in which there was at best a somewhat grudging acceptance that the president would be "interested" in the doings of Congress, it has come to be taken for granted that he *should* regularly initiate and seek to win support for legislative action as part of his continuing responsibilities. The president also has come to be far more active in evaluating legislative enactments with a view to deciding whether to exercise the veto than traditionally was the case.

(2) From a presidency that normally exercised few unilateral powers, there has been a shift to one that is provided—via statutes, court decisions, and informal

*Source: From The New American Political System by Anthony King, ed., pp. 45-85. Copyright © 1978 American Enterprise Institute for Public Policy Research, Washington, D.C. Reprinted by permission.

precedents—with many more occasions for direct policy making through executive orders and other actions not formally ratified by Congress.

(3) From a presidency with extremely modest staff support, there has evolved one in which the president has at his disposal in the Executive Office and "on loan" from elsewhere in the executive branch an extensive bureaucracy to implement his initiatives. It is only because of the rise of a presidential bureaucracy that it has been possible for presidents to follow through on (1) and (2).

(4) Finally, there appear to have been major changes in the quantity and quality of public attention to incumbent presidents. For many Americans the complex, uncertain political world of our times seems to be dealt with by personification, in the form of perceptions of the quality of performance and personal virtue of the incumbent president. Presidents are expected to be symbols of reassurance, possessing extraordinary "nonpolitical" personal qualities that traditionally were associated only with long deceased "hero presidents" of the past, such as George Washington. At the same time they are expected to be politically effective, bringing about favorable national and international social conditions. They have become potential beneficiaries of anything positive that can be attributed to the government, but also scapegoats for social and political discontent.[2]

THE FORMATIVE PERIOD OF THE MODERN PRESIDENCY

The emergence of the physical and symbolic defining characteristics of the modern presidency is evident in the several city blocks surrounding 1600 Pennsylvania Avenue. William Hopkins, who began working as White House stenographer under Hoover in 1931, went on to become executive clerk, and held his White House position until his retirement in the Nixon years, remembers that he had shaken hands with President Hoover the year before going to work in the White House. Hoover still found it possible to carry on the leisurely nineteenth-century New Year's Day tradition of personally greeting any

person who cared to join the reception line leading into the White House.[3]

In Hoover's time, the presidency had not become so central a symbol for public emotions and perceptions about the state of the nation that elaborate procedures for protecting the White House from potentially dangerous intruders were deemed necessary. The White House of our time is surrounded by a high, electronically sensitized fence; its gates are locked and carefully guarded; and the fence extends across West Executive Avenue to the ornate Old Executive Office Building, creating a two-block "presidential compound." In Hoover's time, the lower, unelectrified fence surrounded only the White House grounds and had open gates. Anyone walking east of the White House from what then was not a presidential office building, but rather the site of the State, Navy, and War Departments, customarily did so by strolling across the White House grounds.

Moreover, when Hoover was president, the West Wing of the White House had sufficient space to accommodate the modest presidential staff. The bureaucracy of the modern presidency now occupies not only the building across the street from the West Wing, but also the red-brick, high-rise New Executive Office Building on 17th Street. Extensions of the presidency are to be found in many other nearby buildings, including the Georgian-facade edifices facing Lafayette Square. There is even a house on the square to accommodate and provide office space for ex-presidents.

ROOSEVELT: THE BREAKTHROUGH TO THE MODERN PRESIDENCY.

The first stage in the transformation that accounted for these physical changes was an almost overnight rise in expectations about the appropriate duties of the chief executive. This resulted from the convergence of a deep national (and later international) crisis with the accession and long incumbency of perhaps

the most giftedly entrepreneurial president in American history, Franklin D.
Roosevelt. Nothing was "inevitable"
about the appearance in 1933 of entrepreneurial, innovative presidential leadership. FDR's nomination in 1932 had
not been a sure thing. As president-elect
he barely escaped assassination. It is
impossible to believe that the impact of
the leader next in succession, Vice
President-elect John Nance Garner,
would have been very different from
Hoover's. One can argue that, whether
under Hoover, Garner or the various
other "available" presidential contenders of the time, "social conditions"
would have fostered demands for strong
leadership.[4] But the outcome, if any, of
these demands might well have been
some form of indigenous dictatorship,
such as that described in Sinclair
Lewis's novel It Can't Happen Here.
Crisis was a necessary but far from sufficient condition for the modern presidency that began to evolve under
Roosevelt.

The premodern historical record—
especially the record of the nineteenth
century—contains countless examples
of congressional antipathy to mere
suggestions by the president that particular legislation be enacted.[5] There
were even congressmen who held that
presidential vetoes could not legitimately be used as an expression of policy preference by the chief executive,
but rather must be reserved for occasions when he deemed legislation to be
unconstitutional.[6] FDR promptly established the practice of advocating, backing, and engaging in the politics of winning support for legislation. By the end
of Roosevelt's long tenure in office,
presidential legislative activism had
come to be taken for granted, if not universally approved.

This activism began within four days
of Roosevelt's taking office. The relent-
less succession of "Hundred Days"
legislative enactments passed by the
special session of Congress that met
from noon, March 9, to 1:00 a.m., June
15, 1933—including such major policy

departures as the banking act, the securities act, the Civilian Conservation
Corps, and the National Industrial Recovery Administration—was appropriately viewed as the result of Roosevelt's
leadership. In some cases his leadership
involved bringing about the enactment
of programs that had long been on the
public political agenda, such as the
Tennessee Valley Authority, but which
needed the impetus of the Hundred
Days legislative campaign to achieve
approval. In one case—the Federal Deposit Insurance Corporation—Roosevelt
received praise for passage of a program
that he personally opposed but acceded
to after realizing it had too much congressional support to be defeated.[7]

That FDR was given credit for the initiatives of others points to the fact that
during his administration people tended
more and more to think of the president
as a symbol for government. The public
dealt with the increasing complexity of
government by personifying it. Even before Congress could convene, as the nationally broadcast inaugural ceremony
proceeded, the chief executive was almost instantly transformed from a remote, seemingly inert entity to a vivid
focal point of national attention. FDR's
confident comportment; the high oratory of the inaugural speech, with its
grave warning that he would request
war powers over the economy if Congress failed to act; his ebullience; the
decisiveness of the following day's
"bank holiday" executive order—all of
this elicited an overwhelmingly favorable public response to the new president. William Hopkins, who was then
in the White House correspondence
section, remembers that "President
Roosevelt was getting about as much
mail a day as President Hoover received
in a week. The mail started coming in
by the truckload. They couldn't even get
the envelopes open."[8]

Significantly, the volume of presidential mail has never tapered off. Recent
estimates are that over a million letters
come to the President annually.[9]
Roosevelt evidently was able to wed his

own great powers of personal communication to the general sense of national urgency, channeling what hitherto had been a static patriotic sentiment—American veneration of the great presidents of the past—into a dynamic component of the incumbent president's role. In initiating this characteristic of the modern presidency, he undoubtedly enhanced his ability and that of his successors to muster public support in times of perceived national crisis. But he also undoubtedly established unrealistic and even contradictory standards by which citizens tend to judge both the personal virtue of presidents and their ability to solve the typically controversial social and political problems that arise during their administrations.

FDR also innovated in accustoming the nation to expect that the president would be aided by a battery of policy advisers and implementers. At first these aides were officially on the payrolls of diverse non-White House agencies but were unofficially "the president's men."[10] Best remembered now is the sequence of academic braintrusters who advised FDR as governor of New York and early in his first term; the lawyers who drafted and politicked for the next stage of New Deal legislation; and Harry Hopkins, who served as war-time presidential surrogate in international diplomacy.

Politically attentive Americans tend to regard unofficial presidential advising—for example, Jackson's use of his Kitchen Cabinet and Wilson's of Colonel Edward House—with suspicious fascination. The fascination draws on the titillation of identifying the "real" powers behind the throne. The suspicion arises from the fear of illegitimate, legally irresponsible power—an especially strong concern in a polity in which so many of the political actors are lawyers inclined to invoke constitutional principles, even in debates over matter-of-fact interest-group conflicts.

In any case, in the fishbowl context of American mass communications, grey eminences do not remain grey for long. The two leading young lawyers who were Roosevelt's principal agents during the so-called Second New Deal, Thomas Corcoran and Benjamin Cohen, were pictured on the cover of *Time* magazine. This visibility of the unofficial aides who were essential to maintaining FDR's momentum as policy initiator threatened the legitimacy of his leadership. To the degree that such aides upstaged him, they also detracted from his centrality as a symbol of national leadership. These costs of using visible unofficial advisers must have contributed to Roosevelt's interest in procedures that would provide the presidency with aides who *were* official and who were *not* conspicuous.

Just such a corps of aides was proposed in the 1937 recommendations of the Brownlow committee, the Committee on Administration of the Federal Government that Roosevelt appointed. Arguing that because of the mushrooming responsibilities of the executive branch, "the President needs help," the Brownlow committee proposed that an Executive Office of the President be established, including a White House Office staffed by skilled, energetic aides who were to have "a passion for anonymity." After extensive political bargaining, the Reorganization Act of 1939 was passed and implemented by executive order.[11]

The shift from exclusive use by Roosevelt of behind-the-scenes advisors to use of a staff authorized by statute is recorded in the *United States Government Manual* released in October 1939. Listed immediately following the page identifying the president of the United States is what continues to be the umbrella heading under which presidential agencies are grouped—the Executive Office of the President (EOP). The White House Office (WHO) is listed next. (In October 1939 only three WHO aides had been selected. In the 1970-1971 *Manual*, about the peak year for size of WHO staff, over fifty were listed.)[12]

Each *Manual* since 1939 has listed

next in sequence, following the WHO, the Bureau of the Budget (after 1970, the Office of Management and Budget). BOB/OMB has consistently been by far the most influential Executive Office appendage, except for the White House Office itself. The BOB originally had been established in 1921, after a decade of efficiency-minded lobbying by "good government" reformers who sought to substitute a consolidated and centrally screened executive budget as the communication submitted for congressional action, rather than the disaggregated requests from individual agencies that had been submitted until then. Until the passage of the 1939 Reorganization Act, however, the bureau was not a policy-framing agency, but rather a kind of bookkeeping department which sought to achieve mechanical economies in budgetary requests based, in some cases, on exercises of parsimony as picayune as saving paperclips and pencil stubs. Although officially an agency of the president, the old "green eyeshade" BOB was lodged in the Treasury Department and did not attend to presidential policy goals, apart from the general 1920s policy of holding down budgetary requests and expenditures.

The post-Reorganization Act bureau received a new director, Harold D. Smith, who was both passionately anonymous and assiduously devoted to building an organization of highly able public administrators who would have a continuing responsibility to the presidency, no matter who the incumbent was, as well as serving the man who was in office at the time. Smith's unpublished diaries and the memoirs of the Washington insiders of that period make it clear that he privately assumed an active, if invariably diffident, advisory relationship with President Roosevelt.[13] FDR and Smith conferred regularly. The bureau itself was moved in 1939 from the Treasury Department building to office space in the frequently renamed building directly across the street from

the West Wing of the White House. Smith continued to have similar regular conferences with the new president during the first year of the Truman presidency. Instructively from the standpoint of anonymity, the bureau was rarely discussed in the press, and during his tenure as director, Smith's name appeared only twice—both times in neutral contexts—in the *New York Times Index*.

Because the great changes between 1933 and 1945 in expectations about the magnitude, impact, and nature of the presidency were the outcome not only of the political climate during Roosevent's time in office, but also of FDR's highly personal style, it was not inevitable that what I now confidently describe as "the modern presidency" *had* to continue into subsequent administrations. Roosevelt's personality-centered presidency might simply have been one of many transitory highs in the recurring cycle of presidential passivity and activism, such as the intense but rather brief legislative activism of the early Wilson administration. Roosevelt's monopoly of political attention and his capacity to arouse public feeling were reminiscent of the visibility and appeal of his cousin, Theodore Roosevelt. His use of emergency powers in response to crisis had strong precedents in the Lincoln administration. Therefore, when Roosevelt died, World War II ended, and a virtually unknown "little man" succeeded him, there was reason to expect, fear, or hope that, much as in the Wilson-to-Harding transition, the presidency would again move from center stage in national government to a position closer to the wings.

TRUMAN: INSTITUTIONALIZATION OF THE MODERN PRESIDENCY

Truman's impact on substantive public policies was at best uneven; his impact on the modern presidency as an institution was profound. Under Truman, the presidency did in fact continue to be central in national politics. There was, however, a shift from the ad hoc, personally stimulated policy initiatives of Roosevelt to the methodical development of policy by Truman in consort with WHO and BOB staff members, as well as other public officials. This shift is aptly described by Max Weber's phrase "the routinization of charisma."

As tattered and imprecise as the term "charisma" has come to be, it could not be stretched to describe Truman's leadership, especially the flat, uninspiring impression he communicated during his first eighteen months in office. Truman's initial extremely high Gallup Poll rating (87 percent) expressed national mourning for FDR and sympathy for Truman in what obviously was going to be the monumental task of attempting to succeed Roosevelt. After that first Gallup Poll, Truman's performance as president frequently garnered more disapproving than approving poll responses. This was an effect of the unsettled political times over which Truman presided. (Roosevelt, like Lincoln, died in time not to face postwar problems virtually guaranteed to erode presidential popularity.) Truman's seeming substantive and rhetorical shortcomings as a national leader also contributed to his endemically low popularity. But he had the added burden that would have been faced by any successor of Roosevelt (and perhaps Roosevelt himself had he survived his fourth term)—that of living up to the standard FDR had set in the depression and during the war as an inspirer of public confidence.

Whatever his inspirational inadequacies, Truman was no back-to-normalcy Harding. This was evident as early as September 1945, when in a twenty-one-point reconversion message he anticipated the major themes of what soon evolved into the Fair Deal program.[14] Truman also was not the inexperienced "failed haberdasher" his critics alleged him to be. In leading a major wartime investigating committee that scrutinized the performance of "home front" activities and in his earlier service

on the Senate Appropriations Committee he had over a decade become closely familiar with the operations and policies of the federal government. Moreover, before his entry into the Senate, his extensive experience as a county administrator and his omnivorous reading had left him well furnished with political skills and ideals.

We can see harbingers of the future president in the handful of documents that the Truman Library has been able to salvage from Truman's years in local government. Some of them, in which he methodically accounts for county revenues and expenditures and proposes reforms, anticipate Truman's exceptionally close work with his Budget Bureau staff in examining the many policy issues that quickly fell into the bailiwick of that institution. Other early Truman documents include speeches to patriotic and other civic groups which presage many aspects of his presidential leadership—speeches extolling the centrality of the president in the constitutional system; praising good (that is, decisive, manly, and moral) leaders, including great presidents; and conceiving of social process as the outcome of the triumph of good over bad leaders.[15]

Much of Truman's impact on the presidency is illustrated by comparing his and Roosevelt's ways of dealing with the Bureau of the Budget. In Harold Smith's diaries, a repeated theme during the Roosevelt years is Smith's concern that he would fail to build a continuing staff agency that could serve successive presidencies. So incorrigibly informal was Roosevelt's way of operating that he often treated Smith simply as if he were another of Roosevelt's many unofficial advisers, rather than the head of a statutory presidential staff agency. Smith expressed in his diaries a concern that the agency he was in the process of carefully filling with the most promising administrators he could find would be compromised institutionally by FDR's continuing impulse to make use of the director as a mediator among feuding departments and wartime agencies. He was distressed, as he put it, at being Roosevelt's "Mr. Fixit."

Under Truman, the bureau itself as well as its director became an integral part of the presidency. During Smith's holdover period and the tenure of his exceptionally able successor, James Webb, the bureau rapidly assumed the role of central coordinating institution for framing and formalizing annual presentations of what came to be called "the program of the president." Truman was a direct party to the soon taken-for-granted expanded role of the Bureau of the Budget, the enlargement of the White House Office staff, and the conversion of that staff into a team meeting daily with "the boss," dividing a workload beyond the capacity of the traditional presidency. By 1947 the efforts of the White House staff and of the Bureau of the Budget had become closely coordinated as a result of Truman's, Smith's, and Webb's efforts.

From time to time BOB aides, especially if they developed strong Fair Deal political convictions, "crossed the street" and became White House aides. Meanwhile, the bureau itself continued to develop its joint roles of helping the president to frame his policy program and examining policy proposals in terms of their consistency with the overall outlines of that program as well as their technical feasibility. It was during Truman's first two years in office that the bureau began, as a standard operating procedure, to examine all departmental appropriations requests in terms of their consistency with the president's program. Even more important (and less probable, given the title of the agency), the bureau became centrally involved in the legislative process. It became a regular BOB duty to clear and coordinate all legislative requests originating within federal departments, to help draft legislation emanating from the White House, to clear and draft executive orders, and to do all of this in terms of program of the president. These actions were in addition to the continuation of a bureau function acquired in the late 1930s—review and clearance with other relevant agencies of all congressional enactments with a view to recommending whether they be signed or vetoed.

The annual BOB compilation of proposed legislation and the final budget document provide the basis for what has become the set-piece initiation of each political year—a state of the union message, backed up by draft legislation. Delivered by the president with dignified republican ceremony to a joint session of Congress and other assembled dignitaries, the contemporary state of the union message enunciates the general outlines of the president's program, as well as containing traditional rhetoric about present national conditions and future prospects.

The state of the union message is one of three major presidential communications that go to Congress in January. The second is the budget document itself, accompanied by the budget message and the *Budget in Brief*, complete with graphic illustrations. The third is the report of the president's Council of Economic Advisers (CEA). The CEA, which was provided for in the Employment Act of 1946, is one of two continuing accretions to the Executive Office added during the Truman years. Truman's first council had a chairman who wanted the annual report to be an independent assessment of the economy not coordinated with the political emphasis of the overall presidential program. This view of the role of the CEA did not prevail, however. The council became part of the president's team, and its report and the other two January messages quickly became complementary assertions of the same program. A second statutory body, the National Security Council (NSC), grew out of the legislation that brought about the unification of the armed forces. Initially the NSC was conceived of by many congressmen who had supported unification as a potential check on presidents' autonomy in their commander-in-chief role. Truman, however, "domesticated" the NSC as well as the CEA. Ever since the Truman years both of these, plus numerous transient EOP agencies, have been further institutional underpinnings of the modern presidency.

Just as the professional staff of the BOB acquired some of the qualities of those British civil servants who perennially aid the executive, whatever party is in power, so the president's January communications have become roughly akin to the messages to new British parliamentary sessions, ghostwritten by the government in power for delivery by the monarch. But American presidents face one of the most vigorously autonomous legislatures in any parliamentary democracy. Hence their messages only help set the *terms* of the next legislative session's political debate, whereas the proposals voiced by the British monarch almost invariably are enacted into law. The many legislative defeats Truman received from the 79th through 82nd Congresses illustrate how a presidential program may be consistently blocked by an opposition coalition. In Truman's case the amount of Fair Deal domestic legislation that he succeeded in passing was miniscule, although there were major triumphs in assembling a sufficiently large bipartisan foreign policy coalition to authorize the Truman Doctrine, the Marshall Plan, and other postwar reconstruction and cold war initiatives.

Truman was also responsible not merely for initiating but also for carrying through policy making in areas included in the expanded domain of independent presidential action. Among the most consequential exercises of executive initiative by this believer in a presidency with substantial autonomous powers were the decision to use atomic weapons at the end of World War II, the decision to commit American troops to Korea, and the executive order integrating the military. Many of Truman's au-

tonomous decisions were politically costly, including a number that reflected his commitment to maintaining the independent powers of the presidency—for example, the steel seizure and the relief of General MacArthur.

Despite domestic policy stasis, his low general popularity, and the political costliness of some of his decisions, Truman's practice of executive assertiveness entrenched the tendency of all but the most conservative policymakers to look at the president as the main framer of the agenda for public debate—even when much of the debate consisted of castigation of his proposals. Truman, like Roosevelt, was not alone responsible for the changes in the presidency that occurred during his years in office. Key advisers like Smith and Webb were also influential. Moreover, Truman was operating in an environment of big government, the welfare state, and American international involvement that inevitably tended to place major responsibilities on the executive branch. Nevertheless, like Roosevelt, Truman himself does emphatically seem to have been a major independent influence on the shape of the modern presidency. Not everyone in the postwar period was convinced that the welfare state should continue or that the United States should maintain its international commitments. Conservatives of both parties felt that the New Deal welfare innovations should be repealed or cut back. Conservative isolationists and left-leaning supporters of Henry Wallace's 1948 Progressive party, out of wholly different motivations, opposed American involvement in the international arena. And during the post-World War II years not all democracies acquired assertive, stable executive leadership, the French Fourth Republic being an obvious example of a nation in which the top political executives (although not the permanent bureaucrats) were highly limited in influence and unstable in tenure in office. What then was to be expected of the evolving "center stage" presidency when another president replaced Truman—one who had frequently echoed his newly adopted party's claim that the "balance" of political leadership should be redirected toward Congress?

EISENHOWER: RATIFICATION OF THE MODERN PRESIDENCY

When the Republicans returned to power in 1953 and the institutional changes and role expectations of the modern presidency were not fundamentally altered, the Great Divide had been crossed. As is well known, drawing on his long military exposure to staff work, Eisenhower arranged for the establishment of a White House office that was more formally organized and, incidentally, larger than Truman's WHO. At least in the official scheme of things, the Eisenhower White House was an organizational hierarchy. Directly under the presidential apex was a chief of staff—for the first six years, the zealous Sherman Adams. As the assistant to the president, Adams was listed first in the *Organization Manual*; other White House aides were enumerated in an indented list that visually conveyed their subordination to Adams. Adams's counterpart in foreign affairs—again for the first six years—was Secretary of State John Foster Dulles.

We know from a variety of sources, including the newly opened private and confidential files of the president's personal secretary, that Eisenhower was far from being a mere puppet of Adams and Dulles. He was intimately involved in national security policymaking and had multiple sources of information about domestic as well as foreign affairs. As a domestic political conservative without a strong desire to innovate, except in modest incremental ways, Eisenhower does, however, seem to have left to Adams and his associates a variety of substantive decisions that would have been made by the president himself in the previous administration, as well as making use of Adams as a framer of al-

ternatives under circumstances where Truman would have canvassed alternatives on his own.

Other steps toward formalization in the Eisenhower White House were the regular and systematic practice of holding cabinet meetings (although, as in other presidencies, the cabinet was not a decisionmaking body); the establishment of a Cabinet Secretariat; and the creation of an elaborate National Security Council structure, in which special attention was paid not only to formal presentations in weekly meetings of the NSC, but also to the use of a coordinating mechanism (later scrapped by Kennedy) to attend to the implementation of policy.

Many of Eisenhower's formal mechanics of White House organization were supplemented by informal, unpublicized proceedings. The NSC meetings, for example, which by the end of the 1950s had come to be thought of as mechanical rituals, were in fact coordinating and teamwork-generating occasions. Preceding the official meetings, however, there were off-the-record meetings by the president with a subgroup of the NSC, and these appear to have been occasions for a genuine process of hammering out policy in which the president arrived at decisions after hearing contending points of view.[16] And members of the cabinet had individual access to the president to discuss matters that cabinet members invariably find impolitic to discuss openly in the cabinet room. Moreover, for the first time the White House Office staff acquired an official legislative liaison office (staffed by a skilled lobbying team that Eisenhower "appropriated" from the Pentagon). As Eisenhower came to be more and more aware that even a conservative who wished to put curbs on policy innovation needed effective representation of his views to Congress, this staff became increasingly systematic in its efforts to advance the president's program.

Above all, under Eisenhower there

continued to *be* a president's program. Having talked of "restoring the balance," Eisenhower quickly found himself to be a presidentialist—that is, a defender of the accrued responsibilities of the modern presidency. This ratification of the overall properties of the modern presidency during Eisenhower's two terms is manifested at both the formal and the symbolic levels. On the formal level, his position favoring presidential prerogative is instructive. Eisenhower immediately became intensely active, for example, in the campaign that successfully defeated the Bricker Amendment, which would have made presidential executive agreements with other nations subject to Senate ratification. In terms of maintaining the symbolic function of the office, Eisenhower was able to draw on his longstanding public credit as the most popular figure to emerge from World War II in order to maintain a remarkably consistent high level of prestige and popularity with the electorate, even at times when Washington insiders derided him for his seeming lack of political skill and knowledge. In this sense he was able—with what seems to have been minimum effort—to live up to the high expectations established under FDR that presidents be endowed with virtuous personal qualities but nevertheless be sufficiently politically competent to carry out their tasks in a way that leaves citizens broadly satisfied with the state of the nation.

A third, and from the standpoint of this essay especially consequential, aspect of the Eisenhower presidency was his continued use of the institutional resource that made it possible for there to be a "program of the president"—the Bureau of the Budget. Eisenhower's first bureau director, Joseph Dodge, became attuned to the bureau's procedures before assuming office, taking advantage of Truman's offer of interelection "internships" for Eisenhower appointees. Dodge quickly recognized the high quality of the bureau's senior personnel

and their readiness to shift from shaping a Truman program to shaping an Eisenhower program. Although there was no first-year Eisenhower legislative program, there was one to accompany his January 1954 state of the union message. The requests for proposed legislation from federal agencies were routinely sent out by the bureau's professional staff in 1953. Before the year was over it became evident that an Eisenhower program would be submitted to Congress.

In August 1956 Eisenhower's secretary, Ann Whitman, replied to an inquiry from Milton Eisenhower as to how the president's workload might be reduced. Her letter, from which I quote selectively, suggests how a basically conservative president, working in a tightly staffed White House, allocated his energies. During much of the previous year the president had been recovering from two major health setbacks, so her remarks apply primarily to Eisenhower's practices up to his September 1955 heart attack. We see his very great attention to national security policy and his greater willingness to delegate policy initiation in domestic than in international affairs.

Regular Weekly Meetings:

1. The National Security Council seems to be the most time-consuming, from the standpoint of number of hours *in* the actual meeting, the briefing before the meeting that has seemed to become a routine, and the time that the president must give, occasionally, to be sure that the meetings reflect exactly the decisions reached. . . . [Mrs. Whitman thought that frequently the president was already well informed on the substance of the prior briefings and of the meetings themselves. She noted "he himself complains that he knows every word of the presentations as they are to be made. However, he feels that to maintain the interest and attention of every member of the NSC, he must sit through each meeting. . . ."]

2. The cabinet meetings are not usually so long as NSC, but the president feels in some instances that to fill out an agenda, items are included that are not necessarily

of the caliber that should come before the cabinet. . . .

3. The press conferences. These meetings are preceded by a half to three-quarter hour briefing by staff members. [Mrs. Whitman felt that in most cases Eisenhower was already sufficiently informed to meet the press without briefings, but added "the meetings do serve the purpose of letting him know how various members of the staff are thinking. . . ."]

4. Legislative leaders meetings. When the Congress is in session, these are held weekly, but do not last, on the average, more than an hour and a half and only about five minutes' preparation is required.

5. The president has a weekly meeting with the secretary of defense.

6. The president usually has a half-hour meeting with [economic advisers]\Dr. [Gabriel] Hauge and Dr. [Arthur] Burns. I think he finds these meetings valuable and do not believe the sessions are unduly prolonged.

Mrs. Whitman also noted that the president had a half-hour daily intelligence briefing from Colonel Andrew Goodpaster, and she listed roughly a dozen categories of "other items that occupy his time," some of them taking up very little time (for example, independent agencies), some of them involving him in time-consuming ceremonial duties (receiving ambassadors, meeting dignitaries and civic groups, state dinners, and signatures), and others involving policy and intermittently consuming much time. The latter included the State Department ("meetings with the secretary are irregular, based upon the urgency of the particular crisis of the moment"); additional defense matters ("here is a great time-consuming area. . . . I can't always see why some of the inter-Service problems cannot be resolved before they come to the president"); "other cabinet matters" ("The president is available at all times to any cabinet member for consultation"); "personnel, appointments, domestic matters" ("My general impression is that all such items have been pretty well digested [by Sherman Adams] before they reach the president, and that only his

final judgment is required"); and speeches ("The president spends a great deal of time personally on his speeches, but I don't think that routine can ever be changed. I think only by the process of editing and reworking does the speech become truly his own—and I think the hours—and I guess he spends twenty to thirty on each major speech—are inevitable.")[17]

THE PRESIDENCY SINCE 1960: STRUCTURAL CHANGES, OSCILLATIONS, AND CONTINUITY

In any institution it is difficult in the short run to distinguish between permanent changes and changes that will turn out to have been only ephemeral. Many changes in the post-Eisenhower presidency were thought to have been permanent at the time but from the perspective of the late 1970s appear to have been rather drastic zigs and zags in patterns that had been established during the formative first three modern presidencies. Taking as a combined basis of classification the actual functioning of the presidency and the way in which the more widely read commentators on American politics have evaluated its functioning, the Kennedy-to-Carter years can be divided into three phases.

Phase one is the period beginning with Kennedy's efforts—"vigorous" efforts—to initiate a wide range of policies, some of them long-term inheritances from the Democratic party's New Deal-Fair Deal agenda, others projects with a distinctive Kennedy stamp. This period continues through the enactment of the extraordinary volume of Johnson Great Society legislation by the heavily Democratic 89th Congress. The bulk of commentators on the presidency viewed this as a period during which a previously "stalemated" presidency was steadily increasing both in its impact on public policy and also in the merit of its contribution to the political system. Merit, of course, is in the eye of the beholder. The beholders I have in mind are the politically liberal academics and publicists who provide most of the "serious" commentary on public affairs. During the formative presidencies, as we shall see, most such political commentators had become convinced of the institutional desirability of a "strong" presidency. Experiencing the Kennedy qualities of personal leadership, the posthumous idealization of Kennedy, and the passage of Johnson's sweeping domestic policy program during the period from Kennedy's death to roughly the end of the 89th Congress, these commentators typically felt that the presidency was beginning, in practice, to perform precisely the functions in the political system they had long felt that it ought in principle to be performing.

The period of Great Society legislative enactment overlaps with the second phase, from the advent of serious protest at Vietnam escalation through Watergate and President Nixon's resignation. Even before the end of the 89th Congress, increasing American military involvement in Vietnam began to induce commentary on the presidency, which, as in the first post-1960 phase, stressed the growing capacity of presidents to shape public policy, but which now emphasized "excessive" presidential power. By late in the Watergate sequence, the view that the presidency was a dangerously unchecked institution was no longer monopolized by liberal political commentators. For convenience, I adopt for this period the label that came to be virtually automatic for many writers: "imperial presidency."

The first two phases, that of celebration of presidential strength and that of lamentation about the "imperial" practices of Presidents Johnson and Nixon, have been followed by a phase that, using the most recent catchword, I shall call "postimperial." During the time since President Nixon left office, one

president, Gerald Ford, has joined the select ranks of William Howard Taft and Herbert Hoover as the only twentieth-century incumbents to run unsuccessfully for reelection. Ford's successor, Jimmy Carter, limped through an initial year in office, during which he encountered what could charitably be called limited response to his ambitious legislative and foreign policy goals and a substantial erosion in his Gallup Poll ratings.[18]

Presidential politics in phase three, at the advent of the final quarter of the century, seems remarkably like the pattern of politics of the formative pre-Kennedy modern presidencies as described in Richard Neustadt's influential essay, "The Presidency at Mid-Century."[19] As a former Truman aide who had worked on the unsuccessful Fair Deal domestic program and who was also aware of the inability of FDR to win support for similar policies after 1938 and of Eisenhower's difficulty in achieving even limited policy goals, Neustadt saw the presidency as a highly restrained institution. Granting that modern presidents had acquired far enhanced formal powers and role expectations, Neustadt argued that presidents nevertheless were exceptionally limited in their capacities to turn formal power into effective policymaking. Further, the tension between the demands on them and the limitations on their ability to make policy and hence to live up to expectations put them in a position Neustadt likened to that of "a cat on a hot tin roof."

The rather drastic and rapid alternations since 1960 in the way in which the presidency has functioned and, possibly as important, in the way in which it has been perceived to function are to a considerable extent a consequence of one continuing property of the presidency. Among all American national political institutions, none is so profoundly affected by the personal characteristics and performance in office of the incumbent and of the other personalities he chooses or permits to act as his chief associates. One reason why the Roosevelt, Truman, and Eisenhower presidencies *could* be formative was that their long duration accustomed political actors, including presidents themselves and the public at large, as well as other members of the policymaking community, to broadly consistent practices in the conduct of the presidency. Between 1933 and 1961 the *three* formative modern presidents held office for the equivalent of *seven* four-year terms. Since then *five* presidents have been in office for the equivalent of just over *four* four-year terms.

Just as it was by no means predetermined that the three formative presidents would have the cumulative impact that they did have in shaping the basic qualities of the modern presidency, there was nothing inexorable about the way the institution has developed since. On the contrary, it has been plausibly maintained that each of the post-Eisenhower presidents had a major personal impact on the phases through which the presidency has moved since 1960. Would the three phases described above have occurred if the individual named Richard Nixon had defeated Kennedy in 1960? What would have happened if Kennedy had served two full terms? Or if Nixon had never become president?

Although there is no definite way to answer such questions, it is possible to apply systematic evidence and inference to them. "What if?" questions are the grist of historical explanation. It is only possible to say that *x* caused *y* in a historical sequence by inferring that some plausible non-*x* would have led to a result different from *y*. Putting this concretely, and in terms of the effects of presidential psychology on the evolution of the presidency, we may note that, quite appropriately, there continue to be debates about whether Kennedy would have escalated the Vietnam conflict in the fashion that Johnson did, whether FDR would have presided over the same Truman-led sequence of cold war events that occurred after his death, and so forth. The entire enterprise of psychological interpretation of presidents and their behavior is dependent on such speculation.[20]

By the late 1970s the rapid turnover in presidents had become an important quality of the presidency itself, as well as helping to explain the sequence of cyclical rather than secular changes in certain overall properties of the office. Modern presidents, at least since the Twenty-second Amendment, have generally been recognized by political observers as short-run participants in Washington policymaking, who therefore tend to have a hurried approach to the making of policy. The more enduring fixtures of the Washington political community—senior members of Congress, justices, lobbyists, and Washington attorneys, for example—can better afford to play a waiting game. If the impact a president seeks is policy innovation rather than the maintenance of the status quo, the president's relatively brief tenure of office encourages him to engage in activities that are politically risky: simply to win office he needs to raise aspirations about what he will be able to contribute to the nation; once in office, the difficulty of meeting those aspirations opens up temptations to cut corners—for example, to rush legislation through Congress and leave considerations of practical implementation for later on, or to circumvent slow-moving or otherwise recalcitrant departments and bureaus by moving policymaking into the White House, say, by augmenting the role of the assistant for national security affairs over that of the secretary of state or by establishing a White House "plumbers" group. The temptation to cut corners therefore seems bound to increase.

SHIFTING EVALUATIONS OF THE PRESIDENCY

In describing the circuitous course of what seemed to be the beginning of enduring changes in the post-1960 presidency, I have deliberately merged institutional functioning and prevailing value judgments about institutional functioning. This is because one of the most significant changes that occurred lay precisely in the evaluation of the institution by writers who, to a considerable extent, were actually responding to their own negative assessments of the policies and performance of individual presidents, especially Johnson and Nixon. The change in evaluations of the presidency by the most widely read and listened to commentators on that institution has had two consequences. First, it has helped fuel the political debate that has led, for example, to the presidency-curbing legislation of the 1970s. Second, value judgments affect empirical assessments. Since the "imperial" presidency, actions that might previously have seemed to show normal presidential autonomy have been construed as showing a tendency toward augmented unilateral power. As difficult as it is to separate value and empirical judgments in a context where the first type of judgment has contributed to the state of affairs that one seeks empirically to evaluate, it is useful to try to do precisely that.

William Andrews has carefully documented the shifts during the years of the modern presidency in normative appraisals of the institution by academic and, to a lesser extent, nonacademic commentators.[21] His summary pins down and expands on the point made earlier about the politically liberal perspective that has informed most serious writing on the presidency. By the later Truman years, most of the more widely read writers on the presidency had established an academic, and to a lesser extent a journalistic, orthodoxy about the greater intrinsic merit of the presidency as a political institution as compared with other national political institutions. Conservatives still fulminated about excesses in presidential power, but with the exception of the writings of the Princeton University constitutional law theorist Edward Cor-

win, academic commentary had come to stress the importance of an unfettered, activist president.

The standard themes in both the scholarship and the textbooks of the time[22] are that the president is the nation's single elected official and hence his mandate is broader than the "broken" mirror reflection of public opinion provided by Congress; that the president's institutional vantage point, overlooking other national institutions and facing outward internationally, makes him the most appropriate custodian of the "public interest"; and that the exigencies of an intricately interdependent economy, society, and international environment make it important to have a leader with leeway to act promptly and decisively with a minimum of hindrance and political pulling and hauling. From this standpoint, the major flaw in the presidency is not its susceptibility to the usurpation of power, but its subjection to the political restraints described in Neustadt's "The Presidency at Mid-Century." As we have seen, writers during the first half of the 1960s tended to be delighted that the presidential Gulliver had begun to be freed from the many "parochial" restraints on presidential leadership.

The very same writers who up to the mid-1960s looked to an unfettered presidency as a major positive feature of the political system, during the imperial presidency phase began to sound like the 1940s and 1950s conservatives who had favored the Twenty-second Amendment and the narrowly defeated Bricker Amendment. The bellwether of revisionism on the merits of a strong presidency is Arthur Schlesinger, Jr., whose book (which introduced the term *The Imperial Presidency*) includes an explicit mea culpa for Schlesinger's uncritical celebration of presidential activism in his writings on Jackson, Roosevelt, and Kennedy.[23]

Interestingly, Schlesinger goes out of his way to rediscover and to pay his respects to the main scholar of the presidency whose works focus on the chief executive's "aggrandizement of power," Edward Corwin.[24] Since Schlesinger and the many other liberal writers on the presidency only became preoccupied with the dangers inherent in the institution when they became distressed about particular policies pursued by Johnson and Nixon, it is instructive to note the development of Corwin's own thinking. As Andrews shows, Corwin was sufficiently enthusiastic about strong presidential leadership to be the chief academic supporter of Franklin Roosevelt's proposal to expand the size of the Supreme Court in order to reverse its proclivity to strike down New Deal legislation. The press of the day widely viewed Corwin as a major candidate for membership on the proposed "packed" Court.

In the event, "Court packing" never took place; Roosevelt soon had numerous openings to fill, and he never nominated Corwin. By 1940 the first of the four editions of Corwin's textbook criticizing the rise in presidential power had appeared. Without assuming a crass quid-pro-quo motivation on Corwin's part, one can reasonably surmise that his substantive evaluation of FDR had sharply altered after 1937 and that this change—like the changes in the 1960s liberals' views in response to presidential performance in office—was critical in reshaping his overall evaluation of the degree to which the institution itself was appropriately performing its constitutional responsibilities. In short, people often think they are evaluating the presidency when in fact they are evaluating presidents.

THE USE OF PERSUASION AND COMMAND

Command and persuasion are two pivotal terms in Neustadt's book *Presidential Power*.[25] Published in 1960, this work was quickly acknowledged as the most realistic scholarly account of how the presidency actually functions and what presidents can do to enhance their leadership. We have seen that Neustadt was not impressed with the shift toward greater capacity for policy initiation and unilateral action by modern presidents (these developments he described as the president's "clerkship"). Rather, he was concerned with the likelihood that presidents would fail to be politically effective because of the restraints on them by other elements in the political system and because of their own failure to exercise skilled leadership.

The central leadership skill, in Neustadt's view, was the power of persuasion—a power presidents can exercise by effective bargaining, maintaining their reputations with other policy makers as skilled and popular leaders, and seeking to arrange that other policymakers find it in their own interest to do voluntarily what the president wants them to do. Truman's wooing of Republican Senator Arthur Vandenberg to win bipartisan support for the Truman Doctrine and the Marshall Plan was Neustadt's illustration of effective persuasion. By command Neustadt meant unilateral presidential orders that are intended to be obeyed without defiance because they lie (or at least the president thinks they lie) in the sphere of decision making within which the president is authoritative, whether on a constitutional, statutory, or some other basis. Neustadt's examples of command were three major decisions: Truman's discharge of MacArthur and his seizure of the steel industry and Eisenhower's dispatch of troops to Arkansas to enforce school integration. All three decisions were unpopular; the steel seizure, in fact, was ruled unconstitutional.

Neustadt's inferences were that commands are evidence of presidential weakness rather than strength; that they do not contribute to the president's later effectiveness; and (presumably) that they are likely to be rare. Numerous presidential decisions during the 1960s and 1970s were construed as exercises of command and seemed to belie these inferences about the utility and frequency of presidential command decision making. First, much attention was paid to types of decisions that seemed not to have concerned Neustadt—namely *routine* command decisions. In later years these began to be recognized as politically significant. Second, many observers felt that *major* command decisions—decisions of the sort that did concern Neustadt—were becoming substantially more common.

Examples of routine command are presidential orders affecting White House administrative staffing and staff organization and presidential orders setting in motion the sophisticated travel and communication facilities at the president's disposal. A much more mundane example is the president's instruction to his secretary to carry out a clerical chore. Routine command is an inevitable component of leadership. If *all* presidential decision making were by persuasion and bargaining, as a literalist might conclude upon reading Neustadt, the president undoubtedly would be hopelessly overloaded.[26] Nevertheless, routine commands can be politically consequential—for example, the command to install a voice-activated tape recording system in the president's office or the command to ready the way for foreign travel, as in the 1972 Nixon trips to China and the Soviet Union, which greatly enhanced the president's popularity and made him a sure election winner.

Moreover, major presidential command decisions clearly *seemed* to be becoming more common during the years after Neustadt's book was published—especially during the imperial phase of the post-1960 presidency. Obvious examples are various of Johnson's and Nixon's decisions in connection with the Indochinese conflict; the instances of political espionage and sabotage by Nixon associates that were brought out in the Watergate episode; and numerous Nixon decisions in domestic politics, such as his aggressive use of presidential spending pow-

ers. At least, part of the increase in command during the Johnson and Nixon administrations, however, was simply an increase in perceived command. A liberal internationalist who favored Roosevelt's destroyers-for-bases exchange with Britain in 1940 was not likely to classify this as an act of command. The same liberal, as a Vietnam dove, might well have placed many similarly unilateral Johnson and Nixon decisions in the command category.

It follows that the command decisions that are politically costly are decisions that draw unfavorable attention to the president. For most of the public, such decisions need merely to be unpopular to affect the president unfavorably. For fellow leaders, command decisions by the president may be viewed unkindly not only because such leaders and their constituents disagree with their content, but also because they disagree with their wisdom, or even their legitimacy in constitutional terms. This class of major command decision is emphatically open to the kind of backlash that Neustadt had in mind—especially because decisions of this sort are not shared. The debacles of each of the imperial presidencies document this somewhat modified version of Neustadt's argument.

THE INTRACTABLE POLITICAL ENVIRONMENT OF THE POSTIMPERIAL PRESIDENCY

At what Neustadt called "mid-century," presidents were severely restrained in their ability to affect policy, especially in spheres other than those that permitted unilateral action. They were surrounded by an intractable political environment. As the last quarter of the century begins, after a period during which presidents seemed to be riding high, intractability is back. Many of the restraints on presidents that seemed unnecessarily oppressive to liberals in the 1950s and early 1960s are precisely those that so often restrained Ford and that make Carter's efforts at policy achievement so difficult. The way in which these restraints manifest themselves does seem to have changed, largely as the result of factors that make it even harder in the late 1970s than it was during the three formative modern presidencies for presidents to live up to the continuing belief of many citizens that the president is singly responsible for the state of the entire nation.

The most conspicious obstacle to presidential policy influence is Congress. From the rise of the congressional conservative coalition following the 1938 presidential election through Johnson's landslide election in 1964, the major source of congressional resistance to presidential initiatives was—especially in the Roosevelt, Truman, and Kennedy years—the resistance by conservative Republicans and southern Democrats to liberal presidential policy proposals. Eisenhower's domestic policy conservatism was sufficiently disguised by his advocacy of "modern Republicanism" to make this seem to be the case even during the single Republican presidency of that period.

The 95th Congress, which in Carter's first year in office passed none of his major substantive legislative proposals, had approximately the same one-sided Democratic majority as the 89th Congress, which in a comparable period of time enacted a sizable proportion of Johnson's Great Society program. One major difference between them was that Carter's was operating in an "end of liberalism" climate—a time when the failures of many Great Society programs had produced widespread skepticism about the efficacy of legislative attacks on major social problems. In fact, the phrase "the end of ideology" seems more applicable to the political discourse of the 1970s than it was to the period in which it was coined, the 1950s. In the 1950s there were still many political activists and practitioners who took it for granted that *broadly* liberal or *broadly* conservative political

programs, if only enacted, would rectify what they felt to be the nation's social and political shortcomings. In the present era of economic "stagflation" and of such cross-cutting conflicts as those between liberal policy reformers favoring environmental protection and liberal labor union activists favoring economic growth, clear-cut lines of cleavage and hence the bases for organizing coalitions are harder to identify than they were even in the ostensibly unideological 1950s.

Closely related to the decline of predictable ideological groupings in Congress (as elsewhere in society) is a decline since the 1950s in the ability of congressional leaders to serve as effective intermediaries between their colleagues and the president, knowing that on achieving agreement with the president they can deliver significant blocs of votes and bring about the passage of the desired legislation. Consider the negotiations that shaped the final outcome of the Civil Rights Act of 1957. The point at issue was a provision of the legislation that enabled federal judges to exact fines and prison sentences in cases when state officials deprived citizens of their voting rights. If such cases were not decided by judges, but rather by the lily-white southern juries of the time, there would have been no effective sanction against southern officials who ignored the act's provisions. Through the efforts of the two Texas power brokers who led the majority Democratic party, Speaker Sam Rayburn and Senate Majority Leader Lyndon Johnson, a group of swing congressmen had been won over to the provision, which finally became law: fines as great as $300 and jail sentences up to forty-five days would be acceptable without the requirement of a trial. Johnson, who considered this a more favorable compromise than he had hoped for, telephoned President Eisenhower and

asked the president to see quietly if his boys would agree to that. The president asked for ten minutes. He called [the Republican leaders, William Knowland and Joseph Martin] off the floor; both agreed. . . . [Eisenhower] called Lyndon Johnson back and said everything was okay. He asked for a little time so the proceedings would be in order, which Lyndon agreed to. . . . The President called [his chief of legislative liaison] who was delighted at the compromise.[27]

Even if Carter had managed to establish such solidly grounded bargaining relations with the congressional party leaders of the 95th Congress, there was little likelihood that the leaders themselves would have been able to deliver the goods. . . . no subsequent congressional party leaders have been as skilled at molding coalitions as Johnson and Rayburn were; there has been an increasing tendency for incumbent congressmen automatically to be returned to office if they run for reelection, and this undoubtedly increases congressmen's independence in dealing with both their party leaders and the president; and a massive growth in congressional staffs has further decentralized congressional power by giving congressmen their own decision-making resources. Above and beyond these changes, there appears to be a general post-Watergate congressional resistance to cooperation with the White House.[28]

In the 1950s it was widely taken for granted that Congress was a major check on executive autonomy and that the "weakness" of congressional parties limited the chances that partisanship would serve to "bridge the separation of powers" even when the same party was in control of both branches of government. Who would have thought that a quarter-century later one explanation of a president's difficulties in influencing his party would be a still greater decline in the capacity of congressional leaders to mediate between members of Congress and the president? This decline does seem to have occurred, however, and it parallels still another institutional decline—that of the power of party leaders in the states and localities to mediate between their constituencies and the president, especially in presidential-selection politics.

During the formative period of the modern presidency, the "decentralized" national party system was widely viewed as a restraint on the mobilization around the president of national policymaking coalitions. By the 1970s state and local party organizations were so fragmented that, by contrast, the 1930s through the 1950s seem to have been high points of party government. At least in the earlier period there *were* party organizations and leaders with whom presidents could bargain and who viewed a successful president as a political asset. Accompanying the general decline in the strength of state and local party organizations throughout the 1960s there was a striking decline in candidacies and campaigns using traditional grass-roots party channels. The older decentralized party fiefdoms were at least entities with which presidents could bargain—for example, when the time came for renomination or for influencing the choice of one's successor. Today there is much less to bargain with "out there." Moreover, the change in presidential-selection rules toward multiple primaries, caucus states that are penetrable by disciplined candidate organizations, the disappearance of unit-rule voting at national conventions, and other "democratizing" party reforms further invalidate the textbook description of the president as chief of his party. In 1968, if Johnson had not withdrawn his candidacy, it was by no means certain that he would have been renominated. Ford fought an extremely demanding battle for the 1978 nomination. And while Nixon's renomination was superficially in the traditional pattern of partisan renomination of incumbent presidents, his main resource was the Committee to Re-elect the President, not the Republican party.[29]

Clearly much of what is intractable about the political environment of the late 1970s results from the inability of

presidents to work effectively with institutions that also restrained the early
modern presidents. The difference is in
the nature of this inability. In the past,
the resistance came from institutions
that possessed sufficient structure and
leadership so that bargaining and
negotiation were possible. In the present, institutions are more amorphous,
less responsive to their own leadership
or any other, and are therefore less well
suited for presidential coalition-
building.

This amorphousness also appears increasingly to apply to cabinet departments, as Heclo suggests . . . in his
larger study of the executive branch.[30]
The president's appointees—the cabinet
secretaries and assistant secretaries—
seem less and less likely to be professional politicians or public figures who
have independent bases of political influence. Rather, they are professional
participants in the policy domains that
concern their departments. In this respect they tend to have views that con-
verge with those of the career officials
in the departments—the latter having
increasingly become advocates of the
substantive policy directions of the programs that they administer. Cabinet secretaries have always "gone native" and
civil servants have always had views
about their programs, but if Heclo is
correct, there is now less difference between the political appointees and the
career bureaucrats than there once was.
Above all, the departments are decreas-
ingly available to the president as firm
entities with which he can work out alliances in the course of policymaking
and implementation.

Under the heading of intractability (if
not amorphousness) it also is appropriate to mention the mass media, which
nowadays expose the president to a
kind of scrutiny that probably accounts
both for the evanescent high popularity
of many presidents during their early
months in office and for their subsequent sharp declines in support.
Roosevelt was rarely photographed from

the waist down; many Americans do
not appear to have been aware of the
extent of his physical disability. George
Wallace's physical disability was publicized in minute clinical detail; his
physical limitations and his emotional
state were described in ways that could
scarcely have encouraged support for
his presidential aspirations. In part, microscopic focus on real or attributed
presidential acts and traits (Carter's folk-
siness, Ford's physical ineptness, Nixon's outbursts of temper during the late
stages of Watergate) is a result of the
shift from print journalism to television
newscasting as the principal source relied upon by most Americans for political news.[31] Without accepting the indictment by Nixon loyalists of the "liberal establishment" mass media, I think
that Nixon speech-writer Raymond
Price is undoubtedly right in his comment that

> Television has vastly changed the nature of
> the news business. . . . People turn to the
> news, whether print or broadcast, for both
> information and entertainment. Whereas
> print journalism has tended more toward
> the presentation of information that enter-
> tains, the structure of television news is
> such that it is designed to be an entertain-
> ment that informs.[32]

Media coverage of the president-elect
and the first few months of an administration tends to emphasize the endear-
ing personal touches—Ford's preparation of his own English muffins, Carter's
fireside chat in informal garb. No wonder both of these presidents enjoyed
high poll ratings during their initial
months in office. But the trend can only
go downward. Even if the media coverage simply shifts to rather straightforward reporting of initial administration
efforts to get organized and develop a
program, the impact is bound to be unfavorable in contrast to the idyllic initial
presentations of the president. Further,
after idealizing presidents, the media
quickly search out their warts. More and
more it is the shortcomings in presidential performance that are newsworthy.

Moreover, tough investigative journalism now is a prime means of making a professional mark. Such journalism may have been an invaluable counterweight to Johnson credibility gaps and Nixon stonewalling. For present purposes, however, what needs to be noted is that aspiring Woodwards and Bernsteins constitute still one more environmental obstacle to presidential leadership.[33]

THE PRESIDENTS' REACTIONS TO THEIR POLITICAL ENVIRONMENT

During the years when presidents were widely viewed by liberal political commentators as having an edge over other members of the policy community in their ability to identify and successfully to promote the public interest, some of these commentators were sensitive to the "Caesarist" potential of a politics in which sustained efforts were made to enhance a single leader's influence over other policymakers without providing him with legitimate instruments of leadership.[34] The now barely remembered "responsible party" proposals that were endorsed by many political scientists in the 1950s were designed to domesticate strong presidential leadership by harnessing it to party organizations that would be ideologically cohesive and that would also have a base in widespread participation by idealistic local party members. Needless to say, there has been no move toward strong, responsible political parties along the lines that the party reformers advocated, or along any other lines.

The reformers' concern with Caesarism does, however, seem to have been prophetic. It anticipated the perceived increases in the arbitrary use of presidential command powers during the Johnson, Nixon, and, some would claim, Kennedy years. Some of the excesses of imperial presidential leadership seem to have been attempts to flail out at the very aspects of the political environment that make the presidency a potentially stalemated institution: if bureaucrats seem disloyal, wiretap them; if the media and Congress will surely object to a desired military action, carry it out in secret. Obviously individual presidents differ in the degree to which they perceive their political environment in adversary terms and are prepared to act ruthlessly. Nevertheless, as the authors of an article reporting the sharp policy differences between Nixon supporters and supergrade civil servants comment, "even paranoids have enemies."[35]

GROWTH AND EVOLUTION OF THE PRESIDENTIAL BUREAUCRACY

From early in the 1960s through the end of the Ford administration, the number of people working in the White House Office increased substantially. There have been various published itemizations of the changes, but since practices such as borrowing personnel from other agencies in the executive branch have periodically changed and are difficult to monitor, I simply refer the reader to the several complementary attempts at year-by-year tabulation.[36] There has also been growth in the remainder of the Executive Office of the President, but here the statistics are even less susceptible to summary discussion because the EOP has frequently been used to house agencies that are not engaged in staffing the presidency but have line responsibilities. The most obvious example has been the Office of Economic Opportunity, which for many years was located in the EOP out of a fear that its program would be "absorbed" and that it would lose its innovative aspects and public visibility if it disappeared into the sprawling Department of Health, Education, and Welfare.

Something more than Parkinson's Law has been at work in the growth of the White House staff. In 1961, an administration took office committed to introducing new programs and energizing continuing programs. The Johnson administration was even more activist than Kennedy's, especially if "activism" is used to describe both the monumental outpouring of Great Society programs and also the expansion of hostilities in Vietnam. In these two administrations, the desire to innovate, combined with an impulse to circumvent resistance of the sort discussed in connection with the intractable political environment, led to an increasing tendency "to run the government from the White House." The need to coordinate interdepartmental programs had also expanded greatly. With Nixon, the desire to curb many of the innovations of the previous two administrations in the context of what seemed to Nixon and his associates to be a uniquely hostile environment (a Democratic Congress, administrators committed to carrying out New Frontier–Great Society programs, and mass media that in their view were not disposed to portray the president favorably).led to an even further expansion of the White House Office staff. Nixon's intense concern with foreign affairs and his close cooperation with Henry Kissinger and the much enlarged National Security Council staff, which served as Kissinger's EOP replica of the State Department, further contributed to the size of the bureaucracy attached to the presidency, as did Nixon's concern with domestic political enemies, which came to a head with the Watergate break-in and its aftermath.

Other important changes in the Executive Office of the President, especially changes in the Bureau of the Budget, which eventually led to a renamed agency with a somewhat changed mission, were underway throughout the post-Eisenhower period. We have seen that much of the Truman domestic program was drafted by Bureau of the Budget staff, working closely with Truman's (by present standards) small White House office team, especially the aides of the successive special counsels, Clark Clifford and Charles S. Murphy. The bureau proved to be remarkably capable of shifting gears and of responding to Eisenhower's

deep commitment to budgetary restraint. After the eight Eisenhower years, however, the bureau did not seem to Kennedy and Johnson to be an administrative entity well suited for framing a large volume of new policy, some of it without much precedent. Even before taking office, Kennedy appointed task forces to help shape his legislative agenda. Johnson made regular use of task forces, linking them to a much expanded White House domestic policy staff. Task forces typically were composed of people from the private sector, presidential aides, and federal officials. Use was made of individual Budget Bureau officials, but frequently they acted not in their institutional status as bureau officials, but rather as individuals who were chosen because they were viewed as personally knowledgeable and imaginative.

The Bureau of the Budget and its successor agency, the Office of Management and Budget (OMB), continued to clear legislation and executive orders, but more and more, routine rather than innovative policies bore the agency's imprint. Perhaps the most stable aspect of the bureau's role since 1960 has been its review of congressional enactments with a view to examining their consistency with the president's program and their practical efficacy.[37] There has been no systematic change in presidential responses to OMB's recommendations about whether or not to exercise the veto.

The 1970 reorganization in which the BOB became the OMB was a direct response to the Nixon administration's desire to have a political impact through the assertive use of the executive branch in policymaking—for example, by the impoundment of funds appropriated to maintain Great Society programs. Yet the change was anticipated in Kennedy's and Johnson's view of BOB as too slow-moving and cautious to keep up with their policymaking efforts. Under Kennedy and Johnson and under

Nixon, the bureau seemed ill-equipped to meet presidential desires, whether desires to initiate policy or to retrench.

The most distinctive feature of the OMB (which in many ways did continue to carry out the BOB's basic functions) was the introduction of a "layer" of presidential appointees directly under the OMB director. These officials were, in effect, line officers. Their counterparts were the White House office domestic policy aides. The new layer of politically appointed assistant directors and the bolstered White House staff were intended to make the bureau more systematically responsive to White House directives. During this period, OMB directors also tended to become detached from the professional staffs of their agency. More and more, they were used as personal staff advisers to the president, sometimes physically located in the West Wing and at any rate rarely in touch with the detailed work of the agency in such matters as the legislative clearance of less visible components of the presidential program and the examination of agency budget requests.

At the time of the 1970 transition, a number of long-time senior members of the agency, including some who had held positions of responsibility from as far back as the Smith era, found other employment or went into retirement. At least some of the exodus reflected unhappiness with the agency's changed mission. As Berman's research and other studies show,[38] the OMB is populated with aides who have spent far less time in the agency than was traditionally the case with the BOB and who tend to be reconciled to the notion that their responsibility is directly to the incumbent president. Undoubtedly there is much idealization in the BOB veterans' view that they served both president and presidency and in their feeling of commitment to "neutral competence." Nevertheless, there is reason to believe that the shift from BOB to OMB weakened a valuable restraint on gran-

diose presidential aspirations. One reason why many of the implementation failures of Great Society programs were not anticipated or more promptly detected was that the BOB staff (which has not increased in proportion to the growth of the White House staff) did not have the time and resources to evaluate the cascade of new programs and policy proposals.

Under present circumstances, however, it is far from certain that, even with sufficient resources, the OMB will be as disposed to warn presidents that proposed policies have hidden costs and impracticalities as the BOB traditionally would have been. Further, an agency with few officials who have long records of service and with a rather high rate of personnel turnover is bound to lack what is commonly called "institutional memory"—the ability to evaluate current proposals in terms of its experience with previous endeavors to accomplish the same ends.[39]

Both the change from BOB to OMB and the great expansion of White House staffs in the 1960s and early 1970s clearly arose out of presidential efforts to respond to a sense that, in spite of the center-stage status of the modern president, he is surrounded by a cast of actors more committed to stealing the show from him than to allowing him to live up to the nation's expectations that his performance be the extraordinary one. There is, however, no evidence that a larger White House staff and a more deferential BOB/OMB have in fact made recent presidents more successful. On the matter of White House size, Nixon's experience provides the strongest evidence of a contrary effect, as the innumerable memoirs and other Watergate-induced revelations so extensively document. A White House Office that envelops the entire Old Executive Office building and harbors an armed member of a political espionage unit and a special counsel whose safe contains unaccounted-for cash campaign contributions—in short, an office that leaves room for "White House horrors"—symbolizes the broader problem of a presidential bureaucracy that has expanded to the point where the president is victimized rather than helped by members of a staff whom he himself cannot begin to supervise.[40]

Under Ford, the size of the White House staff did not decline markedly, though one of Nixon's innovations for imposing the presidential will on public policy, John Ehrlichman's Domestic Council, fell into disuse. Carter has sharply cut the size of the White House staff and substituted a domestic policy staff for a council, but the consequences of Carter's reorganization cannot yet be assessed. Much of the reduction is cosmetic—for example, certain personal services are no longer tabulated under the heading White House Office and much White House business will now be conducted by personnel detailed from other agencies. The political layer of OMB has in fact been expanded rather than reduced.

PRESIDENCY-CURBING LEGISLATION

In the days when the Bricker Amemdment was narrowly defeated by a coalition led by a Republican President, the notion that an already politically restrained presidency needed added legal restraints was abhorrent to liberal commentators on American politics. They saw the presidency as the political institution most likely to have a benign impact on public policy. Opponents of the Bricker Amendment in most cases felt that there had already been a recent and unfortunate presidency-weakening constitutional change—the Twenty-second Amendment, restraining the president from running for a third term. Many of these same commentators sympathized with such exercises of presidential prerogative as Truman's deliberate refusal to seek a congressional resolution authorizing American military invervention in Korea—a refusal Truman made with some awareness that

he was increasing his potential political vulnerability, but on the principled gound that he wanted to avoid setting a precedent that, he felt, would weaken future presidents. Yet, as Averell Harriman, who at the time recommended that Truman seek such a resolution, has since noted congressional authorization would have "tied the hands" of many later opponents of "Truman's War."[41]

In connection with the general alterations in views about the presidency that occurred during the Vietnam conflict and Watergate, presidency-curbing legislation came to receive increasing support—much of it from former defenders of a broad construction of the president's power. Largely during the Watergate period, Congress enacted an unprecedented array of presidency-curbing legislation. Most of these laws have not been tested or, when they have been, have not had much effect on existing practices. All told, however, it is hard to believe that their total impact on presidents will be nil. Certainly if the laws had then been in force many past acts of presidential initiative would have had to be carried out with more systematic attention to congressional support than they were. Here are some of the major legislative changes, beginning with one that is a logical consequence of BOB's transformation into OMB, a more explicitly political agency:

● After fifty-three years during which BOB/OMB had existed as an agency wholly in the president's preserve, in 1973 the OMB director and deputy directors for the first time became subject to congressional confirmation. (P.L. 93-250, 88 Stat. 11, 1974.)

● In 1973 Congress allowed the lapse of a presidential power to propose executive branch reorganization plans, which would go into effect unless rejected by Congress within sixty days. In 1977 President Carter succeeded in winning restoration of this power (the Reorganization Act of 1977), but with restraints on the elimination of statutory programs and the provision that no more than three reorganization plans can be pending at any time.

• The Impoundment Control Act of 1974 (Title X of P.L. 93-344) requires that if a president does not want to expend appropriated funds he must report "recission" to Congress. If he wants to *defer* spending funds, he is able to do so unless one house of Congress votes disapproval. Recissions must be approved by both houses within forty-five days.

• The Case Act, passed in 1972 (P.L. 92-403), requires that all executive agreements with foreign powers be reported to the Congress. In fact, however, the Nixon administration failed to report a number of international agreements, notably several made with the government of South Vietnam.

• The War Powers Resolution of 1973 (P.L. 93-148) requires the president to consult with Congress "in every possible instance" before committing troops to combat and to submit a report on his action to Congress, and makes it necessary for the Congress, unless physically unable to meet, to authorize the military action. In the one case to which this has applied, President Ford's rescue of the ship *Mayaguez* and its crew, there was congressional briefing but not consultation, and the episode did not last the sixty days allowed until congressional action was required; most important were the political realities: numerous members of Congress promptly praised Ford's action.[42]

In describing these changes I have used the term commonly applied to them—"president-curbing" legislation. Yet we have also noted the potentially high costs of presidential command actions, especially when these are based on broad interpretations of the extent to which the vague language of Article II entitles the president to engage in autonomous action. At least in the case of Truman and Korea, the War Powers Resolution probably would have yielded the equivalent of the congressional resolution that Harriman urged Truman to seek. And this in turn could have provided Truman with protection from some of the criticism he received as the war lingered on. (Indeed one objection to the resolution by those who felt it did not sufficiently curb presidential war powers was that just such a

possibility might occur.) In the legalistic context of American politics it is possible that more explicitly bounded presidents will be more, rather than less, able to maintain sustained support for their political goals.

SUMMARY AND CONCLUSIONS

Patterson in his analysis of the contemporary Congress . . . notes that if Henry Clay had been resurrected and placed in the 95th Congress he would begin to see that, in spite of many detailed changes in the structure of the institution, it continues to function in ways reminiscent of the period before the Civil War. By contrast, we have seen that even a 1920s president would have difficulty making sense of the modern presidency. The changes that have transformed the traditional presidency were evident by the end of the Eisenhower administration. The turbulent experience of the institution since 1960 has also left a few apparently enduring residues—for example, the legislation just summarized and the changes in the White House Office and Executive Office of the President more generally. During the Kennedy, Johnson, and Nixon administrations, more fundamental changes in the presidency seemed to be underway; but to an extraordinary degree the politics of the post-Nixon presidency have been reminiscent of the severely restrained "mid-century" presidencies.

In commenting on the changes in evaluations of the merits of the presidency as an institution that occurred during the post-Eisenhower years, I have not sought to summarize the views of the institution that have been prevalent in the years since Nixon resigned. There are many views of how Ford and (to date) Carter have comported themselves in office, but the "data base" for evaluating the postimperial presidency as an institution is too thin. Even more important, the intellectual resources for such an evaluation are not yet available.

The older presidency-celebrating imagery of "lonely grandeur" and "awesome power," and of the need for more power, cannot be resurrected. A common prescription during the Johnson and Nixon years—that the presidency be "demystified"—may slowly be coming to pass, particularly if the nation continues to undergo a series of one-term presidencies. Yet presidencies still do seem to be expected to perform wonders.

My own discussion of the president-curbing legislation stressed the possible contributions that a firmer statutory basis of power might make to effective presidential leadership. I cannot imagine, however, that legislative changes will fundamentally alter dilemmas that arise from high expectations of presidential performance and the low capacity of presidents to live up to those expectations.

Today's presidency is an institution in search of new role definitions. This is evident in the actions of the president himself, as we see Carter floundering through episodes of self-conscious image-building, self-imposed demands for policy enactments which do not come to pass, a state of the union message stressing the need for lowered expectations from government, and attempts at tough old-fashioned political arm-twisting in connection with Panama Canal Treaty roll calls. Perhaps a president who had not come up as a political outsider, belaboring standard Washington political practices, would have been off to a more effective start. But even as Washington-wise a President as Johnson, whose administration started with widely acclaimed successes, came to grief.

Taking it for granted that FDR's political skills and the widespread sense of crisis that enabled him to put them to work were sui generis, it may be instructive to consider the view of the presidency held by the last two-term incumbent—Eisenhower. As I noted, archives now available at the Eisenhower Library emphatically refute the image that president-watchers of the time had of Ike as a "captive hero," cherubically soothing the American people with his infectious grin and golfing while others ran—or failed to run— the government. We discover a "modern Republican" whose modernity consisted of being an internationalist and of favoring moderate departures from conservative political principles in the interest of providing the Republican party—or at least its president—with sufficient electoral strength to win the support of an electorate unprepared to see basic New Deal programs, like Social Security, repealed. More interestingly, we see a man for whom leadership had been a life-long preoccupation and who in extensive correspondence with his associates enunciated in detail how he conceived of leadership in general and of the presidency in particular.

In my own reflections on what a contemporary presidential role definition might be, I have found instructive such assertions of Eisenhower's as the following comment in a letter to Henry Luce, written in August 1960, ruminating on his tenure in office:

> The government of the United States has become too big, too complex, and too pervasive in its influence on all our lives for one individual to pretend to direct the details of its important and critical programming. Competent assistants are mandatory; without them the Executive Branch would bog down. To command the loyalties and dedication and best efforts of capable and outstanding individuals requires patience, understanding, a readiness to delegate, and an acceptance of responsibility for any honest errors—real or apparent—those subordinates might make.[43]

Eisenhower, with his popularity and his limited domestic policy aspirations, could make such a statement with more assurance than a normal survivor of domestic political wars, especially one committed to substantial political changes. And one doubts whether Sherman Adams would fully have endorsed the last sentence in Eisenhower's statement. Nevertheless, the gist of his message—that the president is not the political system—might usefully inform political thought today. It may be easier to convince presidents of this than the general public. Presidents have an interest in their own "demystification" if they are to keep from falling into the perennial trap of seeking overachievement and accomplishing dismal underachievement.[44]

Elsewhere in his letter to Luce, Eisenhower commented that, having had for two years a slim Republican majority and for six years a Democratic majority in Congress, "the hope of doing something constructive for the nation . . . has required methods calculated to attract cooperation, although the natural impulse would have been to lash out." This may be no more than a self-serving way of saying that one has practiced the art of the possible. Again, however, I think Eisenhower's comments suggest a point that may contribute to a redefining of the role of the modern president in more workable terms. The most appropriate redefinition would seem to be one that educates both citizens and political leaders (and, in particular, the president himself) to view the office in terms of a realistic assessment of what presidents can in fact accomplish in American politics.

This role definition would make it perfectly clear that the buck—a term that presumably refers to all major policymaking—neither stops nor starts only in the Oval Office. It circulates among many political actors. Depending upon the president's skill, his interest, the nature of the issues being considered, and the state of the national and international political environment, the president can have a major impact on how the buck circulates and with what results. But he neither is, nor can be, nor should be an unmoved mover.

NOTES

1. For further discussion of the differences between the traditional and modern presidencies, see the preface to Fred I. Greenstein, Larry Bergman, and Alvin Felzenberg, *Evolution of the Modern Presidency: A Bibliographical Survey* (Washington, D.C.: American Enterprise Institute, 1977).

2. Fred I. Greenstein, "What the Presidency Means to Americans: Presidential 'Choice' Between Elections," in *Choosing the President*, ed. James D. Barber (Englewood Cliffs, N.J.: Prentice-Hall, 1974), pp. 121-47.

3. William Hopkins, Oral History Interview, June 3, 1964, John F. Kennedy Library, Waltham, Mass. I am indebted to Mr. Hopkins for expanding on his oral history in a personal interview.

4. For a discussion that treats the exigencies of international power politics and other aspects of the international and national environment of the modern presidency as centrally (but not exclusively) responsible for the rise of what I am here calling the modern presidency, see Franz Schurmann, *The Logic of World Power: An Inquiry into the Origins, Currents, and Contributions of World Politics* (New York: Random House, 1974).

5. Note, for example, Senator George Hoar's comments that in the mid-nineteenth century congressmen

> would have considered as a personal affront a private message from the White House expressing a desire that they should adopt any course in the discharge of their legislative duties that they did not approve

and similar congressional assertions quoted in John T. Patterson, "The Rise of Presidential Power before World War II," *Law and Contemporary Problems* 40 (Spring 1976): 39-57. The presidents from McKinley to Hoover were in general more disposed to take an interest in legislative outcomes than their nineteenth-century predecessors and in this respect anticipated the great increase in sustained presidential involvement in the legislative process that began with Franklin Roosevelt. Stephen Wayne, *The Legislative Presidency* (New York: Harper and Row, 1978), pp. 13-16.

6. Charles L. Black, Jr., "Some Thoughts

on the Veto," *Law and Contemporary Problems* 40 (Spring 1976): 87-101.

7. For general background on the initial months of Roosevelt's first term see Frank Freidel, *Franklin D. Roosevelt: Launching the New Deal* (Boston: Little, Brown, 1973); and E. P. Herring, *Presidential Leadership: The Political Relations of Congress and the Chief Executive* (New York: Rinehart, 1940).

8. Hopkins, Oral History Interview. Also see L. A. Sussman, *Dear FDR: A Study in Political Letter Writing* (Totawa, N.J.: Bedminister Press, 1963).

9. Merlin Gustafson, "The President's Mail," *Presidential Studies Quarterly* 8 (Winter 1978): 36.

10. Patrick Anderson, *The President's Men: White House Assistants of Franklin D. Roosevelt, Harry S. Truman, Dwight D. Eisenhower, John F. Kennedy, Lyndon B. Johnson* (Garden City: Doubleday, 1968); and Stephen Hess, *Organizing the Presidency* (Washington, D.C.: Brookings Institution, 1976).

11. President's Committee on Administrative Management, *Report with Studies of Administrative Management in the Federal Government* (Washington, D.C., 1937). B. D. Karl, *Executive Reorganization and Reform in the New Deal: The Genesis of Administrative Management, 1900-1939* (Cambridge, Mass.: Harvard University Press, 1963). R. Polenberg, *Reorganizing Roosevelt's Government* (Cambridge, Mass.: Boston University Press, 1966).

12. Hugh Heclo, *Studying the Presidency* (New York: A Report to the Ford Foundation, August 1977), p. 37. Wayne, *op. cit.*, pp. 220-21.

13. Diary of Harold Smith, Franklin D. Roosevelt Library, Hyde Park, N.Y. Much of the discussion of the Bureau of the Budget and its successor agency, the Office of Management and Budget, in this chapter relies on the comprehensive, archivally based discussion by Larry S. Berman in his "The Evolution of a Presidential Staff Agency: Variations in How the Bureau of the Budget—Office of Management and Budget Has Responded on Presidential Needs" (Ph.D. diss., Princeton University, 1977).

14. Alonzo Hamby, *Beyond the New Deal: Harry S. Truman and American Liberalism* (New York: Columbia University Press, 1973).

15. Harry S. Truman, President's Secretary File, Historical, County Judge Address, 1929-33, Box 239, Harry S. Truman Library, Independence, Mo. Here is Truman on the importance of constitutionalism and leadership in the development of the American Constitution:

> From the Magna Charta to the Declaration of Independence and the American Constitution is a space of some 560 years; and every step forward was the result of the ideals and self-sacrifice of some great leader. . . . We have an idealist in the White House now, the first we've had since Woodrow Wilson, and he's going to show us how to pull ourselves out of our present woes.

Camp Pike, Arkansas, August 1933 (on this occasion Truman was "commandant" of a patriotic gathering of youths, probably a regular program of a veteran's organization). Also see the following undated Washington's Birthday remarks (c. 1932) to a Masonic group. George Washington

> was a human, powerful, straightforward man. He liked horse races, liked to take a chance in friendly games, liked a good drink of liquor once in a while and when necessity called for it could swear as well and as effectively as Alexander, Caesar, Napoleon, or any other great commander of men. Men handled in the mass expect the boss to cuss them out when they need it and they like it.

16. Douglas Kinnard, *President Eisenhower and Strategy Management: A Study in Defense Politics* (Lexington, Ky.: The University Press of Kentucky, 1977).

17. Ann Whitman to Milton Eisenhower, August 28, 1956, Names Series, Box 13, Dwight D. Eisenhower Library, Abilene, Kansas.

18. "Only Half of Americans Praise Carter's First Year," *Gallup Opinion Index*, Report No. 152, March 1978. Also see the April 14, 1978 *New York Times* report "Approval of Carter Drops to 46% in Poll: Rating is Lowest after 14 Months for any President Except Ford in Wake of Nixon Pardon," p. A.10.

19. Richard E. Neustadt, "The Presidency at Mid-Century," *Law and Contemporary Problems* 21 (Autumn 1956): 609-45.

20. Many of the characterizations of twentieth-century presidents by James D. Barber in his *The Presidential Character: Predicting Performance in the White House*, 2nd ed. (Englewood Cliffs, N.J.: Prentice-Hall, 1977), suggest that the personal qualities of an incumbent president were highly consequential for the course of historical

events during their administrations. For an abstract discussion of the circumstances under which political leaders' personal qualities are likely to have an impact on events, see Fred I. Greenstein, *Personality and Politics; Problems of Evidence, Inference and Conceptualization* (New York: Norton Library, 1975), chap 3.

21. William G. Andrews, "The Presidency, Congress and Constitutional Theory," in *Perspectives on the Presidency*, ed. Aaron Wildavsky (Boston: Little Brown, 1975), pp. 24-44.

22. Thomas Cronin, "The Text Book Presidency," in *Perspectives on the Presidency: A Collection*, ed. Stanley Bach and George T. Sulzner (Lexington, Mass.: D. C. Heath, 1974), pp. 54-74.

23. Compare the view of discretionary presidential policymaking in Arthur M. Schlesinger, Jr., *The Imperial Presidency* (Boston: Houghton Mifflin, 1973), with that implicit in Schlesinger's *The Age of Jackson* (Boston: Little, Brown, 1946); *The Age of Roosevelt*, 3 vols. (Boston, Houghton Mifflin, 1957, 1959, 1960); and *A Thousand Days: John F. Kennedy in the White House* (Boston: Houghton Mifflin, 1965).

24. Edward S. Corwin, *The President, Office and Powers, 1787-1957: History and Analysis of Practice and Opinion*, 4th ed. (New York: New York University Press, 1957), originally published in 1940.

25. Richard E. Neustadt, *Presidential Power: The Politics of Leadership with Reflections on Johnson and Nixon* (New York: Wiley, 1976), originally published in 1960.

26. Peter Sperlich, "Bargaining and Overload: An Essay on Presidential Power," in *The Presidency*, ed. Aaron Wildavsky (Boston: Little, Brown, 1969), pp. 168-92 and in *Perspectives on the Presidency*, ed. Aaron Wildavsky.

27. Telephone calls, Conversations between Dwight D. Eisenhower and Lyndon B. Johnson re Civil Rights Bill, August 22, 1957, DDE Diaries, Box 15, Dwight E. Eisenhower Library, Abilene, Kansas.

28. On recent congressional independence of both executive leadership and leadership by congressional leaders see, in addition to Patterson's chapter in this volume, "Congress: Bold and Balky," *Time*, January 23, 1978: Barry M. Hager, "Carter's First Year: Setbacks and Successes," *Congressional Quarterly Weekly Report* 35 (December 24, 1977): 2637-42; and Dom Bonafede, "Carter's first Year: An Assess-

ment," *National Journal* 10 (January 14, 1978): 44-49.

29. On how local party potentates in the past were both a greater restraint on presidents than at present and a greater bargaining asset for makingpolicy, see Richard E. Neustadt, "The Constraining of the President: The Presidency after Watergate," *British Journal of Political Science* 4 (October 1974): 383-97; Lyle W. Dorsett, *Franklin D. Roosevelt and the City Bosses* (Port Washington, N.Y.: Kennikat Press, 1977); David S. Broder, "Of Presidents and Parties," *The Wilson Quarterly* 2 (Winter 1978): 105-14.

30. Hugh Heclo, *A Government of Strangers: Executive Politics in Washington* (Washington: Brookings Institution, 1977).

31. Burns Roper, *Changing Public Attitudes toward Television* (New York: Television Information Service, 1977).

32. Raymond Price, *With Nixon* (New York: Viking, 1977), pp. 185-86.

33. Daniel P. Moynihan, "The Presidency and the Press," *Commentary* 51 (March 1971): 41-52.

34. As the authors of the famous "Schattschneider report" calling for reform of the American party system put it, presidential power not grounded in issue-oriented parties that have a solid base in the electorate

favors a President who exploits skillfully the arts of demagoguery, who uses the whole country as his political backyard, and who does not mind turning into the embodiment of personal government.

Toward a More Responsible Two-Party System: A Report of the Committee on Political Parties, American Political Science Association (New York: Rinehart, 1950), p. 94.

35. Joel D. Aberbach and Bert A. Rockman, "Clashing Beliefs within the Executive Branch," *American Political Science Review* 70 (June 1976): 456-68.

36. See, for example, the sources cited in note 12.

37. Larry Berman, "OMB and the Hazards of Presidential Staff Work: Some Call it TOMB," *Public Administration Review*, forthcoming. Heclo, *Government of Strangers, op. cit.*, p. 81.

38. James F. C. Hyde, Jr. and Stephen J. Wayne, "Partners in Presidential Policy-Making: White House—OMB Legislative Relationships" (Paper prepared for delivery at the 1975 Annual Meeting of the Southern Political Science Association.).

39. Hugh Heclo, "OMB and the Presidency: The Problem of Neutral Competence," *The Public Interest*, no. 38 (Winter 1975): 80-98.

40. The specific illustrations are taken from John Dean, *Blind Ambition* (New York: Simon and Schuster, 1976). For a review of the basic literature on the congeries of events summarized by the term "Watergate," see the bibliographical note to Fred I. Greenstein, "A President is Forced to Resign: Watergate, White House Organization, and Nixon's Personality," in *America in the Seventies: Problems, Policies and Politics*, ed. Allan P. Sindler (Boston: Little, Brown, 1977), pp. 99-101.

41. Francis H. Heller, ed., *The Korean War: A 25-Year Perspective* (Lawrence: The Regents Press of Kansas, 1977), p. 105.

42. For a thorough discussion of current legislation and precedents bearing on the separation of powers, see Louis Fisher, *The Constitution between Friends: Congress, the President, and the Law* (New York: St. Martin's 1977); and Fisher's *Presidential Powers* (Washington, D.C.: Congressional Research Service, Library of Congress, October 25, 1977). Also see Graham T. Allison, "Making War: The President and Congress," in *Law and Contemporary Problems* 40 (Summer 1976): 86-105.

43. Dwight D. Eisenhower to Henry Luce, August 8, 1960. DDE Diaries, Box 33, Dwight D. Eisenhower Library, Abilene, Kansas.

44. For the argument that another of the major constitutionally mandated institutions, the Supreme Court, would be more politically secure if leaders and other citizens had a less idealized, more politically realistic, conception of how the institution functions in the polity, see Martin Shapiro, "Stability and Change in Judicial Decision-Making: Incrementalism or *Stare Decisis?*," *Law in Transition Quarterly* 2 (Summer 1965): 134-57.

42. The Past and Future Presidency*

AARON WILDAVSKY

In the third volume of *The American Commonwealth*, Lord Bryce wrote, "Perhaps no form of Government needs great leaders so much as democracy." Why, then, is it so difficult to find them? The faults of leadership are the everyday staple of conversation. All of us have become aware of what Bryce had in mind in his chapter on "True Faults of American Democracy," when he alluded to "a certain commonness of mind and tone, a want of dignity and elevation in and about the conduct of public affairs, an insensibility to the nobler aspects and finer responsibilities of national life." If leaders have let us down, they have been helped, as Bryce foresaw, by the cynical "apathy among the luxurious classes and fastidious minds, who find themselves of no more account than the ordinary voter, and are disgusted by the superficial vulgarities of public life." But Bryce did not confuse condemnation with criticism. He thought that "the problem of conducting a stable executive in a democratic country is indeed so immensely difficult that anything short of failure deserves to be called a success. . . ." Explaining "Why Great Men Are Not Chosen," in the first volume of his classic, Bryce located the defect not only in party politics but in popular passions: "The ordinary American voter does not object to mediocrity."

Ultimately, Bryce was convinced,

*Source: Reprinted with permission of the author from *The Public Interest*, No. 41 (Fall 1975), pp. 56-76. Copyright © 1975 by National Affairs, Inc.

"republics Live by Virtue"—with a capital "V," meaning "the maintenance of a high level of public spirit and justice among the citizens." Note: "among the citizens," not merely among public officials. For how could leaders rise so far above the led; or, stemming from the people, be so superior to them; or, held accountable, stray so far from popular will? Surely it would be surprising if the vices of politicians stemmed from the virtues of the people. What the people do to their leaders must be at least as important as what the leaders do to them. There are, after all, so many of us and so few of them. Separating the presidency from the people—as if a president owed everything to them and they nothing to him—makes as much sense as removing the people from the government it has instituted.

If the reciprocal relations between political leadership and social expectations could be resolved by exhortation, the problem would long ago have ceased to be serious. If expectations are not being met, it is leaders who are not meeting them, and either lower expectations or higher caliber leadership is required. But both may be out of kilter. Should one or two leaders fail, that may well be their fault. When all fail (Kennedy, Johnson, Nixon, and now Ford), when, moreover, all known replacements are expected to fail, the difficulty is not individual but systemic: It is not the action of one side or the reaction of another but their mutual relationships that are flawed. That the people may reject their presidents is obvious; that presidents might flee from their people is less so. Once presidents discover the embrace of the people is deadly, they may well seek to escape from it. Presidents who tried to exercise powers they did not have might then be replaced by presidents unwilling to exercise the powers they do have. The future of the presidency will be determined not by the presidency alone but by how presidents behave in response to the environment "We-the-People" create for

them. Presidents, we shall learn, can retreat as well as advance.

PRESIDENTIAL POPULARITY

In the future, presidents will be more important but less popular than they are today. The presidency will be more powerful *vis-à-vis* institutional competitors but less able to satisfy citizen preferences than it is now. Unwilling to play a losing hand, future presidents will try to change the rules of the game. If they cannot get support from the people, they can increase the distance between themselves and their predators.

The importance of presidents is a function of the scope of government; the more it does, the more important they become. No one believes that the federal government of the United States is about to do less—to abandon activities in which it is now engaged, to refuse involvement in new ones, to go below instead of above the percent of the gross national product it now consumes. Hence presidents must, on the average, be more important than they used to be. Even if one assumes the worst—a weak president opposed by strong congressional majorities—the president's support will make it easier for proposals to receive favorable consideration and his opposition will make it less likely that legislation will be considered at all or be passed over his veto. Limiting presidential importance would require the one thing no one expects—limiting what government does.

Presidents remain preeminent in foreign and defense policy. Formal authority is theirs; informal authority, the expectations as to who will do what, is almost entirely in their domain. There does not have to be a discernible foreign policy but, if there is, presidents are the people who are expected to make it. The exceptions—the Jackson Amendment on Soviet Jews, restrictions on aid to Cambodia, Vietnam, and Turkey—prove the rule. They show that presidents are not all-powerful in foreign policy; they do not get all they want when they want it. But these incidents are just what they seem—minor. The Turks would not be behaving differently in Cyprus if they continued to receive American aid, and détente, if there ever was such a thing, has evidently not been disturbed by Russian repudiation of their undertaking on the emigration of Soviet Jews. Reluctance to provide funds for Cambodia and Vietnam was, at most, a matter of deciding when—under the present Republican or a future Democratic president—rather than whether these governments would fall. Congress may anger foreign governments and dismay secretaries of state; it may point to itself as evidence of national disagreement; but it will not succeed in making foreign policy. The main recommendation of the congressional delegation to Cambodia, after all, was to send the secretary of state there post haste!

I risk belaboring the obvious because, in the backlash of Watergate, it has become all too easy to imagine a weakening of the presidency. Not so. Does anyone imagine fewer groups will be interested in influencing a president's position in their own behalf or that his actions will matter less to people in the future? The question answers itself. The weakening of the presidency is about as likely as the withering away of the state.

To be important, however, is not necessarily to be popular. Let us conceive of presidential popularity as a vector of two forces: long-term dispositions to support or oppose the institution and short-run tendencies to approve or disapprove what the occupant of the office is doing. Either way, I believe, the secular trend in popularity will be down.

By far the most significant determination of presidential popularity is the party identification of the population. Since the proportion of people identifying with the major parties has shown a precipitous decline, future presidents are bound to start out with a smaller base comprised of less committed sup-

porters. This tendency will be reinforced by a relative decline of the groups—the less educated and the religious fundamentalist—who have been most disposed to give unwavering support regardless of what a president does or fails to do. Education may not make people wise, but it does make them critical. As the number of critical people in the country increases, criticism of presidents will naturally increase. Thus future presidents will have to work harder than have past presidents to keep the same popularity status, so to speak. To offset long-run decline they will count on good news in the short run. But the news is bound to be bad.

PUBLIC POLICY AND POLITICAL RESPONSIBILITY

There is no consensus on foreign policy; the lessons learned from the past have not proved helpful. The 1930s apparently taught the United States to intervene everywhere, and the 1960s to intervene nowhere. Neither lesson is supportable. Under the spell of Vietnam, the instinctive reaction to foreign policy questions is "no." Foreign policy requires faith: Evils must be avoided before their bloody consequences manifest themselves to the doubtful. But there is no faith. As in the parable of the Doubting Thomas, congressmen would not believe the president concerning the situation in Cambodia until they actually went there, plunged their hands into the wounds of the people, and saw they were red. For presidents the adaptive response will be inaction until it is too late, after which there is no point in doing anything.

Reaction to the oil embargo and the manyfold increase in oil prices is a portent of things to come. When it came in the midst of an Egyptian and Syrian invasion of Israel, the United States did not react at all. Why were the American people not told of the inevitable consequences of the oil price increase, from mass starvation to poor countries and financial havoc among allies to inflation at home? Because then the president would have had to do something about it.

Future presidents will allow foreign events to speak for themselves after the fact so they don't have to speak to them beforehand. They may reluctantly give in to popular demands for strong action but they will not act in anticipation. Followership, not leadership, probably will best describe future presidential foreign policy.

There is not today, nor is there likely to be in the near future, a stable constituency in support of social reform. The 1930s through the 1950s were easy to understand. The "haves" did not like to pay, and the "have nots" preferred the benefits they received to the alternative. By the late 1960s, however, the poorer beneficiaries had learned from their leaders that they did not benefit, which led the richer providers to add ingratitude to their list of complaints. Then the extreme passion for equality, against which Tocqueville warned, asserted itself to label anything the government was able to accomplish unworthy of achievement. Too little, too late; or too much, too soon, the result was always the same: a feeling of failure. For as long as directly contradictory demands are made on public policy, governments (and hence presidents) will be unable to get credit for what they do.

Public housing is a good example of how to make an evident failure out of an apparent success. The nation started with a low cost shelter program for the stable working poor. Public policy concentrated the available resources into housing projects, so some people could be helped; and resident managers used their discretion to screen out "undesirables," so tenants could live in peace. It was not necessarily the best of worlds for all, but it was better for some. But all that changed in the 1960s. Screening was condemned as racism and worse: Didn't justice require that the worst-off be given preference? Not long after,

public housing was attacked as a failure for all the crime it attracted. The dynamiting of buildings in St. Louis' Pruitt-Igoe Project symbolized, unfairly but persuasively, the blowup of hopes for public housing.

More medical care for the poor and aged is incompatible with easier access and lower costs for the whole population. By now the poor see doctors about as often as anybody else. This might be considered an accomplishment of Medicare and Medicaid—except that no one wants to accept responsibility for the consequences. Because access increases faster than facilities, the medical system gets crowded; because doctor and patient are motivated to resolve their uncertainties about treatment by using the insurance and subsidies at their disposal, the system gets expensive; because medical care is only moderately related to health, morbidity does not decline and mortality does not decrease in proportion to expenditure. Hence we hear that the system is in crisis because it is overcrowded, too expensive, and doesn't do much to improve aggregate health rates.

Examples of incompatibilities could come from almost any area of public policy—training the hard-core unemployed at low cost or decreasing dependency by increasing payments to people on welfare—but I will content myself with one less obvious example: party reform. The evils besetting our major political parties are supposed to be excessive influence of money and insufficient power of participation. But participation requires more meetings, conferences, primaries; in a word, more money. Told that money is the root of all evil, on the one hand, and required to dig deeper for it to promote participation, on the other, the position of our parties must be as perilous as that of presidents, who are urged simultaneously to limit their powers and to lead the people.

Where will support for presidential power come from? The only time a constituency appears is when there is a threat of curbing or eliminating existing programs. Then one discovers there are really recipients of medical care, aid to dependent children, food stamps, and the whole panoply of subsidies, transfer payments, and tax expenditures. But when they are safe, one could never guess from the torrent of abuse (money matters more than men, forms triumph over functions) and they had something worthwhile to lose. But they do and they will.

The mega-increase in the cost of energy means a decline in our standard of living. We pay more and get less. There will be fewer resources available to support social programs. Race relations may worsen as the poor (and black) do worse. Conservationists and producers will disagree more over strip-mining, oil shale, atomic power plants, and the like. Contradictory demands on government—produce more energy with less damage to the environment at lower cost—will increase.

It will be difficult to reduce defense expenditures because allies and dependents will be poorer and weaker than they were. It will be hard to avoid the threat of force because international events will become more threatening, and it will be difficult to use force because the nation will be torn between recent memories of Vietnam ("No more foreign adventures!") and older recollections of the Second World War ("Intervene before it is too late!"). As foreign news becomes less favorable, government will seek to apply more pressure at home. Is a tariff on imported oil a foreign or a domestic policy? Obviously, it is both. Yet there is no reason to believe that people will become less attached to their lifestyles or less interested in benefits from expensive spending programs. Demands on government will increase as the willingness of citizens to pay for them decreases. Reduction and redirection of consumption will become inevitable. The lot of a president will not be a happy one.

In view of these circumstances, the barest extrapolation from current events, it hardly seems likely that the nation will have to worry about a too powerful presidency, a legislative dictatorship (as President Ford claimed in over-zealous campaign rhetoric), judicial tyranny, or any of the other scare slogans of the day. There will be enough blame for everyone. The complaint will be that our political institutions are too weak in comparison to their responsibilities, not that one is too strong in relation to another.

PRESIDENTIAL POWER

If it is a question of who gets the blame, a president will still be first in war, in peace, and in the hearts of his countrymen, for he will remain the single most visible and most accountable political actor. If it is a question of whose views will prevail on the largest number of important issues over the longest period of time, presidents will still beat out their competitors.

In order to be a consistent competitor Congress would have to speak with a single voice. The days are gone when House Speaker "Uncle" Joe Cannon held so much internal power that Presidents Theodore Roosevelt and William Howard Taft had to deal with him as if he were a foreign potentate. I refer not merely to independent congressional election through a decentralized party system in which no person owes election to another (though it is worth reminding ourselves of this fact of life) but also to the continuing dispersal of power. The tendency of every procedural reform (save one) is to disperse substantive power. The more congressmen are forced to work out in the open, the less they are able to concert with one another in private. The more difficult it is to compromise their differences, the less they are able to oppose the chief executive. The decline of seniority may permit talent to be substituted for age; it also guarantees that

Congress will provide less attractive careers for people with whom presidents have had to deal, not once but indefinitely. Participatory democracy may have many virtues but institutional cohesion is not likely to be one of them. Enhancing the ability of individual legislators to express themselves is not equivalent to uniting them in behalf of a common program.

The exception is the budget reform. If successful, it would, by relating revenue to expenditure, enable Congress to maintain its power of the purse. But the prognosis is problematic. The impetus for change came from the excessive and extreme use of impoundment by President Nixon. Whether this was only a temporary abuse, or represents adaptation to a situation in which congressmen like to get credit for spending but blame presidents for taxation, remains to be seen.

If the new House and Senate budget committees attempt to act like cabinets on the British model, which enforce their preferences on the legislature, they will fail. Cabinets are committees that tolerate no rivals and Congress is composed of rivals. If the budget committees permit too many deviations, or are overruled too often, it will become clear that expenditures are out of control. Power will pass to the executive. Impoundment de facto will be replaced by impoundment de jure, for everyone will know that without fiscal responsibility there can be no financial power. Since future increases are built into present budgets—increases in social security benefits may well take up all the slack for over a decade unless there are to be huge deficits—congressional restraint in the face of desire for social programs may collapse.

Parties would not be anyone's current "man-on-a-horse" to control presidents. The Republican National Committee avoided implication in Watergate because President Nixon was able to brush it aside in order to run his own campaign. Nevertheless, the party must

accept a large share of the blame. If party leaders may be excused for not stopping Watergate before it got started, they must surely be faulted for not halting the cover-up once it became visible. The remarkable thing was the president's perseverance in the pattern of secret . . . forced revelation . . . new secret . . . new forced revelation . . . ad nauseam. Had there been party leaders (congressmen, national committee members, governors, state chairmen, city "bosses") with power in their own jurisdictions, they could have descended on the president en masse and said they would denounce him if he did not do the right thing. They, at least, had to be told the truth so they could judge the truth to tell. But this scenario did not occur. Why not?

The nation lacks party leaders because its parties are weak. The same weakness that allows a Barry Goldwater or a George McGovern, candidates without substantial popular support, to take the nomination for president also makes party leaders ineffective in bringing pressure to bear on their president. At a time when the nation most needs the restraint on office holders exercised by organizations with an interest in the long-term repute of their party, it can no longer call on them. The price of making parties too weak to do harm turns out to be rendering party leaders too useless to do good.

What is in it for anyone to be a hardworking member of a political party? Except for the few who go on to public office, all the party activist can expect is abuse. What used to be candidate selection is now determined in primaries; what used to be patronage is now called civil service; what used to be status has turned into sneer. The politician has replaced the rich man as he who will as soon enter heaven as a camel passeth through the eye of a needle.

Reform, which one might think would strengthen parties, is in fact designed to weaken them. Once a candidate gets financial support from the government, he has less use not only for "fat cat" financiers but for "lean kitten" party politicians. The latest version of "The Incumbent Protection Act" will not make legislators more amenable to party considerations. New rules for party conferences and conventions stress expression at the expense of election. It is as if the Democratic party did not know itself but had to discover who it was at the last minute by descending into the streets. Instead of being a place where the party meets to choose candidates who can win elections, conventions become a site for expressing the delegates' awareness of who they are. The politics of existentialism replaces the existence of politics.

The demise of parties is paralleled by the rise of citizen lobbies like Common Cause whose main thrust is to weaken other intermediary organizations— parties, labor unions, trade associations—that stand between citizen and government. Largely middle-class and upper-middle-class in composition, these "public interest" lobbies seek to reduce the influence of "private interests" by limiting the money they can contribute or the activities they can carry on to mold politicians or shape legislation. The sun that these laws are supposed to bring to politics, however, does not shine equally on all classes. Without strong unions and parties, workers will find that "open" hearings will, in effect, be "closed" to them. Corporations will continue to use lobbyists but they can pack no meetings. Only citizen lobbies combine the cash and the flexible hours of middle-class professionals needed to produce "mass" mobilization aimed at specific targets. Eventually, as intermediary groups decline, the idea will grow that lively citizen lobbies should replace moribund political parties. But as the lobbies weaken the capacity of social interests to bargain, they will discover that they cannot perform the integrative function of parties.

POLITICS IN THE LIBERAL SOCIETY

If party and legislature cannot constrain presidents, can the press do the job? It can do its jobs—to expose and to ventilate—but it cannot do the president's job: to provide leadership in critical areas of public policy. So long as people are concerned with abuse of power, the press will be powerful. Its essentially negative role is then viewed in a positive light. But when the pervasive problem in government is lack of power, the critical virtues of the media of information will become their carping vices.

Today we have become accustomed to certain constants: presidents are rarely satisfied with their portrayal in the media of information, and reporters and commentators constantly complain about attempts to mislead or control them. They never seem to find a president who loves public criticism; he never seems to find a press and television that love him. It is in the president's interest to put the best gloss he can on things, and it is the reporter's vocation to find out what is "really" happening. Presidents are judged on the news and they can't help wishing it were good. But the news cannot be good when conditions are bad. No president in the near future will get good grades and every president will want to flunk the press.

The media, after all, are part of society. They reflect the dissatisfactions with government that grew in the 1960s. Scoops used to go to reporters who played along; today Pulitzer prizes go to reporters who get things they are not supposed to have. The leak of the Pentagon Papers, which did so much to galvanize the Nixon administration in precisely the wrong way, would not have been possible without a public opinion to which challenging government had become infinitely more respectable than it was a decade before. Any reporter in Britain, whatever his party and policy preferences, is more a part of the permanent government (the elites that rule this time or expect to next time) than is any reporter in America, even if his favorite occupies the White House. Newsmen are not merely observers; they are also, in David S. Broder's apt title, "Political Reporters in Presidential Politics."

The perennial quarrel between the press and the president inadvertently points up an aspect of their relationship that is more important than whether one institution gets along with the other: like everyone else in America, the press is fascinated by the presidency. If its exaltation of the incumbent has declined, its fixation on him has not. Whom the press talks about is as important as what it says (if not more so). The media reinforce the identification of the presidency with the political system.

People generally ask why their presidents are doing so little rather than so much. Since America is a liberal society, it is not surprising that its people developed a liberal theory of the presidency. All power to the presidency? We never quite went that far. What is good for the presidency is good for the country—we came near to that. The people wanted a New Deal, and a president gave it to them. They wanted egalitarian social legislation and, on the whole, presidents were disposed to give it to them. The people wanted more, and presidents could promise more. They wanted novelty, and presidents provided it—new frontiers, great societies, fair deals, crusades. . . .

By comparison, Congress appeared confused, courts seemed mired in precedent, and bureaucracies were tangled in red tape. Checks turned into obstructions and balances became dead weights. The separation of powers looked like an eighteenth-century anachronism in a twentieth-century world. In short, we were concerned with results, and unconcerned with institutions. The idea that the presidency was implicated in a system of checks and balances, that the safety of the nation lay not in individual virtue but in institutional arrangements, was, though given lip service, in fact given short shrift. Once again, soon enough, the people will want a strong, action-oriented president to override obstructive courts and dilatory and divided Congresses.

BUREAUCRATIC FRUSTRATIONS

The real rival to the presidency will be the bureaucracy, if not by intent, then through inadvertence. It is not so much that bureaucrats might resist a presidential lead, though they might, but that such leads will be increasingly hard to give. The sheer size of government means that the Executive Office inevitably knows less about what is going on and what to do about it than it has in the past. Nor can any one person, including the president, know more than a small proportion of what his staff knows, which in turn is only part of the picture. The more frequently that government tries to intervene more deeply in society, the less anyone is able to control events and further removed the presidency is bound to be from what is actually going on. When government is overburdened, bureaucracy becomes unbearable; the march of complexity is mainly responsible for the mounting frustration of presidents with "their" bureaucrats.

When Richard Fenno first published his classic study The President's Cabinet in 1959, it appeared that this cadre was at its lowest ebb. Its lack of a collective interest in decisions made by others and its dependence on the president rather than on cabinet colleagues explained why it had never really been strong in the history of American politics. Under Presidents Kennedy, Johnson, and Nixon, however, the cabinet appeared not merely weak but virtually non-existent. Its former low ebb seems, in retrospect, almost to have been its high tide.

What happened? In the old days,

AARON WILDAVSKY

presidents mistrusted the cabinet because they were not entirely free in choosing its members. They had, in effect, to "give away" appointments to important party factions outside the government and to powerful congressmen inside. The decline of party in American political life, however, has meant that recent presidents have not been beholden to it. The increasing diffusion of power within Congress has also meant that there were correspondingly fewer powerful leaders whom presidents have had to cater to in making appointments. Yet their increased freedom in selecting cabinet members apparently has not led presidents to confer greater trust on their appointees. Why not?

Secretaries of the great departments must serve more than one master. They are necessarily beholden to Congress for appropriations and for substantive legislation. They are expected to speak for the major interests entrusted to their care, as well as for the president. They need cooperation from the bureaucracy that surrounds them, and they may have to make accommodations to get that support. A secretary of agriculture who is vastly unpopular with farmers, a secretary of interior who is hated by conservationists, and all secretaries whose employees undermine their efforts, cannot be of much use to the chief executive. Nevertheless, presidents (and especially their personal staffs) appear to behave as if there were something wrong when cabinet members do what comes naturally to people in their positions.

To the White House staff the separation of powers is anathema. They have wonderful ideas, apparently, only to see them sabotaged in the bureaucratic labyrinth. How dare those bureaucrats get in the way! The notion that the departments might owe something to Congress or that there is more to policy than what the president and his men want flickers only occasionally across their minds. It is as if the presidency were THE government. The president's men tend to see themselves not as part of a larger system, but as the system itself.

Alternatively, going to the other extreme, consider the image of a beleaguered outpost in the White House with all the insignia of office but without the ability to command troops in the provinces. As Arthur Schlesinger, Jr., put it when reflecting on his experiences as an adviser to President Kennedy in *A Thousand Days,*

> Wherever we have gone wrong . . . has been because we have not had sufficient confidence in the New Frontier approach to impose it on the government. Every important mistake has been the consequence of excessive deference to the permanent government.

Small wonder, then, that presidents in later times have interpreted discontent with their policies or their behavior not as evidence of the intractability of the policy problems themselves but as another effort by the "big bad bureaucracy" (readily expanded to include the "establishment press") to frustrate the people.

COURTS AND THE CURBING OF POWER

The protection afforded by the courts in the Watergate case really shows how limited their role must be. If we are to depend on future criminal actions to control presidents, if they can do anything they please that isn't plainly illegal, then they can do "most anything." It is no derogation of the courts to say that they are (with a few notable exceptions) reactive. They may tell others what to do after (usually a long time after) the fact, but they cannot compete with executives and legislatures for control of future choices. Indeed, efforts to alter future behavior by writing into law (or interpreting) prohibitions against specific past events are bound to fail.

The legal profession has the right aphorism: hard cases make bad law.

Congress has, after the fact, passed the War Powers Act to restrict presidents in the future. In my opinion, the gesture was futile and possibly dangerous. Basically, the act provides that within 60 days of the commencement of hostilities the president must receive positive congressional approval, or the military action grinds to a halt. Would this law have stopped Vietnam? That is doubtful because of the spirit prevailing at the time of the Gulf of Tonkin Resolution. Will it enable a president to respond when necessary and restrain him when essential? Such judgments, I fear, are more readily made in retrospect than in prospect. My concern is that the War Powers Act can be converted too easily into a permanent Gulf of Tonkin Resolution bestowing a legislative benediction in advance on presidential actions, by which time Congress has little choice left. Now presidents can point to a statute saying that they can do what they want (the Mayaguez affair should dispose of the requirement for consultation) for up to 60 days. The lesser defect lies in trying to anticipate the specific configuration of events by general statutory principles. The greater defect lies in trying to frame general principles on the basis of the most recent horrible event. And the greatest defect resides in treating a systemic problem, whose resolution depends on the interaction of numerous parts in a dynamic environment, as if it were a defect in a single component operating in a static situation.

History shows, to be sure, that constitutions are often written against the last usurper—the United States Constitution against the Articles of Confederation, the Fifth French Republic against the Fourth and the Third, Bonn against Weimar, the United Nations contra the League of Nations. So, too, do generals frequently end up preparing for the last war. But this is not quite so bad as aiming living constitutional provisions at dead targets. The nation has not been well served by the anti-third-term (read

anti-Franklin Roosevelt) amendment, which guarantees that if the people ever find a president they deem worth keeping in office, they will have prohibited themselves from doing so. In the guise of denying power to presidents, it has, in fact, been denied to the people. Were it not for the two-term limitation, moreover, we would be spared the current nonsense of proposing a single six-year term. Why some people think popular control over presidents would be increased by taking them out of the electoral arena after they assume office must remain a mystery.

The difficulties judges face in trying to capture a probabilistic process of institutional interaction in a deterministic principle is nowhere better illustrated than in the recent pronouncement of the Supreme Court on executive privilege. In the old days an assertion of executive privilege had no legal status. No one knew what it meant, which was just the way things should be. Presidents needed confidentiality; Congresses needed information; these self-evident truths were left to contend with each other according to the circumstances of the time and the pulling and hauling of the participants. Eventually an accommodation was reached that lasted until the question was raised again under altered conditions. Richard Nixon changed all that by bending the principle so far that it broke in his hands. Although the Supreme Court could not quite put executive privilege back together again, it went one step beyond by giving legal sanction to a doctrine that never had one. In order to achieve a unanimous opinion that President Nixon had to give up the tapes, the Supreme Court apparently felt it necessary to distinguish this case from all others by declaring that executive privilege might exist in other cases but manifestly not in this one. For the first time, future presidents will be able to cite an opinion to the effect that there is a legal basis for executive privilege.

Suppose all the other institutions—

Congress, courts, bureaucracies, parties—ganged up on the presidency: couldn't they curb presidential power? No doubt they could. But the likelihood of their all getting together is small, unless they face a common threat. Now what president would be so foolish as to attack each and every other institution all at the same time? Nixon, of course—the House on expenditures, the Senate on foreign policy, the media on misinformation, the courts on credibility, and on and on. Are we then to think of Watergate as the modal condition of the presidency? No, it is more like a limiting condition: Many things have to go wrong at once before the presidency enters into a knockabout against all comers. If future presidents have to do all that Nixon did before their wings are clipped, they will win every race against their institutional competitors.

There are, to be sure, contrary trends that might lead to the emergence of demagogic presidents who would hold sway over the multitudes. The decline in party identification leaves latitude for personality differences among the candidates to show up in the form of landslide majorities. And the growing influence of issue enthusiasts in national nominating conventions means that the major parties are more likely to nominate candidates preferred by their extremes but rejected by the population at large. This is what happened to the Goldwater Republicans in 1964 and the McGovern Democrats in 1972. But the popularity of the winners, Johnson and Nixon, did not last long.

It is also possible that the very absence of consensus on foreign policy and the very presence of contradictions at the heart of domestic policy would lead to a call for a leader to overcome (or more accurately, suppress) these disturbing conditions. Under these circumstances, threats to liberty are likely to arise less from a desire for personal presidential aggrandizement, and more from mass insistence that power be exercised to eliminate ambiguity. The presidential problem will not be power but performance.

THE FLIGHT OF THE PRESIDENCY

Perhaps the most interesting events of our time are those that have not occurred—the failure of demagogues, parties, or mass movements to take advantage of the national disarray. Maybe the country is in better shape than we think, or they (whoever "they" are) are waiting for things to get still worse. In any event, it now appears that the United States will have to get out of its predicaments with the same ordinary, everyday, homespun political institutions with which it got into them. How will its future leaders (preeminently its presidents) appraise the political context in which they find themselves? For leadership is not a unilateral imposition but a mutual relationship, in which it is as important to know whether and wither people are willing to be led as why and where their leaders propose to take them.

When you bite the hand that feeds you, it moves out of range. That is the significance of the near-geometric increase in the size of the Executive Office from Truman's to Nixon's time. Originally a response to the growth of government, it became a means of insulating presidents from the shocks of a society with which they could no longer cope.

As government tried to intervene both more extensively and more intensively in the lives of citizens, the executive office, in order to monitor these events, became a parallel bureaucracy. The larger it grew and the more programs it tried to cover, however, the more the Executive Office inadvertently but inevitably became further removed from the lives of the people who were being affected by these new operations. Then the inevitable became desirable and the inadvertent became functional; for as presidents discovered that domestic programs paid no dividends—see Nixon's comment in the Watergate tapes about the futility of building more outhouses in Peoria—insulation from the people didn't seem such a bad idea.

After Watergate, it became necessary to reduce the size of the Executive Office and to increase the number of people reporting directly to the President, so as to show he was as different as possible from his predecessor. Disassociation from Watergate, however, is not the same as organization for action. Faced with a lack of consensus in foreign policy and an absence of support for domestic policy, future presidents may well retreat in the face of overwhelming odds.

In the first months of Richard Nixon's second term, when his administration was at full strength and he was attempting to chart a new course, he tried both to reorganize radically the federal bureaucracy and to alter drastically his own relations to it. In part, the idea was old—rationalize the bureaucracy by creating a smaller number of bigger departments, thus cutting down on the large number of people previously entitled to report directly to the president. Part of it was new—creating a small group of supersecretaries who would have jurisdiction over several departments, thus forming, in effect, an inner cabinet. Part of it was peculiarly Nixonian—drastically reducing demands on his time and attention. Part of it, I believe, is likely to be permanent—adapting to the increasing scope and complexity of government by focusing presidential energy on a few broadly defined areas of policy. Presidents have to deal with war and peace and with domestic prosperity or lack of it. There will continue to be a person the president relies on principally for advice in foreign and defense policy, and another on whom he relies for economic management. The demands on presidents for response to other domestic needs vary with the times—so that there will undoubtedly be one or two other superadvisers, called by whatever names or holding whatever titles, to deal with race relations or energy or the environment or whatever else seems most urgent. The rest will be a residual category—domestic policy supervised by a domestic council—reserved for a vice president or a cabinet coordinator.

The response to ever-increasing complexity will continue to be ever-greater simplicity. This is the rationale behind wholesaling instead of retailing domestic policies; behind revenue sharing instead of endless numbers of categorical grants; behind proposals for family assistance and negative income taxes instead of a multiplicity of welfare policies; behind a transfer to state and local governments of as much responsibility (though not necessarily as much money) as they can absorb. "Here is a lot of trouble and a little money," these presidential policies seem to say, "so remember the trauma is all yours and none of mine."

THE "OFFENSIVE RETREAT"

Future presidents will be preoccupied with operating strategic levers, not with making tactical moves. They will see their power stakes, to use Neustadt's term, in giving away their powers; like everyone else they will have to choose between what they have to keep and what they must give up. Not so much running the country (that was Nixon's error) but seeing that it is running will be their forte. The cabinet, or at least the inner "super-secretary" cabinet, will undergo a visible revival because presidents will trade a little power for a lot of protection. The more prominent a president's cabinet, the less of a target he becomes. When presidents wanted to keep the credit, they kept their cabinets quiet; but they will welcome cabinet notoriety now that they want to spread the blame.

The "offensive retreat" of the presidency will not be the work of a single president or a particular moment in time. Nor will this movement be unidirectional. Like most things, it will be a product of trial and error in which backsliding will be as prominent as forward movement. But as presidents discover there is sickness in health and ignorance in education, they will worry more about their own welfare.

Presidents, and the governments for which they stand, are either doing too much or too little. They need either to do a great deal more for the people or a great deal less to them. They must be closer to what is happening or much further away. At present, they are close enough to get the blame but too far away to control the result; for government to be half involved is to be wholly abused. Which way will it move?

One way is nationalization. The federal government would take over all areas of serious interest; there would be a National Health Service, a National Welfare System, and the like. Industry would not be regulated at a remove—but run for real. The blame would go to the top but so would the power. Presidents would literally be running the country. The danger of overload at the center would be mitigated by mastery of the periphery. Uncle Sam would be everybody's tough Uncle and it would not be wise to push him around. Before it comes to this, however, presidents will try to move in other directions.

Presidents will seek the fewest levers but those with the most consequential effects. They will be money men, manipulating the supply to citizens through income floors and the supply to business through banks. Taxes will vary with expenditures; if government spends more, taxes will go up, and if it spends less, they will go down, with the upper limit set by constitutional limitation. Income will determine outgo. Regulatory activities and agencies will be severed from all presidential connection; why should presidents get into trouble for fixing the price of milk or determining routes for airlines or setting railroad rates? States and localities will undertake whatever supplementary programs they are willing and able to support.

Presidents will handle systemic crises, not ordinary events. They will be responsible for war and peace abroad, and life and death at home, but not much in between. The people will not call on their president when they are in trouble. The president will call on his people when he is in trouble, for presidents will represent the general interest in maintaining essential services and institutions, not the private and personal interests of every individual in his and her own fate.

PRESIDENTIAL PROSPECTS

The framers of our Constitution intended that its overarching structure should restrain each institution through the mutual interaction of its parts. Citizens should now see that their safety lies in that restraint. So long as the presidency is seen as part of the system, subject to its checks and balances, citizens retain hope and show calm. The institutional lesson to be learned, therefore, is not that the presidency should be diminished but that other institutions should grow in stature. The first order of priority should go to rebuilding our political parties, because they are most in need of help and could do most to bring presidents in line with strong sentiments in the country. Had there been Republican "elders" of sufficient size and weight, the president representing their party could not have so readily strayed in his perception of the popular will. Whatever its other defects, a party provides essential connective tissue between people and government. So do the media. So does Congress; strengthening its appropriations process through internal reform would bring it more power than any external threat could take away. The people need the vigor of all their institutions.

Strengthening the political system as a whole will not necessarily weaken the presidency. On the other hand, making the presidency into the government would not only threaten liberty but leave it without support in times of adversity. No one wants to be president of a bankrupt company; chairman of the board of a going concern is more like it. The national objective should be to increase total systemic capacity in relation to emerging problems. One way to do this is to lower people's expectations of what government and its leaders can do for them. Maybe that is what Watergate has tried to tell us. Another way is to depend on leadership. Maybe that is what President Ford's pardon of his predecessor should teach us not to do.

For 30 halcyon days the people of the United States had a president they could trust. This hope and trust was a precious national resource. Its dissipation was a national calamity. For it did not belong to Ford alone but was bestowed upon him by virtue of the circumstance under which he entered office. His task was to husband and preserve it for the dark days ahead. This was not only his but also the nation's most precious stock of political capital and he squandered it with a sudden wastefulness. If it were a question of the former president suffering more and the people less, Ford clearly mistook his priorities.

The voice of Ezekiel—"Son of man, trust not in man"—has a contemporary echo. If only Nixon went, the hope was, a leader would arise among us. Apparently not. The resignation and pardon warn against passive dependence on leaders. The wisdom of a democracy must lie in its "separated institutions sharing power." The virtues of a democracy must ultimately be tested, not in the leadership of its fallible men, but in the enduring power of its great institutions.

But institutions are not everything. They function in a climate of opinion that both limits and shapes what they can do. Those who operate them respond to the rewards and punishments of the environment in which they are situated. A people who punish truthfulness will get lies; a people who reward symbolic actions will get rhetoric instead of realism. So long as the people appear to make contradictory demands for domestic policies, they will be supplied by contrary politicians. Until the country is prepared to support a foreign policy that is responsive to new events, it will continue to nourish old misunderstandings.

Long before the current disenchantment, Henry Fairlie, in his book *The Kennedy Promise,* had questioned whether Americans did not have too exalted an opinion of what politics (and hence presidents) could do. To some, Kennedy's Camelot recedes in the shimmering distance as nobility thwarted, its light tragically extinguished before its time. Fairlie discerned in the Kennedys an excessive conception of what government could do, a sense of politics over society that would come to no good. As he puts it,

> The people are encouraged to expect too much of their political institutions and of their political leaders. They cease to inquire what politics may accomplish for them, and what they must do for themselves. Instead, they expect politics to take the place religion once held in their lives.

When leaders were gods, it is worth recalling, they punished their people.

Public officials need to know they cannot lead by following a people that does not know where it wants to go, or how to get there. They must persuade themselves—and, in so doing, the people they wish to lead—that no one can have it all or at the same time. As officials seek to improve their public performance, they must simultaneously strive to shape popular expectations, for unless the two meet there can be no hope for (and perhaps no distinction between) the leaders and the led. If they fail, leaders will move not with but from their people. If they succeed, then the short-term predictions of this essay—the flight of the presidency from its people—need not become the longer-run prognostication for the larger political system.

NOTES

NOTES

NOTES

NOTES

NOTES

NOTES

NOTES